THE COMPANION TO

Dombey and Son

TREY PHILPOTTS

LIVERPOOL UNIVERSITY PRESS

© Trey Philpotts 2014

ISBN: 978-1-78138-127-4

A CIP catalogue record for this book is available from the British Library.

All rights reserved: No reproduction, copy or transmission of
this publication may be made without written permission.

No paragraph of this publication may be reproduced, copied
or transmitted save with written permission or in accordance with the
provisions of the Copyright Act 1988 (as amended), or under the
terms of any licence permitting limited copying issued by the
Copyright Licensing Agency, 6–10 Kirby St,
London EC1N 8TS.

Any person who does any unauthorised act in relation to this publication
may be liable to criminal prosecution and civil claims for damages.

Published in Great Britain in 2014 by
Liverpool University Press
4 Cambridge Street
Liverpool L69 7ZU
www.liverpooluniversitypress.co.uk

Jacket illustration: 'The Dombey Family' by Hablot K. Browne ('Phiz')

Typeset and layout by Amanda Helm
amandahelm@helm-information.co.uk

Printed and bound by CPI Group (UK) Ltd, Croydon, CR0 4YY

THE DICKENS COMPANIONS

Series Editors: Susan Shatto and David Paroissien

The Companion to *Dombey and Son*

THE DICKENS COMPANIONS

[1]
The Companion to *Our Mutual Friend*
MICHAEL COTSELL

[2]
The Companion to *The Mystery of Edwin Drood*
WENDY S. JACOBSON

[3]
The Companion to *Bleak House*
SUSAN SHATTO

[4]
The Companion to *A Tale of Two Cities*
ANDREW SANDERS

[5]
The Companion to *Oliver Twist*
DAVID PAROISSIEN

[6]
The Companion to *Hard Times*
MARGARET SIMPSON

[7]
The Companion to *Great Expectations*
DAVID PAROISSIEN

[8]
The Companion to *Martin Chuzzlewit*
NANCY AYCOCK METZ

[9]
The Companion to *Little Dorrit*
TREY PHILPOTTS

[10]
The Companion to *Dombey and Son*
TREY PHILPOTTS

To Susan and David

CONTENTS

List of Illustrations	viii
General Preface by the Editors	xi
Abbreviations for Dickens's Works and Related Material	xiii
Bibliographical Symbols and Abbreviations	xiv
Introduction	1
A Note on the Text	8
How to Use the Notes	9
The Notes	11
Select Bibliography	527
Index	554

LIST OF ILLUSTRATIONS

Plate

1. Wrapper for the monthly numbers of *Dombey and Son*: Wrapper Number 11, August 1847. Woodcut, designed in 1846, by Hablot K. Browne — 12

2. Title page from the autograph manuscript — 13

3. 'Fancies' for Mr Dombey, by Hablot K. Browne, from Forster, *The Life of Charles Dickens*, 1872–4, Vol. 2 — 23

4. 'Fancies' for Mr Dombey, by Hablot K. Browne from Forster, *The Life of Charles Dickens*, 1872–4, Vol. 2 — 24

5. The Little Midshipman, The Charles Dickens Museum, London — 59

6. Blue-coat charity school uniform — 91

7. 'Paul and Mrs. Pipchin', by Hablot K. Browne in the third monthly number — 127

8. *Chain Pier, Brighton*, by John Constable, 1826–7 — 160

9. 'Entrance to the London and Birmingham Railway Station', the Euston Arch, *c*. 1838 — 206

10. The London and Birmingham Railway under construction in Camden Town, by J. C. Bourne, 1837 — 207

11. 'Idol of the Sandwich Islanders', *The Mirror of Literature, Amusement, and Instruction*, 8 (12 August 1826): 88 — 230

12. Copp's Royal Hotel, Leamington Spa. Lithograph by W. Rider, 1830 — 249

13. 'Guy's Tower, Warwick Castle', from *Curiosities of Great Britain: England & Wales Delineated*, *c*. 1845 — 249

14. Henry ('Hen') Pearce, 'the Game Chicken', from Pierce Egan, *Boxiana*, 1830, Vol. 1 — 270

15. Fulham from the Thames, 1825, by William Henry Prior, from Thornbury and Walford, *Old and New London*, 6 vols, 1873–8 — 280

16	Woodway House, Teignmouth, Devon, *c.* 1825: a cottage *ornée*	352
17	'London going out of Town; or, the March of Bricks and Mortar', 1829, from George Cruikshank, *Scraps and Sketches*, 1832	356
18	'Political Ravishment, or, the Old Lady of Threadneedle-Street in danger!' by James Gilray, 1797	375
19	'Abstraction and Recognition', by Hablot K. Browne, in the fifteenth monthly number	427
20	'The Railway Dragon', from *George Cruikshank's Table-Book,* 1845	483
21	'The Bell-Toller', from *Courtship, and Marriage, of Cock-Robin and Jenny Wren, c.* 1825	489

GENERAL PREFACE
BY THE EDITORS

The Dickens Companions series provides the most comprehensive annotation of the works of Dickens ever undertaken. Separate volumes are devoted to each of Dickens's fifteen novels, to *Sketches by Boz* and to *The Uncommercial Traveller*; the five Christmas books are treated together in one volume. The series will be completed by a General Index and Book of Maps, making twenty volumes in all.

The nature of the annotation is factual rather than critical. The series undertakes what the general editors of the Clarendon Dickens have called 'the immense task of explanatory annotation' of Dickens's works. Each Companion will elucidate obscurities and allusions which were doubtless intelligible to the nineteenth-century reader but which have changed or lost their meaning in a later age. The 'world' of Dickens passed away more than a century ago, and our perceptions and interpretations of his works can be sharpened by our having recalled for us a precise context or piece of information.

The annotation identifies allusions to current events and intellectual and religious issues, and supplies information on topography, social customs, costume, furniture, transport, and so on. Identifications are provided for allusions to plays, poems, songs, the Bible, the *Book of Common Prayer* and other literary sources. Elements of Dickens's plots, characterization and style which are influenced by the works of other writers are also identified. When an aspect of the text can be shown to have been influenced by Dickens's own experience this is indicated. The work of Dickens's illustrators is also discussed. Finally, although the Companions do not attempt the work of a modern scholarly edition, material from Dickens's manuscripts and proofs is included when it is of major significance.

The main part of the information in each Companion is arranged in the form of notes presented for convenient use with any edition of Dickens's works. The information is thus placed where it is most relevant, enabling the notes to be used to elucidate a local difficulty, or to pursue the use of a certain kind of material or the development of a particular idea. To facilitate the last purpose, the notes are cross-referenced, and each Companion contains a comprehensive index. The introduction to each Companion traces the major influences and concerns revealed by the annotation and, where appropriate, demonstrates their place in the genesis and composition of the text.

Dickens's vital and imaginative response to his culture is a familiar fact, but the Dickens Companions demonstrate and explore this response more fully and in far greater detail than has ever been attempted. Hitherto, Dickens's works have been annotated only on a modest scale. Many modern editions of the novels contain some notes, but there is not space in one volume for both the text of a novel and a comprehensive annotation of the text. Because most volumes of the Dickens Companions are devoted to a single work, the series can provide the full-scale, thoroughgoing annotation which the works of Dickens require. The completed series will comprise a uniquely comprehensive archive of information about Dickens's world, affording the modern reader an unparalleled record of Dickens's concerns and the sources of his artistry. For many kinds of scholar, not merely Dickensians, the Dickens Companions will provide a fundamental tool for future critical and historical scholarship on various aspects of nineteenth-century British culture.

To undertake the 'immense task' of annotation, the Editors have assembled a team of Dickens scholars who work closely with the Editors in order to enhance the depth and scope of each Companion. The series is not a variorum commentary on Dickens: it does not consist of a survey or a selection of comments by other annotators and scholars. Previous scholarship is, in general, cited only when it is considered to identify an important piece of information about the historical, literary and biographical influences on Dickens's works.

The annotation in the Dickens Companions is based on original research which derives for the most part from the writing of Dickens's own time, the reading available to him and the books he is known to have read. The annotation is not perfunctorily minimal: a large number of notes are substantial essays, and all are written in a readable style. Nor does the annotation consist of narrow definitions of what the reader (in the opinion of another reader) 'needs to know' in order to 'understand' the text. Rather, the annotation attempts to open up the actual and imaginative worlds which provided the sources and the backgrounds of Dickens's works in the belief that what interested, engaged and amused Dickens can hardly fail to interest, engage and amuse his readers. Our largest hope for the Dickens Companions is that the volumes will be read with a pleasure akin to that with which Dickens's own writings are read, and that they will be genuine Companions to both his works and his readers.

The idea of providing each of Dickens's major works with a companion volume of annotation originated with the late Professor T. J. B. Spencer. It is to his memory that the series is gratefully and affectionately dedicated.

1980–95   SUSAN SHATTO
MICHAEL COTSELL

After the publication of five volumes, Michael Cotsell retired from the series as Associate Editor. David Paroissien replaces him as co-editor, pledged to continue with Susan Shatto an annotative enterprise devoted to recovering and illuminating the allusive worlds of Dickens's novels and the culture which gave rise to them.

1997   SUSAN SHATTO
DAVID PAROISSIEN

ABBREVIATIONS FOR DICKENS'S WORKS AND RELATED MATERIAL

1. Works: Major

AN	*American Notes*
BH	*Bleak House*
BL	*The Battle of Life*
BR	*Barnaby Rudge*
C	*The Chimes*
CC	*A Christmas Carol*
CH	*The Cricket on the Hearth*
CHE	*A Child's History of England*
DC	*David Copperfield*
DS	*Dombey and Son*
GE	*Great Expectations*
HM	*The Haunted Man*
HT	*Hard Times*
LD	*Little Dorrit*
MC	*Martin Chuzzlewit*
MED	*The Mystery of Edwin Drood*
MHC	*Master Humphrey's Clock*
NN	*Nicholas Nickleby*
OCS	*The Old Curiosity Shop*
OMF	*Our Mutual Friend*
OT	*Oliver Twist*
PI	*Pictures from Italy*
PP	*The Pickwick Papers*
SB	*Sketches by Boz*
TTC	*A Tale of Two Cities*
UT	*The Uncommercial Traveller*

2. Works: Miscellaneous Writings

Bentley's	*Bentley's Miscellany*
CP	*Collected Papers*
MP	*Miscellaneous Papers*
RP	*Reprinted Pieces*
AYR	*All the Year Round*
HW	*Household Words*

HN	*The Household Narrative of Current Events*
CD	*Charles Dickens Edition,* 21 vols (1867–[74])

3. Related Material: Basic Sources

AR	*Annual Register*
BCP	*The Book of Common Prayer*
BPP	*British Parliamentary Papers*
Forster	John Forster, *The Life of Charles Dickens,* 3 vols (1872–4) rptd London: Dent, 1966
HO	*Home Office Papers* (Public Record Office)
Letters	*The Letters of Charles Dickens*, Pilgrim Edition. 12 vols. Oxford: Clarendon, 1965–2002 Vols 1 and 2 ed. Madeline House, Graham Storey, and Kathleen Tillotson. Vol. 3 ed. Madeline House, Graham Storey and Kathleen Tillotson. Vol. 4 ed. Kathleen Tillotson. Vol. 5 ed. Graham Storey and K. J. Fielding. Vol. 6 ed. Graham Storey, Kathleen Tillotson and Nina Burgis. Vol. 7 ed. Graham Storey, Kathleen Tillotson and Angus Easson. Vol. 8 ed. Graham Storey and Kathleen Tillotson. Vol. 9 ed. Graham Storey. Vols 10–11 ed. Graham Storey. Vol. 12 ed. Graham Storey, Margaret Brown and Kathleen Tillotson
Letters: Coutts	*Letters from Charles Dickens to Angela Burdett-Coutts, 1841–1865,* ed. Edgar Johnson (1953)
Letters: MDGH	*The Letters of Charles Dickens*, edited by his Sister-in-law and his Eldest Daughter. Vol 1. 1833–1856 (1880)
Memoranda	*Charles Dickens' Book of Memoranda,* ed. Fred Kaplan (New York: New York Public Library, 1981)
Speeches	*The Speeches of Charles Dickens,* ed. K. J. Fielding (1960, 2nd edn 1988)

BIBLIOGRAPHICAL SYMBOLS AND ABBREVIATIONS

MS	Manuscript
CP	Corrected proofs
< >	Deletion in MS or proof
^ or ^	Addition or substitution in MS
^ OR ^	Addition or substitution in proof
illegible word	Signifies an unreadable word in MS

INTRODUCTION

Dickens began writing *Dombey and Son* in June 1846 after a two-year break from novel writing. This interval, between the publication of the last number of *Martin Chuzzlewit* in June 1844 and the appearance of the first instalment of *Dombey* in September 1846, remains a key one in Dickens's career. This was a period characterized by international travel (a year residing in Italy), disappointment over the sales of *Martin Chuzzlewit* and a growing resolve to play a stronger role in the political life of the nation, culminating in Dickens's short-lived editorship of the *Daily News*. Along with this desire for engagement was a determination to develop as a writer by enlarging his 'stock of description and observation by seeing countries new to me' and by living abroad. Such a move offered an additional advantage: living somewhere he knew 'to be CHEAP and in a delightful climate' would counter his fear of becoming over-exposed and remove the prospect of 'putting myself before the town as writing tooth and nail for bread' (*Letters* 3.587).

These and other comments in letters to John Forster point to the long gestation of Dickens's seventh novel, a work that seems partially an outgrowth of the failure of his editorship of the *Daily News* and his desire to make a new start. On 30 January 1846, only nine days after the publication of the first issue of the *Daily News*, he told Forster that he was already 'revolving plans … for quitting the paper and going abroad again to write a new book in shilling numbers' (*Letters* 4.485). A month later, like the unclean spirit in St Matthew, he was 'seeking rest, and finding none', wandering the streets of London at night as he thought about his new novel (*Letters* 4.510). He soon decided to move with his family to Lausanne for a year. This would put distance between himself and the *Daily News* and allow him to work up 'some Mountain knowledge in all the four seasons of the year' and would provide fodder for future works of fiction. The move would also save him money and give him peace to begin his new long novel, which he believed could be written 'better in retirement' (*Letters* 4.538–9). He arrived in Lausanne on 11 June and spent the first two weeks clearing the decks: he wrote to Lord John Russell about Ragged schools, and to the heiress Angela Burdett Coutts about her 'charitable projects'. He also wrote half of a simplified account of *The Life of Our Lord* for his children, and 'cleared off' much of his correspondence. With these tasks completed, in late June 1846 he emphatically informed Forster: 'BEGAN DOMBEY!' (*Letters* 4.573). One sign was particularly promising: as he was unpacking a box, he took hold of a book, which turned out to be *Tristram Shandy*, and decided that 'whatever passage my thumb rests on, I shall take as having reference to my work'. The passage was 'What a work it is likely to turn out! Let us begin it!' (*Letters* 4.573–4). For his readers *Dombey* marked a return to form. The sales of the early numbers were 'BRILLIANT!' (*Letters* 4.631). As Forster explained years later, 'From this date all embarrassments connected with money were brought to a close' (2.17).

Dickens initially struggled with the writing. It had been two years since he last worked on a novel, and he was composing the opening chapters far from London and its 'numbers of figures': 'the toil and labour of writing, day after day, without that magic lantern, is IMMENSE!! ... *My* figures seem disposed to stagnate without crowds around them' (*Letters* 4.612–13). Moreover, he was trying to do something he had never done before: begin two works at the same time, both *Dombey* and his fourth Christmas story, *The Battle of Life*. He eventually settled down, however, and by the end of October composition was proceeding smoothly. While the interruptions attendant upon life in a foreign country ('these bird-of-passage circumstances') remained a problem, he told Forster on 4 November that he had 'no reason to complain, God knows, having come to no knot yet' and, in fact, he finished chapters nine and ten in five days, a pace that Forster called 'marvellously rapid' (*Letters* 4.653, n. 3).

Dickens spent more time planning the new novel than he had spent on previous works. This is the first of his novels to have detailed number plans for each chapter. It is also the first novel in which he sets out, at length, his original intentions ('Outline of Intentions', p. 16). There are also lengthy directions to Hablot Knight Browne about illustrations, early studies of Mr Dombey's appearance and, as is common with all of Dickens's novels, dozens of epistolary comments about individual scenes and characters. This extra material bears out the claim of John Butt and Kathleen Tillotson that *Dombey and Son* is 'the first of his novels to be thoroughly designed in advance' and thus to achieve the kind of 'artfully interwoven' and 'ingeniously complicated plot' that Dickens insisted in the 1837 preface to *The Pickwick Papers* could not 'with reason be expected' in serial form (73).

This artfulness is manifest in the legion of details that the novel contains and that this *Companion* endeavours to illuminate. As in all his works, there is a fascination with words and the use of language, especially the language of popular culture. This is a world of sentimental songs and nautical melodrama, of street ballads and comic refrains, of florid verse and formulaic phrases, of moralistic tracts and of slang in its many varieties. It is also a novel full of superstitions and fairy tales, of legendary characters and mythical beasts. There are changelings, dragon sentries and 'great monsters', along with the Flying Dutchman and Sleeping Beauty. But Dickens seems equally at home with contemporary scientific theories (of sound and electromagnetism, miasmic air and dreams) as well as the pseudo-sciences (mesmerism, phrenology and physiognomy). Alongside allusions to fairy tales, there are others to recent archeological discoveries, such as the statues found on Easter Island and the stone heads of Honduras.

As might be expected, given Dickens's voracious reading habits, literary allusions abound. There are references to the *Odyssey*, the *Canterbury Tales*, *Don Quixote*, the *Arabian Knights*, the *Divine Comedy*, and *Paradise Lost*, as well as to the works of such major figures as Defoe, Goldsmith, Sheridan, Gay, Thomson, Wordsworth, Coleridge and Byron, and to Dickens's contemporaries, Carlyle, Thackeray, Tennyson, and Browning. Because of the presence of Dr Blimber and his school, *Dombey* also contains scores of classical allusions, though most are familiar anecdotes, memorable quotations and well-known epic motifs, all standard fare for an educated person of Dickens's generation. The most frequently cited works are, predictably, the Bible and the *Book of Common Prayer*.

Dickens also draws on the real world, particularly his own childhood experiences. Like Walter Gay, he delighted in the life of the sea. He was born in a seaport town (Portsea), where his father was a naval pay clerk, and it was in another seaport town (Chatham) that he spent some of the happiest years of his youth. He took his middle name – 'Huffam' – from a naval rigger (his godfather) who, like Captain Cuttle, lived in Limehouse near the London docks. And, as an adult, he owned the complete works of such maritime novelists as Captain Frederick Marryat and James Fenimore Cooper. In the words of his fictional persona, David Copperfield, 'I had a greedy relish for a few volumes of Voyages and Travels ... and for days and days I can remember to have gone about my region of our house, armed with the centre-piece out of an old set of boot-trees – the perfect realization of Captain Somebody, of the Royal British Navy, in danger of being beset by savages, and resolved to sell his life at a great price' (ch. 4).

Dickens makes use of his other experiences as well. The depiction of Staggs's Gardens derives from his painful memories of Camden Town, a suburb to the northwest of London. In 1822, when he was ten, Dickens and his family moved to a small house on Bayham Street, an area that Forster characterized as 'about the poorest part of the London suburbs' and a visible sign of the decline in his family's fortunes (bk 1, ch. 1). Dickens is also inspired by his childhood acquaintances. So Mrs Pipchin is partly based on his memories of Mrs Elizabeth Roylance, who lived in Camden Town, and with whom Dickens stayed in 1824 while his father was imprisoned in the Marshalsea and while the young boy was working at Warren's blacking factory. The prototype of Miss Blimber is Louisa King, one of the daughters of Joseph Charles King, who ran a school attended by two of Dickens's children. And young Paul is probably modeled on his disabled nephew, Harry Burnett, who was said to be 'a singular child, meditative, and quaint in a remarkable degree' (Griffin 426). There was even an inspiration for Mr Dombey, the unidentified 'Sir A — E —, of D —'s' ('the class man to a T', in Dickens's words) though the editors of the Pilgrim *Letters* are right to suggest that any resemblance between the two men was probably 'only a matter of physical likeness' (*Letters* 4.586, n. 3). It is during this same time, the mid- to late-1840s, that Dickens began work on his 'autobiographical fragment', the highly evocative account of his early days at Warren's blacking factory and of his father's imprisonment for debt, which was probably composed between 1845 and 1849. As Alan Horsman remarks in his introduction to the Clarendon edition of *Dombey*:

> There is ... a close relationship between the fragment and *Dombey and Son*, in the time of gestation and composition as well as in part of the content, and, behind both of these, though whether as cause or consequence is uncertain, in the increasing adoption of the child's standpoint as the early part of the novel proceeds. (xxv)

Dombey and Son is also influenced by Dickens's work with Angela Burdett Coutts at Urania Cottage, a home for homeless women in Shepherd's Bush. He first described his ideas for the home in a lengthy letter to Miss Coutts on 26 May, only a few weeks before he began work on his new novel (see *Letters* 4.552–6). Dickens helped arrange the cottage, choose its inmates and establish its rules. He was particularly keen on sending promising women to Cape Town or Australia (a precondition for admittance to the Cottage was a willingness 'to be sent abroad'). This concern with the reclamation of destitute women is reflected in Dickens's sympathetic portrayal of Alice Marwood, the reformed prostitute who has returned from Australia ('where convicts go'). Alice's pleas for both help and forgiveness echo Dickens's plan to tempt the inmates of Urania Cottage 'to virtue' 'by means of affectionate kindness and trustfulness' (*Letters* 5.178, 183). So, too, Dickens's belief in the power of social conditioning, and the importance of raising a child in a loving and safe environment, finds its negative expression in her mother, Good Mrs Brown, who has raised her daughter in squalor and neglect. As Alice says of herself, 'Nobody taught her, nobody stepped forward to help her, nobody cared for her' (ch. 34). As is often the case, however, the influences on Dickens are many. If the characterization of Alice Marwood is informed by his work on Urania Cottage, it is also indebted to one of Dickens's earliest sketches, 'A Visit to Newgate' (*SB*), which records the tense conversations between two sets of aged and haggard mothers and their poor but attractive daughters.

As with all his novels, *Dombey* contains countless topical references. There are allusions to English concerns: the plight of governesses, poisoned air, prostitution, burial practices, the marriage market, emigration, the flooding of the River Thames and the bulls at Smithfield Market. There are others to the world abroad. Dombey has an agent in Barbados and is most likely involved in the West Indies export trade. There are allusions to Peruvian silver mines, trade fairs in Russia, colonial life in India, Australian penal colonies, Russian incursions into 'Oriental countries', as well as to Chinese coolies, Indian thugs and to 'suttee' (widow-burning). Dickens also remarks on popular misconceptions about China, and English prejudices against France. Despite these many topicalities, it is striking that there is not a single allusion to the two major political and social events of the mid-1840s: the repeal of the Corn laws and the Irish potato famine. One led to the resignation of the Prime Minister, and a shift in political power, and the other caused the deaths of one million people. Nor is there any mention of the working-class movement for political reform known as Chartism, a widely-discussed issue in the mid- to late-1840s.

It is also noteworthy that the only public figures specifically mentioned are of the previous generation or dead. So there are derogatory references to several royal figures, including Henry VIII and two brothers of George IV – Frederick, Duke of York and Edward Augustus, the Duke of Kent (and the father of Queen Victoria). Mr Toots imagines that the Duke of Wellington has written him 'an important letter'. And Mr Dombey owns a bronze bust of William Pitt the Younger, who was noted for his reasoned discourse, his knowledge of public finances and his association with commercial interests, and who is thus an appropriate model for a capitalist such as Dombey. But there is little else. Perhaps the public figure with the most influence over the novel is Caroline Sheridan Norton, a probable inspiration for Edith Dombey, though she is never mentioned directly. Mrs Norton had separated from her well-to-do husband in 1836, fleeing with her three children. Her husband countered by accusing her of adultery with Lord Melbourne, the Prime Minister, which led to one of the most sensational court cases of the 1830s. Although the husband's suit was dismissed, Mrs Norton could not get a divorce and was tied to him for the rest of her life. Dickens had reported on the Norton *v.* Melbourne trial in June 1836, and she later became an acquaintance.

One topical issue that does receive sustained treatment is education, which was very much on Dickens's mind in the months leading up to *Dombey*. In September 1845, he began to look for a school for his eight-year-old son Charley. He briefly thought about sending him to a recently established public school, Marlborough, but later settled on King's College School, London, which emphasized a largely classical curriculum (*Letters* 4.466, n. 4; 4.670). Dickens was also thinking about education in a larger context. In March 1846, he urged Dr James Kay-Shuttleworth to work with him 'to try an experimental Normal Ragged School, on a system. It could be done, without reference to the Union, at a very small expense; and surely you and I could set one going, and ascertain, by facts and figures, and regular entries in books, what could be done in Three Months'. This would be a school where 'the boys would not be wearied to death, and driven away, by long Pulpit discourses' (*Letters* 4.527). In June, the same month he began *Dombey*, Dickens wrote a letter to Lord John Russell about Ragged Schools and asked Lord Morpeth if he could help him gain 'some Commissionership, or Inspectorship, or the like, connected with any of those subjects in which I take a deep interest', including 'the Education of the People, the elevation of their character' (*Letters* 4.566; 572).

The public debate in the 1830s and 1840s over the nature and reach of state-sponsored education was highly topical. Proponents of a nationally organized system of education argued that it would prepare the general population to vote, improve the efficiency of industrial society, lower crime rates, and increase literacy. Opponents, such as Dombey, complained of the 'levelling sentiments' implicit in educational reform and believed that 'the inferior classes should continue to be taught to know their position, and to conduct themselves properly' (ch. 5). Dickens is particularly critical in *Dombey* of the 'by rote' method of instruction. Here, we see the influence of Rousseau (in *Emile*) and of nineteenth-century educationalists such as Friedrich Froebel and the English pioneer of infant schools, Samuel Wilderspin, all of whom recommended that children learn through experience, spontaneous play and curiosity and who resisted attempts to prematurely 'force' children to bloom in the 'hothouse' manner satirized in the depictions of the educational regimes of Mrs Pipchin and Dr Blimber.

The other issue that Dickens develops is sanitary reform, which is the subject of the most overtly polemical passage in the novel. It is here, in chapter 47, that Dickens directly addresses the reader, and asks for 'a good spirit who would take the house-tops off' to reveal the plight of the poor. This passage was most directly inspired by a series of letters that appeared in the *Times* in 1847, shortly before the passage was written, warning of a new outbreak of cholera, and by a leading article that followed in support of the letters. The letters and leader were part of a much broader agitation for sanitary reform that marked the mid-1840s, and which was led by evangelicals such as Lord Ashley, 7th Earl of Shaftsbury, and by a variety of pressure groups. This 'good spirit' passage is one of the first times in his career that Dickens took a public stand for sanitary reform and is especially memorable because he powerfully attributes the condition of the poor to social and environmental forces beyond their control.

Dombey also records the social developments of the 1840s, such as the emergence of London suburbs, which was made possible by improved roads and by the growth of commuter rail lines, and which, like other forms of construction, reflected a specific social trajectory. So Mr Carker lives in a picturesque cottage in 'the green and wooded country near Norwood', just southeast of London, whereas his sister Harriet is relegated to a 'blighted' area to the north of London, 'neither of the town nor country', an 'intermediate space' with tall chimneys and brickfields (ch. 33). And there is the growth of towns like Brighton, which Dickens visited during the period he was writing *Dombey and Son* and, closer to London, Kingston-upon-Thames, the attractive market town which is the residence of an unnamed director of the Bank of England who attends Dombey's wedding.

Of course, *Dombey and Son* is most famous for its allusions to the railway. It contains one of the first and most evocative descriptions of travel by rail. And it is the first English novel to record, as a major plot element, the death of one of its protagonists by locomotive accident. There are vivid descriptions of the destruction brought about by the building of rail lines, and of the cleaner and more commercialized world that rises in its place. Dickens is also alive to the sensory experience of train travel – the shrieking and rattling of the locomotive, the trembling of the ground, the heat and the smoking cinders, the variable and confusing signal-lights and the disorienting effects of speed. And, in the character of Mr Toodle, there is information about the conditions of workers on the railway lines, their opportunities for advancement and their housing arrangements. Dickens also makes clear that in the mid-1840s railway construction in England was more advanced than on the mainland of Europe, especially in France, which lagged behind until late in the century. It is revealing that in chapter 54, during her flight to France, Edith travels by steamboat and probably by hired carriage and in chapter 55, Mr Carker is depicted 'in a dim coach-house, bargaining for the hire of an old phaeton, to Paris'. The imagery here is far removed from the rattling locomotive and the smoking cinders: there are ringing horse-bells, 'bad ground', 'loud shouting and lashing', and 'a shadowy postilion muffled to the eyes' (all vividly depicted in Browne's illustration for the chapter, 'On the Dark Road').

While Dickens draws on both private and public experiences, as well as on the minutiae of everyday life, it is also true that when it suits his purpose, he is willing to fabricate details. In chapter four, for instance, Walter Gay enthuses over the romantic stories associated with such ships as the *Charming Sally*, the *Polyphemus* and the *George the Second*. Although the ships' names were popular ones, there is no record of a *Charming Sally* having sunk 'In the Baltic Sea ... on the fourteenth of February, seventeen forty-nine', as Walter claims; nor of a *Polyphemus* captained by 'John Brown of Deptford'; nor of a *George the Second* foundering on 'the coast of Cornwall, in a dismal gale'. In a similar manner, although Dickens often quotes real songs, at other times he conflates motifs from several songs, as in the 'ballad of considerable antiquity ... that set forth the courtship and nuptials of a promising young coal-whipper with a certain "lovely Peg" ' (ch. 9). He also refashions the landscape to fit his fictional needs. So, in chapter 20, in the richly detailed description of Mr Dombey's train ride along the London and Birmingham line, Dickens records, with a remarkable degree of specificity and accuracy, the actual sights and sounds that a real traveller would have experienced along this route. But he also has Mr Dombey ride all the way into Birmingham, when it would have been much quicker for him and his travelling companion, Major Bagstock, to have disembarked at Coventry, only eight miles from Dombey's destination in Leamington (Birmingham is twenty miles away). At other times, though, he meticulously insists on getting his facts straight. In December 1847, for instance, he wrote to Lieut. Augustus Tracey, RN, the Governor of the Westminster House of Correction, 'to ask you a question on one or two little nautical points, in order that I may be quite right in Dombey' (*Letters* 5.205).

Dickens is equally exacting in his ascription of physical ailments to his characters. This is most evident in his depiction of Major Bagstock, who has symptoms that suggest he suffers from several related ailments. His wooden features and his 'very rigid pair of jaw-bones' indicate partial paralysis, or palsy. Palsy, in turn, was sometimes associated with watering in the eyes (cf. 'the Major sat ... watering at the eyes') and, in some instances, with the convulsive disorder known as chorea which may explain the Major's 'rolling' head. The Major's blue (or 'purple') face also suggests that he is suffering from cyanosis, a symptom of emphysema, which is indicated by his chronic wheezing and fits of coughing. And his 'eyes starting out of his head' suggest the condition exophthalmia, which is also associated with watering of the eye. And there are Mrs Skewton's tremors which, along with her paralysis, 'indistinctness of speech' and temporary memory loss, indicate that she suffers from 'the shaking palsy', as described by Dr James Parkinson in 1817. And, when the first Mrs Dombey is said to suffer from 'a certain degree of languor and a general absence of elasticity', Dickens is betokening more than post-pregnancy debility. She is suffering from the condition defined by contemporary medical textbooks as 'nervous shock', which was thought to sometimes lead to death.

Dombey and Son is very much of its time, the mid-1840s, with its railway boom and its growing suburbs. But with its fairy tale motifs and Shakespearean echoes, it also transcends that time. Perhaps the most resonant allusion, accordingly, is one that underlies the main familial relationship in the novel: Paul Dombey, Senior, 'too stern and pompous', is a Lear-like figure who misconceives the love of his daughter and loses everything.

A NOTE ON THE TEXT

The text of *Dombey and Son* quoted throughout this volume is that of the Clarendon Dickens edition of the novel, edited by Alan Horsman (1974) ('Clarendon'). Clarendon uses as its copy text the first, one-volume edition published on 12 April 1848. The notes in the present volume address only those variants I have considered especially relevant to the novel's contexts.

HOW TO USE THE NOTES

To help the reader locate in the novel the word or phrase quoted in an entry, the notes are presented in this way: the opening phrase of the paragraph which includes the entry is quoted as a guide and printed in italics; the entry itself appears in boldface type. This system should also help the reader who turns from the novel in search of a note on a particular word or phrase.

Documentation within the notes is kept to a minimum by the use of an abbreviated form of referencing. Works of literature are referred to by their parts: *Vanity Fair* 12; *Past and Present* 3.2; *The Faerie Queene* 2.12.17.14–16; 'The Idiot Boy' 8–10. Frequently cited works of criticism and other secondary sources are referred to by author, part (where relevant) and page: '(Collins 171–2)', '(Mayhew 3.106–7)'. Complete details are given in the Select Bibliography.

The Work Plans

The notes include transcripts of the sheets of memoranda on which Dickens sketched out his ideas for which monthly number. He folded each sheet once to make two pages, and he referred to the sheets as single 'Mems'. In the present volume, they are referred to as 'work plans'. To distinguish the pages from each other, the left page is described as the 'number plan' and the right page as the 'chapter plan'.

The Notes

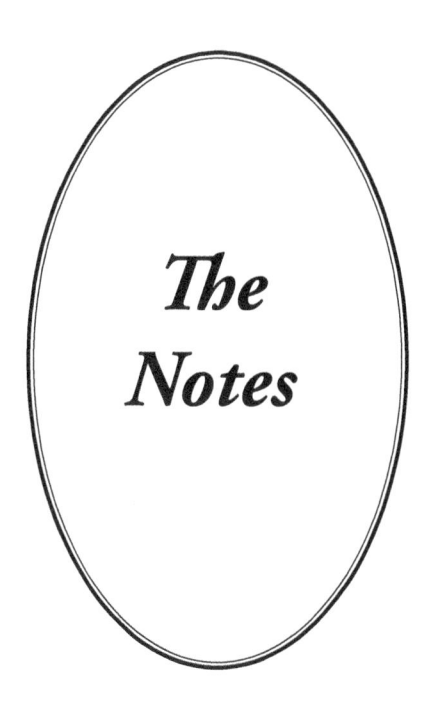

1   Wrapper for the monthly numbers of *Dombey and Son*: Wrapper Number 11, August 1847. Woodcut, designed in 1846, by Hablot Knight Browne ('Phiz'). Each month's wrapper was identical except for part number and month designation.

2   Title page from the autograph manuscript, showing 'Some' before 'Dealings'.

[TITLE]

Dealings with the Firm of Dombey and Son, Wholesale, Retail and for Exportation] This was a usual way for firms and businesses to describe themselves, for example: '*A Catalogue of Valuable Books ... sold wholesale, retail and for exportation, by James Asperne, No 32, Cornhill, October 1805*'; 'Photography, Wholesale, Retail, and for Exportation, Ottewill & Co., 24 Charlotte Terrace, Islington' (a small advertisement in *Notes and Queries*, January 1, 1853, p. 31). See also William Hone, *The Every-day Book and Table Book* (1838):

> It was the common joke of the neighbourhood to designate my aunt, my uncle, and the infant Shakerly, as 'Wholesale, Retail, and For Exportation; and, in truth, they were not inapt impersonations of the popular inscription, – my aunt, a giantess, my uncle a pigmy, and the child being 'carried abroad.' (663–4)

On 18 July 1846, Dickens urged John Forster to impress upon Bradbury and Evans the need to maintain 'the closest secrecy' concerning his new novel's title: 'The very name getting out would be ruinous' (*Letters* 4.586).

[DEDICATION]

THIS STORY IS DEDICATED,
WITH GREAT ESTEEM,
TO
THE MARCHIONESS OF NORMANBY.

The Marchioness of Normanby (1798–1882), *née* the Hon. Maria Liddell, wife of Constantine Henry Phipps, 2nd Earl of Mulgrave, created Marquess of Normanby in 1838. In 1839, the new Queen made Lady Normanby a lady-in-waiting. She gained a reputation as a great Whig hostess and partly inspired Disraeli's Lady Montfort, the political hostess in *Endymion* (1880). Dickens met the Normanby's son, George Augustus Constantine Phipps, the Earl of Mulgrave, on his voyage to America in 1842, and they enjoyed each other's company often during Dickens's tour and subsequently in England. Lord Normanby presided at the farewell dinner in June 1844 in honour of Dickens's departure for Italy, and his son was among the guests. During his sojourn in Paris from November 1846 to February 1847, while he was composing *Dombey and Son*, Dickens met the Normanbys several times, as Lord Normanby had been appointed Ambassador at Paris the previous August. Dickens wrote to Lord Normanby in July 1847 to say that 'in six or seven months' time', he would be writing to Lady Normanby to ask her permission to dedicate the novel to her (*Letters* 3.13, 14n, 16, *passim*; 4.147n; 5.109; *DNB*).

[DICKENS'S OUTLINE OF INTENTIONS]

About a month after Dickens began his new novel, he provided John Forster with an 'outline of my immediate intentions in reference to Dombey'. Forster quoted the passage in his *Life of Dickens* to rebut the charge 'that Paul died at the beginning not for any need of the story, but only to interest its readers somewhat more ... and that Mr. Dombey relented at the end for just the same reason.' In Forster's view, 'While every other portion of the tale had to submit to such varieties in development as the characters themselves entailed, the design affecting Paul and his father had been planned from the opening, and was carried without real alteration to the close' (2.19–20).

> I will now go on to give you an outline of my immediate intentions in reference to Dombey. I design to show Mr. D. with that one idea of the Son taking firmer and firmer possession of him, and swelling and bloating his pride to a prodigious extent. As the boy begins to grow up, I shall show him quite impatient for his getting on, and urging his masters to set him great tasks, and the like. But the natural affection of the boy will turn towards the despised sister; and I purpose showing her learning all sorts of things, of her own application and determination, to assist him in his lessons: and helping him always. When the boy is about ten years old (in the fourth number), he will be taken ill, and will die; and when he is ill, and when he is dying, I mean to make him turn always for refuge to the sister still, and keep the stern affection of the father at a distance. So Mr. Dombey – for all his greatness, and for all his devotion to the child – will find himself at arms' length from him even then; and will see that his love and confidence are all bestowed upon his sister, whom Mr. Dombey has used – and so has the boy himself too, for that matter – as a mere convenience and handle to him. The death of the boy is a death-blow, of course, to all the father's schemes and cherished hopes; and "Dombey and Son," as Miss Tox will say at the end of the number, "is a Daughter after all." ... From that time, I purpose changing his feeling of indifference and uneasiness towards his daughter into a positive hatred. For he will always remember how the boy had his arm round her neck when he was dying, and whispered to her, and would take things only from her hand, and never thought of him. ... At the same time I shall change her feeling towards him for one of a greater desire to love him, and to be loved by him; engendered in her compassion for his loss, and her love for the dead boy whom, in his way, he loved so well too. So I mean to carry the story on, through all the branches and off-shoots and meanderings that come up; and through the decay and downfall of the house, and the bankruptcy of Dombey, and all the rest of it; when his only staff and treasure, and his unknown Good Genius always, will be this rejected daughter, who will come out better than any son at last, and whose love for him, when discovered and understood, will be his bitterest reproach. For the struggle with himself, which goes on in all such obstinate natures, will have ended then; and the sense of his injustice,

which you may be sure has never quitted him, will have at last a gentler office than that of only making him more harshly unjust. ... I rely very much on Susan Nipper grown up, and acting partly as Florence's maid, and partly as a kind of companion to her, for a strong character throughout the book. I also rely on the Toodles, and on Polly, who, like everybody else, will be found by Mr. Dombey to have gone over to his daughter and become attached to her. This is what cooks call "the stock of the soup." All kinds of things will be added to it, of course. (25–26 July 1846; *Letters* 4.589–90)

PREFACE

I cannot forgo my usual

the unbounded warmth and earnestness of their sympathy in every stage of the journey] The early numbers of *DS* received generally strong reviews, which must have heartened Dickens, especially in light of the disappointing sales of *Martin Chuzzlewit* (which ended its run in July 1844); the critical failure of its immediate predecessors, the *Cricket on the Hearth* (1845) and *Pictures from Italy* (1846); and the problems that marred Dickens's editorship of the *Daily News* (January–February 1846). 'The readers of Mr Dickens must be happy to find him again in his proper walk, and as original and amusing as ever', observed *Chambers's Edinburgh Journal* (24 October 1846; 212). According to *The Economist*, 'There was urgent need to paint such a man as Dombey. The world of London is filled with cold, pompous, stiff, purse-proud men like this ... ' (10 October 1846; 215). The *Westminster Review* proclaimed *DS* 'the best' of Dickens's novels and believed 'No other writer can approach Dickens in a perfect analysis of the mind of children' (April 1847; 225). Charles Kent, the reviewer for the *Sun*, avowed that '*Dombey and Son* is assuredly the masterpiece of Charles Dickens' (13 April 1848; 229). (The review was so warm that it earned Kent a note of thanks from Dickens, and led to a close friendship between them.) *The Examiner* (in a review perhaps written by Forster) stated that 'with no abatement of the life and energy which in his [Dickens's] earlier works threw out such forcible impressions of the actual, we have in a far higher degree the subtler requisites which satisfy imagination and reflection' (233).

Privately-expressed responses were sometimes equally strong: Dickens's close friend, the Scottish judge and literary critic, Lord Jeffrey, for example, wrote Dickens several letters in 1846 and 1847, praising effusively the depiction of the Dombey family, and admitting that he cried over the death of young Paul. In his last letter on the subject, he told Dickens, 'You have the force and the nature of Scott in his pathetic parts, without his occasional coarseness and wordiness; and the searching disclosure of inward agonies of Byron, without a trait of his wickedness' (12 September 1847; Lord Cockburn, *Life of Lord Jeffrey, with a selection from his correspondence*, 2 vols, 1852, 2.429). Macaulay, too, wept 'as if my heart would break', this time over the characterization of Florence Dombey in the first number (Trevelyan, 1877, 2.211).

Reviewers singled out for special praise the depiction of Dombey and his relationship to his children, and most were moved by the death of young Paul at the end of the fifth number (for more on the outpouring of emotion consequent upon his death, see the note to chapter 16, pp. 214–15). They were also impressed by the originality of the railway topic. Other readers, though, detected a weakening after number five, a sense that Dickens's grasp on his material had loosened. In the words of Philip Collins, they 'felt that Dickens had shot his bolt too early, and that Dombey, his second wife, and Carker proved a poor substitute for the former interest centring on the children' (212). Still others complained of 'fine writing', poetical 'vagueness' and an over-abundance of wave imagery and compared Dickens unfavourably to Thackeray, whose *Vanity Fair* was being serialized at about the same time (January 1847–July 1848), also in twenty monthly numbers, and for the same publisher. So *The Man in the Moon*, which was established in January 1847 as a rival to *Punch*, urged its readers to 'Read *Vanity Fair*, but avoid comparing it with *Dombey and Son*, or you will never be able to bear the latter again' (January 1848; 220). *The Man in the Moon* also published several lampoons of *DS* in 1847 and 1848, including an 'Inquest on the late Master Paul Dombey' that ridiculed Dickens for exaggeration and a lack of planning (March 1847). In the same vein, the reviewer for *Blackwood's Magazine*, John Eagles, lamented the novel's 'exaggerated' characterization, its 'bitter' satire, 'unnecessarily accumulated', and its 'odious' depiction of the more unsavory parts of life' (230) (quotations are from Collins, 1971, 212–41; also see Collins, 1967, 82–94, and Litvack, 1999, 99–106).

From the outset, sales of *DS* far surpassed expectations. Bradbury and Evans, Dickens's new publishers, conducted an extensive advertising campaign, and the initial print-run of the first number – 25,000 – sold out in hours (at its height, *MC* sold no more than 23,000 per number), with a reprint of 5,000 issued by 10 October. The next day, Dickens gloated to Forster:

> The *Dombey* success is BRILLIANT! I had put before me thirty thousand as the limit of the most extreme success, saying that if we should reach that, I should be more than satisfied and more than happy; you will judge how happy I am! (*Letters* 4.631 and note)

By the third and fourth numbers, the print-run was raised to 32,000, and after young Paul's death to 33,000, and, for the final double number, to 35,000. (In comparison, *Vanity Fair* sold fewer than 5,000 copies per number.) On 17 June 1848, after the end of the serialization, Dickens concluded that 'Dombey has been the greatest success I have ever achieved' (*Letters* 5.341) (Patten, 1978, 182–97).

Chapter 1

First monthly number
October 1846

DOMBEY AND SON

Dickens initially overwrote each of the first four numbers, from one to six pages. '[A]ccustomed to economize at the expense of the comedy', he cut back in the proof stage on the characterization of Mrs Chick and Major Bagstock, though he made other significant cuts as well (for the more important ones, see below, and in the following chapters) (Butt and Tillotson 77–8).

The work plans suggest that Dickens had originally intended the first number to comprise three chapters or thirty-two pages, the usual length for a single number in MS. But he then added a fourth chapter that brought the total length of the first number to forty-two pages (the work plans show that he squeezed in a brief summary of the fourth chapter on the lower-right side of the number plan.) Once he had the proofs in hand, on 7 August, Dickens realized his mistake and decided to write a shorter final chapter for the first number, reserving the original 'ten pages of Wally and Co. entire for number two'. Dickens sent this shorter chapter, which covered slightly more than four MS pages, to Forster, who believed that it weakened the first number. In response, and to accommodate the original fourth chapter, Dickens made cuts in the first three chapters (the newly-written four-page chapter eventually became chapter 7). With Dickens's permission, Forster made additional deletions on the second proof.

In his introduction to the Clarendon edition, Alan Horsman has noted, 'The whole had been written with a remarkable fluency: for page after page the MS presents a far cleaner appearance than in later numbers' (xvi). But he also observes, 'It is unfortunate that Dickens's own cuts are all in the first three chapters which have most to do with the subject of the book as announced by the title, for he thus reduces his emphasis upon the central idea and removes some quite specific anticipations of its later development. ... Forster's further deletions in the second proof tend to compound these losses. ... In extreme contrast, chapter iv remains uncut' (xvi–xvii). Significant deleted passages from this first number are included below, in notes in this chapter and in the next two chapters.

Dombey sat in the corner

Son lay tucked up warm in a little basket bedstead, carefully disposed on a low settee immediately in front of the fire and close to it, as if his constitution were analogous to that of a muffin,]

> When the new-born babe is removed from its Mother, it should be wrapped in warm flannels, having the mouth and nose uncovered. It may be placed in

Sketch of Dombey – Mother confined with long-
expected boy. Boy born, to die. Neglected girl,

Florence – a child   family –
     Mrs Chick –common-mind and, humbug

Wet nurse – Polly Toodlie

    Toodle a stoker.

    Lots of children

Wooden Midshipman
Uncle – adventurous nephew – Captain Cuttle

Mr Dombey keeps his an eye upon Richards.

Dombey and Son.

Miss Tox introduces "the party."

Number Plan

(Dealings with the Firm of Dombey and Son: N.º 1)
_____

chapter I.

~~Dombey and Son~~

~~In which~~ Dombey and Son ~~are presented to the Reader~~.

Death of the mother.

chapter II.

In which timely provision is made for an ~~famil~~ emergency that will sometimes arise in the best regulated families ~~Also Mis~~

Wet nurse introduced.

Chapter III.

In which Mr Dombey, ~~is xxxxxxx in the bosom of his family~~. as a Man and a Father, is seen at the head of the home Department.
Mr Dombey   Miss Nipper.

chapter IV
In which some more first appearances are made on the stage of these adventures.

chapter IV.

In which some more first appearances are
made on the Stage of these Adventures

Chapter Plan

a warm bed or basket near the fire, and should be suffered to remain perfectly still and quiet, a watchful eye being kept over it. (*Plain Observations on the Management of Children*, 1828, 4)

Parents were cautioned that a new-born infant 'ought not to be exposed to any thing that may violently or too suddenly affect the senses; on which account … it should not be exposed either to great heat or cold' (Underwood, 1835, 17). A 'basket bedstead' is a cradle that is neither rocked nor swung.

Contemporary medical advice books recommended that, immediately after childbirth, and after the soiled linen has been removed, the mother should be 'carefully moved to the upper part of the bed', strictly preserving the 'horizontal position' ('*on no account for one moment, must the mother be raised upright*'). Once this has been done, 'the room must be slightly darkened; no conversation, and, least of all, whispering, be permitted; the friend must guard the room from all intruders' (Bull, 1853, 195). During ordinary convalescences, the mother was advised to 'never leave her bed, even to have it made, before the eighth or ninth day' (Churchill, 1857, 562).

Dombey was about eight-and-forty

Dombey was about eight-and-forty years of age. … Dombey was rather bald, rather red, and though a handsome well-made man, too stern and pompous in appearance, to be prepossessing.] While working on the fourth chapter of *DS*, Dickens confided to Forster that he was 'excessively anxious' about 'The points for illustration, and the enormous care required'. He then added, 'The man for Dombey, if [Hablot] Browne could see him, the class man to a T, is Sir A — E —, of D — 's' (unidentified). As the Pilgrim editors suggest, the resemblance between Dombey and 'Sir A — E — can have been only a matter of physical likeness' (*Letters* 4.586 n. 3). In Forster's view,

> A nervous dread of caricature in the face of his merchant-hero, had led him [Dickens] to indicate by a living person the type of city-gentleman he would have had the artist select; and this is all he meant by his reiterated urgent request, "I do wish he could get a glimpse of A., for he is the very Dombey." But as the glimpse of A was not to be had, it was resolved to send for selection by himself glimpses of other letters of the alphabet, actual heads as well as fanciful ones. (2.23–4)

Forster reproduced this 'sheetful' of pencil-drawings of 'actual heads as well as fanciful ones' in his *Life*. As the Pilgrim editors point out, 'Browne had made pencil notes of the leading features of Mr Dombey's appearance – all drawn from No. 1, and mostly from the description at the opening of ch. 1. The arrows against five of the drawings probably indicate CD's preferences' (4.596). See Plates 2 and 3.

The characterization of Mr Dombey has much in common with the description

3   'Fancies' for Mr Dombey, by Hablot K. Browne, from Forster, *The Life of Charles Dickens*, 1872–4, Vol. 2

4   'Fancies' for Mr Dombey, by Hablot K. Browne, from Forster, *The Life of Charles Dickens*, 1872–4, Vol. 2

of 'The Capitalist' in *Heads of the People* (1841). The Capitalist – 'a new species, engendered by a new state of things, and evolved from the invention of funds, and the involutions of commerce' – may be a merchant in one of the 'large wholesale businesses'. He is proud, formidable and reserved, with 'an exaggerated notion of the power and capacity of wealth'. Usually around forty years of age, he works in the City, lives in an elegant and aristocratic house in the West End and 'is often found in a state of widowhood, with one fair child, "sole daughter of his house and heart"' (207–15, *passim*). For more on capitalists, see note to chapter 6, pp. 97–8.

The 'nervous dread of caricature' extended to the Toodle family, and perhaps to Miss Tox, as well: 'Great pains will be necessary with Miss Tox. The Toodle family should not be too much caricatured, because of Polly' (*Letters* 4.586).

Time and his brother Care ... remorseless twins] An allusion to 'Sleep, the brother of Death', used by both Homer (*Iliad* 14.231) and Hesiod (*Theogony* 756). In the *Iliad* 16.672, Homer refers to 'the twin brethren, Sleep and Death'.

Those three words conveyed the one idea

rainbows gave them promise of fair weather;]

> After a long drought, the bow is a certain sign of rain; if after much wet, fair weather. ... If the bow breaks up all at once, there will follow serene and settled weather; if the bow be seen ... at night, fair weather. The appearance of two or three rainbows shews fair weather for the present, but settled and heavy rain, in two or three days' time. (Taylor, 1838, 420)

The rainbow as a metaphor of hope derives from Genesis 9.8–17, where it is a sign that God will never again send a great deluge upon the earth.

He had risen, as his father

Dombey and Son had often dealt in hides,] Dickens is vague about the exact nature of Dombey's business (throughout his career, Dickens tended to be more specific about the dealings of financiers and the stock exchange than about the business of merchants such as Dombey or Anthony Chuzzlewit). The fact that Dombey has an agent in Barbados and that Sol Gills, when he is searching for Walter Gay, visits Barbados, Jamaica and Demerara would indicate that Dombey is a West India merchant. As a modern critic has pointed out, this 'places him in the most distinguished rank of merchants, enjoying a power and prestige far greater than that of any other class of trader' (Russell, 1986, 198). Dombey, who may also have been a shipowner, would have had a share in the West Indies export business: he would have shipped English products to the Caribbean, and filled the holds of his returning ships with raw sugar (see note to chapter 32, p. 347). The 'West India Interest', of which

Dombey would have been a part, exerted considerable influence over rival markets and governmental policies in the eighteenth and nineteenth centuries (Russell, 199).

In 1867, James Greenwood described the demand for leather in Great Britain, which he refers to as a 'passion' and a 'national tendency' from 'time out of mind':

> THE supremacy of leather is, and ever was, maintained by the working Englishman almost as strenuously as Magna Charta, "An Englishman's house is his castle," and "God save the Queen." He regards it with the same implicit confidence as he regards his beer, and will no more accept gutta-percha or india-rubber as a substitute for the former than light French wines or lemonade for the latter. ('The Leather Market', *Illustrated Times* [20 April 1862]: 269–70)

Speculation in leather was rife in the mid-Victorian period, as Greenwood goes on to point out:

> I have been writing hitherto as though it were only among the lowbred and the vulgar – among costermongers and waiters, and tavern boosers – that leather is an article to swear by. We all know different. We all know that within a little year the commercial world – the merchants, and brokers, and bankers – were panic-stricken; that, indeed, many of them were clean knocked off their commercial legs through an earthquake in the leather market. It was not the fault of leather – such an excuse was never attempted; neither did the staunch fabric fail because of a "heavy run" on it. It was simply a case of leather worked to death – of advantage being taken of leather-worship by certain folks whose only aim was, like Jeremy Diddler, to hoodwink the worshippers and fleece them of their money. After all, however, it was probably but a righteous judgment. People – even golden-eyed, mammon-hearted people – were fast sinking into leathern idiotsy. ... The number of bills about with leather soles at that period was wonderful, almost as wonderful – as the sequel proved – as the number of bill-discounters "sold" through trafficking in leather bills. (270)

Norman Russell observes that Dickens seems to lose interest in Dombey's business dealings as the novel proceeds. His expectation, expressed in a letter to Forster, that he would 'carry the story on ... through the decay and downfall of the house, and the bankruptcy of Dombey, and all the rest of it' (25 July, *Letters* 4.590), betrays both uncertainty and a lack of concern about specific details ('and all the rest of it'). Vague references later in the novel to Carker's 'bundle of papers in his hand' (chapters 13 and 23) underscore this imprecision. John Butt and Kathleen Tillotson have observed that this vagueness may reflect a sudden change of plans as Dickens began to place more emphasis on the domestic drama than on the business dealings (Russell, 1986, 199–200).

Family-run businesses such as Dombey's firm were likely to be deemed sound and respectable in nineteenth-century England. Some companies even falsely acquired a family name to gain market respectability and to distinguish themselves from the kind of concern run by shady entrepreneurs from uncertain backgrounds (represented in fiction by such characters as Merdle in *LD* and Melmotte in Trollope's *The Way We Live Now*) (Nenadic 86–91).

that social contract of matrimony: almost necessarily part of a genteel and wealthy station, even without reference to the perpetuation of family firms:]

> A notorious characteristic of English society is the universal marketing of our unmarried women: a marketing peculiar to ourselves in Europe, and only rivalled by the slave merchants of the East. We are a match-making nation; the lively novels of Mrs. Gore have given a just and unexaggerated picture of the intrigues, the manoeuvres, the plotting, and the counterplotting that make the staple of matronly ambition. … Our young men, possessing rather passion than sentiment, form these *liaisons,* which are the substitute of love. … We never go into a ball-room without feeling that we breathe the air of diplomacy. … What schemes and ambushes in every word. … The custom of open match-making is productive of many consequences not sufficiently noticed; in the first place, it encourages the spirit of insincerity among all women, "Mothers and Daughters," – a spirit that consists in perpetual scheming, and perpetual hypocrisy; it lowers the chivalric estimate of women, and damps with eternal suspicion the youthful tendency to lofty and honest love. In the next place, it assists to render the tone of society dull, low, and unintellectual; it is not talent, it is not virtue, it is not even the graces and fascination of manner that are sought by the fair dispensers of social reputation; no, it is the title and the rent-roll. You do not lavish your attentions on the most agreeable member of a family, but on the richest. … Thus society is crowded with the insipid and beset with the insincere. (Bulwer-Lytton, 1833, 188–9)

As Thackeray bluntly observed in *The Newcomes* (1853–5): 'Women sell themselves for what you call an establishment every day, to the applause of themselves, their parents and their world' (ch. 26). Alienation between husband and wife, and father and child, was a common theme in representations of merchants and financiers in mid-nineteenth century novels. In Catherine Gore's *The Banker's Wife* (1843), for instance, the narrator says of the banker Hamlyn,

> His wife knew him to be averse to all display of sensibility; his children were early taught that he detested noise; and the banker's house was, consequently, characterised by the silence, coldness and dullness of the Great Pyramid. (1.2; qtd. in Russell, 1986, 78)

And, of course, in Dickens's own novel *HT* (1854), Mrs Gradgrind, and her daughter, Louisa, pay a psychological price for being alienated from their cold-natured husband and father.

– *To speak of; none worth mentioning.*

In the capital of the House's name and dignity, such a child was merely a piece of base coin that couldn't be invested – a bad Boy – nothing more.] A 'Boy' is presumably a 'yellow-boy', a slang term for a guinea. Hence, a 'bad Boy' is a counterfeit guinea (from 1717, a guinea was worth one pound and one shilling).

Mr. Dombey's cup of satisfaction

Mr. Dombey's cup of satisfaction was so full] From Psalms 23: 'The Lord is my shepherd; I shall not want. ... my cup runneth over.'

The child glanced keenly at

stiff white cravat,] The white cravat, a long, starched neckcloth of lawn, muslin or silk wrapped around the neck with a bow tied in front, went out of fashion with George IV, who discarded it in favour of a black neckcloth for daytime wear. In 1837 the *Gentlemen's Magazine of Fashion* noted that the white cravat was 'effeminate, old-fashioned, and unbecoming', though *de rigueur* for formal evening wear. Mr Barnacle wears a white cravat in *LD* (1.10) (Cunnington, 1966, 138).

her eyes returned to her mother's face immediately, and she neither moved nor answered.] The MS, which continues at this point, adds characterization to Mr Dombey and his view of his first wife: ' "Her insensibility is as proof against a brother as against everything else," said Mr. Dombey to himself. And he seemed so confirmed in a previous opinion by the discovery, as to be quite glad of it'.

"Blockitt, Sir?" suggested the nurse,

the nurse, a simpering piece of faded gentility,] Probably a permanent nurse because she is genteel (cf. Mrs Gamp in *MC*, who is a monthly nurse). The upper nursemaid, who was usually assisted by under nursery-maids, had charge of the nursery. The duties of the upper nursemaid

> commence with the weaning of the child: it must now be separated from the mother or wet-nurse, at least for a time, and the cares of the nursemaid, which have hitherto been only occasionally put in requisition, are now to be entirely devoted to the infant. She washes, dresses, and feeds it; walks out with it, and regulates all its little wants; and, even at this early age, many good qualities are required to do so in a satisfactory manner. Patience and good temper are indispensable qualities; truthfulness, purity of manners, minute cleanliness, and docility and obedience, almost equally so. She ought to be

acquainted with the art of ironing and trimming little caps, and be handy with her needle. (Beeton, 1861, 1013)

Doctor Parker Peps, one of the

one of the Court Physicians, and a man of immense reputation for assisting at the increase of great families, was walking up and down the drawing-room … to the unspeakable admiration of the family Surgeon,] Physicians, especially London physicians, were at the top of the medical profession. The prestige of a university education helped distinguish them from surgeons, for only physicians were required to have a university degree to gain membership of the Royal College of Physicians (members of the Royal College of Surgeons did not need to be graduates). Moreover, physicians, who largely specialised in internal ailments, possessed a theoretical knowledge of medicine which enabled them to diagnose on the basis of close observation. This contrasted with the practical craftsmanship of surgeons, who set bones, treated wounds, amputated limbs and generally confined their work to the outside of the body. Physicians – who, in general, treated only the aristocracy, gentry and upper and middle class – commanded an annual salary of between £800 and £3,000 (in London), with a few earning as much as £10,000. Polished manners and good conversation were necessary if they were to ingratiate themselves with their genteel patrons (Peterson; Digby, 1994, 170–96).

The cachet and character of a 'fashionable physician' are described by R. H. Horne in *Heads of the People* (1840):

> None of the *haut-ton* could be sick without his advice; no sick personage could die happy without his assistance. In short, there were no bounds to the mental satisfaction and substantial "relief" which the aristocracy and rich gentry experienced from paying a series of fees to Sir Courtney Palmoile – the most fashionable physician of his day. … A Fashionable Physician seldom loses the sense of his own dignity, through any inadvertent act of private good feeling. He would see any friend die before him rather than condescend to bleed him with his own hands – for that is expressly the business of a mere surgeon – and these kinds of things are never to be thought of for a moment by a "pure physician!" ('The Fashionable Physician' 63)

"Well Sir," said Doctor Parker Peps

muffled for the occasion, like the knocker;] 'No genteel lady was ever yet confined – indeed, no genteel confinement can possibly take place – without the accompanying symbol of a muffled knocker' (*NN*, ch. 4).

"Good! We must not disguise

there is a want of power in … your amiable lady. … a certain degree of languor, and a general absence of elasticity … the system of our patient has sustained a shock,] Women at the time were expected to suffer from 'nervous shock' immediately after childbirth:

> The sudden alteration of the eye, the diminished or increased sensibility of the brain, the disturbance of the respiratory and circulating systems, the modified secretions, the great exhaustion, &c. are all evidences of a shock to the nervous system, the effects of which are extensively felt. After easy labors the shock is not very remarkable, and the patient soon recovers from it … if the patient be kept free from all excitement and disturbance, and obtain a few hours' sleep. (Churchill, 1857, 555–6)

In rare instances, however, the 'nervous shock' could be

> very severe. In these cases the patient complains of great exhaustion; the senses are either unnaturally dull, or morbidly acute, the breathing is hurried and panting, and the accordance between the respiration and circulation is broken. The aspect of the patient is that of a person in a state of collapse. The countenance is expressive of suffering, anxiety, and oppression. The pulse may be either very slow and labored, or unusually rapid, very small, and fluttering.

Although the patient would usually 'recover from this state of exhaustion or collapse', death would occasionally occur 'in a few hours', if the shock was extreme, even though a post-mortem examination commonly failed to reveal any sign of 'injury or disease'. The only treatments recommended for patients suffering from severe nervous shock were opium (to help the patient rest) and, conversely, moderate quantities of stimulants, such as wine or brandy and water, or ammonia and musk (the latter 'medical' stimulants supposedly worked well with the opium).

Mrs Dombey's symptoms, it should be noted, do not accord with those of what was originally known as 'childbed fever' but was given the name (in 1716) 'puerperal fever', which was 'distinguished by frequency of pulse, oppression, sickness, and headache, by want of sleep, sometimes with delirium; by pain in the belly' (Macaulay, *A Dictionary of Medicine: designed for popular use*, 1831, 454–6).

"So very numerous," murmured the family practitioner

Doctor Parker Peps's West End practice – "] The wealthiest doctors in London practised and lived in the fashionable district of the West End, along with the 'urban gentry' of merchants, lawyers and other professionals. From about 1845, the address most associated with elite London physicians has been Harley Street. (For the location of Mr Dombey's house in the West End, see note to chapter 3, p. 46.)

"Oh!" murmured the family practitioner.

" 'Praise from Sir Hubert Stanley!' "] 'Approbation from Sir Hubert Stanley is praise indeed' (5. 2.151–2), a once-famous quotation from Thomas Morton's comedy, *Cure for the Heartache* (1797). Morton also wrote the successful comedies *The Way to Get Married* (1796) and *Speed the Plough* (1798), which introduced 'Mrs. Grundy' and the idea of Grundyism or extreme moral rectitude.

"You are good enough," returned

our interesting friend] 'To be in an interesting condition' and 'to be interesting' means to be pregnant. An 'interesting event' denotes a birth (*OED*).

"My dear Paul," said Louisa

my very particular friend] 'Closely acquainted, familiar, intimate'. The *OED* cites this example.

The lady thus specially presented

looking at the speakers as if she were mentally engaged in taking off impressions of their images upon her soul,] Presumably an allusion to what was facetiously called 'sitting for your portrait', the practice of prison turnkeys who carefully scrutinized the features of new prisoners to distinguish them from visitors. Mr Pickwick is subjected to the procedure on entering the Fleet (a scene illustrated by Browne in chapter 40). In *BH* the detective inspector Mr Bucket 'looks at Mr. Snagsby as if he were going to take his portrait' (22), and in *LD* the 'demeanour' of Mr Pancks suggests to Amy Dorrit that 'he might be a taker of likenesses, so intently did he look at her' (1.24). In the *HW* article 'A Detective Police Party', Dickens describes how he himself was carefully scrutinized when he first met Mr Bucket's original, Inspector Charles Field, and his fellow detectives:

> Every man of them, in a glance, immediately takes an inventory of the furniture and an accurate sketch of the editorial presence. The Editor feels that any gentleman in company could take him up, if need should be, without the smallest hesitation, twenty years hence. (l.409–10)

Miss Tox's dress, though perfectly

tuckers,] Frills of lace worn around the neck (*OED*).

tippets ... which stood on end in a rampant manner, and were not at all sleek.] A fur or woolen cape or short cloak that covered the shoulders, or the neck and shoulders, often with hanging ends. The *OED* cites this example.

the barrenest of lockets, representing a fishey old eye, with no approach to speculation in it.] In other words, sightless and dead. Macbeth entreats Banquo's Ghost to

> Avaunt, and quit my sight! Let the earth hide thee.
> Thy bones are marrowless; thy blood is cold;
> Thou hast no speculation in those eyes
> Which thou dost glare with. (3.4.113–16)

"Miss Tox, Paul," pursued

a little gift for Fanny ... a pincushion for the toilette table ... I call 'Welcome little Dombey' Poetry, myself."] In 1846, *Punch* remarked on the fashion for decorative pincushions 'whereon were writ the time-old syllables of love and hope – "Welcome, little stranger!" ' ('Mrs. Bib's Baby' 10.53); in 1865, *London Magazine* referred to 'the WELCOME BABY pincushion' as one of the 'everlasting types of babydom. They turn up at the first appearance of little ladies and gentlemen with the regularity of a recurring decimal in life's numeration' ('The Conventionalities of Life' 7.147–8). In the first chapter of *DC*, Betsey Trotwood exclaims ' "Bless the Baby!" ', 'unconsciously quoting the second sentiment of the pincushion in the drawer upstairs'. Thomas Hood alludes to the practice in a letter: 'Our grandmothers worked their autographs in canvass samplers; and I have seen one wrought out with pins' heads on a huge white pincushion – as thus: "Welcome Sweet Babby. Mary Jones" ' (*Poems*, 1846, 150).

"But his deportment, my dear Louisa!"

No portrait that I have ever seen of any one has been half so replete with those qualities. Something so stately, you know: so uncompromising: so very wide across the chest: so upright! A pecuniary Duke of York,] Frederick, Duke of York and Albany (1763–1827), the second son of George III and Queen Charlotte, was notorious for being in debt. Dickens may have in mind the oil portrait of Frederick by Sir David Wilkie (1822–3), in the National Portrait Gallery, though he was probably also aware of the caricatures of the Duke of York by James Gillray and the satirical verses by 'Peter Pindar' (the pseudonym of John Wolcot). By the time he was 24, Frederick's drinking, gambling and association with his brother, the Prince of Wales (later George IV), led him to amass debts that 'were enormous for one so young and inexperienced'. At the time of his wedding, in 1792, he had a debt of £20,000 (Percy, 1882, 2.104, 106). Critics facetiously claimed that his monument, in Waterloo Place, was high enough to keep the Duke out of the range of his creditors. At his death in 1827, the Duke of York was in debt for £2,000,000. Frederick was also a striking failure as a military leader. As the commander of an English contingent of soldiers dispatched to Flanders in 1793, he was defeated by the French army at Tourney. In 1799, his troops in Holland were forced into a humiliating withdrawal and had to give up their prisoners. In 1809, he was dismissed from his post as commander-in-chief on account of having been caught in a scandal with Mary Anne Clarke, who used her intimacy with him to sell army commissions.

Chapter 2

IN WHICH TIMELY PROVISION IS MADE FOR AN EMERGENCY THAT WILL SOMETIMES ARISE IN THE BEST REGULATED FAMILIES

Mrs. Chick made this impressive

Mantua Makers] Milliners and dressmakers. Ladies would visit the mantua-maker in her shop, or the mantua-maker would come to the house. The importance of having stylish mourning is explained in *Fanny Parkinson or, My Brother's Funeral*:

> "My dear friend," said she, "Mrs. Goodprice has sent you at my request, two pieces of bombazine, that you may choose for yourself. – One is more of a jet black than the other – but I think the blue black rather the finest. However, they are both of superb quality, and this season jet black is rather the most fashionable. I have been to Miss Lacings', the mantuamaker, who is famous for mourning. Bombazines, when made up by her, have an air and a style about them, such as you will never see if done by any one else. There is nothing more difficult than to make up mourning as it ought to be. (de Courcy, 1840, 3.46)

Don't you over-exert yourself, Loo,"

Right tol loor rul!] 'Too rul loo rul, loo rul loo rul' was a favourite refrain of comic songs. In *LD*, Mr Meagles notes that Cavalletto's name 'sounds like the chorus to a comic song' ('Caval-looro'), and in *GE*, Biddy pays a halfpence for a comic song having the lines

> When I went to Lunnon town sirs,
> Too rul loo rul
> Wasn't I done very brown sirs,
> Too rul loo rul
> Too rul loo rul.

Mr. Chick invaded the grave silence

the singularly inappropriate air of 'A cobbler there was;'] A popular comic song in seven stanzas which was published in many collections. It describes the perils of falling in love, as illustrated by a cobbler who kills himself because of his unrequited love for a coquette:

> A cobbler there was, and he lived in a stall,
> Which served him for parlour, for kitchen, and hall.
> No coin in his pocket, no care in his pate,
> No ambition had he, nor duns at his gate:
> Derry down, down, down, deny down. [st. 1]
>   (Lamb, 1825, 440)

Mayhew cites 'A Cobbler there was and he lived in a stall ... ' as typifying the songs sung by the street ballad singers of the mid-nineteenth century (1.275).

"Which might be better improved,

Mr. C.," retorted his helpmate,] On the subject of 'How Wives Should Speak of their Husbands, and Husbands of their Wives, etc.', Emily Thornwell's *Lady's Guide to Perfect Gentility* (1856) advises: 'Never use the initial of a person's name to designate him; as "Mr. P.,", "Mr. L.," etc. Nothing is so odious as to hear a lady speak of her husband, or, indeed, any one else, as "Mr. B" ' (151).

the college hornpipe,] Also known as 'the sailor's hornpipe', this was the tune for a 'well-known and spirited' English dance, 'in two sections of 8 bars, each ending with three beats of the foot'. Hornpipe dances, many of which date from the eighteenth century, were performed on the popular stage, and at feasts and wakes and on Saturday nights at village ale-houses (Grove, 1880, 1.753; Emmerson 12). In *DC*, 'To make his example the more impressive, Mr Micawber drank a glass of punch with an air of great enjoyment and satisfaction, and whistled the College Hornpipe' (ch. 12). As a young boy, Dickens was taught to dance hornpipes 'as an accomplishment in great social demand in after-life', by 'a fat little dancing-master', at Wellington House Classical and Commercial Academy ('Our School' 4.51).

rump-te-iddity, bow-wow-wow!"] These two popular refrains appeared in numerous songs and ballads. For example, 'rump-te-iddity iddity, &c.' occurs in 'The Stranger Travestie'; 'King Dick'; 'Holiday Time'; 'The Jubilee'; 'Macbeth'; 'The Ghosts'; and many other titles. 'Bow, wow, wow' was both a familiar air and a refrain (with several variants) in songs such as 'Day and Night Scenes'; 'Mister Manager Stiffdick'; 'Tippling Deities'; 'Guy Faux'; and 'The Chapter on Dogs' (Fairburn, 1826, *passim*).

"It would have occurred to most men,"

it becomes necessary to provide a Nurse."] Scientific evidence from the mid-nineteenth century suggests that it was dangerous to 'dry' nurse a baby (i.e. without benefit of the mother's breast) but that it was also dangerous to 'wet' nurse the baby if the nurse was not the natural mother.

Physicians worried that wet nurses such as Polly Toodle were possible sources of syphilic infection, and social reformers complained that wet nursing allowed the wealthy to prey on the poor. When wet nursing became a necessity, as in the case of the death of the mother, wealthy families made efforts to ensure the health of the wet nurse and provide her with a safe and secure environment.

Because of the importance of wet nurses, and the dangers attendant upon unhealthy ones, wet nurses for the wealthy commanded a good wage, up to £50 a year. Significantly, Mrs Chick gives 'a close private examination of Polly, her children, her marriage certificate, testimonials, and so forth', in order to give her a clean bill of health. Miss Tox is careful to establish that Polly is a married woman and that her name comes from a list at Queen Charlotte's Lying-in Hospital (i.e. she had not given birth to illegitimate children); that she maintains a clean and orderly household, and thus is presumably 'clean' or disease-free herself; and that the blister on the nose of the eldest child is not 'constitutional' (perhaps not syphilic) but accidental, the result of a warm iron.

It is notable, as well, that Polly needs to be isolated from her family once she becomes young Paul's wet nurse. A manual of diet describes the fears surrounding 'poor married' wet nurses:

> A poor married woman, however respectable, is removed from a starving home to sudden abundance, and invariably over-eats herself and it is fortunate if she does not over-drink herself too. She pines and grows anxious about her own child if it is alive, and insists upon having her troublesome husband to see her openly or secretly, on the pretence (a fallacious one) that his visit increases the flow of milk. Moreover, a rich mother cannot but feel some compunction in purchasing for her own offspring what is stolen from another, who is sometimes seriously affected by the fraud, and retires disgusted from this false world. (Chambers, 1876, 143)

In fact, although Dombey worries that Polly might switch infants, his real worry may be that she will nurse her own infant while nursing young Paul, thus potentially spreading infection to Dombey's son (Wiley 217–28). Dickens and Catherine relied on wet nurses after the births of the first and fifth children. Mothers who breast-feed in Dickens's novels include Clara Copperfield and Mrs Micawber. The obdurate Mrs Joe prefers to bottle-feed Pip, who is 'brought up by hand' (*GE* 2).

Running down stairs again

the hackney coach,] A four-wheeled public coach for hire at an appointed stand. It was both popular and relatively cheap and would typically carry three passengers, two inside and another on the box seat. The coachman rode on a nearside horse or, in some cases, on the box seat. Although over 200 hackney-coaches were licensed in London in 1814, by the 1830s the coaches had been superseded, and by 1840 there only remained a few old men with old horses and old coaches. By 1850, according to Mayhew, not one hackney-coach was to be seen in the streets of London (3.347–9).

Nineteenth-century hackney-coaches, frequently the discarded coaches of the nobility, were often shabby and dirty and bore the faded coats of arms of the nobility on their doors. In 'Hackney Coach Stands', Dickens describes a class of hackney-coaches particular to London:

> a great, lumbering, square concern of a dingy yellow colour (like a bilious brunette), with very small glasses, but very large frames; the panels are ornamented with a faded coat of arms, in shape something like a dissected bat, the axletree is red, and the majority of the wheels are green. The box is partially covered by an old great-coat, with a multiplicity of capes, and some extraordinary-looking clothes; and the straw, with which the canvas cushion is stuffed, is sticking up in several places, as if in rivalry of the hay, which is peeping through the chinks in the boot. The horses, with drooping heads, and each with a mane and tail as scanty and straggling as those of a worn-out rocking-horse, are standing patiently on some damp straw, occasionally wincing, and rattling the harness; and now and then, one of them lifts his mouth to the ear of his companion, as if he were saying, in a whisper, that he should like to assassinate the coachman. (*SB*)

"My dear Louisa," said Miss

the Queen Charlotte's Royal Married Females,] Queen Charlotte's Lying-in Hospital was founded in 1752 as the General Lying-in Hospital. After several name changes and relocations, the hospital came under the patronage of Queen Charlotte in 1804 and, in 1813, moved to Old Manor House, Lisson Green (now the Marylebone Road), and thus would have been in the vicinity of Dombey's house in Marylebone during the time frame of the novel, the 1830s and early 1840s. The stated purpose of the hospital was 'to afford an asylum for indigent females during the awful period of childbirth and also to facilitate the repentence of suffering and contrite sinners' (Weinreb and Hibbert, 1993, 646). *The Picture of London* (1802) remarked that such lying-in hospitals provided 'wealthy females' with a 'constant supply of healthy wet-nurses … on application being made to the physician or matron' (208; qtd. in Sanders 960).

"Not at all," returned Miss

(the cleanest place, my dear! You might eat your dinner off the floor),] The connection between housekeeping and morality was a Victorian commonplace. In a passage that was frequently quoted in the nineteenth century, Dr Thomas Southwood Smith expressed confidence that

> A clean, fresh, and well-ordered house exercises over its inmates a moral, no less than a physical influence, and has a direct tendency to make the members of the family sober, peaceable, and considerate of the feelings and happiness of each other. Nor is it difficult to trace a connection between habitual feelings of this sort and the formation of habits of respect for property, for the laws in general, and even for those higher duties and obligations, the observance of which no laws can enforce. (qtd. in Johnson, 1847, 210)

Dickens himself highly valued cleanliness and order. Rather unusually for a mid-Victorian man, he would bathe (or shower) every morning. And before he began to work, he was obsessive about the arrangement of chairs, tables and the items on his writing desk. He was equally vexed by the sloppiness of others, placing notes about untidiness on his daughters' pincushions. Even on holidays by the sea, Dickens explained to a friend, 'Nothing is allowed to be out of its place. Each [boy] in his turn is appointed Keeper for the week, and I go out in solemn procession … three times a day, on a tour of inspection'. He also regularly straightened up after his friends (Collins, 1964, 49; *Letters* 8.145–6).

In *OMF*, Eugene Wrayburn is ironic about the association between cleanliness and morality. He tells Mortimer Lightwood that

> its [a 'very complete little kitchen'] moral influence is the important thing. … See! … miniature flour barrel, rolling-pin, spice-box, shelf of brown jars, chopping-board, coffee-mill, dresser elegantly furnished with crockery, saucepans and pans, roasting jack, a charming kettle, an armoury of dish-covers. The moral influence of these objects, in forming the domestic virtues, may have an immense influence upon me. … In fact, I have an idea that I feel the domestic virtues already forming. (2.6)

"Oh yes," said Miss Tox.

a warm flat iron.] The most widely-used iron, the flat iron (also known as the 'sad iron') varied in size 'from four to nine or ten inches'. Its body was made 'of cast iron, ground smooth at the bottom, and the handle of wrought iron, turned round so as to be hollow.' Irons would generally be heated on detached ironing stoves in the laundry room, or by placing them on a moveable iron shelf hung on the bars of a fireplace grate or in a wall recess, 'like a small chimney, with a hot place and furnace below it' and a flue above, 'to carry out the hot air and prevent it incommoding the laundry'. Large irons retained heat better than small ones (Webster and Parkes, 1855, 1061, 1065).

"Stoker," said the man.

"Stoker ... Steaminjin."] Stokers tended the fire of the boiler of a steam engine. The position is an advance over cleaners (hired to prepared locomotives for service) and represents the first in a series of promotions: 'From cleaner to stoker, from stoker to driver, is the scale which must be ascended by those who aspire to the dignity of driving a locomotive' (*HW* 15.603). Mr Toodle follows this path, rising to an 'Engine Fireman' (ch. 15), the second crew member on a steam locomotive. For more on 'fireman', see note to chapter 15, p. 211.

"Oh! Pretty well, Mum.

The ashes sometimes gets in here;" touching his chest] In 1853, the Actuary of the National Debt Office remarked, 'liability to sickness among persons employed on railways is very great', a fact borne out by statistical tables for 'Members of Friendly Societies'. Although exact numbers should be treated with scepticism, Table XXVI ('Percentage of sick Members of Friendly Societies') shows that, up until the age of forty, railwaymen were more likely to get sick than the average of those men in other dangerous occupations, such as mariners, colliers, miners, painters and police ('Report and Tables by Actuary of National Debt Office on Sickness and Mortality among members of Friendly Societies', 1853, qtd. in Kingsford, 1970, 49–51). Exposure to ashes was apparently such a concern that, according to a source from 1861, 'railway guards, engine-drivers, etc.' had, 'a few years ago – before the fashion became so universal', begun to sport beards and moustaches, to prevent 'the inhalation of the deleterious particles in the air', the 'minute particles of dust, ashes, and carbonaceous matter' to which they were 'constantly' exposed (Adams 159).

"Miss Tox seemed to be so little

entering into a close private examination of Polly, her children, her marriage certificate, testimonials, and so forth.] It was thought best to leave the physical examination of the wet-nurse to a medical practitioner, and the examination of her 'moral' qualities to the parents and close relations. In his *The Maternal Management of Children* (1853), Thomas Bull MD recommended that the following physical traits be considered: 'the general health of the woman: next, the condition of her breast,

– the quality of her milk – its age and her own; whether she is ever unwell while nursing; and, last of all, the condition and health of the child' (64). She should have 'a robust constitution, free from all suspicion of a strumous [scrofulous] character or any hereditary taint'. She should have a 'firm and well formed' breast with a moderately-sized nipple that is 'well developed' and, if the infant to be nursed is newly born, she should have recently delivered a child (which makes her milk more thin and watery, which was recommended). She also should be in her twenties, and have 'one or two children' of her own, 'as she will be likely to have more milk, and may also be supposed to have acquired some experience in the management of infants'. As well, her own newly-born infant should look healthy and seem well-nourished.

Among the moral qualities demanded of a wet-nurse were 'Temperance, cleanliness, a character for good conduct, fondness for children, and aptness in their management', and it was thought that she should possess 'An amiable disposition and cheerful temper' (Bull 64–7). *Domestic Duties; or, Instructions to Young Married Ladies* (1829) recommended that the wet-nurse should have a kind heart, as well as be clean, honest, steady and proper. And 'She ought not to be fond of visiting, and should content herself with such portions of time for relaxation as may be convenient to her mistress, and compatible with the duties of a nursery' (Parkes 142–5).

Besides breast-feeding the infant, the monthly nurse-maid had various duties: 'Day and night she has the care of, and is the companion of, the little ones. She looks after their persons, food, clothing, and apartments, – their amusements, exercise, and rest, – and she must necessarily, more or less, have to do with the formation of their moral character' (Bull 314).

"Oh, of course," said Mr. Dombey.

"I desire to make it a question of wages, altogether. … When you go away from here, you will have concluded what is a mere matter of bargain and sale, hiring and letting: and will stay away. The child will cease to remember you; and you will cease, if you please, to remember the child."] This passage illustrates Carlyle's complaint in *Past and Present* (1843) that 'We have profoundly forgotten everywhere that *Cash-payment* is not the sole relation of human beings; we think, nothing doubting, that *it* absolves and liquidates all engagements of man' (3.2).

Thus arrested on the threshold

the stimulating action of golden shower-baths.] The phrase 'golden shower' denotes a sudden acquisition of wealth: e.g. 'So universally indeed is gold disseminated over the central parts of the Brazils, that a golden shower … might be supposed to have fallen upon them' ('Travels in South America', *The Quarterly Review*, 1825, 32.134). The image derives from the Greek myth of Danae, whom Zeus seduces by transforming himself into a shower of gold coins. In middle-class Victorian houses, shower baths were located in the bedroom or dressing room:

The water is forced up into a cistern, with a perforated bottom, by a syringe, and the bather, by pulling a string, opens a valve, which causes the water to descend suddenly in a shower on his head and body through the perforated bottom. ... The whole is made of tin plate painted, one of the upright supports being hollow, to allow the ascent of the water. The usual price is from £3 to £5. (Webster and Parkes, 1855, 1192–3)

A popular treatment at water-cure establishments, shower baths were widely recommended for general well-being:

> To persons in good health, as well as to the apoplectic and the dyspeptic, the shower-bath offers incalculable benefits. It regulates the action of the stomach and bowels, keeps the body in a pleasant glow in winter, and imparts to it a refreshing coolness in sultry weather; it gives appetite, facilitates digestion, quiets the nerves, and produces a placidity of mind which can exist only under the most perfect action of the animal functions. (*The Magazine of Domestic Economy*, 1837, 2.146)

"Can you read?" asked Mr. Dombey.

"Can you read?" asked Mr. Dombey. "Why, not partick'ler Sir." "Write?" "With chalk, Sir?"] Relatively soon after the introduction of the railway, employees were required to be able to read and write because they had to use printed timetables and instructions and also because literacy was considered a mark of character and discipline (Mitch, 1992, 15, 16, 247). Mr Toodle's desire to better himself seems clear when he tells Mr Dombey that he plans to have one of his children teach him to read and write. When Toodle next meets Mr Dombey, several years have passed, and he says with pride, ' "in the matter o readin' ... them boys o' mine, they learned me, among 'em, arter all. They've made a wery tolerable scholar of me, Sir, them boys" ' (ch. 20). Between 1841 and 1851, relatively few jobs (5%) required male workers to be literate. A Parliamentary report in 1854 claimed that illiteracy prevented many working men from being promoted in occupations which gave opportunity for advancement.

"Mostly underground Sir, 'till I got

when they comes into full play."] The MS continues at this point:

> As he added in one of his hoarse whispers, "We means to bring up little Biler to that line," Mr. Dombey inquired haughtily who little Biler was.
> "The eldest on 'em, Sir," said Toodle, with a smile. "It ain't a common name. Sermuchser that when he was took to church the gen'lm'n said, it warn't a chris'en one, and he couldn't give it. But we always calls him Biler

just the same. For we don't mean no harm. Not we."

"Do you mean to say, Man," inquired Mr. Dombey; looking at him with marked displeasure, "that you have called a child after a boiler?"

"No no Sir," returned Toodle, with a tender consideration for his mistake. "I should hope not! No Sir. Arter a BILER Sir. The Steaminjin was a'most as good as a godfather to him, and so we called him Biler, don't you see!"

Alan Horsman remarks of this deletion, which is in Forster's handwriting:

> [This passage makes] a contrast between Mr. Dombey and Toodle as fathers. Like Mr. Dombey, Toodle has ambitions for his eldest son, but without any of the former's possessiveness and self-complacency. The naming of Biler from his future employment glances back to Mr. Dombey's concern with the connection between the signature of Paul Dombey Junior and the correspondence of the House ... but the important difference is that in Toodle's case the naming is out of gratitude – 'The Steaminjin was a'most as good as a godfather to him'. The cut eliminates this difference and with it some of the significance of Mr. Dombey's misplaced generosity when he comes to upset these plans by making the boy a Charitable Grinder. (Clarendon edn., xvi)

As the last straw breaks

As the last straw breaks the laden camel's back,] The idea goes back to at least 1655: 'It is the last feather may be said to break an Horse's back', as used by J. Bramhall, *Defence of True Liberty of Human Actions* 54 (*The Oxford Book of Idioms*; *The Oxford Dictionary of Proverbs*).

down the room in solitary wretchedness. For] The MS continues at this point:

> It would be harsh, and perhaps not altogether true, to say to him that he felt these rubs and gratings against his pride more keenly than he had felt his wife's death: but certainly they impressed that event upon him with new force, and communicated to it added weight and bitterness. It was a rude shock to his sense of property in his child, that these people – the mere dust of the earth, as he thought them – should be necessary to him; and it was natural that in proportion as he felt disturbed by it, he should deplore the occurrence which had made them so.
>
> Some philosophers tell us that selfishness is the root of all our best loves and affection. Mr. Dombey's infant child was from the beginning, so distinctly important to him as being a part of himself, or which was the same thing, of Dombey and Son, that there is no doubt his parental affection might have been easily traced, like many another superstructure of fair fame, to a very low foundation. But it is certain that there has begun to spring up in his habitually frigid breast, a current of anxieties and cares of which this infant

was the source, that impelled the dominant springs of his character to a new action, and perhaps set one or two others in motion, that had never yet been at work.

Horsman remarks of this deletion, which is in Forster's handwriting:

> To cut what Dickens had so specifically left in – Mr. Dombey's son 'was ... distinctly important to him as being a part of himself', with the generalization that follows from this – forfeits the point of Mr. Dombey's emotion here at the thought of the 'Poor little fellow', and leaves the fact that 'he pitied himself through the child' to be commented on as if it has been already established, when it has not. (Clarendon edn., xvi)

Dickens includes the first part of the second paragraph (from 'Some' to 'foundation') in chapter 8, with a few minor changes.

It may have been characteristic

an ignorant Hind] An old and somewhat dated term for a servant, especially, in later use, for a farm servant or agricultural labourer, with a transferred sense of a rustic or boor (*OED*).

Those words being on his lips,

Now, would it be possible for her to change them?] This worry draws on the changeling superstition. See note to chapter 8, p. 121.

Meanwhile terms were ratified and

Richards being with much ceremony invested with the Dombey baby, as if it were an Order,] An allusion to the honours bestowed by the monarch, such as the Order of the Bath, Order of the Garter, Order of Merit, Order of the Thistle, etc.

"Thank'ee, Mum," said Toodle,

"since you *are* suppressing."] Toodle's pronunciation of 'so pressing'.

Polly cried more than ever

matronly apprehensions that this indulgence in grief might be prejudicial to

the little Dombey ("acid, indeed," she whispered Miss Tox),] 'Everything which weakens the system in general, or the stomach in particular' was thought to be a cause of indigestion, including, grief and anxiety, which *Modern Domestic Medicine* (1827) cites as 'frequent and powerful causes' (Graham 356).

"As to living, Richards,

You will order your little dinner every day; and anything you take a fancy to, I'm sure will be as readily provided as if you were a Lady." ... **"And as to porter! – quite unlimited"** ... **"With a little abstinence ... in point of vegetables." "And pickles, perhaps,"**] This reflects the contemporary belief that 'women, when nursing, require to be much more highly fed than at other times'. *The Maternal Management of Children* recommended that the wet-nurse 'should have a wholesome mixed animal and vegetable diet, and a moderate quantity of malt liquor, *provided* it be found necessary'. It warned, however, against the excessive use of porter and pronounced 'other alcoholic stimulants unnecessary':

> a prevailing notion exists that porter tends to produce a great flow of milk. In consequence of this prejudice, the wet-nurse is often allowed as much as she likes; a large quantity is in this way taken, and after a short time so much febrile action is excited in the system, that instead of increasing the flow of milk, it diminishes it greatly. Sometimes, without diminishing the quantity, it imperceptibly but seriously deteriorates its quality. *As a general rule*, porter, wine, or any stimulant is quite as unnecessary for the wet-nurse as for the nursing mother, if she be in sound and vigorous health. There may be cases benefited by the moderate use of malt liquor, but these are the exceptions. If taken, three half-pint tumblers are as much as any nurse ought to be allowed. (Bull, 1853, 68–9)

Because porter could be produced in large quantities, it became a popular drink with the working class (its name derives from its popularity with river and street porters). In 1844, Andrew Ure observed that, whereas early in the century 'Good hard-beer was the boast of the day', 'Of late years the taste of the metropolis has undergone such a complete revolution ... that nothing but the mildest porter will now go down'. In Ure's view, 'the two greatest porter houses, Messrs. Barclay, Perkins, & Co., and Truman, Hanbury, & Co., have become extensive and successful brewers of mild ale, to please the changed palate of their consumers' (1.113). The *Book of English Trades* (1818) remarked, 'London porter is famous in almost all parts of the civilized world' (46).

Notwithstanding which, however, poor

(known in the family by the name of Biler, in remembrance of the steam engine)]

The cockney pronunciation of 'boiler', the large vessel in a steam-engine, usually made of wrought-iron plates riveted together, in which the water is converted into steam (*OED*). When the water in a boiler gets low, it has a tendency to become increasingly noisy.

A quantity of oranges and half-pence

oranges] Oranges used to be considered dessert fruits as well as 'an agreeable and wholesome article of diet', popular because of their healthy 'cooling' qualities, their relative invulnerability to insects, and their slowness to rot. In 1841, Charles Knight estimated that 'We now consume about two hundred and fifty millions of oranges every year' (132) (*Encyclopedia Britannica*, 11th ed.). Ten years later, Mayhew cited Board of Trade figures which put the number at two hundred million. About 25% of this amount was sold retail on the streets of London by an estimated 4,000 persons, mostly women and children (1.88).

to ride behind among the spikes] Spikes were put on the rear axle of hackney coaches to prevent small boys from stealing rides.

Chapter 3

IN WHICH MR. DOMBEY, AS A MAN AND A FATHER, IS SEEN AT THE HEAD OF THE HOME-DEPARTMENT

'A man and a father' alludes to 'Am I Not a Man and a Brother', the inscription on the anti-slavery medallion made by Josiah Wedgwood in 1787. Often called the 'Emancipation Badge', the white cameo in black relief, showing a kneeling black man in heavy chains, was used for snuff-box covers, buttons, rings, pins and other accessories. The Anti-Slavery Society adopted the medallion in 1823. 'The Home-Department' is a play on the government office responsible for domestic matters.

The funeral of the deceased lady

The funeral of the deceased lady having been "performed," to the entire satisfaction of the undertaker, as well as of the neighbourhood at large, which is generally disposed to be captious on such a point, and is prone to take offence at any omissions or short-comings in the ceremonies,]

It is within the last half century that prodigious funerals, awful hearses drawn by preternatural quadrupeds, clouds of black plumes, solid and magnificent oak coffins instead of the sepulchral elm, coffin within coffin, lead, brick graves, and capacious catacombs have spread downwards far beyond the select circle once privileged to illustrate the vanity of human greatness. (*The Times*, 2 February 1875)

Funeral processions would usually begin with hired mourners, or mutes, carrying funeral trappings. The hearse would follow, pulled by four to six black horses covered in black velvet and topped with plumes of black ostrich feathers. For those with social pretensions, coats-of-arms and other insignia would often be engraved on plates on the hearse. Behind the hearse came the coaches containing the mourners.

Funeral practices were much discussed in the 1840s, especially following the release of Edwin Chadwick's *Report on the Sanitary Conditions of the Labouring Population of Great Britain* and its supplementary report, *The Practice of Interment in Towns* (1843), with its sections on topics such as the 'Expenses of Funerals' and 'Want of Regulation at the Funerals in Crowded Districts'. Dickens himself conducted a lifelong campaign against ostentatious funerals (see *MC* 19, *BH* 53, *GE* 35, 'Trading in Death', *HW* 6.241–5 and his letters of 3 and 19 November 1852 to Miss Coutts, *Letters* 6.794–5, 805). In his Will, he 'emphatically' directed that he 'be buried in an inexpensive, unostentatious, and strictly private manner' with 'not more than three plain mourning coaches', and 'that those who attend ... wear no scarf, cloak, black bow, long hat-band, or other such revolting absurdity' (*Letters* 12, appendix K, 732).

Funeral expenses of the upper-middle-class ranged between £200 to £400, and for persons of 'rank and title' between £800 and £1500 (with children's funerals being less, in both cases). For more on mutes, see chapter 8, p. 124.

the footman] Mrs Beeton details the footman's varied tasks, including attending the mistress; waiting at table; cleaning knives and shoes, the furniture and plate; going out with the carriage; carrying messages or letters and running errands; and answering the bell. In fashionable families, he would often wear powder on his hair, in imitation of eighteenth-century custom. Although it was usual to hire footmen with an impressive stature and build, Mrs Beeton deplored the affectation of making the choice solely on the basis of a footman's 'height, shape and *tournure* of his calf'.

On Richards, who was established

Richards, who was established up-stairs in a state of honourable captivity,] In the words of *The Gentleman's House* (1865), 'the Servants' Department shall be separated from the Main House, so that what passes on either side of the boundary shall be both invisible and inaudible on the other' (67). The kitchen, scullery and the servants' offices and private rooms were for the servants only; the family bedrooms, dayrooms, and the study for family members only. The usual practice in 'superior' houses was to have the nursemaid 'established' on the first floor (the second floor in the U.S.) in the 'nurse's-room', near the nursery (Kerr 67, 145).

Mr. Dombey's house was a large one, on the shady side of a tall, dark, dreadfully genteel street in the region between Portland-place and Bryanstone-square.] Dombey's house is located in the fashionable West End. Most of this area of about 200 acres, bounded by Marylebone Road to the north and Oxford Street to the south, comprised the estate of the Portman family, who developed the land between the 1760s and 1820s. Transforming the landscape of Georgian London, the grand design established a grid of streets of large, elegant family mansions and spacious garden squares – Portman Square (1764), Manchester Square (1770), Bryanston Square and Montague Square (both *c*. 1810). The uniformity of building design, the street lay-out and the choice of architects were dictated by the estate, which then leased the land to private and speculative builders who provided the services.

Portland Place (which borders the Portman estate) was laid out by Robert and James Adam (*c*. 1778) and described as 'the finest street in London' by a fellow architect and contemporary, John Nash. With its great width and uninterrupted vista, Portland Place was 'in the highest fashion' when first built, and in the 1870s reminded Walter Thornbury of the 'broad boulevards of Paris' (Wheatley 108; Thornbury 4.450). The street is lined with stately houses having shallow fronts, recessed windows and fine ornamentation. By the late 1840s, Portland Place had lost its exclusivity, the nobility having abandoned the street to merchants and bankers.

Bryanstone (or Bryanston) Square was a much prized location: together with its companion, Montague Square, it was considered in 1833 one of the two 'best examples of well constructed town residences' (Thomas Smith, *A Topographical and Historical Account of the Parish of St Mary-le-Bone* 201). The tastefully planted squares, surrounded by iron railings, were designed to form pleasant promenades for the residents of the neighbouring mansions. Tastes changed, however, and by 1844 Charles Knight's *London* was more critical:

> Montague Square and Bryanstone Square are twin deformities, the former of which is placed immediately in the rear of Montague House. They are long narrow strips of ground, fenced in by two monotonous rows of flat houses. ... A range of balconies runs along the front of the houses in Bryanstone Square; but the inmates appear to entertain dismal apprehensions of the thievish propensities of their neighbours, for between every two balconies is introduced a terrible chevaux-de-frise. ... These two oblongs, though dignified with the name of squares, belong rather to the anomalous "places" which economical modern builders contrive to carve out of the corners of mews-lanes behind squares, and dispose with a profit to those who wish to live near the great. (6.202–03)

It was a corner house, with great wide areas containing cellars frowned upon by barred windows, and leered at by crooked-eyed doors leading to dustbins. It was a house of dismal state, with a circular back to it, containing a whole suite

of drawing-rooms looking upon a gravelled yard,] Most London terrace houses have areas – small, basement-level yards closed off from the pavement by railings and approached by a flight of steps. This entrance was used by servants and tradesmen. In 1853, a German visitor found the effect unusual:

> A London street is in a manner like a German high-road, which is skirted on either side with a deep ditch. In the streets of London the houses on either side rise out of deep side areas. These dry ditches are generally of the depth of from six to ten feet, and that part of the house, which with us would form the lower story, is here from ten to twelve feet underground. This moat is uncovered, but it is railed in, and the communication between the house door and the street is effected by a bridge neatly formed of masonry. (Schlesinger 3)

two gaunt trees, with blackened trunks and branches, rattled rather than rustled, their leaves were so smoke-dried.] Because coal, the fuel most widely burned in London since 1600, produced a greater quantity of soot and black smoke than any other fuel, it left a black pall over everything. Mayhew quotes an authority on air pollution who gave evidence to a parliamentary committee:

> On one occasion at the Horse Guards the amount of soot deposited was so great that it formed a complete and continuous film, so that when I walked upon it I saw the impression of my foot left as distinctly on that occasion as when the snow lies upon the ground. (2.341)

Cassell's Household Guide told gardeners that they must 'counteract the impurity of a town atmosphere by greater attention [than in the country] to the cleanliness' of their plants: 'At frequent intervals the soot and dust which are sure to settle more or less on the leaves should be entirely washed away, and the plants, if healthy, will immediately repay the attention by their fresh appearance and vigorous growth' (1.20).

water-carts] In order to keep down the dust on the main thoroughfares during the summer, horse-drawn carts released water from a perforated wooden tank or barrel mounted below the rear axle. The practice was so widespread that 'the enormous quantity of water annually poured on the roads of London', according to one observer, constituted 'an important drain upon the water supplied to the metropolis' (see the description of Mr Carker making his way along the 'over-watered road' in chapter 22) (Thomson and Smith, 1877; Ashton, 1906, 215).

the old clothes men, and the people with geraniums, and the umbrella mender, and the man who trilled the little bell of the Dutch clock as he went along.] The buying and selling of old clothes, a characteristically 'Jewish' trade in the early and mid-nineteenth century, was especially lucrative at a time when the urban poor could not afford new clothing. Mayhew estimated that at mid-century there were 500 to 600 Jewish old clothes sellers, though at one time the figure may have been as high as 1,000. The old clothes men would set out about eight in the morning from places like Portsoken Ward, Houndsditch, in the East End, shouting 'Clo! Clo!' as they progressed and bought used clothes from the wealthier population in the West End. In the afternoon, they trudged back to Rag Fair, an open-air market held daily in Rosemary Lane near Tower Hill, to dispose of their purchases to dealers, themselves predominantly Jewish. Most of the second-hand clothes shops run by Jews were located in Seven Dials, part of the parish of St Giles-in-the-Fields, in west-central London ('Seven Dials', *SB*; Mayhew 2.119–21; Endelman 178–83).

Geraniums, which sold in pots ranging in price from 3*d.* to 5*s.*, were one of the flowering plants sold by flower-root sellers at stalls and in barrows, from the end of May to July:

> To carry on his business efficiently, the root-seller mostly keeps a pony and a cart, to convey his purchases from the garden to his stall or his barrow, and he must have a sheltered and cool shed in which to deposit the flowers which are to be kept over-night for the morrow's business. (Mayhew 1.138)

Umbrella-menders – commonly known by the slang term 'mushroom-fakers' or its condensed form 'mushfakers' – were also a frequent London sight. According to Mayhew,

> Men, some tolerably well-dressed, some swarthy-looking, like gipsies, and some with a vagabond aspect, may be seen in all quarters of the town and suburbs, carrying a few ragged-looking umbrellas, or the sticks or ribs of umbrellas, under their arms, and crying "Umbrellas to mend," or "Any old umbrellas to sell?" The traffickers in umbrellas are also the crockmen, who are always glad to obtain them in barter, and who merely dispose of them at the Old Clothes Exchange, or in Petticoat Lane.

Mayhew categorized umbrella-menders as street artisans who would repair any umbrella on the owner's premises, remarking that 'So far there is no traffic in the business, the mushroomfaker simply performing a piece of handicraft, and being paid for the job' (2.115).

German or 'Dutch' clocks (a corruption of *Deutsch*) were invented by Christiaan Huygens in 1656. They were cheap wooden clocks, either free-standing or wall-mounted, with brass wheels, a pendulum and a painted face. Many also had wooden figures that darted inside and shut a door when the hour struck (*OCS* 48). With the lowering of import duties on foreign goods, the popularity of Dutch clocks rose in the 1820s. Second-hand Dutch clocks were hawked in the streets, usually by Dutchmen or Germans and, according to a contemporary, the presence of this type of street-seller often indicated 'prosperity and personal respectability on the part of the working man' (Mayhew 2.23; Porter, 1847, 533).

the bands of music and the straggling Punch's shows going after it, left it a prey to the most dismal of organs, and white mice; with now and then a porcupine, to vary the entertainments;] The Punch and Judy show featured Punch (originally

'Pollicinella' or 'Punchinello'), a fat hunchback with a shrill voice, and his shrewish wife Judy (or Joan). Shows invariably depicted the conflict between Punch and Judy, and frequently the Devil. In a typical plot, Punch becomes angry and kills his own baby, fights with his wife and kills her, kills a number of other characters, attacks a policeman, and tricks the hangman into hanging himself rather than Punch. The show ends with Punch killing the Devil.

Barrel-organs were so common on the London streets in the mid-nineteenth century that they constituted a public nuisance. In 1826, Prince Pückler-Muskau remarked that London barrel-organs 'resound day and night in every street, and are at other times insufferable' (85). The 'white mice' allude to another source of concern for the mid-Victorian public: young Italian boys forced to beg on the streets by their masters. The boys would rent 'fancy' mice in boxes for 1*s* 6*d* a day (and sometimes monkeys, squirrels, dogs, tortoises and even porcupines) which would 'dance' and perform tricks. By the 1830s, the boys began to rent barrel-organs, either plain or with waltzing figures, and began to earn as much as six or seven shillings a day. An 'Exhibitor of Birds and Mice' remarked that 'my mice fetch and carry, like dogs; and three of the little things dance the tight-rope on their hind legs, with balance-poles in their mouths' (Mayhew 3.174–5, 220). In April 1846, Dickens informed a correspondent that 'I talk to all the Italian Boys who go about the streets with Organs and white mice, and give them mints of money per l'amore della bell'Italia' (*Letters* 4.535; Grant 232–4; Zucchi 76–110). For more on street musicians, see notes to chapter 23 and chapter 31, pp. 227, 336.

the lamplighter made his nightly failure in attempting to brighten up the street with gas.] The lamplighter made his rounds at dusk, using a pole with a small oil-lamp at the top to turn on the gas in the lantern. He would then ignite the gas with a small burst of flame from the oil-lamp. Gas lighting was first tried experimentally in London in 1807 and began generally in 1814, following the establishment of the Gas Light and Coke Company in 1810–12. Because the gas companies piped in an inferior, adulterated gas that did not burn cleanly, gas lamps in many areas only had the illuminating power of 14 to 16 candles, though most produced the power of 23 candles. And, before the use of 'Governors' or regulators, gas pressure varied: if the jet was ignited during a period of low pressure, the tap had to be almost completely open to achieve a tolerable flame (Flanders, 2003, 208).

It was as blank a house

the neighbouring mews,]

> The mews of London … constitute a world of their own. They are tenanted by one class – coachmen and grooms, with their wives and families – men who are devoted to one pursuit, the care of horses and carriages; who live and associate one among another; whose talk is of horses. (Mayhew 2.208)

some fragments of the straw that had been strewn before the house when she was ill,] Straw was used to deaden the noise of passing vehicles.

The apartments which Mr. Dombey

the smell of hot-pressed paper,] Servants would iron the newspaper in order to dry the ink and prevent it from smudging before delivering the paper to the master of the house.

"My darling," said Richards, "you wear

you wear that pretty black frock in remembrance of your Mama." "I can remember my Mama," returned the child … in any frock."] Florence's comment reflects Dickens's dislike of the excessive ritualization surrounding mourning (p. 45). Mourning would be worn from the day of the funeral, though in practice it might take time to make or buy the mourning clothes. The fabric would be bombazine – a twilled or corded fabric of silk (or cotton) and worsted – or crape (a silk fabric crimped with irons to dull the surface). Mourning etiquette was complex, and the length of mourning depended on one's gender and relation to the deceased. Young girls would typically mourn their parents for twelve months. For the first six months, the prescribed costume was black with black or white crape (for the first two months of this period, they were not allowed to wear linen cuffs and collars, and jewellery); after six to ten months, they would wear less crape, until finally, in the last few months, they would dispense with black crape altogether, and were permitted to wear jewellery and grey gloves, and colours such as grey, lavender, mauve and black-and-grey. Although mourning clothes were supposed to be drab and plain, and to have dull, unreflective surfaces, dressmakers and retailers capitalized on the vogue for mourning by selling fashionable costumes of rich material and elaborate detail (Morley 63–77; Flanders, 2003, 378–84; also see table in Flanders, 'Mourning Clothes for Women' 386).

"Oh! but begging your pardon, Mrs. Richards

"I may be very fond of pennywinkles … but it don't follow that I'm to have 'em for tea."] A cockney variant of periwinkle, the English name of gastropod mollusk or shore snails, much used for food (*OED*).

"Yes, Mrs. Richards, just come

detached the child from her new friend by a wrench – as if she were a tooth.] In *Principles of Surgery* (1842), James Syme, Professor of Clinical Surgery at the

University of Edinburgh, and Surgeon to the Queen, recommended dentists use 'the tooth-key, as it is called, or powerful forceps, of which the blades are short, concave, and placed obliquely in regard to the handles'. Although 'Many ingenious devices' had been contrived to pull the tooth out perpendicularly from the socket, Syme recommended:

> In order to dislodge the roots, it is necessary that the alveolar processes [the parts of bone that surround and support the teeth] should be broken more or less; and the best way of accomplishing this is to draw the tooth towards that side which makes the least resistance, at the same time raising it from its bed. Both the instruments that have been mentioned [the tooth-key and forceps] enable the operator to exert a force in this oblique direction. (484)

Although nitrous oxide, ether and chloroform were first used for surgical and dental procedures in 1846 and 1847, their adoption took time to gain acceptance.

"Oh! there's a Tartar within

a Tartar] A savage and violent or irritable and intractable person, deriving from the name of one of the tribes under Genghis Khan. Dickens uses the word in *DC* (6): '"I'll tell you what I am," whispered Mr. Creakle … "I'm a Tartar' " and *OMF* (1.8): 'The old man was an awful Tartar' (1.8).

Spitfire seemed to be in

a disciple of that school of trainers of the young idea which holds that childhood, like money, must be shaken and rattled and jostled about a good deal to keep it bright.] An allusion to the pleasures of child-rearing in James Thomson, *The Seasons*, 'Spring' (1728):

> Then infant reason grows apace, and calls
> For the kind hand of an assiduous care.
> Delightful task! to rear the tender thought,
> To teach the young idea how to shoot,
> To pour the fresh instruction o'er the mind,
> To breathe the enlivening spirit, and to fix
> The generous purpose in the glowing breast. (1147–53)

Teaching 'the young idea how to shoot' had evolved into a poetic cliché by the late eighteenth and early nineteenth centuries. Dickens was sensitive to the casual violence inflicted on children and described himself as once having been 'caught in the palm of a female hand by the crown … and violently scrubbed from the neck to the roots of the hair' (*AYR*, 'The Uncommercial Traveller' 3.85).

"It ain't right of you

I may wish ... to take a voyage to Chaney ... but I mayn't know how to leave the London Docks."] With its supposedly quaint, backward culture, China was a popular source of amusement to the British, especially at the time of the first Opium War (1839–41). Dickens makes fun of popular misconceptions of China in *LD* (1.13). A few years earlier, he wrote (or had a hand in writing) two articles that betrayed his antipathy towards the Chinese and their culture ('The Chinese Junk', *Examiner*, 24 June 1848; 'The Great Exhibition and the Little One', *HW*, 3 [5 July 1851]: 356–60).

The London Docks, on the left bank of the Thames between St Katherine's Docks and Shadwell, were the nearest docks to the City in the early nineteenth century. Constructed in 1805, they comprised 'an area of 90 acres – 35 acres of water, and 12,980 feet of quay and jetty frontage, with three entrances from the Thames'. Their impressive nature is conveyed in two *HW* articles:

> If any one would form anything like an adequate conception of the wonders of London, and of the power and wealth of this country, he should pay a visit to the London Docks. ... From near the Tower all the way to Blackwall, a distance of four miles, he will find it a whole world of Docks. The mass of shipping, the extent of vast warehouses, many of them five and seven stories high, all crowded with ponderous heaps of merchandise from every region of the globe, have nothing like it besides in the world, and never have had. The enormous wealth here collected is perfectly overwhelming to the imagination. (Howitt, 'The Queen's Tobacco-Pipe', 2 [4 January 1851]: 354)

> Here, Jack leaps into great life. Ship-chandlers, ship-grocers, biscuit-bakers, sail-makers, outfitting warehouses, occupy the shops on either side. Up a little court is a nautical day-school for teaching navigation. There is a book-stall, on which lies the "Seaman's Manual," the "Shipmaster's Assistant," and Hamilton Moore's "Navigation." There is a nautical instrument maker's, where chronometers, quadrants, and sextants are kept, and blank log-books are sold. The stationers display forms for manifests, bills of lading and charter-parties. Every article vended has some connexion with those who go down to the sea in ships. (Sala, 'Jack Alive in London', 4 [6 December 1851]: 256)

Notwithstanding Mr. Toodle's great reliance

she was a good plain sample of a nature that is ever, in the mass, better, truer, higher, nobler, quicker to feel, and much more constant to retain, all tenderness and pity, self-denial and devotion, than the nature of men.] An expression of mid-Victorian domestic ideology as codified in such works as Sarah Stickney Ellis's bestseller, *The Women of England: Their Social Duties and Domestic Habits* (1839), which defined the 'nature' of middle-class men and women in very different ways. According to Ellis, 'to men belongs the potent ... consideration of worldly aggrandizement' and 'all considerations relating to the acquisition of wealth' (35). In contrast to the 'inborn selfishness' of men, women were considered to be 'clothed in moral beauty', self-denying and spiritually pure:

> The women of England, possessing the grand privilege of being better instructed than those of any other country in the minutiæ of domestic comfort, have obtained a degree of importance in society far beyond what their unobtrusive virtues would appear to claim. The long-established customs of their country, have placed in their hands the high and holy duty of cherishing and protecting the minor morals of life, from whence springs all that is elevated in purpose, and glorious in action. The sphere of their direct personal influence is central, and consequently small; but its extreme operations are as widely extended as the range of human feeling. ... [A]s far as the noble daring of Britain has sent forth her adventurous sons, and that is to every point of danger on the habitable globe, they have borne along with them a generosity, a disinterestedness, and a moral courage, derived in no small measure from the female influence of their native country. (1843 ed., 36–7)

His little daughter hesitated

She looked up in his face once more.] Browne's depiction of this scene, 'The Dombey Family', is the first illustration of Mr Dombey in the novel. For Dickens's views on the visual representation of Dombey, see note to chapter 1, p. 22–5.

So, Polly kept her before his eyes,

He don't want me. He don't want me!"] Although grammarians such as the anonymous author of *The Vulgarities of Speech Corrected* (1826) frowned on the use of 'don't' 'when it follows the words *he, she* or *it* or the name of an individual', it was acceptable, at least colloquially, until at least the 1870s. So Trollope's Vicar of Bullhampton says, 'If he don't take care, he'll find himself in trouble' (17), and an Oxford undergraduate in *Tom Brown at Oxford* comments, 'I put him down as a laster. ... However, it don't matter now' (16) (qtd. in Phillipps 69).

"Oh! Being only a permanency

a excellent party-wall between this house and the next, I mayn't exactly like to go to it,] Susan is punning on the phrases 'to go to the wall' – to give up in a conflict or struggle – and 'party-wall' – a mutually owned wall separating two buildings or pieces of land. Party-walls were the subject of much legal wrangling and legislation in the nineteenth century (*OED*).

Chapter 4

IN WHICH SOME MORE FIRST APPEARANCES ARE MADE ON THE STAGE OF THESE ADVENTURES

As a letter to Forster reveals, Dickens's original intention concerning Walter Gay was

> to disappoint all the expectations that chapter [4] seems to raise of his happy connection with the story and the heroine, and to show him gradually and naturally trailing away, from that love of adventure and boyish light-heartedness, into negligence, idleness, dissipation, dishonesty, and ruin. To show, in short, our ordinary life; to exhibit something of the philosophy of it, in great temptations and an easy nature; and to show how the good turns into bad, by degrees. If I kept some little notion of Florence always at the bottom of it, I think it might be made very powerful and very useful. What do you think? Do you think it may be done, without making people angry? (*Letters* 4.593)

Shortly after completing the third number, Dickens informed Forster that he had changed his mind:

> I see it will be best as you advise, to give that idea up; and indeed I don't feel it would be reasonable to carry it out now. I am far from sure it could be wholesomely done, after the interest he has acquired. (22 and 23 November 1846; *Letters* 4.658)

As Forster explained, 'Walter was reserved for a happier future; and the idea thrown out took modified shape, amid circumstances better suited to the excellent capabilities, in the striking character of Richard Carstone in the tale of *Bleak House*' (*Life* 2.21–2)

Though the offices of Dombey and Son

within the liberties of London, and within hearing of Bow Bells, when their clashing voices were not drowned by the uproar in the streets,] In other words, within the City of London, that part of Greater London administered by the Lord Mayor and City of London Corporation, an area that covers slightly more than one square mile. The City, the financial centre of London, is bounded by Temple Bar on the west, Smithfield and Moorfields on the north, Aldgate and Tower Hill on the east, and the River Thames on the south. The 'liberty' or 'liberties' is the district, extending beyond the bounds of the City, which is subject to municipal control (*OED*). 'Bow Bells' are the bells of the church of St. Mary-le-Bow, on the south side of Cheapside. A person born within the sound of Bow Bells is traditionally said to be

Chapter 4 *In which Some More First Appearances are made . . .* 55

a true Londoner or a Cockney. Bow Bells feature in the story of Dick Whittington: they called him back to London to become Lord Mayor in 1392. The original bells were destroyed in the Great Fire of 1666 and were not fully replaced until 1762. For Dickens's dislike of 'the uproar' of city streets, see note to chapter 23, p. 277.

Gog and Magog] Two colossal wooden statues of these mythical giants dominated the Guildhall, located just north of Gresham Street and to the east of St. Paul's Cathedral. The fourteen-foot-high figures were made of wicker-work and pasteboard and placed on pedestals near the Guildhall's west window. They were carried through the streets in Lord Mayors' Shows and were thought to 'typify the dignity of the City'. According to Augustus Hare, 'There is an old prophecy of Mother Shipton which says that "when they fall, London will fall also" ' (1878, 1.238). Dickens seems to have first seen the statues when he was seven or eight:

> I came into their presence at last, and gazed up at them with dread and veneration. They looked better tempered, and were altogether more shiny-faced, than I had expected; but they were very big, and, as I judged their pedestals to be about forty feet high, I considered that they would be very big indeed if they were walking on the stone pavement. I was in a state of mind as to these and all such figures, which I suppose holds equally with most children. While I knew them to be images made of something that was not flesh and blood, I still invested them: with attributes of life – with consciousness of my being there, for example, and the power of keeping a sly eye upon me. ('Gone Astray', *HW* 7.554)

The British legend of Gogmagog appears in Geoffrey of Monmouth's *Historia Regum Britanniae* (*c.* 1136; 1.16) and is referred to in Spenser's *Faerie Queen* (3.9.50), Milton's *History of Britain* and Blake's *Jerusalem* 98 (52).

This and the subsequent references to the Royal Exchange, the Bank of England and the East India House put Dombey's offices in the heart of the City of London, in the vicinity of Cornhill and Threadneedle Street.

the Royal Exchange was close at hand;] The Royal Exchange, at the juncture of Threadneedle Street and Cornhill, was the traditional place for merchants to conduct their business. Dickens may have in mind the third Royal Exchange building, which opened in October 1844 (the first was built by Sir Thomas Gresham in 1565–67 and destroyed by the Great Fire of 1666; the second was opened in 1669 and destroyed by fire on 10 January 1838). The third Exchange, with its large portico and eight Corinthian columns, was designed by Sir William Tite and modeled on the Pantheon in Rome. In the mid-nineteenth century, the Royal Exchange housed the foreign exchange market and was occupied by Lloyd's Subscription Room; the Royal Exchange Assurance, west; the London Assurance, south; and offices originally planned for Gresham's College (Weinreb and Hibbert 689–91).

the Bank of England, with its vaults of gold and silver "down among the dead

men" underground, was their magnificent neighbour.] The Bank of England, opposite the Royal Exchange in Threadneedle Street, was founded in 1694 to support the public debt during the expensive wars fought by William III. It became the bedrock of the banking system in the first quarter of the nineteenth century. In 1844, it gained the sole right to issue banknotes, placing it at the head of the financial structure and increasing its control over the money supply (Gardiner and Wenborn 62–3). (For the Bank's nickname, 'the Old Lady of Threadneedle Street', see note to chapter 36, page 375). The 'vaults of gold and silver' refer to the Bullion Office, 'a subterranean vault, where they keep the gold and silver bars from Australia, California, Russia, Peru, and Mexico; where they weigh them, sell them, and from whence they send them to the Mint' (Schlesinger, 1853). Dickens and W. H. Wills remarked in 1850 that the bullion in the 'very respectable arched cellars' of the Bank of England 'lately averaged' 'sixteen millions and a half sterling' (*HW* 1 [6 July 1850]: 338, 340). 'Down among the dead men' alludes to the famous toast attributed to the eighteenth-century poet John Dyer: 'And he that will this health deny, down among the dead men let him lie' (*Here's A Health to the King*). 'Dead men' is a slang term for empty bottles, and thus the phrase 'down among the dead men let him lie' means to 'leave him under the table with the empty bottles'.

Just round the corner stood the rich East India House, teeming with suggestions of precious stuffs and stones, tigers, elephants, howdahs, hookahs, umbrellas, palm trees, palanquins, and gorgeous princes of a brown complexion sitting on carpets with their slippers very much turned up at the toes.] Located in Leadenhall Street and several blocks east of the Royal Exchange and the Bank of England, the East India House comprised the principal offices of the East India Company, a trading company chartered in 1600 to develop commerce in the East Indies and India. In the eighteenth century, the East India Company gained administrative control over Bengal and other parts of India, serving as an agent of the British government in India until its powers were transferred to the British Crown in 1858, after the Indian Mutiny. The East India Company was dissolved in 1873.

The East India House was originally founded in 1726 but substantially rebuilt and enlarged in 1798. According to a contemporary observer, the long stone façade of Ionic columns gave the building, 'an air of much magnificence to the whole, although the closeness of the street makes it somewhat gloomy' (Knight 5.61). The adjoining Museum contained 'paintings, prints and drawings, illustrative of Indian scenery and buildings' (Knight 5.62) and much else:

> Hindu idols in silver and gold. Hindu and Goorkha swords. Pair of Gauntlets made at Lahore, sometimes used by the native chiefs and horsemen in India (beautifully elaborate). Sword of the executioner attached to the palace of the King of Candy, (taken at the capture of Candy). Piece of wood of the ship "Farquharson," containing the horns of a fish called the monodon; the largest horn had penetrated through the copper sheeting and outside lining into one of the floor timbers. ... Surya, the Sun, in his seven-horse car. Buddhist idols, and relics. A perfumed gold necklace. The state howdah of Durgan Sal,

usurper of Bhurtpore. Full-length portrait of the famous Nadir Shah.
(Cunningham, 1850)

One large room in the Museum contained 'specimens of Asiatic natural history', including 'Indian, Siamese, and Javanese birds, Sumatran and Indian mammalia, besides butterflies, moths, beetles, and shells'. The Museum also displayed a musical toy, which once belonged to Tippoo Sultan: 'it consists of a tiger trampling on a prostrate man, and about to seize him with his teeth' with a mechanism 'which, when wound up by a key, cause[s] the figure of the man to utter sounds of distress, and the tiger to imitate the roar of the living beast'. A small anteroom was 'occupied by a splendid howdah, or throne, part of it solid silver, adapted for the back of the elephant, in which Oriental princes travel' (Knight 5.63–4). According to Dickens, he first became aware of the East India House when he was about seven or eight and lost in the streets of London:

> Sir James Hogg himself might have been satisfied with the veneration in which I held the India House. I had no doubt of its being the wonderful, the most magnanimous, the most incorruptible, the most practically disinterested, the most in all respects astonishing, establishment on the face of the earth. I understood the nature of an oath, and would have sworn it to be one entire perfect chrysolite. ('Gone Astray' *HW* 7.555)

The East India House was demolished in 1862.

Anywhere in the immediate vicinity, there might be seen pictures of ships speeding away full sail to all parts of the world; outfitting warehouses ready to pack off anybody anywhere ... and little timber midshipmen in obsolete naval uniforms, eternally employed outside the shop-doors of nautical instrument makers in taking observations of the hackney coaches.] In his *Life*, Forster claimed that 'the Little Wooden Midshipman did actually (perhaps does still) occupy his post of observation in Leadenhall Street' (2.35). In an 1881 article in *All the Year Round*, J. Sterry Ashby identified the Wooden Midshipman with a specific nautical instrument shop located at 157 Leadenhall Street, owned by J. W. Norie and Charles Wilson. According to Ashby, the shop was 'first established in 1773' by William Heather 'as a "sea chart, map, and mathematical instrument warehouse"' and 'has but little changed in appearance' since its founding. (J. W. Norie replaced Heather in 1814, and was joined by George Wilson in 1834.) Ashby first 'spotted' the shop as the original of Sol Gills's residence, as a boy, and remarked, without further explanation, that 'It was many years after that I knew, for an actual fact, that this was really the shop that was so graphically sketched in the novel'. Ashby, who visited the shop shortly before it was to be destroyed, found a number of correlations between the actual shop and the fictional shop: the wooden midshipman (Plate 5); '[t]he interior of the shop, with its curious desks and its broad counter' which is described as 'old-fashioned' as the shop's exterior; 'Walter's chamber, with its comprehensive view of the parapets and chimney-pots'; the 'bed-chamber of Sol Gills', 'a cheerful panelled apartment'; and the cellar, 'down a dark narrow flight of steps'. Ashby added, 'a good many extraordinary characters [have been] connected' with the actual shop, including 'an old-fashioned manager, who it is said bore an extraordinary resemblance to Sol Gills' (28 [29 October]: 173–9).

It is presumably the same wooden midshipman over the door of the shop that Dickens recalls in *UT*: 'My day's no-business beckoning me to the east end of London, I ... got past the India House ... and past my little wooden midshipman, after affectionately patting him on one leg of his knee-shorts for old acquaintance' sake' ('Wapping Workhouse', 2 [18 February 1860]: 392). W. E. Milliken, a correspondent to *The Antiquary*, concurred with Ashby that 'there can be little question that the shop soon to disappear from Leadenhall Street was that of Solomon Gills' (1881, 85). Another writer noted in 1903 that the figure that once fronted the shop was 'not ... "a little timber midshipman," but an admiral, whose uniform is said to be exact and complete as worn in the early part of the nineteenth century.' According to this writer, 'The figure was removed from Leadenhall Street when the present owners, Messrs. Norie & Wilson, removed thence to 156, Minories' ('Opticians' Signs' 412).

One problem with any such specific identification, even by Londoners describing the shop forty years after the publication of *DS*, is that, as the passage above makes clear, the area in the 1840s had multiple nautical shops, each with its own wooden midshipman. Was the Norie and Wilson shop simply more long-lived than the rest, at least until 1881?

'The East India and general shipping neighbourhoods, have their headquarters about Cornhill and Leadenhall street; here also outfitters, Utopian land companies, and emigration crimps [brokers], are thick as leaves in Vallombrosa' ('The World of London. Part III', *Blackwood's Edinburgh Magazine*, 50 [July 1841]: 65). Leadenhall Street, which was 'chiefly composed of warehouses and retail shops' formed 'a very great thoroughfare from the centre of the city, to those magnificent proofs of our extensive commerce, the London, and East and West India Docks' (Tallis, *c.* 1838–9).

A midshipman was a naval cadet generally appointed by the admiralty, although one in each ship was appointed by the captain. Before he could become a midshipman, the cadet had to serve one year and had to pass his examinations. 'A midshipman is then the station in which a young volunteer is trained in the several exercises necessary to attain a knowledge of steam, machinery, discipline, the general movements and operations of a ship, and qualify him to command' (Smyth, 1867, 479).

In the early nineteenth century, instrument-making firms were usually family businesses, often passed on from generation to generation. This changed, however, with revisions in company law in 1844 and 1856, which made it easier to form partnerships and joint stock companies. English instrument makers were typically apprenticed, though sometimes for shorter terms and less formally after the repeal in 1814 of the Statute of Apprentices of 1563. They often subcontracted the work because of its specialized nature. The firm of Arnold and Dent, for instance, used 43 different craftsmen in the mid-nineteenth century to produce and put together one instrument. According to a House of Commons paper, there were 25 nautical instrument makers in England and Wales in 1844. Of these, 11 were under 20 years of age, and 14 were 20 or older ('Summary of Occupations' 280).

5   The Little Midshipman in the Charles Dickens Museum, London

Sole master and proprietor of

a Welsh wig] A woolen round, knitted cap, worn by ordinary sailors in the British navy in the eighteenth century (*OED*). Old Fezziwig wears one in *CC*.

midshipmen who have attained a pretty green old age, have not been wanting in the English navy.] From the *Iliad*: 'A green old age, unconscious of decays / That proves the hero born in better days' (trans. Pope, 23.925).
   In the early nineteenth century, midshipmen, who typically entered the English navy at the age of twelve, were promoted to Lieutenant at a very slow pace. A contemporary report estimated in 1835 that, 'at the present rate of promotion', it would take 'between *forty* and *forty-one* years!!' before the 1471 midshipmen in the service 'will all have been promoted', despite the fact that most had served six years and already passed their examinations. 'So that, entering the service at twelve years old, some of the midshipmen will have to attain the age of one hundred and twenty-one years (that is, if they can) before they will obtain their rank!!!' ('Remarks on the English Navy, and the Necessity of a Naval Brevet', *The Metropolitan Magazine* 14

[September–December 1835]: 10–11).

The stock-in-trade of this old gentleman

The stock-in-trade of this old gentleman comprised chronometers, barometers, telescopes, compasses, charts, maps, sextants, quadrants, and specimens of every kind of instrument used in the working of a ship's course, or the keeping of a ship's reckoning, or the prosecuting of a ship's discoveries.] An instrument for measuring time, a chronometer differs from watches in having an improved escapement and a compensation balance, thus allowing sailors to compute longitude at sea, and make other exact observations. It is adjusted to keep accurate time in all ranges of temperature. In the early nineteenth century, reduced production costs and improvements in manufacturing techniques made chronometers more affordable for navigators. A 'ship's reckoning', as used here, is an estimate made of a ship's position, whether by calculation from a log, or the course steered, or by observation of the sun (*OED*). A reckoning is also a record of courses steered and distances achieved since the position of the ship was last marked. It used to be kept on a piece of slate which served as a temporary log of times and distances, and which was wiped clean once the information was transferred to a log book.

Many minor incidents in the household

ship-chandlers] Dealers who supply ships with necessary stores (*OED*).

ships' biscuit] Ships' biscuit was standard fare on long sea voyages. It is described by a visitor to the Navy's victualling department at Portsmouth in 1844:

> We first paid a visit to that part where the ships' biscuit is baked, and stored up. A steam-mill grinds the corn, another kneads the dough for these flat cakes, which when divided and placed upon plates of iron, are again conveyed to the oven by machinery, until the biscuit can be packed in sacks, containing each 120lbs., with which the immense store-rooms are filled. A pound of biscuit is allowed to each man per day. We tasted it, and although it is certainly a pure and nourishing food, we found it so dreadfully hard, that it appeared to us as if the crowning point of English industry were still wanting, namely, a machine to masticate and digest it. (Carus, 1846, 53)

case bottles] Bottles, often square, which were protected by a case; they were commonly used by travellers and sailors.

the Tartar Frigate under weigh, was on the plates;] The *Tartar* Frigate, one of the first British frigates in the modern sense, was 'a scourge to French privateers' during the Seven Years War (1756–63). Its most celebrated victory was 'in pitch darkness' in the English Channel, on 2 November 1757, against the French frigate *Mélampe*, which had been 'fitted out … for the express purpose of catching the Tartar', and which was 'a far more powerful ship', with more guns, men and weight: 'For three hours they smashed round-shot into each other, and at half-past eleven the *Mélampe* ceased firing and hauled down her colours'. During his two-year tenure (1756–8) as Captain of the *Tartar*, John Lockhart and his crew

> had captured nine privateers, from thirty-six guns and three hundred men to eighteen guns and a hundred and seventeen men. They had taken two thousand five hundred prisoners of war, and two hundred and twenty guns; and only five of the Tartar's men had been killed in action. … [Despite 'obstinate and prolonged resistance' by the French,] the Tartar sustained little damage, and her crew little loss.

To honor the famous frigate, several British ships were given its name, and taverns in 'many a south-coast town' bore 'the time-honoured sign of the Tartar Frigate' (Fletcher, 'The Captain of the Tartar', *Macmillan's Magazine,* 86 [September 1902]: 351–4).

When Dickens stayed at Broadstairs, a favourite seaside resort on the east coast of Kent, he apparently frequented one such inn, 'The Tartar Frigate', which was, 'the cosiest little sailor's inn, selling the strongest of tobacco, and the strongest-smelling rum that is to be met with around the coast', according to a contemporary account (Hotten, *Charles Dickens: The Story of his Life*, 1870, 64).

Here he lived too, in

The only change … was from a complete suit of coffee-colour cut very square, and ornamented with glaring buttons, to the same suit of coffee-colour minus the inexpressibles, which were then of a pale nankeen.] 'Inexpressibles', a euphemism for breeches or trousers, was first recorded in 1790 (*OED*). For similar euphemisms, see note to chapter 38, p. 387. 'Nankeen' is a lightweight, pale yellowish cloth originally made in Nanking, China. Nankeen trousers, which were in vogue from the late eighteenth century to the early decades of the nineteenth century, were the customary summer costume of well-dressed men, but were also worn by military men and naval captains.

when gentlemen of England who lived below at ease] From 'The Gallant Seamen', by Martyn Parker (d. 1630):

> Ye gentlemen of England,
> That live at home at ease,
> Ah! little do you think upon
> The dangers of the seas.
> Give ear unto the mariners,

And they will plainly show
All the cares and the fears,
When the stormy winds do blow.
When the stormy, &c. [st. 1]
(*The Melodist, and Mirthful Olio; an Elegant Collection of the Most Popular Songs* 3.59)

It is half-past five o'clock

The usual daily clearance has been making in the City, for an hour or more; and the human tide is still rolling westward.] Offices in the City of London were open from 10 a.m. to 4 p.m. See note to chapter 32, p. 348.

"If I didn't know he

tapping two or three weather glasses with his knuckles. ... "All in the Downs, eh? Lots of moisture!] An allusion to John Gay's ballad, 'Sweet William's Farewell to Black-Eyed Susan' (*Poems*, 1720):

All in the Downs the fleet was moor'd,
The streamers waving in the wind,
When black-eyed Susan came aboard;
'O! where shall I my true-love find?
Tell me, ye jovial sailors, tell me true
If my sweet William sails among the crew.' (11.1–6)

The successful nautical melodrama *Black-Ey'd Susan; or, All in the Downs* (1829) was based on Gay's ballad and contained two renditions of it. The play was written by Dickens's friend, Douglas Jerrold, who performed in Dickens's amateur theatricals and who himself served in the navy. An advertisement for *Black-Ey'd Susan* appears on a poster in Browne's illustration in chapter 60, 'Another wedding'.

The Downs, a sheltered offshore anchorage between the Straits of Dover and the Thames Estuary, provides a refuge for merchant ships during heavy weather. Shipwrecks were not uncommon because the Goodwin Sands to the east tended to shift and were not clearly marked. For more, see note to chapter 23, p. 288.

"Come along then, Uncle!"

"Come along then, Uncle!" cried the boy. "Hurrah for the admiral!" "Confound the admiral!" returned Solomon Gills. "You mean the Lord Mayor." "No I don't!" cried the boy. "Hurrah for the admiral. Hurrah for the admiral! For – ward!"] Walter quotes the cheer bestowed on an admiral after victory in a sea battle when his crew are in the process of boarding a defeated vessel (an admiral, Walter imagines, 'at the head of a boarding party of five hundred men'). This reminds Sol Gills of the shout, 'Hurrah for the Lord Mayor!', that greets the Lord Mayor at ceremonial functions, including the annual ceremonial procession, the Lord Mayor's Show, marking the installation of a new Lord Mayor. The Lord Mayor is the head of the City Corporation and the Chief Magistrate and the Chairman of its two governing bodies, the Court of Aldermen and the Court of Common Council (Weinreb and Hibbert 495–98; 876).

"Oh, is he though!" said

the Sword Bearer's better than him. He draws *his* sword sometimes. … And a pretty figure he cuts with it for his pains,"] The sword-bearer, the most important of the Household Officers of the Lord Mayor, works with the Common Cryer and the Sergeant-at-Arms to administer engagements and daily attendance upon the Lord Mayor. The sword-bearer and mace-bearer accompany the Lord Mayor in the state coach during the Lord Mayor's procession. When the Lord Mayor exits the coach to walk along the streets, the sword-bearer and mace-bearer walk in front of him. The sword-bearer is readily identified by his eight-inch high sable hat, known as the 'Cap of Maintenance' (which may account for the 'pretty figure' irony), and a ceremonial sword in a pearl scabbard, the Sword of State, which was the gift of Queen Elizabeth I. The sword-bearer carries the sword 'upright, the hilt being holden under his bulk, and the blade directly up the midst of his breast, and between his brows' (Smith, 1849, 153).

"For the Lord Mayor, Sheriffs,

Sheriffs, Common Council, and Livery,"] The office of Sheriff is the oldest in the City of London, dating back to the twelfth century. In the early nineteenth century, sheriffs would serve writs of process, attend judges and execute their orders, impanel or summon juries, 'levy and pay into the exchequer all fines to the crown', raise a *posse comitatus* (a group of able-bodied citizens above the age of fifteen) to put down riots and see condemned prisoners executed. They also would attend the Lord Mayor on most official occasions, including meetings of the City Corporation's various Courts, go to the sessions at the Central Criminal Court, and present petitions from the City to Parliament in the House of Commons. Two sheriffs are elected annually for the City of London (*Leigh's New Picture of London*, 1819; Percy, 1824, 259–61; Weinreb and Hibbert, 1993, 805). The Court of Common Council, the major governing body of the City of London since the eighteenth century, is presided over by the Lord Mayor. 'The court's general business is to make laws for the due government of the city, to guide its police, to manage its property; in fact, the court of common council is the city's legislature' (*Leigh's New Picture of London*). The City Livery companies (known as 'liverymen' because they wore a characteristic livery or uniform) annually elect the Lord Mayor and the two sheriffs. *Leigh's New Picture of London* lists 91 livery companies in 1819 (Weinreb and Hibbert, 1993, 166–7).

"Oh! there's not much to

some cards about ships that are going to sail,] In other words, large pasteboard advertisements on walls or windows.

"No bankers' books, or cheque books,

"No bankers' books, or cheque books, or bills, or such tokens of wealth] A bankers' book is 'an authentic record' of cash transactions that allows the user to detect errors in his trade-books (Gilbart, 1871, 596). In *CC*, Scrooge is said to have 'beguiled the rest of his evening with his banker's book' (18). Although at the time a 'cheque book' might be a book in which a bank maintained a register of cheques, the context suggests that Dickens simply means the firm's book of engraved cheque forms and counterfoils, which would have been supplied to the firm by a bank. The 'bills' here may refer either to receipts for goods delivered or services rendered, or to bills of exchange, written orders by the writer (the 'drawer') to someone else (the 'drawee') to pay a specific sum, on a specific date (*OED*).

"Why, Uncle Sol!"

the wonderful Madeira! – there's only one more bottle! ... You shall drink the other bottle ... when you have come to good fortune,] In *A History and Description of Modern Wines* (2nd ed., 1836), Cyrus Redding remarks: 'Madeira wine is one of those which bears age remarkably well, and the wine has not yet been drunk too old. Its flavour and aroma perfect themselves by years' (237). Redding gives further advice in *Every Man His Own Butler* (1839):

> This wine has got into unmerited disrepute, owing to the tricks of dealers in substituting low-priced bad wines, liable to turn acid, for the best wines of the island, while the demand for it ran high. A preference given to sherry by George the Fourth, seems also to have caused this fine wine to get almost wholly out of fashion. The finest East India Madeira is a white wine which has scarcely an equal, nor have the best kinds of Madeira any tendency to acidity. To be secure from fraud, deal with a leading merchant connected with the island. ... The wine should be guaranteed unmixed on the purchase. It should be kept in a warm rather than a cold cellar, and is in its best state for drinking at twenty years old. (24–5)

For how madeira was enhanced by sending it on a voyage, see note below, p. 67.

Chapter 4 *In which Some More First Appearances are made . . .*

"You see Walter," he said,

But competition, competition – new invention, new invention – alteration, alteration – the world's gone past me.] In the late eighteenth and early nineteenth centuries, Great Britain, like other major industrialized countries, was confronted with the social changes wrought by a number of major inventions. The most consequential was the steam engine, which freed power from a dependence on humans or animals and from weather conditions, necessitating the building of large factories, and encouraging monopolies and the concentration of wealth. The steam engine also made possible the passenger railway, which fostered rationalized and regularized modes of social and economic organization, and vastly reduced travel times. The need for better engines, in turn, encouraged improvements in machine crafts, including the invention of the boring machine and boring cylinder and the standardization of parts. Other early nineteenth century inventions included the iron steamboat, the steam printing press, the electro-magnet, the rotating cylinder press, the steam drop hammer and photography, among many others (Mumford 442–45; Landes 41).

These times, Dickens wrote in 1849, 'are marked beyond all others by rapidity of change, and by the condensation of centuries into years in respect of great advances' ('Court Ceremonies', *The Examiner,* 15 December 1849; Slater, 1996, 2.174). In general, Dickens saw material change as positive, insisting that 'we are moving in a right direction towards some superior condition of society' (*HW* 3.356). In darker moments, though, he expressed scepticism about the more zealously chauvinistic rhetoric that exaggerated the case for Britain's material advancement.

"Since you come home from weekly

weekly boarding-school at Peckham,] Apparently, the weekly boarding school in Meeting House Lane, which had been attended by Oliver Goldsmith in the mid-eighteenth century, and which became known as 'Goldsmith's house'. Peckham, about two to three miles southeast of London Bridge, on the south side of the Thames, was a largely rural area in the early nineteenth century, 'a district of market gardens, interspersed with citizens' villas', with a canal used to transport local market garden produce. By 1842, a number of houses had been constructed in Hill Street, their gardens leading down to the canal towpath (Wheatley, 1891, 3.68; Weinreb and Hibbert 605–6).

"Two Uncle, don't you recollect?

a sovereign – "] A British gold coin, first issued in its modern form in 1817, and worth a pound or twenty shillings.

"Why Uncle! don't you call

the woman ... who came to ask the way to Mile-End Turnpike?"] Mile-End Turnpike (constructed in 1717) was the exit from London for Colchester and the northeast. It was located at the junction of Dog Row and Mile End Row. To get to Mile-End Turnpike from the vicinity of the Bank of England, one would need to walk east on Cornhill, which becomes Leadenhall, then northeast up Ludgate High Street, which turns into Whitechapel Road. Whitechapel Road becomes Mile End Road, the turnpike being about a mile east of the starting point. In the nineteenth century, the area was generally respectable and was developed for housing (Weinreb and Hibbert 532).

"Well, Wally," resumed the

"not being like the Savages who came on Robinson Crusoe's Island, we can't live on a man who asks for change for a sovereign,] The 'savages' who come to Crusoe's island turn out to be cannibals: Crusoe first realizes this when he sees 'the Shore spread with Skulls, Hands, Feet, and other Bones of human Bodies; and particularly I observ'd a Place where there had been a Fire made, and a Circle dug in the Earth'. *Robinson Crusoe* (1719) was one of Dickens's favourite books: 'It is a book I read very much; and the wonder of its prodigious effect on me and everyone, and the admiration thereof, grows on me the more I observe this curious fact' (*Letters* 8.153).

"I know it," said Solomon.

"As to the Sea," he pursued, "that's well enough in fiction ... but it won't do in fact; it won't do at all. It's natural enough that you should think about it, associating it with all these familiar things; but it won't do, it won't do."] Sea stories have been popular since at least the story of Jason and his argonauts and Homer's *Odyssey*. Modern sea stories include Defoe's *Robinson Crusoe* and *Captain Singleton* (1720), Smollett's *The Adventures of Roderick Random* (1748) and Frederick Marryat's *Frank Mildmay* (1829), *The King's Own* (1830), *Newton Foster* (1832), *Peter Simple* (1834), *Jacob Faithful* (1834) and *Mr Midshipman Easy* (1836). In several of his novels, 'Captain Marryat', a retired naval commander and a friend of Dickens from 1841, portrayed boy heroes, typically young midshipmen, as embodiments of simple values and the more 'manly' attributes of the British character, frequently rewarding them with advancement and a bride. In *Mr Midshipman Easy*, for instance, Jack Easy joins the service as a boy, and, after a variety of encounters and adventures which portray his courage and willingness to stand up for principles, proves himself as a naval officer and Englishman, and gains a wife and a place in polite society. Other nautical novelists of the 1830s, many of whom were veterans of the Napoleonic Wars, include M. H. Barker, Captain Chamier, Captain Glascock, Edward Howard and William J. Neale. Captain Chamier's motto, representative of the sea story genre as a whole, was 'A sailor's life's the life for me, he takes his duty merrily'. Dickens (and Walter) would also have been influenced by romanticized accounts of Lord Nelson's victories at the Nile in 1798 and at Trafalgar in 1805 – for example, Southey's *Life of Nelson* (1813) and Arthur William Devis's painting, *The Death of Nelson* (1807). The fashion for heroic sea stories faded by the 1840s (Peck 11–29, 50–69; also see Sutherland, 1988, 412-14).

Dickens himself had been fond of nautical melodrama since he first worked as a reviewer of theatrical productions (see, for instance, his review of J. B. Buckstone, *The Dream at Sea*, *Morning Chronicle*, 24 November 1835; rpt Slater, 1996, 2.19-22). Although there were no sailors in his family, Dickens's grandfather, uncle and father had all worked for the Navy Pay Office in Portsmouth, and he took one of his middle names – 'Huffam' – from his godfather, a naval rigger.

Although the nautical sections in *DS* are informed by his knowledge of sea stories and nautical melodrama, Dickens sought outside help when necessary. In December 1847, for instance, he visited the home of Lieut. Augustus Tracey, RN, the Governor of the Westminster House of Correction, Tothill Fields, 'to ask you a question on one or two little nautical points, in order that I may be quite right in Dombey' (*Letters* 5.205).

"Think of this wine for

this wine for instance … which has been to the East Indies and back,]

> Madeira should have an East India voyage; some are satisfied with a West India one. There are also artificial modes of ameliorating this wine; but an assured East India voyage takes precedence of all. The agitation of the wine, as well as the changes of climate, seems essential to its perfect maturity. The additional price of a pipe of Madeira, taken from the island to India, is from three pounds ten to six guineas; to the West Indies, two pounds; and to Brazil, three guineas per pipe, beyond the selling price: such a sum additional is no object to obtain complete excellence. (Redding, 1839, 26)

"Exactly so," said Solomon

when the Charming Sally went down in the – " "In the Baltic Sea … on the fourteenth of February, seventeen forty-nine!"] The details about the loss of an actual vessel in the Baltic, northern Europe's partially landlocked sea, appear to be fictitious. The ship's name, however, was a popular one and was given to at least two ships, one British, the other American, sailing the high seas between the 1760s and 1830s: a 'smuggling vessel' called the *Charming Sally*, laden with spirits for Guernsey, was captured in 1799; and, in January 1777, the Royal Navy captured an American 'rebel privateer sloop' with the same name. The name also found its way onto the London stage: the *Charming Sally* features in *The Beulah Spa: a burletta in two acts*

(1833), by John Miller (*Naval Chronicle* 1.166; *Universal Magazine* 60.106; 'Shipping News', 1761, 9.54, 246, 350, 585, 590, 600).

Shipwrecks were frequent occurrences, often with heavy loss of life. 'Life and Luggage', a *HW* piece from November 1851, reported:

> [L]ast year, six hundred and eighty-one English and Foreign vessels were wrecked on the coasts, and within the seas, of the British Isles. Of these, two hundred and seventy-seven were total wrecks; eighty-four were sunk by leaks or collisions. – As nearly as can be ascertained, seven hundred and eighty lives were lost. … In the single month of March, 1850, not less than one hundred and thirty-four vessels were wrecked on our coasts, or the average for the month of more than *four a day*. … no doubt, many [shipwrecks] occur which never appear in Lloyd's lists or other public records. They are lost at sea with every soul on board. (153)

Detailed accounts of losses at sea and shipwrecks appeared in the shipping intelligence sections of newspapers and in *Lloyd's List* (see note to chapter 22, pp. 266–7), *The Naval Chronicle* (1799–1818) and *Chronicles of the Sea* (1838–40). Shipwreck narratives – usually first-person accounts – were also published separately as single publication books or were collected in anthologies (such as Archibald Duncan's popular *The Marine Chronicle* [6 volumes; 1804]), as well as in broadsides, chapbooks, novels and in the penny press. Both the *Daily News*, which Dickens briefly edited (1846), and the *Household Narrative of Current Events* (1850–5), a monthly supplement to *Household Words*, carried shipping intelligence and descriptions of shipwrecks (Palmer, 1997, 58–9). *Household Words* itself contained a number of articles and fictional works on shipwrecks, including 'The Preservation of Life from Shipwreck' 1 [3 August 1850]: 452–4; 'A Sea-side Churchyard' 2 [7 December 1850]: 257–62; 'Lighthouses and Light-boats' 2 [11 January 1851]: 373–9; 'Life and Luggage' 4 [8 November 1851]: 152–6; 'A Sea-Coroner' 4 [13 March 1852]: 597–8; 'Margaret Fuller' 5 [24 April 1852: 121-4]; 'Down among the Dead Men' 8 [31 December 1853]: 418-24; 'Modern Human Sacrifices' 8 [11 February 1854]: 561–4; 'The Lost Arctic Voyages' 10 [2 December 1854]: 361–5, [9 December 1854]: 385–93, [23 December 1854]: 433–7; 'When the Wind Blows' 11 [24 March 1855]: 188–91; and 'Wrecks at Sea' 12 [11 August 1855]: 36–9. Dickens's most sustained description of the aftermath of a shipwreck is 'The Shipwreck', the first paper in his *UT* series (*AYR*, 28 January 1860); his most famous fictional depiction of a shipwreck is the 'indelible' and 'awful' event described in chapter 55 of *DC*, the death of Steerforth. In 1852, *Littell's Living Age* remarked on the English fascination with shipwreck narratives: 'The narrative of shipwrecks is generally read with a peculiar interest by an insular people, and we see that in this country this interest has continued unabated from the time when Defoe wrote Robinson Crusoe, to the loss of the Amazon and Birkenhead of the present year' ('Wreckage' 35.174).

"Aye, to be sure!" cried

singing, 'Rule Britannia,'] A song of six stanzas from *Alfred: a Masque* (1740), 3.10:

> When Britain first at heaven's command,
> Arose from out the azure main;
> This was the charter of the land,
> And guardian-angels sung this strain;
> [*chorus*]
> Rule, Britannia, rule the waves:
> Britons never will be slaves. [st. 1]

The masque, with words by David Mallett and James Thomson and music by Thomas Arne, was composed at the behest of the Prince of Wales. Shortly after the first performance, the song was published as 'The celebrated ODE, in Honour of Great BRITAIN call'd Rule BRITANNIA'.

"But when the George the Second

"But when the George the Second drove ashore, Uncle, on the coast of Cornwall, in a dismal gale,] Shipwrecks in Cornwall were common because of the rocky coastline and frequent violent storms:

> The shores of Mount's Bay have from time immemorial been remarkable for numerous shipwrecks that have happened on them, attended with scenes of peculiar distress, which none but those who have witnessed such disasters, or have personally suffered from them, can fully describe. From November 1806, to November 1810, no less than eleven ships were wrecked within the immediate vicinity of Porthleaven in this parish. The property thus irrecoverably lost, exceeded £300,000; and what added most painfully to this series of calamities was, upwards of 250 persons were drowned. (Hitchings, 1824, 2.604)

"And when," said old Sol,

"when the Polyphemus – " "Private West India Trader, burden three hundred and fifty tons, Captain, John Brown of Deptford. Owners, Wiggs, and Co.,"] 'Polyphemus' was a name occasionally given to ships, such as the HMS *Polyphemus*, a 64-gun ship of the line that was commissioned in 1782, and the first ship of the Royal Navy (not a private trader, as here) named for the Cyclops Polyphemus in the *Odyssey*. A ship's 'burden' is its carrying capacity, measured in tons. At the beginning of the nineteenth century, the average British ship engaged in the Atlantic trade was about 250 tons.

But an addition to the

a gentleman in a wide suit of blue ... He wore a loose black silk handkerchief round his neck, and such a very large coarse shirt collar ... his rough outer coat ... a hard glazed hat] Seamen's attire varied, though blue was a favourite colour since the late eighteenth century. Dickens described the stage stereotype of a sailor's attire in a letter to Clarkson Stanfield:

> My trousers are very full at the ankles – my black neck kerchief is tied in the regular style – the name of my ship is painted round my glazed hat – I have a red waistcoat on – and the seams of my blue jacket are "paid" [waterproofed] ... with white. In my left hand I hold the baccy box. ... (*Letters* 4.183)

It was common practice for seamen, of almost all nations, to make themselves canvas hats with a brim, and to coat the hats with grease or tar to make them waterproof. These were forerunners of the sou'wester hat, introduced later in the nineteenth century.

with a hook instead of a hand attached to his right wrist;] Hooks for forearm amputations had been in use for centuries, and for above-elbow amputations from the 1840s. Because hooks were considered aesthetically unacceptable, they were primarily worn by men working in manual trades and crafts (Vitali and Robinson et al., 5–6; Kirkup 160).

Like Captain Cuttle, amputees did not wear hooks all the time: in chapter 9, Cuttle 'unscrewed his hook at dinner-time, and screwed a knife into its wooden socket'; and in chapter 49, while dining with Florence, he removes his hook to screw in a fork. Although Cuttle is never shown with an artificial hand, it was usual for amputees to be supplied with a life-like prosthesis of light-coloured and light-weight wood to be worn on social occasions. These were of two types, and both were made by the firm of W. R. Grossmith, a celebrated London manufacturer of artificial limbs in the first half of the century. One type of prosthesis was worn all the time, but the palm contained a socket having a small steel box into which could be screwed a knife, fork, or other small implement; this gave the wearer the appearance of using a real hand. The other type, designed in particular for amputations below the elbow, was removed altogether and replaced by the required implement:

> When the length of stump exceeds five inches from the elbow-joint, [all] the apparatus that is requisite ... consists of the leather stump case, (moulded in its interior to the exact form of the stump, and its exterior shaped to the size and form of the perfect arm) to which is attached the hand I have described. The hand can be taken off at the wrist, at pleasure, and a hook for common purposes, also a fork or knife, flesh brush to wash the sound hand with, and any other instrument instantly affixed to the wrist plate. (Grossmith, 1857, 28)

privateersman,] A member of the crew of a privateer, 'an armed vessel owned and crewed by private individuals, and holding a government commission known as a letter of marque authorizing the capture of merchant shipping belonging to an enemy nation' (*OED*).

"Wal'r!" he said, arranging

Love! Honour! And Obey! Overhaul your catechism] This is the first instance of Captain Cuttle's inveterate tendency to misquote and confuse attributions: he is alluding not to the Catechism but to 'The Solemnization of Matrimony' in the *BCP*. The priest asks the bride in reference to her future husband: 'Wilt thou obey him, and serve him, love, honour, and keep him in sickness and in health; and, forsaking all other, keep thee only unto him, so long as ye both shall live?' 'Overhaul' means 'To examine thoroughly, inspect, scrutinize; esp. to take apart and examine (a piece of equipment, etc.) and repair or modify it if necessary' (for a description of Cuttle's misquotations, see Holt, 1932, 303–08).

The reflection perhaps reminded him

he had better, like young Norval's father, "increase his store."] From John Homes's successful play *Douglas, a Tragedy* (first performed in Edinburgh in 1756 and in London in 1757), which is based on the Scottish ballad of 'Gill Morrice':

> My name is Norval; on the Grampian Hills
> My father feeds his flocks; a frugal swain,
> Whose constant cares were to increase his store,
> And keep his only son, myself, at home. (2.1)

"But he's chockfull of science,"

Up in a balloon? There you are. Down in a bell?] On the coronation of George IV, on 19 July 1821, Charles Green made the first ascent over London in a balloon inflated with coal gas. Eight launches followed in the 1830s; by the 1840s night ascents with displays of fireworks were so common that *Punch* complained it was impossible to go down Piccadilly after dark 'without getting your eyes filled with sand thrown out by the occupants of a balloon car'. Dickens satirized the public insatiability for ballooning spectacles and the 'grand accounts … in the morning papers' in an 1836 sketch, 'Vauxhall Gardens by Day' (Timbs, 1855, 23; *AR*, 1836 , 79, 113, 132, 150; *SB;* Metz, 2001, 142). Diving-bells were used to lower men underwater, often to recover property from foundered vessels, or to repair dock bottoms or landing-piers, or in the construction of breakwater works. In the 1840s, they were commonly made square at the top and bottom, the bottom being a little larger than the top, and the sides slightly diverging from above. The material is sometimes cast iron, the whole machine being cast in one piece, and made very thick. ... Sometimes the diving bell is made of planks of two thicknesses, with sheet lead between them. In the top of the machine are placed several strong glass lenses for the admission of light, such as are used in the decks of vessels to illuminate the apartments below. (Olmsted 172)

A *HW* article, 'Wholesale Diving', describes the descent of a diving-bell off the coast of France (6 [9 October 1852]: 76–81).

"Come! cried the subject of

grog,] 'Grog' consisted of spirits (usually rum) diluted with water and was generally served with a lump of sugar and a slice of lemon. The drink originated in the Navy, either to dilute the rum ration to prevent drunkenness or to mitigate the taste of questionable drinking water.

"Stand by!" said Ned,

"Stand by!"] A nautical phrase meaning 'to be prepared' (Smyth, 1867, 650).

"Yes, yes," said Sol,

Sir Richard Whittington married his master's daughter." ' "Turn again Whittington, Lord Mayor of London, and when you are old you will never depart from it," '] Captain Cuttle conflates the most famous lines from the legend of Dick Whittington with a verse from Proverbs 22.6: 'Train up a child in the way he should go: and when he is old, he will not depart from it'. The biography of the real Richard Whittington (d. 1423) inspired the legend, which is alluded to frequently in *DS*. In the legend, Dick Whittington is a poor orphan from the countryside who believes that the streets of London are paved with gold. He journeys to the city, and is rescued from starvation by Mr Fitzwarren, a rich merchant, who employs him as a scullion. Whittington ventures his only possession, a cat that he has purchased for a penny, as an item to be sold on his master's ship. Cruelly used by the ship's cook, Whittington runs away and walks as far as Holloway. But he turns back when, just outside London, he hears the bells of Bow Church begin to ring, and they seem to say, 'Turn again, Whittington, Thrice Lord Mayor of London'. He returns to London and discovers that his cat has been sold for a large fortune to the king of Barbary whose kingdom has been plagued with rats and mice. This new wealth enables Whittington to marry his master's daughter and 'live in great splendour'. He becomes Sheriff of London, three times Lord Mayor, and is knighted by Henry V. The first known reference to the legend is from a now-lost play, 'The History of Richard Whittington' (1605).

Chapter 5

Second monthly number
November 1846

PAUL'S PROGRESS AND CHRISTENING

Little Paul, suffering no contamination

on the lady thus distinguished.] The MS continues:

> Whether Miss Tox conceived that having been selected by the Fates to welcome the little Dombey before he was born, in Kirby, Beard, and Kirby's Best Mixed Pins, it therefore naturally devolved upon her to greet him with all other forms of welcome in all other early stages of his existence – or whether her over-flowing goodness induced her to volunteer into the domestic militia as a substitute in some sort for his deceased mama – or whether she was conscious of any other motives – are questions which in this stage of the Firm's history herself only could have solved. Nor have they much bearing on the fact (of which there is no doubt), that Miss Tox's constancy and zeal were a heavy discouragement to Richards, who lost flesh hourly under her patronage, and was in some danger of being superintended to death.

Miss Tox was often in

The administration of infantine doses of physic awakened all the active sympathy of her character;]

> One of the greatest errors of the nursery is the too frequent and indiscriminate exhibition by the mother or nurse of *purgative* medicine. Various are the forms in which it is given; perhaps, among a certain class, the "little powder" obtained from the chemist is the most frequent, as it is certainly the most injurious, from its chief ingredient being calomel.

Thomas Bull's *The Maternal Management of Children* (1853) recommended that infants with constipation (a common problem) be given one or two teaspoonfuls of castor oil, cautioning that parents might want to mix it with warm milk or float it 'on peppermint, mint, or some other aromatic water' in order to hide 'its unpleasant flavour'. Bull also recommended one to three drachms of manna, which was 'sweet to the taste, and mild in its operation', again with warm milk or 'in some aromatic water'; and five to ten grains of magnesia, a laxative that 'allays irritability of the stomach', which was especially useful when children were cutting their teeth, and which should be taken with hot milk; and rhubarb, which is especially useful for 'mild cases of diarrhœa'. In order to 'lessen the child's *misery* in physic taking', Bull

Icy christening – Describe the ceremony

Florence lost, and Richards dismissed. Good Mrs Brown.

Make childish romance of Florence being found by Walter –Mr Dombey don't like him.

Number Plan

Chapter 5 *Paul's Progress and Christening*

(Dealings with the firm of Dombey and Son No II)

chapter V.

Paul's Progress and christening

Staggs's Gardens
Biler a charity boy
Miss Tox as a visiting lady. No
The relations in the office
Paul's christening
Major Bagstock.

chapter VI.

Paul's Second deprivation

That is, his nurse.

chapter VII.

A Bird's-eye glimpse of Miss Tox's dwelling place. Also of the state of Miss Tox's affections

Staggs's Grove

Old Major   Polly at home

Miss Tox admires Mr Dombey

Chapter Plan

suggested the use of 'purgative biscuits', a concoction that mixed flour, sugar, eggs and the particular medicine (159–68). Children cutting their teeth would be given such 'soothing' narcotics as Godfrey's Cordial and Dalby's Carminative, both of which contained opium.

A contemporary obstetrician complained of the common tendency to overmedicate infants: 'How often have I been consulted in cases of infants a few days old, because of constipated bowels; and it would severely tax your credulity if I were to name the variety of remedies prescribed for these poor little innocents, without subduing the difficulty, but most certainly impairing the health of the little sufferers' (Bedford 423). Another practitioner put it more succinctly: 'How great a proportion of mankind hate the very name of physic!' ('Some Hints' 585).

Miss Tox was so transported beyond the ignorant present] *Macbeth* 1.5.55–7:

> Thy letters have transported me beyond
> This ignorant present, and I feel now
> The future in the instance.

"Very true, my dear Paul,"

"perhaps that is a reason why you might have the less objection to allowing Miss Tox to be godmother to the dear thing, if it were only as deputy and proxy for some one else.]

> The selection of godparents is often a matter of considerable delicacy and difficulty; for many people are reluctant to accept the office, while others again, who think they have a strong claim to the honour, are offended if they are overlooked. ... The godparents are chosen from the relatives and friends of the parents. ... It is not advisable to choose elderly people for this office; for, although its duties are supposed to cease at confirmation, yet the association often lasts a lifetime, and kindly help and counsel may be given in later days by the godparent of the godchild, should the battle of life prove hard, should parents die, or friends depart. (Lady Colin Campbell, *Etiquette of Good Society*, 1893, 28–9)

"It is not to be supposed,

your husband and myself will do well enough for the other sponsors,] The Anglican Catechism identifies 'Sponsors' as 'the second name for Godfathers and Godmothers'. The Church of England limits the number of godparents to three, requiring that, for every male child, there should be two godfathers and one godmother, and for every female child, one godfather and two godmothers.

Elevated thus to the godmothership

Mr. Dombey further signified his pleasure that the ceremony, already long delayed, should take place without further postponement.] Unless the infant were very sickly and in danger of dying, it was 'usual for the christening to take place, if possible, as soon as the mother is well enough to go out, when her infant is about a month old' (Campbell, 1893, 27). Young Paul's christening takes place some six months after Polly Toodle has been hired (cf. 'During the six months or so, Richards, which have seen you an inmate of this house').

left alone in his library.] The MS continues:

> He had already laid his hand upon the bellrope to convey his usual summons to Richards, when his eye fell upon a writing-desk, belonging to his deceased wife, which had been taken, among other things, from a cabinet in her chamber. It was not the first time that his eye had lighted on it. He carried the key in his pocket; and he brought it to his table and opened it now – having previously locked the room door – with a well-accustomed hand.
> From beneath a heap of torn and cancelled scraps of paper, he took one letter that remained entire. Involuntarily holding his breath as he opened this document, and 'bating in the stealthy action something of his arrogant demeanour, he sat down, resting his head upon one hand, and read it through.
> He read it slowly and attentively, and with a nice particularity to every syllable. Otherwise than as his great deliberation seemed unnatural, and perhaps the result of an effort equally great, he allowed no sign of emotion to escape him. When he had read it through, he folded and refolded it slowly several times, and tore it carefully into fragments. Checking his hand in the act of throwing these away, he put them in his pocket, as if unwilling to trust them even to the chances of being re-united and deciphered; and instead of ringing, as usual, for little Paul, he sat solitary, all the evening, in his cheerless room.

There was anything but solitude

As the knight-errants of old relieved their minds by carving their mistress's names in deserts, and wildernesses, and other savage places] A commonplace in romance literature. For example, in *As You Like It*, Orlando, the son of a knight, records his love for Rosalind on a tree in the Forest of Arden:

> Oh, Rosalind! these trees shall be my books,
> And in their barks my thoughts I'll character,
> That every eye which in this forest looks
> Shall see thy virtue witness'd everywhere.
> Run, run, Orlando; carve on every tree,
> The fair, the chaste, and unexpressive she. (3.2.5–10)

In *Waldemar* (1833; 8), W. H. Harrison refers to reading of 'love-lorn knights wandering through wilds and forests, without carving anything but the names of their cruel or locked-up mistresses on the barks of trees' (99). In 'The City of the Absent' (*UT*), Dickens characterizes the tendency of young City clerks to inscribe the names of their girlfriends on writing pads as 'the legitimate modern successor of the old forest-tree, whereon these young knights (having no attainable forest nearer than Epping) engrave the names of their mistresses' (*AYR*, 8 [18 July 1863]: 495).

"And the child, you see,"

She'll never wind and twine herself about her papa's heart like – " "Like the ivy?" suggested Miss Tox. … She'll never glide and nestle into the bosom of Papa's affections like – the – " "Startled fawn?" suggested Miss Tox.] Clichés of early-nineteenth century sentimental writing. The image of ivy twining itself around a heart occurs in poems such as 'Stanzas' by 'P. B': 'My heart's torn tendrils, vine-like, twine / With fond dependence still on thine' (*Chambers's Journal*, 1 [8 April 1854]: 224) and 'Monterey' by Frances Jane Crosby: 'Still 'round some kindred heart we twine / As clings the ivy to the vine' (Canto 2) (1851). The phrase 'startled fawn' occurs in countless places; for example: 'sprang away like a startled fawn' (1822); 'the first shy, startled fawn-like look of her sister' (1839); 'Timid as a startled fawn' (1835); 'she fled with the swiftness of a startled fawn' (1846). And Letitia Elizabeth Landon, a popular poet of the day, wrote a poem, 'The Indian Girl', with a character known as 'The Startled Fawn', characterized as 'The proud – the shy – the sensitive' (*The Poetical Works of Miss Landon*, 1839, 302–04).

This trivial incident had so

a servant was dispatched to fetch a hackney cabriolet] A hired cabriolet, a light two-wheeled chaise drawn by a single horse, with a large hood of wood or leather and an apron to cover the lap and legs of the passenger. Middle-class Londoners, who could not afford to own a carriage, would frequently hire various sorts of carriage to move about the city:

> Carriages of all kinds, for the conveyance of parties, may be hired at the various livery-stables, with which the metropolis abounds at the following prices – A barouche, or coach, at 1*l*. 5*s*. per day; post-chaise, or chariot, from 1*l*. to 25*s*. per day, with a gratuity (always expected) of 5*s*. to the driver; cabriolets, dennets and tilburies, with horse, at from 18*s*. to 20*s*. per day; saddle horses, at from 10*s*. to 15*s*. per day; any of which, however, if engaged for a longer period, may be obtained at a less price. (*Mogg's New Picture of London*, 1848, 189)

"Have the goodness, if you

take his number legibly."] Because Metropolitan hackney coaches were licensed and regulated, plates were affixed to them 'with the name and abode of the proprietor and number of the licence'. Hackney coaches also had their fares 'distinctly painted' on them, 'as well as the number of persons for whom the carriage is licensed' (*The Supplement* 2.296).

"*Mention to the man, then,*

if he gives her any of his impertinence] Dickens describes one instance of the cab-driver's 'impertinence' in 'The Last Cab Driver' (*SB*):

> In the event of your contemplating an offer of eightpence, on no account make the tender, or show the money, until you are safely on the pavement. It is very bad policy attempting to save the fourpence. You are very much in the power of a cabman, and he considers it a kind of fee not to do you any wilful damage. ... society made war upon him in the shape of penalties, and he must make war upon society in his own way. This was the reasoning of the red cab driver. So, he bestowed a searching look upon the fare, as he put his hand in his waistcoat pocket, when he had gone half the mile, to get the money ready; and if he brought forth eightpence, out he went. ('Second Series', December 1836)

"*You might keep me in*

"You might keep me in a strait-waistcoat for six weeks ... and when I got it off I'd only be more aggravated,] A keeper at Bethlehem Hospital for the insane explained to a Parliamentary Committee in 1815 why his institution did not use strait-waistcoats, unlike some private asylums:

> What are the disadvantages you conceive attending on the use of a strait-waistcoat? – The hands are completely secured, if the strait-waistcoat be tied tightly respiration is prevented or impeded, and it is always at the mercy of the keeper how tight he chooses to tie the waistcoat. If the patient be irritated by itching in any part, he is unable to administer the relief by scratching; or if troubled with flies, in hot weather, it is a painful incumbrance; and, if not changed, is liable to absorb a great deal of perspiration, which renders sometimes the skin excoriated. He cannot wipe his nose, and he becomes a driveller in consequence; he cannot assist himself in the evacuation of his urine or his faeces, or possess personal cleanliness, as long as the strait-waistcoat is applied. Then there is another very curious effect that has resulted from keeping on the strait-waistcoat for a considerable time; in every human hand, accustomed to use the organ of touch, the sentient, or palpitating extremities, or tangent extremities, are deadened, as to their sensibility, from want of use; the nails are pinched up, and I have seen some instances, where patients

have been long kept in the strait-waistcoat, where the nail has resembled the claw of an animal; so that I can pretty nearly judge by the look of the hand of a lunatic, if I do not see his face, whether he has been the subject of a strait-waistcoat a long while. (*Report, together with the Minutes of Evidence ... from the Committee appointed to consider of Provision being made for the Better Regulation of Madhouses in England.* London: House of Commons, 1815, 80–1)

two Griffins,] Also spelled 'griffon' or 'gyphon', these mythological creatures with the body of a lion and the head and wings of an eagle served as fierce protectors and guardians of valuable treasure.

"I'm very much beholden

a mulotter.] Her uneducated pronunciation of 'mulatto' is also used by Mrs Lirripper in 'Mrs. Lirripper's Lodgings': 'she married the ship's cook on the voyage (himself a Mulotter)'.

"It's very easy for some

you naughty, sinful child, if you don't shut your eyes this minute, I'll call in them hobgoblins that lives in the cock-loft to come and eat you up alive! ... Here Miss Nipper made a horrible lowing, supposed to issue from a conscientious goblin of the bull species. ... Having further composed her young charge by covering her head with the bed-clothes, and making three or four angry dabs at the pillow,] In 'Nurse's Stories' (*UT*), Dickens attributes 'most of the dark corners we are forced to go back to, against our wills' to the frightening stories told children by their nurses. One from his own childhood concerned 'a certain Captain Murderer' who cut off his wives' heads, chopped them into pieces and put them into meat pies, which he then sent to the baker, and eventually devoured. His nurse also seasoned the story with physical gestures and sounds: 'The young woman who brought me acquainted with Captain Murderer, had a fiendish enjoyment of my terrors, and used to begin, I remember – as a sort of introductory overture – by clawing the air with both hands, and uttering a long low hollow groan' (*AYR*, 3 [8 September 1860]: 518–9).

Though little Paul was said,

little Paul was said, in nursery phrase, "to take a deal of notice for his age,"] 'To take notice of' was a phrase specifically applied to babies, when they showed curiosity about their surroundings (cf. *CH*: 'Considered, by the doctor, a remarkably beautiful chi-ild! Equal to the general run of children at five months o-old! Takes notice, in a way quite won-der-ful!') (ch. 1; *OED*).

It happened to be an iron-grey

a shrewd east wind blowing –] The association of trouble with the east wind derives from the Old Testament (for example, Genesis 41.4–6, Exodus 10.13, Psalms 48.7, Ezekiel 17.10, 27.26) and had become a commonplace. Dickens refers to the 'East Wind' in a letter of 1849 mentioning the auction of the contents of Gore House to pay off Lady Blessington's debts, and in a speech to the Metropolitan Sanitary Association in 1851 he commented: 'the air from Gin Lane will be carried, when the wind is Easterly, into May Fair' (30 April 1849, *Letters* 5.530; *Speeches* 128). Richard Carstone uses the image to foreshadow trouble in *BH* (ch. 6), as does Mr Jarndyce (ch. 8).

Ugh! They were black, cold rooms

Mr. Pitt, in bronze ... with no trace of his celestial origin about him,] William Pitt, the Younger (1759–1806), the youngest Prime Minister in British history (he was 24 when he took office), served from 1783 to 1801 and again from 1804 until his death in 1806. Pitt was popularly known as 'the heaven-born minister,' an epithet given him by the third Duke of Chandos (see *The Autobiography of Leigh Hunt*, 1850, 1.22). Byron uses it in 'The Waltz; an apostrophic hymn' (1811): 'Oh Germany! How much to thee we owe, / As heaven-born Pitt can testify below'. Critics of Pitt, such as William Cobbett, sometimes used the phrase sarcastically:

> But what has been the modern practice with regard to this property? In the year 1798, the 'heaven-born minister,' Pitt, took away a part of this property; and if he could do so – if the 'heaven-born' minister could do so, surely ungodly fellows like we may make the proposition. (Laughter.) (*Eleven Lectures. ...*, 'Church Property!!! A Seventh Lecture of the French Revolution, and English Boroughmongering', 1830, 6)

The precocious son of a famous father, Pitt was noted for his reasoned and fact-filled speeches, his knowledge of public finances and his association with commercial interests and the urban middle class (making him an appropriate hero for a businessman such as Mr Dombey). His first years as Prime Minister (1783–1792) were marked by success: he restored British prestige following the American War of Independence; established government control over the East India Company; comprehensively addressed Canadian problems; reduced custom duties to stimulate trade; introduced a new sinking fund to deal with the growing national debt; and promoted modest electoral reform. Following France's declaration of war against Britain in 1793, his administration became increasingly repressive – he cracked down on radicals, suspended habeas corpus, supported treason trials in 1794 and tried to counter the influence of revolutionary ideals at home – moves that earned him the opprobrium of caricaturists such as James Gillray, who portrayed him as a fungus on a dungheap, an image later used by the young Coleridge in his radical lectures. Pitt was often criticized for his personal coldness (again, making him an appropriate model for Dombey) and his excessive fondness for drink. He died at 46, his legend influencing the Tory movement in the early nineteenth century (although he considered himself an independent Whig). George Canning's poem, 'The Pilot that Weathered the Storm' (1802), celebrates Pitt as a symbol of British resistance to the French republic and empire, an idea borrowed by Carlyle in *Latter-Day Pamphlets* ('Downing Street', 1850) and alluded to by Dickens in *LD* (1.34) (Cannon, 1997, 752–3; Newman, 1997, 546–8; McCalman, 1999, 648–9).

Bronze and marble busts, statues, medallions, engravings and other mementos of Pitt were common throughout the nineteenth century (for a listing, see the appendix to Edward Gibbon Ashbourne's *Pitt: Some Chapters of His Life and Times*, 1898, 369–92). Browne depicts Pitt's bust in illustrations to the sixteenth number, 'Mr. Dombey and the World' and to the final two-part number, ' "Let him remember it in that room, years to come!" '

guarded the unattainable treasure like an enchanted Moor.] An allusion to one of Dickens's favourite childhood books, Cervantes' *Don Quixote* (1605, 1615). At the inn that Don Quixote mistakes for a castle, he arranges a night-time meeting with the ugly servant-girl Maritornes (whom he believes to be the beautiful daughter of the lord of the castle), but he is beaten up by a mule-driver who has also come to visit her. He tells Sancho Panza that his attacker was no mere mortal: 'I conjecture that the treasure of this damsel's beauty is guarded by some enchanted Moor, and is not reserved for me' (1.17). The fight with the 'enchanted Moor' is frequently recalled (1.43, 45; 2.44).

A dusty urn at each high corner, dug up from an ancient tomb, preached desolation and decay, as from two pulpits;] The increasing number of tourists on the Continent after 1815 gave rise to a flourishing market in antiquities (many of which were faked: see, for instance, Mr Meagles in *LD,* bk 1, ch. 16). The 'two pulpits' are, strictly, a pulpit and a lectern: in the Anglican church, the pulpit stands on the left of the chancel (as viewed by the congregation) and is where the clergyman reads the Gospel lesson and delivers the sermon. On the right stands the lectern, used by lay persons to read the scripture lesson and to lead the congregation in prayer.

And enter that fair enslaver,

fair enslaver,] A romantic cliché, used by writers such as Smollett ('Our hero having prudently submitted to the superior intelligence of his fair enslaver', *Peregrine Pickle* [1751], ch. 53), Fanny Burney ('all that remained to be discovered, was the reception it had meant from his fair enslaver', *Cecilia* [1782], ch. 7), and elsewhere by Dickens (*PP* [54], *OCS* [60], and *OMF* [2.16]).

The baby soon appeared,

in lighter mourning than at first,] For the gradual 'lightening' of the mourning costume, see the note to chapter 3, p. 50.

Once upon the road to church,

the christening party] At Forster's suggestion, Dickens decided to shorten his planned treatment of the christening scene, as a guard against irreverence. He told Forster on 3 October 1846: 'I thought of the possibility of malice on christening points of faith, and put the drag on as I wrote' (*Letters* 4.628). This reluctance to offend probably also explains why Dickens decided against having Browne illustrate the scene.

Arrived at the church steps,

they were received by a portentous beadle.] In 'Our Parish', Dickens refers to the parish beadle as 'the most important member of the local administration', representing him as a combination of indifference and arrogance: 'See him again on Sunday, in his state coat and cocked-hat, with a large-headed staff for show in his left hand, and a small cane for use in the right. How pompously he marshals the children into their places!' (*SB*). A beadle was a subordinate parish official who fulfilled a constabulary function: he maintained order during church services, cleared the streets of beggars, helped collect the poor rate and performed various other policing duties. Beadles were noted for their striking uniform: a three-cornered or 'cocked' hat, a wide-skirted coat trimmed with gold braid, knee-breeches and an official staff. The establishment of the Metropolitan Police in 1829 made the beadle redundant – an issue that was much discussed in the journals and newspapers of the 1840s and 1850s. The most notable fictional representation of a beadle is Mr Bumble in *OT* (2).

Miss Tox's hand trembled

a Babylonian collar.] That is, huge or gigantic (*OED*). George Cruikshank's portrait of a beadle in his *London Characters* (1829) shows the beadle's ceremonial coat as having a tall stand-up collar reaching to his chin and ears. De Quincey used 'Babylonian' in the same sense in *Confessions of an English Opium-Eater* (1821): 'No huge Babylonian centres of commerce towered into the clouds'. Babylon, the largest city in the ancient world, was often in the news from the 1820s onwards, partly influenced by the reports of the antiquarian and traveller, Claudius James Rich, who began excavating in 1811–12 and returned in 1817. He published his discoveries in *Memoir on the Ruins of Babylon* (1815) and *Narrative of a Journey to the Site of Babylon in 1811* (1839). Other scholars and archaeologists carried out subsequent excavations in 1827, 1849 and from the 1850s onwards.

Little Paul might have asked

Little Paul might have asked with Hamlet "into my grave?" so chill and earthy was the place.] To Polonius's aside, 'Will you walk out of the air, my lord?', Hamlet responds, 'Into my grave' (2.2.207–9).

The tall shrouded pulpit and reading desk; the dreary perspective of empty pews stretching away under the galleries, and empty benches mounting to the roof and lost in the shadow of the great grim organ; the dusty matting and cold stone slabs; the grisly free seats in the aisles; and the damp corner by the bell-rope, where the black tressels used for funerals were stowed away ... the strange, unused, uncomfortable smell, and the cadaverous light; were all in unison. It was a cold and dismal scene.] In the *UT* piece, 'City of London Churches' (5 May 1860), Dickens observed of the ageing churches in the City of London:

> There are few more striking indications of the changes of manners and customs that two or three hundred years have brought about, than these deserted Churches. Many of them are handsome and costly structures, several of them were designed by WREN, many of them arose from the ashes of the great fire, others of them outlived the plague and the fire too, to die a slow death in these later days. No one can be sure of the coming time; but it is not too much to say of it that it has no sign in its outsetting tides, of the reflux to these churches of their congregations and uses. They remain like the tombs of the old citizens who lie beneath them and around them, Monuments of another age. (*AYR* 3.89)

The 'grisly free seats' are those 'pews, sittings or benches ... in every such church or chapel, marked with the words "free seats" amounting to not less than one-fifth of the whole sittings ... appropriated for the use of poor persons resorting thereto for ever; upon which pews or sittings no rent shall be charged' (Cripps, 1845, 410). On the large number of churches in the City of London, see note to chapter 56, p. 487.

The very wedding looking

an over-aged and over-worked and underpaid attorney's clerk, "making a search," was running his forefinger down the parchment pages of an immense register (one of a long series of similar volumes) gorged with burials.] He resembles 'the middle-aged copying clerk, with a large family, who is always shabby, and often drunk', one of the lesser of the 'several grades of lawyers' clerks' caricatured in *PP* (ch. 31). The low status of attorney's clerks was proverbial in the nineteenth century. *Blackwood's*, for instance, referred to 'the miserable attorney's clerk', equating him with 'an intriguing Jew' or 'a common cabman' ('Norman Sinclair', 88 [September 1860], 360). In *Heads of the People* (1840), a lawyer's clerk complains of the long hours and pitiful pay for the typical lower-level attorney's clerk:

Every week I worked for sixty hours, obtaining a remuneration of three-pence per hour, and producing an average eight folios in each, for which my employer received two shillings and eight-pence. This discrepancy between the charge of the master and the pay of the labourer, gives birth to the dissatisfaction that englooms the working classes. Supposing my work to have regularly amounted to what I have named, the week's account stands thus:

	Attorney	Attorney's clerk
480 folios, at 4*d*. per folio ...	£8.0.0	£ 0 15 0' (28)

Dickens himself worked as an attorney's clerk, from spring 1827 to autumn 1828, in the office of Ellis and Blackmore, solicitors, at Gray's Inn, and then briefly for Charles Molloy at Symond's Inn. A lawyer's office was, he told a correspondent, 'a very little world, and a very dull one' (*Letters* 1.423).

Churches contained three registers, for births, marriages and deaths. This particular attorney's clerk is searching the burial register, perhaps to trace a pedigree, to locate the heirs of a deceased person or to register a will, this last being among Dickens's own duties while working at Ellis and Blackmore.

After another cold interval,

a wheezy little pew-opener] A church usher, generally an older woman, who assisted at baptisms, marriages and funerals. Douglas Jerrold noted of her attendance at baptisms:

> Here her experience, her knowledge of the world, as picked up and cultivated in the temple of the Lord, stands her in exceeding help. She can at a glance espy the respectable mothers and godmothers, the fathers well to do, and the godfathers of sufficient purse; and, benefiting by her knowledge, she bestows them in separate pews, wide away from the poorer sort. And there are babies whose eyes are blessed by the Pew-Opener with all the prodigality of sudden admiration, the eyes, perhaps, being entirely hidden by the costly lace about them: "darling little angels," whose month or six weeks' noses alone are visible; "cherubs," who have nought in common with the cherubic nature, except indeed in their continual crying. (*Heads of the People*, 1840, 231)

coughing like a grampus.] A type of dolphin, known for its spouting and blowing, and for its ferocity attacking its prey. The term 'grampus' has often been applied to many large fish. In a transferred sense, a 'grampus' is 'A person given to puffing and blowing'. In *PP*, for instance, an unnamed young boy is described as 'a young Grampus!' because 'the boy breathes so very hard while he's eating' (25).

Presently the clerk (the only cheerful

the clergyman ... appeared like the principal character in a ghost-story, "a tall figure all in white;"] A cliché of gothic fiction and other works having gothic motifs. In Matthew G. Lewis's drama *Castle Spectre* (1797), Alice claims to have seen the devil, 'a tall figure all in white extended upon the bed!' (4.1). In Louisa May Alcott's *Little Women* (1868–9), 'A tall figure, all in white, with a veil over its face, and a lamp in its wasted hand' glides 'noiselessly' down 'a corridor as dark and cold as any tomb'. In 'Tramps' (*UT*), Dickens alludes to these kinds of 'old stories', which contain 'a tall figure, all in white, with saucer eyes, coming up and saying, "I want you to come to a churchyard and mend a church clock. Follow me!" ' (*AYR*, 3 [16 June 1860]: 233). The most famous use of the motif occurs in Wilkie Collins's *The Woman in White* (1860).

Even when that event had

Miss Tox kept her Prayer-book open at the Gunpowder Plot,] One of the 'Prayers and Thanksgivings upon Several Occasions' in the *BCP*:

> A Form of Prayer with Thanksgiving,
> TO BE USED YEARLY UPON THE FIFTH DAY OF NOVEMBER,
> For the happy Deliverance of King JAMES I and the Three Estates of
> ENGLAND, from the most traitorous and bloody-intended Massacre by
> Gunpowder.

It was added to the *BCP* in 1605, the year of the failed attempt by a small group of Roman Catholics to blow up the Houses of Parliament, and removed in 1859.

The register signed, and the fees paid, and the pew-opener ... remembered, and the beadle gratified, and the sexton ... not forgotten,] When the baptism has been performed,

> The father accompanies the clergyman to the vestry after the service, in order to give particulars necessary for registration, and also to distribute the proper fees. ... In London these ceremonials are most expensive – so many persons appear on the scene, all of whom expect gratuities. The beadle and the sexton, the woman who sweeps inside the church and the man who sweeps outside, the pew-opener and the clerk, are all ready with itching palms. (Campbell, 1893, 30–1)

During the whole of these proceedings

the clergyman, in delivering ... the closing exhortation, relative to the future examination of the child by the sponsors,] The penultimate paragraph of the Public Baptism of Infants in the *BCP* reads:

> *Then, all standing up, the Priest shall say to the Godfathers and Godmothers this Exhortation following.*

Chapter 5 *Paul's Progress and Christening*

> Forasmuch as this child hath promised by you his sureties to renounce the devil and all his works, to believe in God, and to serve him; ye must remember, that it is your parts and duties to see that this infant be taught, so soon as he shall be able to learn, what a solemn vow, promise, and profession, he hath here made by you. … and that this child may be virtuously brought up to lead a godly and a Christian life; remembering always, that Baptism doth represent unto us our profession; which is, to follow the example of our Saviour Christ, and to be made like unto him; that, as he died, and rose again for us, so should we, who are baptized, die from sin, and rise again unto righteousness; continually mortifying all our evil and corrupt affections, and daily proceeding in all virtue and godliness of living.

When it was all over,

he informed the clergyman how much pleasure it would have given him to have solicited the honour of his company at dinner, but for the unfortunate state of his household affairs.] Lady Colin Campbell's *Etiquette of Good Society* (1893) observes that, whatever the form of entertainment that follows the christening, 'the officiating clergyman is always invited'. The exact nature of the 'entertainment' varied: sometimes, when the christening took place in the morning, the guests would return to lunch, sometimes, 'they separate at the church door, and meet again in the evening at a dinner party in honour of the young stranger' (32).

the sexton]

> The duties of the sexton are determined chiefly by custom, but they are of a similar nature to those of the ancient sacristan. He is the keeper of the church-keys, has general charge of the church, its cleansing and lighting, as also of the vestments and *instrumenta* of Divine Services. … He is also the superintendent of the bell-ringers, and has the care of the churchyard as well as of the church; and he prepares the graves for the burial of the dead, either personally or by his deputies. (Blunt, 1876, 293–4)

There they found Mr. Pitt

Miss Tox produced a mug for her godson, and Mr. Chick a knife and fork and spoon in a case. Mr. Dombey also produced a bracelet for Miss Tox;] Godparents were expected to give their godchild a gift, typically 'a silver mug, a knife, spoon and fork, a handsomely-bound bible, or perhaps a costly piece of lace or embroidery suitable for infants' wear'. Men were usually advised to give something made of silver (Young 286). In 1850, *HW* 'regretted that, at the present time, the grave responsibilities of the sponsors of children is too often considered to end with the presentation of some such gifts as we have enumerated' (1.108).

There was a toothache

He might have been hung up for sale at a Russian fair as a specimen of a frozen gentleman.] The oldest and most celebrated trade fair in Russia was held annually at Nijni-Novgorod, on the Volga. The fair, which dated from the Middle Ages, began in late July and lasted more than a month. It attracted 'merchants from every country and climate – Europeans, Bokharians, Khivans, Kirghizes, Tartars, Armenians, Persians, and even Chinese'. Contemporary accounts of the fair invariably stressed its size ('more than twenty-five miles of streets') and the multiplicity of goods ('every conceivable object of necessity or luxury'):

> Here are mountains of gaudily-painted chests from Kazan, of sizes to suit the wardrobe of each purchaser; there great piles of hides from the Ukraine, bales of cotton goods from the factory of a Russian prince, heaps of fur from the icy regions of Archangel, the wealth of Persia, the treasures of the Ural, tea from China, and iron from Siberia. Each department of commerce had its particular quarter. Thus business is transacted with facility, and bargains are concluded in which millions of rubles are involved, with rapidity which would astonish our richest merchants. (Scott, 1854, 92; *Chambers's Encyclopædia*, 1874, 6.770)

An article on Russian fairs appeared in *Bentley's Miscellany*, which Dickens edited from 1837–9: 'Visit to a Siberian Fair: the Tshuktshi Fair at Ostrovnoie', 7 (1840): 484–96.

Mr. Dombey, in the meanwhile,

Mr. Dombey … had issued orders for the attendance of Richards, who now entered … without the baby;] In its description of the duties of the head nurse, Samuel and Sarah Adams's *The Complete Servant* (1825) states: 'Wages £18 to £25. Perquisites at christenings'. During the entertainment, it was usual for the baby to be exhibited by the nurse, 'either before or after the repast in all the splendour of its christening robe'. She would 'generally' receive 'a present on these occasions – a piece of money is slipped into her hand' (262; Campbell, 1893, 32).

"I am far from being friendly,"

"I am far from being friendly," pursued Mr. Dombey, "to what is called by persons of levelling sentiments, general education. But it is necessary that the inferior classes should continue to be taught to know their position, and to conduct themselves properly.] Throughout the 1830s, Parliament considered a number of educational reforms designed to extend educational opportunities to large portions of the population. Although it rejected four Education Bills in the early 1830s, in 1833 Parliament voted £20,000 to assist School Societies. By the end of the decade, the Committee of Council for Education, the Inspectorate and the Central Society for Education had been established to improve education and widen its reach. It was not until 1870, the year of Dickens's death, that compulsory schooling was established throughout England.

Proponents of a general educational system argued that it would educate the populace to vote; improve the efficiency of industrial society; enable people to read the Bible and have access to cultural resources; lower crime rates; and, as Mr Dombey says, teach 'the inferior classes' to know their place. Dickens generally supported universal schooling: he believed that the state should ensure that all children have access to an education; that it should help pay for the costs; and that it should supervise the standard of teaching. Although he recognized the merit of certain private school initiatives such as the Ragged School Movement, he found them 'at best, a slight and ineffectual palliative of an enormous evil. They want system, power, means, authority, experienced and thoroughly trained teachers' (*HW*, 'Boys to Mend', 5 [11 Sept. 1852]: 596). As he wrote in 'Small Beginnings',

> To endow such Institutions [as the Westminster Ragged Dormitory], and leave the question of National Education in its present shameful state, would be to maintain a cruel absurdity to which we are most strongly opposed. The compulsory industrial education of neglected children, and the severe punishment of neglectful and unnatural parents, are reforms to which we *must* come, doubt it who may. (*HW*, 3 [5 April 1851]: 41–2)

Dickens's most thorough statement in defence of state schooling comes in a letter to Edward Baines, who had publicly opposed such a system:

> I think it right that the State should educate the people; and I think it wrong that it should punish Ignorance, without enlightening or preventing it.
>
> But I would limit its power, and watch it very carefully. I suppose the sense and virtue of the people to have expression in the State; and I do not contemplate the possibility of the Government in England, at this time of day, presuming to tread the minds of the people under its feet.
>
> I apprehend that there are certain sound rudiments of a good education, and certain moral and religious truths, on which we might all agree. I would have those taught in State Schools, to the children of parents of all Christian denominations; favouring no one Church more than another. (*Letters*, 6 [7 June 1850]: 111)

Having the power of nominating a child on the foundation of an ancient establishment, called (from a worshipful company) the Charitable Grinders; where not only is a wholesome education bestowed upon the scholars, but where a dress and badge is likewise provided for them;] Although in one form or another charity schools have existed in Britain since the Elizabethan period, the charity school movement proper began in 1699 when the Society for Promoting Christian Knowledge (SPCK) organised and co-ordinated schools for the poor in every London parish. Charity schools, supported by the donations of private benefactors who often had the right to nominate candidates for the schools, inculcated self-sufficiency, industrious habits and emphasized the Bible, the catechism, 'the three Rs' and the teaching of Anglican doctrine, though sponsors insisted that the children should not be educated above their station. The students, who wore coarse and plain uniforms, attended school for six to seven hours a day and were often provided with training in a craft or trade. Merchants who wanted cheap child labour opposed the charity movement, as did tradesmen who feared that their children would be displaced by apprentices trained in charity schools. Charity schools flourished throughout the eighteenth century and were particularly strong in London and Bristol. In 1729, London had 129 charity schools with 5,225 students. By 1818, 18,400 charity schools existed in England and Wales, with 334,432 students. The early years of the nineteenth century, though, saw the waning of royal support for the schools, and their limited curriculum and poorly prepared teachers brought them into disrepute (*Britain in the Hanoverian Age* 113; *The Oxford Companion to British History* 190).

The precedent for distinctive clothing for charity pupils was set by London's Charity Hospital or Blue-Coat School, which opened in 1553 and provided a model for charitable institutions as late as the nineteenth century (see note to chapter 44, pp. 418–9). In his 'outline' for improving pauper management, Bentham endorsed the concept of distinguishing paupers by their clothing, arguing '*Soldiers wear uniforms*, why not paupers? – those who save the country, why not those who are saved by it' (8.389). Dickens himself criticized charity schools for their inefficiency and for their tendency to stigmatize poor children by forcing them to wear ugly uniforms. In a speech of 5 November 1857, he said of the schools: 'I don't by any means like schools in leather breeches, and with mortified straw baskets for bonnets, which file along the streets to churches in long melancholy rows under the escort of that surprising British monster, a Beadle' (*Speeches* 241). He much preferred the Boston Blind School, which he visited on his tour of America in 1842, for there were 'no charity uniforms, no wearisome repetition of the same dull ugly dress' (3). As Philip Collins has pointed out, Dickens preferred the kind of charity schools 'established, not by the rich for the poor, but by the members of a middle-class trade for the "orphan and necessitous children" of their brethren' (79), charity schools, in other words, that emphasized self-help and avoided patronage (e.g. the Commercial Travellers' School).

Besides Robin Toodle, other Dickensian charity boys include Uriah Heep (*DC*), Grandfather Smallweed (*BH*) and Noah Claypole (*GE*). Like Mr Dombey, Dickens had himself donated enough money to certain institutions to give him the right to nominate candidates, though he believed that the system was humiliating to those who were forced to seek votes, and to donors, who were flooded with requests from supplicants (Collins, 1963, 77–79). 'Worshipful Company' is an honorific title assumed by livery companies and freemasons' lodges (e.g. Carpenters, Goldsmiths, Stationers, Tilers and Bricklayers).

6 Blue-coat charity school uniform. This statue (*left*) is still above the door of what was the Blew-Coat School, Caxton Street, Westminster, 1709. The photograph of a blue-coat schoolboy (*right*) is probably from the 1890s, but the uniform has barely changed. It is still worn today in Christ's Hospital, Horsham, Kent.

"One hundred and forty-seven," said

"The dress ... is a nice, warm, blue baize tailed coat and cap, turned up with orange-coloured binding; red worsted stockings; and very strong leather small-clothes.] Although charity school uniforms varied slightly from school to school, the charity boy would typically wear a single-breasted collarless tail coat, designed in an early-eighteenth-century fashion, which reached to or covered the knees, and which had metal buttons and large flapped pockets (Plate 6). Worn underneath the coat was a long-sleeved waistcoat that could be worn indoors. The shirt had a wide, white collar with long tabs at the front. The boy would also wear leather knee-breeches ('small-clothes') and woollen stockings. The distinctive cap had a flat crown, narrow brim and a red bobble on top. Blue and grey were the most popular colours for the main charity-school garments, and sometimes green and brown. From about 1717, a badge, generally a perforated metal disc made of copper or brass, was worn on the breast of the coat or the waistcoat. The badges would typically bear the child's number and the name of the school (Cunnington and Lucas, 1978, 122–8).

Such temporary indications of

the Dead March in Saul.] The popular name for the funeral march from Handel's oratorio *Saul* (1739), which became a favourite funeral processional, and which was used on state occasions, such as the funeral of the sovereign.

The party seemed to get colder and colder, and to be gradually resolving itself into a congealed and gelid state] Fashionable chaudfroid and aspic dishes were highly ornamental (because the meat, fish or poultry could be seen through the transparent jelly) and difficult to achieve. The principles of preparing the classic aspic dishes are explained by the celebrated French chef, Anton Carême, in his *Le Cuisinier Parisien* (1828), and Mrs Beeton gives a recipe for 'Aspic, or Ornamental Savoury Jelly' (no. 366).

whistled "With a hey ho chevy!"] 'With a heigh ho, chivey / Hark forward, hark forward, tantivy!', originally the chorus of an eighteenth-century hunting song, 'Old Towler', became well known from 1824 because of its inclusion in a frequently reviewed parody of von Weber's opera, *Der Freischutz* (1821), first performed in London at the English Opera House in 1824. The parody, *Der Freischutz Travestie*, by 'Septimus Globus', was published in 1824 and illustrated with twelve etchings by George Cruikshank. The song containing the chorus is entitled 'Skeleton Huntsmen', and reviews of the parody always quoted the lyrics of the song (*The London Literary Gazette and Journal of Belles Lettres, Arts Sciences &c ... for the Year 1824*, 651–2; *The Portfolio*, 1825, 4.86–8; Hone, 1826, 1.648-9; for the lyrics of 'Old Towler', see: *The Musical Banquet of Choice Songs*, 1790, 22–3).

Chapter 6

PAUL'S SECOND DEPRIVATION

Polly was beset by so many

who (like Tony Lumpkin), if she could bear the disappointments of other people with tolerable fortitude, could not abide to disappoint herself,] In the first act of Oliver Goldsmith's *She Stoops to Conquer* (1773), Tony Lumpkin informs his mother that he is going to a local alehouse, the Three Jolly Pigeons. When she comments that he could 'disappoint them for one night at least', he responds, 'As for disappointing *them*, I should not so much mind; but I can't abide to disappoint myself' (5.110).

This euphonious locality was situated

the Strangers' Map of London, as printed (with a view to pleasant and commodious reference) on pocket-handkerchiefs, condenses, with some show of reason, into Camden Town.] Several London maps were especially designed for the use of visitors, such as *Mogg's Strangers' Guide to London* (1837) and *Wallis's Guide for Strangers through London* (1825, 1827, 1841). For the sake of portability and convenience, maps were occasionally printed on handkerchiefs. For instance, John William Steel, in an historical sketch of the Society of Friends (1899), claimed to possess 'a map of the six Northern Counties' of England, 'prepared by James Backhouse of Darlington, in 1773, and printed upon a large silk handkerchief for light carriage and easy reference when travelling' (75).

Camden Town, north-east of Regent's Park between Somers Town and Kentish Town, was laid out in 1788 with construction beginning in 1791. The modest houses, which were intended for industrious artisans who desired to live in the suburbs, deteriorated quickly into 'fourth-rate residences, public and boarding-houses', and were thus considered dispensable when the London and Birmingham Railway company sought land in the 1830s (Kellett, 1969, 247). Camden was originally intended as the terminus for the London and Birmingham Railway, but when Euston Station assumed this function, Camden Town Station and its 'immense warehouses' were

> used chiefly as a kind of supplementary station to that of Euston Square; here, for instance, are kept the engines required for the metropolitan extremity of the line; and here all the heavy goods are set down, with cattle, sheep, &c., thereby leaving the Euston Square station entirely for the accommodation of passengers, and for the receipt and delivery of parcels. (Knight, 1844, 6.313)

When Dickens was ten years old, his family moved from Chatham into a small house in Camden Town, on Bayham Street, parallel to and east of High Street. His memories of the area, recorded by Forster, were altogether unpleasant:

> Bayham Street was then about the poorest part of the London suburbs, and the house was a mean, small tenement, with a wretched little garden abutting on a squalid court. Here was no place for new acquaintances for him; no boys were near with whom he might hope to become in any way familiar. A washerwoman lived next door, and a Bow Street officer lived over the way. Many times has he spoken to me of this, and how he seemed at once to fall into a solitary condition apart from all other boys of his own age, and to sink at home into a neglected state which had always been quite unaccountable to him. (1.1)

In 'An Unsettled Neighbourhood', Dickens characterized early-nineteenth-century Camden, before the railway, as a 'shabby, dingy, damp, and mean' neighbourhood, whose inhabitants 'made a desperate stand to keep up appearances', hiding behind their doors 'to diffuse the fiction that a servant of some sort was the ghostly warder', and never paying their bills until absolutely necessary. As Dickens described it, Camden Town before the railways had few visitors, few shops, and even a cab 'was such a rare sight'. '[I]f ever a man might have thought a neighbourhood was settled down until it dropped to pieces', he remarked, 'a man might have thought ours was' (*HW* 10.289).

The first shock of a great earthquake had,

The first shock of a great earthquake had, just at that period, rent the whole neighbourhood to its centre. Traces of its course were visible on every side. Houses were knocked down; streets broken through and stopped; deep pits and trenches dug in the ground; enormous heaps of earth and clay thrown up; buildings that were undermined and shaking, propped by great beams of wood. ... Everywhere were bridges that led nowhere; thoroughfares that were wholly impassable; Babel towers of chimneys, wanting half their length; temporary wooden houses and enclosures, in the most unlikely situations; carcases of ragged tenements, and fragments of unfinished walls and arches, and piles of scaffolding, and wildernesses of bricks, and giant forms of cranes, and tripods straddling above nothing.] In 1853, Charles Manby Smith described the kind of dislocation and disruption consequent upon the construction of railway lines:

> *Now* ... what do we see? Bricks and tiles, and staring windows, from which, for aught we know, a thousand eyes may be looking down upon us; and there, a few yards or so to the left, the deep gorge of a railway cutting, which has ploughed its way right through the centre of the market-gardens, and burrowing beneath the carriage-road, and knocking a thousand houses out of its path, pursues its circuitous course to the city. (361)

Early calculations of the number of such street demolitions – for instance, the estimates that appear in parliamentary debates of the 1840s – are unreliable: until 1853, railway companies did not provide exact figures, and local or central governments did not assess the extent of the destruction. 'Until the early fifties the real costs of metropolitan improvements were therefore unknown', explains H. J. Dyos, 'for the displaced persons of Early Victorian London remained uncounted and their migrations uncharted', though even approximate numbers would 'seem to show that the figure of 20,000 persons displaced by "metropolitan engineering works", including railways, before 1864, or even that of 50,000 by 1867, are both too low' ('Railways and Housing' 13).

In short, the yet unfinished

the ... Railroad was in progress, and, from the very core of all this dire disorder, trailed smoothly away, upon its mighty course of civilisation and improvement.]
The phrase 'civilisation and improvement', was first used by Goldsmith in his *History of England* (4 vols; 1764, 1771): 'The slave trade was represented in its true light by Mr. Wilberforce, who affirmed, that it produced frequent and cruel wars among the natives of Africa, and greatly obstructed their civilisation and improvement' ('George III', cited in 1806 ed., 14.263). The phrase gained currency in the next few decades and was used by such writers as William Godwin, *An Enquiry Concerning Political Justice* (2 vols 1793; 'Of National Characters', 1.66) and Thomas Malthus, *Definitions in Political Economy* (1827): 'that natural and necessary state of things, which, in the progress of civilisation and improvement, tends continually to increase the quantity of fixed capital employed ...' (chs 5, 32).

A confidence in the power of the railway to civilize and improve was common in the middle of the nineteenth century. John Francis's comments in *A History of the English Railway* (1851) are typical:

> Railways have produced results which the wildest prospectus never dared to exhibit. They have found sources of profit which the most vivid imagination never conceived. They have carried millions instead of thousands, and that at a rate so low as to compel traffic where none previously existed. They have created towns, erected manufactories, built churches, educated children, peopled villages, filled heaths with houses, given the poor man the luxuries of the rich, placed the wealthy on a level with the poor, enforced a punctuality which was before wanting, have taken the townsman from the smoke of the city, have given the yeoman a glimpse of the town paved with the gold of imagination, have shed a light and life over many a country village, and by the power of that great discovery for which Franklin was derided, which Wheatstone has developed, and which Cooke has applied, have made the uttermost parts of the land converse with the speed of light. (1.202)

But as yet, the neighbourhood

But as yet, the neighbourhood was shy to own the Railroad. One or two bold speculators had projected streets; and one had built a little, but had stopped among the mud and ashes to consider farther of it. ... Nothing was the better for it, or thought of being so.] In 1851, John Francis recorded the kind of dark predictions inspired by the construction of the London and Birmingham Railway:

> It was said with great boldness and bitterness of spirit, that the new railway would be "a drug on the country;" that its "bridges and culverts would be antiquarian ruins;" that "it would not take tolls sufficient to keep it in repair;" that "the directors were making ducks and drakes of their money;" that "every hill and valley between the two towns would behold falling arches and ruined viaducts." It was said once more that game would cease to be, and that

agricultural communication would be lost; that not a field existed but what would be split and divided; springs would be dried up, meadows become sterile, agricultural operations would be suspended. Like an earthquake it would create chasms, it would upheave mountains; and it was pathetically added, the railway promoter was like an evil providence, unrighteously attempting that which nature was too kind to effect. (1.174)

It was also said that railways would produce ashes that would ignite homes close to the tracks and smoke that would 'injure' the wool of nearby sheep; that their engines would emit a poisoned gas that would kill the game flying overhead; that they would put 'Hundreds of innkeepers and thousands of horses' out of work, as well as lessen 'labour for the poor'; that they would destroy Britain's canal system; that falling embankments would crush houses; that railways would render useless the 27,000 miles of turnpike roads; that 'the gloom and damp of tunnels, and the deafening peal, the clanking chains, and the dismal glare of the locomotives would be disastrous alike to body and mind' (Williams, 1852, 34–5).

In the wake of the financial crisis of 1825, a number of the more traditional commercial houses of London were initially reluctant to invest heavily in the railway. In the words of John Francis, 'They rarely ventured on anything novel': 'They feared at once to involve their character and their capital, and for a short time they held aloof' (178, 180). By 1846, the year Dickens began *DS*, this reluctance had disappeared, as an early history of the railway explained:

> Up to the year 1843, and during part of 1844, railways may be regarded as honestly working their way through good and evil report into the public appreciation of their value, not only socially and generally, but as a means for the investment of capital. The security and profit they offered were so great that there was a rapid flow of capital in the new direction. The dividends paid by the London and Birmingham, by the Liverpool and Manchester, and by the York and North Midland Companies were at the rate of 10 percent. per annum, while the Grand Junction was paying 11, and the Stockton and Darlington 15 per cent. The temptation of such dividends could not be resisted. Enterprise outran prudence, and railways became for the first time popular beyond every other kind of investment. (Williams, 1852, 39)

In contrast to this emphasis on the initial slowness of change, in 'An Unsettled Neighbourhood' (*HW* 10 [Nov 11 1854]: 289–92), Dickens emphasizes the speed and immediacy with which the residents of Camden Town converted their shops and homes into facilities that would appeal to railway travellers:

> That people who had not sufficient beds for themselves, should immediately begin offering to let beds to the travelling public, was to be expected. That coffee-pots, stale muffins, and egg-cups, should fly into parlour windows like tricks in a pantomime, and that everybody should write up Good Accommodation for Railway Travellers, was to be expected. Even that Miss Frowze should open

a cigar-shop … with a familiar invitation underneath it, to "Take a light," might have been expected. I don't wonder at house-fronts being broken into shops, and particularly into Railway Dining Rooms. … I don't complain of three eight-roomed houses out of every four taking upon themselves to set up as Private Hotels and putting themselves, as such, into Bradshaw. … I don't make it any ground of objection to Mrs Minderson … that, in exhibiting one empty soup-tureen with the cover on, she appears to have satisfied her mind that she is fully provisioned as "The Railway Larder." I don't point it out as a public evil that all the boys who are left in the neighbourhood, tout to carry carpet bags. The Railway Ham, Beef, and German Sausage Warehouse, I was prepared for. (290)

A bran-new Tavern … had taken for its sign The Railway Arms … the Excavators' House of Call] 'Amongst the middle classes of to-day', *The History of Signboards* observed in 1866,

> no institution of ancient times has been more corrupted and misapplied than heraldry. … Good wine and beer were formerly to be had at the Boar's Head, or the Three Tuns; but those emblems will not do now, it must be the "Arms" of somebody or something; whence we find such anomalies as the … *Grand Junction Arms,* (Praed Street, London;) … *Railway Arms,* (Ludlow). (Larwood and Hotten 34–5)

In this case, 'The Excavators' House of Call' would be where the journeymen excavators working on the railway would assemble.

Staggs's Gardens was uncommonly incredulous.

It was a little row of houses, with little squalid patches of ground before them, fenced off with old doors, barrel staves, scraps of tarpaulin, and dead bushes; with bottomless tin kettles and exhausted iron fenders, thrust into the gaps.] The houses in the area were 'third-rate', according to their official description in the leases of 1809; John Nash called the houses 'mean', a disgrace to the northwestern part of the metropolis; for John White, the first of the five hundred houses to be finished were inferior, 'miserable modern erections'. The poor quality of the houses was due to the fact that they had short leases by early nineteenth-century standards (only 40 years, and not 99) and because of their relatively remote location (qtd. in Kellett, 1969, 247).

Some were of opinion that Staggs's Gardens derived its name from a deceased capitalist, one Mr. Staggs, who had built it for his delectation.] A common slang term in the mid-Victorian period, a 'stag' is a speculator in railway shares who expects an immediate return on investment. The term seems to have been introduced in 1845 by Thackeray in an illustrated piece in *Punch*, entitled 'The Stags. A Drama of

To-day' (9.104), and recurred frequently in later issues. In the original piece, Tom and Jim Stag, a 'retired thimblerigger' and a costermonger, apply for railway shares for which they cannot pay, under the name of Victor Wellesley Delancy who resides at 'Staggland, Bucks'. The term can also be found in Cruikshank's *Table Book* of 1845, which has many articles on the 'Railway Panic', and *The Comic Almanack* for March 1846. Fenn's *Compendium of the English and Foreign Funds*, explained, 'A Stag is one who is not a Member of the Stock Exchange, but deals outside, and is sometimes called an "Outsider" ' (109). Frederick S. Williams pointed to the shady reputation of the stag, who 'has long since been in the position of having no character to boast of, having gone through all the several stages of whitewashing, remand, and imprisonment in Whitecross Street, with perhaps some experience in the criminal jurisprudence of his country' (1852, 46).

The term 'capitalist' was widely used but with different connotations. The essay on 'The Capitalist' in *Heads of the People* (1841) describes the type with impartiality (see note to chapter 1, p. 25). In contrast, Carlyle, Isaac D'Israeli and Benjamin Disraeli all censured capitalists. For example, Carlyle ranked 'big Capitalists' alongside 'Railway Directors, gigantic Hucksters, Kings of Scrip' ('The Present Time', *Latter-Day Pamphlets*, 1850). Isaac D'Israeli described capitalists as 'traffickers' in money ('The Poverty of Literary Men', *Miscellanies of Literature* (1840), vol. 1, ch. 17, p. 360). And in Benjamin Disraeli's *Sybil; or The Two Nations* (1845), a working man laments, 'The capitalist flourishes, he amasses immense wealth; we sink lower and lower' (13).

Others ... held that it dated from those rural times when the antlered herd, under the familiar denomination of Staggses, had resorted to its shady precincts.] Early in the nineteenth century, Camden Town maintained its distinctly rural character: 'the rural lanes, hedgeside roads and lovely fields made Camden Town the constant resort of those who ... sought its quietude and fresh air to reinvigorate their spirits'. The eastward extension of the Regent's Park Canal in 1816, bringing coal wharves and some small industry, changed the area (Weinreb and Hibbert, 1993, 118-19).

the master chimney-sweeper at the corner ... had publicly declared that on the occasion of the Railroad opening, if it ever did open, two of his boys should ascend the flues of his dwelling, with instructions to hail the failure with derisive jeers from the chimney pots.] Railways faced a great deal of opposition, especially in their early years (see also pp. 95–7). Some of the opposition was personal and instinctive. So William IV was 'very peremptory in his dislike' of the railways. And Colonel Charles Sibthorp, MP for Lincoln, claimed in 1844 to have fought 'every proposition of every railroad whatever'. Another MP, G. C. Berkeley, wished that 'the concoctions [of all railway schemes] were at rest in Paradise' (Simmons and Biddle, 1997, 359).

The black-eyed was so softened

Chapter 6 *Paul's Second Deprivation*

she caught up little Miss Toodle who was running past, and took her to Banbury Cross] From the nursery rhyme:

> Ride a cock horse to Banbury Cross
> To see a fine lady upon a white horse
> With rings on her fingers and bells on her toes
> She shall have music wherever she goes.

Typically, as the tune was sung, the child would be given a ride on a foot or bounced on a knee.

But first the young Toodles,

a pious fraud,] A deception for a supposedly worthy end. The phrase was originally used by Ovid in *Metamorphoses* (*Pia mendacia fraude*, 11.711) and became relatively common in the eighteenth and nineteenth centuries.

if they could only go round towards the City Road on their way back,] They would have walked south toward the New Road and then northeast along the New Road until they arrived at the City Road, a thoroughfare that runs southeast from the Angel at Islington to Finsbury Square. The City Road was opened on 29 June 1761 (Wheatley, 1891, 1.404).

Now, it happened that poor

the costume of the Charitable Grinders.] For 'Charitable Grinders' see note to chapter 5, p. 89.

the master: a superannuated old Grinder of savage disposition, who had been appointed schoolmaster because he didn't know anything, and wasn't fit for anything, and for whose cruel cane all chubby little boys had a perfect fascination.] The ignorant and incompetent schoolmaster is a recurrent type in Dickens's fiction (e.g. Squeers [*NN*], Creakle [*DC*], Mr Wopsle [*GE*]), drawn from his own educational experience:

> I don't like the sort of school to which I once went myself, the respected proprietor of which was by far the most ignorant man I have ever had the pleasure to know [*laughter*], who was one of the worst-tempered men perhaps that ever lived. ... I don't like that sort of school, because I don't see what business the master had to be at the top of it instead of the bottom. ... (*Speeches* 240)

In the 1848 preface to *NN*, Dickens complained of an educational system that promulgated such a type:

any man who had proved his unfitness for any other occupation in life, was free, without examination or qualification, to open a school anywhere; although preparation for the functions he undertook, was required in ... the whole round of crafts and trades, the schoolmaster excepted; ... a structure, which, for absurdity and a magnificent high-minded *laissez-aller* neglect, has rarely been exceeded in the world.

Surprises, like misfortunes, rarely

Surprises, like misfortunes, rarely come alone.] The proverb, 'Misfortunes seldom come alone' dates from the fourteenth century.

her two young charges, were rescued by the bystanders from under the very wheels of a passing carriage] The major London streets at the time were 'crowded with cabriolets, hackney-coaches, omnibuses, &c. all driving at as furious a rate as if on an unfrequented turnpike road'. A contemporary remarked that 'The stranger fancies every moment that some one will be run over, or that some serious accident will take place from their coming into collision', and expressed surprise that 'so few accidents should occur' (Grant, 1837, 1.8). The author of *How to Make Home Happy* estimated (in 1857) that 'nearly one hundred persons are killed yearly, or injured, in London, by street accidents' (Jones 33).

(it was market day) a thundering alarm of "Mad Bull!" was raised.] The bulls have been transported down the City Road (which is where they encounter Susan, Polly and the children) and are probably going down St John's Street, to Smithfield Market. There were two cattle-market days for Smithfield Market – Monday and Friday – with business being conducted from 4 a.m. to late morning. Smithfield, which adjoined Little Britain, was the world's largest market for the sale of cattle, sheep and pigs. 'Smithfield has had lately to accommodate a quarter of a million cattle,' *Chambers's Journal* estimated in 1854, 'and a million and three-quarters, or more, of sheep, besides a proportionate number of calves, lambs, and pigs, in the year' ('The Last Days of an Old Acquaintance', 2 [2 December 1854]: 362). The cattle, sheep and swine were transported to London by road or rail, and then herded to the market by drovers, blocking traffic and endangering pedestrians. In some instances, 'a few "infuriated" oxen have taken it into their heads to fly off at a tangent from the drovers. They soon make a clear path for themselves. Parts of the market, or the openings of streets leading to it ... are deserted with amazing dispatch, in order to make way for the enraged and affrighted oxen' (Grant, 1842, 2.179). Dickens and W. H. Wills gave dramatic expression to such an incident in 1850:

> "Mad bull! mad bull! mad bull!" resounded from the Smithfield-bars.
> "Mad bull! mad bull!" was echoed from the uttermost ends of St. John Street.
> ... A fine black ox was tearing furiously along the pavement. Women were

screaming, and rushing into shops, children scrambling out of the road, men hiding themselves in doorways, boys in ecstacies of rapture, drovers as mad as the bull tearing after him, sheep getting under the wheels of hackney-coaches, dogs half choking themselves with worrying the wool off their backs, pigs obstinately connecting themselves with a hearse and funeral, other oxen looking into public-houses – everybody and everything disorganised, no sort of animal able to go where it wanted or was wanted; nothing in the right place; everything wrong everywhere; all the town in a brain fever because of the infernal market! ('The Heart of Mid-London', 1 [4 May 1850]: 125)

HW participated in the campaign to close Smithfield Market and published several articles condemning it ('The Cattle-Road to Ruin', 1 [29 June 1850]: 325–30; 'From Mr. Thomas Bovington', 1 [13 July 1850]: 377; 'A Monument of French Folly', 2 [8 March 1851]: 553–8; 'The Smithfield Market of the Model Smithfield', 2 [8 March 1851]: 572–3). The sale of live cattle continued until 1855, when the market was abolished by Parliament (Smithfield Market Removal Act, *14 & 15 Vict., c. 61*). Driven bulls, and their drover with a cudgel, can be seen in the background of Browne's illustration for the final number, 'Another Wedding' (for more on the bulls and Smithfield Market, see Philpotts, 2010, 25–44).

With a wild confusion before

she was quite alone.] In 'Gone Astray' (*HW*, 13 August 1853), Dickens claimed to have become lost in the City of London 'When I was a very small boy indeed, both in years and stature'. According to Dickens,

> The child's unreasoning terror of being lost, comes as freshly on me now as it did then. I verily believe that if I had found myself astray at the North Pole instead of in the narrow, crowded, inconvenient street over which the lion in those days presided, I could not have been more horrified. But, this first fright expended itself in a little crying and tearing up and down; and then I walked, with a feeling of dismal dignity upon me, into a court, and sat down on a step to consider how to get through life.
>
> To the best of my belief, the idea of asking my way home never came into my head. It is possible that I may, for the time, have preferred the dismal dignity of being lost; but I have a serious conviction that in the wide scope of my arrangements for the future, I had no eyes for the nearest and most obvious course. I was but very juvenile; from eight to nine years old, I fancy.

Indulging in romantic fantasies that recall those of Walter Gay, the young Dickens 'made up my little mind to seek my fortune. When I had found it, I thought I would drive home in a coach and six, and claim my bride'. After a visit to the Guildhall, and the two statues of Gog and Magog, the young boy 'began to roam about the City, and to seek my fortune in the Whittington direction'. In the essay, Dickens remarks on his own youthful naïveté: 'The City was to me [as a child] a vast emporium of precious stones and metals, of casks and bales, honour and generosity, foreign fruits and spices. Every merchant and banker was a compound of Mr Fitz-Warren and Sinbad the Sailor' (7.553–5).

She was a very ugly

carried some skins over her arm.] Mrs Brown is a buyer of rabbit skins (she shortly gives Florence 'a rabbit-skin to carry, that she might appear the more like her ordinary companion'). According to Mayhew, such buyers were usually 'poor, old, or infirm people' who had 'been in some street business, and often as buyers, all their lives'. Rabbit-skin buyers, who sold the skins to hat manufacturers or hat furriers, made regular rounds, carried the skins in their hands, and cried, 'Any hareskins, cook? Hareskins'. In Mayhew's estimation, there were 'at least 50 persons buying skins in the street', each of these persons collecting 50 skins per week for 32 weeks of the year ('it was mostly a winter trade, but some collect the skins all the year round'). One hare-skin buyer, a woman 'upwards of fifty', informed Mayhew,

> "I've sold hareskins all my life, sir, and was born in London; but when hareskins isn't in, I sells flowers. I goes about now (in November) for my skins every day, wet or dry, and all day long – that is, till it's dark. To-day I've not laid out a penny, but then it's been such a day for rain. I reckon that if I gets hold of eighteen hare and rabbit skins in a day, that is my greatest day's work. I gives 2d. for good hares, what's not riddled much, and sells them all for 2½d. I sells what I pick up, by the twelve or the twenty, if I can afford to keep them by me till that number's gathered, to a Jew. I don't know what is done with them. I can't tell you just what use they're for – something about hats." [The Jew was no doubt a hat-furrier, or supplying a hat-furrier.] [Mayhew's note] (2.112)

It is notable that, like Mrs Brown, who supplements her meager income by selling rags, bones and 'dust', Mayhew's hare-skin buyer also sells flowers.

They had not gone very far,

a back room, where there was a great heap of rags of different colours lying on the floor; a heap of bones, and a heap of sifted dust or cinders; ... and the walls and ceiling were quite black.]

> The Rag-Gatherers and Bone-Pickers, and "Pure" [dogs' dung] Collectors are different names for one and the same class. Of bone-pickers, rag-gatherers, and pure collectors, it is considered that there are 800 to 1,000 resident in London. My informant judges, he says, from the number he sees about the

streets every morning. One-half of the above number he thinks are to be found in the low lodging-houses of London, and the rest dwell in wretched, half-furnished rooms. In no case has a bone-grubber ever been known to rent even the smallest house for himself. Upon an average, he thinks there must be at least two of the class living at each of the low lodging-houses. This would give 442 as the number there located (the Government returns estimate the number of mendicants' lodging-houses in London at 221); so that, doubling this, we have 884 as the gross number of individuals engaged in this calling. (Mayhew, Letter 15, 7 December 1849, *The Morning Chronicle Survey of Labour and the Poor*, vol. 2)

The bones were sold to dealers who paid a halfpenny per pound of bones, or a penny for three pounds, and the dealers (such as Mr Krook in *BH*) sold them to soap-boilers, who boiled out the fat and marrow for use and then crushed the bones and sold them for manure (*HW*, Horne, 'Dust; or Ugliness Redeemed', 1.380).

"I want that pretty frock,"

"I want that pretty frock … and that little bonnet, and a petticoat or two, anything else you can spare."]

> *Child stripping.* – This is generally done by females, old debauched drunken hags who watch their opportunity to accost children passing in the streets, tidily dressing with good boots and clothes. They entice them away to a low or quiet neighbourhood for the purpose, as they say, of buying them sweets, or with some other pretext. When they get into a convenient place, they give them a halfpenny or some sweets, and take off the articles of dress, and tell them to remain till they return, when they go away with the booty.
>
> This is done most frequently in mews in the West-end, and at Clerkenwell, Westminster, the Borough, and other similar locations. These heartless debased women sometimes commit these felonies in the disreputable neighbourhoods where they live, but more frequently in distant places, where they are not known and cannot be easily traced. This mode of felony is not so prevalent in the metropolis as formerly. In most cases, it is done at dusk in the winter evenings, from 7 to 10 o'clock.

John Binny estimated that there were 97 'larcenies from children' in the City and the 'Metropolitan districts' in 1860, totaling £70 10s in stolen property (Mayhew 4.281–2).

In hurriedly putting on the bonnet,

Good Mrs. Brown whipped out a large pair of scissors, and fell into an

unaccountable state of excitement. ... it was only her hair ... which Mrs. Brown coveted,] Hair was a valuable commodity, fetching between 5s. to £5 per oz. in the early nineteenth century, depending on its weight and beauty. The best hair was 'well fed, and neither too coarse nor too slender' and was at least twenty-five inches in length'. According to the *London Encyclopædia* (1829), 'The hair of the growth of Britain, and other northern countries, is valued much beyond that of Italy, Spain, the south parts of France, &c.' (10.759).

In 1855, *HW* quoted a passage from Philip Stubbes's *The Anatomie of Abuses* (1585) to underscore the similarity between conditions in late-sixteenth century London (which he calls 'Munidnol') and the existence of the predatory 'Good Mrs. Browns' of the mid-nineteenth century:

> ... if any children have fair hair, they will entice them into a secret place, and either by force, or for a penny or two, will cut off their hair; as I heard that one did in the city of Munidnol, of late, who, meeting a little child with very fair hair, invegled [sic] her into a house, promised her a penny, and so cut off her hair, – and besides, took most of her apparel. (*HW* 12.117)

At length, Mrs. Brown,

a great thoroughfare ... she was to go to the left,] If Mrs. Brown's 'shabby little house' is in the vicinity of Smithfield, as seems likely, then the 'great thoroughfare' would be Newgate Street. To get to her father's office, Florence would simply have had to turn left on Newgate Street, follow it eastward until it became Cheapside and then Cornhill. Near the Bank of England, she would have found her father's office. In the novel, however, she gets lost, and wanders further south, until she arrives at the River Thames, where she meets Walter Gay.

All she knew of her

that great region which is governed by the terrible Lord Mayor.] In other words, the City of London. For the boundaries of the City, see note to chapter 4, p. 54. For Lord Mayor, see note to chapter 4, p. 63.

"You're Dombey's jockey, an't you?"

"You're Dombey's jockey, an't you?"] A subordinate or underling.

Obedient to the indication of

at her journey's end,] *Othello* 5.2.270–1: 'Here is my journey's end, here is my butt / And very sea-mark of my utmost sail.'

Mr. Clark stood rapt in amazement:

as the Prince in the story might have fitted Cinderella's slipper on.] The story of Cinderella was one of Charles Perrault's *Contes du Temps Passé* (1696), translated into English by Robert Samber in 1729.

He hung the rabbit-skin over his left arm; gave the right to Florence; and felt, not to say like Richard Whittington – that is a tame comparison – but like Saint George of England, with the dragon lying dead before him.] Legendary instances of success and heroism from British folklore. For Dick Whittington, see note to chapter 4, p. 72. St George (d. *c.* 303), England's patron saint, is said to have been martyred in Palestine in the fourth century and has been known in England since the seventh or eighth centuries. The legend of St George slaying the dragon was popularized in the West by William Caxton's translation and printing of *The Golden Legend* (1483). According to the legend, George is a tribune who rescues a young Libyan Princess from being sacrificed to a dragon by cutting off its head.

"Why, I think it's Mr. Carker,"

Mr. Carker,"] 'Cark' refers to something that burdens the spirit, and hence denotes a 'troubled state of mind, distress, anxiety; anxious solicitude, labour, or toil' (it is also a verb, meaning 'to burden with care' or 'to be anxious') (*OED*).

"Ah! true! more shame for him,"

After a minute's pause … he bestirred himself] The manuscript continues after the word 'he':

> said, "he's the strangest man, Mr. Carker the Junior is, Miss Florence, that ever you heard of. If you could understand what an extraordinary interest he takes in me, and yet how he shuns me and avoids me; and what a low place he holds in our office, and how he is never advanced, and never complains, though year after year he sees young men passed over his head, and though his brother (younger than he is), is our head manager, you would be as much puzzled about him as I am."

This passage presumably became expendable once Dickens decided against having Walter Gay gradually turn toward dishonesty. Butt and Tillotson observe that 'We may be sure that Carker the Junior's "extraordinary interest" in Walter Gay was an interest in a young man who was to fall as he had fallen' (79).

Walter went on to cite various precedents, from shipwrecks and other moving accidents, where younger boys than he had triumphantly rescued and carried off older girls than Florence,] Precedents include the heroes of Fielding's *Tom Jones* (1749) and Smollett's *Peregrine Pickle* (1751) and *The Expedition of Humphry Clinker* (1771), even though all the young men and the girls they fall in love with early in their lives are older than Walter and Florence. *Tom Jones* describes Tom's numerous acts of heroism and generosity whilst suffering violent mishaps and serious wounds, false accusations, arrest and imprisonment. He is eventually reunited with Sophia and married. The heroes of Smollett's picaresque novels endure accidents, misfortunes and imprisonments similar to those of Tom Jones before they, too, are allowed to marry their youthful sweethearts.

Mr. Dombey's glance followed

his mind's eye] *Hamlet* 1.2.183–4:

> *Hamlet*: My father – methinks I see my father.
> *Horatio*: Where, my lord!
> *Hamlet*: In my mind's eye, Horatio.

There they found that Florence,

Then converting the parlour, for the nonce, into a private tyring room,] 'Tyring' or 'tiring' room, an archaic term for a dressing room, specifically the dressing room of a theatre, occurs frequently in seventeenth- and eighteenth-century drama, and is also used by Pepys in his *Diary* and Smollett in his translation of *Gil Blas*.

The entrance of the lost child

Mrs. Chick stopped in her lamentations on the corruption of human nature, even when beckoned to the paths of virtue] Although the phrase 'paths of virtue' occasionally appears in eighteenth-century literature (e.g. in the works of 'Monk' Lewis and David Hume), it was popularized by a children's book, *The Paths of Virtue Delineated: or, the History in Miniature of the Celebrated Pamela, Clarissa Harlowe and Sir Charles Grandison, familiarised and adapted to the capacities of Youth* (1756). This was a version of Richardson's novels abridged for children in one volume by the publisher, Edward Baldwin. It went through many editions and was reprinted in 1813 as *The Beauties of Richardson*.

"Ah Richards!" said Mrs. Chick,

the little child that is now going to be prematurely deprived of its natural nourishment."] For wet-nursing, see chapter 2, p. 35–6.

Chapter 7

A BIRD'S EYE GLIMPSE OF MISS TOX'S DWELLING-PLACE; ALSO OF THE STATE OF MISS TOX'S AFFECTIONS

Miss Tox inhabited a dark

a dark little house that had been squeezed, at some remote period of English History, into a fashionable neighbourhood at the west end of town,]

> at the beginning of the eighteenth century the place [Marylebone] was a small village, quite surrounded by fields, and nearly a mile distant from any part of the great metropolis. ... Indeed, at the commencement of the present [the nineteenth] century Marylebone was a suburban retreat, amid "green fields and babbling brooks." (*Old and New London,* 1878, 5.254)

where it stood in the shade like a poor relation of the great street round the corner, coldly looked down upon by mighty mansions. It was not exactly in a court, and it was not exactly in a yard; but it was the dullest of No-Thoroughfares. ... The name of this retirement ... was Princess's Place;] Miss Tox's house would seem to be very near Portland Place ('the great street round the corner') – thus very close to Mr Dombey's house – and in one of several 'no thoroughfare' mews that run north and south off Devonshire Street.

Miss Tox inhabited a dark

distant double knocks.] A loud double knock was used by two classes of people, which often caused confusion. As implied here, it signaled the arrival of the gentry: 'his birth entitles him to give the double knock which despotic custom has made the peculiar privilege of gentility' (*The Bijou* 3 [1830]: 247). But it was also used by certain members of the working class, including postmen, tax collectors and messengers. Thomas Hood's poem, 'The Double Knock', depicts a young lady's excitement on hearing a double knock downstairs, as she assumes it signals the arrival of her beau;

she is disappointed to learn that the man at the door is actually the tax-collector (*Thomas Hood's Own*, 1839, 201).

Elsewhere in *DS*, the double knock is used by Sir Barnet and Lady Skettles (14), Major Bagstock (31), the guests at Mr and Mrs Dombey's dinner (36) and, comically, by the master chimney sweep in Staggs's Gardens who has come up in the world by getting a job with the railway and buying a bigger house: he is discovered 'knocking a double knock at his own front door' (15).

There was another private house

where the most domestic and confidential garments of coachmen and their wives and families, usually hung, like Macbeth's banners, on the outward walls.] *Macbeth* 5.5.1–3:

> Hang out our banners on the outward walls;
> The cry is still 'They come:' our castle's strength
> Will laugh a siege to scorn … .

At this other private house

a wooden-featured, blue-faced, Major, with his eyes starting out of his head] Major Bagstock is characterized throughout the novel as suffering from a wide range of physical symptoms suggestive of several diseases, some closely related: palsy ('wooden-featured'); exophthalmia ('eyes starting out of his head'); chorea; emphysema; gout; and apoplexy. Dickens names two of the diseases (gout in chapters 10 and 26; apoplexy in chapters 20, 26, 40 and 58), while the others are hinted at in Bagstock's symptoms. In addition to the symptoms mentioned here (wooden features, blue face, protruding eyes), he is also described as suffering from watering eyes; a 'rotatory motion of his head'; wheezing and 'fits of coughing and choking', often after eating; and 'plethoric symptoms'.

Wooden features and his 'very rigid pair of jaw-bones' (7) suggest that Bagstock has palsy, manifested in his face by partial paralysis. The eminent neurologist and anatomist, Sir Charles Bell, described a case of right-sided facial palsy associated with abundant secretions of tears: compare the description of Bagstock as having 'essence of savoury pie oozing out at the corners of his eyes' (20); and 'the Major sat … watering at the eyes' (26) (*The Nervous System of the Human Body*, 3rd ed., 1836, 249). Another case of right-sided facial palsy also involving 'tears perpetually rolling down the cheek' is reported in the *Edinburgh Medical and Surgical Journal*, 1809, 5.27. Palsy was closely associated with apoplexy (*i.e.* cerebral hemorrhage, stroke), and it was usual for apoplexy to occur as the primary malady followed by paralysis (James Copland, *Of the causes, nature and treatment of palsy and apoplexy*, 1850, 120). As Bagstock's 'whole life' is described as 'being a struggle against all kinds of apoplectic symptoms' (20), his characterization suggests that his wooden, rigid features are the result of his having suffered a stroke (for more on apoplexy, see note to chapter 20, p. 238). According to Copland, palsy was also 'closely related' to chorea (involuntary movements): compare Bagstock's frequently 'rolling his head'; moreover, palsy was associated with gout (see note to chapter 10, pp. 149–50).

Bagstock's blue face (sometimes 'purple'), which is repeatedly referred to, indicates cyanosis (also known as blue disorder or blue jaundice), 'a symptom of many different diseases', including emphysema, which is itself hinted at in his chronic wheezing and fits of coughing (see note to chapter 10, p. 150):

> Cyanosis is the name given to a blueish coloration of the skin and mucous membrane, caused by the stagnation of blood in the right cavities of the heart and venous system, in individuals affected with emphysema of the lungs. ... In cyanosis, the skin presents a livid blueish tint of a violet or blackish purple, with stripes or spots of a deeper colour, and of various extent. It is more intense on the face; above all, on the cheeks, nose, lobules of the ears, and upper eyelid. ... It becomes more marked ... during digestion, by the use of stimulants, coughing, crying, walking, and, in general, by any exertion. ... It acquires its highest degree of intensity in paroxysms. ... The face is swelled and tumid. ... There is no disease but what may be complicated with cyanosis. The affections of the heart, of which cyanosis is an external symptom, almost always end in haemorrhages or dropsies. (P. Rayer, *Treatise on diseases of the skin*. ... Trans. from the French by William Dickinson, 1833, 282-4; see also John Forbes, Alexander Tweedie, John Conolly, *Cyclopædia of Practical Medicine*, 1832, 1.500)

Bagstock's 'eyes starting out of his head' – sometimes described as 'lobster eyes' and 'eyes like a prawn's' – suggest the disease of exophthalmia (or exophthalmos):

> *Exophthalmos or protrusion of the eyeball.* This is one of the earliest symptoms of any kind of growth within the orbit. Sometimes the eye is projected directly forwards. ... More frequently the eyeball is pushed forwards and to one side, towards the nose or temple, upwards or downwards. (William Mackenzie. *A Practical Treatise on the Diseases of the Eye*, 1830, 45)

One of the symptoms of the disease is 'a continual ... weeping of the eye' which might account for Bagstock's 'watering at the eyes' (26), although these might also be symptomatic of palsy (see above) (George Frick, *A Treatise on the Diseases of the Eye*. New ed., 1826, 307). According to these authors, the causes of exophthalmia include tumour, a blow to the eyes and syphilis.

At this other private house

a dark servant of the Major's, whom Miss Tox was quite content to classify as a "native," without connecting him to any geographical idea whatever.] 'Native' was used in this period to refer to a member of an indigenous ethnic group, with the suggestion of his inferior status and culture (*OED*). In this case, the 'Native' is from India and is undoubtedly one of Major Bagstock's former colonial servants (the

Major's Indian past is suggested in chapter 20, where we learn that the Major's old friend is 'Bill Bitherstone of Bengal'). In a cancelled MS passage he is called 'Abdallah' (Horsman xxvi).

'Everybody in India has servants', an *AYR* article begins, 'every European, at any rate'. 'Even soldiers in barracks do not attend upon themselves as they do in England. Cavalry troopers have a certain number of *Syces* assigned them to look after their horses; and in the infantry, also, natives do a great deal of the rough work for the men, who have an easy time of it compared with their daily experience in this country'. Moderate physical punishment of Indian servants was legally tolerated though Europeans were supposed to refrain from using their fists, sticks or whips. Although the *AYR* correspondent claimed that 'stories of ill-treatment' were exaggerated, he conceded that Indian servants were often managed 'with more harshness than is necessary' (9.420). Another contemporary observer put it more bluntly: native servants, he said, were 'treated like furniture'. Certainly, Major Bagstock's brutal treatment of the 'Native' would have been incompatible with the 'Moderation, temper, and kindness' that were supposed to be the distinguishing characteristics of the British officer, as defined in general orders issued by Sir John Malcolm in 1821 (Money 2.214; James, 1998, 160). While repeatedly criticizing Indian servants for their deceptiveness and tendency to 'swindle their masters', the *AYR* correspondent concluded, 'As a general rule ... it must be said that the natives are faithful to those whose salt they eat' ('Indian Servants', 9 [27 June 1863]: 416–17). Later in the century, *Chambers's Journal* remarked that 'The submissive air and humble gait of natives of India should alone be sufficient to disarm a European, and prevent him from ever lifting a hand against one of them' ('Indian Servants', *Chambers's Journal* 3 [27 March 1886]: 202–5).

The 'Native' performs in England a variety of functions usually assigned to separate servants in India because of class distinctions and because they were so affordable (he carries bags, cooks, waits at table, opens doors, lights guests to bed, and serves as Major Bagstock's personal attendant and messenger). 'It is not unusual', a contemporary remarked, 'for families of only moderate means [in India] to keep ten or twelve servants' (Kerr, 1873, 97). The most important servant was the 'bearer', who carried palanquins; was 'responsible for his master's clothes'; had 'charge of his keys'; called his master 'at the proper hour to dress for parade, the early walk, or ride'; dusted and arranged his rooms; readied his bath and attended him as he retired to bed. As the head-servant of the house, the bearer 'should always be well dressed, more especially so as one of his functions is to receive visitors at the door' (cf. the Native's ill-fitting 'European clothes' in ch. 20) ('Indian Servants', *Chambers's Journal* 3: 202–5). In 1864, *AYR* complained that the English soldiers in India 'have been so long accustomed to have everything done for them by their cook-boys and other native servants, that they can do nothing for themselves, save clean their clothing and arms, and not always that' ('Military Mismanagement' 10.350).

In *DC*, Julia Mills returns to England from India 'with a black man to carry cards and letters to her on a golden salver, and a copper-colored woman in linen, with a bright handkerchief round her head, to serve her Tiffin in her dressing-room' (ch. 64). For more on 'native' servants, see note to chapter 20, pp. 233, 237.

Perhaps there never was

at his club,] Bagstock's club is in Pall Mall, the location of London's gentlemen's clubs (see notes to chapters 41 and 58, pp. 405, 407, 502). A 'cluster of mansions', some in the style of a 'restored Grecian temple' and others 'a modern Italian palace', the clubs were

> devoted to the unclassical and everyday purposes of eating, drinking, lounging, and reading newspapers. ... Clubs may be generally described as houses combining the characters of restaurants and reading-rooms, for the use of a select number of associated persons, who agree to make an annual payment for their support. ... Originating within the present century, and concentrating a large proportion of the men of fortune, station, and political note in the metropolis ... [t]he main object of modern clubs is ... supplying to their members the necessaries of life at the lowest possible rate. They are, it is admitted, furnished and conducted on a scale which may be called luxurious; but ... [c]onsidering ... the high amount of convenience and comfort they afford, clubs are extremely economical. ('Club-Life', *Chamber's Edinburgh Journal*, 1845, 1.241)

Of the five clubs for military and naval officers, the United Service Club (established 1815) was open to both British Army and East India Company officers of the rank of major and above. Since 1828, it has been housed in a neoclassical mansion (by John Nash) in Pall Mall ('Club-Life' 1.242).

The dingy tenement inhabited by

The greater part of the furniture was of the powdered-head and pig-tail period: comprising a plate-warmer, always languishing and sprawling its four attenuated bow legs in somebody's way;] That is, the furniture is old-fashioned, dating from the eighteenth century. A plate-warmer was a portable cabinet disguised as a piece of furniture but insulated inside to retain heat; folding or sliding doors revealed shelves 'to keep plates, dishes, and viands hot' (*A True and Exact Particular and Inventory ... of Thomas Warren*, 1732, 31; *London Journal of Arts and Sciences*; and *Repertory of Patent Inventions*. 17 [1841]: 74–5).

The description of Miss Tox's plate-warmer 'sprawling its four attenuated bow legs in somebody's way' suggests an allusion to one of the best known anecdotes about the dramatist, Richard Brinsley Sheridan, one which was always referred to as 'Sheridan and the plate-warmer':

> Sheridan was dining at Peter Moore's with his son Tom, who was at that time in a very nervous debilitated state. The servant, in passing quickly between the guests and the fire-place, struck down the plate-warmer. This made a great noise, and caused Tom Sheridan to start and tremble. Peter Moore, provoked

at this, rebuked the servant, and added, "I suppose you have broken all the plates?" – "No, Sir," said the servant, "not one." – "No!" exclaimed Sheridan; "then, damn it! you have made all that noise for nothing." (*Sheridiana; or, Anecdotes of the Life of Richard Brinsley Sheridan*, 1826, 288–9)

Although Major Bagstock had arrived

Although Major Bagstock had arrived at what is called in polite literature, the grand meridian of life,] The phrase 'meridian of life' was a cliché in the late eighteenth and nineteenth centuries, used by authors such as Charlotte Smith (*Emmeline*, 1788), Mary Wollstonecraft (*Mary*, 1788), William Godwin (*Fleetwood*, 1805), Maria Edgeworth (*Patronage*, 1814), James Fenimore Cooper (*The Headsman*, 1833) and Nathaniel Hawthorne (*Twice-Told Tales*, 1837).

he was mightily proud of awakening an interest in Miss Tox, and tickled his vanity with the fiction that she was a splendid woman who had her eye on him. This he had several times hinted at the club: in connexion with little jocularities, of which old Joe Bagstock ... was the perpetual theme. ... "Joey B., Sir, ... is worth a dozen of you. If you had a few more of the Bagstock breed among you, Sir, you'd be none the worse for it.] The depiction of Bagstock as vain, boastful, self-centred and snobbish seems inspired by Thackeray's Indian Army Officer, Major Goliah O'Grady Gahagan, the satiric hero of his own story, *The Tremendous Adventures of Major Gahagan* (1838). Bagstock and Gahagan have many similarities: like Gahagan, Bagstock describes 'the extent to which he had been beloved and doted on by splendid women and brilliant creatures' (22); like Gahagan, Bagstock is an intimate friend of the nobility (he often boasts of his friendship with 'His Royal Highness the late Duke of York'); and both recount their own heroic deeds while in India (see also notes in chapters 10 and 31, pp. 150–1, 337).

Gahagan's opening description of his life is similar in style to Bagstock's references to himself:

> From this slight specimen of my adventures, the reader will perceive that my life has been one of no ordinary interest; and, in fact, I may say that I have led a more remarkable life than any man in the service – I have been at more pitched battles, led more forlorn hopes, had more success among the fair sex, drunk harder, read more, and been a handsomer man than any officer now serving her Majesty. (1)

the Major's stronghold and donjon-keep of light humour,] 'Donjon' is the archaic spelling of 'dungeon' and refers to a castle's great tower or innermost keep. The archaic spelling is used to distinguish this older meaning of 'dungeon' from its modern meaning, a dark, subterranean place of confinement (*OED*).

The major decided, after some

The major decided, after some consideration, that it meant man-traps; that it meant plotting and snaring] Man-traps were used by landowners to deter trespassers who were not poachers. There were modern 'humane man-traps', so called because they snapped the bone of a man's leg smoothly rather than making a compound fracture like the old ones (see 'Market Gardens', *HW* 7.414).

But still, when that day

divers ornaments, cut out of coloured card-boards and paper, seemed to decorate the chimney-piece and tables] There was a great variety of ornamental cut-paper work made by ladies in the eighteenth and nineteenth centuries, partly so that they would not be seen to sit idle and partly in order to occupy their time. Such dainty work also showed off the grace and beauty of their hands when in company. Silhouettes and *papier-maché* were popular. Paper mosaic flower pictures were cut from coloured drawing papers and parchment, and then varnished to stiffen them. Paper-filigree, popular with the gentry and nobility from the mid-eighteenth century, was made from paper or vellum and framed; the craze was for hatchments, coats-of-arms and other small decorative panels. Rolled-paper work was a favourite way to decorate coasters, boxes and tea-caddies: paper or parchment was cut into strips, gilded or tinted red, and then folded into shapes and glued onto the article to be decorated. Advice on cut-flower work gave detailed instructions, including diagrams, for making several varieties of paper flowers (*Cassell's Household Guide*, 1869, 193–5, 264–6; Toller, *The Regency and Victorian Crafts, or, The Genteel Female – Her Arts and Pursuits*, 1969, *passim*).

Miss Tox occasionally practised on the harpsichord, whose garland of sweet peas was ... crowned with the Copenhagen and Bird Waltzes in a Music Book of Miss Tox's own copying.] *The Musical World* remarked in 1836:

> The harpsichord ... has been superseded by the piano-forte, and has disappeared almost as completely as its precursor the spinet. Within our memory an old harpsichord might occasionally be met with in an old house in the country, played upon by an old maiden aunt, who performed the pieces of Handel and Scarlatti, accompanied vocal music from the thorough bass figures, and lamented the decay of musical knowledge among the rising generation.
> (15 July 1836, 66)

The waltz, which began in Germany in the mid-eighteenth century, quickly became popular throughout Europe, although it was considered *risqué* in Regency England because of the close physical contact of the partners (see Byron's satiric poem, 'The Waltz; an apostrophic hymn' [1811]). By the 1820s, the waltz's popularity showed signs of waning in England and France, though the elder Johann Strauss's tour of the two countries in 1837–8 brought renewed attention, and by the 1840s waltzes were popular pieces to play at home (*The New Grove Dictionary of Music* and *Musicians*; *Oxford Companion to Music*). The 'Copenhagen Waltz' (waltzes were customarily named for the location or the occasion for which they were composed) and the 'Bird Waltzes' were both taught to songbirds and were popular with musical amateurs and street musicians in the early nineteenth century. It was common in the nineteenth century for amateurs to copy musical scores for their personal use. David Copperfield, for instance, witnesses Julia Mills 'copying music ... a new song, called Affection's Dirge' (33).

Over and above all this,

Miss Tox had long been dressed ... in slight mourning.] Slight mourning was generally worn by distant relatives of the deceased, or by a widow when a year had elapsed since the death of her husband.

The perseverance with which

froze its young blood] From *Hamlet*, 1.5.15–16: 'I could a tale unfold whose lightest word / Would harrow up thy soul, freeze thy young blood.'

Miss Tox returned no other

making his cockade perfectly flat and limp] A ribbon or knot of ribbons ornamenting baby clothes and caps (*Fraser's Magazine*, 1850, 42.97).

Chapter 8 Third monthly number
December 1846

PAUL'S FURTHER PROGRESS, GROWTH, AND CHARACTER

Dickens was initially uncertain about how quickly to have young Paul grow up. He asked Forster what he thought about making 'number three a kind of half-way house between Paul's infancy, and his being eight or nine years old – In that case I should probably not kill him until the fifth number.' But he also wondered if readers were 'so likely to be pleased with Florence, and Walter, as to relish another number of them at their present age? Otherwise, Walter will be two or three and twenty, straightaway' (*Letters* 4.628–9).

A 'close relationship' between *DS* and Dickens's fragmentary autobiography, which he began writing sometime between 1845–9, has been noted by Horsman. He locates the relationship 'in the time of gestation and composition as well as in part of the content, and, behind both of these, though whether as cause or consequence is uncertain, in the increasing adoption of the child's standpoint as the early part of the novel proceeds' (xxv).

On the downfall and banishment

the nursery may be said to have been put into commission; as a Public Department is sometimes, when no individual Atlas can be found to support it.]

> COMMISSION. In law, an appointment usually by letters patent or warrant to persons as authority to execute certain duties. ... In this mode many offices and departments are filled ... even some of the highest judicial or ministerial functionaries of the realm are appointed thus: as when parliament is not opened by the sovereign in person, a commission is appointed to read the speech, &c.; so also bills which have passed the houses of parliament are often signed for the sovereign by commissioners. (*The Dictionary of Trade, Commerce and Navigation*, 1844)

Atlas, one of the Titans in Greek mythology, is the guardian of the pillars of heaven, which support the sky. As punishment for fighting against Zeus, he was made to hold up the sky himself.

Yet, in spite of his early promise,

every fit of the hooping-cough ... Some bird of prey got into his throat instead of the thrush; and the very chickens turning ferocious – if they have anything to do with that infant malady to which they lend their name –] Until the early nineteenth century, little was known about the whooping cough, and it was not until 1812–13 that physicians recognized the involvement of the upper respiratory tract (though they had understood the infectious nature of the disease since the early eighteenth century). Despite this medical knowledge, Mrs Beeton insisted that the 'hooping cough' is a 'spasmodic' disease that 'is only infectious through the faculty of imitation' (1861). She advised 'keeping up a state of nausea or vomiting', but also recommended a 'moral' cure: 'the parent should endeavour to break the paroxysm of the cough ... by even measures of intimidation' (1058).

Thrush, chiefly a disease of infants, is characterized by white ulcers on the inside of the mouth and on the lips, and is caused by a parasitic fungus. Advice on thrush is given to nurses and nursery-maids in *The Complete Servant* (1825):

> In this disorder nothing avails more than an emetic at first, and then a little

General Mems for N̲o̲ 3.   Tipchin
                            M^rs ~~Whychin~~

                                    Mrs Alchin Mrs Somchin
Mrs Roylance - House at the Seaside.   Mrs Pipchin

Miss Tox's party. Her uncle the Magistrate. -The Major.
                                              To stand over

    Walter?
    Captain Cuttle

Progress of Paul, and growing affection for Florence
    Carker.
        offices in the City
            To stand over

___as if he had taken life: unfurnished, and
the upholsterer were never coming.

Master Bitherstone
    and Miss Pankey

            Bill of Sale - Dogley, the Broker.

        Mirrors -hearth-rugs

Number Plan

Chapter 8 *Paul's Further Progress, Growth and Character*

(Dealings with the Firm of Dombey and Son ~ N.º III.)

chapter VIII.

Paul's further ~~progress~~ progress, ~~and character growth and character. With some account of Mrs Pipchin's Wrychin's establishment~~ growth, and character.

old child – "Papa what's money?"

chapter IX.

In which the wooden Midshipman gets into trouble.

Execution at Old Sol's

Chapter X.

Containing the Sequel of the Midshipman's disaster.

Money borrowed from M.ʳ Dombey to pay out the broker –

Chapter Plan

magnesia and rhubarb, (if there is diarrhoea,) with thin chicken-water as drink. Testaceous powders, or the *absorbent mixture* ... will also be proper. If there is no looseness, it will be proper to give a grain or two of calomel, with three or four grains of rhubarb. The mouth and throat should at the same time be cleansed by gargles. (Adams 264)

Chickenpox appears in most children between the ages of two and eight. 'In the ordinary course of this complaint, the symptoms are so slight as not to require the aid of medicine' 'unless the eruption be of the confluent kind, that is, the pimples being numerous and running into each other, when the danger is to be appreciated from the degree of violence of the concomitant fever'. As for treatment:

> Gentle purges are all that are in general necessary. If the shivering, sickness, head-ache, and pains in the limbs, are severe, an active purge ... should be administered, succeeded by some diluting drink; and the patient should be confined to a quiet, spacious, and well ventilated room, with a cool dress, till the febrile symptoms have left him. (Graham, 1827, 290–1)

Mrs Wickham was a waiter's wife

whose application for an engagement in Mr. Dombey's service had been favourably considered, on account of the apparent impossibility of her having any followers,] 'Followers' is a colloquial term used to designate the young men who courted maidservants. 'There are many stipulations in hiring ... servants', a correspondent in London observed in 1843,

> a very common one is ... that "no followers shall be allowed," that is, no sweethearts; the course of true love must not flow, either smoothly or disturbedly, into kitchens and sculleries; great numbers of "no follower" servants, notwithstanding the prohibition, obtain husbands; marriages between the male and female domestics in large establishments are not unfrequent, while flirtations with milkmen, bakers, butchers, fishmongers, and others, through the area rails, are considered things of course, with policemen most especially of all. ('Letter 13', *Change for the American Notes*, 29)

In *NN*, an employment agency for domestic servants has an advertisement for a cook:

> 'Mrs Marker ... Russell Place, Russell Square; offers eighteen guineas; tea and sugar found. Two in family, and see very little company. Five servants kept. No man. No followers.' (16)

It is hardly necessary to observe,

If he could have bought him off, or provided a substitute, as in the case of an unlucky drawing for the militia,]

> SUBSTITUTE *in the Militia.* A person who voluntarily offers to serve in the room of another that has been chosen by ballot. But if afterwards he should himself be chosen by ballot, he is not exempted from serving again, as principles are, within certain restrictions. Substitutes may be provided for quakers. Every substitute is liable to a penalty for not appearing to be sworn upon due notice being given; and every regularly enlisted soldier who shall offer to serve as a substitute in the militia, is liable to forfeit £10 or to be imprisoned. Substitutes who desert are to serve the remainder of their term when taken. (*A New and Enlarged Military Dictionary*, 1810, vol. 2)

As J. R. McCulloch remarked, 'the military degenerated into a sort of capitation tax; with this oppressive and unjust peculiarity, that it fell with as much severity on the poor as on the rich; so that, while it only imposed a trifling sacrifice on the latter, it often forced the poor man from his house, and compelled him to become a soldier. In consequence, the militia became exceedingly unpopular' (*A Descriptive and Statistical Account of the British Empire*, 1854, 2.456).

Some philosophers tell us that selfishness

Some philosphers tells us that selfishness is at the root of our best loves and affections.] This sentence and the one that follows it are slightly modified versions of a passage that Dickens originally included in chapter one but then deleted because of space limitations. See note on p. 41–2.

'Philosophers' was how the Utilitarians referred to themselves and also how others referred to them. For example, in a review of the works of Jeremy Bentham, J. S. Mill used the term 'utilitarian philosophers' (*Tatler*, 1832, No 431, 62), and *The British Churchman* disparaged the group as 'these soi-disant philosophers of the Utilitarian school' (1844, 1.484). Although the Utilitarians were not the first to connect private and public interest (earlier proponents included Bernard Mandeville, Bishop Butler, the 3rd Earl of Shaftesbury and Adam Smith), the notion became associated with them in the first half of the nineteenth century. Bentham maintained that self-interest motivated human actions and united mankind in a common selfish concern. He remarked in 1824, 'In every human breast ... self-regarding interest is predominant over social interest: each person's own individual interest, over the interests of all other persons taken together' (*Book of Fallacies*, ch. 9). And he proposed in 1830,

> In all human minds, in howsoever widely different proportions, *self-regard,* and *sympathy* for others, or say, *extra-regard,* have place. ... But, in self-regard even sympathy has its root: and if, in the general tenor of human conduct, self-regard were not prevalent over sympathy, – even over sympathy for all others put together, – no such species as the human could have existence.
>
> (*Constitutional Code,* ch. 6)

The narrator's observation in *Dombey* echoes Carlyle's recurrent condemnation of the political economists' promotion of self-interest as the root of benevolence:

> It is contended by many that our mere love of personal Pleasure, or Happiness as it is called, acting on every individual ... will of itself lead him to respect the rights of others, and wisely employ his own: to fulfil, on a mere principle of economy, all the duties of a good patriot. ... Many there are, on the other hand, who pause over this doctrine; cannot discover, in such a universe of conflicting atoms, any principle by which the whole shall cohere: for if every man's selfishness, infinitely expansive, is to be hemmed in only by the infinitely-expansive selfishness of every other man, it seems as if we should have a world of mutually-repulsive bodies with no centripetal force to bind them together. ('Voltaire', 1829)

his parental affection might have been easily traced, like many a goodly superstructure of fair fame, to a very low foundation.] 'Goodly superstructure' was used recurrently from the 1760s onward in discussions on the early formation of character and also in commentaries on the Bible. It became a cliché found in writers such as Washington Irving (*A History of New York*, 1809) and Anne Brontë (*Agnes Grey*, 1847).

feeling as if the boy had a charmed life, and *must* become the man with whom he held such constant communication in his thoughts,] *Macbeth* 5.8.12: 'I bear a charmed life, which must not yield, / To one of woman born'.

Thus Paul grew up to be nearly

he had a strange, old-fashioned, thoughtful way, at other times, of sitting brooding in his miniature arm-chair,] Young Paul seems to have been modeled on Harry Burnett, the disabled son of Dickens's sister, Fanny Burnett, and her husband, Henry. According to their minister, the Reverend James Griffin,

> ... Harry Burnett, was the original, as Mr. Dickens told his sister, of "Paul Dombey." The poor little fellow, with spinal deformity, had been taken to Brighton, as "Little Paul" is represented to have been. He was a singular child, meditative, and quaint in a remarkable degree. He used to lie for hours on the beach with his books, giving utterance to thoughts quite as wonderful for a child as those which are put into the lips of Paul Dombey. Little Harry loved his Bible, and loved Jesus his Saviour. He seemed never tired of reading his Bible, and his hymns, and other good books suited to his age: and the bright little fellow was always cheerful and happy. (426)

Dickens may have borrowed character traits from his nephew, but the death of young Paul could not have been influenced by the death of Harry, since he died suddenly ('after a three day's illness') in January 1849, almost a year after the novel was completed.

he looked (and talked) like one of those terrible little Beings in the Fairy tales, who, at a hundred and fifty or two hundred years of age, fantastically represent the children for whom they have been substituted.] A reference to the folk superstition of changelings, starving or aged imps who were substituted for children (or sometimes adults), supposedly to improve the elfin breed. Changelings were commonly represented as repellent and sinister: they possessed large heads and small, stunted bodies; contorted features; dark or sallow skin, and usually looked aged and wizened. They were notorious for their gluttony, irritability and general maliciousness. Accounts of the terrible consequences that ensued because of a naïve faith in 'fairy abductions' and changeling incidents were common in the journals and newspapers of the day. In one famous case from 1826, a woman drowned a four-year-old boy who was believed to be a changeling because he could not speak or stand. And in 1843, a father was charged with mistreating his young son in the hope that he would be reclaimed by the fairies: the boy was forced into a tree for several hours at Christmas, and then, at the father's command, beaten and starved by his servants. Less credulous Victorians, including many folklorists, assumed that changelings were a survival of the ancient practice of abducting children, or of infant sacrifice. Others assumed they were simply diseased children, and associated their repulsive appearance with childhood afflictions.

Novelists such as Emily and Charlotte Brontë, Elizabeth Gaskell and Dinah Muloch Craik, among many others, frequently drew on the superstition. Besides the direct association with 'those terrible little Beings', Dickens depicts young Paul Dombey as the victim of a 'wasting disease', and he is said to be 'strange, old-fashioned', and to possess an 'old, old face' and a melancholy disposition, and to have a tendency toward 'slyness'. And, typical of changelings, he is essentially unlike his father. Other changeling figures in Dickens include Quilp (*OCS*), and Bart and Judy Smallweed (*BH*) (Silver, 1999, 59–87).

"Papa! what's money?"

"Papa! what's money?" ... "What is money, Paul?" ... "Yes," said the child ... "what is money?" Mr. Dombey was in difficulty. He would have liked to give him some explanation involving the terms circulating-medium, currency, depreciation of currency, paper, bullion, rates of exchange, value of precious metals in the market, and so forth; but ... he answered: "Gold, and silver, and copper. Guineas, shillings, half-pence."] Helping to educate children and general readers about political economy were question-and-answer books such as *A Catechism of the Currency* (3rd ed., 1836):

> What is currency?
> Money of the state, and also bills of exchange, promissory notes, bank

bills and cheques; all which, being accustomed to pass *current* among men in transactions of business, as the representative of value, are hence called *currency* ...

What is money?
Money is a *token,* of certain nominal amount, issued by government in return for value received, and payable into the exchequer for taxes, whence it becomes of necessity a *general legal tender.* (John Taylor, 1836, 1, 29)

The dialogues sometimes took the form of satire, as in 'A Political Catechism' from *The London Magazine* (1750):

Q. What is the chief end of man?
A. To get money.
Q. How do you know this?
A. By the universal practice of my countrymen, especially those in place.
Q. What is money?
A. The sovereign and sole acknowledged disposer of all worldly things.
Q. How is money to be got?
A. As the advantages and uses of it are without number, so are the means of acquiring it. (19 [1750]: 292; for another satirical approach, see *The Spirit of the Public Journals for 1802* 6 [1803]: 229)

Thomas Day's popular moral stories, *The History of Sandford and Merton; a work intended for the use of children* (1783–9), reflect a criticism of Adam Smith's promotion of self-interest among producers in a capitalist society, as expressed in his *Wealth of Nations* (1776). In *Sandford and Merton*, the didactic Mr Barlow uses questions and answers to morally educate the spoilt little Tommy Merton:

Mr. Barlow. What is money?
Tommy. Money, sir, money is I believe, little pieces of silver and gold, with a head upon them.
Mr. Barlow. And what is the use of those little pieces of silver and gold?
Tommy. Indeed I do not know that they are of any use: but every body has agreed to take them; and therefore you may buy with them whatever you want.
Mr. Barlow. Then, according to your last account, the goodness of the rich consists in taking from the poor houses, clothes, and food, and giving them in return little bits of silver and gold, which are really good for nothing.
Tommy. Yes, sir; but then the poor can take these pieces of money and purchase every thing which they want.
Mr. Barlow. You mean, that, if a poor man has money in his pocket, he can always exchange it for clothes, or food, or any other necessary?
Tommy. Indeed I do, sir.
Mr. Barlow. But whom must he buy them of? For, according to your account,

the rich never produce any of these things: therefore the poor, if they want to purchase them, can only do so of each other.
Tommy. But, sir, I cannot think that is always the case: for I have been along with my mamma to shops, where there were fine powdered gentlemen and ladies that sold things to other people, and livery servants, and young ladies
…
Mr. Barlow. But, my good little friend, do you imagine that these fine powdered gentlemen and ladies made the things which they sold?
Tommy. That, sir, I cannot tell; but I should rather imagine not: for all the fine people I have ever seen are too much afraid of spoiling their clothes to work. (qtd. in the 1828 ed., 109)

Mr Dombey was so astonished,

some magnetic attraction.] Different theories of magnetism were discussed from the Middle Ages onward. By the eighteenth century, the term 'magnetic attraction' was familiar enough for Fanny Burney to use it as a metaphor of the emotions in *Camilla* (1796; ch. 9). In 1820, the Danish scientist, Hans Christian Ørsted observed that electric currents induce magnetic fields, and the following year, Michael Faraday's collaboration with Humphry Davy and William Hyde Wollaston resulted in his publishing work on electromagnetic rotation. Throughout the 1820s to 1840s, Faraday's experiments contributed to the development of electromechanical devices. In these decades, numerous books helped to educate the public about the principles of magnetism and electricity: e.g. 'Magnetism', *Notes to Assist the Memory in Various Sciences*. 2nd ed., 1827, 56–60; 'Magnetism', *First Lines of Science; or, A Comprehensive and Progressive View of the Leading Branches of Modern Scientific Discovery and Invention*. 1827, ch. 12.

"With your usual happy

His soul is a great deal too large for his frame.] A 'large soul' (from *amplus animus*) recurs as a literary image from the early eighteenth century onwards; see, for example Pope, *Odyssey* (1726): 'Eurybates! In whose large soul alone / Ulysses viewed an image of his own'; and the description of John Dryden in *Lives of Eminent and Illustrious Englishmen* (1835): 'he was of too large a soul to be permanently cramped and pinioned by ridiculous affectations' (George Godfrey Cunningham, ed., 1835; 4.314).

"I am afraid," said Mr. Dombey,

He is not a living skeleton,] Claude Ambroise Seurat (b. 1797), the Frenchman known as 'the Living Skeleton' or 'the Anatomie Vivante', was exhibited in the

Chinese Saloon in Pall Mall in 1825. Seurat's height was 5 feet and 7 ½ inches, and his weight 78 pounds (35 kg). According to the 'Interesting Account and Anatomical Description', which was sold at the exhibition, and quoted by William Hone in his *Every-Day Book*:

> The ribs are not only capable of being distinguished, but may be clearly separated and counted one by one, and handled like so many pieces of cane; and, together with the skin which covers them, resemble more the hoops and outer covering of s small balloon, than any thing in the ordinary course of nature. ... Seurat is presented to view in a state of nudity, save a mere covering of several inches deep round the loins, through which are cut large holes to admit the hip bones to pass through, for the purpose of keeping it in its place. His general appearance is that of a person almost entirely devoid of muscular substance, and conveys to the mind the idea of a being composed of bones, cellular substance and skin only on. ... There is nothing in Seurat to disgust, as far as I could judge from what I saw or heard of him. (1.511, 516)

'The Living Skeleton' is the basis for one of Sam Weller's 'Wellerisms' in *PP*: 'Here's your servant, Sir. Proud o' the title, as the Living Skellinton said, ven they show'd him' (15).

"I hope so," returned her brother.

We are not ... mutes,] Mutes were professional mourners and attendants, hired to walk in funeral processions, often because of their ability to maintain a sad expression. Dickens, who detested the elaborate ritual associated with Victorian funerals, ridiculed the practice of employing mutes to hold staves draped in black in a *HW* essay of 1850: 'There they stood, for hours, with a couple of crutches covered over with drapery: cutting their jokes on the company as they went in' and breathing strong fumes of rum and water ('From the Raven in the Happy Family' 1.241). For more on Dickens's dislike of such funeral practices, see note to chapter 3, p. 45.

"A daughter of Momus," Miss Tox

Momus,"] One of the classical gods about whom school children were taught:

> THE name of the god Momus is derived from the Greek, signifying a jester, mocker, or mimick; for that is his business. He follows no particular employment, but lives an idle life, yet nicely observes the actions and sayings of the other gods, and when he finds them doing amiss, or neglecting their duty, he censures, mocks and derides them with the greatest liberty. (Andrew Tooke, *Tooke's Pantheon of the Heathen Gods, and Illustrious Heroes, revised for a Classical Course of Education, and adapted for the use of Students*, 1827, 138–9)

"Yes, he did," returned

he recommended, to-day, sea-air. Very wisely, Paul, I feel convinced."] In the early to mid-nineteenth century, infectious diseases were believed to be propagated by a miasma, or effluvia, emanating from bodily exhalations and putrid organic matter. The urban atmosphere was thought to be especially noxious, as William Buchan noted in *Domestic Medicine* (1785): 'The air in cities is not only breathed repeatedly over, but is likewise loaded with sulphur, smoke, and other exhalations, besides the vapours, continually arising from innumerable putrid substances, as dung hills, slaughter-houses, &c. Few things prove more destructive to children than confined or unwholesome air', Buchan remarked. He added, 'I ... have often known the most obstinate diseases cured by removing them from such a situation to an open free air'. While generally supportive of a plan by Joseph Paxton to erect air-controlled sanatoriums, 'which shall contain throughout, whatever climate may be fixed upon', *HW* argued that a change of climate was, by itself, not enough to improve health: 'As a specific, as a sole remedy, no doubt it is, on the whole, as much a quack remedy as Morison's Pill; that pill contains ingredients of use in the right place. Quackery consists, not in any thought or thing, but in the method of employing it' ('Foreign Airs and Native Places', 3 [2 August 1851]: 446–50).

"There is nothing to be made

the air of Brighton,] The seaside resort 51 miles south of London made fashionable by the Prince of Wales (later George IV), who moved there in 1783 and built the Royal Pavilion, 'the nucleus of modern Brighton' according to one contemporary account (*Penny Cyclopædia*, 1836). The population of the town grew rapidly in the early nineteenth century, from 7,339 in 1801 to 40,634 in 1831, with the number of residents in the summer, in 1836, at about 70,000.

Claims for the restorative powers of sea water were first made in England in *A Dissertation on the Use of Sea Water in Diseases of the Glands* (1753) by Dr Richard Russell, under whose direction sea-bathing at such towns as Brighton became fashionable. But the advent of the railway in 1841, which brought hordes of holidaymakers from London, made Brighton less appealing to members of the aristocracy. Queen Victoria, for instance, found its inhabitants to be 'very indiscreet and troublesome' and refused to return after 1843. In 1845, Thackeray surveyed the town and claimed to have observed forty-nine railway directors, thirteen barristers and at least twelve famous actors. In 1847, he counted 300 acquaintances in fifteen minutes, including dandies, City men and Members of Parliament (Pimlott 118–19). (It should be noted that Mr Dombey, Mrs Skewton and Mrs Pipchin all travel by road, and not by rail.)

According to the *Penny Cyclopædia* (1836), 'The number of private schools at Brighton is very considerable, a circumstance owing to the salubrity of the place, and the desire of many parents who live in London to send their children out of the metropolis'. In 1857, Mrs Merrifield concurred, remarking that 'few towns in

England possess a greater number of educational establishments'.

Dickens first visited Brighton at the end of October 1837, shortly after finishing *PP*, and again in February 1841, though the newly opened railway line would have made access easy, and there may have been other unrecorded visits before 1846. He made at least two visits while working on *DS* – in May 1847 and March 1848 – and several visits in the late 1840s and 1850s, and, in the 1860s, gave public readings in Brighton (Davey, 1910, 257–61).

Mrs. Pipchin] Mrs Pipchin is partly based on Dickens's memories of an old family friend, Mrs Elizabeth Roylance, of Little College Street, Camden Town, with whom the twelve-year-old Dickens stayed in the spring of 1824, probably for just a few weeks, during the period that his father was imprisoned for debt in the Marshalsea, and while the young Dickens was working at Warren's blacking factory (Allen, 1988, 84–7). After Dickens's father left prison, the family also may have lodged with Mrs Roylance. Dickens draws attention to the connection in his autobiographical fragment, written between 1845 and 1849:

> I (small Cain that I was, except that I had never done harm to any one) was handed over as a lodger to a reduced old lady, long known to our family, in Little-college-street, Camden-town, who took children in to board, and had once done so at Brighton; and who, with a few alterations and embellishments, unconsciously began to sit for Mrs. Pipchin in *Dombey* when she took in me.

A letter to Forster, on 4 November 1846, confirms the connection, though Dickens seems to misremember his age:

> I hope you like Mrs. Pipchin's establishment. It is from the life, and I was there – I don't suppose I was eight years old; but I remember it all as well, and certainly understood it as well, as I do now. We should be devilish sharp in what we do to children. (*Letters* 4.653)

As well, on the left-hand side of the memoranda for number three, Dickens refers to Mrs Pipchin as 'Mrs. Roylance'. At the top of the same page, he tries different names – 'Mrs Wrychin' (deleted for 'Tipchin'), 'Mrs Alchin', 'Mrs Somchin' – before finally arriving at 'Mrs Pipchin'. Dickens described his time with Mrs Roylance in the autobiographical fragment:

> She had a little brother and sister under her care then; somebody's natural children, who were very irregularly paid for; and a widow's little son. The two boys and I slept in the same room. My own exclusive breakfast, of a penny cottage loaf and a pennyworth of milk, I provided for myself. I kept another small loaf, and a quarter of a pound of cheese, on a particular shelf of a particular cupboard; to make my supper on when I came back at night. They made a hole in the six or seven shillings, I know well; and I was out at the blacking-warehouse all day, and had to support myself upon that money all the week.

Chapter 8 *Paul's Further Progress, Growth and Character* 127

PAUL AND Mrs. PIPCHIN.

7   'Paul and Mrs. Pipchin' by Hablot K. Browne in the third monthly number

There is no evidence that Mrs Roylance mistreated the young Dickens, and she may have let him stay with her free of charge, despite his conviction that he was a 'lodger'. But the period was a dark one for him. He wrote that, except for the money paid for his 'lodgings' (if that were the case),

> I certainly had no other assistance whatever (the making of my clothes, I think, excepted), from Monday morning until Saturday night. No advice, no counsel, no encouragement, no consolation, no support, from any one that I can call to mind, so help me God. ... I know I do not exaggerate, unconsciously and unintentionally, the scantiness of my resources and the difficulties of my life. I know that if a shilling or so were given me by any one, I spent it in a dinner or a tea. I know that I worked, from morning to night, with common men and boys, a shabby child. I know that I tried, but ineffectually, not to anticipate my money, and to make it last the week through. ... I know that I have lounged about the streets, insufficiently and unsatisfactorily fed. I know that, but for the mercy of God, I might easily have been, for any care that was taken of me, a little robber or a little vagabond.
>
> ('Autobiographical Fragment')

According to James T. Fields, Dickens claimed that Mrs Pipchin was based on 'an old lodging-house keeper in an English watering place where he was living with his father and mother when he was but two years old. After the book was written he sent it to his sister, who wrote back at once: "Good heavens! what does this mean? you have painted our lodging-house keeper, and you were but two years old at that time!" ' ('Some Memories of Charles Dickens', 1870, 237). In his introduction to the Clarendon edition of *DS,* Horsman suggests that this story 'is not to be dismissed out of hand' 'Since it is possible, from the evidence presented by William J. Carlton, that Dickens's family was in Southsea in the summer of 1814, when his first brother Alfred was born and died' (xxv).

"In pumping water out of the

"In pumping water out of the Peruvian Mines." ... "Not being a Pumper himself ... but having invested money in the speculation, which failed."] The major Peruvian silver mines were the two veins of Cerro de Pasco, Veta Colquirirca and Veta Pariarirca, located in the Andes. Steam-power was thought to have been introduced to the Pasco mines in about 1814 or 1815. In 1825, the drainage of these mines was undertaken by an English company called the 'Pasco Peruvian'. 'After driving 110 feet in the adit [a horizontal opening by which a mine is entered or drained], at a cost of $40,000, (between September 1825 and January 1827), this company failed, and the government of Peru undertook the work by paying $2,000 a month towards the expenses' (Blake 171). The early pumps, which were vulnerable to acid water, and thus easily rusted and destroyed, were worked by chains and long copper rods. By 1832, only one steam-engine remained functioning. The primary 'pumpers' were

Indian peasants of two classes: those who worked 'in the mines all the year round without intermission' or those who made 'only temporary visits to Cerro de Pasco'.

Although a contemporary source estimated in 1869 that Cerro de Pasco produced nearly 59,000,000 ounces of silver in the late eighteenth and early nineteenth centuries, the *Journal of Mining and Manufactures* cautioned, 'It is impossible to form anything like an accurate estimate of the yearly produce of the mines of Cerro de Pasco; for a vast quantity of silver is never taken to the Callana [the Peruvian smelting house], but is smuggled to the coast, and from thence shipped to Europe' (Blake 171–3; 'Peruvian Silver Mines', *The Merchants' Magazine* 17 [July–December 1847]: 436).

"Not being a Pumper himself,"

Mrs. Pipchin's management of children is quite astonishing.] 'Management' was the term conventionally used to discuss bringing up children; see for example, the advice given by the authority on infant education, Samuel Wilderspin: 'If abilities be necessary to manage children from eight to fourteen years of age, they are infinitely more so for the management of infants; and everything must depend upon the conduct and capabilities of those to whom so precious a charge is intrusted' (1824, 201). See also the note below on Mrs Pipchin as ' "a great manager" '.

"Perhaps I should say of

interesting members of society,] In other words, important, a now obsolete use of the word 'interesting'.

"Why, I really don't know,"

It is not a Preparatory School. ... Should I express my meaning ... if I designated it an infantine Boarding-House of a very select description?"] The distinction here is between the kind of thoroughly inadequate 'Preparatory Day-School' that Dickens attended as a young boy ('Wellington House Classical and Commercial Academy'), and a private boarding school such as Mrs Pipchin runs. In 'Our School' (*HW* 4 [October 11 1851]: 49–52), Dickens describes his unpleasant experiences at 'a Preparatory Day-School' in the Hampstead Road:

> The master was supposed among us to know nothing ... The only branches of education with which he showed the least acquaintance, were, ruling, and corporally punishing. He was always ruling ciphering-books ... or smiting the palms of offenders ... or viciously drawing a pair of pantaloons tight with one of his large hands, and caning the wearer with the other. We have no doubt whatever that this occupation was the principal solace of his existence. (49)

In his *Life of Samuel Johnson* (1775), James Boswell quotes Johnson on an acquaintance who married 'a little presbyterian parson, who keeps an infant boarding school'. Infant boarding schools are also mentioned by Samuel Wilderspin in his *Infant Education* (4th ed., 1829; 151).

This celebrated Mrs. Pipchin

his relict still wore black bombazeen, of such a lustreless, deep, dead, sombre shade, that gas itself couldn't light her up after dark, and her presence was a quencher to any number of candles.] Bombazeen (or bombasine) is a twilled or corded fabric of silk (or cotton) and worsted frequently used in mourning; for it being the height of mourning fashion, see note to chapter 2, p. 33. In the first stage of mourning, garments were not supposed to be shiny or reflect light, hence their oppressive drabness. The mourning clothing of the huge crowd at the funeral of the Duke of Wellington in 1852 was supposedly so dark that it absorbed the newly installed gas light in St Paul's Cathedral (Morley, 1971, 63–4). For more on gas lighting, see chapter 3, p. 49.

She was generally spoken of as "a great manager" of children;] The epithet was widely used to refer to famous actor-managers in the London theatres. For example, 'Great manager Kemble' is the refrain of a comic song about John Kemble, and Thomas Hood's affectionate address to Robert William Elliston, comic actor and manager of Drury Lane Theatre, opens 'Oh! Great Lessee! Great Manager! Great Man!' (*The Covent Garden Journal*, 1810, 663–5; *Odes and Addresses to Great People*. 2nd ed., 1825, 103). The phrase was sometimes used ironically, as in a reference to the actor-manager Thomas Sheridan: 'After much hesitation, she was received by the great manager in the most slovenly of morning costumes, unshaven, and bearing the exhausted, dull look of the overnight's conviviality' (*Tait's Edinburgh Magazine for 1839*, 6.771).

all her waters of gladness and milk of human kindness,] 'Waters of gladness' was a religious cliché, sometimes used in nineteenth-century sermons (e.g. 'These waters of gladness, we look to drawing them out of another well', Frederick William Faber, *The Blessed Sacrament*, 1855). The collocation may derive from the biblical phrase, 'oil of gladness' (Psalm 45.7: 'Thou lovest righteousness, and hatest wickedness: therefore God, thy God, hath anointed thee with the oil of gladness about thy fellows'. A variant occurs in Hebrews 1.9). '[M]ilk of human kindness' echoes Lady Macbeth's thoughts about Macbeth: 'Yet do I fear thy nature; / It is too full o' th' milk of human kindness / To catch the nearest way' (1.5.15–17).

The Castle of this ogress

The Castle of this ogress and child-queller] The depiction of the grotesque Mrs

Pipchin is inspired by the fairytale, 'Hop-o'-my-Thumb', originally published in Charles Perrault's *Histoires, ou Contes du Temps Passé* (1697), the collection first translated into English by Robert Samber as *Histories, or Tales of Time Past* (1729). 'Hop-o'-my-Thumb' recounts how a family of children are abandoned by their parents in 'the very thickest and darkest part of the forest' where they mistake 'the noise of the wind among the trees' for the howling of wolves, and 'every moment they thought they should be eaten up'. (Mrs Pipchin's house 'has a continual reverberation of wind in it', and she is surrounded by frightening plants which move and look like animals.) The children arrive at 'the house of an Ogre, who eats up little boys and girls', but they are protected by the ogre's kind wife (the model for Mrs Pipchin's 'good-natured' niece). As soon as the children have arrived, 'the Ogre asked if the supper were ready' and is served a sheep (compare 'At one o'clock there was a dinner … Mrs. Pipchin … made a special repast of mutton-chops'). Two other fairy tales with the same motifs are 'Puss in Boots' (a castle and an ogre), by Charles Perrault, and 'Princess Zamea and the Prince Almanzon' (a dark forest, and a 'monstrous giant' who lives in a castle), by the French fairy-tale writer, Madame d'Aulnoy (*Fairy Tales and Novels*, translated into English in 1817; 'Hop-o'-my-Thumb' and 'Puss in Boots' cited in John Smith, *The Fairy Book*, 1836).

a steep by-street at Brighton; where the soil was more than usually chalky, flinty, and sterile, and the houses were more than usually brittle and thin;]

> The town is built on a slope, and is defended from the N. winds by the high land of the South Downs, which from Beachy Head as far as the central part of Brighton press close on the sea and form high chalk cliffs. From the central part of Brighton W. the hills recede farther from the sea, leaving a level coast. Thus the town of Brighton in the E. part presents a high cliff to the sea, and in the W. part a sloping low beach. The soil on the South Downs is a calcareous earth resting on chalk: on the steep slopes and some of the flat tops the soil is very thin; in the hollows and occasionally on other parts it is a pretty good loam, capable of producing profitable crops. … In 1831, there were 2,763 houses in the town … taxed at £10 and more, and 8,885 within the parliamentary boundaries. (*Penny Cyclopædia*, 1836, 5.423–4)

snails … holding on … with the tenacity of cupping-glasses.] Cupping was a standard bloodletting procedure and an alternative to using leeches. The glasses, 'of various sizes and shapes, neither very important', were applied to the head, neck, trunk or extremities, depending on the condition being treated. *A Few Practical Observations on the Art of Cupping* (1835) describes the use of cupping-glasses and, after a flame has been introduced, their powerful adherence to the skin on the neck:

> The patient being placed either in or out of bed … the sponge, dipped in water as hot as can comfortably be borne, should be applied to the part intended to be operated upon; then glasses adapted to the volume of the patient's neck, three in number … being held at once in the left hand, the torch dipped

in spirits of wine, and previously lighted, is introduced under each glass in succession, at *the lower edge,* and quickly withdrawn: the air thus exhausted, the glass adheres with amazing force, and the patient may now be said to be dry cupped. (Staples, 1835, 24, 28–31)

Mrs. Pipchin's scale of charges being high,] Mrs Pipchin later boasts: ' "I had a pretty fair connection at Brighton ... little Pankey's folks alone were worth a good eighty pound a-year to me" ' (59). Considering that she has two other boarders along with Paul and Florence, Mrs Pipchin would earn around £300 a year, a sizeable income for a widow. *The Complete Servant* (1825) advises that with £100 (or guineas) annually, '*A Widow* or other *unmarried Lady,* may keep a *Young Maid Servant,* at a low salary; say from 5 to 10 Guineas a year' (5). According to *A New System of Practical Domestic Economy* (1827), an income of £300 can comfortably support a gentleman and his wife, three children and two maid servants given wages of £12 and £8 annually (427).

At one o'clock there was

At one o'clock there was a dinner, chiefly of the farinaceous and vegetable kind ... Miss Pankey ... was regaled with rice;] The contemporary prejudice against giving children meat was condemned by Herbert Spencer in his chapter, 'Physical Education' in *Education: Intellectual, Moral and Physical* (1859; 1861):

> There is an over-legislation in the nursery. ... Not simply a more or less restricted diet, but a comparatively low diet, is thought proper for children. The current opinion is, that they should have but little animal food. ... "Meat is not good for little boys and girls" ... has by repetition grown into an article of faith. ... If, however, we inquire for the basis of this opinion we find little or none. It is a dogma repeated and received without proof ... We have put the question to two of our leading physicians, and to several of the most distinguished physiologists, and they uniformly agree in the conclusion, that children should have a diet not *less* nutritive, but, if anything, *more* nutritive than that of adults. The grounds for this conclusion are obvious, and CHILDREN REQUIRE A NUTRITIVE DIET. (226, 231–2; de Stasio 299–306)

Mrs. Pipchin's niece, Berinthia,] Berinthia is the name of the attractive young widow and coquette in two popular and related plays, John Vanbrugh's *The Relapse; or, Virtue in Danger: a Comedy* (1696) and Richard Brinsley Sheridan's *A Trip to Scarborough: A Comedy* (1777). Although *The Relapse* was performed well into the eighteenth century, it was increasingly criticised for its bawdy language and portrayal of immorality. From 1777, it was replaced on stage by *A Trip to Scarborough,* Sheridan's faithful but more respectable adaptation.

As it rained after dinner,

Mrs. Pipchin knocking angrily at the wall, like the Cock Lane Ghost revived,] The Cock Lane Ghost was a celebrated hoax that fascinated London in 1762 and that subsequently became the subject of a number of literary spoofs and satires lampooning credulousness. *The Gentleman's Magazine* for that year reported on 13 January 'noises and other extraordinary circumstances, attending the supposed presence of a spirit, that for these two years past has been heard at night' at a house in Cock Lane, Smithfield, owned by one Richard Parsons (32.43). The ghost was alleged to be that of a former tenant, a woman who had died two years previously and whose lover had just successfully sued Parsons to recover a loan. Parsons' young daughter appeared to be the channel for the dead woman's communications. The phenomenon attracted crowds, including many eminent persons, who thronged to Cock Lane in the hope of hearing the noises. A committee that included Dr Samuel Johnson was appointed to investigate, and its findings were published in *The Gentleman's Magazine* in February 1762: 'It was therefore the opinion of the whole assembly, that the child has some art of making or counterfeiting particular noise, and that there is no agency of higher cause' ('An Account of the Detection of the Imposture in Cock-Lane', 32.81–2). The subsequent trial found that Parsons, working with others, had pressured his daughter to participate in the deception. Parsons was sentenced to be pilloried and his collaborators were imprisoned.

Dickens was skeptical of the existence of ghosts and publicly ridiculed the spiritualist craze of the 1850s, with its table rappings and séances, though spiritualists continued to make efforts to convert him. In an *AYR* article, 'Rather a Strong Dose', Dickens maintained firmly that Protestants must 'guard with jealousy all approaches tending down to Cock-lane Ghosts and such-like infamous swindles, widely degrading when widely believed in' (9 [21 March 1863]: 87). For his other attacks on spiritualism, see 'Well-authenticated Rappings' (*HW* 17 [20 February 1858]: 217–20) and 'The Martyr Medium' (*AYR*, 9 [4 April 1863]: 133–6).

After tea, Berry brought out

a little work-box, with the Royal Pavilion on the lid,] In 1852, George A. Sala characterized 'the work-box, with a view of the Pavilion at Brighton on the lid' as one of the 'things departed' that he had once loved (*HW* 4.401). The Royal Pavilion, in the centre of Brighton, was the residence of the Prince of Wales (later George IV) between 1787 and 1822. The building developed in stages: originally a farmhouse, it was extended by the Prince into a neo-classical building known as the 'Marine Pavilion'. Between 1815 and 1822, John Nash was commissioned to greatly enlarge it, adding cupolas, pinnacles, domes and scalloped arches, all inspired by a mixture of Chinese and Indian styles.

a great volume bound in green baize,] A Bible; cf. 'The Bible … is taken down from the high shelf, and drawn out of its covering of green baize' and 'Josiah's own Bible and prayer book were not forgotten. Involuntarily the old man paused as he was carefully enfolding the former in its green baize cover' (Bourne Hall Draper, *Sketches* *from the Volume of Creation*, 1830, 155; 'Chapters on Churchyards', *Blackwood's Edinburgh Magazine* 23 [March 1828]: 313).

At last it was the children's

As little Miss Pankey was afraid of sleeping alone in the dark, Mrs. Pipchin always made a point of driving her up-stairs herself, like a sheep; and it was cheerful to hear Miss Pankey moaning long afterwards, in the least eligible chamber, and Mrs. Pipchin now and then going in to shake her.] According to Dickens, in his *AYR* piece, 'Travelling Abroad',

> It would be difficult to overstate the intensity and accuracy of an intelligent child's observation. At that impressible time of life, it must sometimes produce a fixed impression. If the fixed impression be of an object terrible to the child, it will be (for want of reasoning upon) inseparable from great fear. Force the child at such a time, be Spartan with it, send it into the dark against its will, leave it in a lonely bedroom against its will, and you had better murder it.
> (2 [7 April 1860]: 559)

Dickens's daughter Mamie remarked of her father that he had 'such wonderful sympathy for all childish fears and fancies, that he never once "snubbed" his children about such things' (1885, 64).

The breakfast next morning

Master Blitherstone read aloud to the rest a pedigree from Genesis (judiciously selected by Mrs. Pipchin), getting over the names with the ease and clearness of a person tumbling up the treadmill.] In *Praeterita*, John Ruskin describes reading long passages of the Bible with his mother, and then memorizing some of them, with her paramount concern being his ability to pronounce the words with the correct intonation:

> In this way she began with the first verse of Genesis, and went straight through, to the last verse of the Apocalypse; hard names, numbers, Levitical law, and all; and began again at Genesis the next day. If a name was hard, the better the exercise in pronunciation, – if a chapter was tiresome, the better lesson in patience, – if loathsome, the better lesson in faith that there was some use in its being so outspoken. (31)

There are several lists of generations in Genesis, alternately held together by words such as 'begat', 'bare', 'came of' and 'and', used in a chant-like sequence (see 'The genealogy and age of the patriarchs' [ch. 5]; 'Generations of the sons of Noah' [ch. 10]; 'One language' [ch. 11]; 'Wives and generations of Esau' [ch. 36]; 'Jacob moves to Egypt' [46.8–27]). Mrs Pipchin's 'judiciously selected' extracts are, no doubt, her efforts to eliminate the occasional risqué words such as 'concubines', graphic phrases such as 'came out of his loins' and perhaps words associated with conception such as 'begat'.

something else done to him with salt water, from which he always returned very blue and dejected.]

> The acknowledged advantages of sea bathing may be fairly attributed, we think, to the equability, and as respects the average state of the atmosphere in our climate, the high temperature of the water of the ocean. It is a well-known fact, that when persons are accidentally wetted with sea water, they are less liable to take cold than under similar circumstances with fresh water. Whilst it cannot be denied, that salt water operates slightly as a stimulant to the skin, the effect to which we have just alluded is due to its slow rate of evaporation, the deposition of a slight film of salt upon the clothes, and the tendency consequent thereon to carry off heat from the body less rapidly than by the evaporation of fresh water. (*The Saturday Magazine* [29 July 1837]: 36)

Mrs. Pipchin presided over some early readings. It being a part of Mrs. Pipchin's system not to encourage a child's mind to develop and expand itself like a young flower, but to open it by force like an oyster,] For the analogy between the growth of plants and the education of children, see note to chapter 11, pp. 158–9.

the moral of these lessons was usually of a violent and stunning character: the hero – a naughty boy – seldom, in the mildest catastrophe, being finished off by anything less than a lion, or a bear.] An allusion to the story of Harry and Tommy in Daniel Fenning's *Universal Spelling Book*, first published in 1756, and then in successive editions until at least 1847. Dickens first alludes to the book in his early piece, 'Some Particulars Concerning a Lion':

> … one old spelling-book in particular recounts a touching instance of an old lion of high moral dignity and stern principle, who felt it his imperative duty to devour a young man who had contracted a habit of swearing, as a striking example to the rising generation. (*Bentley's Miscellany* 1 [May 1837]: 515)

In the story, Tommy and Harry are brothers whose parents love them excessively but fail to restrain their faults. This has a bad effect on Harry, who associates with 'rude and wicked Boys', begins to swear and lie and repeatedly claims that he 'don't care' for the grief he causes his parents. While apprenticed to his uncle in London, Harry becomes a spendthrift and a dissolute. In contrast, Tommy is dutiful and sober, and is rewarded with a successful career and a virtuous, wealthy wife. After inheriting only a pittance from his father, Harry rejects Tommy's offer to take him into his business, again claiming he 'don't care', and becomes a criminal. After being convicted and sent to Newgate Prison, he escapes and flees overseas, but his ship founders on the Barbary Coast, and he is cast ashore in a wild and desolate place. Although he repents of his behavior, and often '[thinks] upon his old Words, *don't care*', it is too late: 'he at last ... became a Prey to wild Beasts, which God suffered to tear him to pieces, as the just Reward of his Disobedience and misspent Life'. Dickens alludes to the story in *DC* when Steerforth tells David: ' "At odd dull times, nursery tales come up into the memory, unrecognized for what they are. I believe I have been confounding myself with the bad boy who 'didn't care,' and became food for lions – a grander kind of going to the dogs, I suppose" ' (ch. 22; Tillotson, 1983, 31–4).

This kind of didactic literature for children was popularized by Mrs Mary Martha Sherwood (1775–1851), who published nearly one hundred tracts and stories. Her best-known work, *The History of the Fairchild Family* (the first part was published in 1818), included a visit to a gallows as an object lesson for quarrelling children. In a speech in 1857, Dickens observed that among the schools 'I don't like' was included 'that sort of school – and I have seen a great many such in these latter times – where the bright childish imagination is utterly discouraged, and where those bright childish faces ... are gloomily and grimly scared out of countenance' (*Speeches* 241).

Such was the life at Mrs. Pipchin's.

Mr. Dombey came down; and then Florence and Paul would go to his Hotel,] Identified as the Bedford (see note, chapter 10, pp. 152–3).

Mr. Dombey seemed to grow, like Falstaff's assailants, and instead of being one man in buckram, to become a dozen.] Falstaff, one of Dickens's favourite Shakespearean characters, exaggerates the number of his assailants to Prince Hal:

> *Falstaff.* ... a hundred upon poor four of us.
> *Prince.* What, a hundred, man?
> *Falstaff.* I am a rogue if I were not at half-sword with a dozen of them ...
> *Gadshill.* We four set upon some dozen ...
> *Falstaff.* I have pepper'd two of them ... two rogues in buckram suits ... Four rogues in buckram let drive at me. ...
> *Prince.* What, four? Thou saidst but two even now.
> (*Henry IV, Part I* 2.4.155–90)

an aunt's at Rottendean,] More commonly called Rottingdean, 'a pleasant marine village', four miles east of Brighton, 'with a good road thereto, along the margin of the cliff'. Rottendean contained about ninety or a hundred houses in 1827, along with 'many excellent lodging houses ... and a good Inn. The best of the former face the sea, and are let the greater part of the year to visitants, who prefer the rural retirement of the place, to the gaities and bustle of Brighton' (Sickelmore, 1827, 148).

Master Bitherstone, whose relatives were all in India, and who ... suffered so acutely in his young spirits that he once asked Florence ... if she could give him any idea of the way back to Bengal.] By about 1805, British influence extended

Chapter 8 *Paul's Further Progress, Growth and Character*

throughout most of India. The periodic setbacks, such as the first Afghan War (1838–42), did little to slow British expansion. In the 1840s, Great Britain annexed both Sind (1843) and the Punjab (1849) in order to strengthen the northwest frontier against Russian incursions. Bengal – one of the three 'presidencies' of India, along with Madras and Bombay – was 'a large province of Hindustan, which derive[d] much importance from the circumstance of its being the seat of the supreme government in British India'. British influence in Bengal dates from the 1650s, when the East India Company was granted trading rights in the province, 'free from all payment of customs' duties'. From the 1770s, according to the *Penny Cyclopædia* (1835), 'the English have remained undisputed masters of the province of Bengal, the capital of which [Calcutta] has become the seat of government to which the governors of the other presidencies have been made subordinate' (3.232). By the 1840s, the English in 'British India' were said to have reformed their manners and their eighteenth-century reputation for drunkenness, 'irreligion and profligacy', and become 'astonishingly like the upper classes of those at home' (*The British World in the East*, 1846, 1.496).

A long-standing problem was the unhappiness of children sent home to English schools by their families in India:

> "I need scarcely point out to you the amount of mental disquiet connected with their ['the Anglo-Indian community's'] children, suffered by parents resident in our Indian Empire. Let at the most tender and care-wanting age to the guardianship of those who often receive their charge with doubtful willingness, or sent home under the guidance of mothers, they are, in either case, placed probably at the first respectable school which may present itself – their education thus becoming a matter of chance. Our public schools are of so expensive a character, that a father must be wealthy to maintain his son in comfort there, whilst their foundational advantages are only to be enjoyed by those who are resident upon or near the spot, who can make themselves thoroughly acquainted with the mode in which to obtain them, and actively exert themselves for the furtherance of their object. Within the last ten years, much has been done by the formation of proprietary schools to afford the best education at modern expense." (*The Asiatic Journal and Monthly Miscellany.* Vol. 2. Third Series. November-April 1844. 'Correspondence. Education of Children whose Parents Reside in India' 399)

Moreover, teaching the children of Anglo-Indians was considered a special responsibility because of the need to assume the role of parents:

> 'I myself know by experience, and I have frequently heard others complain, that the expense of placing "a child from India" at school, or with a clergyman, in England, is much greater than it would be did his parents reside at home … for a tutor incurs a far heavier degree of responsibility in undertaking the charge of such a pupil, than he would do in receiving one whose parents could exercise a direct superintendence over his habits and progress'
> (*The Asiatic Journal and Monthly Miscellany*, 3.284)

Master Bitherstone may reflect Dickens's recollection of a boy named 'Dumbledon', who attended Wellington House Academy:

> We remember an idiotic goggle-eyed boy, with a big head and half-crowns without end, who suddenly appeared as a parlor-boarder, and was rumoured to have come by sea from some mysterious part of the earth where his parents rolled in gold. He was usually called "Mr." by the Chief, and was said to feed in the parlor on steaks and gravy; likewise to drink currant wine. And he openly stated that if rolls and coffee were ever denied him at breakfast, he would write home to that unknown part of the globe from which he had come, and cause himself to be recalled to the regions of gold. He was put into no form or class, but learnt alone, as little as he liked – and he liked very little – and there was a belief among us that this was because he was too wealthy to be "taken down." ... Some two years afterwards, all of a sudden one day, Dumbledon vanished. It was whispered that the Chief himself had taken him down to the Docks, and re-shipped him for the Spanish Main; but nothing certain was ever known about his disappearance.

'Our school was rather famous for mysterious pupils', Dickens added (*HW*, 'Our School' 4.50).

"Never you mind, Sir,"

the story of the little boy that was gored to death by a mad bull for asking questions."] Unidentified.

From that time, Mrs. Pipchin

She would make him move his chair to her side of the fire, instead of sitting opposite;] Dickens detested Browne's accompanying illustration, 'Paul and Mrs. Pipchin' (see Plate 7, p. 127):

> I am really *distressed* by the illustration of Mrs. Pipchin and Paul. It is so frightfully and wildly wide of the mark. Good Heaven! in the commonest and most literal construction of the text, it is all wrong. She is described as an old lady, and Paul's "miniature arm-chair" is mentioned more than once. He ought to be sitting in a little arm-chair down in a corner of the fireplace, staring up at her. I can't say what pain and vexation it is to be so utterly misrepresented. I would cheerfully have given a hundred pounds to have kept this illustration out of the book. He never could have got that idea of Mrs. Pipchin if he had attended to the text. Indeed I think he does better without the text; for then the notion is made easy to him in short description, and he can't help taking it in. (*Letters* 4.671)

the contracted pupils of his eyes were like two notes of admiration.] That is, like exclamation marks, expressing wonder; an echo of *The Winter's Tale* 5.2.12–14: 'the changes I perceived in the King and Camillo, were very notes of admiration. They seem'd almost, with staring on one another, to tear the cases of their eyes'.

This consolatory farewell, Mrs. Wickham

she indulged in melancholy – that cheapest and most accessible of luxuries –] By the early decades of the nineteenth century, 'the luxury of melancholy' had become a cliché of romantic and sentimental writing (e.g. James Austen, *The Loiterer: a periodical*, 1792, 242), and is part of Dickens's continuing attack on various forms of escapism, usually associated with eighteenth-century fashions that survived into the early to mid-nineteenth century (see notes on pastoralism, medievalism, the picturesque and on Dickens's dislike of romanticized views of the past). By the middle of the eighteenth century, melancholy was celebrated by the graveyard poets, and others, as a unique joy that put one in touch with the infinite, usually through an appreciation of antiquities and ruins. John Dyer wrote of the 'kindly mood of melancholy that wings the soul, and points her to the skies' (*The Ruins of Rome*, 1740), and Thomas Warton the Younger described the pleasures of melancholy as

> … that elegance of soul refin'd,
> Whose soft sensation feels a quicker joy
> From Melancholy's scenes, than the dull pride
> Of tasteless splendor and magnificence
> Can e'er afford. ('The Pleasures of Melancholy', 1747)

Because of its association with heightened states of creative intensity, melancholy proved attractive to the Romantic poets, many of whom celebrated its bittersweet virtues. In 'To a Sky-Lark' (1820), Percy Shelley observed, 'Our sweetest songs are those that tell of saddest thought' (l. 90). For Wordsworth, melancholy was prompted by the 'still, sad music of humanity' ('Tintern Abbey', l. 91,1798), and for Keats, by 'the green hill in an April shroud' ('Ode on Melancholy', l. 14, 1820). From the outset, the fashion for melancholy had its critics and satirists. In 1712, Joseph Addison noted that 'melancholy is a kind of Demon that haunts our island, and often conveys herself to us in an Easterly Wind' (No. 387, 24 May 1712). In 1713, Alexander Pope immortalized the absurdities of the fashion when he added the 'Cave of Spleen' section (Canto IV) to the original version of *The Rape of the Lock* (1712). Thomas Love Peacock also satirized melancholy in *Nightmare Abbey* (1818) (Newman, 1997, 445–6).

Chapter 9

IN WHICH THE WOODEN MIDSHIPMAN GETS INTO TROUBLE

The recollection of those incidents,

Richard Whittington;] See note to chapter 4, p. 72.

a ballad of considerable antiquity, that had long fluttered among many others, chiefly expressive of maritime sentiments, on a dead wall in the Commercial Road: which poetical performance set forth the courtship and nuptials of a promising young coal-whipper with a certain "lovely Peg," the accomplished daughter of the master and part-owner of a Newcastle collier.] Ballads for sale were attached by 'pinners-up' to screens, boards, railings or blank walls. Mayhew noted that there was a 'great demand' for songs such as 'A Life on the Ocean Wave,' and 'I'm Afloat', and that 'Three-fourths of the customers ... were boys', adding that '780 guineas are yearly expended in London streets, in the ballads of the pinners-up' (1.273). The particular ballad of the 'coal-whipper' and 'lovely Peg' seems to be a conflation of familiar elements in sea songs. 'Peg' is a recurrent name in sea songs (along with 'Ned'): e.g. 'Thus to describe Poll, Peg, or Nan, / Each his best manner tried'; 'Young Peg of Portsmouth Common / Had like to have been my wife'; 'I'm Peggy, once your soul's desire, / To whom you prove a rover'; 'His sister Peg her brother loved, / For a right tender heart had she' (*Sea Songs and Ballads*, 1863, 40, 60, 78, 79).

The collier was used as a point of sentimental and satirical contrast in ballads such as 'Collier's Bonny Lassie' and 'The Collier Swell':

> The collier has a daughter,
> And O she's wonder bonny,
> A Laird he was that sought her,
> Rich both in lands and money.
> (*Ancient and Modern Scottish Songs*, 1776, 1.207)

> A collier by trade, but I've changed as you may tell, sir,
> And since a richer purse I've got, I'll be a regular Swell, sir.
> (Ashton, 1888, 385)

The Commercial Road, built in 1803 largely with money from the East India Company, is a long, broad thoroughfare then with a tramway that connected the East India Docks at Blackwall and the Company's warehouses in the City (Wheatley, 1891, 1.448). A 'coal-whipper' whipped coal from the hold of a ship to the deck, using a block-and-tackle. The 'chief business' of Newcastle on the River Tyne in the county of Northumberland was 'the shipment of coals, the produce of the surrounding coal-pits'. In 1838, 2,450,778 tons of coal were sent to the coast, with about one half of the amount going to London (*The Penny Cyclopædia*, 1839).

non-Dominical holidays,] Holidays not on Sunday.

But a frank, free-spirited,

fancy portraits] 'Portraits based upon or drawn from conceptions of the fancy'. The first recorded use of the term is 1800 (*OED*).

In this way, Walter, so far

Sometimes he thought … what a grand thing it would have been for him to have been going to sea … and to have gone, and to have done wonders there, and to have stopped away a long time, and to have come back an Admiral of all the colours of the dolphin, or at least a Post-Captain with epaulettes of insupportable brightness, and have married Florence (then a beautiful young woman) … and borne her away to the blue shores of somewhere or other, triumphantly.] Walter's imaginings resemble Dickens's own account of his boyhood reading, fictionalized through David Copperfield's recollection of the books that 'kept alive my fancy':

> I had a greedy relish for a few volumes of Voyages and Travels – I forget what, now … and for days and days I can remember to have gone about … the perfect realisation of Captain Somebody, of the Royal British Navy, in danger of being beset by savages, and resolved to sell his life at a great price. The Captain never lost dignity. … the Captain was a Captain and a hero. (4)

The earliest novels and stories to romanticize life at sea date from the 1820s to 1840s and were the work of the first generation of marine novelists, James Fenimore Cooper and Captain Frederick Marryat. In his library at Gad's Hill, Dickens had the works of both authors (Cooper's *Novels and Tales*, 40 vols, 1841, and Marryat's *Novels*, 13 vols, n.d.), as well as two collections of 'Voyages and Travels': James Burney, *A Chronological History of Voyages and Discoveries in the South Sea or Pacific Ocean* (5 vols, 1803–17); William Mavor, *A General Collection of Voyages and Travels, from the Discovery of America to the Nineteenth Century* (28 vols, 1810). The stock elements in sea stories were ridiculed by Thackeray in *The Tremendous Adventures of Major Gahagan* (1838):

> The writers of marine novels have so exhausted the subject of storms, shipwrecks, mutinies, engagements, sea-sickness, and so forth, that (although I have experienced each of these in many varieties) I think it quite unnecessary to recount such trifling adventures. (ch. 1)

The genre was revived, however, by Charles Henry Dana's realistic *Two Years Before the Mast* (1840), which recounts life at sea through convincing, authoritative and authentic details.

Until 1864, the Royal Navy used squadron colours to subdivide the fleet, with each rank of admiral being assigned a different colour: the Admiral's squadron wore a red flag; the Vice-Admiral's a white flag; and the Rear Admiral's a blue flag.

Dolphins were popularly thought to change colour as they were dying:

> The changes of hue displayed by the dying Dolphin are peculiar; but have been much exaggerated by the poetical descriptions of travellers. Soon after the fish has been removed from the water, the bright yellow with rich blue spots, which constitutes the normal colour of the animal, is exchanged for a brilliant silver, which a short time after death passes into a dull grey, or lead colour. The original golden hue occasionally revives in a partial manner, and appears above the silver field, producing a very interesting display of colours.
> (Timbs, 1841, 362)

In 1795, epaulettes with thick bullions were added to the dress uniform of some officers, including Admiral and Captain. The 1795 Regulations specified that post captains wear two gold epaulettes with plain straps, while captains with less than three years' experience wear only one epaulette, and that on the right shoulder. After 1812, all senior officers adopted two epaulettes: post-captains, with a silver crown and anchor; junior captains, with a silver anchor only. A Post-Captain 'takes post': he holds a commission as a full-grade captain, which distinguishes him from an officer who has been given the courtesy title of 'Captain' but who is only an acting captain or master and commander of a lower-graded vessel. The term 'Post-Captain' appears to date from 1731–47 in the Naval Regulations, and seems not to have been used officially after 1824. Informally, though, the distinction between 'Post-Captain' and 'Captain' lingered later into the nineteenth century (*OED*).

There lived in those days,

in Bishopsgate Street Without – one Brogley, sworn broker and appraiser, who kept a shop where every description of second-hand furniture was exhibited in the most uncomfortable aspect,] Bishopsgate Street Without is situated north of Camomile and Wormwood Streets or without the walls of the City of London, as opposed to Bishopsgate Street Within, located between Cornhill and Camomile Street, which is within the walls. In 'Brokers' and Marine-store Shops' (*SB*), Dickens described the kind of 'heterogeneous mixture of things' found in the most humble of brokers' shops:

> Our readers must often have observed in some by-street, in a poor neighbourhood, a small dirty shop, exposing for sale the most extraordinary and confused jumble of old, worn-out, wretched articles, that can well be imagined. Our wonder at their ever having been bought, is only to be equalled

by our astonishment at the idea of their ever being sold again. On a board, at the side of the door, are placed about twenty books – all odd volumes; and as many wine glasses – all different patterns; several locks, an old earthenware pan, full of rusty keys; two or three gaudy chimney ornaments – cracked, of course; the remains of a lustre, without any drops; a round frame like a capital O, which has once held a mirror; a flute, complete with the exception of the middle joint; a pair of curling irons; and a tinder box. In front of the shop window, are ranged some half dozen high backed chairs, with spinal complaints and wasted legs; a corner cupboard; two or three very dark mahogany tables with flaps like mathematical problems; some pickle jars, some surgeons' ditto, with gilt labels and without stoppers; an unframed portrait of some lady who flourished about the beginning of the thirteenth century, by an artist who never flourished at all; an incalculable host of miscellanies of every description, including bottles and cabinets, rags and bones, fenders and street door knockers, fire irons, wearing apparel and bedding, a hall lamp, and a room door. Imagine, in addition to this incongruous mass, a black doll in a white frock, with two faces – one looking up the street, and the other looking down, swinging over the door; a board with the squeezed up inscription 'Dealer in marine stores', in lanky white letters, whose height is strangely out of proportion to their width; and you have before you precisely the kind of shop to which we wish to direct your attention.

the shrewd east wind] See note to chapter 5, p. 81.

shrill complainings of a cabinet piano, wasting away,] The upright piano, which was more compact and thus more useful for the home, replaced the square piano in the early nineteenth century. The most common type of upright piano was the cabinet piano-forte, also called the 'bookcase' piano, which was tall and rectangular, and which had shelves to store music in the upper part of the case, to the right of the strings. The compactness of its design tended to diminish sound quality. The *Penny Cyclopædia* in 1840 considered that the cabinet piano 'has long since been superseded and laid aside' (18.142).

Mr. Brogley himself was a moist-eyed,

that class of Caius Marius who sits upon the ruins of other people's Carthages,] The conventional spelling is Gaius Marius (157–86 BC). Plutarch records how the elderly and defeated Roman general and consul sought compassion as a fugitive from the governor of Carthage but was told by a messenger that the governor refused him entry to the city:

> When Marius heard this he wanted words to express his grief and resentment, and for a good while held his peace, looking sternly upon the messenger, who asked him what he should say, and what answer he should return to the

Prætor? Marius replied with a deep sigh; Go tell him that thou hast seen the exiled Marius sitting on the ruins of Carthage: by which noble answer he well represented the fortunes of that city, and his own, as terrible examples of the vicissitude of all human affairs.
(*Plutarch's Lives*. Trans. John Dryden, 1758, 3.152)

Brokers were employed by courts to value debtors' household effects that might be seized if the debtors did not pay their rent or other debts. The courts would place the broker, or the broker's man, in the house to ensure that no goods were removed while the debtor tried to raise the necessary money. 'The Broker's Man' (*SB*) describes the job, as told by Mr Bung, who once worked for a broker:

> ... a broker's man's life is not a life to be envied; ... people hate and scout 'em because they're the ministers of wretchedness, like, to poor people. ... I never liked it, God knows; I always looked out for something else, and the moment I got other work to do, I left it. ... I'm sure the business, to a beginner like I was, at all events, carries its own punishment along with it. I wished again and again that the people would only blow me up, or pitch into me – that I wouldn't have minded, it's all in my way; but it's the being shut up by yourself in one room for five days, without so much as an old newspaper to look at, or anything to see out o' the winder but the roofs and chimneys at the back of the house, or anything to listen to ... it's all this, that makes you feel sneaking somehow, and ashamed of yourself.

Mr Bung's account contains several examples of the misery wrought by brokers and their assistants, especially among the very poor, those who have no chance of paying their way out of debt.

"The fact is," said Mr. Brogley,

"there's a little payment on a bond debt – three hundred and seventy odd, over due: and I'm in possession."] 'BOND, in law, is a deed whereby the party obliges himself, his heirs, executors, or administrators, to pay a certain sum of money to another at a day appointed' (*London Encyclopædia* 4 [1829]: 296).

Captain Cuttle lived on the brink

Captain Cuttle lived on the brink of a little canal near the India Docks, where there was a swivel bridge which opened now and then to let some wandering monster of a ship come roaming up the street like a stranded leviathan.] Probably the 'City Canal', the three-quarters-of-a-mile-long canal that lay south of the West India Docks, and which cut off the large bend of the Thames, connecting Limehouse Reach with Blackwall Reach, and forming the northern boundary of the Isle of Dogs.

The canal, which had a lock and swing bridge at either end, was originally constructed by the Corporation of London 'to enable ships to avoid the circuitous navigation of the Isle of Dogs', but proved unsuccessful as a ship canal, and was sold to the West India Dock Company in 1829. The India Docks comprise the West India Docks, which opened August 1802 and the East India Docks, which opened in August 1806, both located in Blackwall, six miles to the east of the City of London. (The East India Dock Company and the West India Dock Company united in 1838.) 'At the time of construction', the West India Docks were reputed to be 'the most magnificent in the world' (Wheatley, 1891, 3.459). Covering 295 acres, they were 'the most capacious of all the great warehousing establishments in the port of London' (Mayhew, 1851, 3.310). There was both a northern, or import dock, 170 yards long by 166 yards wide, which held 204 vessels of 300 tons each; and a southern or export dock, 170 yards long by 135 feet wide, which held 195 vessels. The much smaller East India Docks had a 19-acre import dock and a 10-acre export dock, and a basin of three acres (*Leigh's Picture of London*, 1819).

Dickens would have known the area since boyhood: from 1822–3 he visited his godfather, Christopher Huffam, who lived near the India Docks, at Church Row, Limehouse.

the erection of flag-staffs, as appurtenances to public-houses;]

> Let any Gentleman ride round the environs of London on a Sunday evening, and in every quarter he would see flags displayed from public-houses, apprising the artisan where he might procure beer and spirituous liquors. ('Admission to Public Institutions', *Hansard* 65 [14 July 1842]: 127)

then came slopsellers' shops, with Guernsey shirts, sou'wester hats, and canvas pantaloons, at once the tightest and loosest of their order, hanging up outside.]
'Slops' originally referred to sailors' baggy trousers ('canvas pantaloons'), but came to mean 'seamen's clothes in general' (*The Synonymous, Etymological and Pronouncing English Dictionary*. Samuel Johnson and William Perry, 1805). Slopsellers sold 'cheap ready-made' garments, 'not at all advantageously to Jack', as opposed to 'show-shops' which sold 'bespoke' garments, those that were made individually (Smyth, 1867, 633). In practice, 'Many of the large tailoring houses at the East-end of London are both show-shops and slop-shops' (Mayhew, 'Letter XVII', *The Morning Chronicle: Labour and the Poor*, 1849–50).

A 'Guernsey shirt' was a thick, knitted, close-fitting shirt or vest, worn by seamen, and usually made of blue wool. A 'sou-wester hat' had a broad brim and was elongated at the back. It was made of a very fine canvas permeated with an oil-based preparation that gave it a glossy surface and made it waterproof (Kemp, 1976).

anchor and chain-cable forges, where sledge hammers were dinging upon iron all day long. … the air was perfumed with chips; and all other trades were swallowed up in mast, oar, and block making, and boat building. Then, the ground grew marshy and unsettled. Then, there was nothing to be smelt but rum

and sugar.] Walter is walking near the West India Docks, on the Isle of Dogs, which *HW* characterized in 1853 as *'terra incognita'* for most Londoners. Of the landscape and industries in the area, *HW* remarked:

> We have called the Isle of Dogs a low, green, swampy field, fringed with industry, and inhabited by a few cows. The industry, as in most other parts of the vicinity of London, is becoming more developed each year. ... there is the ship-yard ... and then there is a busy group of anchorsmiths, copper merchants, mast and block makers, shipping butchers, and ship-chandlers. Then, advancing further south down the western margin, we come to establishments of large size. There are the huge anchors of Messrs. Brown and Lenox, the timber preserving works of Sir William Burnett ... the mast and oar works of Messrs. Ferguson ... and such an array of pitch and tar men, timber men, ship men, lightermen, block and pump men, wire-rope men, galvanized-iron men, ship-tank men, and lime-burning men, as gives a very peculiar character to this district.

Along the north side of the import dock, ran 'extensive warehouses for sugars, coffee, and other dry goods'. Along the south side, there was 'an extensive quay and warehouses for rum; and an eastern and western wood quay and sheds' (Weale, 1854, 343). *HW* estimated that these warehouses, 'have contained at one time a hundred and fifty thousand hogsheads of sugar, half a million bags of coffee, thirty or forty thousand pipes of rum and Madeira, fifteen thousand logs of mahogany, and twenty thousand tons of logwood!' (7.273–5).

The Captain was one of those

one of those timber-looking men, suits of oak as well as hearts,] 'Hearts of oak' was a familiar image in patriotic songs such as 'Hearts of Oak' (1759; music by William Boyce): 'Hearts of oak are our ships, / Hearts of oak are our men'. This song appears in Charles Dibdin's *Songs, Naval and National* (1841), a copy of which was in Dickens's library at Gad's Hill. The collection includes other songs having the image; for example, 'Britannia': 'Her hull is royal heart of oak, / And heart of oak her crew'; 'The British Seaman's Praise'; and 'What Should Sailors do on Shore?'

hard glazed hat ... and the shirt-collar like a sail, and the wide suit of blue,] See note to chapter 4, p. 70.

"Wal'r, my lad!" said Captain

It's washing day."] Washing day, invariably on Monday, was synonymous with upheaval for the household and inconvenience for the man of the house because the mistress and servants had no time to cook or perform the usual daily tasks. The topic was often the subject of comic writing:

Chapter 9 *In which the Wooden Midshipman gets into Trouble* 147

> [W]hat an event a washing day is; how, and when it begins, and when, and how it ends. A washing day, at home, then, is the longest day in the week. … The dreadful "notes of preparation" are first sounded by the splashing of buckets full of water, on the evening previous to the ill-fated day. It would seem as if the second sack of Troy had commenced; the hum of buckets and kettles. … Polly is wanted in the name of the brass kettle, Thomas is required on behalf of the tub, and Betty is principal engineer of empty buckets. Poor Grimalkin is turned out of doors, and Ponto wisely chooses the barn, instead of a scald. ('A Washing Day', *The Mirror of Literature*. 2 [1823]: 508–9)

"A boy that can knock

an Englishwoman's house was her castle] 'A man's (Englishman's) house is his castle' is proverbial; the householder's rights to inviolability were defined by Sir Edward Coke in his *Institutes of the Lawes of England* (4 vols, 1628–44): 'For a man's house is his castle, et domus sua cuique est tutissimum refugium; for where shall a man be safe, if it be not in his house?' (Coke 3.162). In the words of a contemporary,

> What we call in England *a comfortable house* is a thing so intimately identified with English customs as to make us apt to say that in no other country but our own is this element fully understood; or at all other events that the comfort of any other nation is not the comfort of this. The peculiarities of our climate, the domesticated habits of almost all classes, our family reserve, and our large share of the means and appliances of easy living, all combine to make what is called a comfortable home perhaps the most cherished possession of an Englishman. (Kerr, 1865, 69)

whether she was to be broke in upon by "raff."] 'RIFF RAFF. Low vulgar persons, mob, tag-rag and bob-tail' ([Grose] *Lexicon Balatronicum*, 1811). Compare *OT*: 'Ragged children, and the very raff and refuse of the river' (50).

The Captain was dining

He unscrewed his hook at dinner-time, and screwed a knife into its wooden socket, instead,] On this type of prosthesis, see note to chapter 4, p. 000.

But when Walter told him

atomies] The term derives from 'anatomy' and means an emaciated or withered skeleton, as in *2 Henry IV* 5.4.33: 'Ay, come, you starv'd bloodhound. … Thou atomy, thou!'

These directions were not issued

Mrs Mac Stinger glided out of the little back kitchen, like an avenging spirit.] In Greek mythology, the three Eumenides (the Roman Furies) were the avenging goddesses dreaded by both gods and men. Homer represents them as the personification of the curses pronounced upon a criminal, and in punishing men, they took away all peace of mind and led them into misery and misfortune.

"Uncle much hove down, Wal'r?"

hove down,] In other words, he is out of commission; 'HOVE DOWN, properly *hove out* or *careened*. The situation of a ship when heeled or placed thus for repairs' (Smyth, *Sailor's Word-Book,* 1867, 394).

"Walk fast, Wal'r, my lad,"

walk the same all the days of your life. Overhaul the catechism for that advice,] From *BCP,* 'A Catechism, That is to say, an Instruction to be Learned of Every Person, Before He be Brought to be Confirmed by the Bishop':

> Question. What did your Godfathers and Godmothers then for you?
> Answer. They did promise and vow three things in my name. First, that I should renounce the devil and all his works, the pomps and vanity of this wicked world, and all the sinful lusts of the flesh. Secondly, that I should believe all the Articles of the Christian Faith. And thirdly, that I should keep God's holy will and commandments, and walk in the same all the days of my life.

"Gills!" said the Captain, hurrying

"Lay your head well to the wind, and we'll fight through it.] That is, sail into the wind (as close to the wind as possible) in order to use your sails effectively and keep on a safe course.

"Never mind," returned the Captain,

"all's fish that comes to your net,] Proverbial since the sixteenth century, the phrase means everything can be used to advantage.

"Gills," said Captain Cuttle,

"**what's the bearings of this business?**] 'To take one's bearings' is a nautical phrase meaning to determine one's position in relationship to surrounding objects. A 'bearing' is also a line of flotation formed by the water when a vessel is sitting upright 'with her provisions, stores, and ballast, on board in proper trim' (Smyth, *Sailor's Word-Book*, 1867; *OED*).

"Yes, yes – oh yes –

Welsh wig] See note to chapter 4, p. 59.

Captain Cuttle walked up and down

setting parallel rulers astride onto his nose, and amusing himself with other philosophical transactions.] Parallel rulers are linked rulers used by a navigator to advance compass directions to a course drawn on a chart. 'Philosophical transactions' alludes to one of the two oldest scholarly journals, influential from its inception in 1665, the *Philosophical Transactions of the Royal Society of London*, customarily referred to as *Philosophical Transactions*.

Chapter 10

CONTAINING THE SEQUEL OF THE MIDSHIPMAN'S DISASTER

Miss Tox, however, maintaining

Yellow Jack] A slang name for yellow fever, from the yellow flag, or 'jack', that was displayed in naval hospitals and on board quarantined vessels to signal the existence of contagious disease.

It was some time coming

gout,] According to Macaulay's *Dictionary of Medicine Designed for Popular Use* (1831):

> This long known and celebrated disease is one of the few maladies and infirmities of which men are disposed to be proud. As it is a disease chiefly brought on by rich and luxurious living, and as it rarely occurs among the

poor and plebeian, to be afflicted with the gout is supposed to imply a degree of opulence and rank in the patient, which the vanity of man converts into a ground of consolation and pleasure. The paroxysms of gout, however, are sometimes so severe, that patients would be glad to have the reputation without the pain; and the sudden and fatal termination which it sometimes has, render its presence in the constitution by no means enviable. (255)

Gout is one of several maladies Bagstock is represented as suffering (see note to chapter 7, pp. 108–9). Others are 'plethoric symptoms' (*i.e.* an excess of blood in the vessels or of fluid in bodily organs), apoplexy and palsy. Nineteenth-century medical opinion closely associated gout with all these conditions and warned that 'gouty people are suddenly taken off by apoplectic fits' (Wilson, 1833, 27–35, *passim*).

And very tough indeed Master

the Major, with his complexion like a Stilton cheese, and his eyes like a prawn's,] Dickens described his friend, the sculptor Angus Fletcher, in a letter of January 1845:

By the time he had finished this third dinner, his eyes protruded infinitely beyond the tip of that feature [his very long nose]. You never saw such a human Prawn as he looked, in your life. (*Letters* 4.252–3)

As Bagstock's eyes are repeatedly described as protruding (compare his 'lobster eyes' in chapter 20), he would appear to suffer from exophthalmia. The bluish-green streaks of mold that characterize Stilton cheese allude to another of his chronic maladies, cyanosis, in which 'the skin presents a livid blueish tint of a violet or blackish purple, with stripes or spots of a deeper colour' (Rayer, *Treatise on diseases of the skin*, 1833, 282). For a description of exophthalmia and cyanosis see note to chapter 7, pp. 108–9.

"By G –, Sir," said

the British possessions abroad.] In the early 1840s, British possessions included India, Australia, British North America (Canada), Trinidad, Tobago, St Lucia, Mauritius, Malta, Ceylon, Malacca, Singapore, the Cape of Good Hope, New Zealand and Hong Kong.

His Royal Highness the Duke of York observed on more than one occasion, 'there is no adulation in Joey. He is a plain old soldier is Joe.] Name-dropping is one of the characteristics of Thackeray's Major Goliah O'Grady Gahagan, on whom Bagstock is partly modelled (see note to chapter 7, p. 112. The parodic autobiography includes numerous anecdotes of Gahagan's intimacy with such figures as Louis Philippe and his wife, the Duchess of Orléans, various English royals and aristocrats, and Indian princes. For the Duke of York, see note to chapter 1, p. 32–3.

Chapter 10 *Containing the Sequel of the Midshipman's Disaster*

"Here is a boy, here, Sir,"

Bill Bitherstone, formerly of Ours.] That is, of our regiment. In *Vanity Fair*, for instance, Major Dobbin is several times referred to as 'Dobbin of ours' by his fellow officers and the narrator.

"That is what he is,

My little friend is destined for a public school, ... ?" ... "I think not. He is delicate."] Public schools (which are, in fact, private) derive their name from the ancient endowments that permitted intelligent local or 'scholarship' boys to attend. By the middle of the nineteenth century, it had become a necessity for middle-class families with social aspirations to send their sons to public schools. Dickens's public schoolboys are generally lacking in energy and resolution: for instance, Richard Carstone in *BH*, Sydney Carton in *TTC*, and Eugene Wrayburn and Mortimer Lightwood in *OMF*. On the other hand, both Tartar and Crisparkle in *MED* attended public schools, and Dr Strong runs an idyllic public school in *DC*. At the urging of Angela Burdett Coutts, Dickens sent his son Charley to exclusive Eton College (Collins, 1963, 24–5, 32–3, 119; Best 150–1).

Sydney Smith described the kind of harsh treatment that Young Paul could have expected at a typical public school in the early nineteenth century:

> The power which the elder part of these communities exercises over the younger, is exceedingly great – very difficult to be controlled – and accompanied, not unfrequently, with cruelty and caprice. It is the common law of the place, that the young should be implicitly obedient to the elder boys; and this obedience resembles more the submission of a slave to his master, or of a sailor to his captain, than the common and natural deference which would always be shown by one boy to another a few years older than himself. Now, this system we cannot help considering an evil, – because it inflicts upon boys, for two or three years of their lives, many painful hardships, and much unpleasant servitude. These sufferings might perhaps be of some use in military schools; but, to give a boy the habit of enduring privations to which he will never again be called upon to submit ... is surely not a very useful and valuable severity in education. ... he will never again be subjected to so much insolence and caprice; nor ever, in all human probability, called upon to make so many sacrifices. ... Such a system makes many boys very miserable. ('Public Schools', *Edinburgh Review*, 1810; *Works* 182)

"If he's delicate, Sir," said

None but the tough fellows could live through it, Sir, at Sandhurst. We put each other to the torture there, Sir. We roasted the new fellows at a slow fire, and hung

'em out of a three pair of stairs window, with their heads downwards. Joseph Bagstock, Sir, was held out of window by the heels of his boots, for thirteen minutes by the college clock."] Established by royal warrant in 1802 in a temporary house in Great Marlow, The Royal Military College moved in 1812 to its permanent building at Sandhurst, 'one of the most healthy spots in England, situated thirty miles distant from London, through which coaches used to pass at every hour' (Stocqueler, 1853, 241). The College comprised both junior and senior departments, the former being for cadets and the latter for commissioned officers. Bagstock would have been a cadet in the junior department, 'for the education of those sons of meritorious officers (either deceased or in straitened circumstances) who were intended to follow their fathers' profession'. Cadets were admitted between the ages of thirteen and sixteen. Although the Military College originated as a charitable institution (orphan cadets were admitted free of charge and the sons of officers currently in the service for a reduced fee), by the 1820s 'the question of charity was passing out of the general scheme', and fewer cadets were admitted (212 in 1829; 180 in 1832; 145 in 1846) (Mockler-Ferryman, 1900, 10, 23). To have obtained his commission, Bagstock would have had

> to satisfy his examiners to the following extent: – thorough knowledge of Euclid, Books 1–6; well versed in either Classics, French, German, or History; conversant with the 1st and 3rd systems of Vauban; proficient in Military Drawing; general conduct unexceptional. (23)

Under the royal warrant, dated 27 May 1808, gentleman cadets at the Royal Military College were 'subject to the Articles of War, and to such other rules and regulations as are, or may be from time to time, established for the maintenance of good order and discipline at the Institution'. Breaches of discipline were punished with 'expulsion, rustication, detention during the vacation, confinement in the Upper Hospital, in the "Black Hole," or in the lock-up room with bread-and-water and impositions, extra studies, close and open arrests, half-hourly roll calls on half-holidays, and extra guards' (Stocqueler, 1853, 242; Mockler-Ferryman, 1900, 33). Forster reports that James Lamert, 'a sort of cousin' to Dickens, 'who was his great patron and friend in his childish days' had attended Sandhurst (*Life* 1.9). 'Three pair of stairs' is three flights, thus the window was on the third floor.

"I generally come down once

"I stay at the Bedford."] The Bedford Hotel, Brighton, established in 1837, billed itself as a 'First-Class Establishment', 'advantageously and conveniently situated on the West Cliff, removed from the noise of the town', with wine 'of the best quality' and with 'Cuisine ... under the management of an experienced Chef from Paris' ('Murray's Handbook Advertiser', 59, *A Handbook of Rome and Its Environs*, 1864). Dickens often stayed at the Bedford when he visited Brighton and, in fact, visited the hotel from 17–29 May 1847, during the period he was writing *DS*.

Chapter 10 *Containing the Sequel of the Midshipman's Disaster*

In fulfilment of his promise,

Mr. Dombey, having referred to the army list, afterwards called on the Major.] Published by the War Office, the Army List contained the names of all commissioned officers in the British army, organized according to their dates of commissions, along with 'the officers in the East India Company's service – or, *now*, that portion of the Queen's army which belongs exclusively to India', and the officers who hold military honours or staff appointments. The bulk of the List, though, contained 'an enumeration of all the regiments in the Queen's army, and all the officers in each regiment, arranged according to the numerical rank of the regiments'. In all, the Army List for 1859 held the names of about 14,000 commissioned officers (*Chambers's Encyclopædia*, 1868, 1.422).

At length Mr. Dombey,

complimented Miss Tox highly, beforehand, on her neighbour and acquaintance.] After this sentence, MS and the first proof have a long passage that includes the following, revealing Miss Tox's hope of succeeding Mrs Dombey:

> Between the Major and me there is now a yawning chasm, and I will not feign to give encouragement, Louisa, where I cannot give my heart. My affections," said Miss Tox – "but, Louisa, this is madness!" – and departed from the room.

For an earlier unadopted passage on Miss Tox's hopes, see note to chapter 5, p. 73 and Horsman's discussion in the Clarendon edition, p. xvii.

"Half a loaf's better than

"Half a loaf's better than no bread,] A proverb dating from the sixteenth century.

a lad over-flowing ... with milk and honey –] A 'land flowing with milk and honey' is how God, who is speaking to Moses from a burning bush, describes the Promised Land (Exodus 3.8, 13.5).

Chapter 11 Fourth monthly number
January 1847

PAUL'S INTRODUCTION TO A NEW SCENE

For example, there was

an honest grocer and general dealer] Grocers sold miscellaneous 'general goods' not sold in other speciality shops, as explained in Anna Maria Hall's *Marian; or a young maid's fortune* (1840):

> The "grocer and general dealer" displays his literally "dried fruits" mingled with candles, sugar, soap, tea, toys, matches, wine, lollipops, and deals forth his "pennorth of cheese" and farthing candle, in clean bib and linen sleeves.
> (ch. 4; 1.116)

Mrs. Pipchin had kept

The population of the parlour was immediately swept up-stairs as on the wings of a whirlwind,] From the hymn by Charles Wesley, alluding to *2 Kings* 2.11: 'there appeared a chariot of fire ... and Elijah went up by a whirlwind into heaven':

> See, the true Elijah flies,
> Lord of those unfolding skies!
> Swifter than the whirlwind's wings
> Flies the glorious King of kings,
> Girt with flames of living fire,
> Higher still he soars and higher,
> Till he gains his bright abode,
> Carries up our hearts to God! [st. 1]
> (qtd. in *Hymns ... a Supplement to Dr Watts' Psalms and Hymns*, 1812, 406)

"There is a great deal of nonsense

"There is a great deal of nonsense – and worse – talked about young people not being pressed too hard at first, and being tempted on, and all the rest of it, Sir," said Mrs. Pipchin. ... It never was thought of in my time, and it has no business to be thought of now. My opinion is 'keep 'em at it.' "] Contemporary educational reformers, such as the members of the Central Society of Education, favoured a graduated approach to educating children:

[A student] should, if possible, never be burdened with a weight of which he feels the addition sensibly as it is made: he should not be laden with a hundred-weight at once; but should take it grain by grain, till at last he finds that he carries without difficulty a weight which, if it had been originally laid upon him at once, would have borne him to the ground. He should not have a field of many acres assigned him all at once to till; he would be dispirited at the sight of so long and apparently hopeless a task. it should be parcelled out to him small portions time by time, a fresh one as each was completed, till at last, surveying the whole, he would be surprised at the ease with which he had accomplished it. (1837; 267–8)

"My good madam," returned Mr. Dombey

your excellent system of management] For 'management' as used to refer to the education of children, see note to chapter 8, p. 129.

"I have had some communication

the Doctor … does not consider Paul at all too young for his purpose. He mentioned several instances of boys in Greek at about the same age.] It was not uncommon for boys to begin instruction in Latin, often at home, at the age of five or even earlier, and to learn Greek only slightly later. Connop Thirlwall, an exceptional case, read Latin at the age of three and Greek at four. More typically, before he was eight, John Conington could repeat a thousand lines of Virgil. At nine, Roundell Palmer, later the 1st Earl of Selborne, was familiar with Horace and Virgil. At eleven, George Osborne Morgan was reading the *Aeneid* and Xenophone's *Anabasis*, and was writing Latin verses. In perhaps the best-known instance, John Stuart Mill 'had been told' that he had begun to learn Greek when he was three years old, though he did not begin to learn Latin until he was eight:

> At that time I had read, under my father's tuition, a number of Greek prose authors, among whom I remember the whole of Herodotus, and of Xenophon's Cyropædia and Memorials of Socrates; some of the lives of the philosophers by Diogenes Laertius; part of Lucian, and Isocrates ad Demonicum and ad Nicoclem. I also read, in 1813 [at seven years of age], the first six dialogues … of Plato, from the Euthyphron to the Theoctetus inclusive: which last dialogue, I venture to think, would have been better omitted, as it was totally impossible that I should understand it. (*Autobiography*, 1853–4, 5–6; Clarke, 1959, 83)

"Hoity-toity!" exclaimed Mrs. Pipchin

The school – The master – The usher – The ~~ƒƒƒ~~ forcing system.
Mr Dombey's impatience

    Florence & Miss Nipper.

    Paul's Education

    Paul's Holidays

    Paul's Weariness

Paul's gradually increasing coldness to his father, and closer and closer inclining   towards his sister.

             enjoying
Dr Blimber's young gentlemen, as they appeared when ~~amusing~~ themselves.

Send Walter to the West Indies

  Florence & the exercises

 Floorcloth.

  ~~Breasting the window like a little~~ bird

   Mr Dombey haunting the place

    Feeder's room

    Mrs Pipchin

    Toots

      Paul
     sitting on the Stairs
Floorcloth — clock — ~~ƒƒƒ~~ + ƒ breasting
the window like a little bird – sea – sky

Number Plan

Chapter 11 *Paul's Introduction to a New Scene* 157

(Dealings with the Firm of Dombey and Son — N.º IV.)

chapter XI.

Paul's Introduction to a new scene –

Dr Blimber's at Brighton

Pauls introduction

Clock in the hall says "how is my lit tle friend?"

chapter XII.

Paul's Education

Boys Internal economy of Blimber's

Boys at dinner &c

chapter XIII.

Shipping intelligence and office business

Picture of the Counting house – Introduce M^r
Carker the Manager, and his brother. Brother's
story – Walter ordered off

Chapter Plan

to lump it." The good lady apologised immediately afterwards for using so common a figure of speech,] The first recorded use of 'lump' as a colloquial word to mean 'to be displeased at (something that must be endured)' is 1833 (*OED*).

Mrs. Pipchin's system would be

he had formed a plan ... of sending Paul to the Doctor's as a weekly boarder for the first-year, during which time Florence would remain at the Castle, that she might receive her brother there, on Saturdays.] Dr Blimber runs a private venture school, a type that developed in the mid-eighteenth century to cater to middle-class children. Such schools existed in a number of British towns but were especially widespread in London and the surrounding areas with their growing middle-class manufacturing population. The smaller schools might total about twelve students, who usually lived with the proprietor's family and who were taught alongside his own children. The quality of these schools varied considerably, as did their curriculum. Many were taught by non-graduate laymen, a number of whom were self-taught, and others by nonconformist ministers or Anglican clergymen. If some of these schools were poorly managed, others developed high reputations, modeling themselves on grammar schools and endowed public schools and generally confining their curriculum to the classics (Clarke, 1959, 74–84; Lawson and Silver, 1973, 202–5). In 1830, the *Edinburgh Review* published an article highly critical of the narrow curriculum provided by one of the foremost models for private venture schools, Eton College:

> Now, at Eton, no instruction is given in any branch of mathematical, physical, metaphysical, or moral science, nor in the evidences of Christianity. The only subjects which it professes to teach, are the Greek and Latin languages; as much divinity as can be gained from construing the Greek Testament ... and a little ancient and modern geography. (51.67)

In fact, Doctor Blimber's establishment was

Doctor Blimber's establishment was a great hothouse, in which there was a forcing apparatus incessantly at work. All the boys blew before their time. ... Nature was of no consequence at all.] The 'forcing apparatus' is an air-forcing pump. A hothouse, as distinct from a greenhouse or conservatory (the terms were often used interchangeably), was 'for forcing fruits, or for growing plants which are indigenous to tropical regions', and was kept at a high temperature by means of fires (there were no fires in a greenhouse). The oldest way to heat a hothouse was 'by furnaces and flues; the other modes practised are by steam, or by hot water led through the house in tubes, and by hot air admitted into the atmosphere of the house' (*Penny Cylopædia*, 1838, 320; *Chambers's Encyclopædia*, 1883, 5.435). 'Blew' is an older term for bloom or blossom, and was used figuratively to mean to flourish, to bloom or to attain perfection (*OED*).

The association between the growth of plants and the development of human character recalls Jean-Jacques Rousseau's *Émile; or On Education* (1762):

> Nature would have them children before they are men. If we try to invert this order we shall produce a forced fruit immature and flavorless, fruit which will be rotten before it is ripe; we shall have young doctors and old children.
> (Book 2)

Rousseau's work influenced such later figures as the Swiss pedagogue, Johann Heinrich Pestalozzi, his German student, Friedrich Froebel (or Fröbel) and the English pioneer of infant schools, Samuel Wilderspin, all of whom advised that children should learn through experience, spontaneous play and curiosity, and that they need to develop emotionally as well as intellectually. The images of the hothouse and forcing apparatus in this passage are also reminiscent of an article on infant education in Bronson Alcott's *American Journal of Education* (1830):

> Trite and simple as the poetical paraphrase of this passage is, we wish we could see it more impressed on the heart of every mother, "Just as the twig is bent, the tree's inclined".... But let it be understood we speak of "training" not of forcing the child. We would remonstrate against that course of education which considers him as a mere vessel to be filled with ideas and principles.... He should be treated, on the contrary, as a plant of wonderful delicacy.... We should beware that we do not attempt to bring it forward prematurely. All the efforts of misjudging teachers and parents who wish to see their children early prodigies, only sacrifice the fruit in order to produce an earlier expansion of the flower, and resemble the hot-bed in their influence in "forcing" a plant to maturity, whose feebleness or early decay must be proportioned to the unnatural rapidity of its growth, and consequent want and symmetry in its parts. (*NS* 1: 355–7)

In 1855, Henry Morley drew on the plants-human analogy to praise the work of Froebel:

> The first sproutings of the human mind need thoughtful culture; there is no period of life, indeed, in which culture is so essential. And, yet, in nine out of ten cases, it is precisely while the little blades of thought and buds of love are frail and tender, that no heed is taken to maintain the soil about them wholesome, and the air about them free from blight. (*HW*, 'Infant Gardens', 11.578)

There young Toots was, at

like a greatly overgrown cherub who had sat up aloft much too long.] Charles

8 *Chain Pier, Brighton,* by John Constable, 1826–7. By permission of the Tate Gallery, London

Dibdin, 'In the Whim of the Moment':

> And many fine things that prov'd clearly to me
> That Providence takes us in tow:
> For, says he, do you mind me, let storms e'er so oft
> Take the top-sails of sailors aback,
> There's a sweet little cherub that sits up aloft,
> To keep watch for the life of poor Jack. (*A Collection of Songs, Selected from the Works of Mr. Dibdin.* A New Edition, 2 vols; 1814)

The Doctor was a portly gentleman

a portly gentleman in a suit of black, with strings at his knees, and stockings below them.] 'Although trousers were generally worn after 1815, many elderly persons still held out in knee-breeches against all innovations, and till the present day [1874] may occasionally be seen clinging to this eighteenth century piece of dress' (William and Robert Chambers, *Chambers's Information for the People*, 1.798). Knee-breeches were fastened at the knees with a drawstring.

posed a boy,] Posed a question to a boy.

like a sentiment from the sphynx,]

> the reason Oedipus had bent his steps toward Thebes, was that he had heard of Sphinx, a monster ... with the head and breasts of a woman, the body of a dog, the claws of a lion, the wings of a bird, and a human voice: this monster had stationed herself by the road-side, where she stopped all travellers, and proposed a riddle to them, which if they did not solve they were devoured: the oracle on the other hand had declared, that if any one explained her riddle, the Sphinx would immediately kill herself for vexation. (Baldwin, 1814, 260–1)

Miss Blimber, too, although

Miss Blimber ... did no soft violence to the gravity of the house.] She is likened to the goddess of Contentment, the poet's muse in Matthew Green's 'The Spleen' (1737): 'Forced by soft violence of prayer, / The blithesome goddess soothes my care'.

She was dry and sandy with working in the graves of deceased languages.] The prototype of Miss Blimber seems to be Louisa King, one of the daughters of Joseph Charles King, who ran a small school at 9 Northwick Terrace. Dickens's son Charley attended the school in 1844, 1845–6 and 1847; another son, Walter Landor Dickens also went there. Charley refers to this school, and to Louisa King, in the introduction to the Biographical edition of *DS* (1892):

> I was myself ... at a school in St. John's Wood where the master was assisted by his daughter, an amiable young lady and a thorough classical scholar – an arrangement which, in the days when the higher education of women had scarcely been heard of, seemed somewhat eccentric and just suggested the Blimber notion, although in manners of detail there was not the slightest likeness between the two families. (qtd. in Tillotson, 1978, 91)

Dickens may have first met Joseph King in March 1839 and certainly by 17 November 1840 in a dinner at William Macready's home. In his 1911 autobiography, Frederic Harrison described King as 'the ideal schoolmaster ... genial, child-like, earnest and unwearying, his whole mind was with his boys, and his nature was pure and hearty as his mind was alert'. King had the reputation for teaching classical literature in a more direct manner than was typical, and for leaving the rote learning of grammar to oral explanations. He 'enlivened' his lessons 'with anecdotes, illustrations, and pieces of poetry, drawings and the like'. Most unusually, he taught his three daughters Greek and Latin. The daughters seem to have been King's only assistants, with the exception of 'a young mathematical tutor'. Louisa was a 'polished and deeply-versed scholar' who taught Greek, according to Alfred Ainger, who attended the school in 1849. The same year, Macready said of her:

> She is quite equal, without exaggeration, to a degree in Classics at Oxford or

Cambridge & is acquainted with Italian and French, has a pleasing and modest address, and I should think, would prove a prize to any mother wishing to exercise her children's minds at an early age. (qtd. in Tillotson, 1978, 92)

Louisa King published two stories in *HW*: 'Why My Uncle was a Bachelor' (11 February 1854; 8.564–70) and 'Mother and Step-Mother', in three instalments (12, 19, 26 May 1855; 11.341–8; 11.367–76; 11.387–98). Anne Lohrli has noted that 'various literary and classical allusions appear in her two *H.W.* stories, as also a quotation in Latin and one in Greek' (332–3) (Tillotson, 1978, 91–5).

None of your live languages for Miss Blimber. They must be dead – stone dead –] According to Forster, Dickens's mother taught him 'the rudiments, not only of English, but also, a little later, of Latin'. 'She taught him regularly every day for a long time', Forster explained, 'and taught him, he was convinced, thoroughly well' (*Life* 1.1.6). Dickens had some knowledge of Latin by the time he was twelve, for in 1824, while his father was imprisoned for debt in the Marshalsea, he was said to have entertained a local pawnbroker, and his clerk, by conjugating 'a Latin verb, and translat[ing] or declin[ing] his musa and dominus' (*Life* 1.1.22). Dickens continued with Latin as a day pupil at Wellington House Classical and Commercial Academy, run by William Jones, who was the model for Creakle and whose school inspired Salem House in *DC*. In 'Our School', Dickens described the Academy, which he attended for two years, as 'a School of some celebrity in its neigbourhood – nobody could have said why' (though in 1838 he had praised the school as 'a good school' – see *Letters* 1.423). 'We were old enough to be put into Virgil when we went there, and to get Prizes for a variety of polishing on which the rust has long accumulated' (*HW* 4.49). In fact, Dickens won the school's prize for Latin (Allen, 1988, 104–12).

A week's work for sixteen-year-old boys at Eton College is described in the *Edinburgh Review* (1830):

> about seventy lines of the *Iliad*, seventy lines of the *Æneid*, two or three pages of each of the compilations called the *Scriptores Graeci* and *Romani*, thirty or forty lines from another compilation called the *Poetae Graeci*, and twenty or thirty verses of one of the Evangelists or the Acts of the Apostles. All the poetry which is construed is learnt by heart; besides which, there is weekly repeated a lesson of the Eton Greek Grammar, and of a very excellent selection from the Elegiac poetry of Ovid and Tibullus. No other books than these are read by a boy in the fifth form; but he is required also to produce an exercise in Latin prose, generally on some trite moral subject, of at least twenty lines; twenty Latin verses, and five or six stanzas of some Lyric measure. (51.68)

The *Edinburgh Review* criticized the uselessness of Eton's narrow curriculum, condemned the compilations as faulty and inadequate and urged an overhaul of the syllabus and methods of teaching (65-80 *passim*).

Although the classical curriculum was attacked by utilitarians and supporters of scientific education, wealthy merchants and manufacturers valued its social desirability, considering that a classical education gave access to culture, power and the highest levels of society (Mermin 51). Dickens's scepticism about the value of a classical education is expressed in Esther Summerson's remarks on Richard Carstone's ability 'to make Latin verses of several sorts, in the most admirable manner'. 'But', she adds, 'I never heard that it had been anybody's business to find out what his natural bent was, or where his failings lay, or to adapt any kind of knowledge to *him*' (*BH* 13). And Dickens 'quite approve[d]', when, in 1867, his son Edward was advised to give his education 'a practical direction immediately bearing on the way of life before him' and thus had to discontinue his studies in Latin (*Letters* 11.362). Nevertheless, Dickens sent his eldest son to Eton.

Mrs. Blimber, her Mama,

Mrs. Blimber … was not learned herself, but she pretended to be,] Unless they were allowed to study Greek and Latin at home by enlightened parents, or unless they taught themselves in later life, women were excluded from learning ancient languages. But translations of the classics were widely available, most notably those of Homer and Virgil by George Chapman, Pope and Dryden. The growing demand for translations is illustrated by Abraham Valpy's 52 volumes of *The Family Classical Library: a series of English Translations of the Most Valuable Greek and Latin Classics* (1830–6). Other popular works were Lemprière's *Classical Dictionary* (1788) and Alexander Adam's *Roman Antiquities … designed chiefly to illustrate the Latin Classics* (1791), both of which went through many editions. Bulwer-Lytton's novel, *The Last Days of Pompeii* (1834) and Macaulay's poems *Lays of Ancient Rome* (1842) are examples of best-selling works that reinterpreted the classical world to suit contemporary tastes (Vance, 1997, 81–193 *passim*; Hurst, 2006, 10–51 *passim*).

She said at evening parties, that if she could have known Cicero,] An expression used repeatedly by Mrs Blimber (in chapters 11, 24 and 60). Marcus Tullius Cicero (106–43 BC), philosopher, politician and the greatest Roman orator and prose writer, had a famously lucid style. Mrs Blimber would admire Cicero as a model of eloquence. His most widely read works are his orations, the best known of which are those against Catiline and his 'Philippics' condemning Mark Antony. In the early nineteenth century, as well as the many editions of his writings in Latin, extracts from Cicero appeared in English translations and in collections such as *Elegant Epistles … a copious collection … selected for the improvement of young persons and for general entertainment* (1822).

to see the Doctor's young gentlemen go out walking, unlike all other young gentlemen … It was so classical, she said.] The school of philosophy founded by Aristotle in Athens in the 4th century BC was given the name 'Peripatetic' because of a popular tradition that Aristotle taught his students while walking around in the Lyceum. The importance of physical exercise for children was touted by the educational reformer, Samuel Wilderspin, though he was critical of boarding-schools:

It is true that we may sometimes see the children of boarding-schools taking a little exercise, but not really so much as they ought, and when they do, it is turned to no other account than merely for the walk. (*Infant Education*, 1825, 182)

As to Mr. Feeder, B.A.,

a kind of human barrel-organ, with a little list of tunes at which he was continually working, over and over again, without any variation. He might have been fitted up with a change of barrels ... if his destiny had been favourable;] A mechanical organ with a wooden barrel studded with brass staples or pins. When the barrel is rotated, the staples or pins activate keys that open the pipes that emit sound. In the early- to mid-nineteenth century, a single barrel only held a limited number of tunes, about ten to twelve. To play more tunes, the organ-grinder had to change barrels.

In nineteenth-century London, there were so many barrel-organs (usually played by Italian immigrants) that they constituted a public nuisance. In 1826, Prince Pückler-Muskau observed that London barrel-organs 'resound day and night in every street, and are at other times insufferable' (85). Dickens was one of several famous Victorians to sign a letter of thanks to Michael Thomas Bass, Liberal MP for Derby, for bringing in a bill to force street musicians to move on if householders complained. Dickens was particularly bothered by the noise around the house he rented at Broadstairs in 1849. 'Unless it pours of rain, I cannot write half-a-hour without the most excruciating organs, fiddles, bells, or glee-singers. There is a violin of the most torturing kind under the window now (time, ten in the morning) and an Italian box of music on the steps – both in full blast' (*DNB*, 'Bass'; *Letters* 5.162–3).

it was his occupation to bewilder the young ideas of Doctor Blimber's young gentlemen.] From James Thomson, *The Seasons* (1726–30), 'Spring':

> Delightful task! to rear the tender thought,
> To teach the young idea how to shoot,
> To pour the fresh instruction o'er the mind,
> To breathe the enlivening spirit and to fix
> The generous purpose in the glowing breast! (1152–6)

they knew no rest from the pursuit of stony-hearted verbs, savage noun-substantives, inflexible syntactic passages, and ghosts of exercises that appeared to them in their dreams. Under the forcing system, a young gentleman usually took leave of his spirits in three weeks.] In 1837, the Central Society of Education complained of ancient language 'exercises which are in common use':

> A boy is hardly fairly landed in one declension of a noun, or one tense of a verb, before he is hurried off to make the same flying acquaintance with another. He is not allowed time or opportunity for *separate* practice on each

point as it comes before him. Frequently he does not remain long enough in the society of those who are introduced to him to recognize them again. ... In very quick travelling one thing pushes another out of the mind, and only a small portion of what is seen is eventually remembered: so words and phrases when learnt in the way which is here objected to are forgotten almost as soon as learnt. (267)

In *Gaslight and Daylight* (1859), George Augustus Sala complained of 'That amiable system of classical education' that

> taught us ... to look upon everything appertaining to Rome and the Romans with something very much akin to horror; to regard Plautus as a bugbear and Terence as a tyrant; to remember nothing of Horace but the portrait of his schoolmaster – nothing of Virgil but the cruel memory of Juno. (367)

envied Curtius that blessed refuge in the earth,] A reference to the Roman legend of Curtius that attempts to explain the depression or pit in the Roman Forum, which dried up and was paved over in the first century BC. According to the most famous version of the legend, in 362 BC a cleft opened in the Roman Forum that would not close up until Rome's most valuable possession was thrown into it. In order to fulfill the prophecy, a soldier named Marcus Curtius, fully armed and on horseback, leaped into the cleft, which immediately closed again. In an alternate version, Mettius (or Mettus) Curtius, a Sabine who was being chased by Romulus and the Romans, jumped with his horse into a swamp that covered the later site of the Forum, barely escaping with his life. In a third version, the area was enclosed as sacred in 445 BC by the consul, Gaius Curtius, after it had been struck by lightening. Benjamin Robert Haydon depicted the legend in *Curtius Leaping into the Gulf*, a painting first exhibited at the British Institution in 1843.

and at the end of the first twelve-month had arrived at the conclusion, from which he never afterwards departed, that all the fancies of the poets, and lessons of the sages, were a mere collection of words and grammar, and had no other meaning in the world.] In *German Letters on English Education*, Leopold Weise remarked that classical instruction was often 'very mechanical, even in the highest forms', and was reliant largely on grammatical questions 'which have for the most part no reference whatever to the main interest' (1854, 91–4). Howard Staunton, in *The Great Schools of England* (1869), complained that, at public schools, the Greeks and Romans are 'unhappily ... treated as if they and their languages were really dead; and the nomenclature of a lingual anatomy is taught and learned, but nothing more' (xxvi–xxvii). Dickens insisted frequently on the importance of the imagination and play for children. On 6 April 1857, for instance, he complained to the Royal General Theatrical Fund,

> we have schoolmasters constantly demonstrating on blackboards to infant minds the utter impossibility of Puss in Boots; we have all the giants utterly

dead and gone … in these times, when we have torn so many leaves out of our dear old nursery books, I hold it more than ever essential to the character of a great people, that the imagination, with all its innumerable graces and charities, should be tenderly nourished. (*Speeches* 229–30)

'Fancies of the poets' (referring to the work of Greek and Roman poets and also to fairy tales) and 'lessons of the sages' (classical philosophers such as Socrates and Plato) were both contemporary clichés.

For he went on, blow,

blow, blow, blowing] A parody of a drill found in grammar books. For Latin grammars, see note to chapter 12, p. 169.

The Doctor was sitting

a globe at each knee] Pairs of terrestrial and celestial globes were common in schoolrooms. Mr Squeers advertises his academy as giving instruction in 'the use of the globes' (*NN* 3), and Miss Twinkleton has a pair of globes in her Seminary for Young Ladies (*MED* 6).

Homer over the door, and Minerva on the mantel-shelf.] Displayed in order to establish the owner as a man of culture and a connoisseur of art and the classics, copies of famous busts of classical figures were popular domestic ornaments. The bust of Homer most often reproduced is the idealized, blind sculpture dating from the Hellenistic period. Varied and elaborated by the Romans and copied by Renaissance sculptors, the sculpture features in Rembrandt's portrait, 'Aristotle Contemplating a Bust of Homer' (1653). Busts of Minerva usually derive from Roman copies of two lost, larger than life-size Greek statues of Pallas Athena dating from the Hellenistic period. One Roman copy is the 'Minerva of Velletri' (also called the 'Athena of Velletri' or 'Velletri Pallas'). A bust modeled on the statue is represented in Angelica Kauffmann's painting, 'Self-Portrait with a Bust of Minerva' (1780). The other Roman copy of a similar Hellenistic statue is the 'Giustiniani Minerva' (also called the 'Athena Giustiniani'). This statue was particularly admired by Englishmen on the Grand Tour, and a bust modeled on the statue is reproduced in Pompeo Batoni's painting of Charles, 4th Earl of Northampton (1758) (Brilliant, 1991).

"Permit me," said the Doctor,

our young Pilgrim to Parnassus.] *The Pilgrimage to Parnassus* is one of a trilogy of plays produced by Cambridge students between 1598–1602. The plays follow the comical attempts of two young scholars to gain preferment and an occupation.

The Pilgrimage to Parnassus allegorizes the young men's four-year progress through university, represented as a journey to Parnassus (the mountain in central Greece considered sacred and associated with Apollo and the Muses). In the course of the play, the students meet with a series of temptations including drunkenness, ignorance and amorousness.

her young daughter, that fair Sexton in spectacles.] 'Sexton' alludes to Miss Blimber's 'working in the graves of the deceased languages'. For sexton, see note to chapter 5, p. 87.

"Permit me," said the Doctor

My daughter Cornelia] She is named after the renowned Roman matron known as 'Cornelia, Mother of the Gracchi'. Cornelia, daughter of the great Scipio Africanus the Elder, was famous throughout Rome as a model of the selfless love of mothers. After the death of her husband, she devoted herself to the upbringing of her sons, Tiberius and Gaius. She hired Greek tutors for them so that they would become learned in the noble arts, and she taught them to be just, kind, honourable, to hate tyranny and to think noble thoughts and perform noble deeds. Dickens would doubtless have known the painting by Angelica Kauffmann, 'Cornelia, Mother of the Gracchi' (1785).

"Like a bee, Sir,"

"Like a bee, Sir," said Mrs. Blimber ... "about to plunge into a garden of the choicest flowers, and sip the sweets for the first time.] From Isaac Watts, *Divine Songs for the Use of Children* (1715), 'Against Idleness and Mischief' (Song 20):

> How doth the little busy bee
> Improve each shining hour,
> And gather honey all the day
> From every opening flower!
>
> How skilfully she builds her cell!
> How neat she spreads the wax:
> And labours hard to store it well
> With the sweet food she makes.

Virgil, Horace, Ovid, Terence, Plautus, Cicero] The Roman writers who were central to nineteenth-century intellectual culture. Classical prose authors were relatively neglected (Cicero excepted), because contemporary taste, influenced by the Romantic period, favoured classical poetry. While the comedies of Plautus and Terence were widely read, it was (along with Homer) the works of Virgil, Ovid and especially Horace that were memorized at length. In *Childe Harold*, Byron reveals his abhorrence of the rote learning he endured in school and singles out Horace in particular:

> Then farewell, Horace; whom I hated so,
> Not for thy faults, but mine; it is a curse
> To understand, not feel thy lyric flow,
> To comprehend, but never love thy verse. (Canto 4.77)

Likewise, Tennyson admitted: 'It was not till many years after boyhood that I could like Horace. ... Indeed I was so over-dosed with Horace that I hardly do him justice even now that I am old' (Tennyson, 1897, 1.16; Hurst, 2006, 10–13; Vance, 1997, 154, 176; Harrison, 290–304 *passim*). For Cicero, see note above, p. 163.

"But really," pursued Mrs. Blimber,

"I think if I could have known Cicero, and been his friend, and talked with him in his retirement at Tusculum (beau-ti-ful Tusculum!),] Although he was never particularly rich, Cicero had eight country residences, including his villa at Tusculum, a resort for wealthy and noble Romans. Situated high above sea level, about 15 miles southeast of Rome, Tusculum has a commanding view of the Roman Campagna. In *PI*, Dickens describes his brief visit to Tusculum in early 1845:

> Then, there is Frascati, and, on the steep above it, the ruins of Tusculum, where Cicero lived, and wrote, and adorned his favourite house (some fragments of it may yet be seen there), and where Cato was born. We saw its ruined amphitheatre on a grey dull day, when a shrill March wind was blowing, and when the scattered stones of the old city lay strewn about the lonely eminence, as desolate and dead as the ashes of a long-extinguished fire. ('Rome')

A learned enthusiasm is so

a very Davy-lamp] An oil-burning safety lamp used in mines. The small cylindrical lamp is covered with a wire gauze chimney, mounted in a metal cage. The wire gauze allows air to enter but prevents the flame or gases from escaping at a high enough temperature to spark an explosion. Sir Humphry Davy (1778–1829) first recognized the suitability of the wire gauze in 1816, and accurately proportioned the size of the perforations.

"An addition to our little

our little Portico,] The *Stoa Poecile* or Painted Porch, a roofed colonnade or portico in Athens, was frequented by Zeno and his disciples, and was where they taught Stoic doctrine. According to Gibbon, 'From the portico, the Roman civilians learned to live, to reason, and to die' (1778, 44.4.352; qtd. in *OED*).

"If Mr. Dombey will walk

the dominions of the drowsy God."] Morpheus, the Greek god of dreams and the son of Hypnos (Sleep).

Chapter 12

PAUL'S EDUCATION

"How much do you know

"How much do you know of your Latin Grammar, Dombey?"] The most widely used textbook of Latin grammar in the nineteenth century was *The Eton Latin Grammar*. Based on a volume first published in the sixteenth century, the book always referred to as the *Latin Grammar* was constantly revised and went through many editions throughout the following centuries. David Copperfield recalls having his ears boxed with the *Latin Grammar* (4); Thackeray refers to it repeatedly in his works, and in *The Mill on the Floss* (1860), Maggie Tulliver helps her brother study it (2.1). For more on classical education, see notes in chapter 11, pp. 155, 162–3.

"He's a very nice old

the great monsters that come and lie on rocks in the sun. ... There are some creatures ... I don't know how many yards long, and I forget their names ... that pretend to be in distress; and when a man goes near them ... they open their great jaws, and attack him.] There were scores of contemporary accounts of 'sea-serpents' and 'sea monsters', and some creatures were said to range from 30 to 100 feet in length. The one most often reported on was 'the Great American Sea Serpent' frequently sighted off the New England coast from 1800 onwards. Referring to its 'immense jaws like those of the crocodile' and body 'of great length', a geologist reviewing the accounts suggested the serpent might be 'some species of saurian animal' (*Magazine of Natural History*, 1834, 7.246). Another monster sighted in the Red Sea matches little Paul's description in its basking in the sun and cleverly using its huge jaws to trap prey:

I remember often observing, as did also every officer and man in the ship, an enormous sea monster. ... we used to be highly amused by looking at this monster lying basking in the rays of the sun, with the upper jaw of the mouth, which had some resemblance to the great porch door of an old cathedral, but probably much larger, hove back to the angle of 45° from the perpendicular, whilst the lower jaw lay extended on the surface of the sea. In this position, while thousands of gulls (whether attracted by the odour of its breath, or some other cause, I know not) were flying immediately over the throat ... the upper and lower jaws were brought together like lightning, with a clap resembling the report of a great gun, by which means some hundreds of the feathered tribe were entrapped into the stomach. This operation was repeated about every ten minutes, until satisfied, when the animal disappeared. (*Blackwood's Edinburgh Magazine*, 1818, 3.206)

Cornelia took him first to

baize doors,] Baize-covered doors were used to separate the servants' quarters as well as the nursery from the rest of the house; compare Lady Charlotte Campbell Bury, *The Manoeuvring Mother* (1842):

"My dear Isabel ... there is nothing alarming in matrimony. ... If you have a family, it won't much inconvenience you. Shut out the nurseries with baize doors, and you will be free from noise. I managed very well, for sometimes I did not see or hear you children for weeks." (1.2)

Mr. Feeder, B.A., who sat

his Virgil stop on, and was slowly grinding that tune] The 'stop' is the handle or knob that turns the organ's pipes on or off, producing different tunes. Barrel-organs usually have two stops: one for the open pipes of metal, the other for the closed wooden pipe. For more on barrel-organs, see note to chapter 3, p. 49.

Paul having been already

"P. Toots, Esquire,]

The designation of 'esquire' is now commonly understood to be due by courtesy to all persons (not in clerical orders or having any higher title of rank) who are regarded as 'gentlemen' by birth, position, or education. It is used only on occasions of more or less ceremonious mention, and in the addresses of letters, etc. (*OED*)

Dickens mocks the social pretensions implicit in the word 'Esquire' in *LD*: in book 2, chapter 1, the male members of the Dorrit family sign their names in a travellers' book with an 'Esquire' appended, and most of the narrator's mentions of them henceforward mockingly include 'Esquire'. Also see Dinah Maria Mulock, *Two Marriages* (1867), 1.42: ' "Jane, wife of Mr. John Bowerbank" (he was not *Esquire* then)' (*OED*). Dickens's father referred to himself as 'John Dickens, Esq.' in the Portsmouth newspaper announcements of the birth of his son Charles (10 February 1812; Michael Allen 19).

By this time the other

a perfect Miller, or complete Jest Book.] *Joe Miller's Jests: or The Wit's Vade-Mecum* (1739) by John Mottley, a compilation of jests named after the English comic actor, Joseph Miller (1684–1738). By 1751, ten editions had been published, each one larger than its predecessor, and further enlarged editions continued to appear. As a result, the name of Joe Miller became a synonym for a jest or witty anecdote.

Doctor Blimber was already in

bearing them in and out himself on after occasions, like a little elephant and castle.] This image dates from the Middle Ages, when the elephant was nearly always represented with a castle (a fanciful version of the howdah) on its back. Early manuscripts show the elephant with a tower strapped to its back, and inside the tower are five knights in armour with weapons. This image became the crest or sign of the Cutlers' Company, a London craft guild which made knives, scissors and surgical instruments using ivory. In the nineteenth century, 'The Elephant and Castle' was both the name of a celebrated tavern at Walworth, in south London, on the spot where several cross roads meet leading from Westminster, Waterloo and Blackfriars bridges to Kent and Surrey, and the name of the surrounding locality. The tavern was formerly a well-known coaching house converted about 1760 from a blacksmith's which had connections with the Cutlers' Company and used the same name and sign (Larwood and Hotten, 1866, *passim*).

"And when," said the Doctor,

when … the brother of Vitellius prepared for him a feast, in which were served, of fish, two thousand dishes … Of various sorts of fowl, five thousand dishes … And one dish … called, from its enormous dimensions, the shield of Minerva, and made, among other costly ingredients, of the brains of pheasants … Woodcocks … And the spawn of the lamprey, brought from the Carpathian Sea,"] In *Lives of the Caesars*, Suetonius explains that the 'besetting sins' of Aulus Vitellius (AD 15–69), Roman emperor in AD 69, 'were luxury and cruelty':

Most notorious of all was the dinner given by his brother to celebrate the emperor's arrival in Rome, at which two thousand of the choicest fishes and seven thousand birds are said to have been served. He himself eclipsed even this at the dedication of a platter, which on account of its enormous size he called the "Shield of Minerva, Defender of the City." In this he mingled the livers of pike, the brains of pheasants and peacocks, the tongues of flamingoes and the milt of lampreys, brought by his captains and triremes from the whole empire, from Parthia to the Spanish strait. ('Life of Vitellius', *Loeb Classical Library*)

This anecdote about Vitellius, as well as a number of other references to classical stories in *DS*, are recounted in Lemprière's *Classical Dictionary* (1788), Adam's *Roman Antiquities* (1791), Valpy's *Family Classical Library* (52 vols, 1830–6) and Gibbon's *The History of the Decline and Fall of the Roman Empire* (6 vols, 1776–88). Dickens owned the 1825 edition of Gibbon, which he kept in his library at Gad's Hill.

"The sounds of the fish

"The sounds of the fish called scari,"] The plural of scarus (parrot-fish). The 'sounds' they make are caused by their plate-like teeth which grind their food. Scari are often mentioned by the Greek and Roman writers, including Pliny and Ovid. Horace observes that they were expensive in his day, and Petronius, in the *Satyricon*, describes them as a delicacy difficult to obtain.

"And the spawn of the

A Titus ... A Domitian ... A Nero, a Tiberius, a Caligula, a Heliogabalus,] With the exception of Titus, a rogue's gallery of Roman emperors as interpreted by such Latin historians as Suetonius and Tacitus. In his *Lives of the Caesars*, Suetonius remarks on the contemporary suspicions that surrounded the Roman Emperor Titus (AD 39–81; emperor, AD 79–81):

> Besides cruelty, he was also suspected of riotous living, since he protracted his revels until the middle of the night with the most prodigal of his friends; likewise of unchastity because of his troops of catamites and eunuchs, and his notorious passion for queen Berenice, to whom it was even said that he promised marriage. He was suspected of greed as well; ... In short, people not only thought, but openly declared, that he would be a second Nero. ('The Life of Titus' 7, Loeb translation)

'But this reputation turned out to his advantage', Suetonius concludes, 'and gave place to the highest praise, when no fault was discovered in him, but on the contrary the highest virtues'. Titus was succeeded as emperor by his brother Domitian in AD

81. Although he was conscientious in his duties, often adopting a moral stance, and respected religious ritual, Domitian was cruel, autocratic and arrogant, 'excessively lustful' and increasingly ruthless ('The Life of Domitian' 11, 22). Nero (emperor AD 54–68) is one of the most notorious of Roman emperors, known for his debauchery; for supposedly instigating a fire that devastated Rome in AD 64; for murdering his half-brother, his mother and his first wife; and for zealously persecuting the Christians. In Suetonius's judgement, 'he showed neither discrimination nor moderation in putting to death whomsoever he pleased on any pretext whatever' ('The Life of Nero' 37). Tiberius, emperor of Rome from AD 14–37, was notorious for the great number of treason trials and persecutions he carried out, and a time of terror towards the end of his reign ('The Life of Tiberius' 61). In the views of both Tacitus and Suetonius, he had a taste for cruelty and gross depravities. Caligula, the popular name of Gaius Julius Caesar Germanicus (AD 12–41), succeeded Tiberius as emperor in AD 37. An autocratic and capricious ruler who terrified his senators and humiliated his officers, Caligula was thought to be insane, a 'monster' who 'could not control his natural cruelty and viciousness' and, among many other perversions, who 'lived in habitual incest with all his sisters' ('The Life of Caligula' 11, 22, 24). Formerly Marcus Aurelius Antoninus, and sometimes referred to as 'Heliogabalus', Elagabalus (emperor AD 218–22) became notorious for his dissipations, eccentricities and disregard of public affairs, and was eventually murdered, along with his mother. The *Historia Augusta* provides a catalogue of 'the base actions of his life of depravity', characterizing him as one of a group of 'monstrous tyrants', along with Caligula, Nero and Vitellius ('The Life of Elagabalus' 1, 13).

"Gentlemen," said Doctor Blimber,

"Johnson will repeat to me to-morrow morning before breakfast, without book, and from the Greek Testament, the first chapter of the epistle of Saint Paul to the Ephesians.] The first chapter of Ephesians, which consists of 23 verses, testifies to the redemption in Christ and concludes with a prayer for spiritual wisdom. The study of the Greek Testament by public schoolboys was highly recommended in *The Classical Journal* (1813):

> To those who wish well to the interests of religion, and sound morality, it has ever been a subject of sincere regret, that the Greek Testament has not been more generally read in our schools. ... The young student is taught to feel and admire the beauties of Homer ... while the book of inspiration, which contains so many salutary truths, marked with the finger of God, which teaches man his duty, and discovers the glorious prospects beyond the grave, is never opened but with reluctance. ... Some of our schools have of late paid considerable attention to the good old custom of reading the Greek Testament weekly, and sometimes more frequently. On this subject, I have one wish only, that the practice may become universal. (7.138–40)

The young gentlemen bowed,

the young gentlemen, broken into pairs, loitered arm-in-arm up and down a small piece of ground behind the house,] Dickens provided Browne with detailed instructions for the accompanying illustration, 'Doctor Blimber's Young Gentlemen as they appeared when enjoying themselves':

> These young gentlemen, out walking – very dismally and formally (observe; it's a very expensive school). ... I think Doctor Blimber, a little removed from the rest, should bring up the rear, or lead the van, with Paul, who is much the youngest of the party. ... Paul as last described, but a twelvemonth older. No collar or neck-kerchief for him of course. I would make the next youngest boy, about three or four years older than he. (*Letters* 4.678)

Dickens confided to his wife that he found 'Browne's plates for the next Dombey' – 'Doctor Blimber's Young Gentlemen as they appeared when enjoying themselves' and 'Paul's Exercises' – 'much better than usual' (*Letters* 4.681).

Mr. Toots, who had been

the Duke of Wellington,] Arthur Wellesley, the first Duke of Wellington (1769–1852), soldier and statesman, who won spectacular victories in the Indian Campaign (1799–1803), the Peninsular Campaign (1808–14) and who defeated Napoleon at the battle of Waterloo (18 June 1815). Wellington was an ultra-Tory who disliked democratic innovation and opposed the Reform Act of 1832. He served as Prime Minister from 1828–30 and Secretary of State from 1834–5. With a distant demeanour, the 'Iron Duke' inspired many public statues and heroic paintings and became a symbol of British nationalism, much as Lord Nelson had before him.

In the confidence of

Briggs was ridden by his lesson as a nightmare:] An allusion to Fuseli's painting, 'The Nightmare' (1781), exhibited at the Royal Academy in 1782. The painting shows an incubus crouched on a sleeping woman with her arm outstretched. The image was engraved in 1783 and widely circulated; Fuseli capitalized on its fame by painting three more versions; and there were many caricatures by artists such as Rowlandson, Gillray and Cruikshank.

Paul had sunk into a sweet

the real gong was giving dreadful note of preparation,] *Henry V* 4.12–15:

... and from the tents
The armourers, accomplishing the knights,
With busy hammers closing rivets up,
Give dreadful note of preparation.

So he got up directly, and found

a pretty young woman in leather gloves, cleaning a stove.] Cleaning the fires and stoves was one of the first duties performed by a housemaid before the family came down for breakfast. The gloves were kept in the housemaid's box,

> which contains her other implements and materials for cleaning grates, &c, as well as a pair of thick buck leather gloves, which may be purchased at all shops for housemaids' use at one shilling per pair. These gloves are very useful, not only in protecting the hands of the cleaner of the grates from becoming hard, discoloured, and unfit for nicer work, but in securing also fine steel work and fire-irons from the touch of the hands, which, if moist, would injure them. (*An Encyclopædia of Domestic Economy* ... from the late London edition, 1845, 361)

"Now, Dombey," said Miss

"I'm going out for a constitutional."] This was a recently (*c.* 1830) coined colloquialism, originating in the universities, for a walk taken for the benefit of one's health, or constitution (*OED*).

They comprised a little English,

They comprised a little English, and a deal of Latin – names of things, declensions of articles and substantives, exercises thereon, and preliminary rules – a trifle of orthography, a glance at ancient history, a wink or two at modern ditto, a few tables, two or three weights and measures, and a little general information.] Examples of the countless volumes available for teaching children such subjects are: *A Summary of Geography and History, Both Ancient and Modern* (5th ed., 1816); *The Instructor: or, Young Man's Best Companion, containing spelling, reading, writing, and arithmetic* ... , 1811; *Pinnock's Explanatory English Reader* (6th ed., 1827); *Arithmetic Made Easy to Children* (2nd ed., 1805); and the popular source of 'general information', Richmall Mangnall's *Historical and Miscellaneous Questions for the Use of Young People* (1800), known as Mangnall's *Questions*. For the classical syllabus used at Eton College, one of the models for schools such as Dr Blimber's, and for the most popular *Latin Grammar* and compilations of the classics translated into English, see notes to chapter 11, pp. 162–3 and chapter 12, p. 172.

whether twenty Romuluses made a Remus,] Children could learn about the legendary founders of Rome in books such as Lemprière's *Classical Dictionary for Schools and Academies* (1832); *Plutarch's Lives, Translated from the Original Greek*, 6 vols (6th ed., 1801); and *Tales about the Mythology of Greece and Rome* (1839).

troy weight,] The standard system of weights used for precious metals and stones was explained in books such as *A Museum for Young Gentlemen and Ladies* (17th ed., 1806) and *The Young Man's Best Companion* (1811).

hic hæc hoc] For schoolboys learning Latin, this was the most memorable and reverberative of several case gender jingles. *Hic, hæc, hoc* is the start of the declensions in the masculine, feminine, and neuter; nominative, genitive, and dative singular of the demonstrative 'this here': *hic, hæc, hoc; huius, huius, huius; huic, huic, huic* (this man, this woman, this thing; of this man, of this woman, of this thing; to or for this man, etc.). In *The Merry Wives of Windsor*, the Welsh parson, Sir Hugh Evans, quizzes young William on his Latin grammar:

> *Evans.* What is he, William, that does lend articles?
> *William.* Articles are borrowed of the pronoun, and be thus declined: Singulariter, nominativo; hic, hæc, hoc.
> *Evans.* Nominativo, hig, hag, hog; pray you, mark: genitive, hujus. Well, what is your accusative case?
> *William.* Accusativo, hinc.
> *Evans.* I pray you, have your remembrance, child. Accusativo, hung, hang, hog. (4.1.35–43)

whether a verb always agreed with an ancient Briton,] Such books as *A Catechism of the History of England* (1822) describe the 'origin of the first inhabitants of England' and ask the child to reply to questions like: 'Describe the persons of the ancient Britons'; 'What was their general character?'; 'What were their occupations?' (ch. 1).

three times four was Taurus a bull,] In *A Summary of Geography and History, Both Ancient and Modern* (5th ed., 1816), children could learn that Taurus is the name of a constellation of the zodiac as well as a range of mountains in Turkey. *A Catechism of Mythology* (1832) gives additional information: 'April, sign of Taurus (a bull.) He represents that animal whose form Jupiter assumed to carry Europa away'.

Miss Blimber expressed her opinion

a kind of learned Guy Faux, or artificial Bogle, stuffed full of scholastic straw.] On 5 November 1605, Guy Fawkes and other Roman Catholic conspirators plotted to blow up the Houses of Parliament with barrels of gunpowder. The plot was discovered and the conspirators tried and executed. In 1606, an Act of Parliament designated the 5th of November a day of thanksgiving, and it became customary for boys to carry through the streets 'the figure of a man made of straw, with a barber's block for the head, ornamented with a stiff paper cap, a bunch of matches in one hand and a lantern in the other. This is fastened in a chair and carried about by the boys, who, hat in hand, run up to the passengers huzzaing and crying, "Please to remember Guy." ' (*Peter Parley's Almanac for Old and Young,* 1836, 65). A 'bogle' is a frightful figure, or scarecrow.

He acquitted himself very well,

The studies went round like a mighty wheel, and the young gentlemen were always stretched upon it.] Breaking on the wheel was a form of torture and execution once used throughout Europe, especially in Germany and France. The victim would be stretched out across the spokes and hub of a cart-wheel and then would have his limbs broken in several places by an executioner wielding a heavy object, often an iron bar. If the severity of the injuries did not cause death, the executioner would hit the victim once or twice in the chest to finish the job. The punishment, though obsolete in Britain by about the seventeenth century, was employed as late as 1827 in Germany (Farrington 44).

After tea there was exercise

After tea ... there was bed; where ... were rest and sweet forgetfulness.] A poetic cliché by the nineteenth century that derives from the description of Ulysses' companions in Pope's translation of the *Odyssey*:

>They ... end in feasts the day:
>They feed; they quaff; and now (their hunger fled)
>Sigh ...
>Nor cease the tears, 'till each in slumber shares
>A sweet forgetfulness of human cares. (12.62–6)

Pope later applies the phrase to Ulysses himself: 'He ended, sinking into sleep, and shares, / A sweet forgetfulness of all his cares' (23.369–70) (see also Milton, *Paradise Lost* [12.606–7]: ' ... to lose / In sweet forgetfulness all pain and woe'.)

"Why, goodness gracious me,

your Pa, Miss Dombey, never would have learnt you nothing, never would have thought of it,] Although private boarding schools for girls had existed since the late seventeenth century, in the early-Victorian period most middle-class and upper-class girls were educated at home, often under the instruction of a governess or their parents and with the help of their own personal reading. Such an education was usually restricted to genteel 'accomplishments' and moral training, and its main object was to prepare girls for marriage, as well as to inculcate habits of dependency, 'distrusting their own conclusions, and shrinking from responsibility, till they sink into mere puppets, useless to themselves and to others' (Maria G. Grey and Emily Shirreff, *Thoughts on Self-culture, Addressed to Women*, 1850, 30; Lawson and Silver, 1973, 207–8, 306). Literacy rates from the 1830s and 1840s suggest that schooling for girls increased during this period, probably in part because of the expansion of the Sunday school movement.

Not a word of this was

her hair in papers] To curl hair, locks were twisted in wetted strips of brown paper, or sometimes newspaper. Miss Blimber uses a playbill from the Theatre Royal, in chapter 14, see note p. 196.

The only difference was,

He grew more thoughtful and reserved, every day; … He loved to be alone; and in those short intervals when he was not occupied with books,] Forster remarked of the young Dickens,

> He was a very little and a very sickly boy. He was subject to attacks of violent spasms which disabled him for any active exertion. … he had great pleasure in watching the other boys … reading while they played; and he had always the belief that this early sickness had brought to himself one inestimable advantage, in the circumstances of his weak health having strongly inclined him to reading. (1.1.5–6)

Unless young Toots had some

Ideas, like ghosts (according to the common notion of ghosts), must be spoken to a little before they will explain themselves;] An allusion to the opening scenes in *Hamlet*, where the soldiers, Horatio and Hamlet know that they must speak first in order to encourage the Ghost to speak:

> *Marcellus.* Thou art a scholar; speak to it, Horatio …
> *Horatio.* What art thou that usurp'st this time of night …
> By heaven I charge thee, speak! …
> Stay! speak, speak! I charge thee, speak!
> *Marcellus.* 'Tis gone, and will not answer …
> *Horatio.* Let us impart what we have seen to-night
> Unto young Hamlet; for, upon my life,

	This spirit, dumb to us, will speak to him …
	Look, my lord, it comes …
	It beckons you to go away with it,
	As if it some impartment did desire
	To you alone …
Hamlet.	It will not speak; then I will follow it …
	Whither wilt thou lead me? Speak, I'll go no further.
Ghost.	Mark me. … (Act 1, Scenes 1, 4, 5 *passim*)

Some mist there may have been … which … would have become a genie; but it could not; and it only so far followed the example of the smoke in the Arabian story, as to roll out in a thick cloud, and there hang and hover.] An allusion to 'The Story of the Fisherman' from *The Arabian Nights Entertainment*. A fisherman catches a vessel in his net, which he opens with a knife. He places the vessel before him, and views it attentively:

> The smoke ascended to the clouds, and extending itself along the sea and upon the shore formed a great mist, which we may well imagine filled the fisherman with astonishment. When the smoke was all out of the vessel, it re-united and became a solid body, of which was formed a genie twice as high as the greatest of giants. (Scott ed., 1811)

The child looked at him

Mr. Toots, feeling himself called upon to say something about this boat, said "Smugglers." But … he added "or Preventive."]

> In 1822 and 1823 the country was at an enormous cost to prevent smuggling. For this purpose the Preventive Service and the Coast Blockade were organised, and the vessels of the royal navy were in active co-operation with a fleet of fifty-two revenue cruisers. In the above two years the total captures on the coasts of England was 52 vessels and 385 boats. (*The Penny Magazine*, 1840, 9.230)

The Preventive Service (also known as the Preventive Water-Guard) operated on land and at sea, and their confrontations with smugglers were frequently reported in newspapers and journals and discussed in Parliament.

Chapter 13

SHIPPING INTELLIGENCE AND OFFICE BUSINESS

Mr. Dombey's offices were in

an old-established stall of choice fruit at the corner: where perambulating merchants, of both sexes, offered for sale at any time between the hours of ten and five, slippers, pocket-books, sponges, dogs' collars, and Windsor soap; and sometimes a pointer or an oil painting.] According to Mayhew, the 'itinerant costermongers' – those who sold fish, fruit and vegetables – had 'regular rounds, which they go daily, and which extend from two to ten miles.' The longest were 'those which embrace a suburban part; the shortest are through streets thickly peopled by the poor, where duly to "work" a single street consumes, in some instances, an hour' (1.7). 'Choice fruit' had two meanings: particular types of fruit and the best specimens of any fruit. In *The Food of London*, George Dodd describes pineapples as a 'choice fruit', a category that also included other imports such as 'grapes, and French and Dutch soft fruit'. 'Choice fruit' was usually associated with Covent Garden because it sold the most expensive produce. A stroller through the market in 1829 recalled: 'I have lounged through it on a summer's day ... looking upon choice fruit, smelling delicious roses'. Although oranges were generally cheap in London, the best specimens were reserved for Covent Garden, where they were 'dignified as "choice fruit" '. 'Choice fruit!' was also one of the traditional cries of London street-sellers, though the cry was considered 'almost extinct' by 1827 (Dodd, 1856, 389, 393; *The Mirror of Literature*, 1829, 13.121; Knight, *Once Upon a Time*. 2nd ed., 1859, 436; Hone, *The Every-day Book and Table-Book*, 1841, 3.588).

Two accounts suggest that slippers were sold by only the very poor: Mayhew describes an unemployed old man 'who was set up in the streets by a charitable lady on a stock of gentlemen's slippers'; and in a Sunday market in the Minories, 'a number of poor creatures were arranged before and around as many boards covered with boots, and shoes, and slippers, busily employed in blacking and polishing their several wares' (Mayhew 1.324; *Evangelical Magazine and Missionary Chronicle*, 1829, 7.537).

Among the street-sellers of 'Stationary, Literature, and the Fine Arts' were those who sold paper and various paper-related products, including 'almanacs, pocket-books, memorandum and account-books' (1.215). Mayhew believed that the sales of pocketbooks had declined considerably over the last ten years (from 1841 to 1851): 'The reason assigned for the decline is that almanacks, diaries, &c., are so cheap that people look upon 1s. as an enormous price, even for a "beautiful morocco-bound pocket-book," as the street-seller proclaims it' (1.271).

Street-sellers of sponges carried them

in baskets, the bearer holding a specimen piece or two in his hand. Smaller pieces are sometimes carried in nets, and nets were more frequently in use for this purpose than at present. It is nearly all sold by itinerants, in the business parts as well as the suburbs, the purchasers being "shopkeepers, innkeepers, gentlemen, and gentlemen's servants." (1.443)

The 'well-known old brown Windsor' soap was, according to *Cassell's Household Guide* (1877–8), among 'the best of all the soaps made, considered from a medical point of view' (1.45). Visiting London in 1825, an American marvelled at the streets crowded with old clothes sellers, beggars and 'lying knaves, with cakes of Windsor soap'. Perhaps they were selling it at an inflated price: although 'a good perfumed soap', Windsor soap could be made at home easily and cheaply (*Boston Monthly Magazine*, 1825, 1.238; *The Family Recipe Book*. 2nd American ed., 1819, 319).

Mayhew counted twelve dogs'-collar men in London in 1851: 'Of the regular hands, one, two, and sometimes three sell only dog-collars (with the usual adjuncts of locks, and sometimes chains, and key-rings), but even these, when their stock-money avails, prefer uniting to the collars some other trifling article' (such as dog-whistles, keys and key-rings, shaving brushes and razors). Two of the primary dogs'-collar men sold their wares 'at a corner of the Bank [of England]' and 'in the neighbourhood of the Old Swan Pier, off Thames-Street'. 'Of the entire number' of dogs'-collar men, 'half are either itinerant on a round, or walk up and down a thoroughfare and an adjacent street or two', as is the case here. Others would 'hang their wares against the rails of any public or other building in a good situation, when they can obtain leave' or 'have stalls, with "a back," from the corners of which hang the strings of dog-collars, one linked within another'.

There were about twenty-five dog sellers on the streets in 1851, Mayhew records. Because 'the purchasers are all of the wealthier class', dog-sellers frequented the well-to-do areas in London, particularly the Quadrant and Regent-Street, though also the Royal Exchange and the Bank of England, as is the case in this passage. Spaniels constituted more than half the street trade, with terriers becoming more fashionable at mid-century (2.53). Hunting dogs such as 'fox-hounds, harriers, pointers, setters, cockers' were 'unknown' to the street trade, in Mayhew's opinion (2.55).

Images of all sorts were sold on the streets of London, everything from prints and engravings to cheap 'coloured pictures in frames' that depicted religious scenes or political figures or members of the royal family. 'Some of the higher-priced pictures are painted purposely for the streets, but are always copies of some popular engraving, and their sale is not a twentieth of the others'. Such paintings were principally sold 'piled on a small stall or carried under the arm', usually 'at the street-markets on Saturday evenings' (1.305).

The pointer always came that way,

Stock Exchange, where a sporting taste (originating generally in bets of new hats) is much in vogue.] The Stock Exchange, Capel-court, Bartholomew Lane, is situated near both the Bank of England and the Royal Exchange. Its members (about

650 in 1851) dealt in 'stocks and shares of all kinds, ranging in solidity from British consuls, the steadiest of all, to Greek coupons and Spanish passives, – railway shares, mining shares, and shares and bonds of joint-stock companies of all kinds' (Patterson, 1865, 144).

Wagers on sporting activities of all kinds were common among members of the Stock Exchange, which was a place

> where bulls and bears in white hats and cutaway coats are now frantic about the chances of the Derby favourite, and the next pigeon match at the Red House; now about three and a quarter for the account and Turkish scrip; now about a "little mare," name unknown, that can be backed to do wonderful things, anywhere, for any amount of money. ... (Sala, 1861, 37)

The Gentleman's Magazine observed, 'it is an open question even now [1873] whether more money does not change hands on the Stock Exchange in the course of a single fortnight in what are really and truly gambling transactions than changes hands at Tattersall's [the primary auctioneer of race horses in the United Kingdom], and on all the racecourses in England, in a year' (Pebody 47). The betting of one's hat seems to have become a particularly clichéd example of this informal wagering: in 1876 a broker claimed to have remarked to a fellow member: 'I'll bet you a new hat (we always bet new hats on 'Change) ... that you don't know so much of any stock you like to name as I of Greek or Latin, and yet it's next to nothing that I know' (Pinto 246).

Cheapside –]

> Cheapside remains now what it was five centuries ago, the greatest thoroughfare in the City of London. Other localities have had their day, have risen, become fashionable, and have sunk into obscurity and neglect, but Cheapside has maintained its place, and may boast of being the busiest thoroughfare in the world, with the sole exception perhaps of London-bridge. Here the two great arteries of Oxford-street and Holborn and of the Strand and Fleet-street from the west, and of Bishopsgate and Leadenhall from the east, together with a mighty stream of traffic from Moorgate on the north and King William-street on the south, are all united, and the great flow of traffic is constantly blocked and arrested by the cross tide ... from Southwark-bridge up Queen-street. (Dickens, Jr, 1879)

The ticket-porter,] A member of a body of porters in the City who were licensed by the Corporation and had the exclusive right of porterage of every description within the precincts of the City. To show that they were licensed, they displayed a document (or ticket) as a badge, and they also usually wore white aprons (Mayhew 3.364–7). Trotty Veck in *The Chimes* is a ticket-porter.

The clerks within were not

the row of leathern fire-buckets hanging up behind him.] Before the advent of water-hoses for the purpose, water was supplied to fire-engines by fire-buckets. A contemporary described their appearance and use ('about 1817–18'):

> By one of the city ordinances, in force at that period, every housekeeper was obliged, under a penalty, to keep four fire-buckets, each of which held more than half a gallon of water, hanging in his hall, or other convenient place. On each bucket were painted the name and residence of the owner. So soon as the cry of fire was heard, the housekeeper, with whatever hands he had, ran with his buckets, in the direction in which the fire was said to be. There the people ranged at convenient distances from the pumps – before we had hydrants – to the fire-engines. Thus it was the engines were supplied with water. (Binns, 1854, 267)

When Perch the Messenger,

When Perch the Messenger, whose place was on a little bracket, like a timepiece,] When not carrying his watch with him, a Victorian gentleman would place it in a pocket watch stand, made of wood, metal, bevelled glass or pottery and often ornamental. The stand, which was usually kept on a desk or chimney-piece, held the watch upright and allowed the time to be read easily.

some title as used to be bestowed upon the Caliph Haroun Alraschid,] In *The Arabian Nights*, Haroun Al-Rashid, the Caliph of Baghdad, roams the city in disguise in order to expose vice and reward virtue.

As this honour would have

You are the Light of my Eyes. You are the breath of my Soul. You are the Commander of the Faithful Perch!] These epithets occur frequently in Persian and Eastern literature. For example: ' "Light of my eyes," he exclaimed, "give ear! ... We shall cease being of little importance in Ispahan" '; 'Adieu, fair princess, light of my eyes!'; 'I perceived that the breath of my soul did not reach them, that the flame of my zeal could not kindle the damp faggots of their spirits' (*The Mirza*, 1841, 2.58; 'The Popular Songs of Russia', *Eclectic Magazine*, 1855, 36.814; *The Gulistan: Being the Rose-garden of Shaikh Sa'di*, trans. Edwin Arnold, 1899, 97).

a waxen effigy, bald as a Mussulman in the morning, and covered, after eleven o'clock in the day, with luxuriant hair and whiskers in the latest Christian fashion,] Wax busts or wooden blocks displayed wigs in the windows of barbers' shops. Muslim men ('Mussulman' is an archaism) traditionally shaved their heads but let their beards grow. A nineteenth-century account describes the practice:

> The Koran makes it honorable for a man to wear a beard, but commands the shaving of the head. There are two great sects among those who accept the Mohammedan faith, the Sheas and the Sunnees. The latter are all Turks and they shave their whole crown, excepting a tuft in the centre by which the archangel may draw them out of the grave. But the Persians are Sheas, and they shave the centre of the head, from the forehead to the neck, leaving a long curl on each side. It is curious to see even little boys with their heads thus polished. (qtd. in Smith, 1888, 386)

In England, fashionable men wore longish curled hair in the 1840s, along with moustaches, sideburns and beards.

Between Mr. Dombey and the

Mr. Carker, as Grand Vizier.] The chief minister of the Ottoman Sultan, the Grand Vizier acted for the sultan in military and civil matters, presided over his royal court, and was, in times of war, the supreme military commander. Both the Grand Vizier and the Sultan figure prominently in 'Aladdin; or the Wonderful Lamp', and other tales from *The Arabian Nights*. The Grand Vizier also featured frequently in the British press and other contemporary accounts during Napoleon Bonaparte's campaign against Egypt (begun in 1798); from 1829 into the 1830s, when Russia undertook a second campaign against Turkey, and, in 1841, during a British naval action against Egypt in defence of Syria and the Ottoman empire (see, for example, Charles Napier, *The War in Syria*, 1842).

The gentleman last mentioned was

He was a great musical amateur in his way – after business; and had a paternal affection for his violincello, which was once in every week transported from Islington, his place of abode, to a certain club-room hard by the Bank, where quartettes of the most tormenting and excruciating nature were executed every Wednesday evening by a private party.]

> Islington – This village, once described as a pleasant country town, is now only separated from London by name: the situation is very healthy and the salubrity of the air, with its vicinity to the metropolis, have long rendered it a favourite retirement of the citizens. The Regent's Canal passes through this parish, and is conducted under the village by means of a tunnel above half a mile in length. (*Mogg's New Picture of London and Visitor's Guide to it Sights*, 1844)

As a seventeenth-century village and popular resort about one and a half miles north of London, Islington used to be considered remote until it began to expand towards the city in the nineteenth century. By the 1830s, it had merged into the metropolis (Wheatley 2.266).

Mr. Carker was a gentleman

two unbroken rows of glistening teeth, whose regularity and whiteness were quite distressing. It was impossible to escape the observation of them, for he showed them whenever he spoke; and bore so wide a smile upon his countenance (a smile, however, very rarely, indeed, extending beyond his mouth)] The unusual perfection and whiteness of Mr Carker's teeth, especially for a Victorian who is 'thirty-eight or forty years old', may signal that he has false teeth. If so, they were probably porcelain or 'mineral-paste' teeth, which did not yellow or rot or promote bad breath, the way that ivory, animal, or human bone false teeth tended to do. Though porcelain teeth were fashionable in the early nineteenth century, they 'had a very artificial appearance in the mouth and made a grating sound when brought together. They were over-white and brittle' (Woodforde 1–3).

"Talking of Morfin," resumed

"he reports a junior dead in the agency of Barbados,] The 'West Indian Fever', or 'as it is generally called, yellow fever', was endemic in the West Indies and reports of deaths and new outbreaks appeared in the newspapers and journals continuously. According to the *London Medical Gazette* in 1838: 'Scarcely a season passes during which, in some portion of the Caribbean chain, or adjacent shores, more or less of a fever will not be found' (22.275). An outbreak in Barbados in 1836 killed hundreds of inhabitants, and the fever also had a lethal effect on ships' crews. Some medical writers suggested that the fever was transmitted by ships coming from Africa and that quarantine of newly arrived ships was essential, but because the means of transmission and prevention were disputed, the topics were a source of debate in medical journals (*The Medico-Chirugical Review*, 1824, 979–1009).

But in taking them with

The letters were post-letters;] Letters sent through the post (and thus paid for by the sender) and not delivered by hand. A letter 'was interpreted to mean a single piece of paper, provided it did not exceed an ounce in weight', and the average rate for a 'general-post letter' sent within England or within London was 6–7 pence (*Penny Cyclopædia*, 1840, 18.455). In 'Symbols' (*Sartor Resartus*, 1833–4), Carlyle rejoiced: 'Wondrous truly are the bonds that unite us one and all … Post Letters, more or fewer, from all the four winds, impinge against thy Glass walls', and J.S. Mill wrote to a friend in 1847: 'If I did pay postage I should not grudge it for your letters, but in fact I do not. The India House pays all my letters, except penny post letters which everybody pays before sending' (to John Austin, 13 April 1847; cited in *The Letters of John Stuart Mill*, vol. 1, ed. Hugh S. R. Elliot, 1910).

But it was true, and

Did he think he could arrange to send home to England a jar of preserved Ginger, cheap, for Mrs. Perch's own eating, in the course of her recovery from her next confinement?] According to Mrs Beeton:

> Preserved Ginger comes to us from the West Indies. It is made by scalding the roots when they are green and full of sap, then peeling them in cold water, and putting them into jars, with a rich syrup; in which state we receive them.
> (note to recipe 1432, 'Ginger Cream')

'As a medicine [ginger] is highly useful', remarked *An Encyclopædia of Domestic Economy* in 1845, 'and an essence or essential of ginger is prepared as a more convenient mode of applying it' (523).

Chapter 14

Fifth monthly number
February 1847

PAUL GROWS MORE AND MORE OLD-FASHIONED, AND GOES HOME FOR THE HOLIDAYS

On ?31 December 1846, Dickens informed Forster of his intentions for this chapter:

> It occurred to me on special reflection, that the first chapter should be [perhaps Forster's error for 'end', the Pilgrim editors suggest] with Paul and Florence, and that it should leave a pleasant impression of the little fellow being happy, before the reader is called upon to see him die. I mean to have a genteel breaking-up at Doctor Blimber's therefore, for the Midsummer vacation; and to show him in a little quiet light (now dawning through the chinks of my mind), which I hope will create an agreeable impression. (*Letters* 4.687–8)

In the number plans for this chapter, Dickens noted of young Paul: 'His illness only expressed in the child's own feelings – Not otherwise described –' (see p. 189).

When the Midsummer vacation approached,

Midsummer vacation] Also known as the 'long vacation', this was summer vacation in the law courts and the universities, so called to distinguish it from the Christmas and Easter vacations. The vacations come in between the three terms of Michaelmas, Hilary and Trinity. This calendar was also observed by the public schools, as well as private schools like Doctor Blimber's.

Tozer, who was constantly galled

a starched white cambric neck-kerchief, which he wore at the express desire of Mrs. Tozer, his parent, who, designing him for the Church, was of opinion that he couldn't be in that forward state of preparation too soon –] A white neck-cloth was a distinguishing feature of the dress of a clergyman in the Church of England, one of the 'passports to clerical dignity', according to *The Church of England Quarterly Review* ('Last Glimpses of Convocation', 33 [1853]: 482).

Tozer's Essay on the subject, wherein he had observed "that the thoughts of home and all its recollections, awakened in his mind the most pleasing emotions of anticipation and delight,"] The observation attributed to Tozer echoes the doctrine of associations, developed by David Hartley in his *Essay on the Origin of the Passions* (1741), and the theories of the emotions explained by David Hume in his *Treatise of Human Nature* (1739) and *Dissertation on the Passions* (1757). Joseph Addison's reference to 'all those pleasing emotions' (*The Guardian*, 1767, 1.215) and a discussion of 'the association of pleasing emotions' in the *Analytical Review* (1793, 15.388) are examples of how the ideas of Hartley and Hume became popularized. By the early nineteenth century, 'pleasing emotions' had become a literary cliché.

had also likened himself to a Roman General, flushed with a recent victory over the Iceni, or laden with Carthaginian spoil, advancing within a few hours' march of the Capitol,] A reference to two sweeping Roman victories. The Iceni, a tribe of ancient Britons, were incited by their queen, Boadicea, to rebel against the Romans, who were attempting to annex Iceni territory in AD 60. The Iceni sacked Colchester, London and St Albans before being brutally suppressed by the Roman governor. Carthage was destroyed by Rome in the Third Punic War (149–46 BC). Children could learn about these victories in such books as *A Catechism of the History of England* (1822), Mangnall's *Historical and Miscellaneous Questions* (1800) and *A Summary of Geography & History, Both Ancient & Modern* (5th ed., 1816).

carried him to see a Giant, or a Dwarf, or a Conjuror] The popularity of 'General Tom Thumb' (Charles Sherwood Stratton), who toured England in 1844–6 under the management of P. T. Barnum, initiated a craze for midgets and dwarfs, who descended on London from Scotland, Holland and Spain. More numerous than dwarfs were giants (in girth more often than in height), although 'Monsieur Louis', the

Packing up his books.

Desire to shew Florence – in wishing for the party – that he is happy there, ~~and~~ that they like him.

"and now."

Did Papa cry?

I am ~~very~~ glad of that. I am very glad Papa didn't cry, Floy.

The River that is always running on

Number Plan

(Dealings with the Firm of Dombey and Son — N.° V)

chapter XIV.

Paul grows more and more old-fashioned, and goes home for the holidays.

Party at Dr Blimber's – Paul's desire to be affectionately remembered – His illness only expressed in the child's own feelings – Not otherwise described – Goes home for the holidays

~~News of Paul's illness No~~

Chapter XV.

Amazing artfulness of Captain Cuttle, and a new pursuit for Walter Gay.

Captain Cuttle – qy Introduce his friend – Mr Bunsbey

Not Yet.

Staggs's Gardens after the Railroad

Polly brought to see him.

chapter XVI.

what the waves were always saying

Walter brought into the room

Paul's Death the old, old, fashion. But there was an older fashion yet, before it
"And so," said Miss Tox, drying her eyes, "Dombey and Son's a daughter, after all!"

Chapter Plan

'French giant', was almost eight feet tall. A Londoner in 1826 reported that M. Louis was being exhibited with 'two Lapland dwarfs'. Other giants were the 'Celebrated Canadian Giant' and a 'Swiss giantess' who could lift three hundredweight with one hand (*Blackwood's Edinburgh Magazine* 19 (1826): 467–8; Mrs Bray, *Legends, Superstitions and Sketches* (1844) 3.157; Altick, 1978, 253–6).

Among the many conjurors performing in London theatres in the 1840s was the Scottish magician, John Henry Anderson, who advertised himself as 'The Great Caledonian Conjuror' and 'The Great Wizard of the North'. Having toured Britain in the late 1830s, he moved to London in 1840 and opened the New Strand Theatre, where his success enabled him to open a new show at the Covent Garden Theatre in 1846. But a review in the *Times* considered Anderson not as good as a visiting German conjuror:

> The entertainments lately given at several of the theatres of a necromantic description bid fair to be outrivaled by the performance of Herr Döbler. ... his illusions are of such a surprising character ... so inexplicable are the mysteries he practises. ... Anderson, the "Great Wizard of the North," who figured at the Strand, and who was followed by Jacobs, another celebrated conjuror ... was unequal to Herr Döbler. (16 April 1842, 6)

As to Briggs, his father

the friends of the family (then resident near Bayswater, London) seldom approached the ornamental piece of water in Kensington Gardens,] Bayswater, 'a vague name for the district extending from the Gravel Pits to the north-west corner of Hyde Park', was a newly-developed area in the 1840s. A contemporary characterized Bayswater as a 'splendid new town', explaining that 'The whole district of streets, squares, terraces, and crescents sprung into existence in the course of about ten years – between 1839 and 1849. Bayswater was noted of old for its springs, reservoirs, and conduits, supplying the greater part of the City of London with water' (Thornbury, 1872–8, 5.183). Because it was close to the City, Bayswater's four- and five-storey stucco-faced mansions were popular residences for wealthy merchants and fashionable families.

An American visitor described the popular appeal of Kensington Gardens, the large parkland attached to Kensington Palace, in 1838:

> There is no place, however, so delightful as Kensington, and that on account of its beautiful gardens, open to the public from sunrise to sunset. ... Kensington Gardens, for beauty, are hardly to be matched. The grand promenades, the green lawns, the shaded walks, the secluded bowers, and the forest and lake scenery, though in miniature, are all beautiful; and finally the long twilights render the scene more enchanting, as they afford so much time for enjoyment after the fiery sun has called in his hot and lurid rays. (*London in 1838*, 1839, 149–50)

The Serpentine, a series of artificial ponds built by Queen Caroline between 1730 and 1733, 'gained its inappropriate name from the single curve which distinguished it from the rectangular ponds in vogue at the time it was formed'. Adding to the 'ornamental' effect may have been the recent changes described by Charles Knight in 1841: 'A new bridge has been thrown across the Serpentine, and more ornamental buildings [have] been erected on its bank to serve for a powder-magazine and the house of the Humane Society, (beautiful antithesis!)'. The Serpentine was frequented by bathers in the summer months and ice skaters in the winter (Knight 1.212; Brown, 1881, 116; Weinreb and Hibbert, 1983, 47–8, 436–7).

"I must beg you not to

A repetition of such allusions would make it necessary for me to request to hear, without a mistake, before breakfast-time to-morrow morning, from *Verbum personale* down to *simillima cygno.*"] She refers to the rules of syntax, which pupils beginning Latin were required to memorise. The rules include the agreement of the verb and the subject in number and person: '*Verbum personale concordat cum nominativo numero et persona*'. *Rara avis in terris, nigroque simillima cygno* ('an extremely rare bird, and very like a black swan'), from Juvenal, *Satires* 6.165, was a popular quotation which was used as a standard example of the rule of syntax concerning 'if an adjective or participle govern a word' ('The General Rules of Construction Exemplified', Rule 5, *The Latin Primer in Three Parts*. 4th ed., 1806; see also: *New Latin Primer*, 1809; *A Dictionary of Select and Popular Quotations*, 1818). An article discussing the advantages of teaching children the classics reflected:

> Probably it will be necessary to the end of time … to teach very young lads the Latin grammar by the good old rule and simple plan of driving it into their memories by pertinacious and conscientious drudgery. The father and mother, the governess, the usher at the private school, must of course go on for some years patiently grinding *hic hac hoc* and *verbum personale concordat cum nominativo*, into the very soul of the pupil by almost mechanical processes if he is to do any good at a public school. (*The National Review*, 1864, 19.293)

" 'Analysis of the character of

"the word analysis as opposed to synthesis, is thus defined by Walker. 'The resolution of an object, whether of the senses or of the intellect, into its first elements.'] John Walker's *A Critical Pronouncing Dictionary and Expositor of the English Language* (1791) defines 'analysis' as 'A resolution of any thing, whether an object of the senses or of the intellect, into its first elements; it stands opposed to Synthesis' (B. H. Smart, *Walker Remodelled. A New Critical Pronouncing Dictionary of the English Language*, 1836, 24). Dickens owned a copy of this edition of Smart's *Walker Remodelled* (Stonehouse, 1935, 116). Walker's *Critical Pronouncing Diction-*

ary was one of the first books to indicate pronunciation and went through twenty-eight editions by 1826.

There were some immunities,

the butler ... had sometimes mingled porter with his table-beer to make him strong.] For porter, see note to chapter 2, p. 43. Table-beer, or small-beer, contained an insignificant amount of alcohol, was cheap to produce and was considered safer to drink than water, which might be contaminated. Recipe books included instructions for brewing it because it was frequently made at home and drunk by families and children (e.g. Maria Eliza Ketelby Rundell, *A New System of Domestic Cookery*, 1824, 340). In his *Zoonomia* (1792–6), Erasmus Darwin recommended table-beer as part of a diet against 'gaol fever' (typhus), and in 1833, Edwin Chadwick's Report on *The Poor Laws in London and Berkshire* noted that convicts on the hulks were allowed one pint of table-beer a day. In 1843, Dr Jonathan Pereira reported that table-beer was part of the diet in London hospitals and in institutions for paupers, lunatics and children (*Treatise on Food and Diet, with observations on the dietetical regimen suited for disordered states of the digestive organs ...* , 1843, 147, 256). Mrs Beeton includes table-beer in her recipe for Hodge-Podge and notes that it is: 'nothing more than a weak ale, and is not made so much with a view to strength, as to transparency of colour and an agreeable bitterness of taste' (recipe 191; see also: Hornsey, *A History of Beer and Brewing*, 2003; Kiple and Ornelas, *The Cambridge World History of Food*, 2000, 703; Webster, 1845, 575).

Over and above these extensive

an unsuccessful attempt to smoke a very blunt cigar; one of a bundle which that young gentleman had covertly purchased on the shingle from a most desperate smuggler, who had acknowledged, in confidence, that two hundred pounds was the price set upon his head, dead or alive, by the Custom House.] Mr Toots has been tricked by a 'turnpike sailor' (i.e. someone in the guise of a sailor):

> He accosts you in the streets mysteriously, and asks you if you want "a few good cigars?" He tells you they are smuggled, that he "run" them himself, and that the "Custom-'us horficers" are after him. I need hardly inform my reader that the cigar he offers as a sample is excellent, and that, should he be weak enough to purchase a few boxes he will not find them "according to sample." Not unfrequently, the cigar-"duffer" lures his victim to some low tavern to receive his goods, where in lieu of tobacco, shawls, and laces, he finds a number of cut-throat-looking confederates, who plunder and illtreat him. (Mayhew 4.417)

Dickens implies the poor quality of the cigar, and thus the fraudulent nature of the 'smuggling', by emphasizing that they are hard-to-light and 'very blunt'. As a cigar-seller observed,

> Everybody likes a smuggled thing. ... In my time I've sold what was smuggled, or made to appear as sich, but far more in the country than town, to all sorts – to gentlemen, and ladies, and shopkeepers, and parsons, and doctors, and lawyers. Why no, sir, I can't say as how I ever sold anything in that way to an exciseman. But smuggling'll always be liked; it's sich a satisfaction to any man to think he's done the tax-gatherer. (1.441)

Cigars were introduced to Britain by officers returning from the Peninsular Wars (1804–13) and soldiers returned from India. Although they had become 'very common all over Europe' by 1830, they were much more expensive than unrolled tobacco. Fashionable men and dandies often smoked cigars, but they were also popular with gentlemen from the 1830s (*The Mirror of Literature, Amusement and Instruction*, 1830, 16.429; *Golden Rules for Cigar Smokers*, 1833; 'Joseph Fume', *A Paper: – of Tobacco*, 1839).

The Custom House, located in Lower Thames Street, just east of Billingsgate dock, attended to vessels coming in and going out of London. Its approximately 600 employees (in the 1850s), working in 170 departments, inspected incoming and outgoing goods, received warrants to show that duties on the goods were paid, gave permits for the landing of cargo and took bonds for the delivery of goods shipped to the coast.

a Spanish Grammar] Many different ones were available; some early editions were: *A Spanish Grammar* (1800); *A New Spanish Grammar* (1809); and *A New, Easy and Complete Grammar of the Spanish Language* (1810).

But Mr. Feeder's great possession was

Mr. Feeder's great possession was a large green jar of snuff, which Mr. Toots had brought down as a present ... for which he paid a high price, as having been the genuine property of the Prince Regent.] Once again, Mr Toots has been duped. Glass snuff bottles, typically coloured olive green or amber, generally lacked the prestige associated with expensive snuff-boxes, many of which were finely-wrought and made from precious materials. George IV, formerly the Prince Regent, was an avid snuff-taker who possessed a collection of labeled jars, bottles and canisters, displayed on shelves in a special chamber at Windsor Castle. Inhaling snuff became fashionable in England around 1680, although it had long been popular in Ireland and Scotland. During the eighteenth century, all classes took up the habit, but it began to decline in the nineteenth century, being gradually replaced by cigar-smoking and then cigarette-smoking.

Neither Mr. Toots nor Mr. Feeder could partake of this or that other snuff ...

without being seized with convulsions of sneezing. Nevertheless it was their great delight to moisten a box-full with cold tea, stir it up on a piece of parchment with a paper-knife, and devote themselves to its consumption then and there.] In *Gaslight and Daylight* (1859), George Augustus Sala described the unfortunate demise of one handicapped snuff-lover: 'after a too copious dose of snuff ... he had fallen into a violent fit of sneezing; and, in the midst of his convulsive movements, had been precipitated from his chair into the bath, and so asphyxiated' (110–11). Some types of snuff required moistening before use. The 'application of a drop or two of green tea, unimplicated by sugar or cream, draws out the fine flavour' (*A Pinch of Snuff* 22). For snuff-boxes, see note to chapter 24, p. 290.

Paul, looking at it, found,

an early party on Wednesday Evening the Seventeenth Instant ... the hour was half-past seven o'clock; and ... the object was Quadrilles.] 'The Seventeenth Instant' is an elliptical way of saying 'the seventeenth of this month'. The quadrille, a popular ballroom dance originating in France, was introduced to London at Almack's Assembly Rooms in 1815. Consisting of five parts or figures, it was danced by sets of four, six or eight couples to lively music adapted from popular songs or stage works. According to a dancing manual of 1856:

> The Quadrille of all the fashionable dances, still retains the possession of the ball-room ... It is not only the most social, as it admits of agreeable conversation and exchange of partners, but it is also the most simple, natural, and elegant in its movements, and the various figures into which it successively transforms itself.
>
> The Quadrille, is adapted to all ages; the stout and the slender, the light and the ponderous, may mingle in its easy and pleasant evolutions with mutual satisfaction. Even a slight mistake committed by the unskillful in this dance, will not incommode a partner, or interrupt the progress of the movement. (Charles Durang, *The Fashionable Dancer's Casket, or, the Ball-Room Instructor*, 1856, 24; see also Sadie, 2001)

There was a certain calm

a certain calm Apothecary, who attended at the establishment when any of the young gentlemen were ill,] Previously little more than a specialized form of shopkeeper, apothecaries had recently acquired a new status in the medical hierarchy on account of the Apothecaries Act of 1815, which required certification based on examination, evidence of sufficient medical education, and a five-year apprenticeship. According to the *Book of Trades* (1837), 'Few persons now apply to a physician till they have tried the skill of an Apothecary'. The practice of consulting an apothecary was especially prevalent in the country, where scarce and expensive physicians were typically called in only as specialist consultants. The public viewed the apothecary as an 'ambiguous animal', 'the connecting link between the professor of physic, and the dealer and general chapman' (Whittock *et al.*, 1840, 385–6; Peterson, 1978, 11; Newman 21–81).

there was a want of vital power … and great constitutional weakness.] Phrases from contemporary medical language which were often used in conjunction, for example: 'In the greater number of instances of irritation, the vital powers are enfeebled; and this constitutional weakness is the reason why the excitement does not become general and pass to the state of fever or inflammation' (*Cyclopædia of Practical Medicine*, 1833, 2.882).

The workman on the steps

the Curfew Bell of ancient days,] Curfew bells were used throughout Europe in the Middle Ages to compel the inhabitants of a town to extinguish their fires and retire to rest. Bells were also used in medieval churches and monasteries to call parishioners to prayer, to mark the 'canonical hours' and to indicate that someone was close to death. They tolled, as well, for funerals, the anniversaries of deaths, and at celebrations, such as weddings, public festivals and national events. The choice of which bell to ring, for how long, and in what manner, signaled exactly which event had occurred. Although it was commonly thought that the custom was introduced by William the Conqueror who ordered that, with the ringing of the curfew bell at 8 p.m., all lights and fires should be extinguished, in fact, curfew bells may have been rung in Oxford during the reign of Alfred the Great (*Encyclopedia Britannica*, 11th ed.; Simpson and Roud, 2000).

King Alfred's idea of measuring time by the burning of candles] Dickens explains in *CHE* that, as a means of telling time exactly, King Alfred 'had wax torches or candles made, which were all the same size, were notched across at regular distances, and were always kept burning. Thus, as the candles burnt down, he divided the day into notches, almost as accurately as we now divide it into hours upon the clock' (147).

He had to think of a portrait

a print that hung up in another place, where, in the centre of a wondering group, one figure that he knew, a figure with a light about its head – benignant, mild, and merciful – stood pointing upward.] Probably Rembrandt's 'Christ Healing the Sick' (*c.* 1647–9), also known as 'the Hundred Guilder Print', an illustration of Matthew 19.2 ('And great multitudes followed him; and he healed them there'). In this image a standing Christ is shown as the radiant central figure surrounded by a halo of light against a dark background. His left hand points upward while his right hand is extended towards the sick and lame figures reclining and kneeling before him. The success of the engraving led Rembrandt to make two more copies, and the image became the most famous of Rembrandt's prints throughout the eighteenth century and much of the nineteenth century. In Britain, 'Christ Healing the Sick' was widely known through the work of the Irish engraver, Captain William Baillie (1723–1810). Baillie purchased Rembrandt's original plate, and his copy of it was published with those of other Old Masters in two folio volumes, *The Works of Captain William Baillie after Paintings and Drawings of the Greatest Masters* (*c.* 1761–7).

Not the least allusion was

though Miss Blimber showed a graceful bunch of plaited hair on each temple, she seemed to have her own little curls in paper underneath, and in a playbill too: for Paul read "Theatre Royal" over one of her sparkling spectacles, and "Brighton" over the other."] The Theatre Royal in Brighton opened its doors on 27 June 1807 with a performance of *Hamlet*, starring Charles Kemble. Playbills from the theatre advertised such plays as *Richard III* and *Paul the Pilot* (9 December 1839) and *The King's Fool* and *Jack Sheppard* (16 December 1839) ('The Theatre Royal, Brighton'; 'Special Collections: Playbills'; for the 'curls in paper', see note to chapter 12, p. 178). Miss Blimber's hairstyle (shown in Browne's illustration, 'Paul goes home for the holidays') is typical of the early to mid-1840s: her hair is flat on the top and smoothly drawn back to a knot. Plaits or braids were frequently adopted, at the back or in various coronet arrangements over the top, or, as here, on the temples (de Courtais, 1973, 114).

There was a grand array

such a smell of singed hair ... But it was only the hairdresser curling the young gentlemen, and overheating his tongs]

> The employment of hot irons to aid in curling the hair, is said to be very injurious to its growth, and Madame Voiart says, she has seen the finest hair become thin and fall off from this destructive practice. ... We cannot, however, see that the irons can have any effect beyond the part of the hair which they touch; and if care be taken that they are not applied too hot, so as actually to destroy the hair, we see no material objection to their occasional use. (*The Art of Preserving the Hair*, 1825, 140)

A writer in *AYR* remarked on 'the torment of curling-irons, wielded by a ferocious hairdresser, who twisted, twirled, and scorched my locks till the tears ran down my cheeks' ('Gardens by Gaslight' 4.519).

But notwithstanding this modest

whether … it was best to wear his wristbands turned up or turned down. Observing that Mr. Feeder's were turned up, Mr. Toots turned his up; but the wristbands of the next arrival being turned down, Mr. Toots turned his down.] Seamstresses were advised to make the full depth of a wristband on a man's shirt 'about five inches' (*Magazine of Domestic Economy*, 1840, 5.242). While it was important that a certain amount of wristband show below the coat sleeve, exactly how much to show was a moot point in the 1840s. The elderly Lord Feenix in chapter 31 wears his wristbands 'almost covering his hands', but this look could also be considered a trait of the seedy or low-class, like the unshaven lawyer's clerk in *Heads of the People* (1840) who wears 'wristbands of check-calico drawn down over his knuckles' ('Tavern Heads'). It was clearly not acceptable to wear them as Dick Swiveller does in *OCS*: 'his dirty wristbands were pulled down as far as possible and ostentatiously folded back over his cuffs' (2). The preferred style was to wear 'the wristbands turned up', like the young London tailor dressed 'to the utmost perfection' in 'The Diurnal Revolutions of Davie Diddledoft', and like the elegant schoolmaster at a 'fashionable metropolitan school for young gentlemen': 'Smellingbottle having completed the trimming of his nails, and turned up both wristbands of immaculate whiteness, so as to make them of an exactly uniform altitude, takes up his pen and begins to write' (*The London Magazine, Charivari and Courier des Dames*, 1840, 1.188, 272).

All the young gentlemen, tightly

the young gentlemen … pumped,] In 'The Dancing Academy', Dickens makes fun of the fashion:

> Mr. Augustus Cooper went away to one of the cheap shoemakers' shops in Holborn, where gentlemen's dress pumps are seven-and-sixpence, and … bought a pair of the regular seven-and-sixpenny, long-quartered, town mades, in which he astonished himself quite as much to his mother, and sallied forth to Signor Billsmethi's [the dancing master]. (*SB*)

Mr. Baps, the dancing-master,] The ability to dance well, and the etiquette that accompanied dance, were important markers of social distinction in the nineteenth century, and thus accorded the dancing master a privileged position among the social elites, and those members of the middle class who aspired to elite status. Dancing masters, who were generally male, taught dance steps, technique and etiquette, arranged and supervised balls and assemblies, and created new dances. They also composed the many dance manuals popular in the nineteenth century (Buckland 4–5). Dickens makes fun of the pretensions to gentility associated with dancing and dancing masters in 'The Dancing Academy', first published in *Bell's Life in London*, 11 October 1835, and later collected in *SB*.

what you were to do with your raw materials when they came into your ports in return for your drain of gold.] The ability to engage in effective 'small talk' was frequently commented on by etiquette manuals and popular magazines. Subjects of small talk – 'the coin that will pass current in any society' – typically fell within a narrow range: 'The weather – the health of your friends – the funds – any accidents which have happened to any of your acquaintances, such as deaths or marriages – the King – Bonaparte – Lord Byron – the cheapness of meat – any watering-place – the corn-bill – the author of Waverly – and the theatre'. Such manuals and magazines warned against 'inveterate small-talkers', whose 'discourse makes one's head ache', and those talkers who talked over the heads of their listeners, or outside the range of their interests ('A Few Thoughts on Small-Talk', *New Monthly Magazine*, 1823, 5.217).

It was Sir Barnet Skettles,

his father, who was in the House of Commons, and of whom Mr. Feeder had said that when he *did* catch the Speaker's eye (which he had been expected to do for three or four years,)] An MP must try to 'catch the Speaker's eye' in order to speak during a debate, and MPs can only speak if called to do so by the Speaker. MPs try to attract the Speaker's attention by standing, or half-standing, to show that they wish to speak.

he would rather touch up the Radicals.] 'To touch up' means to strike lightly or sharply, as with a whip (*OED*). 'Radicals' in this context refers to the parliamentary advocates of fundamental political reform on democratic lines. Following the Reform Act of 1832, other issues endorsed by Whig ministers included ending duties on imported corn, increased support for the education of young children and the further improvement of working conditions by factory legislation. Dickens himself recalled hearing as a child

> of the existence of a terrible banditti called *the radicals*, whose principles were that the prince regent wore stays; that nobody had a right to any salary; and that the army and navy ought to be put down; horrors at which he [Dickens] trembled in his bed, after supplicating that the radicals might be speedily taken and hanged. (Forster, *Life* 1.10)

From his nest among the pillows,

but supposing Russia stepped in with her tallows ... why then you must fall back upon your cottons,] In the early and mid-nineteenth century, tallow, which was used primarily for soap and candles, was imported almost exclusively from Russia (Oddy, *European Commerce*, 1805, 649). In 'Our Russian Relations', a *HW* article published during the early stages of the Crimean War, John Capper remarked on

Britain's favourable trade balance with Russia, noting that the 'principal exports to Great Britain are grain and flour to the value of three and a half millions sterling per annum; tallow two and a quarter millions; flax and linseed two and a half millions; hemp one million; sundries one million'. In contrast, Russia imported British goods that were worth overall 'not more than four millions in value', about a third of which 'consists of manufactured goods of silk, cotton, linen and wool' (333).

Sir Barnet Skettles looked after

whether he had ever been in the Board of Trade. ... "Of something connected with statistics, ... Figures of some sort,]

> The Board of Trade consists of a committee of the privy council, composed of all the great officers of state. The business is principally conducted by the president, deputy president, and the chief of the clerks. It is, properly speaking, a board of reference, to which all difficult or doubtful cases relative to trade or our colonial possessions, exclusive of the East Indies, are referred. The apartments which are occupied by this Board of Trade, are in the northern part of the old building called the Treasury, in Whitehall. (Ackermann, *et al.*, *Microcosm of London* [1808–10])

The science of statistics emerged in Britain in the 1830s with the establishment of the statistical section of the British Association for the Advancement of Science and the Statistical Society of London. Statistics provided political economists with numerical data with which to analyze and address contemporary social problems.

Dickens had opposed his contemporaries' obsession with quantification and statistical societies from early in his career: see 'Section C. – Statistics' of 'The Full Report of the First Meeting of the Mudfog Association for the Advancement of Everything' (1837) and 'Section D. – Statistics' of 'The Full Report of the Second Meeting of the Mudfog Association for the Advancement of Everything' (1838). In late December 1854, as the first revelations about maladministration in the Crimea began to appear in *The Times*, Dickens characterized 'those who see figures and averages, and nothing else' as 'the representatives of the wickedest and most enormous vice of this time' (*Letters* 7.492).

Paul was amazed to see

He even went so far as to D Mr. Baps]

> If it be indelicate to mention a thing, let it never be mentioned by any name whatever; if it be not indelicate to mention it, it cannot be so to use its ordinary proper name. ... That same habit of demi-swearing is another bit of pretension, which, if it cannot be called vulgarity, is certainly Pharisaical. ...

So, too, your man who would cut his throat sooner than use a bad word, will nevertheless write it "d – n," as if everybody did not know what two letters were left out. There is great hypocrisy about these things. (*The Habits of Good Society*, 1860, 53)

There was another thing that

negus,] Mrs Beeton remarks that 'this beverage is more usually drunk at children's parties than at any other'. To make negus, port wine ('allow 1 pint of wine … for a party of 9 or 10 children'), the juice and rind of a lemon and grated nutmeg are steeped in a jug of boiling water and cooled. Sherry or sweet white wine could be used instead of port wine (recipe 1835). Captain Cuttle makes spiced negus in chapter 49.

**"Had I a heart for falsehood framed,
I ne'er could injure You!"**] Richard Brinsley Sheridan, *The Duenna* (1775):

> Had I a heart for falsehood framed,
> I ne're could injure you:
> For though your tongue no promise claimed,
> Your charms would make me true;
> To you no soul shall bear deceit,
> No stranger offer wrong;
> But friends in all the aged you'll meet,
> And lovers in the young. (1.5)

Diogenes was the dog

Diogenes was the dog:] Diogenes (*c.* 400–*c.* 325 BC), the Greek philosopher who founded the Cynic school of philosophy, eschewed social conventions and cited the model of dogs, praising their virtues and advising his contemporaries to study their behaviour. He was thus given the nickname 'the dog', from which the term 'Cynic' derives.

Not even the influence of

such ebullitions of feeling, uncommon among those young Chesterfields.] Philip Dormer Stanhope, 4th Earl of Chesterfield (1694–1773), statesman, politician, literary patron, is best known for his *Letters … to his Son* (1774), in which he gives advice on how to succeed by sustaining a cultivated façade. In several instances, Dickens attacked Lord Chesterfield's amorality through characters in his books. In *BR*, Chesterfield's *Letters* are the favourite reading of Sir John Chester, the gentlemanly hypocrite. In *BH*, Mr Turveydrop, the dandiacal hypocrite, is partly modeled on Lord Chesterfield.

And in *LD*, William Dorrit comports himself like 'a great moral Lord Chesterfield' (1.19). Dr Johnson, who probably influenced Dickens's view of Chesterfield, wrote that Chesterfield taught 'the morals of a whore and the manners of a dancing master' (Boswell's *Life of Johnson*, 1791, entry for 1751–4).

Chapter 15

AMAZING ARTFULNESS OF CAPTAIN CUTTLE, AND A NEW PURSUIT FOR WALTER GAY

It was not unpleasant to

the ministry of the Reverend Melchisedech Howler, who, having been one day discharged from the West India Docks on a false suspicion ... of screwing gimlets into puncheons, and applying his lips to the orifice, had announced the destruction of the world for that day two years, at ten in the morning, and opened a front parlour for the reception of ladies and gentlemen of the Ranting persuasion, upon whom ... the admonitions of the Reverend Melchisedech had produced so powerful an effect, that, in their rapturous performance of a sacred jig ... the whole flock broke through into a kitchen below,] Melchizedek was the king of Salem and the priest of 'the most high God' who blessed Abraham and received a tithe from him (Genesis 14.18–20; also see Psalms 110.4). Early Christian commentary speculated variously that he was Shem, son of Noah; an angel; the Holy Ghost; or a prefiguration of Christ. Carlyle mentions him in *Sartor Resartus* (1833–4).

The West India Import and Export docks offered quayside accommodation for 600 ships and huge warehouses that provided storage for cargoes of West Indian produce. According to a contemporary source, 'There have been known to be at one time on the quays, and in the warehouses and vaults of this Import Dock, colonial produce to the value of £20,000,000 sterling, including 35,158 pipes of rum and Madeira' (Bird 85, 127–8; *Handbook of London* 459). For more on the India Docks, see note to chapter 9, p. 144–6.

'Ranters', the epithet given to Primitive Methodists, were an evangelical group that broke away from the main body of Wesleyans in 1811. They were notorious for their open air, fire-and-brimstone style of preaching, along with their revivalist meetings in tents and their propensity to 'jump' or break into dance during services. In the early nineteenth century, their fiery rhetoric and open-air informality had an especal appeal for members of the working-class, though in the 1840s Primitive Methodists became more 'respectable' and conservative. In 1842, membership was nearly 80,000. A decade later, there were over 100,000 Primitive Methodists, particularly in the Potteries, and the coalfields of Durham, Northumberland, Yorkshire, Lincolnshire and Norfolk (Cannon, 1997). 'Ranters' were also zealous teetotalers. The Reverend Howler's announcement of 'the destruction of the world' reflects the millenarianism often associated with the evangelical movement, and such prominent figures as Edward Bickersteth, Dr Thomas Chalmers and the Reverend Samuel Marsh, though millenarian views were not generally popular among Primitive Methodists.

This the Captain, in a moment

Lovely Peg,] See note to chapter 9, p. 140.

the lawful beadle] See note to chapter 5, p. 83.

"Keep her off a point

"Keep her off a point or so!"] The usual way to instruct a sailor steering a ship, for example, ' "Keep her away, een half point!", said he to the helmsman' ('The Earthquake of Caracas', *Waldie's Select Circulating Library*, 1833, 2.595). A point is a division of the circumference of the magnetic compass card, which is divided into 32 points, each of 11°15'. A point of the compass was, in the days of the older square-rigged ship, about the smallest division to which an average helmsman could steer by wheel, but with the growing efficiency in the rig of these vessels it was possible for a good helmsman to hold a course between two points (*An A–Z of Sailing Terms*, 1992).

"Wal'r, my boy," replied the Captain,

"in the Proverbs of Solomon you will find the following words, 'May we never want a friend in need, nor a bottle to give him!'] The proverb is not from the Bible but an English proverb dating from the sixteenth century, 'A friend in need is a friend indeed'. Cuttle conflates this with the song by Thomas Dibden, 'May we ne'er want a friend, nor a bottle to give him':

> Since the first dawn of reason that beam'd on my mind,
> And taught me how favour'd by fortune my lot,
> To share that good fortune I still was inclined,
> And impart to who wanted what I wanted not.
> 'Tis a maxim, entitled to every one's praise,
> When a man feels distress, like a man to relieve him;
> And my motto, though simple, means more than it says,
> "May we ne'er want a friend, nor a bottle to give him!"
> The heart, by deceit or ingratitude rent,
> Or by poverty bow'd, though of evils the least,

The smile of a friend may invite to content,
And we all know content is an excellent feast.
      'Tis a maxim, entitled &c. ... [st.1]
          (*Universal Songster*, 1825, 1.115)

"Aye!" replied Walter, laughing,

"For the Port of Barbados, boys! / Cheerily! / Leaving Old England behind us, boys! / Cheerily!] This seems to be an allusion to 'Cheerily Man' (sometimes 'Men'), one of the oldest of the anchor-raising shanties, and 'The Farewell', by the popular writer Richard Cobbold. In *AN*, Dickens describes hearing 'the sturdy chorus of "Cheerily men, oh cheerily!" ', as the anchor of his ship was being raised. 'Cheerily Man' has many variants, but the verses quoted are those sung when raising the anchor:

    'Cheerily Man'

Haul all together,
Chorus. Cheerily man!
Haul for good weather,
Chorus. Cheerily man!
She's light as a feather.

We'll haul again.
Chorus. Cheerily man!
With might and main,
Chorus. Cheerily man!
Pay out more chain. [st. 1, 3]
    (cited in Stan Hugill, *Shanties from the Seven Seas*, 1961; 1979)

    'The Farewell'

Farewell to the girl of my heart! ah! farewell!
That pang may be felt, which the tongue cannot tell!
The sailor is leaving Old England once more;
And the girl of his heart must lament on the shore.

Farewell my dear Love, ah! my bosom will burn,
For prosperous voyage and happy return;
The clouds, and the winds, and the waters will rise,
And swell my sad heart with anxieties sighs.

Farewell my dear maiden! O do not despair,
The waters are calm, and the winds they are fair;
My vessel is Hope, and the Pilot above
Will guide me in safety again to my love.

> Farewell then Farewell! thou art brave, thou art true,
> Dear friend of my heart, my kind sailor adieu!
> The boatswain is ready; the parting is o'er;
> The maiden is left to lament on the shore.
> (Richard Cobbold, *Valentine Verses: or, Lines of Truth, Love and Virtue*, 1827)

"There's a friend of mine,"

coasting round to Whitby,] Located 243 miles northwest of London in Yorkshire, Whitby was 'still a very considerable seaport in 1843'. In 1842, there were 291 registered vessels above 50 tons at Whitby, carrying a burthen estimated at 47,837 tons. The *Penny Cyclopædia* characterized the town's inner harbour as 'capacious and secure, with dry docks for building and repairing' (1843, 27.335).

deliver such an opinion on this subject, or any other that could be named, as would give Parliament six and beat 'em.] Cuttle uses cricket terminology to say that his friend's knowledge is superior to that of anyone in Parliament. 'To hit it for six', or 'to knock them for six' occurs when the batsman hits the ball over the boundary without the ball bouncing, thus scoring six runs.

"If you was to take

the buoy at the Nore,"] A buoy placed at the mouth of the River Thames, to direct mariners how to avoid a dangerous sand (*New Encyclopædia, or Universal Dictionary*. 1807, 4.484). The Nore anchorage lay to the east opposite Sheerness, where the Medway joins the Thames estuary and the sea. The Nore lightship was a floating beacon 'always to be illuminated at sun set, or sooner, if the gloominess of the weather should require it'. The earliest light, in 1730, was two large lanterns suspended at each end of a sloop. This was replaced by a single powerful light in 1825, which, in turn, was replaced by a revolving light in 1850 (*Dickens's Dictionary of the Thames*, 1880).

In fact, Captain Cuttle was labouring

"it only wants a word in season] 'A man hath joy by the answer of his mouth: and a word spoken in due season, how good is it!' (Proverbs 15.23).

Walter little imagined why the

a massive gold ring with a picture of a tomb upon it, and a neat iron railing, and a tree, in memory of some deceased friend.] Mourning jewelry in the form of gold rings, bracelets or brooches often employed iconographic devices traditionally associated with death: tombs, willow trees, wreaths, etc. (Morley, 1971, 66–9).

ankle-jacks,] Lace-up boots reaching just below the knee.

The Captain's walk was more complacent

all the jolliest-looking flowers that blow] An allusion to Wordsworth, 'Ode: Intimations of Immortality' (1802–04): 'To me the meanest flower that blows can give / Thoughts that do often lie too deep for tears' (202–3).

His way was nowhere in

He knew no better fields than those near Hampstead, and no better means of getting at them than by passing Mr. Dombey's house.] Hampstead Heath is 'a broad elevated, sandy tract occupying the summit and northern slopes of Hampstead Hill', 'one of the highest hills round London' and 'famous for its … pure air, and fine scenery' (Thorne, 1876, 278, 291). In 1851, *HW* remarked of the surrounding area: 'these fields are always pleasant, and become more so as you approach Hampstead: though bricks and mortar … are rapidly doing mischief' (4.15). In 1831, *The Penny Cyclopædia* characterized the Heath as 'extensive' with 'some large ponds, or reservoirs of water, used for supplying Camden Town and the adjacent parts with water'.

The parish of Hampstead is located northwest of London 'on the outer edge of the metropolitan boundary' (Thorne 278). Walter walks west, from Solomon Gills's shop on Leadenhall, probably taking Cheapside to Holborn to Oxford Street, and then north up Portman Square to Dombey's house just south of Regent's Park. He would then walk east to Hampstead Road, and then northwest to Hampstead Heath. Mr Dombey's house would thus have only been slightly out of Walter's way.

There was no such place

There was no such place as Staggs's Gardens. It had vanished from the earth. Where the old rotten summer-houses once had stood, palaces now reared their heads, and granite columns of gigantic girth opened a vista to the Railway world beyond. The miserable waste ground, where the refuse-matter had been heaped of yore, was swallowed up and gone; and in its frowsy stead were tiers of warehouses, crammed with rich goods and costly merchandise.] The 'granite columns of gigantic girth' refers to the grand Doric portico (designed by Philip Hardwick) that fronted Euston Station, the London terminus of the London and Birmingham Railway. The huge portico, which 'may be considered the largest in Europe, if not the world', according to a contemporary source, symbolized the railway's role as London's gateway to the Midlands. It was matched by a similar

9   'Entrance to the London and Birmingham Railway Station', the Euston Arch, c. 1838

gateway in Birmingham (Roscoe, *The London and Birmingham Railway*, 1839, 38) (see Plate 9).

Once passengers passed through the booking offices in the portico, they would enter 'an extensive yard, covered with a beautifully constructed and elegant roof, supported on iron columns, under which the carriages [would be] placed on their arrival and departure' (39). Railway warehouses, which were primarily designed to accommodate the customers' storage needs, had multiple stories for the sake of compactness and were solidly built, with cast-iron columns to support the floors and outer walls of brick or stone (Simmons and Biddle, 1997, 184).

Before the harmful social consequences of housing demolitions were fully known (see note to chapter 6, p. 94), such 'improvements' were sometimes welcomed as a way to revitalize decaying central areas and to develop the suburbs and planned towns. One contemporary observer expected, for instance, that such demolitions might remove from central London the 'ill-ventilated *culs de sac* and dens of wretchedness in the vicinity of Shoe Lane and Saffron Hill – the nurseries of vice, the nuclei of filth and disease' (T. Hammond, *A Few Cursory Remarks on Railways* [1835], qtd. in Dyos, 1855–6, 14).

the new streets that had stopped disheartened in the mud and waggon-ruts, formed towns within themselves, originating wholesome comforts and conveniences belonging to themselves, and never tried or thought of until they sprung into existence. Bridges that had led to nothing, led to villas, gardens, churches, healthy public walks. The carcasses of houses, and beginnings of new

10   The London and Birmingham Railway under construction in Camden Town, by J. C. Bourne, 1837

thoroughfares, had started off upon the line at steam's own speed, and shot away into the country in a monster train.] Samuel Lewis's *A Topographical Dictionary of England* (1848) described the recent improvements to Camden Town, as a result of railway construction:

> The principal part has been erected within the last few years; the houses are in general well built and regular, and the crescent, terrace, and other ranges in the upper part of it, are of handsome appearance, and command a partial, but pleasing, view of the Hampstead and Highgate hills. Among the most recent improvements, those in the direction of the road to Holloway, along the sides of which many elegant residences are still in progress of erection, are particularly deserving of notice, and, together with the formation of buildings in other parts of the neighbourhood, have contributed greatly to increase the importance and enlarge this appendage to the western part of the metropolis. The streets, which are wide and regularly formed, are lighted and partially paved; and the inhabitants are supplied with water from a conduit, into which it is conveyed from Hampstead. The Camden-Town Station of the Birmingham railway forms one of the most extraordinary assemblages of buildings in the country. Besides twelve acres of Euston-square, thirty acres are occupied here by the company, who have lately made most extensive alterations in their works, and just completed new buildings of remarkable size, at this station.

'Camden Town ... is now of portentous dimensions, stretching out to shake hands with Islington', *The Gentleman's Magazine* reported in 1854. 'The increase in the last few years has been immense' ('The Map of London', 42 [July 1854]: 22). For more on Camden Town, the model for the fictional Camberling Town, see note to chapter six, pp. 93-4.

As to the neighbourhood which

There were railway hotels, coffee-houses, lodging-houses, boarding-houses; railway plans, maps, views, wrappers, bottles, sandwich-boxes, and time tables; railway hackney-coach and cab-stands; railway omnibuses, railway streets and buildings, railway hangers-on and parasites, and flatterers out of all calculation.] The London and Birmingham Railway Company built twin hotels at Euston Station in 1839 – the Victoria Hotel and the Euston Hotel – on opposite sides of the grand Doric portico that fronted the Railway Station. The Victoria Hotel was built to be a 'dormitory' and the Euston Hotel to have first-class accommodation and a coffee-room licensed to sell wine and spirits. In *About Railways* (1865), William Chambers characterized the twin hotels as 'simple erections as regards architecture, being nothing more than white painted walls, pierced with numerous windows, of which there are no less than 350 on the several frontages' (qtd. in Binney and Pearce 120). These were the first railway hotels to be built by a railway company (the first railway hotel of any sort opened at Crewe Station in 1837). In the years that immediately followed, railway hotels were built at Normanton (1840), Derby (1841), Gateshead (1844), Hull (1851) and Paddington (1852), the latter containing 103 bedrooms, making it the largest railway hotel in the country (Simmons and Biddle, 1997, 212).

In 'An Unsettled Neighbourhood', Dickens remarked on the various railway shops and rooms that developed around a railway junction: there were 'Railway Dining Rooms', 'The Railway Ham, Beef, and German Sausage Warehouse', 'The Railway Pie Shop', 'The Railway Hat and Travelling Cap Depot', 'The Railway Hair-cutting Saloon', 'the Railway Bakery', 'the Railway Oyster Rooms and General Outfitting Establishment' and so forth (*HW* 10 [11 November 1854]: 289–92).

There was even railway time observed in clocks, as if the sun itself had given in.] The development of railways led to a standardized method of timekeeping. Before the railways, local time varied from town to town. Plymouth, for instance, was about 20 minutes ahead of London, 220 miles to the east. Because varied times created scheduling confusion, the Great Western and the London & South Western – the two trunk lines from east to west – adopted Greenwich Mean Time as the standard in 1838-41 (Greenwich Mean Time was also referred to as 'London Time' or 'Railway Time'). In 1840, the Great Western Railway began to display large clocks outside each of its stations, clocks that would be visible from passing trains. A year later, the company began using timetables advertising its adherence to London Time and describing the time differences between London and various stops on its line. In 1845 Parliament failed to pass a measure that would have standardized time throughout England, though the electric telegraph, with its ability to instantaneously transmit time signals, made standardization inevitable. Although some towns resisted the change – Bath, Bristol, Cambridge and Norwich were notable holdouts – by 1852, Greenwich time was established along the railway lines throughout Britain (McKenna, 1980, 244–7; Simmons and Biddle, 1997, 512–13).

Among the vanquished, was the master chimney-sweeper, whilom incredulous at Staggs's Gardens, who now lived in a stuccoed house three stories high, and gave himself out, with golden flourishes upon a varnished board, as contractor for the cleansing of the railway chimneys by machinery.] '[R]ailway Chimneys' refer to the funnels that carry off the smoke or steam from a locomotive engine (*OED*). The early years of the railway, in particular, saw a large number of patents for various railway and locomotive improvements. Between March and December 1840, for instance, the British and Foreign Patent Office granted twenty-one separate patents 'for improvements in railways, and locomotion thereon', including, in December, a patent for 'turning the waste steam into the chimney; cleaning out the fire tubes by a jet of steam and hot water' (Hebert, 1846, 2.543).

To and from the heart

Crowds of people and mountains of goods, departing and arriving scores upon scores of times in every four-and-twenty hours, produced a fermentation in the place that was always in action.] From their inception, trunk lines were used to carry goods, gradually replacing roads and canals as the primary means of transport, though the railway companies maintained a horse-drawn cartage system to transport goods from most goods stations. In the early years, the railway companies relied, at least in part, on established road carriers such as Pickford and Co. to organize and run the goods business. The railway companies made more money from their passenger trade than their goods business until 1852, at which point the trend began to reverse. Warehousing was also available at a number of stations.

Wonderful members of Parliament, who, little more than twenty years before, had made themselves merry with the wild railroad theories of engineers, and given them the liveliest rubs in cross-examination, went down into the north with their watches in their hands, and sent on messages before by the electric telegraph, to say they were coming.] Early railway development aroused opposition from many quarters, including Parliament. For example, there was an incredulous Parliamentary reaction to the proposals of the engineer George Stephenson to construct a railway line between Liverpool and Manchester in 1825:

> it was no easy task for him to bring home his convictions, or even to convey his meaning, to the less informed minds of his hearers, in the face of the sneers, interruptions, and ridicule of the opponents of the measure, and even of the Committee [of the House of Commons], some of whom shook

their heads and whispered doubts as to his sanity. (Williams, *Our Iron Roads*, 1852, 17)

To Stephenson's proposal that railway tracks cross the wet and barren waste of Chat Moss, one member of Parliament derisively remarked, 'The making of an embankment out of this pulpy wet moss is no very easy task. ... It is ignorance almost inconceivable. It is perfect madness'. Another member concurred: 'No engineer in his senses ... would go through Chat Moss if he wanted to make a railroad from Liverpool to Manchester'. After thirty-eight days of testimony and thirty-seven witnesses, the Bill was eventually carried by a vote of 88 to 41 (18).

The electric telegraph was patented in 1837 by William Fothergill Cooke and Charles Wheatstone, who installed a trial system on the London and Birmingham line, between Euston and Camden, though the system was costly and crude, and ultimately undeveloped. The Great Western Railway Company had its own system installed between Paddington and Hanwell in 1839, which, after some initial setbacks, was extended to Slough in 1843. The telegraph gained widespread acceptance in 1845, after it was used to apprehend an escaping murderer who was attempting to flee to London (Simmons and Biddle, 1997, 302). *The British Metropolis in 1851* described the reach and speed of the electric telegraph at mid-century:

> These telegraphs are now connected with most of the railways. They are substituted at the Admiralty for the old semaphore telegraphs ... they are also adopted at the Post-office, and at many of the public offices. The machinery can be seen in operation at the Euston-square or the Shoredich railway stations; and the Company has a central station at Lothbury. The telegraph extends at present over about 2353 miles of railway, which are traversed by upwards of 9600 miles of wire, communicating with 266 stations. As many as 52 words have been communicated in a minute by electric telegraph; the more usual number is about 30 per minute. (163)

But Staggs's Gardens had been

But Staggs's Gardens had been cut up root and branch.] In the 'Root and Branch Petition', presented to the House of Commons in 1640, radical reformers expressed their demands to abolish the episcopacy 'roots and branches'. The signatories became known as 'root-and-branch men', and the expression came to apply to any thoroughgoing policy.

Oh woe the day! when "not a rood of English ground" ... is secure!] A conflation of Goldsmith, *The Deserted Village* (1770) – 'A time there was, ere England's griefs began,/When every rood [quarter acre] of ground maintained its man' (57–8) – and Wordsworth, 'On the Projected Kendal and Windermere Railway' (1844) – 'Is then no nook of English ground secure/From rash assault?' (1–2).

He lived in the Company's

He lived in the Company's own Buildings … Toodle, Engine Fireman,] In order to attract workers to remote locations, often distant from established towns, railway companies early on recognized the need to provide accommodation for their employees. In other instances, companies had to provide housing for stationmasters and gate keepers to enable them to live near their station or gate. Even before the Stockton and Darlington Railway – the first public railway – had opened in 1830, the company constructed houses for the enginemen of its stationary engines. And, in 1841, the Newcastle & Carlisle line provided housing for thirty-five men, mostly stationmasters. Before long, company housing became customary and almost a right of condition of service for some positions. The most commonly housed groups of employees were the stationmasters, agents and clerks; houses for gatekeepers were also common. Other employees, such as firemen, were also housed, but much less frequently. Typically, railway employees lived in new dwellings built cheaply with old materials, though sometimes other buildings were converted. Some company housing, such as that provided by the London and Birmingham Railway, came with sanitation and good water supplies. The Railway's smallest terraced houses at Wolverton, for example, had a parlour, kitchen, hot water boiler and two or three bedrooms (Kingsford, 1970, 121–7; Simmons and Biddle, 1997, 213).

A fireman was the second crew position on a steam locomotive. In the early days of the railway, he was simply a stoker, someone who lit the fire and kept it going vigorously enough to produce an adequate amount of steam. Once the steam pressure began to fall, the fireman would fill up the firebox with fuel, and then watch as the fire recovered, usually working in ten-minute cycles. Not until the 1850s did the fireman have any control over the water level in the boiler, which was the duty of the driver, the immediate superior of the fireman. The driver had sole charge of the locomotive, and he told the fireman what to do. Firemen were classified, and paid, according to what type of train they worked on. A fireman on an express passenger train made more than a fireman working on an express goods train; a fireman working on trains that only traveled short distances made more than a shed fireman, who earned the lowest pay. In the 1840s, a fireman earned, on average, about 3 shillings and 4 pence a day, with the range running from 2 shillings and 6 pence to 4 shillings and twopence – about two shillings less than what a driver was paid (Kingsford, 1970, 98; McKenna, 1980, 137; Simmons and Biddle, 1997, 161–2).

"Yes, Mrs. Richards, it's me,"

Mr. Toodle, who had just come home from Birmingham,] Mr Toodle works for the London and Birmingham Railway, a 112-mile line, and one of the first major trunk lines constructed in Britain (in 1846, the London and Birmingham Railway merged with the Grand Junction Railway and the Manchester and Birmingham Railway to form the London and North Western Railway). The London and Birmingham, which was the first significant project of the great early-Victorian engineer, Robert

Stephenson, was authorized in 1833 and was opened gradually in 1837–8. In 1838, the company established locomotive and carriage works at the village of Wolverton, Buckinghamshire, and a town was built for employees. From 1840 to 1850, the London and Birmingham carried all rail traffic between London and central and north-east England, as well as the north-west.

Although the original London terminus was supposed to be in Camden Town, this was changed to Euston. There were eight tunnels along the line, the most formidable being the tunnel one-and-a-third miles long at Kilsby, south of Rugby. Because of deep cuttings at several spots along the line, the London and Birmingham Railway earned the reputation of being the best-graded railway in Britain, once past the steep hill in Camden (Simmons and Biddle, 1997, 281–2).

"Polly! cut away!"] That is, stop crying.

Chapter 16

WHAT THE WAVES WERE ALWAYS SAYING

"Don't be so sorry for me,

Indeed I am quite happy!'] Although children's attitudes toward death are especially difficult to determine, testimonies and diaries from the mid-Victorian period suggest a considerable amount of equanimity on the part of some young children toward their impending ends, largely because of their religious faith and because of the omnipresence of death, both in their daily lives and in their reading. Archibald Campbell Tait, Bishop of London in 1856, and later Archbishop of Canterbury, and his wife Catherine, watched five of their daughters die from scarlet fever, in quick succession. But both parents observed, several times, that none of the children seemed afraid of death for themselves, though the parents acknowledged their own struggle to submit to God's will. When, for instance, nine-year-old May was about to die, she asked that her sister be kept away from her (scarlet fever is infectious), and had her mother find a hymn, which May then asked be read aloud, several times. In her father's words, 'Her dear mind had plainly been much fixed on death', and she preserved a 'calm view of death' up to the end. May herself told her parents that she would not be sorry to die, and said that she happily awaited her new life in heaven. 'From her earliest babyhood', her mother maintained, 'death had seemed to my May a great and blessed reality, the way by which she was to attain her real life'. When another daughter was dying, five-year-old Chattie, she told her parents, very simply, 'I must go away' (Jalland, 1996, 132–5).

"Show me that old nurse,

"Show me that old nurse, Floy, if you please!"] Throughout the death scene to follow, Dickens draws on some of the conventions associated with the Evangelical ideal of the 'good Christian death', an ideal promulgated in religious tracts, journals and in fiction and that influenced depictions of death that were not strictly Evangelical in nature. Ideally, death should occur at home, with the dying person making farewells to each family member. He or she should be conscious until the end, bearing any pain or suffering with fortitude, and resigned to the will of God. In attendance would be immediate family members, an important nurse or servant and sometimes a doctor, though the deathbed would not be crowded, as it might have been in early modern England or eighteenth-century France. Compared with strictly Evangelical accounts, Dickens places less importance on the religious aspects of the 'good death', relying mostly on light and water imagery to convey a vague sense of an afterlife, though he does have young Paul pray and look up at an image of Jesus on the wall. Because the last words of dying persons were held to be particularly significant, it was essential that they be lucid in their final moments. Victorian novelists would reinforce the 'good death' ideal by surrounding the dying character with imagery suggesting the salvation to come. The characters might hear heavenly music, exhibit rapturous countenances, or see a divine light. William Roundell, an Anglican, describes his wife's final hours in the early 1850s – a typical representation of the 'good death' ideal:

> The Manner of her Death was what she had always prayed for, her Illness was short, and not attended with Pain, and her Intellects were perfect. From the first she was sensible her Time was come, and she desired not to continue, but said I am ready to go or stay as seems best to the Allmighty (*sic*). I am in Charity with all human Beings, and I commend myself to the Mercy of God, trusting to the Merits and Intercession of Jesus Christ for the forgiveness of all my Sins. And having so said, she expired without a groan, or single struggle. (Selborne Papers, MS Eng. misc. c. 690, fo. 106; quoted in Jalland, 1996, 35)

"Mama is like you, Floy.

the print upon the stairs at school, is not Divine enough.] A copy of Rembrandt's engraving, 'Christ Healing the Sick' described in chapter 14. See note, p. 195–6.

The golden ripple on the wall

until our race has run its course, and the wide firmament is rolled up like a scroll. The old, old fashion – Death!] An allusion to passages from the Bible:

> And all the host of heaven shall be dissolved, and the heavens shall be rolled

together as a scroll: and all their host shall fall down, as the leaf falleth off from the vine, and as a falling fig from the fig tree. (Isaiah 34.4)

And the heaven departed as a scroll when it is rolled together; and every mountain and island were moved out of their places. (Revelation 6.14)

Dickens told Angela Burdett Coutts on 18 January 1847: 'Between ourselves – Paul is dead. He died on Friday night about 10 o'Clock; and as I had no hope of getting to sleep afterwards, I went out, and walked about Paris until breakfast-time next morning' (*Letters* 5.9). In the preface to the Cheap Edition (1858), Dickens wrote that 'when I am reminded by any chance of what it was that the waves were always saying, I wander in my fancy for a whole winter night about the streets of Paris – as I really did, with a heavy heart, on the night when my little friend and I parted company for ever.'

"Dear me, dear me! To think,"

"To think ... that Dombey and Son should be a Daughter after all!"] This paragraph, which appeared in the first edition and monthly parts (1846–8) and in the 1858 Cheap Edition of the novel, was omitted from the last two editions published in Dickens's lifetime, the 1859 Library edition and the 1867 Charles Dickens edition (Horsman xlvii–viii, 225). Miss Tox's words reflect Dickens's desire, as stated in the number plans 'to throw interest of Paul, at once on Florence'. But it is not known why they were omitted from the 1859 and 1867 editions.

In the 1840s, the death rate in England and Wales for boys aged five to nine ranged from 8.2 per 1000 (1845, 1846) to 11.2 per 1000 (1849) (*The Registrar's General's Statistical Review of England and Wales*, cited in Mitchell, 1988, 60, 62). Sentimentalized depictions of the death of children were conventional in the early- and mid-nineteenth century, and recur frequently in Dickens – in part, no doubt, because of the high juvenile mortality rate. As Philip Collins points out, to take one example: 'no Ragged School meeting was complete without a few anecdotes of edifying juvenile deathbeds, and obituaries on Ragged School stalwarts often contained such a passage as this: "Mr French had his reward in a remarkable deathbed scene of one of his scholars (duly recounted)"' (179). Besides young Paul Dombey, the most notable dead children in Dickens include Smike (*NN*), Little Nell (*OCS*), who Ruskin remarked 'was simply killed for the market, as a butcher kills a lamb' (*Works* 34.275), and Jo (*BH*), along with minor figures such as Oliver Twist's workhouse friend, 'poor little Dick', Dr Marigold's first daughter Sophy, the Darnays' son in *TTC* and little Johnny in *OMF*. Dickens's presentation of child death, especially of the death of young women, owes much to his grief over the death of his seventeen-year-old sister-in-law, Mary Hogarth, who died in his arms in 1837.

In his unsigned review for the *Examiner* (28 October 1848), John Forster summed up the powerful popular reaction to the death of young Paul:

There was probably not a family in this country where fictitious literature is read, that did not feel the death of young Paul Dombey as something little short of a family sorrow. What was said of it by the author of the *Two Old Men's Tales*, that it flung a nation into mourning, was hardly an exaggeration; and perhaps the extent and depth of the feeling was a surprise to even the author himself. (692–3; the author was Mrs Anne Marsh [later Marsh-Caldwell]; cf. *Life*: 'threw a whole nation into mourning' [2.27])

Francis Jeffrey, Lord Jeffrey, who famously wept over the death of Little Nell (*OCS*), wrote Dickens that he had 'so cried and sobbed over it [the death of young Paul] last night, and again this morning; and felt my heart purified by those tears, and blessed and loved you for making me shed them'. 'I have a feeling', he concluded, 'that you will have nothing in the sequel, if indeed in your whole life, equal to the pathos and poetry, the truth and the tenderness, of the four last pages of the number, for those, at least, who feel and judge like me' (31 January 1847; qtd. in Collins, 1971, 216–7). Thackeray's response was equally strong, according to George Hodder:

> Putting No. 5 of *Dombey and Son* in his pocket, he hastened down to Mr Punch's printing-office, and entering the editor's room, where I chanced to be the only person present except Mr Mark Lemon himself, he dashed it on to the table with startling vehemence, and exclaimed "There's no writing against such power as this – one has no chance! Read that chapter describing young Paul's death: it is unsurpassed – it is stupendous!" (*Memories of my Time*, 1870, 277; qtd. in Collins, 1971, 219)

But there were also negative responses. The *North British Review* complained of the 'affectations of style' (7 [May 1847]: 116). And, in 1870, R. H. Hutton dismissed the sentiment surrounding Paul's death as 'pathos of the Adelphi Theatre ... feasting on itself' (Hutton, 'The Genius of Dickens', rpt. in Roscoe, 1906, 56–7).

Chapter 17 — Sixth monthly number, March 1847

CAPTAIN CUTTLE DOES A LITTLE BUSINESS FOR THE YOUNG PEOPLE

The chapter plan shows that the present Chapter 18, 'Father and Daughter', originally preceded this chapter (see p. 217). Dickens reversed their order while working on the proofs (Stone, 69).

Mems

Great point of the Nº to throw the interest of Paul, at once on Florence

Not to make too much of the scene with the father, or it may be too painful.

Illustrations

~~Mr Toots calls with~~ A friend of little Paul's

Florence and Diogenes.

Let him remember it in that room, years to come

children over the way.

Brother and Sister – Walter & Floy.

Captain Cuttle's big watch.

Number Plan

(Dealings with the Firm of Dombey and Son — N̰º VI.)

chapter   XVII.

Father   and   Daughter.
The state of mind of the household.
The progress of Florences grief

The children over the way
The Dog Diogenes, and Mʳ Toots.
The Scene with her father

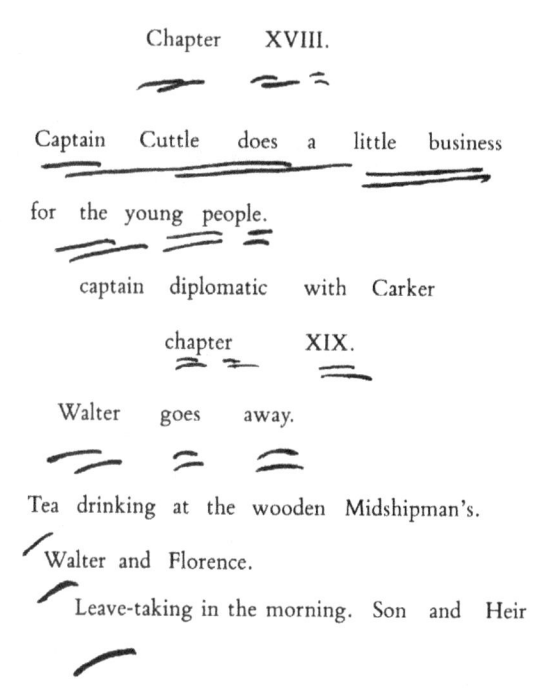

Chapter   XVIII.

Captain   Cuttle   does   a   little   business
for   the   young   people.

captain   diplomatic   with   Carker

chapter   XIX.

Walter   goes   away.

Tea drinking at the wooden Midshipman's.
Walter and Florence.
Leave-taking in the morning. Son   and   Heir

Chapter Plan

Florence's age.–Mems:

N̲o̲. 6. Page 181. Florence was little more than a child, in years – not yet fourteen. ~~child in his own room and his~~ after that, comes Mr Dombey's journey to Leamington, and his courtship, and his return to town, and his marriage, –say, in all, a space of One Year.

After that, comes their journey to Paris, and their return home, and their dinner-party, and Mr Carker's first interview with Edith about Florence, and Mrs Skewton's first attack of Paralysis – say, in all, a space of ~~nine~~ six months.

after that, comes the interval described in the chapter, headed "Domestic relations"—(page 397), and the scene between Mr Dombey and Edith, where he rejects Edith's proposal, and they become Strangers to each other, and the departure to Brighton for Mrs Skewton's

Additional memos pasted onto the verso of the Number Plan (Stone, 71)

Chapter 17 *Captain Cuttle does a little Business for the Young People*

health – the lapse of time at Brighton — and the period of Mrs Skewton's death, and the period after Mrs Skewton's death – say, in all, a space of One Year.

after that comes the Interview between Carker and Mr Dombey at the former's house, where they speak of the period before Mrs Skewton's death, and Mr Dombey's hurt on the same day, and Carker's interview with Her, immediately afterwards, and the interval between those descriptions, and the resumption of the Family in No 15 – say, in all, a space of – six months.

making Florence in N⁰ 15 nearly seventeen.

Before Mr Carker goes down to Leamington, and there meets the Major and Mr Dombey's Intended, Uncle Sol disappears.

And a year is said to have taken place between Uncle Sol's disappearance, and Mrs Skewton's first attack of Paralysis.
which seems to agree, perfectly, with this calculation.

Additional memos pasted onto the verso of the Number Plan (Stone, 71)

Captain Cuttle, in the exercise

lay their heads well to the wind] He is advising the family to confront their problems head on. 'Head to the wind' is a nautical term denoting 'the situation of a ship or boat when her head is pointed directly to windward. The term is particularly applied in the act of tacking or while lying at anchor' (Smyth, 1867, 376).

When Walter returned home on

like those Chinese sages who are said in their conferences to write certain learned words in the air that are wholly impossible of pronunciation,]

> We have heard that the Chinese language is so imperfect, that men are obliged, in conversation, in order to explain their meaning, to trace, with their fingers, in the air, the figure of written characters. This is exaggerated. We have seen sensible and intelligent Chinese, who have assured us that they never are at a loss to explain their ideas by spoken words. (Lieber, 1835, 7.416)

Captain Cuttle, however, becoming

Ned would fetch up with a wet sail in good time, and carry all before him.] To 'fetch up [or 'to come up'] with a wet sail' means to make rapid progress to victory, like a ship whose sails have been wetted to keep close to the wind (*OED*). Cf. Smollett, *Roderick Random*: 'telling me at parting, that he would soon fetch up all my leeway with a wet sail' (ch. 64; 1748); and *The Reprisal* (1757): 'A will fetch up his leeway with a wet sail, as the saying is' (Act Two, 'scene the last') .

Solomon Gills was at first

But the Captain flashed such golden prospects before his dim sight: hinted so mysteriously at Whittingtonian consequences:] For the legend of Dick Whittington, see note to chapter 4, p. 72.

Mr. Carker the Manager,

the empty fireplace, which was ornamented with a castellated sheet of brown paper,] An example of contemporary paper-covered chimney-boards, for instance: 'in summer, when the large fireplace is hidden by a chimney board, covered with Chinese paper, on which is painted a peacock, with its tail spread out'; 'Whatever air might have been introduced through the fire-place, was effectually excluded by a thick chimney-board, covered with a square of wall-paper, representing King George

IV visiting his cameleopard' (Tayler, 1822, 166; *The Mirror of Literature*, 1834, 24.445).

"Thank'ee kindly, my lad,"

Wal'r is as trim a lad as ever stepped; but he's a little down by the head] A 'trim' vessel is properly balanced in the water. If a vessel is 'down by the head', its bow is lower in the water than its stern, often because of a heavy load.

wore round a bit, and I can come alongside of him,] To 'wear' or 'wear round' is to change direction by turning the vessel's bow away from the wind.

All the world and his

the world and his wife, as the saying is,"] An idiomatic expression meaning 'everyone', first recorded in Swift, *Polite Conversation* (1738).

"I'd bet a gill of old Jamaica,"

a gill of old Jamaica,"] A 'gill' is a quarter pint, though in some districts of England it is a half pint, with the quarter pint being called a 'jack' (*OED*). Jamaica, which was under British control from 1655, was the centre of the English supply for rum. Because of its cheap price, the heavy, dark and full-bodied Jamaican rum was particularly popular with seamen and the working class (for more, see note to chapter 32, p. 347).

"There's a general in-draught

a general in-draught ... "Wind and water sets in that direction,] Cuttle means that there is an attraction between Walter and Florence; an 'indraught' is an inward flow of water or air, '*esp.* a current setting towards the land or up an estuary, etc.' (*OED*).

"Pass the word, and there's

a quotation he was preparing for a final burst, "who – comes from Sol Gills's daily, *to* your business, and your buzzums."] 'Business and bosoms' became current from the seventeenth century onward because of the Epistle Dedicatory in Bacon's *Essays* (1625): 'I doe now publish my *Essayes*; which, of all my other workes, haue beene most Currant: For that, as it seemes, they come home, to Mens Businesse, and Bosomes'.

Mr. Perch, who seemed to remember

"Wal'r!" ... there was once a poet of that name,] Edmund Waller (1606–87), Royalist and Restoration poet whose poems were published 1664–86.

if he had proposed to put a poet's statue up – say Shakespeare's for example – in a civic thoroughfare,] Public statues were a widely debated topic in the late 1830s and throughout the 1840s. In 1838, an article in the *Times*, 'The Statues of the Metropolis', commented:

> One feature which more particularly distinguishes the continental cities from our own, and which at once strikes the English traveller, is the number of statues erected in public places, in the open air, to the memory of their kings, or ... to those who either as statesmen, leaders, or philosophers, have proved themselves the benefactors or the ornaments of their country. (1 September 1838, p. 6; see also 7 September 1838, p. 6)

This article, and several that followed, criticized both the dearth of public statues in London and their quality. The author of 'The Living Sculptors of Great Britain' (*London and Edinburgh Magazine*, 1841) disparaged the work of the most famous British sculptors, Sir Francis Chantry and Sir Richard Westmacott, and rather than commissioning them to make more sculptures, advocated 'throwing the execution of public statues open to competition' (243). The general debate was given further significance by the government's decision to commission new statues and busts for the rebuilt Houses of Parliament, which opened in 1844 following the fire in 1834. A Parliamentary committee was established to inquire into 'promoting and encouraging the fine arts' by erecting in the Palace of Westminster 'public monuments in sculpture and painting to men distinguished for eminent literary, scientific, and civil services'. The committee's 'List of Distinguished Persons to Whose Memories Statues Might be Erected' included Chaucer, Spenser, Shakespeare, Milton, Addison, Richardson, Johnson and Sir Walter Scott (*Times*, 15 October 1845, p. 8; see also: *Times* 9 September 1844, p. 5; *Literary Gazette*, 1844, 500; 'Public Statues' in: Charles Knight, *London*, 1844, 6.65–80).

Carlyle continued the general discussion in 'Hudson's Statue' (*Latter-Day Pamphlets*, 1850), where he complained that England was burdened by an 'extraordinary population of Brazen and other Images which at present dominate the market-places of towns, and solicit worship from the English people. The ugliest images, and to the strangest class of people, ever set-up in the world'. He was particularly offended by the fact that so many represented men of business and capitalists: 'They are your lucky (or unlucky) Gamblers swollen *big*. Paltry Adventurers for most part; worthy of no worship; and incapable forever of getting any, except the soul consecrated to flunkyism'.

Mysterious and incomprehensible the Captain,

Mrs. MacStinger (who might have been brought up at Doctor Blimber's, she was such a Roman matron) fortified herself ... behind the open street-door, and refused to come out to the contemplation of her blessed infants] Although there were many famous Roman matrons (such as Volumnia, mother of Coriolanus, and Lucretia), the mention of Mrs MacStinger's children indicates that the allusion is to Cornelia, known as the Mother of the Gracchi (see note to chapter 11, p. 167). As a widow with twelve children,

> she devoted herself solely to their education, and rejected the most splendid offers of marriage. All her children died young except the two famous tribunes Tiberius and Caius Gracchus, and a daughter. ... A pleasing anecdote is related of her; on being visited by a lady of high rank, the stranger displayed to her with much ostentation, her jewels and other ornaments, expecting that Cornelia would do the same, but the Roman matron brought out her children as her brightest jewels. (Watkins, 1806, n. p.)

CHAPTER 18

FATHER AND DAUGHTER

There is a hush through

She promises a little fry for supper, and struggles ... against her feelings and the onions.] Lamb's fry (offal, especially testicles, or liver) could be 'bought very cheap'. The standard recipe appears in Kitchiner's *The Cook's Oracle* (1836): 'Fry it plain, or dip it in an egg well beaten on a plate, and strew some fine stale bread-crumbs over it; garnish with crisp parsley'. He advises serving it with a sauce made with the juices, a sliced onion or shallot, butter, flour and wine (293; see also 250).

At the offices in the City,

Ball's Pond] In the 1840s, Ball's Pond was a 'populous' hamlet in Islington, consisting 'principally of uniform ranges of houses'. *Mogg's New Picture of London* (1844) remarked,

> the situation is very healthy and the salubrity of the air, with its vicinity to the metropolis, have long rendered it a favourite retirement of the citizens. The Regent's Canal passes through this parish, and is conducted under the village by means of a tunnel above half a mile in length. (240)

Ball's Pond was named after John Ball, a tavern-keeper during the Restoration, and was once the location of a large pond much frequented by duck-hunters (Lewis, 1848).

Now the rosy children living

four black horses at his door, with feathers on their heads; and feathers tremble on the carriage that they draw; and these, and an array of men with scarves and staves, attract a crowd.] Funeral feathers, which were on the hearses and horses, and worn on the head of a man in the procession, were probably introduced in the years immediately following the Restoration. The man who headed the procession would wear a scarf, as would other people in the procession, and there would be men carrying staves. Dickens mocked the fashion for real or imitation ostrich feathers in 'From the Raven in the Happy Family': 'Because there were not feathers enough yet, there was a fellow in the procession carrying a board of 'em on his head, like Italian images'. He was accompanied by mutes, 'about five-and-twenty or thirty other fellows ... dressed up in scarves and hat-bands, and carrying shut-up fishing rods, I believe' (*HW* 1.241). For more on funeral processions, see note to chapter 3, p. 45.

The juggler who was going to twirl the basin,] Jugglers constituted one type of London street performer in the early to mid-nineteenth century, along with acrobats, balancers, tumblers, conjurors and fire-eaters. Mayhew interviewed one juggler who performed his act on stilts, including balancing a basin on a pole: 'I next took a wooden pole, and on the top of it a wash hand basin – the pole was 7 feet high, and on the top of the pole, still on my stilts, I kept the basin spinning round' (*The Morning Chronicle*, 25 May 1850, 'Letter LIII'). Another juggler observed:

> there ain't above twenty jugglers in all England – indeed, I'm sure there ain't – such as goes about pitching in the streets and towns. I know there's only four others besides myself in London, unless some new one has sprung up very lately. You may safely reckon their earnings for the year round at a pound a-week, that is, if they stick to juggling; but most of us joins some other calling along with juggling, such as the wizard's business, and that helps out the gains. (Mayhew, 1851, 3.107)

And now, among the knot

the knot of servants dressed in mourning,] The custom of a well-to-do family paying for their servants' mourning clothes when a member of the family has died is illustrated in John Galt's *The Ayrshire Legatees; or, the Pringle Family* (1821). The Scottish minister's wife Mrs Pringle, who is renowned 'both for economy and management', sends instructions to her friend Miss Glencairn:

I beg you will go to Bailie Delap's shop, and get swatches of his best black bombaseen, and crape, and muslin, and bring them over to the manse ... If you cannot come yourself, and the day should be wet, send Nanny Eydent, the mantuamaker, with them; you'll be sure to send Nanny, ony how, and I requeesht that, on this okasion, ye'll get the very best the Bailie has. ... You will get, likewise, swatches of mourning print, with the lowest prices. I'll no be so particular about them, as they are for the servant lasses, and there's no need, for all the greatness of God's gifts, that we should be wasteful.

(Letter 1)

tumble in the mud.] Mayhew recorded the experiences of a crossing-sweeper who also worked as a street tumbler at night: 'We're always sure to make money if there's mud – that's to say, if we look for our money and ask; of course, if we stand still we don't. ... At night-time we tumbles – that is, if the policeman ain't nigh' (2.496).

The feathers wind their gloomy way

All of him that is dead,] A variant of 'all that is mortal', a phrase often used in epitaphs and one that had become a cliché by the early nineteenth century.

The chief thing that they

"it seems like Sunday." They can hardly persuade themselves but that there is something unbecoming, if not wicked, in the conduct of the people out of doors,] Everything closed down on Sundays during the early years of Victoria's reign. So-called 'Sabbatarians', middle-class and primarily Evangelical reformers, sought to prohibit most Sunday activities – public entertainment, transport, drinking, trading, labour, the postal service and the Sunday press. From the outset of his career, Dickens had assailed such prohibitions, which he believed were 'directed exclusively ... against the amusements and recreations of the poor'. Particularly pernicious were the 'general gloom and austerity' that accompanied Sunday closings, blighting the one day in the week when the working class, freed from labour, could enjoy itself (*Sunday Under Three Heads*, 1836, 649). In the 1830s and 1840s, the Sabbatarian movement was spearheaded by figures such as Sir Andrew Agnew, a Scottish Whig hailed by Evangelicals as 'the hero of the Sabbath', and by groups such as the Lord's Day Observance Society. Sabbatarian activity increased in the 1850s: on 30 May 1850, Lord Ashley successfully moved to end postal delivery and collection on Sunday; in 1854, the government put further restrictions on the Sunday opening hours of public houses, and, in 1855, Lord Robert Grosvenor introduced a Trading Bill prohibiting Sunday trading in London, with a five-shilling penalty for each illegal sale. Massive crowds protesting such restrictions assembled in Hyde Park on three consecutive Sundays in June and July 1855. It is at this time that Dickens 'said to any one in Parliament whom I know or have happened to see ... they [the people] have suffered an amount of cruel denial through the last Sunday bill [the Beer Act of 1854], which you don't or won't understand; and it is wonderful to see you rushing on to riot and disturbance as you are' (Pope, 1978, 42–95; *Letters* 7.659–60).

an altered and blameless existence as a serious green-grocer in Oxford Market.] 'Serious' here means earnest in matters of religion; the term was usually associated with Nonconformists, as in *Nicholas Nickleby*:

> 'Three serious footmen ... Cook, housemaid, and nursemaid; each female servant required to join the Little Bethel Congregation three times every Sunday – with a serious footman. If the cook is more serious than the footman, she will be expected to improve the footman; if the footman is more serious than the cook, he will be expected to improve the cook.' (ch. 16)

Oxford Market (also known as 'Portland Market') was a small covered market for meat, fish and vegetables. It would have been close to Mr Dombey's house as it was south of Portland Place, on the corner of Great Titchfield Street and Market Place. The market was established in 1731 and opened three days a week. The ground and buildings were sold in 1876 and destroyed in 1880 (Wheatley, 1891, 2.620).

Mrs. Chick approved of this resolution,

disparaged Miss Tox as a crocodile; yet her sympathy seemed genuine,] The sixteenth-century phrase 'crocodile tears' describes tears that are feigned, or shed only in order to deceive. It derives from the belief that crocodiles wept while devouring or luring their prey.

But it is not in the nature

the sacred fire of Heaven, is as gentle in the heart, as when it rested on the heads of the assembled twelve, and showed each man his brother, brightened and unhurt.] The Pentecostal fires are described in Acts 2.1–4:

> And when the day of Pentecost was fully come, they were all with one accord in one place. And suddenly there came a sound from heaven as of a rushing mighty wind, and it filled all the house where they were sitting. And there appeared unto them cloven tongues like as of fire, and it sat upon each of them. And they were filled with the Holy Ghost, and began to speak with other tongues, as the Spirit gave them utterance.

"I say," he proceeded, "Miss Dombey!

I could have had him stolen for ten shillings,] Dog-stealing was a lucrative business: ladies' small spaniels and lap-dogs were particularly prized and might fetch £50 or £60. More common dogs fetched much less, usually between £1 to £5. The thief would keep the dog for a day or two at a public house and then deposit it at a dog-dealer with whom he was connected. If the owner failed to advertise for the dog, a 'restorer' would attempt to extort money from the owner directly, offering 'to restore the dog if terms could be come to'. In some cases, the thief might even threaten to torture the dog or cut its throat, though there seems to have been no evidence that such threats were actually carried out. Sir Robert Peel, Lord Cholmondeley, Earl Stanhope, Count D'Orsay and the Bishop of Ely all paid money for the return of their dogs. One of the small bronze figures that Dickens had on his writing desk, and that he had with him in Lausanne in June 1846 (i.e. as he began to write *DS*) was a dog thief/salesman with 'lots of little dogs in his pockets and under his arms' (Mayhew, 1851, 2.48–51; 4.326; Charles Collins, 'Charles Dickens's Study', *The Graphic* 1870, qtd. in Slater, 2009, 256).

In fact, Diogenes was

as if he had come express to a Dispensary to be examined for his health.] Dispensaries, together with general medical hospitals and medical charities, comprised a quarter of the 500 charitable institutions in London in the first half of the nineteenth century. Affording free treatment to the destitute sick, the dispensaries included the London Dispensary, City of London Dispensary, Islington Dispensary, General Dispensary and Royal Universal Dispensary (review of Highmore's *Philanthropia Metropolitana* in *Gentleman's Magazine*, 1822, 92.340). An article in *HW* in 1851, 'Twenty-four Hours in a London Hospital', describes how patients are rapidly examined on admission and then either treated, or given prescriptions or sent to another department for further examination and admission as in-patients (2.457–65).

Diogenes the man did not

Diogenes the man did not speak plainer to Alexander the Great] An anecdote from 'The Life of Alexander' in *Plutarch's Lives*:

> the Grecians, being assembled at the Isthmus, declared their resolution of joining with Alexander in the war against the Persians, and proclaimed him their general. While he stayed here, many public ministers and philosophers came from all parts to visit him and congratulated him on his election, but contrary to his expectation, Diogenes of Sinope, who then was living at Corinth, thought so little of him, that instead of coming to compliment him, he never so much as stirred out of the suburb called the Cranium, where Alexander found him lying alone in the sun. When he saw so much company

near him, he raised himself a little, and vouchsafed to look upon Alexander; and when he kindly asked him whether he wanted anything, "Yes," said he, "I would have you stand from between me and the sun." Alexander was so struck at this answer, and surprised at the greatness of the man, who had taken so little notice of him, that as he went away he told his followers, who were laughing at the moroseness of the philosopher, that if he were not Alexander, he would choose to be Diogenes. (Dryden's translation)

Diogenes ... devoted himself to her service.] For Diogenes and his nickname, 'the dog', see note to chapter 14, p. 200. Dickens himself loved and admired dogs and owned several over the years. His friend James T. Fields recalled:

> He always had much to say of animals as well as of men, and there were certain dogs and horses he had met and known intimately which it was specially interesting to him to remember and picture. ... He was such a firm believer in the mental faculties of animals, that it would have gone hard with a companion ... if a doubt was thrown ... on the mental intelligence of any four-footed friend. ... Quite a colony of dogs has always been a feature at Gad's Hill. When Dickens returned home from his last visit to America, these dogs were frequently spoken of in his letters. ('Some Memories of Charles Dickens', *Atlantic Magazine*, August 1870)

Among his own dogs were Linda, a St Bernard acquired as a puppy at Tavistock House; Turk, a mastiff; and two Newfoundlands. His eldest daughter described the day at Tavistock House when she was given a gift of 'a little white Pomeranian, with black eyes and nose', but

> From this very first moment Charles Dickens took to the little dog and made a pet of her, and it was he who gave her the name of Mrs Bouncer. ... He had a peculiar voice and way of speaking for her, which she knew perfectly well and would respond to at once. ... To be stroked with a foot had great fascination for Mrs Bouncer ... and Charles Dickens would often and often take off his boot of an evening and sit stroking the little creature – while he read or smoked – for an hour together. ... He loved the dog, and was always greatly touched by [her] truly wonderful devotion. (Mamie Dickens, 'Charles Dickens at Home', *New York Times*, 6 April 1884)

If anything had frightened her,

she stood and looked at him as if stricken into stone.] Dombey is being compared to Medusa, the most famous of the Gorgons, the three frightful monsters from Greek mythology whose heads were covered with hissing serpents. Medusa, the only mortal Gorgon, was so hideous that everyone who looked at her was turned to stone.

Chapter 19

WALTER GOES AWAY

The wooden Midshipman at the

his elfin small-clothes] His tiny breeches (see Plate 5, p. 59).

caring as little for what went on about him, terrestrially, as Archimedes at the taking of Syracuse.] An anecdote from 'The Life of Marcellus' in *Plutarch's Lives*:

> But what gave Marcellus the greatest concern was the unhappy fate of Archimedes who was at that time engaged in study ... that he neither heard the noise and hurry of the Romans, nor perceived that the city was taken. While he was thus employed, a soldier came suddenly upon him, and commanded him to follow him to Marcellus; which he refusing to do till he had finished and demonstrated his problem, the soldier, in a rage, drew his sword and killed him. (Dryden's translation)

Such a Midshipman he seemed

But no fierce idol with a mouth from ear to ear, and a murderous visage made of parrot's feathers, was ever more indifferent to the appeals of its savage votaries, than was the wooden Midshipman to these marks of attachment.] Apparently one of the feathered idols collected during the important voyage of the HMS *Blonde* to the Sandwich Islands (Hawaii) and the South Pacific in 1824. A contemporary article, 'Idol of the Sandwich Islanders', includes an illustration (Plate 11) and a description:

> The idol is composed of wicker work covered over with red, black, and yellow feathers, which are esteemed by the natives as sacred, the mouth consists of two rows of dog's teeth, and the eyes are pieces of mother of pearl with a nut stuck in the centre of each; the neck is surrounded by a string of European beads, probably left by captain Cook; the idol altogether is nearly three feet in height, and though distorted, still bears a resemblance to the features of the islanders. The morai, or temple, out of which it was taken, and the only remaining one now existing in the Sandwich Islands, was the celebrated "Hare o Keave," or House of Keave, the depository of the remains of departed kings and princes of Owhyee. (*The Mirror of Literature, Amusement, and Instruction* [12 August 1826]: 88)

11   'Idol of the Sandwich Islanders', *The Mirror of Literature, Amusement, and Instruction* 8 (12 August 1826): 88

But that ancient mariner might

that ancient mariner] Although the phrase was occasionally used from the seventeenth century onward, this is probably an allusion to Coleridge, 'Rime of the Ancient Mariner', first published in *Lyrical Ballads* (1798).

"Goodness knows," exclaimed Miss

Mrs. Pipchin as a overseer would come cheap ... and if a knowledge of black slavery should be required,] Slaves and their overseers were topical in the 1840s. Two books published in 1846 contained the autobiographies and stories of freed slaves, describing their lives on plantations and the brutal treatment of overseers: *Interesting Memoirs and Documents Relating to American Slavery* and *The Life of a Negro Slave*. After publication of the first edition in England, *The Life of a Negro*

Slave (first published in New York in 1832) was reviewed in *Eclectic Review*, 1847, 21.64–8 and abridged at length in *Chambers's Miscellany*, 1847, 17.1–32. Other contemporary books included Andrew Steinmetz, *A Voice in Ramah; or, Lament of the Poor African* (1842) and *Slavery and the Internal Slave Trade in the United States of North America* (The Committee of the British and Foreign Anti-Slavery Society; 1841). According to *Slavery and the Internal Slave Trade*,

> "Overseer" is the name which designates the assemblage of all brutal propensities and fiendish passions in one man. An overseer must be the lowest of all objects, consenting to be loathed and detested by the master who employs him; and at the same time he must be the most callous of all reprobates, in order to inflict tortures, from the sight of which the planter himself sometimes recoils with horror. (76)

Dickens expressed disgust for slavery in *AN*, calling it 'that most hideous blot and foul disgrace' (ch. 3), as well as in *MC*, and in his correspondence and private conversations. He predicted, while he was in the United States, that 'I shall be able to say one of these days, that I accepted no public mark of respect in any place where slavery was; – and that's something' (*Letters* 3.90; 24 February 1842).

"There was no reason," said

If I do my duty, I do what I ought,] Perhaps an allusion to two of Lord Nelson's most famous statements: 'England expects every man will do his duty' (a signal at the Battle of Trafalgar, 1805), and 'Thank God, I have done my duty' (repeated as he lay dying) (Robert Southey, *The Life of Horatio, Lord Nelson*, 1813). Mr Pecksniff quotes Nelson in *Martin Chuzzlewit*: ' "It is our duty so to do. Let us be among the few who do their duty. If … as the poet informs us, England expects every man to do his duty…" ' (43).

Bright rose the sun next

Bright rose the sun … and up rose Walter] An allusion to John Dryden's translation of Chaucer's *The Knight's Tale*, 'Palamon and Arcite; or, the Knight's Tale' published in 1700 as part of *Fables, Ancient and Modern*: 'Now morn with rosy light had streak'd the sky / Up rose the sun, and up rose Emily' (bk 3). The image was much admired by literary critics and also frequently adapted by many writers, including Shakespeare, Byron and Scott.

"Hear him!" cried the Captain.

Train up a fig-tree in the way it should go, and when you are old sit under the

shade on it.] A conflation of Proverbs 22.6 – 'Train up a child in the way he should go: and when he is old, he will not depart from it' – and Micah 4.4 – 'But they shall sit every man under his vine and under his fig tree; and none shall make them afraid: for the mouth of the Lord of hosts hath spoken it'.

heave a-head] 'To advance the ship by heaving in the cable or other rope fastened to an anchor at some distance before her' (Bowditch, *New American Practical Navigator*, 1823, 294).

The relentless chronometer at last

in a hackney coach to a wharf, where they were to take steam-boat for some Reach down the river, the name of which, as the Captain gave it out, was a hopeless mystery to the ears of landsmen.] For hackney coach, see note to chapter 2, p. 36. A 'reach' was a section of the river that could be seen in one view, and included, eastward on the Thames from London, Upper Pool, Lower Pool, Limehouse Reach, Deptford Reach, Blackwall Reach, and so forth. Soon after the first steam boat entered the River Thames in 1815, steam-powered vessels began offering short-range services. 'Countless thousands' annually passed up and down the Thames 'in steam-packets', Porter recorded in 1836, so that 'within the last five years [steam vessels] have, in a great degree, superseded the use of sailing vessels' (2.46–8).

they were boarded by various excited watermen] Their steamboat is crewed by licensed Thames watermen who ferried passengers and cargo along and across the river. For more on the Company of Watermen and Lightermen, see note to chapter 28, p. 317.

men in red shirts running barefoot to and fro,] Sailors wore red shirts and went barefoot (only officers wore shoes). In 'Loss, by fire, of the Hibernia', the ship on fire hoists 'a sailor's red shirt as a signal of distress', and 'The Sailors' Home' mentions a 'merchant seaman in a red shirt' (*The Mariner's Chronicle*, 1834, 177; *HW* [22 March 1851]: 2.613).

black caboose] 'The cook-room or kitchen of merchantmen on deck; a diminutive substitute for the galley of a man-of-war. It is generally furnished with cast-iron apparatus for cooking' (Smyth, 1867).

Chapter 20

Seventh monthly number
April 1847

MR. DOMBEY GOES UPON A JOURNEY

Major Bagstock delivered himself

the ill-starred Native had already undergone a world of misery arising out of the muffins, while, in connexion with the general question of boiled eggs, life was a burden to him.] Eggs and muffins were common 'camp fare': one military man referred to muffins as 'great favourites in India' (Doveton, 1844, 108). The Native is performing the role of the *khitmutghar* (see note to chapter 7, p. 110):

> One of his most important duties is to be able to cook fairly well when called upon to do so, more especially when his master may move into camp either on the march or on a shooting expedition. Then he is expected to show his powers in the culinary art; and, generally speaking, Mohammedan cooks acquit themselves admirably in this respect. They are especially clever at making omelettes, soufflets, and such-like. ('Indian Servants', *Chambers's Journal* 3 [27 March 1886]: 203)

The Major's purple visage deepened

The Major's purple visage deepened in its hue, and the Major's lobster eyes stood out in bolder relief,] For Bagstock's suffering from cyanosis and exophthalmia, and numerous other complaints, see notes to chapter 7, p.000 and chapter 10 (gout), p. 000; for his chorea and apoplexy, see notes below.

With a rotatory motion of his head,] Bagstock is later described as 'rolling his head like a harlequin' (26). This involuntary movement suggests he has chorea, which according to James Copland, 'is closely related to palsy', another of Bagstock's complaints (see note to chapter 7, p. 108; *Of the causes, nature and treatment of palsy and apoplexy*, 1850, 181). In his account of chorea, John Eberle describes how the 'head is sometimes thrown from side to side, or backwards and forwards' (*A Treatise on the Practice of Medicine*, 1835, 2.78). For Mrs Skewton's shaking palsy, see note to ch 21, p. 261.

as he shook Mr. Dombey by the hand, imparting to that peaceful action as defiant a character as if it had been the prelude to his immediately boxing Mr. Dombey for a thousand pounds a side and the championship of England.] The 'thousand pounds' is an exaggeration. Although the most celebrated of early nineteenth century boxers might, on rare occasion, fetch £500 a side (as in a match between Josh Hudson

Mems:

The mother and daughter. The mother, and her cant about "heart", and nature – Daughter who has been put through her paces, before countless marrying men, like a horse for sale – Proud and ~~disgusts~~ weary of her degradation, but going on, for it's too late now, to try to turn back – These to be encountered at Leamington.

The Railroad Ride. Take care of the Major.

Harriet Carker, the Sister.

Toots's greatness

Toots looking forward to Florence
Conciliating Nipper
Illustration with Diogenes laboring under a mistake.

Number Plan

(Dealings with the Firm of Dombey and Son _ N.º VII.)

Chapter XX.

N~~ew Faces~~ M.ʳ Dombey goes upon a journey.

Chapter XXI.

New Faces.

Chapter XXII.

A trifle of management by M.ʳ Carker the Manager.

Rob the Grinder employed as a spy, and sent to live with old Sol Gills

Chapter Plan

and Tom Cannon), or 500 guineas a side (as in a match between Hen Pearce ['the Game Chicken'] and Jem Belcher), such prizes were extraordinary. A modern historian of prizefighting has estimated that £50 'was usual for the more important fights and many fights were arranged for much less'. The Pugilistic Club would frequently supplement the stakes with an additional purse of £5 to £50 (Ford, 1971, 94).

"No, Sir," said the Major,

"Devil a bit!] 'Not at all!' (Davies, *A Supplemental English Glossary*, 1881, 180).

Joe might have been, by this time, Lieutenant-General Sir Joseph Bagstock, K.C.B.,] The abbreviation of Knights Commander of The Order of the Bath, the second level of the fourth most senior Order in the British honours system. The Order of the Bath, originally conferred to reward military service, was established in 1725 by George I. Until 1815, there were no more than thirty-six Knights of the Bath. After Waterloo, the Order was divided into two divisions and membership was increased. There was a civilian division, with one class (until 1847), Knights of the Order of the Bath, and a military division, with three classes, the middle one being KCB.

Mr. Dombey, in his estimation

the Major as an officer and a gentleman,] A popular phrase drawn from *The Articles of War; Rules and Articles for the Better Government of His Majesty's Horse and Foot Guards*, etc. (1762), section xv, art. xxiii: 'Whatsoever commissioned Officer shall be convicted before a general Court-martial, of behaving in a scandalous infamous Manner, such as is unbecoming the character of an Officer and a Gentleman, shall be discharg'd from Our Service'. The phrase recurs repeatedly in popular periodicals (e.g. *Blackwood's Edinburgh Magazine* [67 (1850): 276–7], which described cases from 1801 and 1814; and *The Dublin Review* [10 (February 1841): 155], which gave details of the much publicized courts-martial of Capt Reynolds, 11th Hussars, and the Earl of Cardigan).

a no less becoming sense of it, than the beadle of the Royal Exchange.] The Royal Exchange had its own beadle (*Further Report of the Commissioners ... House of Commons Papers*, 1820, 5.113).

But these were lonely thoughts

Mr. Dombey was disposed to regard him as a choice spirit] *1 Henry VI*, 5.3.1: 'ye choice spirits that admonish me'; *Julius Caesar* 3.1.164: 'The choice and master spirits of this age'; Bunyan, *Pilgrim's Progress*, 'In the Similitude of a Dream', part 2: 'He was a man of a choice spirit'.

The Native, who had no

The Native, who had no particular name, but answered to any vituperative epithet,]

> An Englishman [in India] very seldom troubles himself about the names of his servants. He calls them generally by the names of their respective offices – Bearer, Syce, &c. Their individual designations he may pick up by degrees, as he does their physiognomies, but it is by no means imperative that he particularises thus far. ('Indian Servants', 9 [27 June 1863]: 417)

"Dombey," said the Major,

a devilled grill, a savoury pie, a dish of kidneys,] Devilled dishes, which were grilled with hot condiments, may have been introduced by British soldiers returning from India. *The Cook and Housewife's Manual* ('Meg Dods', 4th ed., 1829) describes 'Devils' in detail:

> they are most commonly considered as provocatives and stimulants … The only indispensable attribute … is scorching heat and tear-compelling pungency. Devils are made of the legs, rumps, backs, and gizzards of cold turkey, goose, duck, capon; and of all kinds of game … and also of venison, veal, and mutton-kidney, fish-bones … and of biscuits or rusks … The seasonings, which consist of salt, pepper, cayenne; and curry, mushroom, anchovy, or truffle-powder, must be administered at the discretion of the consumer. It is a good mode to have the things seasoned at table, and then sent to the kitchen fire. The devils must be broiled on a strong clear fire, and served in a hot-water dish, or one with a spirit-lamp. (recipe 550)

Savoury pies might consist of beef-steak, poultry or game, rabbit, mutton, mince, or veal and ham. Broiled kidneys were a breakfast or supper dish. Mrs Beeton's recipe is for fresh sheep kidneys, skinned and placed on a skewer 'over a nice clear fire'. They are served on a very hot dish and seasoned with salt, pepper and a little butter (recipe 724).

"Very excellent fare, Major,"

ate rather more of rich meats than was good for him, insomuch that his Imperial complexion was mainly referred by the faculty to that circumstance.] The 'faculty' refers to the medical profession, as in Thomas Hood, *Up the Rhine* (1840): 'Fat bacon … was once in vogue amongst the faculty for weak digestions' ('Letter from Mr Frank Somerville to Gerard Brooke'; *OED*, 10).

Old Joe, Sir," said the Major

But Joe has had his day. J. Bagstock is extinguished – outrivalled – floored,] From the proverb, 'Every dog has his day', as in, for example, *Hamlet* 5.1.286: 'The cat will mew, and dog will have his day'; Carlyle, *French Revolution* (1837), 3.1.1: 'How changed for Marat, lifted from his dark cellar … ! All dogs have their day; even rabid dogs'.

"That woman, Sir," said the

His Royal Highness the late Duke of York … at a levee,] For the Duke of York, see note to chapter 1, pp. 32–3. A levee was a ceremonial interview between the British monarch and a select group of notables, held in the early afternoon about once a week when Parliament was in session. The occasion was more than social: 'Privileges are solicited by public corporations, and bestowed; honours and dignities conferred upon individuals; favours granted; and such other acts of condescension, grace, and courtesy rendered' (Colton, 1835, 1.291).

"Dombey," said the Major

his whole life being a struggle against all kinds of apoplectic symptoms,] Bagstock's apoplexy is closely associated with his 'usual plethoric symptoms' – an 'overfulness of the blood vessels' – referred to later in the chapter:

> The tendency to apoplexy is given, in the first place, by certain conformations of body. … A large head, a short thick neck, a florid complexion, broad shoulders, short stature, with a tendency to corpulency, are the prominent features of the apoplectic figure. … The predisposition to apoplexy is connected, in the second place, with a certain period of life. … A predisposition to apoplexy is further given by such habits of life as tend to produce plethora generally, to drive the blood in more than ordinary quantity upon the vessels of the brain, or to prevent its free return to the heart. Hence it is, that full living, habitual intoxication, sedentary pursuits … have always been accused of leading to apoplexy. *Exciting causes.* – The principal of these are, the distension of the stomach by a full meal, the immoderate use of wine or spirits … very long or loud speaking, severe fits of coughing. (George Gregory, 1835, 359–60; *Works of William Cullen*, 1827, 2.355).

For Bagstock's other medical problems, see note to chapter 7, pp. 108–9; for his gout, see note to chapter 10, pp. 149–50.

"And, now, Dombey, as you

Chapter 20 *Mr Dombey goes upon a Journey*   239

Leamington,] See note below, pp. 250–1.

The Major being by this time

the departure of the railway train to Birmingham,] They are leaving for Euston Station (also known as Euston Grove and, sometimes, Euston-square Station), the London terminus of the London and Birmingham Railway. The 112½ mile line, which opened in its entirety in September 1838, served as 'a grand trunk from the metropolis towards the northern part of England', and passed through the counties of Middlesex, Hertfordshire, Buckinghamshire, Northamptonshire, Worcestershire and Warwickshire (Roscoe, 1839, 7). For more on Euston Station, see note to chapter 15, pp. 205–6.

The Native got him into his great coat ... and buttoned him up ... then handed him separately ... his wash-leather gloves, his thick stick, and his hat;]

> Your native servant is rather displeased, if you do not allow him to put on your coat or jacket in the morning when you dress. I have know Europeans who carried this point of etiquette much further, and never by any chance pulled on their own stockings, but had a native servant to assist them. ... One of the most energetic men I have known in India, regularly employs a servant to draw on his socks, and makes a boast of it. He does it deliberately, on the ground that, in this exhausting climate, we should husband our strength and reserve it for other and higher duties. (Kerr, 1873, 99)

this unfortunate foreigner (currently believed to be a prince in his own country),] This was a claim made about African slaves as early as the seventeenth century:

> I told you our house was for all Guests ... there came a Person of Honour, who had been a Traveller, and among his Attendants a Negro, or Black-man, which he had brought from *Guiana*. This Black-more was reported by his Master and others, to be the Son of a Prince in his own Country. (*The English Rogue* ... Richard Head, 1674, 3.17–18)

In Frederick Marryat's *Mr Midshipman Easy* (1836), the ship's steward, a former slave, 'claimed the rank of prince in his own country, with what truth could not of course be substantiated' (9).

who aimed at him from the pavement with those great missiles like a Titan,] Dickens confuses the Titans and the gods in the Titanomachy, the battle between the Titans and the Olympians described in Hesiod's *Theogany*. In the battle, the gods are assisted by giants with a hundred hands who throw rocks, a hundred at a time, at the Titans:

> Terrible, strong, of force enormous; burst
> A hundred arms from all their shoulders huge;
> From all their shoulders fifty heads upsprang
> O'er limbs of sinewy mould. They then array'd
> Against the Titans in fell combat stood,
> And in their nervous grasp wielded aloft
> Precipitous rocks. (887–93)

The Titans were defeated by Zeus and the Olympian gods and imprisoned in Tartarus.

But before the carriage moved away,

before the carriage moved away,] After entering Euston Station through the grand portico, a passenger on the London and Birmingham line would proceed to the booking offices and apply for his ticket:

> Stating his name, the place to which he is journeying, and the quantity of luggage ... he pays his fare, and receives a ticket from the clerk corresponding to the class of carriage he has chosen. If the ticket be for the first class, it will be numbered to correspond with a seat in the carriage which he must occupy. If it be for the second class, the traveller is free to take possession of any seat in that train which may be unoccupied. (Wyld, 1838, 1)

After passing through the booking offices, the passenger would enter

> an extensive yard, covered with a beautifully constructed and elegant iron roof, supported on iron columns, under which the carriages are placed on their arrival and departure. This shed is 200 feet long and about 50 span, and at night is brilliantly lighted with gas. Even when it happens that a train arrives from the country just as another is leaving town, and when hundreds of persons are enclosed in the area under the shed, all is regularity and facility for departure. (Roscoe, 1839, 39)

His marked behavior seemed to afford the Major ... unbounded satisfaction; and he sat for a long time afterwards, leering, and choking, like an over-fed Mephistopheles.] On 10 March 1847, Dickens informed Browne:

> I should premise that I want to make the Major, who is the incarnation of selfishness and small revenge, a kind of comic Mephistophelean power in the book. ... But a great deal will come of it: and I want the Major to express that, as much as possible in his apoplectico-Mephistophelean observation of the scene, and in his share in it. (*Letters* 5.34–5)

Chapter 20 *Mr Dombey goes upon a Journey*

Dickens is drawing on the sixteenth-century German legend of Faust, with Mr Dombey as Faust and Major Bagstock as Mephistopheles, the demon who tempts Faust and to whom Faust sells his soul. The most notable treatments of the legend are Christopher Marlowe's *Doctor Faustus* (1604) and Goethe's *Faust* (part 1, 1808; part 2, 1832). The Faust legend was popular on the London stage: there were productions of different versions at the Prince's Theatre in 1840, the New Strand Theatre in 1841 and Sadler's Wells Theatre in 1842 (*Times*, 22 May 1840, 5; 2 June 1841, 5; 21 September 1842, 5).

"No Sir," said Toodle,

rubs on."] To struggle on. The idiomatic phrase is 'to rub on with the world' (or 'through the world') (*OED*).

The simple father was beginning

a brute jobbed into his place of schoolmaster] 'To job' means to use one's public office or trust for private advantage, usually by advancing undeserving favourites. In 'Our Commission', Dickens says ironically, 'Job was the only article he had found in England, in a perfectly unadulterated state' (*HW* 12.26).

the Major being heavy to hoist into Mr. Dombey's carriage, elevated in mid-air, and having to stop and swear ... every time he couldn't get his foot on the step,] In the 1840s, rolling stock was set quite high above the wheels. To enter a railway carriage, passengers would step onto a narrow running-board or slender iron step and lift themselves into the car, a decidedly difficult feat for someone as heavy as the Major. Although it has been suggested that Dombey's 'chariot' is being lifted onto a railway truck, the syntax indicates that it is the Major who is hoisted 'into' a 'carriage'. Moreover, at the end of the journey, they hire a post-chaise to take them to Leamington. Had they travelled with Mr Dombey's own carriage, they would not have needed a post-chaise. Nor would such a short trip have required transporting one's personal carriage. For two divergent opinions on the carriage, see Billington, 1932, 205–08 and 1932/33, 230; and Read, 1932/33, 25–30.

He found no pleasure or relief

The very speed at which the train was whirled along,] In 1840, *Bradshaw's Guide* records the average train speed on the London and Birmingham Railway to be 27.5 miles per hour. *The London and Birmingham Railway Guide* (1839) estimates that speeds varied between 20 and 40 miles per hour (Roscoe 43). Overall, in 1840, it took less than five hours to get from London to Birmingham by rail, compared with about eleven hours by road. In 1841, eleven trains ran each day between London and

Birmingham, with the first-class fare being £1 10*s*, the third-class £1 (*A History of the County of Warwick*, vol. 7).

The power that forced itself upon its iron way – its own – defiant of all paths and roads, piercing through the heart of every obstacle,] This kind of imagery was common in the 1830s and 1840s. *The London and Birmingham Railway Guide* (1838), for instance, remarked that the train, 'the iron-hearted monster, to whom alike are desert, rock, and flowery mead, drags us along, unaffected by the poetry of Nature, and the wood-girt slope, and meandering water' (Wyld 53).

With its numerous bridges, tunnels, embankments and cuttings, the London and Birmingham line was relatively level, despite the fact that the country between the two cities consisted of 'a series of basins or low districts, separated from each other by considerable ridges of hills' (10). The *Guide* pronounced the section between the towns of Watford and Coventry (which would have constituted the vast majority of Dombey's trip), 'the very best the country would admit of, and an unobjectionable line for locomotive engines, having no rise greater than one foot in three hundred thirty, or sixteen feet per mile'. Overall, 'Thirteen miles of the Railway are laid level – fifty-two at an inclination varying from one foot to fourteen feet in a mile – and forty-seven at inclinations varying between fourteen and sixteen feet per mile. ... The longest continued length of level rails is about four miles' (Roscoe, 1839, 30, 96n).

Away, with a shriek,

a shriek, and a roar, and a rattle,] The shriek of the engine's whistle, and other noises associated with the moving train, were the cause of much complaint. In E. J. Burbury's *Florence Sackville* (1852), for instance, the narrator remarks on the engine's 'unearthly, wailing shriek', which she compares to 'nothing so much as the cry of a tortured fiend' (84). And *Chambers's Edinburgh Journal* complains that the 'profound silence' of a Sunday morning in Manchester was 'broken occasionally by the wild shriek of a locomotive, and the thundering noise of the luggage-train by which it is followed, or by the sharp ringing of iron on the pavement' ('Saturday Evening in Manchester', 13 [16 March 1850]: 167). Another problem was vibration, which was so bad on the early trains that it was thought to cause health problems, especially for firemen and engine drivers:

> In the locomotive workers these shocks express themselves as a continuous tremor in all the joints of the body that is only interrupted by sudden vertical jolts or sideways motions: this tremor is so intense and rapid that if the engine-driver or fireman were to attempt to rest his body on its bone structure in a rigid fashion by planting his feet firmly on the floor, it would be impossible for him to stand even for a short time. (*Wieck Deutsche Illustrirte Gewerbezeitung*, v. 25, Leipzig, 1860; qtd. in Schivelbusch 115)

The vibration was typically caused by the railway carriage's 'lateral swinging to the right and to the left between the rails', and by 'a rocking motion, arising partly from

[this] lateral vibration, and partly from the irregularity of the level of the rails, either side of the carriage alternatively sinking and rising, either as the relative levels of the rails change, or as the conical tires of the wheels mount upon them and descend by the lateral vibration', as well as by an 'alternate vertical shaking common to the whole body of the carriage' ('Progress of Civil Engineering', *Journal of the Franklin Institute of the State of Pennsylvania*. [May 1839]: 355).

The passage that follows anticipates 'A Flight', another detailed description of a train journey, this time from London to Paris, which Dickens wrote for *HW* a few years after the publication of *DS* (3 [30 August 1851]: 529–33).

Away ... from the town, burrowing among the dwellings of men and making the streets hum, flashing out into the meadows for a moment, mining in through the damp earth, booming on in darkness and heavy air, bursting out again into the sunny day] A passage that underscores the contemporaneity of the novel's action. Until 1844, train carriages at Euston were manually fastened to ropes in the track and pulled up the steep ascent, at about twenty miles per hour, by stationary steam-engines located 1¼ miles away, at Camden Depot. 'The train is generally drawn up this length of railway in three or four minutes, during which time the passenger passes under several very handsome stone and iron bridges and galleries'. Once the train had arrived 'at the Iron Bridge which carries the line over the Regent's Canal, the carriages are detached from the rope, and allowed to run along the line until they meet the locomotive engine by which it is afterwards propelled' (Roscoe, 1839, 42).

The train then passed 'under the bridge which carries Chalk Farm Lane over the Railway' and arrived at 'an excavation leading to Primrose-Hill Tunnel, which he enters at a depth of forty-five feet below the surface'. 'After clearing the tunnel and excavation', a contemporary guidebook remarked, 'the traveller almost universally experiences a sensation of freedom and elasticity, like to that which the pilgrim feels when he has surmounted the heights that have long engaged his toiling steps'. Overall there were seven tunnels on the line, three 'tunnel bridges' and 150 bridges (Wyld, 1838, xiii; Roscoe, 1839, 41, 44–5).

through the chalk, through the mould, through the clay, through the rock,]

> The district through which the line passes is peculiarly interesting in a geological point of view, and from the railway crossing the different strata at nearly right angles, it probably intersects a greater number of formations than any other line will do in the same distance.
>
> The strata which are crossed extend from London clay to the borders of the Coal Measures, and the various deep cuttings and tunnels show most interesting sections of each formation. They have considerable attractions for geologists, and have been numerously visited.

The London clay, which had 'a close, compact, and dry appearance', was visible at Primrose Hill Tunnel. 'At Watford, near Colne, the chalk first made its appearance underneath the plastic clay' (Roscoe, 1839, 31–2).

Through the hollow, on the

Through the hollow, on the height, by the heath, by the orchard, by the park, by the garden, over the canal, across the river, where the sheep are feeding, where the mill is going, where the barge is floating, where the dead are lying, where the factory is smoking, where the stream is running, where the village clusters, where the great cathedral rises, where the bleak moor lies,] This scene seems partly real, partly imaginative. Although the London and Birmingham Railway crossed several canals, the reference may be to the Grand Junction Canal, which the line crossed at several points and sometimes ran alongside. The 'mill' and the 'factory' suggest that the train has reached one of the many market-towns along the line, perhaps Two Waters, near Boxmoor station, about twenty-four miles from London. Immediately before arriving at Two Waters, the train crossed the river Gade and the Grand Junction Canal. Passengers would then have seen, on the right, 'the tall chimneys which appear above the copse', which would have been 'those either of the iron works, at which great quantities of iron are forged into bars, and thence carried by canal to various parts of the kingdom, or of the paper-mills, where much paper is manufactured to supply the demands of the respective wholesale stationers in the metropolis'. There are no 'great cathedrals' on this line, but Dickens may have had in mind the 'high octagonal spire' of the 'ancient Norman structure', the church 'dedicated to St. Mary', which was located in Hemel Hempstead, a nearby market-town visible in the distance on the right (the churches at St Albans and Coventry were not elevated to cathedrals until 1877 and 1918, respectively).

Breasting the wind and light,

great works and massive bridges crossing up above,] Perhaps the bridges located just west of Tring station, near the village of Pendley, and about 32 miles from London. This area contained 'one of the most stupendous cuttings to be found in this country': 'As far as the eye can range, one immense chasm through the earth appears before the observer, and at intervals are bridges carrying roads across the Railway at a fearful height' (Roscoe, 1839, 67).

mansions, rich estates,] Such as Woburn Abbey, the seat of the Duke of Bedford, in the market-town of Woburn, 41 miles from London:

> The mansion is built in a quadrangular form, having the principle front towards the west, and is of the Doric order, with a rusticated basement. ... The park, surrounded by a wall twelve miles in circumference, is well stocked with deer and game. It is beautifully diversified with hill and dale, and ornamented at the terminations of the different avenues with grottoes, Chinese temples, and ruins. (Wyld, 1838, 57)

Also along the line was Stowe Park, 'the magnificent seat of the Duke of Buckingham, and one of the finest palatial structures of which England can boast', and Whitley Hall, the seat of Lord Hood, 'a spacious stone structure', just visible 'upon a bosky eminence to the left' of the tracks (Wyld, 1838, 63, 98).

Away, with a shriek,

plunging down into the earth again, and working on in such a storm of energy and perseverance, that amidst the darkness and whirlwind the motion seems reversed, and to tend furiously backward, until a ray of light upon the wet wall shows its surface flying past like a fierce stream.] Suggestive of Kilsby Tunnel, about 75 miles from London. At 1¾ miles, it was 'the longest subterranean excavation in the course of the line' and 'one of the most extraordinary works of the present day' (Wyld, 1838, 86; Roscoe, 1839, 103). Lengthy underground tunnels were a new and disorienting experience for the first rail travellers, and were considered by many to be dark, noisy, damp and generally unhealthy, as well as vulnerable to collapse. Thomas Roscoe, the author of *The London and Birmingham Railway Guide* (1839), felt compelled to assure his readers that the directors of the London and Birmingham line, 'in order to quiet the minds of the public', had visited one of the tunnels on the line and decided 'that the apprehensions which had been expressed, that such tunnels are likely to prove detrimental to the health, and unpleasant to travellers, were perfectly futile and groundless' (98).

pausing for a minute where a crowd of faces are … sometimes lapping water greedily, and before the spout at which it drinks has ceased to drip upon the ground, shrieking, roaring, rattling through the purple distance!] Steam locomotives stopped periodically to replenish their supply of water. At Watford Station, for instance, the first 'principle' station out of London on the London and Birmingham line, 'a ten-horse steam engine … with suitable pumps and machinery' would supply the train's tender with water (a 'tender' was a specially constructed carriage that carried the fuel and water). Alternatively, the description may refer to the water pumping engine much farther along the line, at Rugby Station, 83 miles from London (Roscoe, 1839, 55, 112). 'Purple distance' was a poeticism; for example, William Mason, *The English Garden: a poem* (1772): 'e'er yet yon closing boughs / Blot out the purple distance' (3.331–2).

Louder and louder yet, it

Everything around is blackened. There are dark pools of water, muddy lanes, and miserable habitations far below. There are jagged walls and falling houses close at hand, and through the battered roofs and broken windows, wretched rooms are seen, where want and fever hide themselves in many wretched shapes, while smoke, and crowded gables, and distorted chimneys, and deformity of brick and mortar penning up deformity of mind and body, choke the murky

distance.] Rail travellers heading to Leamington Spa from London would have typically disembarked at Coventry Station, which is 94 miles from London and only eight miles from Leamington (whereas Birmingham is eighteen miles farther along the line, and more than twenty miles from Leamington). However, the imagery here, and the phrasing (e.g. the fact that the town is described as the 'goal of the line'), would strongly suggest that Dickens is thinking of Birmingham.

The London and Birmingham Railway Guide (1838) describes what travellers would have seen as they entered Birmingham:

> Through the arch of this bridge ['a massive viaduct'] we obtain our first glimpse of "the great forge of Europe," imperfectly discernable through the murky vapours in which it is constantly enshrouded. Having passed beneath the aforesaid arch, we enter on an elevated embankment, from which, as we run merrily onwards to our destination, is seen, more comprehensively and perfectly the *Vul*canic [*sic*] city, rising on the hills before us, with its thousand Cyclopean furnaces, sending up their dingy fumes,
>
> "To furrow heaven's gloom with blackening frowns,
> And seare with gloom the smiling god of day." (Wyld 154–5)

Osborne's London & Birmingham Guide (1840) furnishes more details:

> To the left, the suburban gardens of the industrious artizans may be seen by the canal side, and a little closer to the town, are some of those rusty looking buildings called manufactories, which constitute a portion of the machinery for the production of hardwares. From the end of the embankment, the line is carried on a series of splendid arches over the [River] Tame and Lawley-street, and the traveller in the train can look down upon the house-tops from this elevated viaduct, at the end of which is a small embankment, and then a bridge over the canal, across which the London and Birmingham and Grand Junction lines run side by side, and then curving away from each other, enter their separate stations. We now pass the Engine House, a large sixteen-sided building, on the left, and after sundry joltings, resulting from the crossing of different lines of rails, enter beneath the spacious shedding of the Birmingham Terminus, and stop at the Arrival Parade, which is on our left side, and from which there are numerous conveyances to all parts of the town. (196–7)

In the eighteenth century, Birmingham established itself as the commercial focus of the Midlands and the leading metal manufacturing centre in Great Britain. By the 1840s, it had also become 'a grand centre of railway communication' with four distinct railway lines arriving in the city by the Rea valley (several more opened in the 1850s and after), and with the two terminal stations, at Curzon Street and Lawley Street, in close proximity. Its train station for the London line (which opened on 17 September 1838) was situated at the northeastern end of the town, '250 feet above the level of the London terminus', and 'adjoining the station of the

Liverpool Line' (Lewis, *A Topographical Dictionary*, 1848). Although in the 1840s the town had 'few large factories', there were 'a vast number of workshops, more or less extensive, in each of which portions of the work are done'. These required a large number of steam engines that consumed an enormous amount of coal, leaving much of the country black with soot (240 tons of coal were consumed per day in 1839, 380 in 1849) (Knight, 1866, 1.1109). In 1807, Robert Southey, writing as 'Espriella', characterized the 'filth' of Birmingham as 'active and moving, a living principle of mischief, which fills the whole atmosphere and penetrates every where, spotting and staining every thing, and getting into the pores and nostrils. I feel as if my throat wanted sweeping like an English chimney' (*Letters from England* 71). In 1835, Alexis de Tocqueville designated Birmingham 'an immense workshop, a huge forge, a vast shop. ... One might be down a mine in the New World. Everything is black, dirty and obscure, although every instant it is winning silver and gold' (*Journeys to England and Ireland* 94).

Just before he arrived at the Birmingham terminus, a rail passenger from London would have noted 'a black sluggish stream, which is the river Rea, made the receptacle of the sewers of the town'. The 'filthy condition of the river near the railway station', a Committee of Physicians and Surgeons noted, 'is a subject of constant and merited animadversions, and ... requires especial attention lest it should become a source of disease'. This same committee found the major streets to be 'well drained', though remarking that this was 'far from the case with respect to many of the inferior streets, and to many, or rather most, of the courts, which, especially in the old parts of the town, are dirty and neglected, with water stagnating in them' (*Report ... into the Sanitary Condition of the Labouring Population of Great Britain*, 1842, 305–06, 332).

Because of a rapid increase in population in the early nineteenth century (from 71,000 in 1801 to 233,000 in 1851), about two-thirds of the working-class houses in Birmingham (by 1850) had been built in the low-cost 'back to back' style (i.e. terraces of houses with two houses sharing a back wall). Although in some ways an improvement over earlier forms of working-class accommodation, 'back to back' houses had doors and windows only at the front (because three of their four walls were shared with other houses), so they had little light, ventilation or privacy, and were crowded together in densely populated areas (Burnett, 1986, 73–4). In 1835, *The History of Birmingham* remarked on the inferior quality of housing in Birmingham, and of the tendency of housing to collapse: 'One would think, if a man can survive a house, he has no great reason to complain of the shortness of life' (Hutton 78–9).

The descriptions here, and in chapter 27, are doubtless informed by Dickens's trip through the area during the last few days of October 1838. On 29 October, Dickens and Hablot Browne travelled by coach to Leamington, where they stayed at Copp's Hotel. The next day, they went to Kenilworth Castle by post-chaise, and then visited Warwick Castle and thence to Stratford, where they spent the night. On 31 October, they moved on to Shrewsbury 'by way of Birmingham and Wolverhampton, starting at eight o'Clock through a cold wet fog, and travelling when the day had cleared up, through miles of cinder-paths and blazing furnaces and roaring steam engines, and such a mass of dirt gloom and misery as I never before witnessed' (*Letters* 1.447–8). It is this trip through Birmingham and its environs that Dickens drew on in *The Old*

Curiosity Shop (ch. 44–5), as he told Forster: 'You will recognize a description of the road we travelled between Birmingham and Wolverhampton' (*Letters* 2.131–2).

The Major, who had been blowing

the post-horses had been harnessed and the carriage ready.]

> Conveyances ... of all kinds, from the truck to the fly and omnibus, will be found outside the gates of the [Birmingham] station, to convey luggage and passengers to various parts of the town. (Wyld, 1838, 155)

Travellers in a hurry often hired post-chaises, light four-wheeled carriages pulled by a team of horses. Two passengers could travel inside and two more outside on the 'dicky' at the back. A post-boy rode astride one of the horses. Post-chaise travel was more expensive because the passenger personally contracted for it and because relays of horses were used for speed. The mention of the 'post-horses' would seem to provide further evidence that Mr Dombey does not convey his 'chariot' on the train. A chariot is a light four-wheeled carriage with only back seats, and with a coach-box, distinguishing it from a post-chaise. It was driven by a coachman on a box and not by a postilion. There is also no evidence, when Mr Dombey and Major Bagstock arrive in Leamington, and when they tour Warwick and Kenilworth, that they are using Mr Dombey's chariot.

In this flow of spirits

his usual plethoric symptoms,]   See note on apoplexy above, p. 238.

the Royal Hotel,] Copp's Royal Hotel in Leamington Spa opened in June 1827, on the south side of the High Street between Court Street and Clemens Street (Plate 12, p. 249). *Fairfax's New Guide and Directory to Leamington Spa and its Environs* (1835), described the hotel as an 'elegant structure, which in taste and magnificence surpasses every other public edifice in Leamington'. The front of the hotel, which extended to 111 feet and had a striking entrance, was 'cased in Roman cement, and of the Grecian style of architecture'. Copp's Hotel had many private apartments in addition to its public rooms, along with more than 100 'bed chambers, fitted up with every attention to comfort and convenience', and was generally thronged with visitors, including 'first families among the nobility and gentry'. The hotel was officially declared bankrupt in 1841, changed hands several times, and was demolished in 1847 (*Fairfax's New Guide and Directory*, 52–3; Homer, 1991).

Dickens and Browne stayed the night at Copp's Royal Hotel on 29 October 1838, on Dickens's first visit to Leamington, and next day took a coach to Kenilworth Castle (the two were en route for Birmingham to investigate the working conditions of children employed in cotton mills in Manchester). Dickens called the Royal Hotel

Chapter 20 *Mr Dombey goes upon a Journey*

12   Copp's Royal Hotel, Leamington Spa. Lithograph by W. Rider, 1830

13   Guy's Tower, Warwick Castle. From *Curiosities of Great Britain: England & Wales Delineated, c.* 1845

an 'Excellent Inn' in his Diary (*Letters* 1.634), and wrote his wife, 'We found a roaring fire, and elegant dinner, a snug room, and capital beds all ready for us at Leamington after a very agreeable (but *very* cold) ride' (*Letters* 1.447).

He not only arose next morning

like a giant refreshed,] 'So the Lord awaked as one out of sleep: and like a giant refreshed with wine' (*BCP*, 'The Psalter', Psalm 78:66).

Mr. Dombey would prefer remaining in his own room, or walking in the country by himself, on that first day of their sojourn at Leamington; but next morning he would be happy to accompany the Major to the Pump-room, and about the town.] Located 98 miles northwest of London, Leamington was an 'unnoticed village' until the end of the eighteenth century, when its springs began to attract national attention. By the 1830s, its population had grown from 315 (in 1801) to more than 6000, and its reputation as a health resort had become well established. To meet the growing influx of visitors, eight major hotels were built, including Copp's Royal Hotel and three boarding houses. Leamington was renowned for its wells, having a total of eleven, each offering mineral waters. There were also seven baths, with the 'main attraction' being the Royal Pump Room and Baths, a 'most splendid pump room and suite of baths' erected in 1813 at the cost of £25,000. 'This elegant edifice, one of the most admired objects in the town, consists of a central mass, extending one hundred and six feet in length, and rising to the height of thirty feet'. The building had two wings, each thirty feet long and was surrounded on three sides 'by a spacious colonnade, formed by duplicated pillars of the Doric order'. Fairfax judged it 'the most complete and magnificent structure, of the kind, in the kingdom'. Patrons took the waters and promenaded in the Pump Room from 7 to 10 in the morning. In the immediate neighbourhood, there were 'many inviting paths and agreeable walks, suitable for the invalid or the pedestrian'. Although the Royal Pump Room and Baths was profitable in its early years, by the late 1840s the fashion for 'taking the waters' had begun to wane. In 1862, a new company bought the spa building and carried out extensive renovations (Fairfax, 1835, 9, 28–9, 89; 'History of Royal Leamington Spa').

An anonymous writer described the attractions of Leamington Spa in a letter to the Editor, published on 20 February 1847 in the *Royal Leamington Spa Courier and Warwickshire Standard*:

> The chief attractions of Leamington have always appeared to me to consist in the beauty and architectural ornaments of the streets, the capacity and cleanliness of the streets themselves, and their ample accommodation for the large and increasing traffic. ... During a great portion of the year, Leamington is the resort, not of the gay and frivolous, not of the hunter or the steeple chaser, but of the ailing, the weak, the old, who resort hitherto to recruit their tottering health, by the aid of those waters Nature has so lavishly bestowed

upon the Spa. (qtd. in Homer, 1991, 23)

Dickens made at least three visits to Leamington. He stayed overnight with Browne in 1838 (see above), and returned on 2 November 1858 to give two public readings at the Music Hall. He noted of his reception, 'Little Leamington came out in the most amazing manner yesterday. We took £130, and turned away hundreds upon hundreds of people. They are represented as the dullest and worst of audiences. I found them very good indeed – even in the morning'. His last reading in Leamington, again at the Music Hall, was on 1 January 1862. On 15 March 1847, while he was working on *DS*, Dickens proposed that he and Browne pay a visit to Leamington, though there is no record that they ever made the trip, and in May 1848 contemplated putting on one of his private theatricals in the town, though he finally decided against it (*Letters* 8.693; Dexter, 1928, 179; *Letters* 5.34, 5.314).

The Major ... swaggered up and down through all the public places: looking into subscription books to find out who was there,] Subscription books listed the names of contributors and the amount each had donated to the town's several libraries, reading rooms, galleries, meeting places for scientific and literary matters and other 'fashionable and inviting places of resort', with which Leamington was well endowed (*Moncrieff's Guide to Leamington Spa, and its Vicinity*, 1833, 49). Looking through subscription books to find out 'who was there', was a common practice at health resorts. In *Humphry Clinker* (1771), Matthew Bramble 'consulted the subscription-book' in Bath, finding 'the names of several old friends' ('Bath, May 5').

It was surprising how much

Mr Dombey ... who had rarely, at any time, overstepped the enchanted circle within which the operations of Dombey and Son were conducted,] The magic circle is part of magical lore: the possessed person was often guarded from the attack of fiends by being placed in the middle of an enchanted circle, through which no spirit could supposedly break. The circle was thought to be about nine feet in diameter and was usually formed at midnight 'in the midst of some dark forest, churchyard, vault, or other lonely and dismal spot'. 'Without the protection of this circle, the magician, it was believed, would have been carried off by the spirits' (*Chambers's Encyclopædia*, 1883, 3.42). A well known example of the magic circle is from the climax of *The Tempest*, where Prospero persuades the king and his followers to enter the magic circle which he has made, and where they stand charmed:

> Here enters ARIEL *before;* then ALONSO, *with a frantic gesture, attended by* GONZALO; SEBASTIAN *and* ANTONIO *in like manner, attended by* ADRIAN *and* FRANCISCO. *They all enter the circle which* PROSPERO *had made, and there stand charm'd; which* PROSPERO *observing, speaks.* (Act 5, Scene 1)

In *DC,* David, thinking of Dora Spenlow, imagines that 'some grim enchanter had drawn a magic circle round the innocent goddess of my heart' (ch. 38).

Chapter 21

NEW FACES

In this manner the Major

the Major and Mr. Dombey were walking arm-in-arm ... when they beheld advancing towards them, a wheeled chair, in which a lady was seated, indolently steering her carriage by a kind of rudder in front,] In order to help Browne illustrate this passage, Dickens first provided him with a summary of the plot, which included characterizations of several of his protagonists and a detailed description of the illustration, 'Major Bagstock is delighted to have the opportunity':

> The first subject which I am now going to give, is very important to the book. *I should like to see your sketch of it, if possible.*
> I should premise that I want to make the Major, who is the incarnation of selfishness and small revenge, a kind of comic Mephistophelean power in the book; and the No. begins with the departure of Mr Dombey and the Major on that trip for change of air and scene, which is prepared for in the last Number. They go to Leamington, where you and I were once. In the Library, the Major introduces Mr. Dombey to a certain lady, whom, as I wish to foreshadow, dimly, said Dombey may come to marry in due season. She is about thirty – not a day more – handsome, though haughty-looking – good figure – well dressed – showy – and desirable. Quite a lady in appearance, with some of a proud indifference about her, suggestive of a spark of the Devil within. Was married young. Husband dead. Goes about with an old mother who rouges, and who lives upon the reputation of a diamond necklace and her family. – Wants a husband. Flies at none but high game, and couldn't marry anybody not rich – Mother affects cordiality and heart, and is the essence of sordid calculation – Mother usually shoved about in a Bath chair by a Page who has rather outgrown and out-shoved his strength, and who butts at it behind, like a Ram, while his mistress steers herself languidly by a handle in front – Nothing the matter with her to prevent her walking, only was once sketched (when a Beauty) reclining in a Barouche, and having outlived the beauty and the barouche too, still holds on to the attitude, as becoming her uncommonly. Mother is in the machine, in the Sketch. Daughter has parasol.
> The Major presents them to Mr. Dombey, gloating within himself over

what may come of it, and over the discomfiture of Miss Tox. Mr. Dombey (in deep mourning) bows solemnly. Daughter bends. The Native in attendance, bearing a camp-stool and the Major's great coat. Native evidently afraid of the Major and his thick cane. If you like it better, the scene may be in the street or in a green lane. But a great deal will come of it: and I want the Major to express that, as much as possible in his apoplectico-Mephistophelean observation of the scene, and in his share in it. (*Letters* 5.34–5)

After reviewing Browne's preliminary sketch of the scene (apparently not extant), Dickens asked that, if possible, the Major be depicted as 'older, and with a larger face' and insisted that the

> Native – who is so prodigiously good as he is – must be in European Costume. He may wear ear-rings, and look outlandish, and be dark brown, but his fashion must be of Moses, Mosesy – I don't mean old testament Moses, but him of the Minories [a reference to E. Moses & Son, tailors, of 154–7 Minories]. (*Letters* 5.35)

As Dickens indicates, Mrs Skewton is sitting in a Bath chair, an early version of the wheel-chair invented by James Heath of Bath around 1750. Designed to convey invalids to the Pump Room or to bathe in the Roman Baths, bath chairs gained in popularity and by 1830 had replaced the sedan chair as the usual mode of hired transport in Bath.

she was very blooming in the face – quite rosy –] Cosmetics, including rouge and a heavy white face-paint, 'were in plenty' until very early in the nineteenth century, according to the journalist Cyrus Redding (3.349–50). By the mid-century, however, they were pronounced 'almost out of fashion' as well as morally compromising and harmful to the skin. 'Genuine *Eau de Cologne* and *pâte d'amande,* are the only cosmetics young ladies should use; rouge may be suitable for actresses, but not for modest females in private life' (Webster, 1855, 1014; Bureaud-Riofrey 305). *The Cornhill Magazine* lamented the fact that, despite such warnings,

> Old men and women, who would resist the irresistible *fact* of age, will never be brought to acknowledge the *beauty* of age; they want another beauty; they cling to the remembrance of departed charms. If the rouge-pot and the hair-dresser can help them to dead *simulacra* of those charms, they are welcomed; and although they keenly see through the like pretences in others, they cannot be argued out of the wisdom of employing such pretences themselves. ('Aids to Beauty, Real and Artificial', 1863, 7.392)

When women did use rouge, they were supposed to use it with discretion. In Robert Smith Surtees' novel *Mr Romford's Hounds* (1865), for instance, Miss Hazey applies only 'the slightest touch of rouge' to remove her pallor upon awakening (ch. 44, 218). *The Cornhill Magazine* noted, 'Both rouge and pearl-powder are much oftener used in drawing-rooms than is suspected – rouge is even used by men – but the moderation with which they are employed causes them to escape general notice' (1863; 7.393).

The 'several kinds of rouge' were all 'composed of some vegetable colour, and talc, or powdered French chalk', though the most common variety derived 'from the colouring matter of the safflower' (Webster, 1855, 1014).

The Major no sooner heard

butting at the carriage with his head to urge it forward, as is sometimes done by elephants in Oriental countries.]

> The elephant ... can push along a very heavy weight, or break through a strong paling, by the dead pressure of its snout. Where tame elephants are used, this property is often turned to account; and those elephants which are in the service of Indian merchants, may often be seen doing the work of a dozen of porters, in pushing about bales and boxes, and rolling heavy casks. (*The British Cyclopædia of the Arts, Sciences ...*, 1838, 7.399)

Britain had established hegemony throughout almost the entire Indian subcontinent by the early nineteenth century, which meant that descriptions of India and its animals were pervasive in British culture by the 1840s.

"And can you be a day,

settling her false curls and false eyebrows with her fan, and showing her false teeth, set off by her false complexion,] *The Cornhill Magazine* complained in 1863 that, in addition to cosmetics, ageing men and women resorted to false hair such as wigs, toupees and hair pieces; false eyebrows; and belladona, which was used to artificially 'brighten' eyes ('Aids to Beauty, Real and Artificial', 7.393–7).

Such 'artificial aids', the magazine explained,

> are open to the twofold objection of *not* successfully effecting their purpose, and by this failure producing moral disgust. We see through the pretence, resent the fiction, and despise the vanity. The man or woman whom we should simply not have admired becomes an object of ridicule or contempt. Painfully is this forced upon us in the too common attempt to disguise age, and to dress old mutton like spring lamb. No one is deceived for a moment, and the reaction of disgust endures. (7.392)

Other writers agreed. Mrs Amelia Opie, for instance, included 'false hair, false bloom, false eyebrows, and other artificial aids to the appearance' as representative of 'Illustrations of Lying' (1843; 3.495), and Thomas Hood complained that false friends were 'as common ... as false hair, false eyebrows, and false teeth' (*The Comic*

Annual for 1842, 133). Mr Carker's false teeth are also relevant in this respect (see the note to chapter 13, p. 185). This is the first of two times in the novel that Mrs Skewton fixes her false eyebrows (see note to chapter 26 and note on p. 303).

"in the Garden] A sign reading 'To the Pump Room' in Browne's illustration suggests that this meeting occurs close to the Royal Pump Room and Baths, whose proprietors had 'laid out several acres of land in beautiful and spacious walks and shrubberies, enclosed in the front by iron pallisading on one side by a strong fence, on the opposite side by the river' (Fairfax 30). For Pump Room, see note to chapter 20, p. 250.

The discrepancy between Mrs. Skewton's

a barouche,] A stylish carriage since the late eighteenth century, a barouche had a half-hood behind that could be raised or lowered, a seat in front for the driver and seats inside for two couples to sit facing each other. It usually had four wheels and was pulled by four horses in pairs. In 1837, William Bridges Adams noted that the barouche was 'formerly a very fashionable carriage for the summer season, though little adapted for winter, or for travelling purposes. Of late years Britzschkas have taken the place of Barouches' (*English Pleasure Carriages* 227–8).

a then fashionable artist who had appended to his published sketch the name of Cleopatra in consequence of a discovery made by the critics of the time, that it bore an exact resemblance to that Princess as she reclined on board her galley.] An allusion to Enobarbus's description of Cleopatra:

> The barge she sat in, like a burnish'd throne,
> Burn'd on the water. The poop was beaten gold.
> … For her own person,
> It beggar'd all description. She did lie
> In her pavilion, cloth-of-gold, of tissue,
> O'erpicturing that Venus where we see
> The fancy out-work nature. On each side her
> Stood pretty dimpled boys, like smiling Cupids,
> With divers-colour'd fans, whose wind did seem
> To glow the delicate cheeks which they did cool,
> And what they undid did. (2.2.195–209)

'Fashionable' eighteenth-century portrait painters, such as Reynolds, Romney and Gainsborough, often painted society ladies dressed as idealized mythical, classical, historical or literary heroines, and the paintings were engraved in large numbers for popular distribution. Early Victorian images of Cleopatra, such as Kenny Meadows's engraving from 1839, typically portray her seductively posed. The Victorian view of Cleopatra as a dangerous flirt, threatening to men, is embodied in Tennyson's lines from *Maud*: 'She meant to weave me a snare / of some coquettish deceit, Cleopatra-like' (1.215–16).

Shakespeare's *Antony and Cleopatra*, based on the final part of Plutarch's life of Marcus Antonius, was not very popular in the nineteenth century. J. P. Kemble's acting version of the play in 1813, which incorporated passages from John Dryden's *All for Love* (Dryden's treatment of *Antony and Cleopatra*), and William C. Macready's version in 1833 were notable failures. Samuel Phelps produced an abbreviated version of the play at Sadler's Wells in 1849, though this too was commercially unsuccessful (Wells, 1998; Dobson and Wells, 2001).

Dickens may have made the decision to compare Mrs Skewton and Shakespeare's Cleopatra at the last minute. He neither mentions Cleopatra in his number plans nor in his detailed instructions to Browne for the illustration that accompanies her introduction (Gager, 1996, 204; 'Shakespeare's Unruly Women', Georgianna Ziegler *et al.* Exhibition Catalogue. Folger Shakespeare Library, 1997).

"*No, we have been to*

To Harrowgate and Scarborough, and into Devonshire.] The fashionable spa towns of Harrowgate (now Harrogate) and Scarborough would have appealed to someone with Mrs Skewton's pretensions. In the early nineteenth century, Harrogate was one of the major watering-places in England. Located 200 miles from London in north Yorkshire, Harrogate had a population of 4,785 in 1841. Hotels and lodgings were abundant, and there was a theatre, promenade-rooms, news-rooms, billiard-rooms and ball-rooms. The railway reached Harrogate in 1848 and Scarborough, just to the east on the north Yorkshire coast, in 1845. *The Penny Cyclopædia* described the overall appeal of the genteel seaside resort in 1841:

> Scarborough combines the advantages of sea-bathing and of mineral baths, and owes to these natural advantages its past celebrity and present prosperous condition. Its neighbourhood presents a course of the finest sands in England, undulating into a variety of beautiful bays, and sheltered by lofty cliffs and bold projecting headlines. Its own bay is spacious and open to the sea, and the water pure and transparent. (21.12)

Just as Dickens was writing *DS*, the South Devon Railway Company was making the rural county of Devon (then widely but incorrectly called Devonshire), in the southwest, accessible to tourism. Between May 1846 and June 1847, the first sections of the line were opened between Exeter, Teignmouth, Newton Abbot and Totnes. The railway and its celebrated engineer, Isambard Kingdom Brunel, were much in the news during this time (e.g. *Times* 13 October 1846, 5; 31 October 1846, 6; 28 January 1847, 5). John Murray's *Handbook for Travellers in Devon and Cornwall* (1851; 6th ed revised, 1865) describes Devon's notable geology and antiquities and considers it 'preeminently the beauty of the western counties':

> The lanes are steep and narrow, and bordered by tangled hedges. ... In the deep

shadowy combes the villages lie nestled, with roseate walls of clay and roofs of thatch, and seldom far from one of those crystal streams which enliven every valley of this rocky county. ... For those who relish less cultivated scenes, Dartmoor presents a waste of rock-capped heights and dark morasses, most truly forlorn and wild. But the tints of the moor are of surpassing beauty, the air most exhilarating, and the grandeur of its lonely hills calculated to impress the most apathetic tourist. (xlvi)

"My Dearest Edith," returned Mrs. Skewton,

Nature intended me for an Arcadian.] In classical and Renaissance legends, Arcadia (a remote mountainous region of Greece) was associated with the wholesome, simple life of its shepherds and shepherdesses. The rustic area served as the location of Sir Philip Sydney's pastoral romance, The *Arcadia* (*c.*1583–4; 1590). Dickens uses Mrs Skewton to parody the contemporary fad for pastoralism, much as he uses Mrs Merdle in *LD* (who is 'pastoral to a degree, by nature', 1.33). Pastoral writing originated with the *Idylls* of Theocritus (*c.* 270 BC), describing rural life in his native Sicily, and with the *Eclogues* of Virgil (70–19 BC), set in an imaginary Arcadia. Neglected during the Middle Ages, pastorals were revived during the Renaissance by Petrarch and his imitators and were especially popular in the sixteenth and early seventeenth centuries with dramatists (Tasso, Guarini, Fletcher) and writers of prose romances (Cervantes, Sidney, Sannazar). Alexander Pope, inspired by Virgil's *Eclogues*, was one of the last true pastoralists (see his two collections of pastorals, 1704 and 1708). Later writers burlesqued the pastoral (Gay, *Shepherd's Week*, 1714) or made it more realistic (Wordsworth, 'Michael', 1800), though pastoral language, with its talk of 'swains' and 'shepherds' continued to find its way into popular verse and song.

Dickens frequently mocks pastoralism in *LD*: e.g. the narrator ironically characterizes the sewers and wells of London as 'Arcadian objects' (1.3), young John Chivery is 'a young Swain' who imagines 'pastoral domestic happiness' with Little Dorrit (1.18) and who likes to sit in his 'groves' of drying linen (1.22); Old Mr Nandy sings 'pale and vapid little songs, long out of date, about Chloe, and Phyllis, and Strephon' (1.31); and, in the ultimate comic deflation of the pastoral ideal, one wall of the Plornishes' shop-parlour has been 'poetically heightened' to represent a thatched cottage, with sun-flowers and holly-hocks and a 'faithful dog' and 'a pigeon-house enveloped in a cloud of pigeons'. See also 'Arcadian London', *AYR*, 29 September 1860.

Cows are my passion. What I have ever sighed for, has been to retreat to a Swiss farm, and live entirely surrounded by cows – and china.] She wishes to imitate Marie Antoinette, who sought to escape the formality of the Court of Versailles by living at the model farm, which included a dairy, mill and dovecote, constructed for her in the 1780s. These were part of an ersatz peasant *hameau* at le Petit Trianon in the grounds of Versailles that had been inspired by other artificially rustic hamlets being built by the French aristocracy. Dressed as shepherdesses and milkmaids and using milkpails of Sèvres porcelain, the queen and her ladies milked carefully washed cows that had been chosen for their gentle temperaments. From the 1770s, the gardens surrounding *Le Hameau* were transformed from classical, geometric designs into a natural-looking landscape, influenced by Rousseau's cult of natural simplicity and the growing taste for romantic and picturesque scenery. Mrs Skewton's mention of 'china' alludes to Marie Antoinette's huge collection of Sèvres porcelain. Continuing a tradition of royal patronage established by Louis XV, the queen patronized the Sèvres factory, and its records show that two months' work was required to produce just one plate for one of the many services she commissioned.

This curious association of objects,

suggesting a remembrance of the celebrated bull who got by mistake into a crockery shop,] The phrase, 'a bull in a china shop', seems to derive from a pantomime and a comic song (*London Review and Literary Journal*, 1812, 61.53; *Theatrical Inquisitor and Monthly Mirror*, 1817, 10.345). 'The extraordinary spectacle of a *Bull in a China Shop*, afforded great entertainment' in a pantomime at the Lyceum Theatre on 23 December 1811, and in 1817, the famous actor John Kemble, playing a clown, 'encored his song of the "Bull in a China-shop" ':

> A bull who got into a china-shop.
> … With his right leg, left leg, upper leg, under leg …
> He popp'd in by chance at the china-shop door,
> Where they very soon found that the bull was a bore;
> The shopman to drive him out tried with much care,
> The floor being covered with crockery-ware;
> And among it, resenting the shopman's taunt,
> The bull began dancing the cow's carrant.
> … With his right leg, left leg, &c.
> (lines 6–15, cited in *Universal Songster*, 1825, 88)

"Stop a moment, Withers!"

calling … with all the languid dignity with which she had called in days of yore to a coachman with a wig, cauliflower nosegay, and silk stockings.] This was the livery of a coachman in the late eighteenth century and Regency periods. The floral nosegay was worn in the lapel. Wilkie Collins expresses nostalgia for the costume in 'The Last Stage-Coachman':

> The Last Stage-Coachman! It falls upon the ear of every one but a shareholder in railways with a boding, melancholy sound. In spite of our natural reverence for the wonders of science, our hearts grow heavy at the thought of never again beholding the sweet-smelling nosegay, the unimpeachable top-boots

and fair white breeches, once so prominent as the uniform of the fraternity. (*The Illuminated Magazine*, May 1843, 1.209)

"Genteel, Sir," said the Major,

"The Honourable Mrs. Skewton ... is sister to the late Lord Feenix, and aunt to the present Lord. The family are not wealthy – they're poor, indeed – and she lives upon a small jointure;] The courtesy prefix 'The Honourable' (usually abbreviated 'The Hon.') indicates that she is the daughter of a viscount or baron. Because her husband was a commoner, she retains the title after marriage. A 'jointure' is a provision made by the husband before the marriage to support his wife after his death. Among other conditions, a jointure was required to begin immediately on the husband's death; to extend for the duration of the wife's life; and to be given to the wife herself and not to trustees acting for her. 'The mode of giving a jointure is usually by way of a rent-charge on the husband's real estate, the effect of which is to allow her to remain in possession of the estate, or part of it, after the husband's death, so long as she lives' (*Chambers's Encyclopædia*, 1883, 5.737).

"Was there any family?"

"Was there any family?" ... "Yes, Sir, ... There was a boy." Mr. Dombey's eyes sought the ground, and a shade came over his face. "Who was drowned, Sir," ... "Indeed?" said Mr. Dombey, raising his head.] Mr Dombey's gloom on learning of Edith's son suggests that he has already considered marrying her and realizes that their marriage would result in his stepson having a possible claim on his estate when he dies. News of the son's death enables Dombey to continue contemplating marriage.

The Honourable Mrs. Skewton

lodgings that were fashionable enough and dear enough,] *Fairfax's New Guide and Directory to Leamington-Spa and its Environs* (1835) lists 43 lodging-house keepers. In this list are included 'the names of those persons only whose houses are devoted exclusively for the accommodation of Visitors; and not the names of respectable Tradesmen, a portion of whose houses are generally appropriate for the same purpose' (167).

a neighbouring milk-shop ... a shed belonging to the same dairy] Milk-shops or dairies in towns and cities distributed fresh milk delivered to them twice a day by large dairies on the outskirts and, from the 1840s, by railway (Dodd, *The Food of London*, 1856, 268–97). A *HW* article on the provision of fresh milk in London describes several unscrupulous practices: shops frequently adulterated milk with water from the pump, and many shops were supplied with milk from cows kept 'in dark, damp dens. ... Other cow-keepers have sets of cellars, and other underground places; others pack them in yards, dirty lanes, or any holes and corners, and often in company with swine'. But this was not the practice of a dairyman who kept a 'neat little shop' near High Holborn and boasted: ' "My cow-keeper's cows don't live in such places ... they live in proper sheds, with plenty of air, good drainage, and lots to eat" '. This dairyman employed Welsh girls to distribute his milk from his shop:

> This shop, or dairy, had a low-fronted window, in which were seen several tin cans, ranged round a small slanting board, whereon appeared the portrait of a red and white cow, between whose legs and the window glass was thrust a little basket, containing five eggs and a cobweb. (9 November 1850, 2.145)

the stone of that young Sisyphus,] A symbol of futility from Greek mythology, Sisyphus was reputed to be the craftiest of men and was punished for his misdeeds by endless labour in the underworld. He was forced to roll a stone to the top of a hill, only for it to roll back down; he then had to begin again.

donkey-cart,] A two-wheeled vehicle of a lighter, more elegant make, with springs, drawn by a single horse.

Mr. Dombey and the Major

Mrs. Skewton arranged, as Cleopatra, among the cushions of a sofa: very airily dressed: and certainly not resembling Shakespeare's Cleopatra, whom age could not wither.] Another allusion to the description by Enobarbus (see above), including his further praise: 'Age cannot wither her, nor custom stale / Her infinite variety' (2.2.239–40).

"Devil a bit, Ma'am,"

tough and blunt old Joes ... plain red herrings with hard roes,] Red herrings are herrings which have been smoked (and which can thus be dry and tough). Mrs Beeton gives a recipe for red herrings and hard roe:

> The best way to cook these is to make incisions in the skin across the fish, because they do not then require to be so long on the fire, and will be far better than when cut open. The hard roe makes a nice relish by pounding it in a mortar, with a little anchovy, and spreading it on toast. If very dry, soak in warm water 1 hour before dressing. (recipe 267)

"The man has no sensitiveness,"

Without that gleam of sunshine on our cold cold earth," said Mrs. Skewton,] 'Cold earth' had become a poetical cliché by this time. It occurs frequently in Spenser's *The Faerie Queene* (1590, 1596), for example, 'The cold earth was his couch' (bk 3, st. 53), and appears in eighteenth-century drama: Nicholas Rowe's *The Tragedy of Jane Shore* (1714): 'Receive me, thou cold earth' (line 259). 'Cold earth' is also common in the Romantic poets – e.g. Wordsworth, 'On the Power of Sound' (1835): 'The little sprinkling of cold earth that fell' (10.156), Shelley, 'Lines' (1823): 'The cold earth slept below' (1), Byron, *The Prisoner of Chillon* (1816): 'And scoop'd for him a shallow grave / Even from the cold earth of our cave' (150–1).

her lace tucker,] A narrow strip of lace, often quite straight, worn around the top of the bodice from the seventeenth century to the early nineteenth century. It was often added to fill in a low décolletage during the day.

"My dearest Edith rallies me,

shaking her head: which shook a little of itself sometimes, as if the palsy twinkled now and then] Her tremors, along with her paralysis, 'indistinctness in her speech' and temporary memory loss (in chapter 37), suggest that Mrs Skewton is suffering from the neurological disease first described by James Parkinson in *Essay on the Shaking Palsy* (1817). 'So slight and nearly imperceptible are the first inroads of this malady, and so extremely slow its progress', he wrote, 'that it rarely happens, that the patient can form any recollection of the precise period of its commencement'. Parkinson placed the greatest emphasis in his essay on *paralysis agitans* or the *shaking palsy*:

> The first symptoms perceived are, a slight sense of weakness, with a proneness to trembling in some particular part; sometimes in the head, but most commonly in one of the hands and arms. These symptoms gradually increase in the part first affected; and at an uncertain period, but seldom in less than twelvemonths or more, the morbid influence is felt in some other part. Thus assuming one of the hands and arms to be first attacked, the other, at this period becomes similarly affected. After a few more months the patient is found to be less strict than usual in preserving an upright posture: this being most observable whilst walking, but sometimes whilst sitting or standing. Sometime after the appearance of this symptom, and during its slow increase, one of the legs is discovered slightly to tremble, and is also found to suffer fatigue sooner than the leg of the other side: and in a few months this limb becomes agitated by similar tremblings, and suffers a similar loss of power. (3–4)

For more on 'the shaking palsy', see note to chapter 37, p. 382–3.

"You have almost reason

a variety of landscape drawings, of which he had already recognized several as representing neighbouring points of view,] Drawing was 'one of the first accomplishments in the world', according to J. W. Alston's *Hints on Landscape Painting* (1804; qtd. in Lichten 203). Students of drawing, who canvassed the British Isles for romantic locales that represented the picturesque ideal, began by imitating picturesque prints, or learned from textbooks or drawing masters. They would frequently practise stylized 'touches', artistic exercises based on prescribed hand movements. There were specific 'touches' for each species of tree, for instance, which give a decorative quality to many early nineteenth century amateur landscapes. Especially influential with amateur artists in the 1830s were the drawing manuals and collections of views of Samuel Prout (1783–1852) and J. D. Harding (1798–1863). Such artists favoured landscapes, coastal scenes, cottages, castles and moss-covered ruins though, inevitably, they excluded anything ugly or unpleasant from the representation (Lichten, 1950, 201–08). For the picturesque, see note to chapter 27, pp. 308–9.

"And you play, I already know."

"And you play ... And sing? ... You have many resources against weariness at least,"] Although such accomplishments – together with drawing, dancing, conversation and deportment – had been traditionally considered desirable in ladies, by the first half of the nineteenth century advice on women's education was criticizing the acquisition of such skills and urging instead the importance of developing the intellect. This was the opinion of *The Mother the Best Governess: a practical system for the education of young ladies* (1839):

> Unfortunately, the present state of things in, what is called, good society ... requires an unnatural predominance to be given to a very inferior branch of education, – the teaching of *accomplishments* ... The external (and how often mechanical!) actions of playing, singing, dancing, and painting, are held to be absolutely necessary ... whilst the habits of thinking connectedly, reasoning soberly, sympathizing properly, and of acting in a manner consistent with the high prerogative of being moral and religious agents, are, for the most part, left to nature or accident to teach, or else a *secondary* place is given to them in the course of instruction. (1839, 14–15)

The Major, who was quite forgiven

picquet] 'Piquet' (the most usual spelling) is a rather complicated 'fashionable' card game dating from the sixteenth century. Two players use a shortened deck of thirty-two cards. Twelve cards are dealt to each player, two or three at a time, with the remaining eight cards (the talon) being spread out, face down. Players then discard cards and draw from the talon to improve their hand, declare various classes of scoring combinations (point, sequence and set) and then play the cards in tricks. A game consists of six deals, a *partie* ('Laws of the game of Piquet, as played in the most fashionable circles', *Hoyle's Games*, 1807, 109–29).

"Yes. It's very nice,"

undeveloped recollections of a previous state of existence –] An allusion to Wordsworth, 'Ode: Intimations of Immortality from Recollections of Early Childhood' (1807):

> Our birth is but a sleep and a forgetting:
> The Soul that rises with us, our life's Star,
>   Hath had elsewhere its setting,
>   And cometh from afar:
>   Nor in entire forgetfulness,
>   And not in utter nakedness,
> But trailing clouds of glory do we come
>   From God, who is our home:
> Heaven lies about us in our infancy! (58–66)

Chapter 22

A TRIFLE OF MANAGEMENT BY MR. CARKER THE MANAGER

It was in the writing

expanding his mouth, as if it were made of India Rubber:] Toys were among the many uses found for India rubber:

> Look at this little India-rubber gentleman, just purchased bran-new from a toy-shop: you may open his jaws to any extent you please, you can make him laugh, cry, yawn, grin, frown, simper, stare, doze—it is all one to him: he returns into himself again and to the original expression of his countenance, when the pressure from without is removed. (*HW*, 'India-Rubber', 7 [12 March 1853]: 29)

Also called *caoutchouc*, India rubber was distilled from certain trees and plants native to South America, Africa and the East Indies. It was used to erase black lead pencil marks, to make waterproof boots and clothing, life-preservers, invalid beds, surgical instruments, bandages, tents, portable boats, and many other products. India rubber, a contemporary noted, 'is remarkable for the flexibility and elasticity ... Pieces of it may be stretched, after being soaked in warm water, to seven or eight times their original length' ('Wonderful Trees', *Robert Merry's Museum*, 1849, 132).

"Work, young Cain that you

"Work, young Cain that you are! ... An't you the idlest vagabond in London?"] After the murder of his younger brother Abel, Cain learns that he will be 'cursed' by men and made 'a fugitive and vagabond ... in the earth' (Genesis 4.11–12).

The Central Society of Education described the damage done to young children by the charity school system:

> The very act of sending a child to a charity school ... has a tendency to defeat one of the most important objects of education, namely, the cultivation of a spirit of self-reliance and independence. ... He is made to feel that he is a receiver of alms, and learns to consider it no shame. The first spark of honest pride ... dies away within him; the first exercise of his reasoning powers only leads him to discover that there are other means of getting through the world than by self-exertion, and he becomes a tame, spiritless, nerveless creature. Or perhaps (for the system sometimes produces a species of reaction which is equally mischievous,) the severity of the discipline, and the pain and weariness arising from the mechanical drudgery of an ill-conducted school, tempt him to break through all restraint, and to become a vagabond for life. (*Central Society of Education. Second Publication. Papers.* 1838; 340–41)

"I an't indeed Sir," whimpered

I've been a-going wrong Sir, ever since I took to bird-catching and walking-matching. ... nobody knows ... what they bring you down to."] There were about 200 bird catchers in London in 1851. They caught birds in the fields surrounding London and then sold them to shopkeepers or to houses or peddled them in the streets (see note to chapter 33, p. 355). Rising very early, they often walked great distances to lay their nets. Bird-catchers often took to the trade 'evidently from natural inclination, ... its being the best and most healthful means of subsistence' available. Mayhew interviewed one bird-catcher who confessed '... father didn't seem to like my growing up and being a bird-catcher, like he was'. But the young man 'never felt well' in the trades and, on his father's death, 'took to the catching at once and had all his traps'. When Mayhew asked the bird-catcher if he liked bird-catching, he responded, 'Well, I'm forced to like it, for I've no other to live by' (2.64–66). In 'Shy Neighbourhoods' (*UT*), Dickens remarked on 'the bad company birds keep. ... British birds are inseparable from low associates' (*AYR*, 3 [26 May 1860]: 156). For Rob's trapping other people's pigeons, see note to chapter 23, p. 280–1.

Rob has also helped rig foot races or 'walking-matches'. A typical ploy involved the passing of false information, as in a 'cross match footrace' between 'Captain Barker and Calfmeat', which

> was made with a predetermination that the "captain" should lose; for he, indeed, could not win, if he would. He was not known, however, at Doncaster, so he was industriously puffed off, as capital, and odds on him offered, at the very commencement, by some of the knowing ones, and accepted to large nominal amounts by others of the same party. In the midst of large companies there, and in London, the foot race was hourly broached by them; it occupied everybody's attention, and large sums were ostentatiously placed in the hands of third persons for security sake, but in reality to gammon the flats. These manoeuvres succeeded: the Captain (whom none knew to be such, but a marker) entered the lists, decidedly the favourite; the party backed him to the last, but with none save each other or their associates, in order to throw dust in the eyes of the bystanders. The racers started, the Captain lost to a nicety, Calfmeat's backers received the stakes, if he really had any besides the London party; and these, upon making up their receipts and payments, found a balance of £4600, to be divided into certain shares, between the worthies, Messieurs Grampias, Bronteman, Grouch, Priestby, and Barker. (Bee, 1828, 257–8)

a cove] According to Jon Bee's *Slang. A Dictionary of ... the Sporting World*, a 'cove' is 'any body whatever, masculine; thus we may have a rich cove, a 'gentry cove,' or a poor one. ... He is, however, understood to be one who frequents the haunts of low-bred people, or of seeing life in its varieties' (Badcock, 1823).

They seemed to have brought

a velveteen jacket ... a particularly small red waistcoat like a gorget, an interval of blue check,] It was common for sportsmen and gamekeepers to wear velveteen. In 'Shy Neighbourhoods', Dickens notes that birds will 'do things for people in short-skirted velveteen coats with bone buttons ... which they cannot be persuaded by the respectable orders of society to undertake' (*AYR* 3.156). A gamekeeper interviewed by Mayhew is said to have worn 'a large velveteen jacket, [and] a cloth waistcoat which had once been green', which is characterised as 'the gamekeeper style of dress' (1.124). A 'gorget' is the patch of colour on the throat of a bird. Brightly-coloured waistcoats were fashionable in the early- to mid-nineteenth century. As a young author, Dickens could be seen strolling around London in a red or green waistcoat with a gold watch chain and tight trousers.

"You're a nice young gentleman!"

"There's hemp-seed sown for *you*, my fine fellow!"] Hangman's nooses are made of hemp fibres.

"Wag, Sir. Wagging from school."

**"Wag, Sir. Wagging from school."
"Do you mean pretending to go there, and not going?" said Mr. Carker.
"Yes, Sir, that's wagging, Sir ... I was chivied through the streets, Sir, when I went there, and pounded when I got there."**] 'To wag it', 'to play the wag' and 'to hop the rag' – all are phrases meaning 'to play truant'. The *OED* cites this example as the first recorded use of the term, as well as one from Mayhew: 'The object before you, gentlemen, is a transverse section of cane, – common cane, – such, mark you, as is used by schoolmasters for the correction of boys who neglect their tasks, or play the wag' (3.87). 'Chivied' means to be chased or pursued. Both Rob's truancy and his punishment seem to have been typical occurrences for charity school children. The Central Society of Education instances one fifteen-year-old boy, Thomas Batt, whose father had been transported for life:

> Boy cannot read and write; went for a year to a charity school in the Mile-end-road; the boys there wear red coats and waistcoats, with corduroy knee-breeches. Used to play truant sometimes, and was then punished with two or three cuts on the hand; after playing truant, used to be afraid of going to school, because he knew he should get 'whapped.' (*Central Society of Education. Second Publication. Papers.* 1838, 366)

The Son and Heir has not

"The Son and Heir has not been spoken, I find by the list,"] *Lloyd's List*, the newsletter that supplies shipping intelligence, has been published since 1734 by Lloyd's, the 'Society of Underwriters or Marine Insurers'. Lloyd's took its name from Edward Lloyd, the proprietor of a London coffee house, where, in about 1688, underwriters began to conduct business. By 1774, Lloyd's had moved to 'Subscription Rooms over the Royal Exchange, where merchants, shipowners, and underwriters obtain shipping intelligence, and where business of marine insurance is carried on through the medium of underwriters'. The *List*, which was issued each afternoon in the mid-nineteenth century, depended on a large number of agents, scattered at major seaports throughout the world, to supply 'first-rate' information (according to *HW*), including 'the arrivals and departures of ships; all accidents or disasters relative to shipping or cargoes; the appearance of enemies' cruisers in time of war ... and generally ... every kind of information likely to prove of service to the underwriters'. This information would arrive at Lloyd's 'by every mail or post', and then would be sorted and posted in one of the public rooms. 'Simultaneously with this registering', a 'rough copy' of the list would be 'printed on slips of paper', which would be 'marked with the hour and minute when issued' and then posted and checked. 'Towards the afternoon the various printed slips, with any corrections that may be needed, together with all electric despatches received' were then compiled into *Lloyd's List*. *HW* remarked that one of the 'fullest' *Lists*, published in 1850, 'covered fifteen pages in the Arrivals and Loss books for one day, giving the names of about four hundred and sixty vessels', adding that this was six times the number from 1800. *HW* concluded that 'Not a storm can rage in the wide oceans of the South, without a record at Lloyd's. No hurricane can rush through eastern seas, without a chronicle at Lloyd's. Every gale, every squall, let it be where it may, is felt at Lloyd's' (Cunningham, 1850; *HW*, 'Underwriting' 5 [4 September 1852]: 585–9). For more on Lloyd's, see note to chapters 26 and 32, p. 300–1, 348–9.

This attention, however flattering,

working himself along by the elbows after the most approved manner of professional gentlemen who get over the ground for wagers.] An allusion to the characteristic posture of race walkers:

> The competitors in the race started with straight knees and upright figures. Their shoulders were well back and their heads erect. Such an attitude as that shows off a well-proportioned man; but then comes the feature which makes the defect, from a spectator's point of view, in a walking match – the arms are bent at the elbow and the hands point upward. This destroys much grace, but for speed and the avoidance of fatigue is absolutely necessary. ('Young England's College Sports', *London Society* 5 [April 1864]: 382)

The prodigal son was evidently

The prodigal son] An allusion to the parable of the prodigal son in Luke 15.11–32: having wasted his inheritance on debauchery and fallen into poverty, the profligate son of a well-to-do man is welcomed home by his father with feasting and celebration.

Nothing doubting now that the

Mr. Ketch] Jack or John Ketch (d. 1688) was a government executioner who took office around 1663 and who earned a reputation for 'excessive and inhuman barbarity' (*DNB*).

"He has been a little wild Sir," replied Polly

the baby, who was making convulsive efforts with his arms and legs to launch himself on Biler, through the ambient air] 'Ambient air' is a poeticism; cf. for example, Milton, *Paradise Lost*: 'All space, the ambient air wide interfused / Embracing round this florid earth'; Congreve, 'The Birth of the Muse': 'He launched the world to float in ambient air'; Shelley, 'Alastor': 'And sound from the vast earth and ambient air'.

This Mr. Carker did, in his

Mr. Carker, was the be-all, and the end-all of this business.] *Macbeth* 1.7.1–7:

> If it were done when 'tis done, then 'twere well
> It were done quickly. If th' assassination
> Could trammel up the consequence, and catch
> With his surcease success: that but this blow
> Might be the be-all and the end-all, here,
> But here upon this bank and shoal of time,
> We'd jump the life to come.

More affable and pleasant yet,

the cold perspective of tall houses,] For the 'tall, dark, dreadfully genteel street in the region between Portland-place and Bryanstone-square' and a contemporary description of the area, and its 'two monotonous rows of flat houses', see note to chapter 3, p. 46.

Mr. Toots, emancipated from the

a divan,] A smoking-room (*OED*).

Mr. Toots devoted himself to the cultivation of those gentle arts which refine and humanize existence, his chief instructor in which was an interesting character called the Game Chicken, who ... knocked Mr. Toots about the head three times a week, for the small consideration of ten and six per visit.] Boxing in England flourished from about 1815 to the mid-1820s. Typically, boxers were illiterate immigrants, most commonly Jews, and the Irish or blacks who were employed in the more lowly-paid trades (a number were butchers). They came from large urban areas (Bristol and Birmingham especially), mostly because boxing was organized and promoted in towns, and because boxers would come to towns and cities, especially London, to earn their reputation. In the view of George Smeeton, London was 'in a pre-eminent degree the metropolis of pugilistic science, the grand centre of amateurs and performers' (qtd. in Ford, 1971, 41).

Chapter 22 *A Trifle of Management by Mr Carker the Manager*

Boxing skills were one of the 'accomplishments' expected of young gentlemen at the time. In the words of a boxing manual from 1840, 'Self-defence ... is essential to the safety of man as a social being; nor is it less requisite for him as an individual' (Walker 35). The most famous instructors of amateurs were Gentleman John Jackson and William Fuller. Jackson, who conducted lessons at 13 Bond Street three times a week, counted among his clientele 'all the elite of the fashionable world ... noblemen and gentlemen of the highest rank', including Lord Byron. Fuller, who opened a subscription room at Valenciennes, instructed many Frenchmen before moving to Chicago and opening a gymnasium there. Besides Jackson and Fuller, there were other ex-prizefighters who became instructors, including the famous pugilist, Daniel Mendoza, of whom it was said that 'he knocked the heads of the noble lords and right honourables about with as much indifference as if they had been barber's blocks, in order to beat instructions into their pericraniums' (Ford, 1971, 131).

Such instruction was not reserved for 'noble lords and right honourables', but was also available to the middle class. In *His Recollections and Experiences* (1884), Edmund Yates, a correspondent for *HW*, recalled his boxing instruction, in the period between 1847 and 1852,

> I was also exceedingly fond of sparring, which I learned first from old Nat Langham, in an empty room of a tavern in the Strand, where the barracks of the Commissionaires now are, and afterwards from young Alec Keene, a mighty pretty fighter. I never had much science, but being strong and very long in the reach, and being able to take a good amount of "punishment," I was rather an awkward customer. (1.174)

The ten shillings and sixpence per thrice-weekly visit can be usefully compared with the 30 shillings a week made by Pancks in *LD* (2.34), the 12 shillings a week made by Tip Dorrit in the office of an attorney at Palace Court (1.7), and the 15 shillings a week made by Bob Cratchit, Scrooge's Clerk.

Pugilists usually adopted nicknames – in *DS*, there are 'the Game Chicken', 'the Nobby Shropshire One' (ch. 32), 'the Larkey Boy' (ch. 44) – or the nickname was 'put upon them by the slang-whang reporters, who, when a new man appears, inquire "what name he will go by?" ' (Bee, 1823, 203). The names might allude to the boxer's trade: 'the Bath Butcher' (Sam Martin), 'Coachey' (Jack Holmes), 'Sailor Boy' (Harry Jones). Or to his home: 'West-country Dick' (Richard West), 'the Brummagem Youth' (Phil Sampson). Or to the boxer's physical appearance: 'No Neck' (Duggan), 'White-headed Bob' (Ned Baldwin). Some titles were honorific: 'the Champion' (Tom Cribb), 'the Inimitable' (George Head), 'the Nonpareil' (Jack Randall). Other nicknames involved puns, such as 'the Great gun of Windsor' (Tom Cannon), 'Tom Spring' (Tom Winter). Other boxers were accorded prefixes, such as 'Gentleman' or 'Sir' (Richard Humphries, John Jackson and Dan Donnelly), and a host of other names: 'Young Rumpsteak' (Peter Crawley), 'Young Ruffian' (Jack Firby), 'the Pet of the Fancy' (Dick Curtis) (a list culled from Ford, 1971, 54–6). In a letter from February 1841, Dickens delights in imagining Angela Burdett Coutts protected from an unwanted suitor by boxers named 'the Pet of the Fancy', 'the Slashing Sailor Boy' and 'Young Sawdust' (*Letters* 2.207–08).

There were many 'Chickens' and 'Pets', including, famously, 'the Game Chicken' or 'the Bristol Game Chicken', which were the punning nicknames of Henry or 'Hen' Pearce (1777–1809) (plate 14 below). Pearce, who was 'about five feet nine inches' and had a 'round' chest that 'denoted considerable strength' (172), was a 'tremendous hard hitter', noted for striking his opponents with a left blow under their ears (172). Pearce defeated one of the most famous of all English boxers, James Belcher, near Doncaster, in a 'terrible battle' of eighteen rounds, on 6 December 1805, during which Pearce 'displayed ... great science and courage' (*DNB*; Egan, 1812, 170). Earlier victories included Pearce's triumphs over Jem Bourke and Elias Spray and John Gulley, the latter contest lasting 59 rounds or 'ONE HOUR AND TEN MINUTES!' (Egan, 1812, 165). In *Boxiana* (1812), Pierce Egan said of Pearce:

14   'Hen' Pearce, 'Game Chicken', from Pierce Egan, *Boxiana* (1830), vol. 1

> His pretensions as a Pugilist stand upon a proud eminence, that few, indeed, can ever expect to attain. In possessing a thorough knowledge of the science he was equal, if not superior, to all his competitors; and supported with strength, almost Herculean, that enabled him either to receive the attacks of his adversary with the most steady composure, or put in his hits with giant-like force; his wind so truly excellent, that in all his battles he was scarcely ever seen much distressed; and for game or bottom unquestionably unrivalled, that his noble and daring spirit never drooped to cry ENOUGH! (146–7)

Egan also remarked on Pearce's 'fine athletic form, strength, wind, and agility ... manly courage and sublime feeling ... and ... greatness of soul' (146) and recorded two heroic and successful rescues of young women (from fire and from attackers) in 1807. After he retired, Pearce was plagued by problems with 'incontinence' (presumably a reference to his drinking and womanizing [see below]), and 'went to different country towns, exhibiting sparring, and teaching the arts of self-defence' (171). He died in April 1809, 'the miserable victim of a consumption', 'considerably reduced' and in need of charity, at 31 years of age (171, 174).

Dickens's fictionalized 'Game Chicken' is no doubt intended to represent some latter-day imitator of the famous Hen Pearce, whose career flourished in the very early nineteenth century, long before the 1840s, when *DS* ostensibly takes place.

who was always to be heard of at the bar of the Black Badger,] Boxers were notable drinkers, a habit that sometimes affected their careers and reputation. Jack Randall and Tom Hickman were known as aggressive drunks, and Tom Molyneux, Dan Donnelly, Dutch Sam, Jack Randall and Josh Hudson owed their deaths to drink. In the case of George Head, 'His predilection for blue ruin was the ruin of himself – and scarce three weeks elapsed since he boasted he would drink 16 glasses of gin without disturbing his intellects. That this propensity hastened his final exit, no one can doubt' (obituary in *Bell's Life*, qtd. in Ford, 1971, 54). Henry Pearce himself, 'the Game Chicken', was said to have 'poured down copious libations at the shrine of Bacchus' during his residence in London, which, 'added to the fond caresses of the softer sex, among whom he was a most distinguished favourite', impaired his health, 'and he retired to his native place [Bristol], to enjoy peace and the comforts of domesticated life; and by the advice of his friends, immediately relinquished the profession of a pugilist for that of a victualler' (Egan, 1812, 151). Dickens may have modeled the name of the pub, 'Black Badger', on the Black Bull, West Smithfield, which was managed in 1820 by Tom Shelton, a famous boxer of the day.

wore a shaggy white great-coat in the warmest weather,] Edmund Yates remarked of this fashion of the 1830s and 1840s, 'The great-coats of those days were no misnomers. They were really enormous garments, adorned with several capes and deep pockets; they were Chesterfields, Petershams, Taglionis, Sylphides' (*His Recollections and Experiences*, 1884, 1.46).

The Game Chicken, who was

The Game Chicken ... was quite the Apollo of Mr. Toots's Pantheon,] Depicted as young and beautiful, Apollo is the Greek god of the sun, archery and prophecy, and the patron of musicians, poets and physicians. The Pantheon in Rome is the temple consecrated to all the gods, built by the Emperor Hadrian in AD 117–38.

a marker who taught billiards, ... a Life Guard who taught fencing, ... a job-master who taught riding, ... a Cornish gentleman who was up to anything in

the athletic line, and two or three friends connected no less intimately with the fine arts.] A billiard-marker marks the points made by each billiards player and keeps track of the progress of the game. 'The Marker', a *HW* article, gives a first-person account of the marker's 'bitter' and lonely life:

> nobody trusts me; nobody interests himself in me in the least, or considers me as anything beyond a peripatetic convenience for getting at your ball when it is out of reach. Nobody ever gets familiar with me, except Mr. Crimp [a cant term for a type of cheating], and I am the dumb witness, daily, of innumerable frauds. (13 [26 April 1856]: 360)

Tip Dorrit is a billiard marker for a while in *LD* (1.20).

The Life Guards are one of two regiments of cavalry that form, with the Royal Horse Guards, the household cavalry. Because these regiments took precedence over all other corps, commissions in them were sought after by fashionable young men. Retired Life Guards frequently taught fencing, as Mr George does in *BH*. A job-master keeps a livery stable and lets out horses and carriages for a specific period of time (*OED*).

But however it came about,

leaving cards at Mr. Dombey's door.] Visiting-cards were left in two ways: either visitors gave the card to a servant and departed, or they first asked for the master or mistress, and, if they were not receiving or not at home, simply left the card. Social propriety demanded that the cards be left between three and six in the afternoon (in London) and that calls 'from a slight acquaintance' be returned 'the next day, or at longest within three days, unless the distance is too great'. For a newly-independent young man such as Mr Toots, the presentation of his visiting cards would have been a minor rite of passage. Mr Toots's would have had his title and last name –'Mr Toots' – printed in the centre of the white pasteboard card, with his address in the bottom left-hand corner. It was expected that 'A well-bred person always receives visitors at whatever time they may call, or whoever they may be; but if you are occupied and cannot afford to be interrupted by a mere ceremony, you should instruct the servant beforehand to say that you are "not at home" ' (*The Habits of Good Society*, 1869, 834, 837–8).

the British Dominions – that wide-spread territory on which the sun never sets,] The phrase, 'El imperio en el que nunca se pone el sol' (The Empire on which the sun never sets) was first used to describe the Spanish empire in the sixteenth century. Its English application may derive from the Scottish literary critic, John Wilson (Christopher North): 'His Majesty's dominions, on which the sun never sets' (*Noctes Ambrosianae* [no. 20], *Blackwood's Magazine* [April 1829]).

Chapter 23 *Florence Solitary, and the Midshipman Mysterious*

Now it is certain that Mr. Toots

an acrostic on Florence,] The practice of praising a lady by writing an acrostic using her name was established in 1599, when Sir John Davies wrote twenty-six 'Hymns to Astroea' in honour of Queen Elizabeth, each poem an acrostic using the name 'Elisabetha Regina'. Although better poets, such as Dryden and Addison, condemned them, acrostics became popular, particularly in the nineteenth century, when a huge number of acrostic books were published (Augarde, 1986, pp. 33–6). An acrostic on Dickens's name appeared in Charles Grinfield's *A Century of Acrostics on the Most Eminent Names in Literature, Science, and Art, Down to the Present Time: Chronologically Arranged* (1855):

> **D**elightful Novelist! lov'd by youth and age.
> **I**n 'many-colour'd life' how rich thy page!
> **C**omic, pathetic scenes alike to thee;
> **K**indliest benevolence in all we see,
> **E**nnobling humble worth, and struggling poverty,
> **N**o sickly sentimental trash we find;
> **S**weet sympathy pervades thy bright, thy glowing mind. (50)

Chapter 23　　　　　　　　　　　　　　　Eighth monthly number
　　　　　　　　　　　　　　　　　　　　　　May 1847

FLORENCE SOLITARY, AND THE MIDSHIPMAN MYSTERIOUS

Florence lived alone in the

the blank walls looked down upon her with a vacant stare, as if they had a Gorgon-like mind to stare her youth and beauty into stone.] See note to chapter 18, p. 228.

No magic dwelling-place in magic

No magic dwelling-place in magic story, shut up in the heart of a thick wood, was ever more solitary and deserted] This is the first of several allusions in this chapter to 'The Sleeping Beauty in the Wood', one of Charles Perrault's *Contes du*

⌒   Her education in the great mansion –
⌒ Florence – Like an enchanted house.

⌒ Captain Cuttle going aboard Bunsby's ship.

⌒ Carker going down to Leamington?   No 9?

⌒ or Mrs Skewton in the Major's dressing room? N^o
                                                    9?

⌒ The Barnet Skettleses. Florence's study there.

⌒ Polly – The boy of Paul's age?

⌒ John Carker the Junr, and his sister .

⌒ Uncle Sol to die?

    No. Run away, to look after Walter

        Pipchin
         Blimbers
       Good Mrs Brown.
        Mr Feeder and Mr Toots.

Number Plan

(Dealings with the Firm of Dombey & Son — Nº VIII)

Chapter XXIII.

Florence solitary, and the Midshipman mysterious

Chapter XXIV.

The Study of a loving heart.

Chapter XXV.

Strange news of Uncle Sol.

Chapter Plan

Temps Passé, avec des moralités: Contes de ma mère l'Oye (1696), translated into English in 1729 by Robert Samber as *Mother Goose's Tales*. After the Princess has been put into a deep slumber by the fairies, the King and Queen

> having kissed their dear daughter without waking her, quitted the Castle, and issued a proclamation forbidding any person, whosoever, to approach it. These orders were unnecessary, for in a quarter of an hour there grew up around the Park so great a quantity of trees, large and small, of brambles and thorns, interlacing each other, that neither man nor beast could get through them, so that nothing more was to be seen than the tops of the Castle turrets, and they only at a considerable distance. (trans. J.R. Planché, 1858)

There were not two dragon sentries

There were not two dragon sentries keeping ward before the gate of this abode, as in magic legend are usually found on duty over the wronged innocence imprisoned;]

> We frequently find the dragon, both in ancient and modern fable, in the capacity of a guard to enchanted castles, subterranean abodes of magicians, hidden treasures, &c. Thus, in the Grecian mythology, the Golden Apples of Hesperides are watched by a dragon that sleeps neither night nor day; so, also, is the Golden Fleece, which occasioned the Argonautic expedition. ('Romantic Fables and Popular Superstitions', *The National Magazine* 1 [July 1852]: 34)

a glowering visage, with its thin lips parted wickedly, that surveyed all comers from above the archway of the door,] A decorative neoclassical carved stone mask placed above the keystone of the arch in the masonry of the doorway.

a monstrous fantasy of rusty iron curling and twisting like a petrifaction of an arbour over the threshold, budding in spikes and corkscrew points, and bearing, one on either side, two ominous extinguishers,]

> It was customary, in the Hogarthian era, and until the close of the last century, to bestow much cost on the iron-work about aristocratic houses. The lamp-irons at the doors were often of highly enriched design in wrought metal; many old and curious specimens still remain in the older streets and squares at the west-end of our metropolis. Fig. C depicts one of these in Manchester Square, and the reader will observe the trumpet-shaped implement attached midway. This is an extinguisher, and its use was to put out the flambeau carried lighted by the footman at the back of the carriage, during a night-progress in the streets. (*The Book of Days*, 1832, 2.410–11)

"Who enter here, leave light behind!"] An allusion to the inscription above the gate of Hell in Dante, *Divine Comedy*, 'Lasciate ogni speranza voi ch'entrate' (All hope abandon, ye who enter here) ('Inferno', 1.1).

The brass band that came into the street ... a poor little piping organ of weak intellect,] In 'The Monster Promenade Concerts', W. H. Wills blamed much of 'the madness existing and wrought in this County of Middlesex' on street music:

> In retired streets, squares, terraces, or "rows," where the more pleasing music of cart, coach, and cab wheels does not abound, the void is discordantly filled up by peripatetic concerts, which last all day long. You are forced, each morning, to shave to the hundredth psalm groaned out from an impious organ; at breakfast you are stunned by the basses of a wretched waltz belched forth from a bass trombone; and your morning is ruined for study by the tickling of a barrel piano-forte; at luncheon acute dyspepsia communicates itself to your vitals in the stunning *buldering* of a big-drum; tuneless trumpets, discordant cornets, and blundering bass-viols form a running accompaniment of discord to your afternoon walk; hurdy-gurdies, peradventure, destroy your dinner; fiddles and harps squeak away the peace of your whole evening; and, when you lay your distracted head on your pillow you are robbed of sleep by a banditti of glee singers, hoarsely croaking, "Up rouse ye then, my merry, merry men!" (*HW* 2.95)

Dickens was one of several famous men to sign a letter of thanks to Michael Thomas Bass (Liberal MP for Derby) for bringing in a bill that would force street musicians to move if householders complained. Dickens was particularly bothered by the noise around his holiday home in Broadstairs in 1849: 'Unless it pours of rain, I cannot write half-an-hour without the most excruciating organs, fiddles, bells, or glee-singers. There is a violin of the most torturing kind under the window now (time, ten in the morning) and an Italian box of music on the steps – both in full blast' (*DNB*, 'Bass'; *Letters* 5.162–3). For more on street musicians, see notes to chapters 3 and 31, pp. 48–9, 336–7.

automaton dancers, waltzing in and out at folding doors,] In his account of London street performers, Mayhew lists the 'Street Showmen' who demonstrated 'mechanical figures' (1.6). These were probably similar to those described in 'Popular Toys':

> A whole volume might be written on the subject of street toys and the ingenuity and characteristic eloquence of the itinerant merchants who sell them. There is a little humble stand behind some railings at the top of Cheapside which has been in existence ever since the oldest city man can recollect. ... Hopping-frogs, "transformation cards," acrobatic spiders, Jacks-in-the-box, and snakes of restless activity may all in turn be bought for a penny on the *trottoirs* of Oxford Street. (*Every Saturday*, 1866, 1.151)

A visitor to an American museum in 1843 remarked on the 'mechanical dancing figures. ... The mechanical figures were such perfect imitations of life, and went through so many wonderful evolutions, that they might well surprise even those accustomed to the marvels of mechanism' (*Letters from New York*, 1852, 1.265).

The spell upon it

The spell that used to set enchanted houses sleeping once upon a time, but left their waking freshness unimpaired.] In 'The Sleeping Beauty in the Wood' (see above), the good fairy

> touched with her wand everybody that was in the castle (except the King and Queen): governesses, maids of honour, women of the bedchamber, gentlemen, officers, stewards, cooks, scullions, boys, guards, porters, pages, footmen. ... As soon as she had touched them, they all fell asleep, not to wake again until the time arrived for their mistress to do so, in order that they might be all ready to attend upon her when she should want them. Even the spits that had been put down to the fire, laden with partridges and pheasants, went to sleep, and the fire itself also.

But Florence bloomed there,

But Florence bloomed there, like the king's fair daughter in the story.] Despite having been asleep for a hundred years, the Princess in 'The Sleeping Beauty in the Wood' is unchanged in appearance when the Prince awakens her:

> He entered a chamber covered with gold, and saw on a bed, the curtains of which were open on each side, the most lovely sight he had ever looked upon – a Princess, who seemed to be about fifteen or sixteen, the lustre of whose charms gave her an appearance that was luminous and supernatural. He approached, trembling and admiring, and knelt down beside her.

Her father did not know –

She was very young, and had no mother,] An echo of Browning's play, *A Blot in the 'Scutcheon*. In 1842, Forster had sent Dickens the manuscript of the play to get his opinion, and Dickens's response was enthusiastic:

> Browning's play has thrown me into a perfect passion of sorrow. To say that there is anything in its subject save what is lovely, true, deeply affecting, full of the best emotion, the most earnest feeling, and the most true and tender source of interest, is to say that there is no light in the sun, and no heat

in blood. It is full of genius, natural and great thoughts, profound, and yet simple and beautiful in its vigour. I know nothing that is so affecting, nothing in any book I have ever read, as Mildred's recurrence to that "I was so young – I had no mother." I know no love like it, no passion like it, no moulding of a splendid thing after its conception, like it. And I swear it is a tragedy that MUST be played; and must be played, moreover, by Macready. (*Letters* 3.381–2)

Dickens had been thinking about *DS* since 1843, the year that Browning's play was first performed (Horsman xiii; Goffe-Stoner 97–9).

Miss Nipper, who was perhaps

a plea in bar] A rather complicated image to indicate the forcefulness of her gesticulations, which are likened to a 'plea in bar', a plea that alleges the existence of some new fact in order to limit or stop an action or prosecution (also known as a 'special plea') (*OED*).

"I am not very anxious to

Fulham,]

> This place is situated on the north bank of the Thames, and consists of several irregularly-built streets, and various handsome detached houses, and ranges of modern buildings. … it is partially paved, lighted with gas … and amply supplied with water from the river and from springs. … In the vicinity of Fulham are several extensive nursery-grounds, and much of the land is occupied by market-gardeners, who are noted for the cultivation of asparagus. There are a manufactory for brown stone-ware, and an extensive malt-kiln.
> (Lewis, *A Topographical Dictionary of England,* 1848)

W. J. Loftie remarked that Fulham 'is too far for the regular London visitant, and too near for a special excursion', and noted the 'sleepy air' about the parish: 'The little red court, the quiet gardens, the dark trees, slumber in the summer sunshine: in winter they seem to hibernate' (1875, 169). For the picturesqueness of the Thames at Fulham, see note to chapter 24, p. 289.

"If I hadn't," said Susan Nipper,

I may not be a Amazon, Miss Floy, and wouldn't so demean myself by such disfigurement,] The mythical race of female warriors believed by the ancient Greeks to be living in Scythia or some other remote location. It was erroneously believed that

FULHAM CHURCH, IN 1825.

15   Fulham from the Thames, 1825, by William Henry Prior. From Thornbury and Walford, *Old and New London* (6 vols, 1873–8)

the Amazons cut off their right breasts so that they would not interfere with the use of their bows and javelins.

As Polly had been to tell

That sporting character ... whistled ... and then yelled in a rapture of excitement, "Strays! Whoo-oop! Strays!" which identification had such an effect upon the conscience-stricken pigeons, that instead of going direct to some town in the North of England, as appeared to have been their original intention, they began to wheel and falter;] As well as being a bird-catcher (who sells live birds: see note to chapter 22, pp. 264–5), Rob also makes money from trapping pigeons to sell to poultry dealers:

> This fancy is a great favourite with certain of the lower classes in the Metropolis, and perhaps too generally injurious to their better interests. Their common method of entrapping stray pigeons, the property of other people, does not well consist with an honest principle, takes up too much of the time of those who practise it, and leads to loose and irregular habits. (*A Practical Treatise on Breeding, Rearing and Fattening All Kinds of Domestic Poultry*, 1816, 181)

Rob's pigeon loft on the roof of the Wooden Midshipman's is described in chapter 32 as 'sundry tea-chests and other rough boxes'. While keeping pigeons was a popular pastime, Rob's practice of decoying other people's birds was reprehensible:

> Many persons in London convert the spaces between the garrets and the roofs of their houses into lofts, by making an aperture in the tiling, which opens on a platform, fixed on the outside. ... Any place, in fact, that is dry, light, airy, and sufficiently commodious, may be converted into a good loft. The trap or aery is fixed on the outside upon a platform of wood, at the common entrance of the birds ... Traps are, for the most part, square, with one, two, and sometimes three entrances; each of which is furnished with a door contrived in such a manner, as to allow a person concealed within the loft, or any other place whence he can obtain a view of the trap, effectually to close the entrance in a second, by merely pulling a piece of string. ... The trap is frequently used, by depraved persons, for the purpose of catching stray pigeons, which they decoy into it either by some of their own birds, or by baits of hemp, rape, canary-seeds, or otherwise. (William Clarke, *The Boy's Own Book,* 1829, 201)

Mayhew's enquiries revealed that live pigeons were never sold by street hawkers of birds, but dead pigeons were bought by poultry-hawkers, who paid 1*s.* 9*d.* a dozen for undressed pigeons. In an average year, 383,000 pigeons were sold in London markets (compared to the same number of ducks, 124,000 turkeys and a million geese) (1.128, 132, 134, 135).

While he was yet busy

swivel-bridges,] Swivel-bridges, or swing-bridges, can be opened to allow the passage of barges and masted boats, and are used on canals, rivers, at the entrance to locks, and at railway crossings.

It happened by evil chance

Mrs. Mac Stinger was knocked up by the policeman at a quarter before three in the morning,] Policemen or night-watchmen would wake up factory workers and others wanting to rise early, as described in Disraeli, *Sybil; or, The Two Nations* (1845; ch. 13):

> A man muffled up in a thick coat, and bearing in his hand what would seem ... to be a shepherd's crook, only its handle is much longer ... touches a number of windows with great quickness as he moves rapidly along. A rattling noise sounds upon each pane. The use of the long handle ... becomes apparent ... enabling him ... to reach the upper windows of the dwellings whose inmates he has to rouse.

pattens] Sandals made of wood, metal and leather worn to raise the ordinary shoe out of the mud or wet. The wooden sole, secured to the foot by a leather strap over the instep, was mounted on an iron ring that raised the wearer an inch or two off the ground. Indoors, pattens were worn by servants when doing jobs such as mopping floors; outdoors they were worn in the rain, and for walking on unpaved and undrained roads. The sounds heard on a rainy night in 'The Streets – Night' (*SB*), are 'the constant clicking of pattens on the slippy and uneven pavement, and the rustling of umbrellas'.

"Who says he don't live here?"

cast pearls before swine!"] From the Sermon on the Mount, Matthew 7.6: 'Give not that which is holy unto the dogs, neither cast ye your pearls before swine, lest they trample them under their feet, and turn again and rend you.'

The Captain in his own apartment

everything ... was wet, and shining with soft soap and sand: the smell of which dry-saltery impregnated the air.] Drysalters dealt in various chemical products (dyes, glues, oils, drugs, preserved foods) that contained salt. Salt mixed with vinegar was a general cleaning agent, as was sand:

> For Scouring Floors. Dry some fuller's earth, and with boiling water make it into a thick paste; mix it with one-third of its quantity of very fine sand, sifted; sprinkle this mixture over the floor, and with a scrubbing-brush and cold water, scrub the boards ... and finish by scrubbing with plenty of cold water. ... Equal proportions of spirits of salt, and of vinegar, mixed, will extract all stains out of floors. (Mrs Dalgairns, *The Practice of Cookery adapted to the business of everyday life*. 3rd ed., 1830, 449)

the Captain...looked round on the waste of waters with a rueful countenance,] Sancho Panza introduces his master as 'the perplexed and downtrodden Don Quixote de la Mancha, alias the knight of the rueful countenance' (1811 ed., 2.10). 'Rueful countenance' is used repeatedly as Quixote's epithet.

But when the Captain, directing

he had looked for no rarer visitor than the potboy or the milkman;] Potboys, who served drinks in public houses, went round the neighbourhood in the morning to collect the empty pewter or tin pots hung on the area railings by customers who had taken their beer home with them. Public houses also sent their potboys to sell pints of beer around working-class districts in the evening: 'The Baker and Potboy' describes a potboy who 'glides through the dark streets with his lantern and beer-trays, like a glow-worm' (*The Mirror of Literature*, 1828, 9.431). Empty milk cans were also hung on the railings for the milkman to fill on his next round.

the Captain stood up, aghast, as if he supposed her ... to be some young member of the Flying Dutchman's family.] He imagines Florence to be an apparition, like the legendary ill-fated phantom ship, the *Flying Dutchman*, which was condemned to sail the stormy seas off the Cape of Good Hope and was excluded from every port. Sir Walter Scott explains in a note to *Rokeby; a Poem* (1813, canto 2, st. 11) that his lines about the 'Phantom Ship' and 'Daemon frigate' were founded on 'the well-known nautical superstition concerning a fantastic vessel, called by the sailors The Flying Dutchman'. The legend also inspired the story 'Vanderdeeken's Message Home', about a seventeenth-century Dutch captain sailing around the Cape of Good Hope and supposedly in league with the Devil (*Blackwood's Edinburgh Magazine*, 1821, 9.127–31). The details of this story in turn inspired many subsequent writers, including Captain Marryat's *The Phantom Ship* (1839).

Instantly recovering his self-possession,

Captain Cuttle ... raised the hand of Florence to his lips, and standing off a little ... beamed on her from the soap and water like a new description of Triton.] In Greek myth, Triton, the son of Poseidon and Amphitrite, is a sea god usually represented as half man and half fish, carrying a trident and blowing on a conch shell. He had the power to calm the ocean and abate storms.

"No, Heart's-delight," said Captain Cuttle,

Heart's-delight,"] Captain Cuttle is probably alluding to a song by Thomas Dibden, 'Sweethearts and Wives' (sometimes entitled 'Saturday Night, or Push the Grog About'), although 'Heart's Delight' was a poetic cliché, appearing in dozens of ballads, going back to the Middle Ages. The relevant lines from Dibden's song concern a sailor's toast to his sweetheart:

> I'll give, cried I, my charming Nan,
> Trim, handsome, neat, and tight;
> What joy so fine a ship to man,
> She is my heart's delight!
> So well she bears the storms of life,
> I'd sail the world throughout,
> Brave ev'ry toil, for such a wife:
> Then push the grog about.
> (*Songs of the Late Charles Dibdin*. 3rd ed., 1850, 34)

a out'ard and visible sign of a in'ard and spirited grasp,] From the Catechism (*BCP*): 'an outward and visible sign of an inward and spiritual grace given unto us; ordained by Christ himself'.

"Not a bit," returned the Captain,

"who I'll stand by, and not desert until death doe us part, and when the stormy winds do blow, do blow, do blow – overhaul the Catechism," said the Captain, parenthetically, "and there you'll find them expressions –] Another misquotation: the lines – 'till death do us part' – are not from the Catechism but from the marriage service (*BCP*), which Captain Cuttle conflates with the opening stanza of 'Ye Mariners of England, a Naval Ode', by Thomas Campbell:

> Ye Mariners of England
> That guard our native seas,
> Whose flag has braved, a thousand years,
> The battle and the breeze –
> Your glorious standard launch again
> To match another foe!
> And sweep through the deep,
> While the stormy winds do blow, –
> While the battle rages loud and long,
> And the stormy winds do blow.
>
> (*The Poetical Works of Thomas Campbell, 1837*)

Again the Captain clapped

without any note of preparation,] From *Henry V* 4.12–15 (quoted in note to chapter 12, pp. 174–5).

However, they got to the corner

that terrible fire-ship,] 'A vessel filled with combustible materials, and fitted with grappling-irons, to hook and set fire to the enemy's ships' (Smyth, 1847, 298–9). Fire-ships featured frequently in the news in the 1820s because they were used by the Greeks against the Turkish fleet in the Greek War of Independence (see, for example, *Times*, 4 August 1821, 2; *Nile's Weekly Register*, 1822-3, 23.405).

Captain Bunsby's vessel, which was called the Cautious Clara, and was lying hard by Ratcliffe.] Ships were more usually given bold, adventurous names, such as 'Alert', 'Challenger', 'Valiant' etc. (see *Lloyd's Register of Shipping*). Ratcliffe is a hamlet in the parish of Stepney, on the north bank of the Thames between the marshes of Wapping and the Isle of Dogs. Ships were built in the area in the fourteenth century, though later it was mainly used for the fitting out, repairing and victualling of ships. Ratcliffe was devastated by fire in 1794, but was soon rebuilt and, by 1810, the Commercial Road had been cut through the area. The Limehouse Basin of the Regent's Canal opened in 1820 and, shortly after, the land north of the Commercial Road was developed for housing. Between 1801 and 1861, the riverside hamlet's population tripled, to 17,000. According to a late-nineteenth-century observer, it 'is still for the most part occupied by marine men and those dependent upon or connected with them. But the buildings are rather places of business than dwellings, and the building space has been largely encroached upon for docks and yards' (Wheatley, 1891, 3.149; Weinreb and Hibbert, 1985, 656–7).

The boy then shoved out a plank

standing rigging,] The fixed part of a vessel's rigging, that which is 'made fast'. The 'standing rigging' supports the masts and is not hauled upon, unlike the 'running rigging' (Smyth, 1867, 650; *OED*).

Immediately there appeared, coming

one stationary eye in the mahogany face, and one revolving one, on the principle of some light-houses.] Such as the lighthouse on the coast of Northumberland known as 'The Scares, or Fern Isles', which had 'Two revolving and one stationary light' (*Edinburgh Encyclopædia*, 1832, 12.54) The lighthouse optic (lenses and prisms) had four panels arranged in a square so that when the optic was rotated, it gave out four flashes during the period of rotation. An article in *HW* published in 1851 notes that foreigners were struck with admiration at a coastline so well provisioned ('Lighthouses and Light-Boats', 2.373). Advances in civil engineering and the development of reflector lamps helped meet the demand for the construction of lighthouses on Britain's coasts owing to increased shipping from the end of the eighteenth century onwards.

decorated with shaggy hair, like oakum,] Oakum, the loosely twisted fibres obtained by untwisting and picking old hemp rope, is used especially as a caulking material in the seams of wooden ships (*OED*).

The head was followed by a perfect desert of chin, and by a shirt-collar and neckerchief, and by a dreadnought pilot coat, and by a pair of dreadnought pilot trousers, whereof the waistband was so very broad and high, that it became a succedaneum for a waistcoat:] 'Dreadnought' denotes both a stout woolen cloth with a thick long pile and the thick coat of which the cloth is made, a coat that is usually worn in very bad weather. A 'pilot coat' (also known as a pea-jacket) is a short, stout woolen overcoat commonly worn by sailors. A 'succedaneum' is an object that substitutes for something else: in this comical image, the waist of Bunsby's trousers is so high that they look like a waistcoat.

"Bunsby," said the Captain,

science, which is the mother of inwention, and knows no law.] Captain Cuttle confuses two proverbial phrases: 'necessity is the mother of invention' and 'necessity knows no law'. The former phrase seems to have been first used in its modern form in R. Franck, *Northern Memoirs*, 1694, 44 – 'Art imitates Nature, and Necessity is the Mother of Invention' – though the same idea occurs much earlier in Persius, *Satires*, Prologue 10 – 'magister artis ingeniique largitor venter' (the belly is the teacher of art and the giver of wit). The latter phrase derives from a Latin saying – 'necessitas non habet legem' – and seems to have been first used in English in Langland, *Piers Plowman*, B. xx. 10: 'Nede ne hath no lawe, ne neure shal falle in dette' (1377) (Speake, 2003).

Bunsby, will you wear, to oblige me, and come along with us?"] To 'wear', originally a nautical term for turning around with the head away from the wind in order to sail on another tack (*OED*):

> in veering or wearing, especially when strong gales render it dangerous, unseamanlike, or impossible, the head of the vessel is put away from the wind, and turned around 20 points of the compass instead of 12, and, without strain or danger, is brought to the wind on the opposite tack. (Smyth, 1867, 710)

"Here is a man," said

a man ... that has had more accidents happen to his own self than the Seamen's Hospital to all hands; that took as many spars and bars and bolts about the outside of his head when he was young, as you'd want a order for on Chatham-yard to build a pleasure-yacht with;] In 1821, the Seamen's Hospital was established by the Seamen's Hospital Society on board the *Grampus*, a 50-gun ship at Greenwich. When more space was needed, it was moved in 1830 to the *Dreadnought*, with 104 guns, and, in 1857, to the *Caledonia*, with 120 guns. According to a contemporary source, the Seamen's Hospital was

> the only establishment for the reception of sick seamen arriving from abroad, or to whom accidents may happen in the river. It receives sick and disabled seamen of every nation, on presenting themselves alongside, no previous recommendation being necessary, who are maintained, and, when necessary, clothed, until entirely convalescent. (Richardson 122–3)

Between 1821 and 1844, the Seamen's Hospital admitted 41,055 patients and dispensed its medical stores to 16,834 outpatients (*The Metropolitan Charities*, 1844, 9). 'Although much good was done in these floating hospitals, the drawbacks inseparable from ship-life were found to be serious. Questions of ventilation, of light, of quiet, and of access, became, at last, so pressing that the committee of the society were only too glad to take the opportunity of the vacation of Greenwich Hospital by the pensioners and to move their patients ashore in April, 1870' (*Dickens's Dictionary of the Thames*, 1880, 189).

In 1842, Chatham dockyard was located just north of Chatham, on the right bank of the River Medway. There were

> four docks and seven building slips at Chatham, most of which are covered with immense roofs. To the south-westward of the docks there is a long range of storehouses facing the river, and having in front a spacious quay, part of which is occupied as an anchor wharf. Behind this line of buildings, which is upwards of a thousand feet in length, is the ropery, where cables and all other kinds of ropes are manufactured for the use of ships of war. Beyond the docks, to the northward, are the mast-ponds and sheds for storing timber. ... At the smiths' shop anchors and other articles of iron work are made for the use of the navy; and towards the north-eastern extremity of the yard is the saw-mill, erected by Mr. Brunel. (*The Ports, Harbours, Watering-Places, and Coast Scenery of Great Britain* 1.125)

Dickens's father, a clerk in the Navy Pay Office, was attached to the dockyard at Sheerness in early 1817, and shortly thereafter, to the dockyard at Chatham. For more on Dickens's familiarity with the county of Kent, see note to chapter 56, p. 487.

Bunsby, whose eye continued

Gravesend,] For Gravesend, see note to chapter 56, p. 487.

"Whereby," proceeded the voice,

Awast then!"] 'AVAST. A term of command at sea, signifying, hold, stop, stay' (Crabb, 1830, 42).

"Do I believe that this

If a skipper stands out by Sen' George's Channel, making for the Downs, what's right ahead of him? The Goodwins.] To 'stand out' is a nautical term meaning 'to sail in a direction away from the shore, hence generally, to start on a journey' (*OED*). St George's Channel is the channel between England and Ireland. The Downs is a sheltered offshore anchorage for merchant ships during heavy weather, located between the Straits of Dover and the Thames Estuary, and protected on the west by the coast and on the east by the Goodwin Sands. The Goodwin Sands – sandbanks 'about seven miles from the coast, ten miles long, and two or more in breadth' – presented a hazard to ships (more than 1000 shipwrecks have been recorded) because the land was constantly shifting, or not clearly marked, or because of storms, especially from the south. *The Ports, Harbours, Watering-Places, and Coast Scenery of Great Britain* (1842) explained,

> The Goodwin Sands ... consist of a more soft, fluid, porous, spongy, but withal tenacious substance, than the neighbouring sands, and are consequently of such a quality, that when a ship strikes upon them, there is but very little chance of her getting off; the nature of the sand being to swallow its prey in a few hours, while the surf, which breaks over them, frustrates all attempts to approach the ill-fated vessel. When the tide, however, has ebbed sufficiently, these sands become so hard and firm that cricket-matches have been played upon them. But woe to him who does not quit so treacherous a field at the proper moment; for on the return of the tide they are instantly converted into quicksands, that float to and fro with the waves. (2.142)

The Goodwins are just south of Broadstairs, which Dickens frequently visited, and which he referred to in a *HW* piece, as 'Our Watering Place' (3 [2 August 1851]: 433–6). For his first mention of 'the Downs', see note to chapter 4, p. 62.

The students of the sage's

the main leg of the Bunsby tripod ... some other oracular stools –] Bunsby is likened to the sibyl Pythia at Delphi who was consulted in advance of all important undertakings. She was inspired by sulphurous vapours issuing from a hole in the ground, over which she sat on a three-legged stool, the tripod. But because of the raving, convulsive manner in which she delivered her oracles, her statements required interpretation by the priests.

Hope's own anchor, with good roads to cast it in.] The image of the anchor as a symbol of hope dates from Hebrews 6:19: 'Which hope we have as an anchor of the soul, both sure and steadfast'. By the nineteenth century the image had become a literary cliché. 'Good roads' refers to a sheltered area of water near the shore where vessels could safely lie at anchor (*OED*).

Chapter 24

THE STUDY OF A LOVING HEART

Sir Barnet and Lady Skettles,

a pretty villa at Fulham, on the banks of the Thames;] In *Rambles by Rivers: The Thames* (2 vols, 1849), James Thorne remarks of Fulham,

> The Thames just here is remarkably picturesque. On one side is a line of irregular buildings; on the other, the stately trees of the Bishop's Walks. In front is a rude many-arched wooden bridge, having a weather-beaten church at either end of it. Altogether Putney bridge with the two churches and the surrounding scenery is one of the more remarkable views on the lower part of the Thames. (2.209)

For more on Fulham, see note to chapter 23, p. 279.

a rowing-match]

> A well-contested rowing-match on the Thames, is a very lively and interesting scene. The water is studded with boats of all sorts, kinds, and descriptions; places in the coal-barges at the different wharfs are let to crowds of spectators, beer and tobacco flow freely about; men, women, and children wait for the start in breathless expectation; cutters of six and eight oars glide gently up and down, waiting to accompany their *protegés* during the race; bands of music add to the animation, if not to the harmony of the scene; groups of watermen are assembled at the different stairs, discussing the merits of the respective candidates; and the prize wherry, which is rowed slowly about by a pair of sculls, is an object of general interest. ('The River', *SB*)

the occasional appearance of the river in the drawing-room,] The Thames periodically flooded during heavy rains and sudden thaws, causing damage and sometimes death. On 16 February 1826, for example, 'the water was higher than ever known before and rose above two feet in Westminster-hall ... and came into the cellars and ground rooms near the river on both sides, and flowed through the streets of Wapping and Southwark', as well as covering 'all the marshes and lowlands in Kent, Essex, Suffolk, Norfolk, and Lincolnshire' (Hone, 1837, 2.232). And, on 24 November 1852,

> The land-waters meeting the high tides of the Thames, have flooded those parts of the metropolis which lie upon its banks. The streets on the Surrey side have been laid under water. Lambeth, Bermondsey, and Rotherhithe

have been some feet under water, and the inhabitants have been driven to the upper floors, or have left their houses in waggons and boats. Great exertion was required, in many cases, to prevent the tide from rushing into the furnaces of gas-works, iron-foundries, and breweries. The Temple Gardens were repeatedly covered. (*The Annual Register,* 1853, 198)

Sir Barnet Skettles expressed his

Sir Barnet Skettles expressed his personal consequence chiefly through an antique gold snuff-box, and a ponderous silk pocket-handkerchief,] Taking snuff required a handkerchief to sneeze into after inhaling: see notes to chapter 14, pp. 193–4. Expensive and highly ornamental snuff-boxes, which were sometimes made of gold or goldplate, were a sign of consequence. Thomas Carlyle, for instance, recorded that Friedrich II of Prussia 'was very expensive about his snuff-boxes; wore two big rich boxes in his pockets; five or six stood on tables about; and more than a hundred in store, coming out by turns for variety. The cheapest of them cost £300… he had them as high as £1,500' (*History of Friedrich II of Prussia* 4.279). Napoleon was another noted collector of snuff-boxes.

like a sound in air, the vibration of which, according to the speculation of an ingenious modern philosopher, may go on travelling for ever through the interminable fields of space,] In *The Ninth Bridgewater Treatise: A Fragment* (1837), 'On the Permanent Impression of Our Words and Actions on the Globe We Inhabit', Charles Babbage (1792–1871), the English mathematician and inventor, theorized that sound waves have a permanent existence, even after they are no longer audible to the human ear:

> The waves of air thus raised, perambulate the earth and ocean's surface, and in less than twenty hours every atom of its atmosphere takes up the altered movement due to that infinitesimal portion of the primitive motion which has been conveyed to it through countless channels, and which must continue to influence its path throughout its future existence. … Every atom, impressed with good and with ill, retains at once the motions which philosophers and sages have imparted to it, mixed and combined in ten thousand ways with all that is worthless and base. The air itself is one vast library, on whose pages are for ever written all that man has ever said or woman whispered. There, in their mutable but unerring characters, mixed with the earliest, as well as with the latest sighs of mortality, stand for ever recorded, vows unredeemed, promises unfulfilled, perpetuating in the united movements of each particle, the testimony of man's changeful will. (ch. 9, 35–6)

Babbage acknowledges his debt to Laplace's *Théorie analytique des probabilitiés* and its description of the path taken by 'une simple molécule d'air ou de vapeurs' (35), though he was also influenced by William Wollaston, whose work Babbage cites in chapter

14 (see Wollaston, 'On Sounds Inaudible by Certain Ears', *Philosophical Transactions of the Royal Society*, 110 [1820]: 306–14). Dickens, who owned a first edition of *The Ninth Bridgewater Treatise* (Stonehouse 9), paraphrased Babbage's theory of sound in his speech on 27 September 1869 at the Birmingham and Midland Institute:

> It has been suggested by Mr. Babbage, in his *Ninth Bridgewater Treatise*, that a mere spoken word – a mere syllable thrown into the air – may go on reverberating through illimitable space for ever and for ever, seeing that there is no rim against which it can strike: no boundary at which it can possible arrive. Similarly it may be said – not as an ingenious speculation, but as a steadfast and absolute fact – that human calculation cannot limit the influence of one atom of wholesome knowledge patiently acquired, modestly possessed, and faithfully used. [*Applause.*] (*Speeches* 399)

Dickens also alludes to Babbage and his theory in 'Night Walks', an *UT* piece originally published in *AYR* (21 July 1860):

> When a church clock strikes, on houseless ears in the dead of the night, it may be at first mistaken for company and hailed as such. But, as the spreading circles of vibration, which you may perceive at such a time with great clearness, go opening out, for ever and ever afterwards widening perhaps (as the philosopher has suggested) in eternal space, the mistake is rectified and the sense of loneliness is profounder. (3.31)

Dickens knew Babbage personally: he attended one of Babbage's famous soirées in 1840 and corresponded with him as early as 1841 (Toynbee, ed., *Diaries of William Charles Macready, 1833–1851*, 1912, 2.59; *Letters* 2.307) (Picker, 2003, 15–17, 158).

In the early nineteenth century, the word 'philosopher' was still applied to someone learned in the physical sciences (physicists, scientists, naturalists), as well as to someone versed in the metaphysical or moral sciences (*OED*).

coming to the end of his mortal tether] *Hamlet* 3.1.66–7: 'For in that sleep of death what dreams may come, / When we have shuffled off this mortal coil'.

Sir Barnet was proud of

Ptolemy the Great.] Ptolemy I Soter ('Saviour') (367/6–282 BC), a major Macedonian general and childhood friend of Alexander the Great. Following the division of Alexander's empire, Ptolemy was given Egypt in 323 BC, and became king in 305 BC. He moved the capital of Egypt from Memphis to Alexandria, created the famous library and is responsible for bringing Egypt into the Hellenic mainstream. Ptolemy founded the Ptolemies (hence, 'the Great'), the Macedonian dynasty that ruled Egypt from 323 BC to 30 BC.

killed a brace of birds with one stone,] The idiomatic phrase is 'to kill two birds with one stone'.

Skettles Junior, much stiffened as

invited on a visit to the parental roof-tree,] 'The main beam or ridge-pole of a roof', a phrase sometimes used figuratively (*OED*).

he would have preferred their passing the vacation at Jericho.] In other words, 'at a great distance' or 'far away' – a slang or colloquial reference to Jericho, the city north of the Dead Sea that was destroyed by Joshua at the beginning of the Israelite invasion of Canaan (Joshua 6.20–1). Thackeray uses the phrase in a similar way in *The Virginians*: 'She may go to Bath, or she may go to Jericho for me' (16; 1859) (*OED*).

"You are very kind, Sir

What does Terence say? Any one who is the parent of a son is interesting to *me*."] A version of an oft-cited line from Terence's comedy, *Heauton timorumenos*: 'I am a man, and nothing that concerns a man do I deem a matter of indifference to me' (1.1.25). The play was adapted from a Greek comedy by Menander and produced at Rome in 163 BC. For Terence, see note to chapter 11, p. 167.

Mrs. Blimber replied, with a

if Sir Barnet could have made her known to Cicero,] See note to chapter 11, p. 163.

"Has she no other brother?"

"Has she no other brother?" "None." "No sister?" "None." "I am very, very sorry!" said the little girl.] An echo of Thomas Hood, 'The Bridge of Sighs' (1844):

> Who was her father?
> Who was her mother?
> Had she a sister?
> Had she a brother?
> Or was there a dearer one
> Still, and a nearer one
> Yet, than all other? (st. 8)

Allusions to 'The Bridge of Sighs' are used in *BH* to add pathos to Esther and Mr Bucket's search for Lady Dedlock (chs 57, 60).

The flowers that Florence held

The flowers that Florence held to her breast began to fall when she heard those words,] Reminiscent of Adam's response in *Paradise Lost* to Eve's confession that she has eaten of the tree of knowledge:

> On th' other side, Adam, soon as he heard
> The fatal trespass done by Eve, amazed,
> Astonied stood and blank, while horror chill
> Ran through his veins, and all his joints relaxed;
> From his slack hand the garland wreathed for Eve
> Down dropped, and all the faded roses shed. (9.888–93)

She did so always.

what a heap of fiery coals was piled upon his head!] The command ascribed to Solomon – 'If thine enemy be hungry, give him bread to eat; and if he be thirsty, give him water to drink: For thou shalt heap coals of fire upon his head, and the Lord shall reward thee' (Proverbs 25.21–2) – and quoted by St Paul:

> Dearly beloved, avenge not yourselves, but rather give place unto wrath: for it is written, Vengeance is mine; I will repay, saith the Lord. Therefore if thine enemy hunger, feed him; if he thirst, give him drink: for in so doing thou shalt heap coals of fire on his head. Be not overcome of evil, but overcome evil with good. (Romans 12.19–21)

There was one man whom

roaming about the banks of the river when the tide was low, looking out for bits and scraps in the mud;] Work characteristic of a 'mud-lark', someone who searched for potentially valuable items 'such as coals, bits of old-iron, rope, bones, and copper nails that drop from ships while lying or repairing along shore'. In Mayhew's view, mudlarks, who would 'wade sometimes up to their middle through the mud left on the shore by the retiring tide',

> are certainly about the most deplorable in their appearance of any I have met with in the course of my inquiries. They may be seen of all ages, from mere childhood to positive decrepitude, crawling among the barges at the various wharfs along the river; it cannot be said that they are clad in rags, for they are scarcely half covered by the tattered indescribable things that serve them for clothing; their bodies are grimed with the foul soil of the river, and their torn garments stiffened up like boards with dirt of every possible description. (2.155)

Disturbed as Florence was,

Florence was seized with such a shudder as he went, that Sir Barnet, adopting the popular superstition, supposed somebody was passing over her grave.] If a person shudders without cause, it is supposedly because someone has walked over his (future) grave. The first known written evidence for this popular superstition occurs in Jonathan Swift, *Polite Conversation* (1738, Dialogue 1).

Chapter 25

STRANGE NEWS OF UNCLE SOL

Captain Cuttle, though no

Captain Cuttle, though no sluggard, did not turn out so early on the morning after] An allusion to 'The Sluggard', one of Isaac Watts's *Divine and Moral Songs for Children* (1720):

> 'Tis the voice of the sluggard; I hear him complain,
> 'You have wak'd me too soon, I must slumber again.'
> As the door on its hinges, so he on his bed,
> Turns his sides, and his shoulders, and his heavy head.
> 'A little more sleep and a little more slumber.'

In *The Childhood and Youth of Charles Dickens* (1883), Robert Langton quotes a 'Mrs Gibson', who knew Dickens when he was a boy: 'A rather favourite piece for recitation by Charles at this time was "The Voice of the Sluggard" from Dr. Watts, and the little boy used to give it with great effect, and with *such* action and *such attitudes*' (26). For Captain Cuttle's own allusion to the song, see note to chapter 56, p. 490.

"Keep her free, then," said the Captain,

"Keep her free, then," said the Captain, impressively, "and ride easy."] 'Keep her free' means to keep water out of a ship to prevent sinking, and to 'ride easy' is to float gently. See, for example, *The Annual Register* (1836): 'The Athol steamer ... was struck by a tremendous sea, which ... caused her to strain so much that the crew could not keep her free, after labouring at the pump all night' (139); *Chronicles of the Sea* (1838): 'There was no possibility of getting nearer the wreck ... she was continually filled with water; and all their efforts to keep her free were unavailing'

(1.83); *The Law Times* (1843): '15 more fathoms of chain were given out in order that she might ride easy' (154).

Not a station-house, or bone-house,

bone-house] A charnel house. Bone houses were sometimes incorporated below ground in churches, or church-yards, to receive the bones removed from graves which had to be exhumed.

it went gleaming where men were thickest, like the hero's helmet in an epic battle.] A gleaming helmet, *micans galea*, is frequently associated with heroes in battle in the many stories of Jason and the Argonauts' quest for the Golden Fleece and in Homer's *Iliad*. For example, Jason is described in the *Argonautica*, by Apollonius Rhodius: 'he took the gleaming helmet of bronze filled with sharp teeth, and his sword girt round his shoulders, his body stripped, in somewise resembling Ares and in somewise Apollo of the golden sword' (1278–1325). The *Iliad* describes the 'rich gear' of Nestor, King of Pylos: 'Shield, two spears, and gleaming helmet / … he always wore / When he armed to lead his men into battle' (10.74–7). Hector is similarly described going into battle: 'Hector, son of Priam, equal to man-slaughtering Mars, led the van, and held before him his shield … and round his temples his gleaming helmet was shaken' (13.774–806).

the Captain read of all the found and missing people in all the newspapers and handbills,] The kind of notices that appeared in newspapers, often with a catchphrase and key words printed in large capital letters. A personal advertisement from *The Times* is typical:

> LEFT her HOME (4, Regent's place, Battersea-rise), on Wednesday morning, the 6th ult., a GIRL, about 14 years of age, very short of her age, and a scar over one of her eyes: had on a white straw bonnet, with blue and white pearl riband, check shawl, and drab-coloured frock. Any person giving INFORMATION of her to her disconsolate parent, at the above address, will be REWARDED for the trouble. (4 March 1856, 1)

Mayhew records that, in 1841, 1000 persons were reported lost or missing to the London police, with 560 of them eventually being 'restored'. 'For twenty years [from 1841 to 1860] the number of persons reported lost, stolen, strayed, and missing has been steadily increasing', Mayhew added ('Extra Volume' 265).

"Now, look ye here, my lad,"

turn-to, and open the door. … whatever time it is, turn-to and show yourself smart with the door."] That is, set to work (*OED*).

"You'll continue to be rated

"You'll continue to be rated on this here books,"] His name and wages will continue to be listed in the account books ('To be subjected or liable to payment of a certain rate; to be valued for purposes of assessment, taxation, or the like', *OED*).

"A nice small kidney-pudding now,

"A nice small kidney-pudding now, Cap'en Cuttle," said his landlady: "or a sheep's heart.] Mrs Beeton gives a recipe for beef-steak and kidney pudding in a suet crust (recipe 605). A sheep's heart could be stuffed with a considerable quantity of chopped bacon in the stuffing, boiled for a little while and then baked in the oven and served with gravy (Hale, 1852, 126).

"Have a roast fowl," said Mrs. Mac Stinger,

"Have a roast fowl," said Mrs. Mac Stinger, "with a bit of weal stuffing and some egg sauce.] Mrs Beeton's recipe for roast fowl notes that 'mushroom, oyster, or egg sauce are very suitable accompaniments to roast fowl' (recipe 952). 'What is commonly called veal stuffing', according to *The Family Friend and Domestic Economist, for Midsummer* (1866), is an equal amount of bread crumbs and chopped suet, mixed with salt and pepper, chopped onion and parsley and enough egg to make 'a soft thick pudding'. This was used to stuff fowls and hare as well as veal (214).

"Well, Ma'am," rejoined the Captain,

a quarter's rent] On quarter days (25 March, 24 June, 29 September and 25 December) tenants paid their rent and servants and other employees received their wages (see note to chapter 35, p. 366).

"You might say – if you liked,"

"You might say ... that you'd read in the paper that a Cap'en of that name was gone to Australia, emigrating,] By the mid-nineteenth century, Australia had earned a reputation for giving opportunity to people willing to work hard and apply themselves. Openings existed for both free settlers and convicts alike. According to Samuel Sidney, author of the weekly publication, *Sidney's Emigrant Journal*, 'Action is the first great requisite of a colonist; to be able to do anything, to need the least possible assistance, to have a talent for making shift'. Prior knowledge of agriculture, he added, is 'quite unnecessary on an Australian stock or sheep farm'. Men from cities who had never noticed a sheep before, except in a butcher's shop, made good shepherds or hut-keepers (*Sidney's Australian Handbook* 40, 44). An anonymous publication, *Australia: Who Should Go; How to Go; What to Do When There* (1852), vigorously promoted the concept of self-improvement and the need to seize opportunities that the new continent offered: to succeed in Australia, 'a man must be steady, industrious, and wide awake' (2). Dickens provides a brief portrait of a group of emigrants crowded aboard a ship off Gravesend in *DC* (57); Australia, for the Micawbers and Mr Peggotty's family, is a land where blessings fall on them and they all do 'nowt but prosper' (63).

After effecting these improvements, Captain Cuttle,

As a tradesman in the City, too, he began to have an interest in the Lord Mayor, and the Sheriffs, and in Public Companies; and felt bound to read the quotations of the Funds every day, though he was unable to make out, on any principle of navigation, what the figures meant, and could have very well dispensed with the fractions.] For the City, the Lord Mayor and 'the Sheriffs', see notes to chapter 4, pp. 54–5, 63–4. The 'Funds' – public securities against the national debt purchased by small investors – were popular because they were backed by the government and usually paid a healthy 5 per cent return. Miss Rugg invests in the Funds in *LD* (1.25).

Chapter 26 Ninth monthly number
June 1847

SHADOWS OF THE PAST AND FUTURE

"Dombey," said the Major, defiantly,

the Colossus] One of the Seven Wonders of the Ancient World, the Colossus of Rhodes, the bronze statue of the sun god Helios, was built *c*. 292–280 BC. The Colossus, which was supposedly 32 metres high, stood in the harbour of the ancient Greek city of Rhodes until destroyed by an earthquake in 224 BC. In *LD*, Mr Merdle is said to be 'a commercial Colossus' (2.12).

The dinner hour is a sharp seven,] In his essay, 'Dinner, Real and Reputed' (1839), Thomas de Quincey gives a detailed account of the changing times of the hour for dinner:

> In 1700, a large part of London took a meal at two, P. M., and another at seven or eight, P. M. In 1839, a large part of London is still doing the very

Mems.

To bring on the marriage gradually – connect Carker with Edith, <u>before the wedding,</u> and get in Florence

Number Plan

(Dealings with the Firm of Dombey & Son   N͟o͟ IX.)

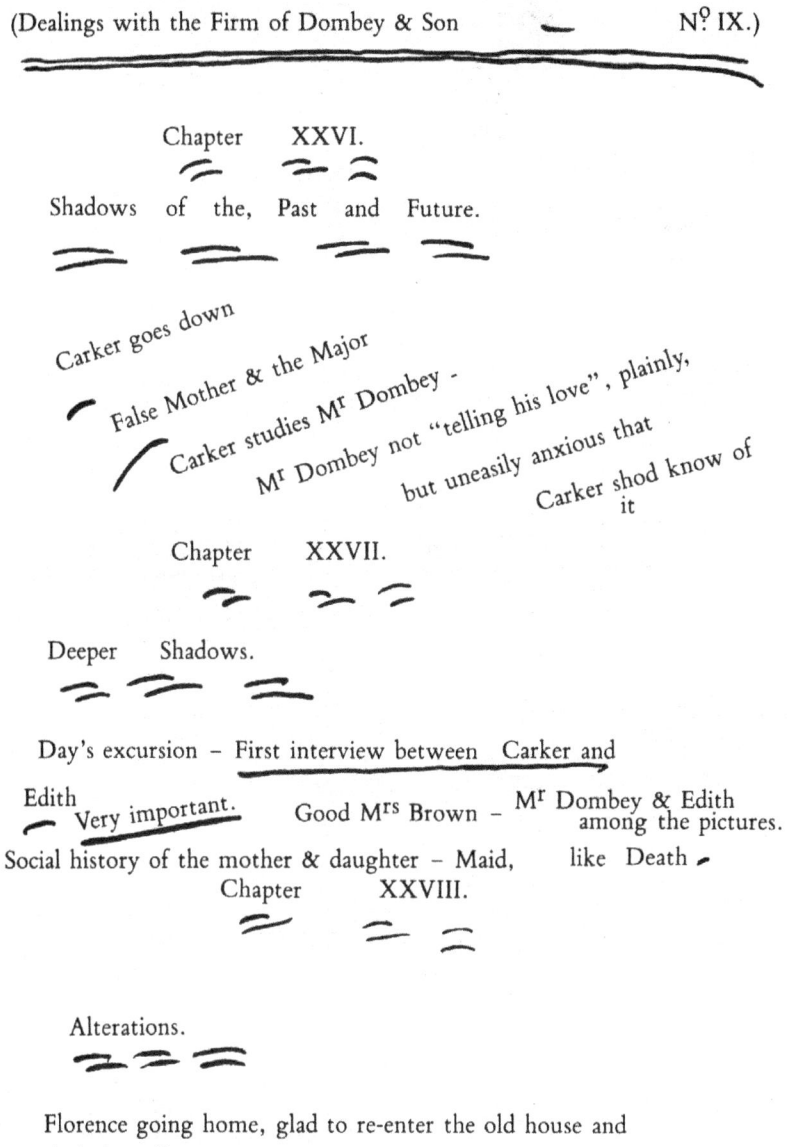

         Chapter   XXVI.

Shadows of the, Past and Future.

Carker goes down

False Mother & the Major

Carker studies M͟r Dombey –

M͟r Dombey not "telling his love", plainly, but uneasily anxious that Carker sho͟d know of it

         Chapter   XXVII.

Deeper Shadows.

Day's excursion – First interview between Carker and Edith
   Very important.   Good M͟rs Brown – M͟r Dombey & Edith among the pictures.
Social history of the mother & daughter – Maid, like Death –
         Chapter   XXVIII.

    Alterations.

Florence going home, glad to re-enter the old house and hide herself
        Susan "— Where's our house!"
    Preparations and repairs – Edith kind to Florence.

Chapter Plan

same thing, taking one meal at two, and another at seven or eight. But the names are entirely changed: the two o'clock meal used to be called *dinner*, and is now called *luncheon*; the eight o'clock meal used to be called *supper*, and is now called *dinner* ...

[From the 1690s to the 1740s] [p]eople now dined at two. So dined Addison for his last thirty years; so dined Pope. Precisely as the rebellion of 1745 arose, did people (but observe, very great people) advance to four, P. M. ... Some things advance continuously, like a flood or a fire. ... Thus advanced dinner, and by these fits got into the territory of evening. And ever as it made a motion onwards, it found the nation more civilized ... and raised them to a still higher civilization. ... Cowper, in his poem on *Conversation* [1782] ... speaks of four o'clock as still the elegant hour for dinner ... [I]n Oxford, about 1804–5 ... colleges ... now dined at four [or] five. These continued good general hours, but still amongst the more intellectual orders, til about Waterloo. After that era, six, which had been somewhat of a gala hour, was promoted to the fixed station of dinner-time in ordinary; and there perhaps it will rest through centuries. For a more festal dinner, seven, eight, nine, ten, have all been in requisition since then. (*Blackwood's Magazine*, 1839, 46.829–30)

"There is very little," returned

At Lloyd's, they give up the Son and Heir for lost.]

A just idea of the importance attaching to shipping advices by underwriters and others, may be formed from the number of casualties of all kinds occurring on the seas in all parts. The documents existing at Lloyd's show these were, in the year 1847, not less than about two thousand two hundred; of which as many as eight hundred were instances of ships abandoned at sea, or wrecked. ... These figures do not include steam-vessels. ... Amongst the casualties, there were in the year 1847, not less than forty-nine ships reported as having put to sea, of which no further tidings were heard; these must, of course, have gone down with all hands. (*HW*, 'Underwriting' 5 [4 September 1852]: 585–9)

Information about arrivals and losses was found in the Underwriters' Room:

The doors of this room open at 10 and close at 5. Immediately within the bar, at the entrance, are two high tables, containing large ledger-looking books; the one on the right hand recording the daily intelligence of the arrivals of all ships at their destined port; while that on the left hand is the casualty, or "double-line" book, where the losses and accidents are recorded, and which, after a heavy gale of wind, or the arrival of an Indian mail, is an object of much interest to the anxious underwriter. At the further end of the room is the Anemometer, an ingenious and delicate instrument, which keeps a perpetual record of the force and direction of the wind, and of the quantity of rain which has fallen, the machinery for which can be observed from Cornhill, above the roof of the Exchange. Beyond this is the reading-room, containing the lists of sailings and arrivals. Each list from the coast, as soon as it is received, is pasted on a board, so as to be easily accessible, while the foreign lists are pasted into separate books, appropriated for each port, so that the shipping intelligence at any port in the world can be obtained at a minute's notice. (Cunningham, 1850)

In September 1852, *HW* remarked on 'those who, hoping against hope, look long, though vainly, in each coming mail for tidings which will never come', noting that 'when long months have passed, the name is scored from off the books at Lloyd's' (5.589). For more on Lloyd's, see notes to chapters 22 and 32, pp. 266–7, 349.

"Sit down," said Cleopatra, listlessly

I am frightfully faint and sensitive this morning] These complaints, together with Mrs Skewton's 'wanting in that energy' and 'languishing' on the sofa in a dark room are symptomatic of what contemporary medicine classed as 'a morbid irritable condition of the nervous system' and specifically defined as hysteria (Eberle, 1835, 2.112). In 'Of the Predisposing Causes of Nervous, Hypochondriac, and Hysteric Disorders' (1768), Robert Whytt remarked on women's vulnerability to nervous disorders: 'Women, in whom the nervous system is generally more moveable than in men, are more subject to nervous complaints, and have them in higher degree' (*The Works of Robert Whytt*, 1768, 540). As Whytt's essay demonstrates, doctors recognized a link between hysteria and hypochondria:

> Although *hypochondriasis* and hysteria are distinct diseases, yet they frequently approximate each other, or are even associated in females; indeed, most hysterical females may be said to be hypochondriacal, especially if hysteria has become habitual or confirmed. (James Copeland, *A Dictionary of Practical Medicine*, 1845, 2.324; see also Eberle 2.104 and John Robertson, 'On the Origin and Nature of Hysteria', *The Register and Library of Medical and Chirurgical Science*, 1835, 1.410)

Moreover, well-to-do women, who laid claims to sensitivity and excitability as emblems of refinement, were supposedly most liable to suffer from hysteria:

> Its fundamental condition would appear to consist in an extremely sensitive and excitable state of the whole nervous system, and a consequent inordinate activity of the various organic sympathies. ... The *predisposition* to hysteria depends sometimes on a peculiar constitutional habit. ... Like gout, it is

much more commonly encountered in the mansions of the rich and luxurious, than in the hovels of the poor and laborious. Indolence, sedentary habits, a pampered and luxurious mode of living, the too early and overstrained exercise of the mind, the habitual excitement of the imagination ... are among the most common and influential causes of the nervous or hysteric predisposition. (Eberle, 2.104)

Dickens had previously represented the nervous invalid in Mrs Wititterly in *NN* (39), whose symptoms are described by her husband: ' "This violent strain upon the nervous system. ... A sinking, a depression, a lowness, a lassitude, a debility" ' (see also Janet Oppenheim, *'Shattered Nerves': Doctors, Patients and Depression in Victorian England*, 1991, 209).

Here the Major, under cover

rolled his head like a Harlequin,] This involuntary movement of the head suggests he suffers from chorea: see note to chapter 20, p. 233. The action was typical of the comic pantomime character. For example, in *AN* (1842): 'The black driver recognises him by twirling his head round and round like a harlequin' (9). The actor Edmund Kean included a rolling head in his performances, as recounted in the *Life of Edmund Kean* (2 vols, 1835), which describes the actor after a performance, drunk, and angry with a man who had criticised him:

> He left the room accordingly, and ran to his lodgings for the weapons, having on his Harlequin costume .... He mounted the door-steps, entered the house ... and without ceremony jumped, Harlequin fashion, right through a glass-door. ... Fronting them all ... stood the tipsy Harlequin. That personage now threw himself into a position, set his arms a-kimbo, began rolling his black head round and round – quick – quicker – quicker still – they thought he would never stop. (1.168–70; qtd. in 'Life of Edmund Kean', *Monthly Review*, 2 [1835]: 356)

The rolling head is also referred to in 'Mr P's Visit to London' in *New Monthly Magazine* (1822), in which 'Mr P' describes a bizarre dream: 'The figure that first caught my eye was a harlequin, rolling his head over his own shoulders, and then leaping over the shoulders of others' (3.405).

Pantomimes in which Harlequin was the main attraction (harlequinades) were frequently performed in the early nineteenth century. For example, in London theatres such as Drury Lane, Sadler's Wells, Astley's, the Adelphi and the Princess's Theatre, there were performances of: 'Harlequin and King Pepin; or, Valentine and Orson' (1843); 'Harlequin Hogarth; or, the Two London 'Prentices'; 'Harlequin and the Yellow Dwarf; or, the Enchanted Orange Tree and the King of the Golden Mine'; and 'Harlequin Billy Taylor; or, the Flying Dutchman and the King of Raritonga' (all performed in 1851) (Southern 36–9).

apoplexy] For his suffering from this disease, see note to chapter 20, p. 238.

"Major Bagstock, although I know

the world ... is a false place: full of withering conventionalities: where Nature is but little regarded, and where the music of the Heart, and the gushing of the Soul ... is seldom heard, –] For Mrs Skewton's romanticism and pastoralism, see notes to chapters 2 and 27, pp. 1 and 308–10.

Mrs. Skewton, tracing the outline of her eyebrow with her forefinger,] The second time in the novel that Mrs Skewton adjusts her false eyebrows. In a similar way, in *LD*, Mrs Merdle is said to have 'traced the outline of her left eyebrow, and put it right' (1.20). So, too, in Trollope's *Can You Forgive Her?* (1864–5), Mrs Arabella Greenow, a wealthy widow affecting sorrow over her late husband's death, 'smoothed her eyebrows with her handkerchief after her last ebullition of grief' (2.47.72). See note to chapter 21, p. 254.

"Mr Dombey," said Mrs. Skewton, when

it is my failing to be the creature of impulse, and to wear my heart, as it were, outside.] As Iago does in *Othello* 1.1.65–6: 'But I will wear my heart upon my sleeve. / For daws to peck at. I am not what I am'.

"To beat up these quarters,

"To beat up these quarters,] To hunt out where one lives, to visit unceremoniously. The phrase was formerly a 'military term signifying to make an unexpected attack on an enemy in camp' (Brewer 111).

"The agony I have endured,"

garnered up her heart] *Othello* 4.2.59–62:

> But there where I have garnered up my heart,
> Where either I must live or bear no life,
> The fountain from which my current runs
> Or else dries up – to be discarded thence!

"This morning, Ma'am," returned the Major.

For Dombey is as proud ... as Lucifer."] 'As proud as Lucifer' is a proverb dating from the fourteenth century.

"Well, Ma'am," said the Major.

Warwick Castle, and to Kenilworth,] See notes to chapter 27, pp. 307–8 and following, 315.

The Major, like some other

he shone resplendent at one end of the table, supported by the milder lustre of Mr. Dombey at the other;] Hanging on the wall of Browne's illustration for the scene, 'Joe B is sly Sir; devilish sly', is a painting of the 'wooing' of Uncle Toby and the Widow Wadman in *Tristram Shandy* (1759–67), probably derived from C. R. Leslie's painting of the subject, now in the Victoria and Albert Museum (Steig, 1978, 95).

But the Major, having

a choice spirit] See note to chapter 20, p. 236.

like a stately showman who was glad to see his bear dancing well.] An old London showman described the characteristic movements of a dancing bear, one of the street performers of the early to mid-nineteenth century:

> The bear had been taught to roll and tumble. She rolled right over her head, all round a stick, and then she danced round about it. She did it at the word of command. Michael [an Italian who trained the bear] said to her, 'Round and round again.' (Mayhew, 1861, 3.72)

Peter Parley's Annual for 1864 designated the dancing bear, 'the poor beast who is led by the nose by some Savoyard through the streets of London, and who generally has a disagreeable monkey on his shoulders, the whole presenting a picture of hideous and comical misery truly odd, especially when we think of the poor bear being taught to dance on a hot iron' ('Bears and Bear-Hunting' 232–4). In 1859, George Sala referred to the dancing bear 'with his piteous brown muzzle and uncouth gyrations', as one of the 'street arts' that was 'among the things departed' (*Gaslight and Daylight* 62).

Yes, I play picquet a little,"

picquet] See note to chapter 21, pp. 262–3.

It might be only

the white teeth were prone to bite the hand they fawned upon.} 'To bite the hand that feeds one' is an expression first recorded in Edmund Burke's *Thoughts on the Cause of the Present Discontents* (1770).

Chapter 27

DEEPER SHADOWS

But he found he was mistaken

some kindred monster of the ancient days before the flood,] An allusion to the wicked time before the great flood by which God punished sinful humanity, saving only Noah and his family, along with two of every animal, in an ark built according to God's instructions: 'And God saw that the wickedness of man was great in the earth, and that every imagination of the thoughts of his heart was only evil continually' (Genesis 5).

A withered and very ugly

dressed not so much like a gipsy as like any of that medley race of vagabonds who tramp about the country, begging, and stealing, and tinkering, and weaving rushes, by turns, or all together . ... "Let me tell your fortune, my pretty lady,"] The distinction is between gypsies, who were typically represented as dressing in patches and rags, and the somewhat more respectably dressed vagabonds. 'For the most part', Mary Russell Mitford remarked in the early nineteenth century, gypsies 'have a preference for rags, as forming their most appropriate wardrobe, and being a part of their tools of trade, their insignia of office'. In contrast, unemployed skilled workers looking for employment would 'travel about the country in shabby-genteel attire, stating that they have been well off formerly but are reduced by recent misfortune ... [including] first-class workmen out of work, owing to the bankruptcy of their employers' ('The Young Gipsy', *The Works of Mary Russell Mitford, Prose and Verse*, 1841, 147; *Monthly Review* 2 [1839]: 340).

In his *UT* piece, 'Tramps', Dickens characterizes the variety of tramps who wander through the English countryside in the summer. These include the disreputable tramps – 'the tramp of the order savage' who 'has no occupation whatever'; 'the slinking tramp ... of the same hopeless order'; the ingratiating, begging tramp; the tramp 'whose stock-in-trade is a highly perplexed demeanour', and 'the tramp who pretends to be a gentleman' – and the 'tramp handicraft men' – the chair-menders, clock-menders and bricklayers. There are also 'the many tramps who go from one oasis of town or village to another, to sell a stock in trade', 'the tramping soldier', 'the tramps with carts or carriages – the Gipsy-tramp, the Show-tramp, the Cheap Jack' – and finally 'the haymaking and harvest tramps'.

The 'weaving of rushes' was to mend chairs or make baskets: 'Very agreeable, too, to go on a chair-mending tour. What judges we should be of rushes, and how knowingly (with a sheaf and a bottomless chair at our back) we should lounge on bridges, looking over at osier-beds'. Dickens imagined the tramp handicraft men to have a particularly enviable lot: 'Where does the lark sing, the corn grow, the mill turn, the river run, and they are not among the lights and shadows, tinkering, chair-mending, umbrella-mending, clock-mending, knife-grinding? Surely a pleasant thing ... to grind our way through Kent, Sussex, and Surrey' (*AYR* [16 June 1860]: 230–4).

In addition to telling fortunes, genuine gypsies made a living primarily by hawking small, home-made goods and by tinkering (repairing pots and pans). They followed other trades, such as mending chair-bottoms, making baskets ('weaving rushes'), rat-catching, wire-working, selling fruit, fish and earthenware, and mending bellows. They would also do seasonal farm-work, harvesting fruit and vegetables (Mayall 32–49).

"Let me tell your fortune,

the Death's Head] A symbol of mortality and the vanity of life in Western culture, the death's head evolved from the *transi*, the decomposing and worm-infested cadaver that figured in macabre iconography of the fourteenth to sixteenth centuries. In the sixteenth century, the clean skeleton, and the skull most prominently, replaced the decaying corpse as the most common image of death. It is at this time that the *memento mori* becomes fashionable, the skull as a grim reminder of the inevitability of death, and an expression of a new sensibility that emphasizes the centrality of death in human affairs. Probably the most famous instance of the death's head tradition in English literature is Hamlet's soliloquy on Yorick (5.1) (Ariès, 1981, 113, 327–33; Laderman, 2001). For the related 'Dance of Death' tradition, see below, p. 315–6.

Munching like that sailor's wife

Munching like that sailor's wife of yore, who had chestnuts in her lap, and scowling like the witch who asked for some in vain,] *Macbeth* 1.3.3–9:

> A sailor's wife had chestnuts in her lap,
> And munched, and munched, and munched. 'Give me,' quoth I.
> 'Aroint thee, witch,' the rump-fed runnion cries.

>Her husband's to Aleppo gone, master o' th' Tiger.
>But in a sieve I'll thither sail,
>And like a rat without a tail
>I'll do, I'll do, and I'll do.

In spite of himself, the Manager

pointed with her finger in the direction he was going,] *Macbeth* 2.1.42–3: 'Thou marshall'st me the way that I was going, / And such an instrument I was to use'.

"What was that you said,"

Bedlamite?"] The priory of St Mary of Bethlehem (established in 1247 in Bishopsgate, London) was the first public institution for the care of the mentally ill in Britain. Bethlehem Hospital, popularly known as 'Bedlam', was transferred to Moorfields in 1676 and then moved to a new building in St George's Fields, Lambeth, in 1812–15.

"Really," cried Mrs. Skewton,

say, like those wicked Turks, there is no What's-his-name but Thingummy, and What-you-may-call-it is his prophet!"] A reference to the *Shahadah,* one of the central teachings of the Koran, the sacred Book of Islam: 'There is no God but Allah, and Mohammed is His Prophet'. The Shahadah is the first of the 'Five Pillars of Faith', recited by most Muslims at least daily.

"I am quite rejoiced,

lady-mother,] 'Lady' prefixed to a designation of relationship (here, 'mother') is an archaic genteelism denoting respect but used ironically here.

"Oh!" cried Mrs. Skewton,

"the Castle is charming! – associations of the Middle ages – … Don't you dote upon the Middle ages, Mr. Carker?"] Warwick Castle, on a cliff above the River Avon, was originally a motte and bailey fort constructed by William the Conqueror in 1068. In the thirteenth century, stone replaced wood in the castle construction. In the fourteenth and fifteenth centuries, Guy's Tower and Caesar's Tower and Dungeon were added, both influenced by French models, along with an elaborate gatehouse and barbican (Plate 13, p. 249).

According to a contemporary visitor's guide (1824), Warwick Castle was 'shown to strangers every day in the week, from seven in the morning until six in the afternoon, during the absence of the Earl and Countess of Warwick. When the family is residing at this Seat, the building cannot be inspected after half-past ten in the morning, except on Saturdays, when it is open from one o'clock till four'. There were many apartments open to the public: the Hall, the Dining Room, Ante-Room, Cedar Drawing Room, the Gilt Room, State Bed Room, State Dining Room. Also on view were the Compass Window, Chapel Passage and Chapel. To the east end of the Great Hall were the Private Apartments: the Breakfast Room, Library, and several other 'private, or family apartments' (*The Warwick Guide* 31, 33, 43, 45).

Dickens was much less enthusiastic about the Castle than Mrs Skewton, describing it parenthetically as 'an ancient building newly restored and possessing no very great attraction beyond a fine view and some beautiful pictures' (*Letters* 1.447, 1 November 1838).

Medievalism marked a Romantic reaction against neoclassical concepts of good taste and decorum, and proved hugely influential in all aspects of British culture throughout the nineteenth century. It is during the early nineteenth century that the 'Middle Ages' gains prominence as a distinct historical period occurring between antiquity and modernity (the word 'medieval' is first recorded by the *OED* in 1827), reflecting a new sense of history found in the work of Leopold von Ranke and Barthold Georg Niebuhr. An early statement of architectural medievalism is Batty Langley's *Gothic Architecture Improved by Rules and Proportions* (1742); major prose expressions of the idea occur in Richard Hurd's *Letters on Chivalry and Romance* (1762) and Thomas Percy's *Reliques of Ancient English Poetry* (1765). Percy's *Reliques* proved particularly influential with the Romantic poets: notably, Wordsworth ('White Doe of Rhylstone'), Coleridge ('Christabel') and Scott (*Marmion*). In the early nineteenth century, the medieval fashion gained impetus from the popular novels of Scott, especially *Ivanhoe* (1819), and found further expression in history painting and medieval costume events such as the Eglinton Tournament (1839). In politics, the medieval impulse emphasizes the interdependence of social classes and the close relationship between landowner and tenant. Major mid-Victorian expressions of the medieval ideal occur in Carlyle's *Past and Present* (1843) and Ruskin's *The Stones of Venice* (1851–3), both of which favourably contrast medieval conditions with those of the modern industrial city (Baldick, 1996; McCalman, 1999).

"Such charming times!" cried Cleopatra.

"Such charming times!" cried Cleopatra. "So full of Faith! So vigorous and forcible! So picturesque! So perfectly removed from commonplace! Oh dear! If they would only leave us a little more of the poetry of existence in these terrible days!"] Mrs Skewton's medievalism is of a piece with her pastoralism and her fondness for the 'picturesque', all expressions of late-romanticism, and the contemporary fashion for images and styles from the distant past. Dickens's dislike of medievalism is reflected in his invariably sarcastic treatment of Roman Catholicism, Disraeli's Young England Movement, the Oxford Movement and the Pre-Raphaelite Brotherhood.

Throughout his career, Dickens castigated what he believed was a naïve tendency to romanticize the past and to condemn the 'degeneracy' of the present. 'If ever I destroy myself', he wrote Douglas Jerrold on 3 May 1843, 'it will be in the bitterness of hearing those infernal and damnably good old times, extolled' (3.481). In the same letter, he informed Jerrold that he was writing 'a little history of England' for his son Charley; this was the work that became *A Child's History of England*, serialized in *HW* from January 1851 to December 1853. The purpose of the history, he explained in August, was that his son 'may have tender-hearted notions of War and Murder, and may not fix his affections on wrong heros [*sic*], or see the bright side of Glory's sword and know nothing of the rusty one' (*Letters* 3.482; 3.537–9). In a later letter, Dickens complained of the 'parrots' who overlooked the brutalities associated with Venice's political history to disparage the modern age of the railway:

> ... past and gone as they are – these things stir a man's blood, like a great Wrong or Passion of the Instant. And with them in their minds; and with a Museum there, having a chamber full of such frightful instruments of torture, as the Devil in a brain Fever could scarcely invent, there are hundreds of parrots who will declaim to you in speech and print by the hour together, on the degeneracy of the times in which a Railroad is building across the Water to Venice! (*Letters* 4.220)

Dickens was equally critical of the fashion for the picturesque, which had been given life in the writings of William Gilpin (*On Picturesque Beauty; On Picturesque Travel, On Sketching Landscape*, 1792); Uvedale Price (*Essays on the Picturesque*, 1794); and William Payne Knight (*The Landscape*, 1794). The picturesque came to denote vivid and striking pictorial effects usually rendered in landscape scenes characterized by broken textures, intricacy, sudden variation, rich natural colours and the play of light and shadow, scenes that included such objects as ruins, mountain crags, withered trees and shaggy animals. Because the overall pictorial effect was more important than close attention to detail, the picturesque implied a freedom from neoclassic 'rules', and superiority to merely 'intellectual' renderings, and over time became synonymous with 'character'. Almost immediately, critics attacked the picturesque as a superficial and insincere manipulation of surface effects: in 1809, Thomas Rowlandson and William Combe satirized the popular enthusiasm for the picturesque in *The Tour of Dr. Syntax in Search of the Picturesque*; in 1849, Ruskin designated the picturesque 'the Parasitical Sublimity' (*The Seven Lamps of Architecture*, ch. 4). Dickens lampooned the picturesque in *SB* ('The Boarding-house'), *PP* (2, 6, 19), *NN* (27), and *BR* (81) (Hill; Hollington, 1984, 138–52). In *LD*, it is notably the villain Rigaud who claims to 'love and study the picturesque in all its varieties. I have been called picturesque myself' (1.30). In Naples, in 1845, Dickens complained that

> The condition of the common people here is abject and shocking. I am afraid the conventional idea of the picturesque is associated with such misery and degradation that a new picturesque will have to be established as the world goes onward. (*Letters* 4.266)

The tendency of the picturesque to transform age and decay into something apparently beautiful – ruins were especially popular as picturesque subjects – make it ironically appropriate for Mrs Skewton (see note to chapter 27, pp. 308–9).

"Pictures at the Castle, quite

"Pictures at the Castle, quite divine!"] *The Visitors' New Guide to the Spa of Leamington Priors, and its Vicinity* (1824) includes four pages listing the 'many valuable pictures' at Warwick Castle. There were, for instance, numerous portraits of English and European monarchs, noblemen, warriors and titled ladies by van Dyck, Rubens, Tintoretto, Murillo, Holbein, Rembrandt and Veronese. There were also landscapes by Salvator Rosa and Poussin. However, as the *Visitors' New Guide* notes, 'it is found impossible to present such a list of the paintings in each apartment as will prove constantly accurate, since alterations in the disposal of many of the pictures are frequently taking place, by direction of the noble proprietor' (165–8).

"Damme, Sir!" cried Major

the admirable Carker,] An allusion to 'the admirable Crichton', James Crichton (1560–82), a Scottish adventurer, linguist, man of letters and scholar who was known for his excellence in a number of different pursuits, both intellectual and physical. (The term 'admirable' was first applied to him in 1603 in John Johnston's *Heroes Scotici*.) In 1837 Dickens's friend William Harrison Ainsworth published a novel about the Scotsman, *Crichton*, which was very favourably reviewed in the journal Dickens was editing at the time, *Bentley's Miscellany*, 1837, 1.416–18.

"We are all enthusiastic,

"We are all enthusiastic, are we not, Mama?"] 'Enthusiasm' had a pejorative connotation in the late eighteenth century, as shown in John Byrom's preface to his 'Enthusiasm, a Poetical Essay' (1773): '*Enthusiasm* is grown into a fashionable Term of Reproach, that usually comes uppermost, when any thing of a deep and serious Nature is mentioned' (22). Although 'enthusiasm', in the sense of excessive religious emotion, was disapproved of by Puritans and Methodists, the term was adopted by writers of sentimental poetry and novels to describe intense feelings and reactions. This usage in turn was satirized, as in William Beckford's parody of the conventional sentimental novel, *Modern Novel Writing, or The Elegant Enthusiast; and Interesting Emotions of Arabella Bloomville. A Rhapsodical Romance; Interspersed with Poetry, in Two Volumes* (1796). In the guise of 'the Right Hon. Lady Harriet Marlow', Beckford mocked melodramatic sentimentality:

> As the matchless Amelia uttered the foregoing enthusiastic rhapsody with

almost superhuman energy, so it suddenly overpowered her weak nerves, and she again fell senseless to the floor, while the sympathising Arabella wiped a lambent tear from her finely suffused eye, with a clean cambric handkerchief, and then again administered her benign relief to the fair evanescent stranger. (1.10)

"Too much so, for our

If ... the sword wears out the what's-its-name – "] Byron, 'So We'll Go No More A-Roving' (1817):

> So we'll go no more a-roving
> So late into the night,
> Though the heart be still as loving,
> And the moon be still as bright.
>
> For the sword outwears its sheath,
> And the soul wears out the breast,
> And the heart must pause to breathe,
> And Love itself have rest.
>
> Though the night was made for loving,
> And the day returns too soon,
> Yet we'll go no more a-roving
> By the light of the moon.

Mrs. Skewton heaved a gentle

that dagger of lath,] An allusion to *Twelfth Night* 4.2.124–8: 'Like to the Old Vice ... Who, with dagger of lath, / In his rage and his wrath, / Cries ah, ha! to the devil' and to *1 Henry IV* 2.4.130–1: 'If I do not beat thee out of thy kingdom with a dagger of lath'. A 'dagger of lath' is the wooden stage dagger worn by the character of Vice in the Morality plays. Dickens uses a stage prop to highlight Mrs Skewton's self-dramatising tendencies. He also makes the point that, as a sentimental romanticist, she indulges in melancholy ('Mrs. Skewton heaved a gentle sigh, supposed to cast a shadow ... '), an emotion that Dickens had earlier in the novel characterized as 'that cheapest and most accessible of luxuries' (chapter 8; see note, p. 139).

Mr. Dombey, having nothing

The Major gorged, like any Boa Constrictor –] In 1841, the *Times* reported on a curious event at London zoo:

VORACITY OF A BOA CONSTRICTOR. – A singular instance of the voracity and power of appetite of this reptile occurred a few days since at the Zoological Gardens in the Regent's-park. Two fine tiger boa constrictors were ... presented ... to the menagerie on the 4th of September last. They were respectively 11 feet and 9 feet in length, and had lived in harmony together in their cage until last week, when the smaller one, being sickly, would not eat at the usual time of feeding. The larger one had just eaten a rabbit and three guinea pigs, when it appears he made a gorge of his more weakly companion, which was proved by the sudden disappearance of the latter, and the more bulky size of the former, which exceeded 3 feet in diameter in the greatest proportion of his body. So singular a case of the carnivorous power and propensity of this reptile is not on record. (5 April 1841, 6)

A young David Copperfield is said to be 'like a boa constrictor who took enough at one meal to last him a long time' (5).

Mr. Carker cantered behind the

over distant landscape,] The county of Warwickshire, situated in the centre of England, was renowned for gentle, rural scenery, with walks and jaunts to nearby places of note and roads made pleasant by avenues of trees and wayside benches. Warwickshire's association with Shakespeare and English history added to the charm, a county full of 'magnificent castles and baronial residences' (*Guide to Kenilworth and its Neighbourhood*, 1858, 3). *The Mirror of Literature, Amusement and Instruction* described the romantic associations that would have made the county so popular for someone with the tastes of Mrs Skewton:

> what olden glories and tales of other times are associated with this county. How many of its sites are connected with high-minded men and great and glorious actions. To the antiquary, the poet, and the philosopher, every foot is hallowed ground; and even the cold calculations of the commercial speculator treat with regard a county whose manufactures add to the stock of national wealth and importance. How many stories of love, war, and chivalry are told of its halls, castles, and monasteries, their lords and ladies and maidens of high birth. (28 March 1829, 13.1)

"We have no Faith left, positively,"

"We have no Faith in the dear old Barons, who were the most delightful creatures – or in the dear old Priests, who were the most warlike of men – or even in the days of that inestimable Queen Bess, upon the wall there which were so extremely golden. Dear creature! She was all Heart!] 'Baron' is a term that came in with the Norman Invasion (1066) and originally referred to one who received land or property from the king, in return for military or other honourable service. The title was eventually restricted to those who attended the Great Council or, after Henry III, were summoned to Parliament. Dickens uses the word 'barons' somewhat variously in *CHE* (it appears 65 times), though generally it refers to powerful, landowning nobles whose interests are frequently at odds with the monarch. The 'dear old Priests, who were the most warlike of men', may be a reference to the upper clergy of the late medieval church described in chapter 11 of *CHE*, 'England under Matilda and Stephen': 'The clergy sometimes suffered, and heavily too, from pillage, but many of them had castles of their own, and fought in helmet and armour like the barons, and drew lots with other fighting men for their share of booty'. In *CHE*, Dickens described Queen Elizabeth (1533–1603) as 'clever, but cunning and deceitful', as well as 'very vain and jealous' (31). Of the Elizabethan period generally, Dickens concluded,

> That reign had been a glorious one, and is made for ever memorable by the distinguished men who flourished in it. Apart from the great voyagers, statesmen, and scholars whom it produced, the name of Bacon, Spenser, and Shakespeare, … will always impart (though with no great reason, perhaps) some portion of their lustre to the name of Elizabeth herself. It was a great reign for discovery, for commerce, and for English enterprise and spirit in general. It was a great reign for the Protestant religion and for the Reformation which made England free. The Queen was very popular, and in her progresses, or journeys about her dominions, was everywhere received with the liveliest joy. I think the truth is, that she was not half so good as she has been made out, and not half so bad as she has been made out. She had her fine qualities, but she was coarse, capricious, and treacherous, and had all the faults of an excessively vain young woman long after she was an old one. On the whole, she had a great deal too much of her father in her, to please me. (31)

Mrs Skewton is referring specifically to a painting of Queen Elizabeth wearing her Coronation Robes, richly embroidered in gold, now in the National Portrait Gallery (*Warwick Castle* 33, 43).

And that charming father of hers! I hope you dote on Harry the Eighth!" … **"So bluff!" cried Mrs. Skewton, "wasn't he? So burly. So truly English. Such a picture, too, he makes, with his dear little peepy eyes, and his benevolent chin!"**] She refers to Holbein's painting of Henry VIII (1530) in the Warwick Castle collection (*Warwick Castle*, 43). Dickens had particular contempt for Elizabeth's father, whom he described in *CHE* as 'a big, burly, noisy, small-eyed, large-faced, double-chinned, swinish-looking fellow in later life'. In Dickens's view, Henry was 'a most intolerable ruffian, a disgrace to human nature, and a blot of blood and grease upon the History of England'. The 'mighty merit' of the Reformation in England, Dickens insisted, 'lies with other men and not with him' (27).

They were not interchanging

Grim knights and warriors looked scowling on them.] There were a number of 'Grim knights and warriors' at Warwick Castle, including one of its most famous paintings, Rubens's *Ambrosio, Marquis de Spinola*, 'a fine portrait, in half amour, with high ruff, and an embroidered scarf round the left arm' (Cooke, 1849, 46).

A churchman, with his hand upraised, denounced the mockery of such a couple coming to God's altar.] The 'churchman' is probably a reference to Rubens's *St Ignatius Loyola*, a full-length portrait posed by an altar and set against a stormy sky:

> The left hand is laid upon a volume (supported by a pedestal) … the right raised as if in the act of prayer; the eyes lifted to a bust [*sic*] of light in the midst of dark clouds; the countenance fine, and deeply marked by enthusiasm; the action dignified and natural; the right foot advancing and so beautifully foreshortened as to appear projecting from the canvass; and the robes magnificent, and disposed with easy grace. The painter has been particularly happy in depicting this visionary enthusiast. … (Cooke, 1849, 54)

Quiet waters in landscapes, with the sun reflected in their depths, … Ruins cried, "Look here, and see what We are, wedded to uncongenial Time!"] Perhaps a reference to one of the two Poussin landscapes in Warwick Castle at the time. Although neither *The Visitors' New Guide to the Spa of Leamington Priors, and its Vicinity* (1824) nor *An Historical and Descriptive Guide to Warwick Castle* (1849) provides details about these landscapes, Poussin's work was notable for including classical ruins. There were also landscapes by Salvator Rosa at Warwick, but these depicted 'savage and uncultivated nature' (Cooke 63).

Animals, opposed by nature, worried one another, as a moral to them.] Perhaps a reference to 'Two Lions', showing two angry-looking lions beside each other. Attributed to Rubens, the painting was located at the time above the fire-place in the breakfast room (Cooke, 1849, 77; Ormond, 1983, 132–3).

Loves and Cupids took to flight afraid,] According to *An Historical and Descriptive Guide to Warwick Castle* (1849), there was a painting entitled 'Cupid', 'a copy from Vandyck', over the east door of 'a splendid little apartment' known as the Compass Room (1849, 70).

Martyrdom had no such torment in its painted history of suffering.] Such as the *Decapitation of Martyrs*, 'by a Spanish painter', which was in the Warwick collection in 1849 (Cooke, 1849, 82).

They made the tour of

the walls, crow's nest,] Warwick Castle, with its elaborate gatehouse, fortified walls and crenellated towers, gives the effect of a crown. Two turrets (Clarence Tower and Bear Tower) flank the gateway to the castle. A 'rare example of a crow's nest' projects from the wall joining Clarence Tower with a third Tower, Guy's Tower. The 'crow's nest … may date from Norman times, and would have been used to enable the Castle guard to watch the town for infringements of the curfew' (*Warwick Castle* 19).

A stroll among the haunted ruins

A stroll among the haunted ruins of Kenilworth, and more rides to more points of view:] About five miles from Leamington, Kenilworth was 'a small but pleasant market town' in the early nineteenth century, particularly famous 'on account of its venerable Castle, so highly celebrated in English history', which was located to the west of the town on rising ground. This 'most magnificent and stately edifice', dating from the twelfth century, passed down to Elizabeth I and then on to the Stuarts, James I and Charles I. It remained 'a mighty structure' until it was seized by Cromwell during the English Civil War, who gave it to his officers. In the early nineteenth century, 'This noble Castle, which measured seven acres within the walls, once the boast of pride … is now a heap of ruins; there still however remain many fragments of dismantled towers, mouldering rooms, gates, and walls, broken battlements, shattered stair-cases, arches, and windows, some of which are beautifully ornamented with tracery …' (Nightingale, 1821, 49; *Fairfax's New Guide*, 1835, 112–13).

Kenilworth Castle gained increased popularity following the success of Walter Scott's romance, *Kenilworth* (1821): 'the effect has been to render thousands interested in a name which was formerly interesting only to antiquarians and architects', *The Penny Magazine* claimed (1). The piece concludes with a quotation from Scott's *Kenilworth* that describes the castle in the 1820s, and provides a moral: 'The bed of the lake is but a rushy swamp; and the massy ruins of the castle only serve to show what their splendour once was, and to impress on the musing visitor the transitory value of human possessions, and the happiness of those who enjoy a humble lot in virtuous circumstances' (31 July 1835; *Kenilworth*, ch. 25).

Dickens himself first visited Kenilworth on 30 October 1838, declaring it 'delightful – beautiful beyond expression'! – Mem: what a summer resort!' (*Letters* 1.634). In November 1858, on his second visit, he gave two public readings at the Music Hall in Leamington ('Little Leamington came out in a most amazing manner yesterday. We took £130', *Letters* 8.693).

Thus they remained for a long

a skeleton, with dart and hour-glass,] At the age of eleven, Dickens was lent Holbein's *Dance of Death* series (1538), and in the early 1830s it was one of the works he consulted on his visits to the British Museum. In March 1841 he purchased Francis Douce's 1833 edition of Holbein's *Dance of Death*, which included the first scholarly introduction. Among the predecessors of Holbein's series, Douce lists a French engraving of 'Death and the lady. He holds an hour-glass and dart, and she a flower in her right hand' (162). In literature, this image was disparaged in 'Personifications in Poetry': 'The common skeleton figure of Death, with his dart and hour-glass, is a very vulgar and trivial conception' (*Monthly Magazine and British Register*, 1799, 8.709).

The tradition gained new impetus in the early nineteenth century with the publication in serial form of Thomas Rowlandson's prints, *The English Dance of Death* (1814–16), which also included an accompanying text. Other versions of the tradition published during the Regency period include *The British Dance of Death* (*c.* 1825), *Death's Doings* (1826) and *Death's Ramble* (1827). In the first inset story of *PP* (3), 'Dismal Jemmy' describes the Dance of Death figures as 'the most frightful shapes that the ablest painter ever portrayed on canvas' (Hollington, 1978, 67–75). For "Death's Head', see earlier note in this chapter, p. 306.

Chapter 28

ALTERATIONS

"Not, Miss, but what

hint at little Pitchers,] 'Little pitchers have large ears' is proverbial since at least the sixteenth century. One of the earliest recorded uses is Shakespeare, *Richard III*: 'Good Madam, be not angry with the child. – Pitchers have ears' (2.4.37).

"And that Mr. Carker has

washiest] A variant of 'washy', meaning lacking in force or vigour, feeble and exhausted, washed-out (*OED*); perhaps a pun on 'Perch', a type of fish, and an alternate meaning for 'washy': overly wet or water-logged.

After your Pa, the Emperor of India is a child unborn to Mr. Carker."] In other words, Mr Dombey and even the Emperor of India are innocents compared to Carker. Susan's mention of the Emperor of India seems pure hyperbole: although the term was current, it was used to refer only to Mughal emperors in previous centuries. Bahadur Shah II (1775-1862), the contemporary Mughal emperor, was not proclaimed 'Emperor of India' until 1857. 'As innocent as the child unborn' was a phrase in use from the seventeenth century; compare *Tristram Shandy*: 'She knows no more at present of it ... said my uncle Toby – than the child unborn' (1765, vol. 8, ch. 28).

Again, Florence, in pursuit

she ... hoped that patient observation of him and trust in him would lead her bleeding feet along that stoney road which ended in her father's heart.] The 'stoney road' recalls the Via Dolorosa, the route in Jerusalem that Christ is believed to have followed from Pilate's judgement-hall to Calvary.

Doctor and Mrs. Blimber,

his fellow pilgrims to Parnassus] See note to chapter 11, pp. 166–7.

There was one guest,

whist] An early form of bridge, whist is usually played by four people, two against two as partners. At the beginning of the game, thirteen cards are dealt face down to each player, and one of the suits is designated trumps. The player to the left of the deal leads. It is necessary for the other players to follow suit if possible. If a player cannot play a card of the same suit, he must play another card, including a trump. The player putting in the highest card or trump wins the trick (one card played in rotation by each player). The winner of the trick leads the next trick.

Mr. Toots, likewise, with the

Mr. Toots ... had established a six-oared cutter, manned by aquatic friends of the Chicken's and steered by that illustrious character in person, who wore a bright red fireman's coat for the purpose,] Six-oared cutters, rowing boats about 34 feet long, crewed by six oarsmen and a helmsman, were used by amateur rowing clubs on the Thames who held regular races from about 1818. The boats were also used by Thames watermen to ferry passengers and cargo. The uniform of licensed watermen, members of the Company of Watermen and Lightermen, was a red coat (and red knee-breeches), and a silver badge. This custom began on 1 August 1715 when the actor, Thomas Doggett, organised a race from London Bridge to Chelsea for six watermen just out of their apprenticeship. He gave the winner a bright crimson coat and a silver arm-badge. What became known as 'Doggett's Coat and Badge Race' has been held annually every summer since 1715.

In his attempt to win the heart of Florence, Mr Toots models himself on Tom Tug, the hero of Charles Dibdin's ballad opera, *The Waterman: or, the First of August* (1774). A candidate for Doggett's prize, Tom sings the song, 'The Jolly Young Waterman':

>And did you not hear of a jolly young waterman,
>Who at Blackfriars-bridge used for to ply;
>He feather'd his oars with such skill and dexterity,
>Winning each heart and delighting each eye ...

And yet, but to see how strange things happen,
As he row'd along, thinking of nothing at all,
He was plied by a damsel so lovely and charming,
That she smiled, and so straightaway in love he did fall.

And, would this young damsel but banish his sorrow
He'd wed her to-night before to-morrow:
And how should this waterman ever know care
When he's married, and never in want of a fare? (1–4, 17–24)

Watched by his mistress on the river-bank, Tom Tug wins Doggett's coat and badge, and so wins her heart. The song is discussed and quoted in Hone, *The Every-Day Book and Table Book* (1838, 2.1063), and Dickens himself quotes the song in *PP* (ch. 33).

During the eighteenth and early nineteenth centuries, the insurance companies of London and the provinces provided the main fire-fighting force. The London insurance companies drew their part-time firemen from the ranks of the Thames watermen. To distinguish the different fire brigades, uniforms were brightly coloured – red, green, blue, brown and so on. For example, around 1810, Norwich Union Insurance Company firemen wore a coat of bright red and green, red knee-breeches, and a silver arm-band like that of the watermen (Wright 3–4).

There was a labyrinth of

great rolls of ornamental paper] At the time, interior decoration and painting were usually undertaken by a professional firm – for wealthier clients by a big company such as J. G. Crace & Sons – for those with less money, by local firms. Such companies would be adept at a wide-range of tasks: paperhanging, marbling, stenciling, graining, gilding and staining, along with distempering and varnishing. The paperhanging and upholstery trades were connected in the early Victorian period, largely because the origins of wallpaper lay in fabric wall hangings, which usually matched the draperies and upholstery of the house. Wallpaper became much more common in the 1840s, once it began to be mass-produced, and duties were lifted and prices fell (the mass-produced paper was made by printing from engraved cylinders onto large rolls of paper, as presumably would have been the case here). As for the quality of the paper, it varied considerably, everything from plain papers with simple patterns to satin and flock papers with elaborate designs. Harriet Martineau, writing in 1852, remarked that 'Star patterns are eternal in popular favor; and so are lobby patterns – granites and marbles' (*HW* 5.517). The most luxurious papers were French pictorial papers. Even individually produced, 'private' papers could be commissioned, designed especially for the wealthiest consumers. From about 1835, wallpaper was pasted directly onto the plaster, instead of onto canvas, as had previously been the case (Thornton, 2000, 223).

an upholsterer's wagon] Upholsterers performed a number of tasks: they made curtains, wall hangings and furniture upholstery; selected and supplied carpets and sometimes ornaments. By the early nineteenth century, '[s]ome of our modern' ones made it part of their trade to 'rent large houses of the nobility and gentry, and fit them up' completely in order to rent them by the week or month 'to families occasionally sojourning in town'. To that end, they employed a variety of craftsmen, mechanics and the like, including painters, carvers, gilders and porters 'who understood best the transit of this description of fragile merchandise' (*Complete Book of Trades* 458–9).

As the nineteenth century progressed, seats and sofas became more deeply padded, and hence more comfortable, a trend facilitated by the increased use in the 1830s of spiral spring upholstery and in the 1850s of deep buttoning (Banham, 1991, 14–19).

In a long and amusing letter to Forster in 1839, Dickens describes his (successful) efforts to find a cottage for his parents at Alphington, 'exactly one mile beyond Exeter' and to engage an upholsterer:

> Of my subsequent visit to the Upholsterer recommended by Mrs. Pannell – of the absence of the upholsterer's wife and the timidity of the upholster [*sic*], fearful of acting in her absence – of my sitting behind a high desk in a little dark shop calling over the articles in requisition and checking off the prices as the upholsterer exhibited the goods and called them out – of my coming over the upholsterer's daughter with many virtuous endearments to propitiate the establishment and reduce the bill – of these matters I say nothing … (*Letters* 1.520)

Florence passed him as if

"this room in panel. Green and gold."] In the second quarter of the nineteenth century, interior walls were usually light in colour, especially in the drawing-room, which was thought of as a distinctly feminine space. In about 1830, *The Paper-Hanger's and Upholsterer's Guide* described the colours associated with the paneling of a drawing-room of the period: 'the walls paneled with watered silk, of pearl white, of *light* tints of pink, or lavender' surrounded by a gilt moulding'. The *Villa Companion* (1838) notes that 'light, warm, sunny tints are much more suitable' than 'deep crimson'. Strong and more sombre colours became fashionable in the 1850s (Thornton, 2000, 222–3).

The staircase was a labyrinth of posts and planks like the outside of the house, and a whole Olympus of plumbers and glaziers was reclining … on the skylight.] That is, the great height of the wooden scaffolding in the hall, reaching up the stairwell through all the floors of the house to the skylight, make the tradesmen seem like gods reclining on Mount Olympus. At the time, plumbers (so-called from working with *plumbum*, lead) cast lead pipes, joined them, made cisterns, erected water-closets and lined kitchen sinks. Outside, they fitted sheet-lead to rain-gutters, covered roofs and inserted slips of lead 'into various ledges of buildings, or between brick-work'. In London, plumbers confined their trade solely to work of this nature; but in the suburbs and smaller places, they also practised 'painting and glazing' (*Complete Book of Trades* 382–3). By mid-century, most middle-class houses in London were connected to a water supply via pipes, and usually the water would be piped to the kitchen. From the 1840s, the more expensive houses would have hot water piped to the upper floors.

Chapter 29 Tenth monthly number
July 1847

THE OPENING OF THE EYES OF MRS. CHICK

Miss Tox, all unconscious of

one little pot of tea, wherein was infused one little silver scoop-full of that herb on behalf of Miss Tox, and one little silver scoop-full on behalf of the teapot – a flight of fancy in which good housekeepers delight;] Mrs Beeton remarks: 'There is very little art in making good tea. ... The old-fashioned plan of allowing a teaspoon to each person and one over, is still practised' (recipe 1814). See also *Bentley's Miscellany* (1841):

> "I don't know how it is," said Mrs. B. "but you *do* make the best dish o' tea as ever I tasted anywheres."
> "Glad you like it," replied Mrs. Jenks. "I always make it a rule to allow one spoonful a-piece for my company and one for the pot – that's my maxum – and I b'lieve it's a good un." (Hal Willis, 'The "Pop" Visit', 9.154)

to water and arrange the plants,] By the end of the Industrial Revolution, indoor pot plants and flowering plants had become an essential decorative accessory, one particularly favoured by town and city-dwellers who lacked a garden of their own. Plants were displayed on balconies, window-boxes and just inside the windowsill, as well as on plant stands throughout a room. Window gardening was thought particularly suitable to ladies' small hands. In the early decades of the nineteenth century, the popularity of indoor gardening was reflected in the number of publications offering advice and instructions to the middle-class amateur who had little knowledge of plant care. These included: J. C. Loudon's *Encyclopædia of Gardening* (1822), which went into many further editions; Elizabeth Kent's *Flora Domestica, or the Portable Flower-Garden with directions for the treatment of Plants in Pots* (1823), followed by two further editions; Loudon's *Gardener's Magazine* (1826–45); and the *Ladies' Magazine of Gardening*, published in the 1840s. Plants recommended for indoor cultivation included all types of bulbs, anemones, auriculas, begonias, camellias, chrysanthemums, cinerarias, ferns, ficus, fuchsias, geraniums, gloxinias, herbs, ivies, pelargoniums, pinks, polyanthus, roses, violas, wallflowers and many more.

Miss Tox endued herself with

paper fly-cages,]

> All over the world where flies abound and the apartments of the houses have white ceilings, it is the custom to withdraw the attention of the fly from the ceiling by paper fly-cages or long strips of white tape placed underneath and a little removed from the ceiling, and on these the flies congregate, and avoid this. ('Notes, Queries, and Replies', *The Medical Times and Gazette*, 1 [16 April 1881], 448; see also *OT*, ch. 37)

Miss Tox was slow in coming

Legends in praise of Ginger Beer, with pictorial representations of thirsty customers submerged in the effervescence, or stunned by the flying corks, were conspicuous in the window of the Princess's Arms.]

> Some of the stalls at which ginger-beer is sold – and it is the same at the coal-sheds and the chandlers' shops – are adorned pictorially. Erected at the end of a stall is often a painting, papered on a board, in which a gentleman, with the bluest of coats, the whitest of trousers, the yellowest of waistcoats, and the largest of guard-chains or eye-glasses, is handing a glass of ginger-beer, frothed up like a pot of stout, and containing, apparently, a pint and a half, to some lady in flowing white robes, or gorgeous in purple or orange. (Mayhew, 1.186)

Ginger beer was a fermented and effervescing drink made of cream of tartar, lemon juice, sugar, yeast and water, and flavoured with ginger. According to Mayhew, ginger beer, which was first sold on the streets of London in the 1820s, had developed into 'a very considerable trade' by mid-century. Considered a 'cooling' beverage, it was typically sold during the summer months in bottles from shops or from barrels at street stalls, and it could be made at home. From about mid-century, it was also sold from portable 'fountains ... fixed on a wheeled and moveable truck' (*OED*; 1.186–8).

They were making late hay ... and though the fragrance had a long way to come, and many counter fragrances to contend with among the dwellings of the poor ... yet it was wafted faintly into Princess's Place, whispering of Nature and her

qy. Two chapters, or Three?   Three

Mrs Chick and Miss Tox. Miss Tox to dawn

as an ~~honest~~ honest toady, in so far as Mr

Dombey is concerned.

Mr Carker the Junior, and his sister.—Next No.

Marriage appointed and coming off.
   Mr Dombey musing at table – Dead sea of mahogany, with
The Marriage   plates and dishes riding at anchor

Carry on the Servants as a sort of odd

chorus to the story.

Number Plan

Chapter 29 *The Opening of the Eyes of Mrs. Chick*   323

(Dealings with the Firm of Dombey and Son   N$^{\circ}$ X)

    Chapter XXIX.

The eyes of Mrs Chick are opened.

Princess's Place, on summer morning.
Miss Tox's meditations
 Mrs Chick's policy
  Miss Tox excommunicated.
    Chapter XXX.

The interval before the Marriage.

    Preparation for Cousin Feenix
Edith ~~lying~~ kneeling on the ground, and lying her head on the pillow beside Florence

    Chapter XXXI.

    The Wedding

Begin with cold dawn – wind and rain – day coming on.
Mr Sownds the Beadle and Mrs Miff the Pew opener
 Mr Dombey, the Major, and Carker
 ~~The/Major~~ Cousin Feenix —Speech.
 The Servants – Breakfast up-stairs and down.
 Edith's Departure Back to dawn again – "To have and to hold from this day forward" – &c – Carker riding into town, saying so

Chapter Plan

wholesome air, as such things will, even unto prisoners and captives, and those who are desolate and oppressed, in very spite of aldermen and knights to boot: at whose sage nod – and how they nod! – the rolling world stands still!] 'Counter fragrances ... among the dwellings of the poor' alludes to one of the two opposing theories of disease that influenced sanitary reformers. The miasma (or zymotic, or effluvia) theory held that contagion existed as a miasma in the atmosphere, lurking in decaying animal and vegetable matter until it spread by a process analogous to fermentation. Because of the supposed connection between these miasmic clouds and the spread of 'infectious' diseases such as cholera, typhus, influenza and yellow fever, it was commonly thought that 'all smell is disease', as Edwin Chadwick memorably put it in 1846 (testimony to parliamentary committee, qtd. in Johnson, 2006, 114). Although the miasmic theory gradually lost ground in the 1840s to the discoveries by bacteriologists and analytical chemists that proved that disease is spread either through contact or by germs that are airborne or waterborne, in 1851 Dickens worried that animal blood and viscera from the slaughterhouses near Smithfield Market would be dumped into the sewers of London and engender an 'immense mass of corruption ... to rise in poisonous gases, into your house at eight, when your children will most readily absorb them' ('A Monument of French Folly' [8 March 1851]: 2.534; Frazer *passim*; Finer *passim*; Wohl *passim*). For Dickens's involvement in the sanitary reform movement, and for more on the miasma theory, see notes to chapters 8 and 47, pp. 125, 431.

Newspapers frequently published detailed accounts of the worrisome stench that permeated the dwellings of the poor in such places as St Giles's:

> Of the stench which pervades these vermin haunted, mouldering, noisome abodes; of the exhalations which arise from the stagnant pools lying iridescent on the unpaved surface of the ground – from the refuse thrown, for want of dust-bins, into the street – and from the soil itself, saturated, as it is, with perennial accumulations of ordure – we spare the reader a detailed account. ... That the neighboring inhabitants of New Oxford Street strive to shut out, by boardings twenty feet high, the loathsome exhalations of this urban jungle; and that they have fenced up the thoroughfares as if against noisome and dangerous vermin, are circumstances of terrible significance, but on which we have not room at present to dilate. The point to which we would call attention is this – that the money-cost of this appalling squalor exceeds the money-cost of decent comfort. ... We invite the proprietor of these neglected abodes [Sir John Hanmer] to weigh carefully these facts and figures. The harvest which he now reaps from crime and squalor is but a meagre harvest; and it is accompanied with an awful responsibility. (*Report from the London Committee of Health*, cited in *Journal of Prison Discipline and Philanthropy*, 1850, 5.15–17)

The Carlylean rhetoric in the passage from *DS* underlines how Dickens shared Carlyle's disbelief in the ability of Parliament to ameliorate social abuses. Forster remarked on this in his discussion of *The Chimes* in 1844:

I had noticed in him the habit of more gravely regarding many things ... the hopelessness of any true solution of either political or social problems by the ordinary Downing-street methods had been startlingly impressed on him in Carlyle's writings; and ... he had come to have ... little faith for the putting down of any serious evil. (2.120–1).

(may God reward the worthy gentlemen who stickle for the Plague as part and parcel of the wisdom of our ancestors, and do their little best to keep those dwellings miserable!)] Dickens describes the 'horrors' of the Great Plague of London in 1665 in *CHE*:

> The disease soon spread so fast, that it was necessary to shut up the houses in which sick people were, and to cut them off from communication with the living. ... The streets were all deserted, grass grew in the public ways, and there was a dreadful silence in the air. When night came on, dismal rumblings used to be heard, and these were the wheels of the death-carts, attended by men with veiled faces and holding cloths to their mouths. ... The corpses put into these carts were buried by torchlight in great pits: no service being performed over them. ... In the general fear, children ran away from their parents, and parents from their children. Some who were taken ill, died alone, and without any help. Some were stabbed or strangled by hired nurses who robbed them of all their money, and stole the very beds on which they lay. Some went mad, dropped from the windows, ran through the streets, and in their pain and frenzy flung themselves into the river. (35).

The phrase 'The Wisdom of our Ancestors' was a cliché, used by such writers as Thomas Dibden (*The Jew and the Doctor*, 1800), James Fenimore Cooper (*The Bravo*, 1831), Benjamin Disraeli (*Coningsby*, 1844) and by Dickens himself in *CC* (1843). Among the titles Dickens invented in 1851 to be printed on book spines for display in his library in Devonshire Terrace was a series entitled '*The Wisdom of Our Ancestors. Vol I, Ignorance. Vol II, Superstition. Vol III, The Block. Vol. IV, The Stake. Vol. V, The Rack. Vol VI, Dirt*'.

Miss Tox sat down upon

Mr. Tox, of the Customs Department of the public service;] In Dickens's day, almost one half of the people working for the Civil Service were employed in Customs. The Custom House, located on Lower Thames Street, had been erected between 1814 and 1817 (modified *c.* 1850). The major departments were 'the Secretary's, the Survey-General's, the Law Officers', the Comptroller of Accounts', the Statistical, and the Long Room'. The 'out-door' department comprised 'surveyors, assistant-surveyors, examining officers, gaugers (with inspectors and assistant-inspectors)'. The major customs-producing items were sugar, tea, tobacco, wine and brandy (Cunningham, 1850; Dickens, Jr., 1879).

Sitting on the window-seats

a man with bulgy legs, and a rough voice, and a heavy basket on his head that crushed his hat into a mere black muffin, came crying flowers ... making his timid little roots of daisies shudder] Mayhew found the root-sellers (i.e. those selling rooted flowering plants) to be 'among the best-mannered and the best-dressed of all the street-sellers ... but that only as regards a portion of them' and 'more attached to their trade than others of their class'. As for the location and nature of the street sales, he explained:

> Hackney is the suburb most resorted to by the root-sellers. The best "pitches" for the sale of roots in the street are situated in the Newroad, the City-road, the Hampstead-road, the Edgeware-road, and places of similar character, where there is a constant stream of passers along, who are not too much immersed in business. Above three-fourths of the sale is effected by itinerant costermongers. For this there is one manifest reason: a flower-pot, with the delicate petals of its full-blown moss-rose, perhaps, suffers even from the trifling concussion in the journey of an omnibus, for instance. To carry a heavy flower-pot, even any short distance, cannot be expected, and to take a cab for its conveyance adds greatly to the expense. Hence, flower-roots are generally purchased at the door of the buyer. (1.137)

In the early 1850s, daisies, whether 'single or wild', were 'coming to be more asked for, each 1*d.*' According to Mayhew, root trade was at its height, 'Towards the close of May, in an early season, and in the two following months', and he estimated that there were about 500 root-sellers in London (1.138). Apart from street sales, flowers and various potted plants would commonly be purchased at Covent Garden, London's main fresh produce market since the seventeenth century.

as though he had been an ogre, hawking little children,] The ogre in 'Hop-o-my-Thumb' eats children (see note to chapter 8, p. 131).

summer recollections were so strong upon Miss Tox, that she shook her head, and murmured she would be comparatively old before she knew it –] A common association. Mayhew noted that

> Perhaps the pleasantest of all cries in early spring is that of "All a-growing – all ablow-ing" heard for the first time in the season. It is that of the "root-seller" who has stocked his barrow with primroses, violets, and daisies. Their beauty and fragrance gladden the senses; and the first and, perhaps, unexpected sight of them may prompt hopes of the coming year, such as seem proper to the spring. (1.132)

He also noted, in a conventional association, that 'The fondness for flowers in London is strongest in the women, and, perhaps, strongest in those whose callings are in-door

Chapter 29 *The Opening of the Eyes of Mrs. Chick*

and sedentary. Flowers are to them a companionship' (1.132).

"If my brother Paul had consulted

You might have led me to the block] The chopping block used in a beheading by axe, a method of execution usually reserved for the upper class. Beheading, apparently introduced into England by William the Conqueror, continued as a form of state execution until the mid-eighteenth century. Dickens, who generally opposed capital punishment, witnessed the beheading of a murderer in Rome on 8 March 1845 ('It was an ugly, filthy, careless, sickening spectacle; meaning nothing but butchery': 'Rome', *PI*).

Miss Tox made no verbal

whose face and figure were dilated with Mephistophelean joy.] See note to chapter 20, p. 240–1.

But none of that gentle

Mrs. Chick drew off as from a criminal, and reversing the precedent of the murdered king of Denmark, regarded her more in anger than in sorrow.] Horatio informs Hamlet that the ghost of his father had 'A countenance more in sorrow than in anger' (1.2.232).

"If any one had told

The scales ... have fallen from my sight.] A cliché borrowed from Acts 9.18: 'And immediately there fell from his eyes as it had been scales: and he received sight forthwith, and arose, and was baptized'. The biblical passage marks the moment at which Saul of Tarsus has his sight restored and becomes a Christian.

"The idea!" said Mrs. Chick,

"The idea! ... of your having basked at my brother's fireside, like a serpent, and wound yourself, through me, almost into his confidence,] A traditional fable about treachery, mentioned by Edmund Spenser: 'now hee playeth like the frozen snake, who being for compassion relieved by the husbandman, soone after he was warme began to hisse, and threaten danger even to him and his' ('A View of the Present State of Ireland', published 1633). Mrs Chick's words are strikingly similar to those in a novel by the popular author, Catherine Ward, *The Cottage on the Cliff, a Sea-Side Story* (1823):

'who would have thought such a thing of Mr. Craftly? a base, vile young man, to come and warm himself by my poor master's fireside, like the snake did with the husbandman, only to sting him to the heart by ruinating his child!' (ch. 36)

While poor excommunicated Miss Tox,

watered her plants with her tears,] Psalm 6.6: 'I am weary with my groaning; all the night make I my bed to swim; I water my couch with my tears'.

Chapter 30

THE INTERVAL BEFORE THE MARRIAGE

The Honourable Mrs. Skewton,

she set her face against Death altogether, and objected to the mention of any such low and levelling upstart –] 'Death is the grand leveler' is a proverb dating from the sixteenth century.

Mrs. Skewton ... had borrowed a house in Brook-street, Grosvenor Square, from a stately relative] Brook Street extends from Hanover Square to Grosvenor Square. With its spacious houses, 'some of rubbed bricks with stone finishings', and its proximity to Hyde Park, Grosvenor Square was one of the most fashionable squares in London, attracting 'more dukes, marquesses, earls, and viscounts' than any other part of the city. Dickens himself referred to Grosvenor Square's 'aristocratic gravity' in *NN* (37), and he described the area in *LD* (1.10). His paternal grandmother was a servant to Lady Blandford, who resided in Grosvenor Square, and his friend Bulwer-Lytton had a house in the area. For the most part, the aristocracy lived in a broad band through the middle of the estate in the area between Brook Street and Upper Brook Street and Grosvenor Street and Upper Grosvenor Street (Timbs, 1867, 749; *Survey of London*, 1977; Kennedy, 1986).

It being necessary for the credit of the family to make a handsome appearance at such a time, Mrs. Skewton, with the assistance of an accommodating tradesman resident in the parish of Mary-le-bone, who lent out all sorts of articles to the nobility and gentry, from a service of plate to an army of footmen, clapped into this house a silver-headed butler ... two very tall young men in livery,]

> Does a fashionable gentleman wish to give a dinner party; he sends to Gunter, or some other professor of gastronomy, and tells him to provide a splendid entertainment for a given number of persons, to have every thing in and out of season, and to see that every thing is *recherché* in the extreme. He has then no further trouble. Gunter takes the whole direction; provides waiters, attendants, plate if it be necessary, in short every thing. So in respect to suppers and balls. Is it the intention of the proprietors to make their apartments resemble green rooms? choice shrubs and exotics are brought; the place is decorated; the supper table is set out with plate, china, glass, and edibles; rout chairs are provided, all at a given expense; and the day after the rout or ball has been given, these ornaments and relics are taken away by the persons who provided them, and the house restored to its usual appearance probably while the proprietors are sleeping from the effects of fatigue. (*London in 1838,* 1839, 108–09)

Such confectionary and catering establishments as Gunter, which were essential to fashionable social functions, made frequent appearances in the fashionable or 'silver fork' novels of the 1820s to the mid-1840s, and in Thackeray's novels of the 1840s and 1850s. In *The Newcomes* (1855), for instance, the narrator moralizes,

> The true pleasure of life is to live with your inferiors .... With a shilling's worth of tea and muffins you can get as much adulation and respect as many people cannot purchase with a thousand pounds' worth of plate and profusion, hired footmen, turning their houses topsy-turvy, and suppers from Gunter's. (9.1.96–7; Altick, 1991, 220–7)

Originally 'St Mary's by the bourne', Marylebone included 'Portman and Cavendish Squares, and Bryanstone and Montague Squares, Portland Place and the Regent's Park'. It was 'The largest and most populous of the suburban parishes', containing 'a considerable number of wealthy inhabitants and tradesmen of the first class, and persons connected with the City, from the wealthy merchant to his clerks and warehousemen' (Chambers, 1849, 2.216; Knight, 1851, 6.271).

As the head domestic servant, the butler was responsible for managing the other servants, paying the domestic bills and ensuring that the house ran smoothly. He presided over arrangements for breakfast, lunch, tea and dinner, and served at these meals; cleaned and stored the household plate; maintained his master's hunting equipment; and, perhaps most importantly, looked after the wine cellar. At dinner, the butler placed the silver and plated articles on the table, carried in the first dish, announced dinner and then took his place behind his master's chair on the left during grace, in preparation for the removal of the dish covers. He would then attend at the side-table, offering wine and setting and arranging later courses. The butler would also make sure that the fires and lighting in the public rooms were in order, ready to receive the family and guests after dinner. The most fashionable butlers, like the most fashionable footmen (see note to chapter 3, p. 45), were tall and generally statuesque (Beeton 962–4; Horn 91–4).

Cleopatra skipping off her couch

one of the very tall young men on hire, whose organ of veneration was imperfectly developed, thrusting his tongue into his cheek,] An allusion to the pseudo-science of phrenology, the method of reading character from the size and contours of the cranium developed by Franz Joseph Gall (1758–1828) and his disciple Johann Gaspar Spurzheim (1776–1832), and popularized in England by the brothers George and Andrew Combe. Different propensities, such as 'veneration', 'benevolence' and 'combativeness', were believed to be located in different 'organs', or regions, of the brain. A well developed region would indicate a correspondingly well developed aptitude. In *A System of Phrenology* (5th ed., 1853), perhaps the most popular book written on the subject, George Combe located 'veneration' 'in the middle of the coronal region of the brain' (i.e. at the crown of the head), explaining that it was 'the source of natural religion, and of that tendency to worship a superior power, which manifests itself in almost every tribe of men yet discovered' (1.399, 401). Dickens himself confessed that 'I hold phrenology, within certain limits, to be true' and claimed a belief in phrenology, 'in the main and broadly, as an essential part of the truth of physiognomy', though in his novels he often presents the subject in a humorous and ironic light (Taylor and Shuttleworth 30; 'A Little Dinner in an Hour', *AYR*, 21.109; 21 February 1860, *Letters* 9.215–16).

In the eighteenth and nineteenth centuries, thrusting the tongue into the cheek was a common gesture of derision and contempt.

"Yes, madam," replied Mr. Dombey;

"the deed of settlement ... is now ready, and ... Edith has only to ... suggest her own time for its execution."] Deeds of settlement were customary only among the wealthy middle class, the gentry and the aristocracy. According to *A Guide to the Unprotected in Every-day Matters Relating to Property and Income* (1863), the deed of settlement comprised

> the lady's fortune, and a certain proportion of the gentleman's, which are placed in the hands of trustees, to secure a certain income for the lady and her children, in case of her husband's death or bankruptcy. No prudent woman should marry without this provision, as, if it is made before her marriage, however much in debt her husband may become, from extravagance or misfortune, her settlement money cannot be made liable. The friends of the lady should *insist* upon a proper marriage settlement to the satisfaction of her Lawyer being signed *before the marriage.* ...
>
> The Trustees of a Settlement ... are responsible for the loss or misapplication of the money entrusted to them, if any is lost through their carelessness. ... A Trustee, or his co-Trustee, should have the Marriage Settlement and all Deeds, Share and Stock Certificates, etc., connected with the Trust, in his hands, or in those of his Lawyer, and never leave them in the husband's keeping. ... It

Chapter 30 *The Interval before the Marriage*

is usual to have two or more Trustees of a Marriage Settlement; one is selected by the lady and the other by the gentleman. (108–10)

So thought Mr. Dombey, when

black-hatchments of pictures] Hatchments – square or lozenge-shaped wooden shields bearing the coat-of-arms of a recently deceased well-to-do person – were fixed to the front of a house to signify that the household was in mourning, as in *Vanity Fair*, ch. 26: 'If we are gentlefolks they will put hatchments over our late domicile, with gilt cherubim, and mottoes stating that there is "Quiet in Heaven" '.

The week fled fast. There

Florence was to cast off her mourning, and to wear a brilliant dress on the occasion.] See note to chapter 3, p. 50. For the practice of young women slighting their mourning on the occasion of a wedding, compare *A Father's Love and a Woman's Friendship. A Novel* (1825):

> They were all however yet in slight mourning for their father, although he was full a year dead when the wedding took place; and that fortunate event having occasioned an alteration in their apparel, Mrs. Granby was satisfied the two girls with her should no longer wear the insignia of death. (Mosse, 1825, 1.55)

"My dear Dombey," returned

I feared you were going, with malice aforethought, as the dreadful lawyers say] 'Malice aforethought' is the state of mind for murder to be charged, involving an intent to kill or cause serious physical harm; e. g. William Blackstone, *Commentaries on the Laws of England*, 1769, 4.14: 'Murder is therefore now thus defined, or rather described, by Sir Edward Coke, "when a person, of sound memory and discretion, unlawfully killeth any reasonable creature in being and under the king's peace, with malice aforethought, either 'express or implied' " '.

Because my charming Florence

quite a Bashaw."] Quite an imperious man. 'Bashaw' is an earlier form of the Turkish title, pasha, used especially in the case of military commanders (*OED*).

Drawn nearer, nearer, nearer yet;

Its touch was like the prophet's rod of old upon the rock.] That is, like a miracle. Compare Exodus 17.5-6:

> And the Lord said unto Moses, Go on before the people, and take with thee of the elders of Israel; and thy rod, wherewith thou smotest the river, take in thine hand, and go. Behold, I will stand before thee there upon the rock in Horeb; and thou shalt smite the rock, and there shall come water out of it, that the people may drink. And Moses did so in the sight of the elders of Israel.

Chapter 31

THE WEDDING

Dawn, with its passionless

Dawn, with its passionless blank face. ... Night crouches yet, upon the pavement, and broods ... dawn moans and weeps ... night returns refreshed,] The personification of nature in the opening and final paragraphs of the chapter continues Dickens's use of fairy tale elements in the novel: the literary device is most associated with fables and fairy tales (Aesop, Perrault, the Brothers Grimm).

the countless ripples in the tide of time that regularly roll and break on the eternal shore,] 'Time and tide wait for no man' is a proverb dating from the fourteenth century.

And now, the mice, who have

the beadle ... the sexton; and Mrs. Miff, the wheezy little pew-opener – ... a thirsty soul for sixpences and shillings.] For beadle, sexton and pew-opener, see notes to chapter 5, p. 83, p. 85 and p. 86. A pew-opener at a wedding is sketched by Douglas Jerrold in *Heads of the People* (1840):

> ... in her delicate duty of locking and unlocking doors; in the serene self-possession with which she at times advances one hand, and then, as if nothing had happened, returns it to her pocket. She has, however, her times of professional gladness; when, to smirk and smile, and tread quickly about the church, to be very busy when there is nothing to be done, to be greatly interested at what, to her, is a dull repetition of a dull scene, is her duty, being

one of the sources of her profit: we speak of weddings. Observe, how gladly good Mrs. Spikenard smiles upon the happy couple, and the crowd of friends, as she meets them at the door; what approving gladness at the solemnity about to be performed is in every look: how quickly she trips along the aisle, and ushers them to the pew. ... She hovers about the bride and bridegroom, the bridesmaids, and, indeed, the whole nuptial party, as if she had positively a personal interest in the matter, assures the young couple that the clergyman will not be long; and, at length, when the good man is gowned, and ready for the service, comes, with her wrinkled face all smiles and satisfaction, to tell the gladsome news that Mr. Tie'emtight is quite prepared. (230)

Busy is Mrs. Miff

the Beadle ... an admirer of female beauty, observes ... she is a spanker – an expression that seems somewhat forcible to Mrs. Miff] 'Spanker' was a colloquialism mostly used by sporting and military men for a woman of superior quality, as in the account of an army officer meeting a young lady at an assembly: 'Miss O'Brien was what Rattigan called a spanker. She was dressed in a blue silk lute-string gown, with a plume of ostrich feathers, flesh-coloured stockings, and red satin shoes' (from a review of *Stories of Waterloo; and Other Tales* [1829], qtd. in *The London Literary Gazette; and Journal of Belles Lettres, Arts, Sciences, etc.*, 1829, 678).

In Mr. Dombey's house, at this

the cook says ... that one wedding makes many,] A proverb dating from the seventeenth century.

a foreigner with whiskers (Mr. Towlinson is whiskerless himself) ... he never knew of any good that ever come of foreigners; and being charged by the ladies with prejudice, says, look at Bonaparte who was at the head of 'em, and see what *he* was always up to!]

> There is an inborn and inbred distrust of "foreigners" in England – continental foreigners ... The word "foreigner" in England, conveys exclusively the idea of a dark-complexioned and whiskered individual, in a frogged coat and distressed circumstances. (*The Parterre of Fiction, Poetry, History, and General Literature*, 1835, 3.70)

Although beards and moustaches had been widely worn on the Continent from the 1830s, they were only acceptable in Britain (until 1853–4) on cavalry officers: the few civilians who dared to sport them were considered swells, or sham foreign counts. A beard, in particular, was 'an abomination in English eyes, and was never seen, unless occasionally in aged eccentrics ripe for Bedlam, or on the chins of ancient

Hebrews' ('The Beard and Moustache Movement', *Illustrated London News* 24 [4 February 1854]: 95). For more on this prejudice, see note to chapter 59, p. 508.

'It is extraordinary what nonsense English people talk, write, and believe, about foreign countries', Dickens remarked on 6 December 1846 (*Letters* 4.676). Even English artists, he complained, maintained excessively narrow and provincial views of the French: 'They seem to me to have got a fixed idea that there is no natural manner but the English manner ... and that unless a Frenchman ... is as calm as Clapham, or as respectable as Richmond-hill, he cannot be right' (*Letters* 7.744).

Hostility to the French, and to foreigners more generally, was a common sentiment in England throughout the nineteenth century. This xenophobia was fuelled by the violence of the French Revolution and the destruction wrought by the Napoleonic Wars, the competitive imperial ambitions of Britain and Russia following the wars, and, later, the revolutions of 1848 and the *coup d'état* of 1851, by which Louis Napoleon revived the French Empire. The particular hatred of Napoleon Buonaparte is reflected in Tennyson's poem of 1833, 'Buonaparte': 'He thought to quell the stubborn hearts of oak, / Madman! ... / We taught him lowlier moods ... / We taught him: late he learned humility, / Perforce'. The French were portrayed as a dangerously destructive, atheistic and impious people whose immorality threatened English values. The actress Fanny Kemble, for instance, lamented the French people's 'selfish disregard of others, which manifests itself in a rudeness of deportment quite as offensive as the sullen mixture of pride and shyness which so long distinguished traveling English', and she observed that 'the common opinion of English people' in 1847 was that the French 'have very much departed from the affable and courteous manner which were once a sort of national characteristic among them' (Butler 80–1).

Dickens frequently used *HW* to attack British provinciality and complacency. He was, for instance, impressed by the openly idiosyncratic manners of the French people, who dressed according to convenience and personal inclinations, wore facial hair and sat in their 'six square feet of yard' without embarrassment. As well, he believed that the French had better laws than the British, recognized the existence of social problems and painted 'vivacious' pictures. In 'Insularities', a *HW* article of 1856, Dickens warned his readers that 'it is of paramount importance to every nation that its boastfulness should not generate prejudice, conventionality, and a cherishing of unreasonable ways of acting and thinking' (13.1).

Mr. Towlinson ... being rendered something gloomy by the engagement of a foreigner ... who has been hired to accompany the happy pair to Paris, and who is busy packing the new chariot.]

> It is notorious that English servants taken for the first time to the Continent, and ignorant of every language but their own, are worse than useless – they are an encumbrance. The traveller who requires a servant at any rate, had better take a foreign one. (*A Handbook for Travellers on the Continent*, 1838, xxi)

Although a foreign servant, or 'courier', was expensive (£8 to £10 a month, according to one estimate), he was regarded as indispensable for travellers who were not fluent in the language of the countries they were visiting. As the *Handbook* remarked, 'He relieves his master from much fatigue of body and perplexity of mind, in unraveling the difficulties of long bills and foreign moneys, sparing his temper the trials it is likely to endure from disputes with innkeepers, postmasters, and the like'. A courier supervised the packing and unpacking of luggage, secured 'clean and well-aired beds', ordered meals and arranged for post-horses when they became necessary. He also examined his employer's carriage each evening for needed repairs, and performed 'all the services of waiting and attendance, cleaning and brushing clothes, &c.' (xxi–xxii).

Only the rich could afford to take their private carriages to the Continent, as Mayhew remarked: 'This was the aristocratic style of travelling, and its indulgence was costly' (3.321). The practice was discouraged by the 'Roving Englishman' (Grenville Murray) in his 'Hints to Travellers':

> A carriage has now [1852] become almost a useless incumbrance; nevertheless, where one is still necessary, it is a silly increase of expense to drag one from England to the place where it is wanted … good travelling carriages may be hired anywhere. (*HW* 6.212)

France began to be fashionable with the British in the late eighteenth century, particularly because French literature, manners and culture were setting the standard for the rest of Europe. The vogue in England for French fashions, which started at the beginning of the nineteenth century, further established France as a favourite destination of the British, for whom a visit to Paris was the chief attraction (Maxwell, 1932, 1–45 *passim*).

Dickens himself knew Paris well, having first visited it in 1844 on his way to Italy. While writing *DS*, he lived with his family for three months in 1846–7 in the Faubourg Saint-Honoré, and throughout the rest of his life he made frequent excursions there with one or another of his friends, always seeming to find stimulation in the excitement and bustle of the city.

The pastry-cook is hard

One of the very tall young men already smells of sherry … and informs his comrade that it's his "exciseman." The very tall young man would say excitement, but his speech is hazy.] Excisemen were customs officials who collected excise duties and tried to prevent smuggling and other illegal activities. They were frequently the butt of comedy, as in Robert Burns's song, 'The Deil's Awa' wi' the Exciseman'; see also a later comic song, 'The Exciseman', in *Universal Songster*, 1834, 1.193.

The men who play the bells,

The men who play the bells … the marrow-bones and cleavers too; and a brass band … put themselves in communication … with Mr. Towlinson, to whom they offer terms to be bought off;] A variety of street musicians, of which there were about 1000 at mid-century. According to a performer on the bells,

> When I first played them, I had my 14 bells arranged on a rail, and tapped them with my two leather hammers held in my hands in the usual way. I thought next I could introduce some novelty into the performance. The novelty I speak of was to play the violin with the bells. I had hammers fixed on a rail, so as each bell had its particular hammer; these hammers were connected with cords to a pedal acting with a spring to bring itself up, and so, by playing the pedal with my feet, I had full command of the bells, and made them accompany the violin, so that I could give any tune almost with the power of a band. ... Of all my plans, the piano, and the bells and violin, did the best, and are the best still for a standard. I can only average 12*s.* a-week, take the year through, which is very little for two. (Mayhew 3.161)

Marrow bones and cleavers were 'the principal instruments in the band of rough music: these are generally performed on by butchers, on marriages, elections, riding skimmington, and other public or joyous occasions' (Grose, 1811). Characteristically, street-performing brass bands, which averaged about four members in each band,

> take up their position in front of a gin-shop, and peal out waltzes, polkas, and operatic novelties, with all the force that cornets-a-piston and trombones can give, to large surrounding crowds. The *enterprise*, in this case, is of comparative magnitude, and the members of the band have a certain position. They may be seen, on other occasions, in the orchestra of a cheap public ballroom, on board the Richmond or Gravesend steamers, or possibly heading an election procession. Nay, we have at times detected some of the *troupe* as beef-eaters, or anomalous foreigners, in caps of sham tiger-skins shaped like flower-pots, and robes of bed-curtain chintz ... blowing away all their energies in front of a menagerie or dancing-show at a large fair. (Gavarni, 1849)

Performers in street bands generally could not read music, which prevented them from being employed in the theatres or other places that required a musical education. In the view of one contemporary observer, however, 'numbers of street musicians (playing by ear) are better instrumentalists than many educated musicians in the theatres' (Mayhew 3.163). Mayhew divided street musicians into two categories:

> the tolerable and the intolerable performers: some of them trusting to their skill in music for the reward for their exertions, others only making a *noise*, so that whatever money they obtain is given them merely as an inducement for them to depart. ... Indeed, many of these people carry with them musical instruments, merely as a means of avoiding the officers of the Mendicity Society, or in some few cases as a signal of their coming to the persons in the neighbourhood, who are in the habit of giving them a small weekly pension. (3.159)

For more on street musicians and Dickens's dislike of their noise, see notes to chapters 3 and 23, pp. 49, 277.

Battlebridge;] Or Battle Bridge, a small village north of London, at the junction of Gray's Inn Road with the Pentonville and Euston Roads and now known as King's Cross (from a statue of George IV, erected in 1836 and taken down in 1845) (Wheatley, 1891, 1.130). In *OMF*, Dickens locates the dust-heaps at Belle Isle, near Battle Bridge (1.4, see Cotsell, 1986, 45–6, 58). (There was another 'Battle Bridge' ['Battlebridge Stairs'], near Tooley Street in Southwark, though Dickens is most likely referring to the Battle Bridge north of London: this Battle Bridge is closer to Brook Street, and is in the vicinity of Ball's Pond, which Dickens mentions in the same paragraph.)

Ball's Pond,] See note to chapter 18, pp. 223–4.

Cousin Feenix has come over

Long's Hotel, in Bond-street.] Long's Hotel was a first-class hotel in the West End, 'patronised by the best county people of the day' and near many clubs ('One of the Old Brigade', 1908). Bond Street, along with Regent Street, is one of the main arteries between the major thoroughfares of Oxford Street and Piccadilly, and, since the eighteenth century, has been renowned for its fashionable shops.

"Dombey," says the Major,

That is the hand, of which His Royal Highness the late Duke of York, did me the honour to observe, Sir, to His Royal Highness the late Duke of Kent,] Like his elder brother, Frederick, the Duke of York and Albany (1763–1827), Edward Augustus, the Duke of Kent and Strathern (1767–1820) – the fourth son of George III and the father of Queen Victoria – was a notable failure as a military leader, and frequently in debt. He served, for a brief period, as commander-in-chief of the forces in British North America, and as governor of Gibraltar, and was gazetted field-marshal in 1805, before eventually retiring to Brussels in 1815. According to the *DNB*, 'his pedantic, almost superstitious, insistence upon minutiæ of military etiquette, discipline, dress, and equipments, made him unpopular in the army' (11.20). For the Duke of York, see note to chapter 1, p. 32–3; for Bagstock's name-dropping as one of the attributes he shares with Thackeray's Major Gahagan, see notes to chapters 7 and 10, pp. 112, 150–1.

up-to-snuff,] Slang, synonymous with 'flash', that is, 'knowing' (*Grose's Classical Dictionary of the Vulgar Tongue*, 1823).

"And if she is to be

"And if she is to be Mrs. Dombey this morning, Sir ... it's high time we were off!"] English canonical law dating from the seventeenth century stipulated that marriages had to be performed between the hours of 8 a.m. and 12 noon; otherwise, they were uncanonical (but not invalid).

Forth, in a barouche, ride

the fat leg of a cherub on a monument, with cheeks like a young Wind.] In Baroque architecture and decoration, cherubs are represented with wings and often have their cheeks puffed out and their lips pursed. The association derives from Psalm 18.10: 'And he rode upon a cherub, and did fly: yea, he did fly upon the wings of the wind'.

he's as stiff a cove as ever he see, but that it is within the resources of Science to double him up, with one blow in the waistcoat.] For 'cove', see note to chapter 22, p. 265. 'Science' was a term sometimes applied to pugilism, often in a jocular manner (*OED*); cf. 'The contest lasted 29 minutes, and it was acknowledged, there never was more skill and science displayed in any boxing match in this kingdom' (*Pancratia, or, a History of Pugilism,* 1812, 76).

Again, the good mother presses

the party in their proper places at the altar rails.] Immediately after 'rails' appeared this passage in the MS and first proof (A):

> The sun is shining down, upon the golden letters of the ten commandments. Why does the Bride's eye read them, one by one? Which one of all the ten appears the plainest to her in the glare of light? False Gods; murder; theft [<theft false witness> A *corr.*]; the honour that she owes her mother; which is it that appears to leave the wall, and print itself, in glowing letters, on her book! (Horsman 427)

" 'Who giveth this woman

" 'Who giveth this woman to be married to this man?' "] From the 'Solemnization of Matrimony' (*BCP*).

Cousin Feenix does that.

Baden-Baden] A fashionable spa in the Black Forest with extensive pleasure-grounds, gardens and promenades, and bathing establishments. Baden-Baden 'is considered one of the most fashionable German watering-places', its healing waters reputed to cure rheumatism and gout, paralysis, neuralgia, skin diseases, and various internal ailments. 'The months of July and August are the *season* when the baths are most frequented, but visitors are constantly coming and going from May to October, if the weather be fine'. *A Handbook for Travellers on the Continent* noted in 1838, 'The number of English visitors has increased so much of late that the place assumes the appearance of a settlement of our countrymen' (485). The *Handbook* quoted 'W. M. T.' (presumably William Makepeace Thackeray) who remarked that Baden-Baden 'may be advantageously resorted to by those amongst our countrymen whom economy or convenience has induced to make the continent their temporary home' (485).

The German spas were preferred by the British to Bath, Cheltenham, Leamington and Malvern and were also cheaper. British visitors predominated at Baden-Baden in the first half of the nineteenth century and frequented the other spas renowned for their gambling casinos as much as for their water-cures. Dickens substituted Baden-Baden for 'near the Pyrenees' in proof.

And will they in the sight

And will they in the sight of Heaven … they plight their troth to one another,] From the 'Solemnization of Matrimony' (*BCP*).

The carriages are once more

the twenty families of little women … every one of whom remembers the fashion and the colour of every article of dress from that moment, and reproduces it on her doll, who is for ever being married.] This is like Jenny Wren's habit of using 'great ladies' to model the dresses of her dolls: 'When I see a great lady very suitable for my business, I say, "You'll do, my dear!" and I take particular notice of her, and run home and cut her out and baste her' (*OMF* 3.2). In 'Dolls', *HW* remarks on the mid-century fashion for dolls of all types, including the most expensive and delicate dolls – which were finely articulated and 'made of yielding and manageable calico, stuffed with saw-dust, hair, or wool, according to its quality', and which were typically produced by 'many hands', working separately on individual parts – and the much more cheaply-made wooden dolls. Doll makers made every effort to keep the dolls' dresses fashionable: 'Unquestionably there is a fashion in dolls and doll's dresses, as in the attire of breathing mortals – the Marionettes, both living and dead, pay visits to Vanity Fair' (7.352–6).

Horses prance and caper; coachmen and footmen shine in fluttering favours, and new-made liveries.] In G. P. R. James's novel *The Step-mother* (1846), a character remarks that 'new carriages and liveries, and wedding favors' are among 'the *et ceteras* of a smart bridal' (264). In *PP,* Sam Weller attends the marriage of Mr

Snodgrass, wearing a white favour in his button-hole and 'clad in a new and gorgeous suit of livery invented expressly for the occasion' (ch. 57). In a tale from 1860, the 'bride elect', who desires to 'keep up appearances', jealously informs her fiancé that an acquaintance has 'a couple of coaches, a pair of greys to each, outriders in liveries, and white favours' and wonders why they should 'do the thing less respectably?' The narrator sardonically remarks, 'This reasoning was conclusive; the world required them, and coaches, greys, outriders, liveries, and white favours were agreed upon' (P. M. R., 'Why John Thrifty Didn't Get Rich' 455; *The Odd-Fellows Magazine. New Series*. 2 [October 1860]: 454–6).

Now, the carriages arrive at

Mr. Punch, that model of connubial bliss, salutes his wife.] Mr Punch, the puppet-show figure, was traditionally at odds with his wife, who attacked him when she discovered he had killed their child in a fit of anger. He wrested the weapon from his wife and then killed her. See note to chapter 3, pp. 48–9.

The pastry-cook has done

a rich breakfast is set forth.] 'Breakfast', after the marriage ceremony, was a meal eaten in the middle of the day at which soup, entrées and game were commonly served.

Cousin Feenix rises, when

wristbands almost covering his hands] For the different styles of wearing wristbands, see note to chapter 14, p. 197.

"Present," repeats Cousin Feenix

at whom the finger of scorn can never –] *Othello* 4.2.54–6:

> ... but, alas! to make me
> The fixed figure for the time of scorn
> To point his slow unmoving finger at!

The image had become a literary cliché by the mid-nineteenth century. Dickens also uses it in *OT* 5, *OMF* 2.3 and *MED* 4.

"I have not," says Cousin Feenix,

it has been my misfortune to be, as we used to say in my time in the House of Commons, when it was not the custom to allude to the Lords … to be … in another place!"] 'In another place' is the formulaic phrase used by members of the House of Commons to refer to proceedings in the House of Lords; e.g. 'It was not for him to allude to what passed in another House of parliament, except as a matter of history; but, he would say, that he had heard of passages delivered in another place which gave him alarm' (*Hansard* 13, [26 April 1825]: 208).

"But I know sufficient

a sadder and a wiser man,] From Coleridge, *The Rime of the Ancient Mariner* (1798):

> He went like one that had been stunned,
> And is of sense forlorn:
> A sadder and a wiser man,
> He rose the morrow morn. (ll.622–5)

By the mid-nineteenth century, the phrase had become a cliché, used by Charlotte Brontë, George Eliot, Wilkie Collins and Arthur Hugh Clough, among others.

All the servants, in the meantime,

Mr. Towlinson, whom to know is to esteem,] This phrase seems to have first appeared in 1805 in the anonymous *The Two Pilgrims, a Romance* ('you know this charming woman; to know is to esteem her'; vol. 2, ch. 2.26) and gained currency in the 1820s and 1830s.

all he hopes, is, he may never hear of no foreigner never boning nothing out of no travelling chariot.] 'To bone' is thieves' or beggars' jargon for to seize or steal (*Grose's Classical Dictionary of the Vulgar Tongue*, 1823; *OED*).

Mrs. Skewton sleeps up-stairs

heel-taps,] The liquor left at the bottom of a glass after drinking (*OED*).

pensive jellies, gradually resolving themselves into a lukewarm gummy soup.] A facetious allusion to one of Hamlet's soliloquies: 'O, that this too too solid flesh would melt, / Thaw, and resolve itself into a dew!' (2.1.129–30).

escorting that lady home by the next omnibus.]

> An omnibus is a kind of coach mounted on four wheels, in shape resembling

an oblong box, with windows at the sides, a seat in front for the driver, and a door with steps behind for the entrance of passengers. The seats are along each side, and both will usually accommodate twelve or fourteen persons. The outside of the vehicle has a well-finished coach-like appearance, generally with its name blazoned in large gold letters on the sides. The interior is tastefully fitted up with coloured cloth or red plush; the seats are stuffed; sometimes there is a carpet for the feet; and the whole has quite a comfortable and respectable appearance. The omnibus is drawn by two horses. ('The Omnibuses', *Chambers's Edinburgh Journal*, 4 April 1835, 77)

The first regular omnibus service in London, which was established by George Shillibeer on 4 July 1829, ran from Paddington Green to the Bank of England. An omnibus was legally designated 'a Metropolitan Stage-carriage' as distinguished from a 'cab', which was designated a 'Metropolitan Hackney'. As a 'Stage-carriage', an omnibus 'pursue[s] a given route, and the passengers are mixed, while the fare is fixed by the proprietor'. In contrast, 'the hackney-carriage plies for hire at an appointed "stand," carries no one but the party hiring it, and the fare for so doing is regulated by law'.

There were about 3000 omnibuses in London at mid-century, the majority of which would begin to run 'at eight in the morning, and continue till twelve at night, succeeding each other during the busy part of the day every five minutes'. According to Mayhew, 'The principle routes lie north and south, east and west, through the central parts of London, to and from the extreme suburbs'. On average, an omnibus would travel six miles each way, 'at the rate of from five to six English miles an hour (seldom six)', and carry fifteen passengers (though nearly all vehicles were licensed to carry twenty-two – 'thirteen inside and nine out'). Passengers would typically pay one of two fares: '3*d.* for part of the distance, and 6*d.* for the whole distance'. Between 150,000 and 225,000 Londoners used the omnibus daily, in Mayhew's estimation (3.336–47; *AYR* 2.31–2).

The Major don't know; that's

Long's,] For Long's Hotel, see note above, p. 337.

Chapter 32 Eleventh monthly number
August 1847

THE WOODEN MIDSHIPMAN GOES TO PIECES

"Ah!" said Captain Cuttle darkly,

sheer off,] Turn aside or change direction, a nautical phrase.

stand off and on, … "The horse-road?" … Go away a bit and come back again alternate – d'ye understand that?"] 'When a ship is beating to windward, so that by one board she approaches towards the shore, and by the other stands out to sea, she is said to stand *off and on* shore' (Bowditch, 1823, 258). A 'horse-road' is one wide enough for horses, in contrast to a footpath (*OED* 'horse' IV.27.c.).

Nevertheless, the Captain did not

the lady's attendance on the ministry of the Reverend Melchisedech rendered it peculiarly unlikely that she would be found in communion with the Establishment.] As Primitive Methodists (see note to chapter 15, p. 201), Melchisedech Howler's flock would not be members of the Church of England, the Established church; in particular, they would not be communicant Anglicans – persons who subscribe to the doctrine of the Holy Trinity and who regularly receive Communion.

Captain Cuttle descended slowly

Hope's anchor] The anchor is an Early Christian symbol of hope, deriving from Hebrews 6.19: 'Which hope we have as an anchor of the soul, both sure and steadfast'.

melancholy truth was at the bottom of that well,] 'Truth lies at the bottom of a well' is a proverb dating from classical antiquity.

"There ain't no drain of nothing

"There ain't no drain of nothing short handy,] 'DRAIN. Gin: so called from the diuretic qualities imputed to that liquor'; 'SHORT. A dram unlengthened by water' (*Grose's Classical Dictionary of the Vulgar Tongue*); compare 'Ginshops', *SB*: 'those two old men who came in "just to have a drain" '.

Mr Carker the Manager.
and.
Mr Carker the Junior with Harriet
} Companion pictures.

Captain Cuttle in his fortified retreat.

The Captain mourns for Walter.

Rob the Grinder.

Mr Toots and the chicken – q^y

Good Mrs Brown and her daughter.   q^y Yes.

Any news of Uncle Sol q^y No

Mr Morfin – q^y.   Yes. (with a view to the future)

Number Plan

(Dealings with the Firm of Dombey and Son — N͟o̱ XI.)

Chapter   XXXII.

The wooden midshipman goes to pieces

M͟r Toots & Captain Cuttle – Toots's love

Disclosure of the loss of the Son and Heir. By Toots.

Glimpse of the Chicken.

Captain Cuttle finds he has mistaken M͟r Carker – Goes there, and is ordered out with ignominy.

The Captain reading the burial service, at night; committing Walter's body to the deep.

Chapter   XXXIII.

Contrasts

~~Contrast of the two~~

Contrast of the two homes – Carker the Manager, and Carker the Junior –

Harriet Carker.

Good M͟rs Brown's daughter comes home from beyond seas – Her conversation with Harriet Carker, who relieves her.

Chapter   XXXIV.

Another Mother and Daughter.

Good M͟rs Brown. To her, her daughter –

Indication of a contrast to M͟rs Skewton and Edith.

Good M͟rs Brown's daughter, finding who has relieved her, to return the money, and curse the giver.

Chapter Plan

"Cap'en Cuttle is my name,

"Cap'en Cuttle is my name, and England is my nation, this here is my dwelling place, and blessed be creation – Job,"] Versions of the motto were inscribed in Bibles and religious tracts, engraved on tombstones and stitched into samplers. The following example, written in a childish hand, comes from the inside cover of an 1838 tract:

> Peter Ingray is my name
> England is my nation
> Bassingbourn is my living place
> And Christ is my salvation.
> ('The Story of Joseph and his Brethren')

Captain Cuttle seems to confuse the popular motto with a verse from Job: 'Naked came I out of my mother's womb, and naked shall I return thither: the Lord gave, and the Lord hath taken away; blessed be the name of the Lord' (1.21).

"Why, I ask you as a

I ask you as a feeling heart,"] 'Feeling heart' was a literary cliché found in religious and sentimental writing from the seventeenth century; compare, for example, Henry Mackenzie, *The Man of Feeling* (1771): ' "You have a feeling heart, Mr. Harley; I bless it that it has saved my child" ' (ch. 29).

"Well," pursued Mr. Toots,

I went up as far as Finchley first, to get some uncommonly fine chickweed that grows there, for Miss Dombey's bird.] In the mid-nineteenth century, Finchley, eight miles north of London, was 'a pleasant rural village' of a few thousand people. It was chiefly known for its extensive but 'uncultivated' Commons, the site of numerous highway robberies in the eighteenth century. (In *OCS*, Kit lives with Mr and Mrs Garland at Abel Cottage in Finchley [ch. 21]). Mayhew lists chickweed as one type of the 'green stuff' 'required for cage-birds', along with 'groundsel, plantain and turf' (Thorne, 1876, 216–17; Mayhew 1.145).

The Captain making a sign

Shipping Intelligence:] 'Shipping Intelligence' was the heading of a regular column in newspapers which listed arrivals, departures and other shipping information relating to the major British ports.

Chapter 32 The Wooden Midshipman goes to Pieces

" 'Southampton. The barque Defiance,

" **'Southampton. The barque Defiance ... arrived in this port to-day, with a cargo of sugar, coffee, and rum, reports ... being becalmed on the sixth day of her passage home from Jamaica,]** Southampton, a major port on the south coast of England, about 70 miles from London, lies on a peninsula between the estuaries of the River Test and Itchen. In the middle of the nineteenth century, the principal trade of Southampton was 'with Portugal and the Baltic, and with the islands of Guernsey and Jersey. Hemp, iron, and tallow are imported from Russia; tar and pitch from Sweden; and from Portugal, wine and fruit' (*The Ports, Harbours, Watering-Places, and Coast Scenery of Great Britain*, 1842, 2.136). Steamers left Southampton for Jamaica twice a month, on the 2nd and 17th, and reached Kingston in about 19 days. They returned to England on the 27th and 12th. The main exports from Jamaica were sugar, rum, molasses, ginger, pimento and coffee (Ripley and Dana, 1860, 9.702–03).

Jamaica, seized from Spain in 1655, was the largest and most important British possession in the West Indies. The introduction of sugar cane as a plantation crop in the seventeenth century led to Britain's near-monopoly and to the establishment of a refining business at home that supplied sugar to North America and much of Europe. 'Sugar is more extensively used in this country [England] than in any other on the globe, and until of late years the refining business has been almost entirely confined to us' (*Dictionary of Trade*, 1844).

Rum, made from the distilled liquor obtained from the fermented juice of the sugar cane, or molasses, was another major export until high duty, temperance activity and unsettled conditions in the West Indies cut rum consumption in Britain by about a third. Additional commodities imported from the West Indies included coffee, cotton, chocolate nuts, ginger, pimento, indigo and various hard and soft woods. In return, British merchants exported wrought iron, copper, brass, pewter, silver, watches, cotton and woollen goods, and 'every article of food and clothing, furniture, ship chandlery, military stores, coals for firing, and every article of accommodation and luxury' (Adolphus, 1818, 2.152–3). By the nineteenth century, coffee was popular among all classes and one of the nation's principal beverages. For Dombey's commercial interests in the West Indies, and its sugar trade, see note to chapter 1, pp. 25–6

" *– latitude,*" *repeated Mr. Toots,*

an English brig, of about five hundred tons burden,] A brig is a two-masted vessel, square-rigged on both masts. The 'burden' is a ship's carrying capacity, stated as a certain number of tons. A spar is 'The general term for any mast, yard, boom, gaff, &c.' (Smyth, 1867, 641; *OED*).

"And Sol Gills," said the Captain,

gave the go-by to] Gave the slip to, eluded (*OED*).

broadside-to you broach, and down you pitch, head-foremost!"] In other words, Sol is like a ship that has 'broached' – veered suddenly so as to turn a side to the wind – and has then been hit by a 'broadside', a discharge of all the cannon on one side of an enemy ship – an attack that causes him to sink (Bowditch, 1821, 236).

"My lad," said the Captain,

the ship's log, and that's the truest book as a man can write.] The ship's record book or journal in which was entered navigation data, speeds, weather, sightings, the names of watch-keepers and all the important events on board. Before being recorded in the log, 'the direction of the wind and the course of the ship, with all material occurrences, together with the latitude by observation' would be recorded on the log-board, two boards divided into columns that shut together like a book. This information, 'together with any other circumstances deserving notice' would, on a daily basis, be transcribed into the log-book, the 'intermediate divisions or watches [of which] are usually signed by the commanding officer' (Smyth, 1867, 452).

"Thank'ee Captain Gills," said

The hollow crowd, you know ... suppose me to be happy;] From the sentimental poem by the popular poet, Mary Anne Browne, 'The Moorland Child' (1839):

> She knew her dreams were disallowed,
>   That she must act a part,
> But 'midst the false and hollow crowd,
>   She took her moorland heart.
>   (*Tait's Edinburgh Magazine*, 1839, 6.583)

As soon as the City offices

As soon as the City offices were opened,] Presumably, businesses in the City kept the same hours as the Bank of England, 10 a.m. to 4 p.m. The opening times of other types of offices, such as government offices and those connected with the legal system, differed widely (James Elmes, *A Topographical Dictionary of London and its Environs*, 1831, *passim*).

"Yes," said Mr. Carker,

The under-writers suffer a considerable loss.] The underwriters have provided accident insurance on the lost vessel. They would have transacted business in their own 'spacious, handsome room' at Lloyd's Subscription Rooms, with seats and tables on both sides and down the centre, and with their own 'particular' seat. As described by Peter Cunningham's *Handbook of London* (1850):

> The insurance broker offers to him [the underwriter] the "risk" for his consideration, and he either accepts or declines it, according as he thinks the "premium" adequate or insufficient. There are about 180 underwriters, but they do not all attend the room, as one individual frequently acts for two or three. To attain success in this branch of business, requires experience, knowledge, and prudence. (293)

In the view of two contemporaries, 'The life of the underwriter, like the stock speculator, is one of great anxiety, the events of the day often raising his expectations to the highest, or depressing them to the lowest pitch; and years are often spent in the hope for acquisition of that which he never obtains' (Thornbury and Walford, 1873–8, 1.513). Also, see notes to chapters 22 and 26, p. 266–7, 300–1.

"Come, come, Captain Cuttle,"

your day's allowance,] The daily rations allowed each sailor in the Royal Navy. From the 1790s, these included: meat; garden peas or chickpeas; cheese; butter; ship's biscuit ('hard tack'); and a gallon of beer. In port, the ship might be provisioned with fresh meat and baked bread (instead of ship's biscuit), and fresh fruit and vegetables.

"My lad," returned the Captain,

what can't be cured must be endoored –] A proverb dating from the fourteenth century.

But the Captain was not

the Captain ... repairing to one of those convenient slopselling establishments of which there is abundant choice at the eastern end of London, purchased on the spot two suits of mourning –] Mourning for men who were close family members required a black suit and hat-band. For slopsellers, see note to chapter 9, p. 145.

a species of hat, greatly to be admired for its symmetry and usefulness, as well as for a happy blending of the mariner with the coal-heaver; which is usually termed a sou'wester;] Both the coal-heaver's hat and the 'sou'wester' were fantail hats (that is, they had fan-shaped brims at the back). The coal-heaver's hat was a close-fitting skull-cap of stout and serviceable leather, from which depended a shapely flap of the same durable material, which covered the breadth of his back, and while in its black and highly-polished condition, it served as an ornament of which the sturdy bearer might well be proud, it answered the doubly useful purpose of protecting his shoulder-blades from being too cruelly indented by angular and awkward 'nobbles,' contained in the two-hundred-weight sack-load, while, at the same time, it screened his jacket from being chafed into holes. (Greenwood, 1872, 333)

Others noticed the resemblance between a sou'wester and a coal-heaver's hat, for example, Earl, *The Eastern Seas*, 'a large black southwester, (a chapeau bearing a close resemblance to a coal-heaver's hat)' [1837, 102]). For more on the 'sou'wester', see note to chapter 9, p. 145.

In this altered form,

when night comes on a hurricane and seas is mountains rowling, for which overhaul your Doctor Watts,'] An allusion to 'The Sailor's Consolation', by Charles Dibdin:

>One night it blew a hurricane,
>The sea was mountains rolling.
>When Barney Buntling turn'd his quid,
>And said to Billy Bowling,
>"A strong north-west is blowing, Bill,
>Ah! don't you hear it roar now?
>Lord, help us, how I pity all
>Unhappy folks a-shore now." [st. 1]
>>(*The Norwich Minstrel; containing several hundred of the most admired and approved songs,* 1831)

The works of Dr. Isaac Watts contain similar storm passages, for example:

>Now the rude air, with noisy force,
>Beats up and swells the angry sea,
>They join to make our lives a prey,
>And sweep the sailor's hopes away,
>Vain hopes to reach their kindred on the shores!
>>('Fire, Air, Earth, and Sea, Praise Ye the Lord', 181;
>>*The Beauties of the Late Rev. Dr. Isaac Watts,* 1821)

Isaac Watts (1674–1748) published four collections of verse, *Horae Lyricae* (1706), *Hymns and Spiritual Songs* (1707), *Divine Songs for the Use of Children* (1715) and *The Psalms of David Imitated* (1719).

When Rob had turned in,

opened the prayer-book at the Burial Service ... committed Walter's body to the deep.] From 'At the Burial of their Dead at Sea' in 'Forms of Prayer to be used at Sea' (*BCP*):

> We therefore commit his body to the deep, to be turned into corruption, looking for the resurrection of the body (when the Sea shall give up her dead,) and the life of the world to come, through our Lord Jesus Christ.

Chapter 33

CONTRASTS

Dickens is doubtless borrowing this rhetorical use of 'contrasts' from Augustus Welby Pugin and Thomas Carlyle, both of whom contrasted the spirituality and harmony of the medieval world with the materialism and degradation of modern industrial life. In *Contrasts, on a Parallel between the Architecture of the Fourteenth and Fifteenth Centuries and Similar Buildings of the Present Day* (1836), Pugin placed illustrations of 'a Catholic town in 1440' beside 'the same town in 1840' to show 'the Present Decay of Taste'. In *Past and Present* (1843), Carlyle contrasted life in the medieval monastery at Bury St Edmunds with the nineteenth-century workhouse to emphasize the need for strong leadership in the modern world.

The first is situated in the

the green and wooded country near Norwood.] Norwood, located in Surrey, six miles southeast of London, 'is situated on a series of beautiful valleys and hills, the latter rising, it is said, to the height of 300 feet above the level of the sea at low water'. In 1842, it had a population of less than 3000 and contained 'a number of scattered villa residences; a mineral spring, the Beulah Spa, in a pleasure-ground delightfully laid out; two episcopal churches, one of Grecian, the other of Gothic architecture; and a large public cemetery, with episcopal and dissenting chapels for performing the burial service'. As the presence of the Royal Beulah Spa and Gardens suggests, Norwood developed a reputation for its salubrity and, in the nineteenth century, was often prescribed by physicians for their patients needing fresh air and a healthy climate. In 1851, *Tallis's Illustrated London* characterized Norwood as

16   Woodway House, Teignmouth, Devon, c. 1825: a cottage *ornée*

> ... the most picturesque district in ... Lambeth ... situate in a delightful vale. ... The surpassing beauty of its scenery has tended to attract residents, and during the present century building has rapidly progressed here, terraces, villas, and hotels, having been erected; but ... speculation has not been permitted to injure the landscape. Norwood still abounds in large uncultivated tracts of forest land. (qtd. in Olsen 191)

In 1852, *The British Gazetteer* remarked that 'The villas of the resident gentry are numerous, and some of the grounds by which they are surrounded exceedingly pleasing'. In 1857, Charles Manby Smith found 'a select circle of genteel people' residing in Norwood. Mr Spenlow has a house in Norwood in *DC*, with 'a lovely garden', 'charming lawn' and 'perspective walks' (26) (Thornbury, 1872–8, 6.315; Inwood 507, 586; *Penny Cyclopædia*, 1842; Thorne, 1876, 453; Clarke, 1852, 3.317; *The Little World of London*, 19).

It is not a mansion; it is of no pretensions as to size; but it is beautifully arranged, and tastefully kept. The lawn ... the flower-garden, the clumps of trees ... the conservatory, the rustic verandah with sweet-smelling creeping plant entwined about the pillars ... though all upon the diminutive scale proper to a mere cottage, bespeak an amount of elegant comfort within, that might serve for a palace.]
'The term cottage has for some time past been in vogue as a particular designation for small country residences and detached suburban houses, adapted to a moderate scale of living, yet with all the attention to comfort and refinement' (*Supplement*

to the Penny Cyclopædia, 1845, 1.426). The particular style of Carker's house is the *cottage ornée* (also called a *ferme ornée*; Plate 16), a picturesque style which flourished from the 1770s–1830s and which was influenced by Horace Walpole's gothic fantasy, Strawberry Hill. According to the landscape authority, John Claudius Loudon, in his *Encyclopædia of Gardening* (1860),

> A *cottage ornée* is a villa on a small scale, which may be characterised by the garden-front opening into a picturesque lawn varied by groups of trees. The cottage is generally low in proportion to its extent, and the roof, which is frequently thatched, has projecting eaves. The walls should be covered with climbing plants, and there is generally a veranda round the house. (484)

Such cottages in fashionable suburbs were a form of social aspiration, offering a lifestyle in imitation of the landed gentry and an escape from the dirt, disease, noise and anxiety of urban life. An 1805 book of designs by R. Lugar, entitled *Architectural Sketches, for Cottages, Rural Dwellings, and Villas in the Grecian, Gothic, and Fancy Styles*, is subtitled '*suitable to persons of genteel Life and moderate Fortune*'. For those who worked in London, living in the suburbs became easier because road improvements made travel more convenient. *The Builder* commented on the flight to the suburbs in 1848:

> East, west, north, and south our cities and towns are extending themselves into the country. ... Houses spring up everywhere, as though capital were abundant, as though one-half the world were on the look-out for investments, and the other half continually in search of eligible family residences, desirable villas, and aristocratic cottages. ('The Building Mania', [14 October 1848]: 500–1)

Dickens also draws on the traditional contrast between the cottage and the palace; see, for example, Horace, *Odes*, Ode 4.15–16: 'With equal foot, rich friend, impartial Fate / Knocks at the cottage and the palace gate'; and the proverbs dating from the sixteenth century: 'Content lodges oftener in cottages than palaces', 'Love lives in cottages as well as in courts'.

It is Mr. Carker the Manager

A gaudy parrot in a burnished cage ... tears at the wires with her beak,] Mayhew describes the trade in parrots, 'paroquets' and cockatoos brought back by sailors returning from the West Indies and Africa. The birds were sold to shop-keepers and street-sellers and fetched between five shillings and thirty shillings each, although a parrot that had been taught to speak would fetch between £4 and £10, depending on its proficiency. Parrots were purchased by 'the wealthier classes who can afford to indulge their tastes'. Mayhew warns against the unscrupulous practice of 'parrot-duffing', in which sellers brightened up the feathers by painting them: ' "the more outlandish you make them look, the better's the chance to sell" ' (2.70–2). In *LD*, the description of Mrs Merdle's parrot is modeled on Carker's (1.20).

Perhaps it is a Juno;

Perhaps it is a Juno; perhaps a Potiphar's Wife; perhaps some scornful Nymph –] This is one of the 'Contrasts' alluded to in the title of this chapter: Juno, the wife and sister of Jupiter in Roman mythology, is the special protectress of marriage and of women, and presides over childbirth. In Genesis 39.7–23, Potiphar's wife seduces Joseph but accuses him of rape. She thus became a type of the 'shameless woman', used frequently to 'recommend chastity as the noblest male qualification', in the words of Joseph Addison (*Guardian*, No. 45). She appears in Bunyan's *The Life and Death of Mr Badman* (ch. 4) and *Pilgrim's Progress* (in the allegorical figure Wanton), and is alluded to in Fielding's *Joseph Andrews* (Lady Booby), Sheridan's *School for Scandal*, Byron's *Don Juan* (1.186), Sir Walter Scott's *Woodstock* (ch. 25) and in Trollope's *The Last Chronicle of Barset* (ch. 51) (Jeffrey, 1992, 625–6). As Janet Larson points out, the story of Potiphar's wife echoes significant plot elements in *DS*: 'the dissatisfied wife of the master, … the foiled seduction, and revenge, all in the context of a business relation between a master and his slave promoted to overseer', though, as she notes, there are also significant transformations (78). In *LD*, it is Mrs Merdle who evokes Juno (21).

The second home is on

The second home is on the other side of London, near to where the busy great north road of bygone days is silent and almost deserted, except by wayfarers who toil along on foot.] The location of Harriet's home in Middlesex to the northwest and 'on the other side of London' stands in marked contrast to leafy Norwood in the southeast, where her brother lives. On opposite banks of the Thames, both homes are 'wide apart' but 'within easy reach of the great city of London.' The description also evokes one of the so-called 'low density' suburbs characteristic of Holloway, Islington and Highgate in the vicinity of the Great North Road. Following the introduction of the railway (1830), road traffic decreased along this principal route in and out of the City from the north. A journalist described the area in 1839:

> The main road [the Great North Road] keeps right through Islington and Holloway: – the latter, in fact, is the name given to the houses on either side of the spacious road from Holloway toll-bar to the foot of Highgate hill. The road has the appearance of a continuous street up to the toll-bar; but from thence the shops begin to disappear, – the road is more country-like, and many of the houses occupied by people in the middling ranks of life are inscribed as "cottages," or at least have the appearance of villas in miniature. At some distance before us the steeple of Highgate church peeps out among trees. Though this is one of the great outlets of the metropolis, there is no

extraordinary hustle; a carriage or a gig, a stagecoach or omnibus, may roll past now and then, but they arrest without distracting the attention. ('Walks in the Neighbourhood of London', *London Saturday Journal* 1.193)

The 'great north road' was the designation given to the highway that passed through Islington, Highgate, Finchley, Barnet and Ware heading towards York and the north of England. The road, which developed in the early part of the eighteenth century, was a slight variant of the original Roman artery to York, which bypassed Ware and ran a little further to the west, via Hatfield, Welwyn, Stevenage and Baldock. The Great North Road also enters the City from the south at London Bridge, crossing north over the bridge and up King William Street, via Prince's Street to Moorgate and then northwards to Islington.

The neighbourhood ... has as little of the country to recommend it, as it has of the town. It is neither of the town nor country. The former, like the giant in his travelling boots, has made a stride and passed it, and has set his brick-and-mortar heel a long way in advance; but the intermediate space ... as yet, is only blighted country ... and here, among a few tall chimneys ... and among the brick-fields, and the lanes where turf is cut, and where the fences tumble down, and where ... the bird-catcher still comes occasionally ... this second home is to be found.] The giant's 'brick-and-mortar heel' alludes to the speculative building of new suburbs resulting from the construction of the railway through Camden Town (see note to chapter 6, pp. 95–7). Such development of previously rural land is satirized in George Cruikshank's 1829 cartoon, 'London going out of Town; or, the March of Bricks and Mortar' (Plate 17, p. 356).

Different kinds of factories, including dyeing and calico-printing, and many brick-fields, were located on the open ground through which the Great North Road passed. Because the heath land offered roosting places for birds, it was frequented by bird-catchers, who sometimes also worked in the brick-fields (Mayhew 2.65; for bird-catchers, see note to chapter 22, p. 264–5). Before the mechanization of brick-making became widespread in the 1850s, it was a craft-centered trade that was most highly developed in or near towns, mostly in the eastern counties.

The heath, or 'turf', on the open ground was popular with turf-cutters, who cut it into small sods and sold it to bird-sellers for 2*d*. – 2½*d*. per dozen as food for the caged birds of London (*Penny Cyclopædia*, 1839, 15.197; *The Newspaper*, 8 April 1848, 119). Mayhew names Shepherd's Bush, Notting Hill, the Caledonian Road, Hampstead, Highgate, Hornsey, Peckham and Battersea as 'the principal places for the cutting of turf ... at present'. Mayhew describes how one could see on this heath land

> a half-illegible board, inviting the attention of the class of speculating builders to an "eligible Site" for villas. Some of these places are open, and have long been open, to the road; others are protected by a few crazy rails, and the turf-cutters consider that outside the rails, or between them and the road, they have a *right* to cut turf. ... (1.163–5)

17   'London going out of Town; or, the March of Bricks and Mortar' (1829), from George Cruikshank, *Scraps and Sketches* (1832)

In Charles Perrault's 'Hop-o'-my-Thumb', an ogre wearing seven-league boots is said to stride 'from mountain to mountain, and [to skip] across rivers as if they were streams' in pursuit of seven brothers, the children of a poor faggot-maker. Eventually, one of the children, the very tiny hero of the tale, steals the boots from the giant while he is sleeping.

Yes. This slight, small,

This slight, small, patient figure ... indicating nothing but the dull, household virtues, that have so little in common with the received idea of heroism and greatness, unless ... any ray of them should shine through the lives of the great ones of the earth, when it becomes a constellation and is tracked in Heaven] Domesticity and piety were a contemporary ideal of womanhood, with literary influences dating from the eighteenth century (see the following note). This type is contrasted with another contemporary concept, the hero. In *On Heroes, Hero-Worship, and the Heroic in History* (1841), Carlyle describes heroes as 'the modelers, patterns, and in a wide sense creators, of whatsoever the general mass of men contrived to do or to attain' (1.1). The constellation imagery seems to derive from Dryden's panegyric in honour of the late Countess of Abingdon, 'Eleonora' (1692):

> For where such various virtues we recite,
> 'Tis like the milky way, all over bright,
> But sown so thick with stars, 'tis undistinguish'd light.
> Her virtue, not her virtues let us call;
> For one heroic comprehends them all:
> One, as a constellation is but one,
> Though 'tis a train of stars, that rolling on,
> Rise in their turn, and in the zodiac run:
> Ever in motion; now 'tis faith ascends,
> Now Hope, now Charity, that upward tends,
> And downwards with diffusive good descends. (143–53)

Her pensive form was not

There was daily duty to discharge, and daily work to do – for such common-place spirits that are not heroic, often work hard with their hands –] Praise for female domestic virtues and simple piety was a common sentiment from the eighteenth century into the mid-nineteenth century. In 'Truth' (1787), for instance, William Cowper describes the 'content of the ignorant but believing cottager':

> Yon cottager, who weaves at her own door,
> Pillow and bobbins all her little store;
> Content though mean, and cheerful if not gay,
> Shuffling her threads about the livelong day,
> Just earns a scanty pittance, and at night
> Lies down secure, her heart and pocket light;
> She, for her humble sphere by nature fit,
> Has little understanding and no wit,
> Receives no praise; but, though her lot be such,
> (Toilsome and indigent) she renders much …
> Oh, happy peasant! Oh, unhappy bard!
> His the mere tinsel, her's the rich reward;
> He praised perhaps for ages yet to come,
> She never heard of half a mile from home. …

The idea is also influenced by such works as Cowper's *The Task* (1785), George Crabbe's *The Village* (1783) and by Thomas Gray's 'Elegy Written in a Country Churchyard' (1751). For a discussion of this topic, see Edgecombe 73–89.

such low natures, who are not only not heroic to their valets nor waiting-women] 'No man is a hero to his valet' is a remark attributed to Mme Cornuel, the French social hostess (1605–94): 'qu'il n'y avoit point de héros pour les valets de chambre'. It became proverbial in English through such authors as Dr Johnson (*Idler* no. 84) and Byron (*Beppo* 33), but Dickens's reference here may derive from Carlyle's mention in

On Heroes, Hero-Worship, and the Heroic in History: 'We will also take the liberty to deny altogether that of the witty Frenchman, that no man is a Hero to his valet-de-chambre. ... No man can be a *Grand-Monarque* to his valet-de-chambre'.

"It is the mirror of truth,"

the mirror of truth,"] A cliché used by writers such as Dante and Goethe, as well as by English theologians, which probably derives from biblical imagery: 'For if any be a hearer of the word, and not a doer, he is like unto a man beholding his natural face in a glass: For he beholdeth himself, and goeth his way, and straightway forgetteth what manner of man he was' (James 1:23–4); 'For now we see through a glass, darkly; but then face to face: now I know in part; but then shall I know even as also I am known'(1 Corinthians 13:12); 'But we all, with open face beholding as in a glass the glory of the Lord, are changed into the same image from glory to glory, even as by the Spirit of the Lord' (2 Corinthians 3:18).

"I am sure," said the gentleman,

One don't see anything, one don't hear anything, one don't know anything;] For the colloquial use of 'don't', see note to chapter 3, p. 53.

She often looked with compassion,

Day after day, such travellers crept past, but always ... in one direction – always towards the town.] London in the nineteenth century drew more migrants than anywhere else in the country. According to Francis Sheppard, 'it has been calculated that in the decade 1841–51 ... some 330,000 new migrants came to the capital, representing no less than 17 per cent of the total population of London in 1841'. In the first half of the century, most came from the south and east of England, with a smaller proportion from elsewhere, but the attractive force of the capital was felt throughout the country (*London 1808–1870: The Infernal Wen*, 1971, 2).

She was in the act

a dauntless and depraved indifference to more than weather: a carelessness of what was cast upon her bare head from Heaven or earth: that, coupled with her misery and loneliness, touched the heart of her fellow woman. She thought of all that was perverted and debased within her, no less than without: of modest graces of the mind, hardened and steeled, like these attractions of the person;] Estimates about the extent of prostitution in London varied widely in the nineteenth century. In 1844, James Beard Talbot, secretary to the London Society for the

Protection of Young Females, calculated the number of known brothels to be 3,335 (excluding the City). But the estimates of Sir Richard Mayne, the Commissioner of the Metropolitan Police, were much lower. In 1838, he put the number of prostitutes in London and the surrounding areas at under 7,000 (excluding the City), a number typical of other police estimates, which fluctuated between 5,500 and 9,500. As for the number of prostitutes in England as a whole, these varied widely as well, from almost 500,000 to police totals of around 30,000. An authoritative modern account concludes that, while 'the police totals err on the low side ... as a calculation of the numbers of women who made a poor or modest living from sex with casually acquired clients they are probably not far from the truth, and surely nearer the truth than figures such as 80,000 for London's prostitutes' (Mason, 1995, 80).

James Beard Talbot outlined two principle stages through which prostitutes passed, losing first their pure feelings of love and tenderness, and then their physical well-being. In the second phase, most victims were tormented by disease and drunkenness, after which they were often arrested by the police. Many careers on the street concluded with the victim 'a blighted wreck of a once finely-formed and handsome woman' (*Miseries of Prostitution*, 1844, 44–5). William Tait described a young woman's downfall in *Magdalenism* (1842):

> The plump rosy cheek soon assumes a pale and sickly aspect. The eyes, once so bright and sparkling, look dim and languid, and seem as if sunk in their sockets. Their skin every where exhibits a sallow, withered appearance; and their whole body becomes feeble and enervated.
>
> In the final stage of dissolution, hectic flushes, perspiration, pale skin, chills and the loss of appetite predominated, before venereal disease brought on even greater suffering. (225)

In *Life in London* (1821), Pierce Egan concluded, 'The life of a PROSTITUTE is of itself a severe punishment, independent of *disease* and *imprisonment*. A volume would not unfold the *miseries* allied to such a character' (2.2.143).

Thinking of this, she did

she did not turn away with a delicate indignation – too many of her own compassionate and tender sex too often do –] Harriet's response (like Rose Maylie's response in *OT* [ch. 40]) counters the contempt for prostitutes that permeated all levels of English society, especially by those who believed that 'women who have once become harlots, having lost their character, are cut off from all hope of retrieving it'. William Hale typified this contempt when he wrote that 'a harlot is one who from awful depravity, from a principle of lust, idleness, profligacy, or avarice, deliberately chooses to prostitute herself to any man' (*Considerations on ... Female Prostitution* 7; Paroissien, 1992, 238). Dickens had a more charitable view: he believed that it was 'reasonably probable' that 'fallen' women (here he is thinking of the ones at Urania Cottage – see below) 'are sensible of the sinfulness and degradation of their lives –

that nothing else but that, has been impressed upon them by society since they began those lives' (*Letters* 5.182).

Harriet uttering an expression

the traveller looked up with a contemptuous and incredulous smile.] Writing about the 'natural' causes of prostitution, William Tait noted irritability of temper as one of the prostitute's defining traits: 'Prostitutes not infrequently give themselves up to the most violent fits of passion; and this is so common to the great majority of them, that it must be attributed more to some natural defect in their character than to the accidental circumstances in which they are placed' (116).

She held up her hair

her hair ... a heap of serpents.] An allusion to the Gorgons, the three frightful female monsters in Greek mythology whose heads were covered with hissing serpents. See note to chapter 18, p. 228.

"Very far. Months upon months

"I have been where convicts go,"] She has been transported to Australia. The practice of transportation originated with an Elizabethan statute in 1597–8 permitting the banishment of dangerous rogues and vagabonds (39 Eliz. I, c. 17) and grew in frequency under James I, who was the first to have felons sent to America. Following further statutes under Charles II in 1666 (18 Chas. II, c. 3) and George I in 1717 (4 Geo. I, c. 2), the transportation of felons became a common means of crime control and a deterrent until a Royal Commission in 1863 recommended discontinuing the practice of sending criminals to distant British colonies. When the War of Independence (1775–83) made it impossible to transport criminals to America, prison colonies in Australia replaced the former American colonies as the main destination for convicts. Sentences varied from transportation for life to lesser periods of seven to fifteen years (Mayhew and Binny 92; Paroissien, 2000, 249).

One of the preconditions for admittance to Urania Cottage (see below) was a willingness 'to be sent abroad' ('Home for Homeless Women', *HW* 7.161). Dickens told Angela Burdett Coutts that he believed, 'the power of beginning life anew, in a world perfectly untried by them [the 'fallen' women], would be so important in many cases, as an effectual detaching of them from old associates, and from the chances of recognition and challenge, that it is most desirable to be, somehow or other, attained' (*Letters* 4.555).

"Ah! Heaven help me and

"**If man would help some of us a little more, God would forgive us all the sooner perhaps.**"] At this time, Dickens was himself active in providing a better life for reformed prostitutes. In 1847, he began a ten-year association with the heiress Angela Burdett Coutts to administer Urania Cottage, a home for 'fallen' and destitute women in a detached house in Shepherd's Bush. They hoped to provide a safe and domestic environment in which to educate the women in household duties and religion, and in self-discipline. As he told Miss Coutts, he intended to appeal to them 'by means of affectionate kindness and trustfulness': 'these unfortunate creatures are to be '*tempted to virtue. They cannot be dragged, driven, or frightened*' (28 October 1847; *Letters* 5.178, 183). Dickens helped to arrange the cottage, choose the women and establish the rules, and he supervised a plan to send promising women to Cape Town or Australia. He even chased after prostitutes on the street to interview them. Dickens's most sympathetic fictional treatment of a prostitute is Nancy in *OT.*

Talbot's *Miseries of Prostitution* lists several other London asylums working to rehabilitate prostitutes. Among those operating in the nineteenth century were the Magdalen Hospital (1758), the Lock Asylum for the Reception of Penitent Female Patients (1792), the London Female Penitentiary (1807), the Guardian Society (1812), the London Female Mission (1836), the British Penitent Female Refuge (1845) and the South London Penitentiary (1843) (64). Each was privately funded and ran on a small scale similar to Urania Cottage.

"I think I have a mother.

"**I think I have a mother. She's as much a mother, as her dwelling is a home,**"] Contemporary studies of prostitution showed that a very large number of prostitutes had lost one or both parents, and that those prostitutes who were not actually orphans were frequently raised in homes where the father had deserted the family or where the parents were separated. Sixty-four percent of the female patients at the Lock Asylum in 1849, for instance, were either half or full orphans (Walkowitz 16–7, 261).

Chapter 34

ANOTHER MOTHER AND DAUGHTER

There was no light in

A heap of rags, a heap of bones,] For Mrs Brown's trade in rags and bones, see note to chapter 6, p. 102–3.

she looked as if she were watching at some witch's altar for a favourable token;]
Witches initiated signs or prophesies by casting spells at their altar, as described by the eighteenth-century poet William Mickle in 'The Sorceress; or, Wolfwold and Ulla':

> 'A happier spell I now shall try;
> Attend, my child, attend,
> And mark what flames from altar high,
> And lowly floor ascend.
> If of the rose's softest red,
> The blaze shines forth to view,
> Then Wolfwold lives – but hell forbid
> The glimmering flame of blue!' (*The British Poets*, 1822, 66.84)

The witch's altar most frequently described by early nineteenth-century writers was the odd-shaped granite mass given that name near the summit of the Brocken, the highest of the Hartz mountains. The Brocken, which was associated with innumerable superstitions, is described in John Murray's *A Handbook for Travellers on the Continent* (1839, Route 73: 'The Hartz'). The same witches' altar was often mentioned in German romances published in English and in contemporary periodicals, such as *Edinburgh Magazine* (1819), *Amulet* (1828) and *Schoolmaster, and Edinburgh Weekly Magazine* (1832).

"It's my gal! It's my Alice!"

It's my handsome daughter, living and come back!"] After their sentence had expired, convicts could leave Australia, though they had to pay for the voyage back to England, usually by having money sent to them or perhaps by earning it as free labourers. The majority of former convicts, however, would remain either because wages were good and work plentiful, or because they could not afford the cost of the return passage (*Mirror of Parliament*, 1840, 4.3130; *Penny Cyclopædia*, 1843, 27.19; Mitchell 100).

"It sounds unnatural, don't it?"

I have heard some talk about duty first and last;] Presumably a reference to the biblical phrase, 'the whole duty of man', from Ecclesiastes 12.13 ('Let us hear the conclusion of the whole matter. Fear God, and keep his commandments: for this is the whole duty of man'); and the title of a popular devotional work (possibly by Richard Allestree) published in 1658. Dickens was particularly fond of the phrase, almost always using it ironically. In a letter to Mrs Richard Watson, for example, he complained that it is 'the whole Duty of Man' to attend the Crystal Palace, and in *HT*, the narrator explains that profit 'comprised the whole duty of man' (*Letters*

7.453; 2.1). The phrase 'First and last' is a formulation common in First and Second Chronicles. For more on the concept of duty, see note to chapter 19, p. 231.

"There was a child called

"born, among poverty and neglect, and nursed in it. Nobody taught her, nobody stepped forward to help her, nobody cared for her."] In *Miseries of Prostitution* (1844), James Beard Talbot cited extreme poverty and abandonment as two principle reasons forcing so many girls into prostitution. On one of his visits to the poorest neighbourhoods in London, he described the conditions that breed prostitutes:

> In one room, destitute of furniture, I found about fifty children, of both sexes, all under the age of fifteen or sixteen years, grouped together, ragged and dirty. These neglected children, during the day, were occupied in thieving, and at night sheltered in the manner described. In another large room I discovered a great number of straw beds, placed upon the floor, only separated from each other by a board, about eight inches high, placed between each bed. These beds were tenanted by between seventy and eighty individuals. (9)

Dickens himself often attributed the corruption of the poor to social conditioning. 'It is dreadful to think how some of these doomed women have no chance or choice', he told Miss Coutts in reference to the 'fallen' women at Urania Cottage. 'It is impossible to disguise from one's self the horrible truth that it would have been a social marvel and miracle if some of them had been anything else than what they are' (*Letters* 5.185). He similarly praised William Hogarth's illustration 'Gin Lane' because, while it exhibits 'drunkenness in the most appalling forms', it 'also forces on attention a most neglected wretched neighbourhood, and an unwholesome, indecent abject condition of life that might be put as frontispiece to our sanitary report of a hundred years later date' (Forster 2.42). And, in *LD*, Dickens made a distinction between a very young prostitute who 'spoke coarsely' but who had 'no naturally coarse voice' (1.14). Elsewhere, however, Dickens depicts poor people who rise above their social conditioning, perhaps most notably Oliver Twist and Lizzie Hexam (*OMF*).

Dickens may well have had in mind his early sketch, 'A Visit to Newgate' (*SB*), when he conceived of the relationship between Mrs Brown and her daughter. In the sketch, he describes difficult conversations between two sets of aged, haggard mothers and their poor but good-looking daughters. In the first instance, the mother is visiting her imprisoned daughter:

> In one corner of this singular looking den [a sort of protective 'cage' separating visitor from prisoner], was a yellow, haggard, decrepit old woman, in a tattered gown that had once been black, and the remains of an old straw bonnet, with faded ribbon of the same hue, in earnest conversation with a young girl – a prisoner, of course – about two-and-twenty. It is impossible to imagine a more poverty-stricken object, or a creature borne down in soul and body, by excess

of misery and destitution, as the old woman. The girl was a good-looking robust female, with a profusion of hair streaming about in the wind – for she had no bonnet on – and a man's silk pocket handkerchief loosely thrown over a most ample pair of shoulders. The old woman was talking in that low, stifled tone of voice which tells so forcibly of mental anguish; and every now and then burst into an irrepressible sharp, abrupt cry of grief. ... The girl was perfectly unmoved. Hardened beyond all hope of redemption, she listened doggedly to her mother's entreaties ... and ... took no more apparent interest in the conversation than the most unconcerned spectators.

In the second instance, it is the mother who is imprisoned:

> ... a squalid-looking woman in a slovenly, thick-bordered cap, with her arms muffled in a large red shawl, the fringed ends of which straggled nearly to the bottom of a dirty white apron, was communicating some instructions to *her* visitor – her daughter evidently. The girl was thinly clad, and shaking with the cold. Some ordinary word of recognition passed between her and her mother when she appeared at the grating, but neither hope, condolence, regret, nor affection was expressed on either side. ... The dialogue was soon concluded; and with the same careless indifference with which they had approached each other, the mother turned towards the inner end of the yard, and the girl to the gate at which she had entered.

As is the case with Alice Marwood, Dickens blames this young woman's degradation on her upbringing:

> Barely past her childhood, it required her a glance to discover that she was one of those children, born and bred in neglect and vice, who have [*sic*] never known what childhood is: who have never been taught to love and court a parent's smile, or to dread a parent's frown. The thousand nameless endearments of childhood, its gaiety and its innocence, are alike unknown to them.

"I am going on," returned the

What came to that girl, comes to thousands every year.] For the estimated number of prostitutes in mid-Victorian London, and England as a whole, see note to chapter 33, p. 358–9.

"She'll soon have ended,"

the strong arm of the Law –] A common variant of 'The long arm of the law', a cliché by the end of the eighteenth century. The image seems to derive from one of the proverbs of Erasmus ('Multae regum aures atque oculi. An nescis longas regibus esse manus') first translated into English by Richard Taverner in 1539: 'Kings have long arms, they have also many eyes and ears' (*Proverbs or Adages ... of Erasmus*, London, 1539).

"So Alice Marwood was transported,

transported ... where there was twenty times less duty, and more wickedness, and wrong, and infamy, than here.] For the transportation of 'the criminal classes' to Australia, see note to chapter 33, p. 360.

and there will be an end of her;] According to Edward Gibbon Wakefield, English prostitutes 'die like sheep with the rot; so fast that soon there would be none left, if a fresh supply were not obtained equal to the number of deaths' (*England and America*, 1833; Prichard 352).

Lost and degraded as she was,

there shone through all her wayworn misery and fatigue, a ray of the departed radiance of the fallen angel.] An angel that has been banished from Heaven as a punishment for disobeying or rebelling against God. The usage is attributed to various Biblical passages, including Isaiah 14.12 ('How you are fallen from heaven, O day star') and Revelation 12 ('Satan ... was cast out into the earth and his angels were cast out with him').

"Sometimes, Ally – in a

I have tramped about the country,] For people 'on the tramp', see note to chapter 27, p. 305–6.

"He will thrive in spite

"He will thrive in spite of that,"] Although prostitutes were treated with widespread contempt, the men who patronized them remained free from censure. A Lord High Chancellor, remarked Edward Gibbon Wakefield,

> may also keep a mistress, or more than one, without incurring the slightest odium; any man of fortune may change from prostitute to prostitute without forfeiting any of the high respect which is paid to him as a man of fortune; no one, in short, suffers any thing by encouraging prostitution, provided he can afford the expense. Women, on the contrary, whose poverty drives them to sin against religion and morality – prostitutes for bread – are regarded with

the sort of scorn which a Turk expresses when he says – 'dog of a Christian!' (*England and America*, 1833; Prichard 351)

Chapter 35 Twelfth monthly number
September 1847

THE HAPPY PAIR

The dark blot on the street

The saying is, that home is home, be it never so homely. If it hold good in the opposite contingency, and home is home be it never so stately, what an altar to the Household Gods is raised up here!] 'Home is home though it's never so homely' is a proverb from the mid-sixteenth century. The representation of home as the source of virtue and emotion played a central role in the creation of a Victorian ideology of domestic life. In ancient Rome there were two types of household gods: the *lares*, who protected the house and deified ancestors or heroes; and the *penates*, who brought wealth and plenty and who personified the natural powers.

Mrs. Skewton, prepared to greet

her quarterly stipend] On quarter days (25 March, 24 June, 29 September and 25 December) servants and other employees were paid their wages. Domestic servants usually also received food and lodging as compensation for services provided. According to Samuel and Sarah Adams' *The Complete Servant* (1825), the annual wages of a lady's maid ranged from 18–25 guineas (239).

Where are the happy

Do steam, tide, wind, and horses, all abate their speed,] For travelling between England and France, see note to chapter 54, p. 468–9.

"And how my dearest Dombey

"And how . . . did you find that delightfullest of cities, Paris?" " . . . I thought it dull," said Mr. Dombey.] Dickens's own initial visit to Paris, for two days in July 1844, elicited a very different response:

I cannot tell you what an immense impression Paris made upon me. It is the most extraordinary place in the World. I was not prepared for, and really could not have believed in, its perfectly distinct and separate character. My eyes ached and my head grew giddy, as novelty, novelty, novelty; nothing but strange and striking things; came swarming before me. I cannot conceive of any place so perfectly and wonderfully expressive of its own character; its secret character no less than that which is on its surface; as Paris is. I walked about the streets – in and out, up and down, backwards and forwards – during the two days we were there; and almost every house, and every person I passed, seemed to be another leaf in the enormous book that stands wide open there. I was perpetually turning over, and never coming any nearer the end. There never was a place for a description. If I had only a larger sheet of paper … I am afraid I should plunge, wildly, into such a lengthened account of these two days as would startle you. (7 August 1844; *Letters* 4.166–7)

Dickens had extended stays in Paris in November 1846 to February 1847, during the period he was writing *DS*, and again from October 1855 to May 1856, when he was writing *LD*. The stay in 1846, 'during that last year of Louis Philippe's reign', evoked a complex reaction. According to Forster, 'He saw almost everywhere signs of canker eating into the heart of the people themselves'. In Dickens's view, Paris was 'a wicked and detestable place, though wonderfully attractive; and there can be no better summary of it, after all, than Hogarth's unmentionable phrase' (Hogarth was reported to have said that 'French houses were gilt and b-sh-t' [*Biographia Britannica* on Sir James Thornhill, VI, part 2, Supplement 1766, p. 172]) (*Letters* 4.669). Dickens also 'reported badly' on the condition of the Parisian streets and on its dangerous quays, after dark (Forster 1.445).

But dinner was announced, and

Mr. Dombey led down Cleopatra; Edith and his daughter following.] In Georgian and Victorian houses, the drawing room is on the first floor and the dining room on the ground floor. Prince Pückler-Muskau, a German visitor to England in 1829, noted that 'The gentlemen lead the ladies into the dining-room, not as in France, by the hand, but by the arm; and here, as there, are emancipated from the necessity of those antiquated bows, which even in some of the best society in Germany, are exchanged every time one hands out a lady'. The Prince did complain, however, of the 'most anxious regard to rank' in the dinner procession (28). The etiquette is explained by Mrs Beeton:

> Dinner being announced, the host offers his arm to, and places on his right hand at the dinner-table, the lady to whom he desires to pay most respect, either on account of her age, position, or from her being the greatest stranger in the party. If this lady be married and her husband present, the latter takes the hostess to her place at table, and seats himself at her right hand. The rest of

Mems.

The Altered* house, and its expression, as it were, of Edith.

Florence's purpose. Remember her old loneliness, and observe her present state of mind.

Mrs Pipchin installed as housekeeper?   Not yet.

Mrs Dombey at home. First Illustration.

Be Patient with Carker—   Get him on very slowly, without incident.

Anything of Miss Tox? Yes. The Toodle family. Second Illustration.

Plan changed afterwards, and the No divided into four chapters. First being too long.

Chapter 35 *The Happy Pair*

(Dealings with the Firm of Dombey and Son — N?. XII.)

chapter XXXV.

The Happy Pair.

M͟r͟/D͟o͟/ The coming home.

Mr Dombey's discovery of what Edith can be. –Turns him against Florence. Tortures himself.

A͟t͟/h͟o͟m͟e͟ The at home, and the dinner before it. Bank Director, East India Director, mild men, Cousin Feenix and his story –. before Carker – Mrs Skewton's artful preparation First quarrel for the future

Chapter XXXVI.

More Warnings than One

Carker's warning to Edith — progress of that incident.

Death's warning to Mrs Skewton – Her paralysis – The change it makes in her

chapter XXXVII.

Miss Tox cultivates an old acquaintance.

Open with the Toodles' at home.

She goes there, i͟n͟/h͟e͟r͟/o͟l͟d͟ to have someone with whom she can talk about Mr Dombey and old times –

Pleasant family scene – Miss Tox and Rob the Grinder.

Chapter Plan [After drawing up this plan, Dickens divided chapter 35 into two, creating a new chapter 36, 'Housewarming'. Subsequent chapters were then renumbered at proof stage.]

the company follow in couples, as specified by the master and mistress of the house, arranging the party according to their rank and other circumstances which may be known to the host and hostess. (13)

She trembled, and her eyes

Unnatural emotion in a child, innocent of wrong! Unnatural the hand that had directed the sharp plough, which furrowed up her gentle nature for the sowing of its seeds!] For Dickens's treatment of the word 'Natural', see note to chapter 47, p. 430.

In her sleep, however, Florence

In her sleep ... Florence could not lose an undefined impression of what had so recently passed. It formed the subject of her dreams, and haunted her;] It was commonly believed that dreams reflected recent impressions, particularly those of the dreamer immediately before sleep, an idea derived from David Hartley's *Observations on Man* (1749) and restated in works such as Dugald Stewart's *Elements of the Philosophy of the Human Mind* (1792–1827), a later edition of which Dickens owned (Stonehouse 105; Bernard 197–214). In fact, Dickens was somewhat skeptical of this idea, asking Thomas Stone, a medical doctor, to revise a piece on dreams for *HW* to make it 'a little less recapitulative of the usual stories in books':

> In the first place I would suggest that the influence of the day's occurrences, and of recent events, is by no means so great (generally speaking) as is usually supposed. I rather think there is a kind of conventional philosophy and belief, on this head. (2 February 1851; *Letters* 6.276)

The similarities in Dickens's letter to the published version of 'Dreams' (2 [8 March 1851]: 566–72) show that Dickens substantially rewrote Stone's manuscript. While the opening of the article retains a bit of the 'conventional philosophy' (in the anecdote of a parrot who remembers, the following morning, the words he had been taught the previous night), later paragraphs echo the letter of 2 February:

> There can be no doubt that the dreams of many persons are very greatly influenced by the reflections and emotions they have experienced the preceding day; but this is by no means invariably the case. (568)

Chapter 36

HOUSEWARMING

Many succeeding days passed in

there were numerous visits received and paid, … If none of the new family were particularly at home in private, it was resolved that Mrs. Dombey at least should be at home in public,] Social convention insisted that, the day after the wedding, the bridesmaids would gather at the house of the bride's father to arrange to send out the new couple's wedding cards (based on lists previously furnished by the groom and bride), one card with the groom's name on it, one with the bride's. If the couple wished to maintain a visiting acquaintance with the recipient, then 'At home' would be added to the bride's card, or sometimes a home address (a practice that was going out of fashion by 1860). On the return of the married couple from their wedding tour, they were expected to be 'At home'. If 'reception days have been fixed, the bride, with her husband and bridesmaids, will sit "at home" ready to receive those to whom cards have been sent, the bride wearing her wedding dress, and the company invited to partake of wedding cake and wine to drink the health of the bride'. The bride and her husband, or the principal bridesmaid if the groom is too busy, were expected to 'return all the wedding visits paid to them', with the exception of those people who paid a visit inappropriately, that is, without having first received a wedding card. 'These return visits having been paid, the happy pair cease to be spoken of as *bride* and *bridegroom*, but are henceforward styled the "newly-married couple" ' (*Routledge's Manual of Etiquette*, 1860, 190).

Accordingly Mr. Dombey produced

Mr. Dombey produced a list of sundry eastern magnates who were to be bidden to this feast, on his behalf; to which Mrs. Skewton, acting for her dearest child, … subjoined a western list,] '[E]astern' refers to the City of London and 'western' to the areas west of the City, such as Mayfair and Kensington.

Baden-Baden,] See note to chapter 31, p. 339.

The proceedings commenced by Mr. Dombey,

in a cravat of extraordinary height and stiffness,] This would be wound twice around the neck and tied in a large bow and would have been high enough to hide everything but the rim of the tall collar. For more on cravats, see the note to chapter 1, p. 28.

punctual to which, an East India Director, of immense wealth, in a waistcoat apparently constructed in serviceable deal by some plain carpenter, but really engendered in the tailor's art, and composed of the material called nankeen, arrived,] Mrs Beeton impressed on her readers that 'If an invitation is accepted, the guests should be punctual, and the mistress ready in her drawing-room to receive them' (12; for the dinner hour, see note to chapter 26, pp. 297, 300). The East India Company, chartered on 31 December 1599, eventually became a huge joint-stock company that, until 1813, had monopoly trading rights east of the Cape of Good Hope. Its main focus was commercial activity in India, though the East India Company maintained major trading posts in Sumatra and at Canton, on the east coast of China. The Company was managed, in England, by a Court of Proprietors, a Court of Directors, and a Board of Control. The Court of Directors, with a term of office of four years, consisted of twenty-four members elected from the Court of Proprietors, each owning at least £2000 of stock. According to the *Penny Cyclopædia* (1837),

> The power of the directors is great: they appoint the governor-general of India and the governors of the several presidencies; but as these appointments are all subject to the approval of the crown, they may be said to rest virtually with the government. The directors have the absolute and uncontrolled power of recalling any of these functionaries. All subordinate appointments are made by the directors, but as a matter of courtesy a certain proportion of this patronage is placed at the disposal of the President of the Board of Control. (9.249)

In the mid-eighteenth century, the East India Company developed territorial ambitions and a large army, and became so influential in Indian politics and administration that the British government was compelled to intervene, culminating in the Charter Act of 1813, which ended the Company's trading monopoly in India (it lost its China monopoly in 1833). From this point, the Company 'survived somewhat anomalously as a quasi-department of the British state until the Indian Mutiny of 1857' (Black and Porter, 1996, 210; Cannon, 1997, 320).

The next stage of the proceedings was Mr. Dombey's sending his compliments to Mrs. Dombey, with a correct statement of the time;] Compare Mrs Dombey's glaring absence before the dinner with what was expected of her. Not only is she not 'ready in her drawing-room' to receive her guests (see above), but, according to Mrs Beeton, the 'half-hour before dinner has always been considered as the great ordeal through which the mistress, in giving a dinner-party, will either pass with flying colours, or, lose many of her laurels.' Although this is a 'trying time', 'The mistress ... must display no kind of agitation, but show her tact in suggesting light and cheerful subjects of conversation'. Mrs Beeton advises her to 'remember that it is her duty to make her guests feel happy, comfortable, and quite at their ease' (12).

The next arrival was a

a Bank Director, reputed to be able to buy up anything –] In the mid-nineteenth century, the Bank of England employed a Governor and a Governor-General, and twenty-four Directors, who collectively constituted the Court of Directors, which conducted regular business on Thursdays. The Directors, who were required to own at least £2000 of stock, were ostensibly elected each year by stockholders, though the real control over their selection rested with the Court of Directors itself. In the view of a contemporary history of the Bank, they had 'full cognizance, either by direct weekly communication or otherwise, of every transaction carried on in the Bank' (Hankey, 1867, 118). For the Bank of England generally, see note to chapter 4, p. 56.

his "little place" at Kingston-upon-Thames,] 'Little place' was a euphemism for a country house, as in Theodore Hook's *Jack Brag* (1837):

> 'Not at home,' is always the answer. 'Out of town?' is the next question; – 'Yes,' is the next answer. – 'Where?' comes next. – 'Down at his little place in Surrey.' That finishes it … 'Little place in Surrey!' said Mrs Brag; – 'why, what d'ye mean? – have you a country-house too?' (ch. 1)

In his *HW* piece 'A Little Place in Norfolk', W. H. Wills remarked on Jack Brag's use of the phrase, then added, 'The Guardians of the Guiltcross poor have good reason to be proud of *their* little place in Norfolk [a small estate with several acres of land]' (1.575).

Kingston-upon-Thames, an attractive municipal borough and market town, is about three miles south of Twickenham and eleven miles from London Bridge. The town, which had a population of 5,989 in 1831, was said in 1842 to be 'irregularly laid out' and to have houses of 'ordinary appearance' and 'houses extending, with little interruption, a considerable distance from the town along the roads to London and to Portsmouth'. The railway reached Kingston-upon-Thames in 1838 (*Penny Cyclopædia*, 1842, 23.318).

a pinery,] A place where pineapples are grown. Growing pineapples was a pastime of the wealthy and required considerable expertise: in his *Encyclopædia of Gardening* (1824), John Claudius Loudon devotes more than twenty pages to the construction of the hothouse, the correct compost, temperature, methods of watering, propagation and so forth ('Culture of the Pinery' 514–35).

mention being made of the Opera … he said he very seldom went there, for he couldn't afford it.] Probably, Her Majesty's Theatre, Haymarket, which was reported to be 'the largest theatre in Europe, except that of La Scala at Milan', accommodating about 2,500 people (Cunningham, 1850). The boxes were 'the private property of the subscribers, or are let out for the season'. In 1844, regular prices for admission were 21 shillings for the pit stalls; 10 shillings, 6 pence for the pit; 5 shillings for the gallery stalls; and 3 shillings for the gallery. According to *Mogg's New Picture of London* (1848),

The performances, which chiefly consist of Italian Operas and French Ballets, are only regularly exhibited on Tuesdays and Saturdays, from about January to July or August. The performers are the most accomplished singers, and elegant dancers, of the Italian, German, and French stages. The Orchestral band is one of the finest in the world. ... (172–3)

Modern historians of London have remarked of Her Majesty's Theatre, 'The years between 1830–50 were the golden age of the opera house. Even the audience in the pit had to wear evening dress'. The theatre closed in 1852, having lost most of its customers to the Royal Opera House, Covent Garden, though it reopened in 1856 after Covent Garden had been destroyed by fire (Weinreb and Hibbert, 1993, 384).

Though less likely, Dickens may also have in mind the Royal Opera House, which adapted Walter Scott's novels for opera and which held the first performances in English of Mozart's *Don Giovanni* (1817), his *Marriage of Figaro* (1819) and Rossini's *Barber of Seville* (1818). The theatre suffered from financial troubles in the late 1820s and was managed by Dickens's close friend, William Charles Macready from 1837 to 1839. In 1847, Giuseppe Persiani, the Italian composer, bought the lease of the theatre, made alterations and reopened it as the Royal Italian Opera (Weinreb and Hibbert, 1993, 209–10).

In 1859, George Augustus Sala, a frequent contributor to *HW*, placed Her Majesty's Theatre, Haymarket, which he called a 'magnificent theatre, glorious with beauties and with riches', above several world famous opera houses, including La Scala, and 'Above the late Royal Italian Opera House, in Bow Street, Covent Garden, London, which was simply a big theatre, ill-built, and undecorated'. As for the crowds at Her Majesty's Theatre, he remarked that 'Here are gathered the mighty, and noble, and wealthy, the venerable and wise, the young and beauteous of the realm' (*Twice Round the Clock*, 254).

The arrivals quickly became numerous.

elderly ladies carrying burdens on their heads for full dress,] In the late 1820s, enormous hats of silk, satin or transparent gauze, loaded with trimmings of the same material were fashionable in the evening. This style was very out of date in the 1840s, when young women preferred hair decoration to head covering (Cunnington, 1970, 435).

there was no sympathy between them, Mrs. Dombey's list, by magnetic agreement, entered into a bond of union against Mr. Dombey's list,] For contemporary theories of magnetism, see note to chapter 8, p. 123. For magnetism used as a synonym for mesmerism, see note to chapter 42, pp. 410–11.

When dinner was announced,

Mr. Dombey took down an old lady like a crimson velvet pincushion stuffed with bank notes, who might have been the identical old lady of Threadneedle-street, she was so rich, and looked so unaccommodating;] Although by the 1840s 'the Old Lady of Threadneedle-street' was a familiar nickname for the Bank of England (the Bank is in Threadneedle Street), this is probably a specific allusion to the cartoon by James Gillray that occasioned the nickname (Plate 18). The cartoon satirizes the Bank's suspension of gold payments by showing the Prime Minister, William Pitt the Younger, pretending to woo the Bank, which is represented as a horrified old lady wearing a dress of £1 notes and sitting on a locked treasure chest. She is protesting 'Murder! Murder! Rape! ... O you villain! ... Ruin!!!' The caption reads: 'Political Ravishment, or The Old Lady of Thread-needle-Street in danger!' (published 1797).

18   'Political Ravishment, or, The Old Lady of Threadneedle-Street in danger!', by James Gillray, 1797

Now the spacious dining-room,

Now, the spacious dining-room, with the company seated round the glittering table, busy with their glittering spoons, and knives and forks, and plates, might have been taken for a grown-up exposition of Tom Tiddler's ground, where children pick up gold and silver.] In the children's game known as Tom Tiddler's Ground, one child assumes the role of Tom and guards territory that he cannot leave, marked by a line on the ground and supposedly strewn with lumps of gold and silver. When the other children enter the area and mimic picking up the pieces, singing 'We're on Tom Tiddler's ground, picking up gold and silver', the child who pretends to be Tom tries to catch them. If he succeeds, the first (or sometimes the last) caught takes his place. 'Tom Tiddler's Ground' is the title Dickens gave to the 1861 Christmas number of *All the Year Round*.

and the long plateau of precious metal frosted, ... whereon frosted Cupids offered scentless flowers to each of them,]

> A centre ornament, whether it be a *dormant*, a *plateau*, an *epergne*, or a *candelabra*, is found so convenient, and contributes so much to the good appearance of the table, that a fashionable dinner is now seldom or never set out without something of this kind. (Bregion and Miller, *The Practical Cook*, 1845, 25)

Such elaborate silver and silver-gilt candelabra and centre-pieces have ornate cast and applied decorations of swags, fruit, flowers, animals and figures. Often more than twelve inches tall and twelve inches wide, epergnes have extending arms or branches that support shallow dishes for holding fruit, flowers and sweetmeats.

"Why upon my life," said

man who sat for somebody's borough. We used to call him in my parliamentary time W. P. Adams, in consequence of his being Warming Pan for a young fellow who was in his minority.] A warming pan, as used here, denotes 'A person who temporarily holds a place or employment until the intended occupant is ready to take it' (*OED*). See, for instance, Disraeli, *Tancred* (1847): 'Hungerford is not a warming-pan; ... he never was originally; and if he had been, he has been member for the county too long to be so considered now' (2.1). And, James Payn, 'Her First Appearance', a story in *HW*: 'The old gentleman had indeed been put in [as rector] at seventy-four by Mr. Swete's father, the patron, as a warming-pan for his son, and he had already taken five years longer to keep the place warm than was expected of him' (19 [11 December 1858]: 29).

Mr. Dombey, who was as

Guy Fawkes,] See note to chapter 12, p. 176–7.

Hessian boots!" ... "Tops!"] Hessian boots, which were first worn by Hessian troops, had tassels in front at the top and were fashionable during the Regency period (*OED*). By the 1830s, Hessian boots were considered passé. In 'Thoughts about People' (*SB*), published in 1835, Dickens referred to 'generally old fellows with white heads and red faces, addicted to port wine and Hessian boots ... '. In 1859, George Augustus Sala deemed Hessian boots one of the objects 'departed' from contemporary society: 'The Hessians of our youth are gone. The mirror-polished, gracefully-outlined, silken-tasselled Hessians exist no more – those famous boots, the soles of which Mr. Brummel caused to be blacked, and in the refulgent lustre of which the gentleman of fashion immortalised by Mr. Warren was wont to shave himself' (*Gaslight and Daylight* 62). 'Tops' refers to top-boots, high boots with tops of white or light-coloured or brown leather (or something similar), once 'habitually worn by gentlemen, yeomen, and farmers, in riding or country dress; now by hunting men, jockeys, grooms, and coachmen' (*OED*).

"In point of fact,

Barkshire?" ... "Shropshire,"] In the nineteenth century, the county of Berkshire, to the west of London, was sometimes spelled as it is pronounced, 'Barkshire'. The county of Shropshire is to the northwest, about 50 miles west of Birmingham.

"Was it? Well! In point

the lobby of the House of Commons]

> The lobby of the House of Commons itself is a very fine apartment, square in plan, about forty-five feet each way, and having a doorway in each side. It forms the chief vestibule to the House of Commons, and by a short corridor communicates with the great octagonal hall in the centre of the palace, which, in fact, forms the only entrance to the lobby. Each side of the lobby is alike in its general features, being divided into three equal parts, the central portion containing a deeply recessed and lofty doorway, and the others being divided into two stories. In this hall, the messengers of the House sit waiting to be dispatched, either to Government officers for documents, or, in the event of a division, to hunt out for members, however late it may be, or, rather, however early in the morning. (Robinson 3)

She **is regularly bought, and you may take your oath** *he* **is as regularly sold!' "**] For the marriage market in England, see note to chapter 1, p. 27.

In his full enjoyment

The shudder, which had gone all round the table like an electric spark,] The subject was topical because of continuing advances on the discoveries made in the 1820s by Hans Christian Ørsted, Michael Faraday and others (see note to chapter 8, p. 123). Faraday's discovery of magnetic induction (the inverse of the Ørsted effect) and the rotation of a plane of light by magnetism, along with James Prescott Joule's discovery in 1843 of the mechanical equivalent of heat, added to the understanding of electromagnetism.

Since the mid-eighteenth century, electrostatic machines and the Leyden jar had been used to produce dramatic displays of electrical sparks and shocks, which were often the highlights of popular lectures by natural philosophers and others. Electric shocks were also administered to cure paralysis and for nervous disorders, again before large public audiences. In the 1830s and 1840s, Faraday's discoveries were popularized by such showmen as Charles Sloman. At the Royal Colosseum Saloon in Albany Street, he mounted a display that included a 'plate machine' with an 'electric surface of upwards of 80 square feet ... so constructed as to give a striking distance or length of spark, hitherto unattainable' (*Mirror* 34 [1839]: 18; *The Times*, 17 June 1839). Other exhibitions included one that ran from 1839 to 1842 in the Adelaide Gallery off the Strand. This was Faraday's South American eel, forty inches long, from which he could induce 'a most intense electric spark' (Timbs 589). The characteristics of static electricity also became known through public shows featuring the inventions of British electricians who were using both static and galvanic electricity in a variety of electrical techniques and instruments. Electricity was also in the news in the 1840s because of its first practical applications, in electroplating and in the electric telegraph (Morus *passim*; Altick, 1978, 152, 379).

Through the various stages

Through the various stages of rich meats and wines, continual gold and silver, dainties of earth, air, fire, and water, heaped-up fruits, and that unnecessary article in Mr. Dombey's banquets – ice – the dinner slowly made its way:] The theory that matter consisted of four elements, earth, air, fire and water, was introduced by the fifth century BC philosopher, Empedocles, and was generally accepted in Europe until the seventeenth century.

The 'various stages', the 'continual gold and silver' (i.e. replacements of plates and dishes) and the slowness of the dinner suggest that it was served *à la Russe*, the French style which was adopted – together with French cuisine – in fashionable circles in the 1820s. In dinners *à la Russe*, Mrs Beeton explains, 'dishes are cut up on a sideboard, and handed round to the guests'. The guest could politely decline or take a perfunctory helping, until he was presented with something he preferred ('Bills of Fare', notes to sections 2137, 2138: 'Service a la Russe'). This contrasts with the more 'ordinary' way of serving practised in the eighteenth and early nineteenth centuries, the informal and convivial *à la Française*, which was characterized by the numerous dishes for each course being laid out at the same time. A guest dining *à la Française* could only eat what was within easy reach, which he would also offer to his neighbour. In place of this 'very troublesome custom', Prince Pückler-Muskau observed in 1829, 'some of the most elegant travelled gentlemen [in England] have adopted the more convenient ... fashion of sending the servants round with the dishes' (*Tour in England, Ireland, and France* 28). In fact, in May 1849, the Dickenses gave a dinner for Elizabeth Gaskell that was served *à la Russe*: 'The dinner was served up in the new fashion – not placed on the table at all – but handed round – only the desserts on the table and quantities of *artificial* flowers ...' (Jane Welsh Carlyle, *Newly Selected Letters* 143).

In her note on the subject, Mrs Beeton observes that dinners *à la Russe*:

> are scarcely suitable for small establishments; a large number of servants being required to carve, and to help the guests; besides there being a necessity for more plates, dishes, knives, forks, and spoons, than are usually to be found in any other than a very large establishment. Where, however, a service *à la Russe* is practicable, there is, perhaps, no mode of serving a dinner so enjoyable as this. (955)

For a dinner of six or more guests, professional caterers would be employed, and at larger parties guests often brought their own footmen to assist at table. Richard Dolby's very successful *The Cook's Dictionary and Housekeeper's Directory* (1830) was the first cookery book to feature French recipes and to include specimen menus illustrating service *à la Russe*. Dolby's model 'Bill of Fare for Eighteen Persons', which would have been served at fashionable London dinners in the 1830s, shows a series of 32 dishes served in succession and divided into two great courses: the first course comprised soups, fish, *entrées* (side dishes) and roasted meats; the second course comprised game and poultry, followed by elaborate sweets and savoury dishes (*entremets*), ices, and dessert. Sherry, Madeira and champagne were the usual wines.

Frozen confections, such as ice cream or sorbets ('ice'), were served during the dessert stage, which 'at an English table' commonly consisted

> of two dishes of fine fruit, filberts, &c. for the corners or sides, and a cake for the middle, with ice-pails in hot weather. Liqueurs are at this stage handed round; and the wines usually drunk after dinner are placed decanted on the table, along with the dessert. The ice-pails and plates are removed as soon as the company finish their ice. (Joseph Bregion and Anne Miller, *The Practical Cook*, 1845, 38)

London confectioners made all types of frozen desserts for the gentry and aristocracy, but from the 1840s there were also many kinds of 'freezing pots', 'ice pots' or 'freezers' to enable ice creams and water-ices to be made at home. Ironmongers sold decorative moulds for presentation. Coffee was served after dessert and before the ladies withdrew (Acton 475–6; Burnett, 1979, 83–95; David 310–21).

incessant double knocks, announcing the arrival of visitors, whose portion of the feast was limited to the smell thereof.] For double knocks, see note to chapter 7, p. 107. Less important guests were invited after dinner. Invitations were sent out at least three weeks in advance. The evening of the dinner, the guests' arrival

> will vary according to their engagements, or sometimes will be varied in

obedience to the caprices of fashion. Guests invited for the evening, are, however, generally considered at liberty to arrive whenever it will best suit themselves, – usually between nine and twelve, unless earlier hours are specifically named. By this arrangement, many fashionable people and others, who have numerous engagements to fulfill, often contrive to make their appearance at two or three parties in the course of one evening. (Beeton 14–15)

When Mrs. Dombey rose, it was a sight to see her lord ... hold the door open for the withdrawal of the ladies;]

> When fruit has been taken, and a glass or two of wine passed round, the time will have arrived when the hostess will rise, and thus give the signal for the ladies to leave the gentlemen, and retire to the drawing room. The gentlemen of the party will rise at the same time, and he who is nearest the door, will open it for the ladies, all remaining courteously standing until the last lady has withdrawn. (Beeton 13–14)

Mr. Dombey was a grave sight,

the Duke of York] See note to chapter 1, pp. 32–3.

Cousin Feenix ... smoothed his long wristbands and stealthily adjusted his wig.] For the different styles of wearing wristbands (Feenix wears his turned down), see note to chapter 14, p. 197. Wigs had fallen out of fashion in the late eighteenth century, though old gentlemen in the 1830s and 1840s sometimes still wore black or powdered ones. Wigs were also acceptable if a gentleman visited Court or if he was in the law or the church (Cunnington, 1970, 75, 95, 151).

But she was not the

the very linkmen outside] Before oil and gas street lighting, link-men or link-boys carried torches of tow and pitch to light pedestrians, sedan chairs and carriages along the street at night: 'Few and far between are the link-boys in this present 1852. The running footmen with the flambeaux have vanished these many years' ('Things Departed', *HW* 4.401). Although the practice was associated with the past (London had gas street lighting from early in the nineteenth century), link-boys were still in use in the mid-century during fogs:

> Blackest darkness and a terrible gloom broods over the fog-enveloped streets. ... Here you meet with the link-boys proper, costermongers with nothing else to do, that try to turn an honest penny by lighting to their homes belated wayfarers ... overpowered by the fog. 'Link-boy, sir – link-boy.' – 'Light 'e

'ome, sir?' ... Look at this: here is a smart man of fashion that must needs drive through the fog in a patent hansom, and cabby won't start without a couple of link-boys to light him along. ('Observations in a London Fog', *Hogg's Instructor*, 1855, 5.53–5)

"*That any difference between you*

Mamas-in-law (that odious phrase, dear Dombey!)] Mothers-in-law were often the butt of jokes, as illustrated by the frequent mentions in *Punch* during the 1840s. For example, a notice for an auction describes how the successful bidder of a particular lot will become possessed of a

LIFE OF DOMESTIC BLISS.
The circumstances under which he will be placed affording extensive capabilities, if cultivated with the smallest portion of tact, for the foundation of
A PARADISE ON EARTH;
which will be not inconsiderably enhanced by
The Certain Absence of a Mother-in-Law!
(*A Bowl of "Punch", or, Selections from the London Charivari*, 1844, 42)

I never shall attempt to interpose between you, at such a time, and never can much regret, after all, such little flashes of the torch of What's-his-name – not Cupid, but the other delightful creature."] By 'the other delightful creature', Mrs Skewton means Venus. As an attribute of both Cupid and Venus, the torch signifies the fire of love.

Chapter 37

MORE WARNINGS THAN ONE

Florence, Edith, and Mrs. Skewton,

For Cleopatra had her galley again now,] See note to chapter 21, p. 255–6.

The hair of Withers was radiant with pomatum, in these days of down, and he wore kid gloves and smelt of the water of Cologne.] All signs of Withers' incipient dandyism: for example, in 1839, the celebrated dandy Count d'Orsay wore his 'hair oiled and curling ... [and] gloves scented with eau de Cologne ... primrose in tint, skin in tightness' (Madden, 1855, 1.341). Pomatum, a scented ointment used for dressing the hair, was made 'by perfuming lard or suet, or a mixture of wax, spermaceti, and oil', 'some or all' of which were blended together (Piesse, 1857, 214). Eau de Cologne is 'a celebrated perfume, invented long ago by the Farina family in Cologne, and since manufactured chiefly by members of the same family. It consists principally of spirits of water, along with numerous essential oils harmoniously mingled together, so as to produce a refreshing and grateful scent' (*Chambers's Encyclopædia*, 1870, 746).

They were assembled in Cleopatra's room.

The Serpent of Old Nile] '[M]y serpent of Old Nile' (1.5.25) is Antony's affectionate name for Cleopatra. Dickens added the descriptive headline, 'The Daughter of the Serpent of Old Cleopatra', in his 1867 edition of *DS*.

sipping her morning chocolate at three o'clock in the afternoon,] From the eighteenth century, chocolate was a fashionable and expensive drink. Thought by some to be the 'perfect food' and by others to be difficult to digest and of insufficient nourishment, chocolate was mixed with milk or water and frequently consumed as a beverage after breakfast. *The Lancet* recommended chocolate as 'a good sustaining food' and as 'mildly stimulating and exhilarating to the nervous system when "run down" through fatigue and worry'. A German physician recommended it to 'the weak, debilitated, and infirm; to children and women' (qtd. in *Cocoa and Chocolate* 46–7, 42).

a peach-coloured velvet bonnet; the artificial roses in which nodded to uncommon advantage, as the palsy trifled with them, like a breeze.] For her tremors, paralysis and other symptoms, see note to chapter 21, p. 261. The description here is a precisely observed detail that reflects Mrs Skewton's worsening condition:

> As the debility increases and the influence of the will over the muscles fades away, the tremulous agitation becomes more vehement. It now seldom leaves him [the patient] for a moment; but even when exhausted nature seizes a small portion of sleep, the motion becomes so violent as not only to shake the bed-hangings, but even the floor and sashes of the room. (Parkinson, 1817, *An Essay on the Shaking Palsy*)

They took her to pieces

Doctors were sent for ... Powerful remedies were resorted to;] She is shortly described as having suffered a 'paralytic stroke'. The contemporary 'powerful remedies' were acknowledged to be ineffective:

> *Palsy*, or a *Paralytic Stroke*. – This may be considered as a partial apoplexy,

and is generally occasioned by the same cause, viz. pressure on the brain from effused or extravasated blood. ... The cure of palsy must be attempted on the same principles as apoplexy, by promoting absorption from the brain, by bleeding, blistering, purging, &c. It is usual in paralytic affections to endeavour to rouse the affected muscles to action by external stimulants, as spirits, mustard, electricity, &c. but when we consider that neither these, nor internal stimulants can possibly remove the pressure on the brain, we have little to expect from them beyond a negative assistance. (Bickersteth, 1829, 67)

The rose-coloured curtains blushed

an indistinctness in her speech, which she turned off with a girlish giggle, and on an occasional failing in her memory, that had no rule in it, but came and went fantastically;] Besides the tremors, which he gives the most attention to, Parkinson also noted that 'impediment to speech' could be a symptom of 'the shaking palsy'. James Copland's *A Dictionary of Practical Medicine* (1858), described the broader impact of the disease on the nervous system:

> The disorders of the nervous system, and of the general health accompanying *palsy*, are various in different cases according to the seat of the malady. ... In *hemiplegia* and palsy of any of the organs of sense, the memory, and in severe or prolonged cases, even the intellectual powers are more or less impaired; the palsy extending even to the mental powers. ... [I]n some cases, the memory chiefly of words or of names, is impaired or perverted, so that the patient substitutes those which either are inappropriate or have an opposite meaning to that which he wished to convey. (3.1.26)

Chapter 38

MISS TOX IMPROVES AN OLD ACQUAINTANCE

The forlorn Miss Tox, abandoned

no delicate pair of wedding cards,] See note to chapter 36, p. 371.

the Bird Waltz] See note to chapter 7, p. 114.

Still, Miss Tox was lonely,

her milky nature,] An allusion to *Macbeth* 1.5.13–14: 'yet do I fear thy nature; / It is too full o' the milk of human kindness / To catch the nearest way'.

she was fain to seek immediate refuge in a pastry-cook's, and there, in a musty little back room usually devoted to the consumption of soups, and pervaded by an ox-tail atmosphere,] Pastry-cook shops were one of the few places a lady could acceptably dine out in London on her own:

> A lady, or a party of ladies, with or without a gentleman, come up to London for the day to do some shopping, to visit the picture galleries, or to pay some visits, and, perhaps, to hear Jenny Lind in the evening. They do not want their dinner the less for spending an active bustling day. But where are they to get it? They must either go to a pastrycook's, where they may have a basin of viscid soup and some oily pastry, or they must go to an hotel and hire an apartment, if they can. The one is very uncomfortable, the other is very expensive. ('The Hotel Guide', *North British Review* 24 [1856]: 275)

Ox-tail soup, according to Eliza Acton's *Modern Cookery* (1845), is 'inexpensive' and 'very nutritious' but 'insipid in flavour without the addition of a little ham, knuckle of bacon, or a pound or two of other meat' (43).

At all events, towards the Toodle

tearing through the country at from twenty-five to fifty miles an hour,] Contemporary accounts of train speed are suspect because locomotives were not usually equipped with speedometers until the twentieth century. In general, though, speed along the early trunk lines was about 25 mph including stops. As for the fastest recorded times, two of the more reliable estimates indicate that trains down the Madeley incline on the Grand Junction Railway achieved speeds of just over 50 mph in 1842 and that the Grand Western Railway's *2-2-2 Ixion* averaged 54.6 mph between Paddington and Didcot in the 1840s. In contrast, the fastest recorded times for stage-coaches were between about 10 to 12 mph (Simmons, 1991, 310–11; Simmons and Biddle, 1997, 464–5).

"You see, my boys and gals,"

If you find yourselves in cuttings or in tunnels, ... Keep your whistles going, and let's know where you are."] Whistles were sounded for safety reasons when a train approached a cutting or tunnel, and were repeated in long tunnels.

"Polly, old 'ooman," said

What a Junction a man's thoughts is,"] In railway terminology, 'junction' can mean either the place at which two routes diverge or the end-on meeting-point between the lines of two companies. It can also refer to the junction station itself (Simmons and Biddle, 1997, 244). Mr Toodle's comparison of the human mind to a railway junction reflects, in a reduced and comic form, the tendency, since the eighteenth century at least, to compare the organization of the human nervous system to a network, whether to a spider's web, a circulatory system, or, most commonly in the nineteenth century, to a modern communications system such as the electric telegraph (Otis, 2001). There were instances, as well, in which the workings of the human mind were compared to a railway system:

> The arrangement [of the nervous system] may thus be seen to resemble the course of a railway train. The various central masses ['nervous masses'] are like so many stations, where the train drops a certain number of passengers and takes up others in their stead, whilst some are carried to their final terminus. (Bascom, 1869, 289)

> ... the first object tends to recal [*sic*] the second by their common part. This common element is like a railway junction, where two or more lines converge; and when the train of thought arrives there, it depends merely upon the particular position of the points, (this being determined by the Law of Contiguity) to decide upon which line its course shall be continued. (Barratt, 1869, 315–16)

Mr. Toodle, in the midst

conveying the two young Toodles on his knees to Birmingham by special engine,] Special engines were not part of the scheduled service but were laid on for a specific purpose. For example, a French minister visiting England in 1833, 'after halting at Birmingham ... was welcomed at Liverpool by the Directors of the Railway, who had a special engine in attendance to convey him along the line' (*The Mechanics' Magazine*, 1833–4, 20.47). Special engines were frequently used for the postal service, as in a letter from a railway official in 1841: 'I regret to find ... that it will be impracticable to ... convey the bags by any of our trains now running, but make it requisite to put on a special engine' (*Report from the Select Committee on Postage, Appendix*, 1843, 130).

This was intended for Mr. Toodle's

whose withers were not unwrung,] A comical turn on lines spoken by Hamlet:

'Tis a knavish piece of work, but what o' that? Your Majesty, and we that have free souls, it touches us not. Let the galled jade wince, our withers are unwrung. (3.2.235–8)

"Not in that place p'raps,"

friends at court] An expression dating from the seventeenth century (e.g. Ben Jonson, *Epicœne, or The Silent Woman*, 1605) and much used by eighteenth-century writers such as Addison, Pope and Swift.

The ill-starred youngest Toodle

The ill-starred youngest Toodle ... born under an unlucky planet,] 'Ill-starred' occurs frequently in Shakespeare. 'To be born under an unlucky planet' is the English translation of the Latin adjective, *astrosus*. 'Unlucky planet' has been in use from the eighteenth century.

"Hearty, Ma'am, thank'ee," replied

Do the rheumaticks keep off pretty well, Ma'am? We must all expect to grow into 'em, as we gets on. ... Many people at your time of life, Ma'am, is martyrs to it.] As the *Penny Cyclopædia* remarked in 1843, 'The term rheumatism, whether properly or not, has been applied to various afflictions which have very little resemblance to one another, except in being attended with pain' (152). Medical books of the time divided rheumatism into two types: acute rheumatism (rheumatic fever), 'which consists in pain, inflammation, and fulness [*sic*] usually about the larger joints and surrounding muscles' and which 'often wander[s] from one part to another'; and chronic rheumatism, which 'differs from the *acute* in being attended with little or no fever or inflammation, the chief symptoms being pain and swelling in the large joints, and in the course of certain muscles'. Mr Toodle is most likely thinking of chronic rheumatism, which was a disease of 'debility'. Acute rheumatism was considered an 'inflammatory' disease, thought to strike people in the prime of life, between puberty and thirty-five (Graham, 1827, 490–9).

"This here, Ma'am, said Toodle,

leathers –] 'Leathers' is a colloquial name for one who wears leather breeches or leggings (*OED*). For the uniform of charity-school pupils, see note to chapter 5, pp. 91–2.

The bargain was ratified on

a youth whom Mr. Dombey had first inducted into those manly garments which are rarely mentioned by name,] The primness about the use of 'trousers' and 'breeches', which originated at the end of the eighteenth century, was almost invariably mocked. For example, in a footnote in his *Poems, Miscellaneous and Humorous* (1791), Edward Nairne explained:

> I have retain'd the word BREECHES, as they art known by no other name amongst country folk. – The change from vulgarity to refinement, in cities and towns, has introduced other appellations; there they are generally called SMALL CLOTHES; but some ladies of high rank and extreme delicacy call them INEXPRESSIBLES. (77)

And in *Poems on Various Subjects* (1800), Samuel Bishop joked: 'Our smarts (so much refin'd the modern speech is) / Say "Inexpressibles," instead of Breeches' (2.183). (Uncle Sol's trousers are called 'inexpressibles' in chapter 4.) By the 1840s, even though the prudery continued to be ridiculed and 'trousers' and 'breeches' remained the words most usually used, a great variety of euphemisms had been coined:

> Ill-used but most beloved, unfortunate but most indispensable habiliment, how many times has it changed its name, and how short a time did the newest and purest name continue bearable – … from the first alias small clothes to tights … to inexpressibles … to unspeakables … to unmentionables … to shorts … to etceteras … to continuations, and so on through antifeminines, remainders, masculines, and nether integuments down to the quaker periphrase lower garments! (Alfred Butler, *Elphinstone*, 1841, ch. 4)

He drew out so bright

He drew out so bright, and clear, and shining … The more Miss Tox drew him out, the finer he came – like wire.] In wire-drawing, a process dating from the fourteenth century, a piece of ductile metal (such as brass, copper, iron, steel, gold, silver) is passed through a series of holes, successively diminishing in diameter, thus lengthening the wire while lessening its thickness. In the nineteenth century, wire-drawing was carried out extensively in the manufacturing districts, with Birmingham having the largest share of the trade. Wire-drawing produced many different types of wire for a whole range of industrial, scientific, agricultural and domestic applications, including telegraph wires; bridge cables; under-sea cables; wire rope; nautical ropes; telescopes; wire netting and fences; safety lamps; garden chairs and bedsteads; venetian blinds; fireguards; spectacle frames; birdcages; needles; fish-hooks; musical instrument strings; watch frames; jewellery and other ornaments (*Penny Cyclopædia*, 1843, 27.476–9; Bechmann 1.414–24; 'Wire-drawing', *HW* 9 [22 April 1854]: 217–21).

Who ran sniggering off

tossed it away with a pieman.] Mayhew identified the gambling game to 'toss the pieman' as 'a favourite pastime with costermongers' boys and all that class':

> If the pieman win the toss, he receives 1*d.* without giving a pie; if he lose, he hands it over for nothing. The pieman himself never "tosses," but always calls head or tail to his customer. At the week's end it comes to the same thing, they say, whether they toss or not, or rather whether they win or lose the toss: "I've taken as much as 2*s.* 6*d.* at tossing, which I shouldn't have had if I had'nt done so. Very few people buy without tossing, and the boys in particular. Gentlemen 'out on the spree' at the late public-houses will frequently toss when they don't want the pies, and when they win they will amuse themselves by throwing the pies at one another, or at me. Sometimes I have taken as much as half-a-crown, and the people of whom I had the money has never eaten a pie. The boys has the greatest love of gambling, and they seldom, if ever, buys without tossing." One of the reasons why the street boys delight in tossing, is, that they can often obtain a pie by such means when they have only a halfpenny wherewith to gamble. If the lad wins he gets a penny pie for his halfpenny. (1.196)

But they never taught honour at the Grinders' School, where the system that prevailed was particularly strong in the engendering of hypocrisy.] Compare Uriah Heep and his father, who had both attended a charity school and learned 'a good deal of umbleness', and earned 'the monitor-medal by being umble'. Upon hearing this, David Copperfield realizes, for the first time, 'this despicable cant of false humility might have originated out of the Heep family. I had seen the harvest, but had never thought of the seed' (*DC* 39).

many of the friends and masters of past Grinders said, if this were what came of education for the common people, let us have none. Some, more rational, said, let us have a better one. But the governing powers of the Grinders' Company were always ready for *them*, by picking out a few boys who had turned out well in spite of the system, and roundly asserting that they could have only turned out well because of it.] For contemporary criticisms of the charity school movement, see chapter 22, p. 264.

Chapter 39 Thirteenth monthly number
October 1847

FURTHER ADVENTURES OF CAPTAIN EDWARD CUTTLE, MARINER

The captain did not, however,

as the Captain implicitly believed that all books were true,] 'These books are true' was a familiar phrase deriving from the traditional Christian theological claim about the authority of the Bible. For example:

> Christians got these books from the Jews, and the Jews to this day support the veracity of these books, at least those of the law of Moses, the prophets and Psalms ... and principally those parts that speak of Christ. These are the writings by which Christians prove the Christian religion to be the work of God; and although the Jews know this and still oppose the Christian religion, yet they persevere in bearing witness that these books are true and wrote by men inspired by God. ('A Layman's Reply to Paine's Age of Reason', *Walker's Hibernian Magazine or Compendium of Entertaining Knowledge for the Year 1796*, Part I, 233–37 [p. 233])

The phrase was often used by Christian missionaries in discussions with the indigenous peoples; see, for example, *The Missionary Register for 1822*, 342; and *The Baptist Magazine for 1824*, 225. The phrase even found its way into poetry and children's literature; for example, 'Puzzle': 'My second, third and fourth, to do ... / Seven, eight, nine, ten – if books are true – ' (*Robert Merry's Museum*, 1842, 3.31, ll. 3, 5).

the Captain always read for himself, before going to bed, a certain Divine Sermon once delivered on a Mount;] The Sermon on the Mount (Matthew 5–7), the source of a great number of allusions in Dickens's works, including in *DS* (see notes to chapters 23 and 47 pp. 282, 432). For Dickens's preference for the New Testament, see note to chapter 58, p. 506–7.

Rob the Grinder, whose reverence

Rob the Grinder, whose reverence for the inspired writings, under the admirable system of the Grinders' School, had been developed by a perpetual bruising of his intellectual shins against all the proper names of all the tribes of Judah, and by the monotonous repetition of hard verses,] Rote-learning was the prevailing method of education in the nineteenth century and included information about

Mems.

Dismissal of Susan Nipper   –No. Next Nº

Mrs Pipchin installed as housekeeper – Yes.

Major Bagstock.

Progress of domestic unhappiness.   Extravagance –

Rob and the Captain
Mr Toots.   qy Mr Feeder.   Mr Toots & the Captain

qy a Doctor Blimber chapter, with no~~body in it~~ dialogue in it?

Bunsby and Mrs Mac Stinger.

qy Mr Toots going to call at Dr Blimber's.

Alice Marwood & her mother?   Yes. A glimpse

Carker family — Mr Morfin.   No.

Mem: open next Nº with Carker at home.

Number Plan

(Dealings with the Firm of Dombey and Son — N? XIII)

chapter XXXIX.

Further adventures of Captain Edward Cuttle, Mariner.

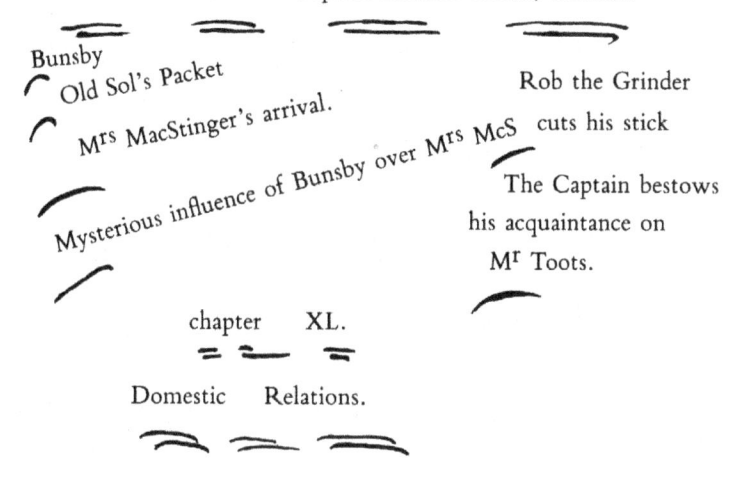

Bunsby
Old Sol's Packet
Mrs MacStinger's arrival.
Mysterious influence of Bunsby over Mrs McS
Rob the Grinder cuts his stick
The Captain bestows his acquaintance on Mr Toots.

chapter XL.

Domestic Relations.

Mr Dombey's determination — Phases of his pride.
Edith's proposal to him – The scene in her boudoir –
How will all the things look when he sees them next?
So to Mrs Skewton, and the chance meeting

Chapter XLI.

New Voices in the waves.

Blimber's –
Toots ∧ Feeder
Mr Dombey & Mrs Pipchin
and so come to Edith at night

Mrs Skewton's Death, in contrast with Paul's —

qy Cousin Feenix and the Mausoleum

Yes. Room enough.

Chapter Plan

the Bible and ancient civilizations. Two of the most popular authors of schoolbooks were Mrs Sarah Trimmer (1741–1810) and Miss Richmal Mangnall (1769–1820), whose works were published in innumerable editions throughout the century. Mrs Trimmer's *Sacred History, Selected from the Scriptures ... particularly calculated to facilitate the study of the Holy Scriptures in Schools and Families* (2 vols, 1817) contains several mentions of 'the tribes of Judah', including:

> The standard of the camp of Judah was first; it consisted of the tribes of Judah, Issachar, and Zebulun ... the standard of Judah being raised, the three tribes which belonged to it set forward. (7th ed., 1817; 2.43–4)

Dickens's use of 'all the tribes of Judah' is slightly misleading because, in the many contemporary references to the subject, the phrase invariably includes other tribes as well. For example, and in addition to Mrs Trimmer's mention, see 'the tribes of Judah and Benjamin' (Lucy Barton, *Bible Letters for Children*, 1831, 81; and W.C. Taylor's *The Student's Manual of Ancient History* (1845, 122): 'the tribes of Judah, Benjamin, Dan, and Simeon'. In the 1848 'new edition' of Miss Mangnall's *Historical and Miscellaneous Questions, for the Use of Young Persons*, the section entitled 'Observations on the Map of Canaan, or the Holy Land' first sets out the facts and then gives a list of questions about them:

> The following were the several divisions and situations of the tribes of Israel, as settled under Joshua: – THE TRIBE OF JUDAH, the largest territory ... THE TRIBE OF SIMEON ... THE TRIBE OF BENJAMIN ... THE TRIBE[S] OF DAN ... EPHRAIM ... ASSHUR ... ISSACHAR ... NAPHTALI ... ZABULON ... MANASSEH ... GAD ... REUBEN.
>
> *Questions.* – 1. How was Canaan divided in the time of Joshua? Name them. How were they respectively situated? The tribe of Judah? Simeon? Benjamin? Dan? Ephraim? Asshur? Issachar? Naphtali? Zabulon? Manasseh? Gad? Reuben? (26)

On biblical history being taught in charity schools, see also *BH* where Grandfather Smallweed's father 'had been bred at a Charity School, in a complete course, according to question and answer, of those ancient people the Amorites and Hittites, [and] he was frequently quoted as an example of the failure of education' (ch. 21). For more on the rigorous demands of religious instruction, see note to chapter 8, p. 134–5.

the parading of him at six years old in leather breeches,] For Dickens's dislike of the sight of 'long melancholy rows' of charity boys 'in leather breeches, ... which file along the streets to churches ... under the escort of that surprising monster, a beadle' (*Speeches* 240), see note to chapter 5, p. 83.

Captain Cuttle also, as a man

Chapter 39 *Further Adventures of Captain Edward Cuttle, Mariner*

the day-book] 'Day-book' can mean both a ship's log-book and a book used to record a shop's commercial transactions.

"If you're in arnest, you see,

clemency is the brightest jewel in the crown of a Briton's head, for which you'll overhaul the Constitution, as laid down in Rule Britannia, and, when found, *that* is the charter as them garden angels was a-singing of, so many times over.] 'Clemency is the brightest jewel in a monarch's crown' was a popular saying in the early to mid-nineteenth century, appearing in many moral tracts and encyclopedias. It was sometimes attributed to L. M. Stretch in this form:

> Clemency is not only the privilege, the honour, and the duty of a prince, but it is also his security, and better than all garrisons, forts, and guards, to preserve himself and his dominions in safety. It is the brightest jewel in a monarch's crown. As meekness moderates anger, so clemency moderates punishment. (L. M. Stretch, *The Beauties of History; Or, Pictures of Virtue and Vice*, 1808, 40)

In fact, though, the phrase goes back to at least the mid-eighteenth century: 'As Clemency is the most valuable jewel in the crown of a monarch, it should always show its luster in controlling the afflicted, and in relieving the distressed' ('Supplement to Volume II', *The Oxford Magazine*, 1769, 241). Captain Cuttle is presumably confusing the phrase with Henry Hallam's observation that 'Clemency ... is the standing policy of constitutional governments, as severity is of despotism' (*The Constitutional History of England*, 1827, 2.584). According to the patriotic song, 'Rule Britannia':

> This was the charter of the land,
> And guardian angels sang this strain:
> 'Rule, Britannia! rule the waves:
> Britons never will be slaves.'

For more on 'Rule Britannia', see note to chapter 4, p. 69.

"My lad," said the Captain,

"a man's thoughts is like the winds, and nobody can't answer for 'em for certain, any length of time together.] John 3.8: 'The wind bloweth where it listeth, and thou hearest the sound thereof, but canst not tell whence it cometh, and whither it goeth: so is every one that is born of the Spirit'.

Oh! I beg your pardon,

you mayn't be in want of any pigeons, may you, Sir?"] For Rob's keeping pigeons on the roof of the Wooden Midshipman, see note to chapter 23, p. 281.

"Oh! It's very hard

It an't because I'm a servant and you're a master, that you're to go and libel me.] Poor references were not, in fact, considered legally libelous:

> A bona fide character given of a servant that she was saucy, &c., if there be no malice, (which must be directly proved), will not ground an action of slander, though the servant was prevented from getting a place thereby. (*Edmondson v. Stevenson*)

> So a servant cannot maintain an action against his former master for words spoken, or a letter written by him, in giving a character of the servant, unless the latter prove the malice as well as falsehood of the charge, even though the master make specific charges of fraud (*Weatherston v. Hawkins*). (Starke, 1830 1.298; see also the entry on 'Libel' in *Penny Cyclopædia of the Society for the Diffusion of Useful Knowledge*, 1839, 13.458)

In the same composed, business-like

Leadenhall Market] Located between Gracechurch Street and the East India House, Leadenhall Market was 'A large market for butchers' meat, fish, poultry, vegetables, leather, hides, bacon and such like' (282). In 1844, *Mogg's New Picture of London* designated it as 'the greatest market in London for the sale of country-killed meat, particularly beef'. In 1850, though, Peter Cunningham's *Handbook of London* remarked that 'Leadenhall is no longer celebrated for its beef, but is deservedly esteemed as the largest and best poultry market in London' (283).

effected an arrangement with a private watchman on duty there, to come and put up and take down the shutters of the Wooden Midshipman every night and morning.] In the early days of London's first professional police force (established in 1829), when it was felt that police coverage was inadequate, especially along back streets, market owners and merchants hired private watchmen to protect their merchandise. Watchmen sometimes performed other duties as well, such as waking people early in the morning or, as here, putting up and taking down shutters. A Mr Wall, one member of a deputation from the parish of St Luke's, complained of private watchmen in 1834: 'There is no authority or control over them; people continue to employ them because they call them up of a morning' (*Report from the Select Committee on the Police of the Metropolis*, House of Commons, 13 August 1834, 255; see also note to chapter 48, p. 440).

Chapter 39 *Further Adventures of Captain Edward Cuttle, Mariner* 395

From this bed Captain Cuttle

with the solitary air of Crusoe finishing his toilet with his goat-skin cap; and although his fears of a visitation from the savage tribe ... were somewhat cooled, as similar apprehensions on the part of that lone mariner used to be by the lapse of a long interval without any symptoms of the cannibals, he still observed a regular routine of precautions, and never encountered a bonnet without previous survey from his castle of retreat.] Robinson Crusoe fashions 'a cap, made of a goat's skin', with a flap hanging down behind, to protect himself from the sun and rain. Shortly after discovering the human footprint on the shore, he begins to worry that cannibals from the mainland are using his island, but he calms himself with the realization that

> I had been here now almost eighteen years, and never saw the least footsteps of human creature there before; and I might be eighteen years more as entirely concealed as I was now, if I did not discover myself to them, which I had no manner of occasion to do; it being my only business to keep myself entirely concealed where I was. ... Yet I entertained such an abhorrence of the savage wretches that I have been speaking of, and of the wretched, inhuman custom of their devouring and eating one another up, that I continued pensive and sad, and kept close within my own circle for almost two years after this ... for the aversion which nature gave me to these hellish wretches was such, that I was as fearful of seeing them as of seeing the devil himself. ... if I had happened to have fallen into their hands, I knew what would have been my lot.

Bunsby, who was one of those

Who being instructed to deliver those words and disappear, fulfilled his mission like a tarry spirit, charged with a mysterious warning.] Bunsby's boy is likened to Ariel, who has just fulfilled a task for Prospero in *The Tempest*:

Ariel [aside to Prospero]	Sir, all this service
	Have I done since I went.
Prospero [aside to Ariel]	My tricksy spirit! ...
Ariel [aside to Prospero]	Was't well done?
Prospero [aside to Ariel]	Bravely, my diligence. Thou shalt be free. (5.1.225–41)

The Captain, well pleased to receive

the listening ear] Poetic diction popularized by Cowper and Byron, among many others. See, for example, *The Task* (1785), 'Tall spire, from which the sound of cheerful bells / Just undulates upon the listening ear' (bk 1); and Canto 4 of *Childe Harold's Pilgrimage* (1818): 'And the retiring strains are hurrying past, / The listening ear then dwells upon the last' (stanza 22).

"Bunsby!" said the Captain,

a man as can give an opinion as is brighter than di'monds – and give me the lad with the tarry trousers as shines to me like di'monds bright, for which you'll overhaul the Stanfell's Budget,] From an English folk song that exists in multiple versions:

> As I was a-walking one May summer's morn,
>   The weather being fine and clear,
> There I heard a tender mother,
>   Talking to her daughter dear.
>
> Says she, "Daughter, I would have you marry,
>   And live no longer a single life";
> "No," said she, "I'd sooner tarry,
>   For my jolly sailor bright."
>
> "Daughter! sailors are given to roving,
>   And to foreign parts they go,
> Then they leave you broken-hearted,
>   And they prove your overthrow."
>
> "Oh, sailors they are men of honour,
>   And they do face their enemy,
> When the thundering cannons rattle,
>   And the bullets away they fly."
>
> "I know you would have me wed a farmer,
>   And not give me my heart's delight;
> Give me the lad whose tarry trowsers
>   Shines to me like diamonds bright." (qtd. in Ley, 1931, 265–6)

The nautical meaning of 'overhaul' is 'to pull asunder for the purpose of examining in detail'. A 'Budget' is a collection or stock, as in 'a Budget of plays' (*OED*). In context, then, Captain Cuttle is telling Bunsby to look into a collection of songs, or songbook, called 'Stanfell's Budget' for the lines 'the lad with the tarry trousers as shines to me like di'monds bright'.

In a letter of 2 March 1849, Dickens explained to Frank Stanfell, a Lieutenant in the Royal Navy since November 1840, and an acquaintance of Dickens, that 'the passage in question refers to a joke between myself and my friend Mr. Stanfield, the celebrated Marine Painter – whose name, in Captain Cuttle's mouth, changes accidentally to yours' (*Letters* 5.503–4). Clarkson Stanfield (1793–1867) was a prosperous marine and landscape painter, and a member of the Royal Academy. Dickens first met Stanfield in the late 1830s, and he helped to illustrate four of Dickens's Christmas books and worked on the scenery for several of the amateur theatricals put on by Dickens (*LD* is dedicated to Stanfield).

Chapter 39 *Further Adventures of Captain Edward Cuttle, Mariner* 397

" '— in forlorn search of intelligence

There he lays, all his days – " Mr. Bunsby, who had a musical ear, suddenly bellowed, "In the Bays of Biscay, O!" which so affected the good Captain, as an **appropriate tribute to departed worth,**] From the song 'The Bay of Biscay O', with words by Andrew Cherry and tune by John Davy. The first verse runs:

> Loud roared the dreadful thunder!
> The rain a deluge showers!
> The clouds were rent asunder
> By lightning's vivid pow'rs!
> The night was drear and dark,
> Our poor devoted bark,
> Till next day, there she lay,
> In the Bay of Biscay, O!
>   (*The Universal Songster; or, Museum of Mirth*, 1825, 1.227)

Variations on the last two lines of this stanza serve as a refrain for the remaining three stanzas. The Bay of Biscay was notoriously difficult to navigate because of its changing currents and many inlets.

departed worth,] An eighteenth-century cliché associated with eulogies, funerals and epitaphs; for example: 'The hearse was accompanied by two mourning coaches, in which were some gentlemen, who admired and esteemed him when living, and were solicitous of paying this last tribute to departed worth' (*New Annual Register … for the Year 1797*, 1798, 25).

"Well, well!" said the Captain

"Affliction sore, long time he bore. … "Physicians," observed Bunsby, "was in vain."] These are formulaic phrases used on gravestones, such as one for a child 'who died July 22, 1789, aged 13 years, 5 months, and 25 days':

> Affliction sore long time I bore,
> Physicians strove in vain,
> Till God was pleased to give me ease
> And took away my pain.
>   (qtd. in *The History of the Town of Lyndeborough … New Hampshire*, by D. Donovan and Jacob A. Woodward, 1906, 590)

The phrases were among a number of inscriptions ridiculed as being 'so very faulty … in general sameness' in an article entitled 'Epitaphs' in 1791:

> The difficulty … of finding discriminating and appropriate terms in which to mention the dead, and remind us of mortality, occasions the constant

repetition of certain phrases and rhimes in our church-yards – Readers, in general, are desired to *stop here,* and *shed a tear* – for whom? for a man or woman they never saw or heard of. ... or perhaps we read that *beautiful stanza* beginning with, "Afflictions sore, long time I bore, / "Physicians were in vain, &c."

It is impossible for the most sympathetic heart to be touched with the continued repetition of such jingles, and as grave-stones of the plainest kind are expensive, I wonder that the *burying clubs* do not purchase a piece of ground for the interment of their members with one large stone in common, signifying that they *were all* loving wives, affectionate husbands; and then might be added the above lines to serve as a kind of funeral *chorus,* "Afflictions sore, long time WE bore &c." (*The Lady's Magazine for September 1791,* 466–7)

Bunsby, descrying no objection,

affixed his sign-manual] An autograph signature that authenticates a document (especially applied to a sovereign's signature) (*OED*).

But no. Bunsby was accompanied

he was three sheets in the wind, or, in plain words, drunk.] '*Three-sheets* in the wind. – Naval, but naturalized ashore, and means *drunk,* but capable of going along – like a ship – which has three sheets braced – main, mizen, and foresail' (*Slang, a Dictionary of the Turf ...* 1823, 265). In other words, if three sheets (ropes or chains) are loose and blowing in the wind, the sails will flap and the ship lurch about; compare, 'Some o' the crew had managed to get at a puncheon o' rum, and swearing they would die jolly, had got "three sheets in the wind," and were tumbling about the deck' (*Gentleman's Magazine,* 1839, 5.244).

"Cuttle," said the Commander,

traps?"] His personal effects, baggage or belongings. The first recorded use of the colloquial term is 1813 (*OED*).

Chapter 40

DOMESTIC RELATIONS

It was not in the nature

The evil that is in it finds equally its means of growth and propagation in opposites.] Read in the context of this paragraph, this alludes to the opening remarks of Mark Antony's speech on the death of Julius Caesar: 'The evil that men do lives after them; / The good is oft interred with their bones' (3.2.75–6).

as hard a master as the Devil in dark fables.] This seems to have been a proverbial or religious phrase; see, for example, the moral tract, *The Cottager's Monthly Visitor*, 1832: 'And the devil is a hard master! For how does he reward his followers?' (12.21). It also occurs in Charles Kingsley's *Westward Ho!* (1855), 'and so the slaves fight like a bull in a tether, no farther than their rope, finding thus the devil a hard master, as do most in the end' (ch. 16, 'The Great Armada'). Stories and legends about the Devil date from the time of the Early Church through to the Middle Ages and the Renaissance. This phrase may refer in particular to the idea of making a contract with the Devil (*e.g.* the Faust legend): the Devil was always careful to write a faultless legal document.

He did not design accompanying

she seemed upon the wane, and turning of the earth, earthy.] 'The first man is of the earth, earthy: the second man is the Lord from heaven' ('Burial of the Dead', *BCP;* cf. 1 Corinthians 15.47).

Without having undergone any decided

Among other symptoms of this last affliction, she fell into the habit of confounding the names of her two sons-in-law, the living and the deceased; and in general called Mr. Dombey, either "Grangeby," or "Domber," or indifferently, both.] For palsy, its symptoms and how it impairs speech, see notes to chapter 21, p. 261 and chapter 37, pp. 382–3.

But she was youthful, very youthful

a fly-away bonnet] A fashionable loose bonnet, one that was apt to 'fly away', worn by young women.

"Tell Joseph, he may

"Tell Joseph, he may live in hope ... or he'll die in despair."] 'Better to live in hope than die in despair' is proverbial (Henderson, 1832, 106).

"I'll tell you what, Sir,"

"a fair friend of ours has removed to Queer Street."] An idiomatic expression used since the early nineteenth century to indicate various types of misfortune, including illness, though it most often betokens financial ruin (*OED*).

After imparting this precious piece

the Major, who was certainly true-blue ... coming within the "genuine old English" classification, which has never been exactly ascertained,] This joke about Bagstock's suffering from cyanosis or 'blue jaundice' (see note to chapter 7, p. 108) leads to wordplay on synonyms for loyalty and nationalism. 'True-blue' derives from the seventeenth-century Scottish Covenanters (who had adopted blue as their colour to distinguish them from the royalists' red) who sought to maintain Presbyterianism as the sole religion in Scotland, as opposed to Roman Catholicism; compare, for example: *The Presbyterian Letany*, 1647: 'a Good, Honest, Sound, Presbyterian ... a True-blue Loyalist'; Scott, *Heart of Midlothian*, ch. 7: 'This was a tough true-blue Presbyterian, called Deans' (*Tales of My Landlord*, 1818, 1.190). 'Genuine old English' had two different applications when it first occurred in the eighteenth century. In *The Humours of Whist: a Dramatic Satire* (1743), the phrase is used to distinguish whist from French and Irish games: 'Now *Whist*, my Lord, is the only genuine old *English* Game, which shews the Genius of the Nation as to its Understanding--as much as *Chevy Chace*, or *Britons Strike home* does as to its Music'. Three decades later, Smollett used it when discussing dialects:

> He proceeded to explain his assertion that the English language was spoken with greater propriety at Edinburgh than in London. – He said, what we generally called the Scottish dialect was, in fact, true, genuine old English, with a mixture of some French terms and idioms, adopted in a long intercourse betwixt the French and Scotch nations. (*The Expedition of Humphry Clinker*, 1771, 2.181)

The phrase later became used in various contexts: for example, in a letter of 1801 Walter Scott referred to 'the genuine old English model' of dramatic composition (Lockhart 60).

Cleopatra, at one time fretful

a more potent skeleton than the maid ... watching at the rose-coloured curtains,]
For the image of death with dart and hourglass, see note to chapter 27, p. 315.

The greater part of

the younger woman carried knitted work or some such goods for sale;] For the items gipsies sold and how they made a living, see note to chapter 27, p. 306.

"Yes, my Lady," with a

Warwickshire.] One of England's midland counties, which included, in 1843, the cities of Coventry and Birmingham, the attractive towns of Stratford-upon-Avon, Kenilworth and Leamington and several pretty market towns. In 1841, Warwickshire had a population of 402,121, a figure that had nearly doubled since the beginning of the nineteenth century (*Penny Cyclopædia* 83–4, 88). For Mrs Skewton's visit to Warwick Castle and the surrounding area, see notes to chapter 27.

Chapter 41

NEW VOICES IN THE WAVES

And gentle Mr. Toots, who

his great mill with the Larkey Boy.] 'Mill' is slang for a boxing-match or fist fight; for example, Pierce Egan, *Boxiana; or, Sketches of Ancient and Modern Pugilism* (1824): 'He did not wish to be *smashed* in his outset, nor enter indiscriminately into every *mill* that might be offered to him' (2.46). 'Larky' means 'ready for a lark', frolicsome, sportive. So-called 'swells' sometimes wore 'larkey' waistcoats, multi-coloured waistcoats with flowers embroidered on them. For the nicknames given to prizefighters, see note to chapter 22, p. 269.

No doubt Diogenes is there,

he comes straightway at Mr. Toots's legs, and tumbles over himself in the desperation with which he makes at him, like a very dog of Montargis.] William Barrymore's translation of Guilbert de Pixérécourt's melodrama *The Forest of Bondy; or, The Dog of Montargis*, a favourite of Dickens's childhood, was first performed on 30

September 1814, at the Theatre Royal, Covent Garden. The story involves a rivalry between two soldiers. One of them, Aubri, receives a promotion, angering the other soldier, Macaire, whose jealousy leads him to murder his rival in the Forest of Bondy. Somewhat later, Aubri's greyhound attacks Macaire, provoking a trial by combat, in which the dog attacks the murderer a final time, forcing him to confess his guilt. In his childhood, Dickens, along with several schoolfriends, put on a production of *The Dog of Montargis* with white mice at Wellington House Academy. Dickens wryly noted, 'one white mouse ... even made a very creditable appearance on the stage as the Dog of Montargis' (John, 2001, 84; *HW*, 'Our School', 4 [11 October 1851]: 49–52). He later briefly alluded to the story in 'A Christmas Tree' (*HW*, 2 [21 December 1850]: 289–95]); other mentions occur in *HW* 15.614 and *AYR* 13.203.

And here is Doctor Blimber,

working like a sexton in the graves of languages.] See notes to chapter 5, p. 87 and chapter 11, p. 167.

the "new boy" of the school;] Although *OED* cites this as the earliest instance in print of 'new boy', the term is used in this sense by Mr Squeers in *NN* (38) and occurred as early as 1787 in *The Literary World* 59.67, referring to a boy at Rugby School.

"You will like," says

I think we have no new disciples in our little Portico,] 'Portico' refers to Aristotle's Lyceum and is probably an allusion to the building depicted in Raphael's painting 'The School of Athens'. Mrs Blimber earlier compared her husband's taking the boys for walks to Aristotle's peripatetic school of philosophy in the Lyceum (see note to chapter 11, p. 163),

New to Florence, too, almost;

Bitherstone, born beneath some Bengal star of ill-omen,] In chapter 8, we learn that Bitherstone's parent's 'were all in India'. See note, p. 137.

his Lexicon has got so dropsical from constant reference, that it won't shut,] In 1843, the Oxford clergymen Henry George Liddell and Robert Scott published two volumes, *A Greek-English Lexicon* and *A Lexicon Chiefly for the Use of Schools* (2nd ed., 1846). Both volumes went through numerous later editions throughout the century. According to Thomas John Graham's *Modern Domestic Medicine* (1827), dropsy is 'a preternatural collection of serous or watery fluid in the cellular membrane, beneath the skin, or in different cavities of the body' (309).

He'd precious soon find himself carried up the country by a few of his (Bitherstone's) Coolies, and handed over to the Thugs, he can tell him that.]
Coolies and Thugs were topical in the 1830s and 1840s. In 1833, Britain abolished the practice of slavery, and plantation owners in the West Indies and the British colony of Guiana, and later in Peru, Cuba and Mauritius, began importing Coolies – Chinese labourers who signed contracts which trapped them in a system of virtual slavery. By the 1840s, tens of thousands of Chinese and Indian workers (India was the other source of supply for field workers) were caught up in what was called the 'coolie trade'. The public became aware of the extent and evils of the traffic in 1844, when Guiana encouraged Chinese emigration, Peru began importing Chinese workers and the Indian Government approved emigration to the West Indies. In Britain, Lord Brougham and the old anti-slavery party denounced the trade as a return to slavery. The worst abuses of the system were ended by Act of Parliament in 1855 (*Parliamentary Papers*: 'Reports from Committees, Session 18 November 1847–5 September 1848', vol. 17, part IV; 'Discussion in the House of Commons on Tuesday, 1 March 1842', reported in the *Sydney Morning Herald*, 19 August 1842, p. 2; David Hollett, *Passage from India to El Dorado: Guyana and the Great Migration*. 1999, p. 55.)

Also frequently mentioned in the news and books of the 1830s and 1840s were the members of the Indian religious sect of Thuggee, whose worship of the goddess Kali obliged them to commit ritual murder. As explained by a contemporary article on the subject:

> The Thugs are a Hindoo race who infest the roads in India, for the purpose of robbing travelers. … Ostensibly, they are simple cultivators of the ground; but for eight months of the year, they move in gangs along the roads, under various disguises and pretexts, murdering and robbing every party whom they think they can empower without danger to themselves. …
>
> At length the private signal is given; each traveller is caught round the neck by a handkerchief, which the wretch who threw it twists as hard as he can, while two of his companions hold the hands of the victim. … They then select the most secret place in the neighbourhood for the interment of the bodies. … Parties of two, four, and nearly as high as twenty, are thus disposed of. …They display the greatest caution in the selection of their victims. … The government runners are seldom attacked by them, because their fate could not fail to become a subject of inquiry. For the same reason, and from a dread of resistance, they rarely make up to Europeans. (*The Public Ledger*, 9 February 1836: 'The Thugs', p. 4)

In 1839, Captain Meadows Taylor published his first-hand account of the sect, *Confessions of a Thug*, a book that made the British public familiar with Thugs. Also in 1839, Captain W.H. Sleeman, Superintendant of Thug Police in the Indian Military Service, published *The Thugs, or Phansigars of India*, in which he describes how the Thugs had been suppressed in many parts of India by 1839 (52–91).

Briggs is still grinding in

with his Herodotus stop on just at present, and his other barrels on a shelf behind him.] The phrasing is picked up from chapter 12, in which Mr Feeder is said to have 'had his Virgil stop on, and was slowly grinding that tune to four young gentlemen' (for 'stop', see note, p. 170). The 'barrels' are the revolving cylinders of a barrel-organ, in which are fixed pins that strike the keys (*OED*). Herodotus, the Greek historian who lived in the fifth century BC, was called 'the father of history' by Cicero and others. His *Histories,* an account of the Persian Wars, is notable for its rich details and its grand scope, and for including the transcribed conversations of a number of participants. For John Ruskin's early reading of 'the whole of Herodotus', see note to chapter 11, p. 155.

A mighty sensation is created,

one who has passed the Rubicon,] 'To cross or pass the Rubicon' is to take a decisive or final step, to pass the point of no return, an expression current since the seventeenth century. The reference is to the stream in northeastern Italy that marked the ancient boundary between Italy and Cisalpine Gaul. In 49 BC, Julius Caesar irrevocably committed himself to a war against the Roman Senate and Pompey once he conducted his army across the Rubicon into Italy, thereby breaking the law that prohibited a general from leading his army out of his province.

Bewildering emotions are awakened also

dine with him to-day at the Bedford; in right of which feats he might set up as Old Parr, if he chose, unquestioned.] Mr Dombey stays at the Bedford in chapter 10, see note, p. 153. Thomas Parr, commonly known as 'Old Parr, 'whose extreme and almost antediluvian age has become proverbial', was supposedly born in 1483 in Winnington, Shropshire, the son of a farmer, and was buried on 15 November 1635 in Westminster Abbey, at the age of 152 years. His death is reputed to have been brought about by fatigue and the change of air and diet consequent on a journey to London to see Charles I. After he died, Old Parr's body was examined by Dr William Harvey, who found it to be remarkably stout and healthy and without obvious signs of decay. The principal authority for the history of Old Parr is John Taylor, 'the Water Poet', who published a pamphlet on Parr during the few months he resided in London in 1635, entitled *The Olde, Olde, very Olde Man; or the Age and Long Life of Thomas Parr.* As late as the 1870s, *Chambers's Book of Days* claimed that the age of Old Parr 'rests on such well-authenticated grounds, that no reasonable doubt can be entertained as to its truth' ('November 15', *Chambers's Book of Days,* 1879, 2.581–2).

Florence then steals away and

the Doctor, with his round turned legs, like a clerical pianoforte,] The furniture trade began to adopt mechanization in the 1840s, and turning was possibly the earliest process of mechanical shaping. The piece of wood being turned was placed in motion by means of a steam engine, which replaced the treadle or lever ordinarily operated by the worker's foot. *Chambers's Encyclopædia* (1874) remarked that 'The pianoforte has in modern times attained a widespread popularity beyond that of any other musical instrument' (7.624). In the estimation of George Dodd's *Dictionary of Manufactures, Mining, Machinery, and the Industrial Arts* (1869), there were roughly 23,000 pianofortes made annually in London in 1851 (280). Dickens resorts at least two other times to the images of the turned pianoforte leg: in *HT*, Mr McChoakumchild, along with 'some one hundred and forty other schoolmasters' is said to have 'been lately turned at the same time, in the same factory, on the same principles, like so many pianoforte legs' (1.2); in *BH*, Mr Quale is said to have 'a great deal to say for himself about Africa, and a project … to teach the natives to turn pianoforte legs and establish an export trade' (4).

Intelligence of the event is

Baden-Baden),] See note to chapter 31, p. 339.

Brooks's –] Brooks's Club, at 60 St James's Street, Pall Mall, was 'the great Whig Club; some of the most distinguished political characters have held their meetings here', including Fox, Wilberforce, Palmerston and Hume. In 1854, the number of members was restricted to 575; the entrance fee was £9. 6s., with an annual subscription of £11. 6s. Brooks's Club was notorious for heavy gambling (Weale, 1854, 305; Weinreb and Hibbert, 1983, 101). For other London clubs, see note to chapter 7, p. 110; for Pall Mall, see note to chapter 58, p. 503.

"Well, upon my life,"

stroking his chin, which he has just enough of hand below his wristbands to do;] For the different styles of wearing wristbands, see note to chapter 14, p. 197.

"There's an uncommon good church

"There's an uncommon good church in the village … pure specimen of the early Anglo-Norman style, and admirably well sketched too by Lady Jane Finchbury – woman with tight stays – but they've spoilt it with whitewash,] Antiquarianism and the search for the picturesque by English tourists helped to popularize the Anglo-Norman style of architecture in the early nineteenth century. Well-known books for travellers and antiquarians, copiously illustrated with engravings, included detailed descriptions of Anglo-Norman antiquities, castles and churches, for example: John

Britton's *The Beauties of England and Wales, or delineations, topographical, historical, and descriptive* (1801–16); J. N. Brewer's *The Picture of England; or, historical and descriptive delineations of the most curious works of nature and art in each county: calculated as an agreeable companion to the tourist, or a class book for the student* (1820); and Edward Brayley's *The Graphic and Historical Illustrator, or: an original miscellany of literary, antiquarian, and topographical information* (1834).

Cousin Feenix is probably mistaken to call the church a 'pure specimen of the Anglo-Norman style' because, according to *The Penny Cyclopædia* (1840), 'there are very few buildings in this style throughout, though there are many which retain detached parts and features' (16.275). But his remark on the whitewash reflects how churches of this period could be disfigured or covered up in later centuries. Describing the church of St Mary Overy in Southwark in 1833, William Taylor remarked, 'This beautiful specimen of the Anglo-Norman style of Architecture, was, till within a few years of the present time, hid from view by a coating of brickwork; with which a large portion of the exterior of the Nave is still disfigured' (*Annals of St Mary Overy: an historical and descriptive account* (1833, 46). According to the *Penny Cyclopædia*, other churches with vestiges of the Anglo-Norman style include the small churches at Barfreston in Kent, New Shoreham in Sussex, Iffley in Oxfordshire and Steetly in Derbyshire, as well as the older parts of the cathedrals of Canterbury, Winchester, Gloucester, Ely, Durham, Norwich, Lincoln and Oxford (275).

The characteristics of the style are described in an introduction to *The Beauties of England and Wales*:

> the style ... is marked by the uniform prevalence of the semicircular arch; by massy columns, standing on a strong plinth, or ... having "a kind of regular base and capital," which are usually square. ... by the massive contours of the mouldings; and by walls of great thickness, without any very prominent buttresses ... one distinguishing mark of the Anglo-Norman churches, when compared with those described as having existed in the island previous to the Conquest, consists in the magnitude and grandeur of their dimensions. (370–1) (James Norris Brewer, *Introduction to the Original Delineations, topographical, historical, and descriptive, intitled The Beauties of England and Wales*, 1818)

At the appointed time, Cousin Feenix

Man with cork leg, from White's.] Cork legs, which were articulated with springs and joints at the knee and ankle, were an advance in prosthetics in the first half of the nineteenth century. Because they were both complicated in construction and designed to be aesthetically pleasing, they were expensive and beyond the reach of the poor, who wore common peg legs (see note to chapter 57, p. 499). Cork legs were also an English invention, according to one of the foremost inventors and manufacturers of prostheses, William Robert Grossmith:

To our nation alone belongs the credit of the introduction of "Cork Legs" as they are called; but this term is an anomaly, as the framework of the English legs has always been constructed in wood, cork being merely used for the external shaping. Many of my patrons express their astonishment on being informed that such an article as a Cork Leg never yet was made, but any person possessing the smallest mechanical idea will perceive that an acting joint made of cork would crumble to pieces with the slightest weight.

The substitution of wooden sockets fitted to the stump, and a very light frame of wood covered with cork for the lower part of the limb, (in lieu of the heavy steel uprights and coverings of thick leather used in other nations,) constituted the great feature of improvement in the English legs, and caused them soon to become popular, as they still are in all parts of the world.

(*Amputations and Artificial Limbs*, 1857, 8)

White's Club, the oldest and most impressive of the St James's gentlemen's clubs, was notorious for high-stakes gambling, and for the presence, in the early nineteenth century, of Beau Brummell, who would sit at the club's celebrated bow window. Originally established as a chocolate-house in 1693 by an Italian named Francis White, White's was destroyed by a fire in 1733. In 1736, it reopened as a private club, and, in 1755, moved to 37 and 38 St James's Street. Although it originally welcomed both Whig and Tory members, towards the end of the eighteenth century it became the home of William Pitt and his supporters (in contrast to Brooks's Club [see note above], which welcomed Charles Fox and his supporters). When the Carlton Club was founded in 1832 as a home for committed Conservatives, White's Club lost much of its Conservative cast and regained its original reputation as a general social club. In 1854, the number of its members was limited to 550 (Weale, 1854, 305; Weinreb and Hibbert, 1983, 988–9). For other London clubs, see note to chapter 7, p. 111.

So Edith's mother lies unmentioned

So Edith's mother lies unmentioned of her dear friends, who are deaf to the waves that are hoarse with repetition of their mystery, and blind to the dust that is piled upon the shore, and to the white arms that are beckoning, in the moonlight, to the invisible country far away. But all goes on, as it was wont, upon the margin of the unknown sea; and Edith standing there alone, and listening to its waves, has dank weed cast up at her feet, to strew her path in life withal.] The allegorical treatment in this passage may have been influenced by the lower-right-hand side of the cover-design for the monthly parts, with its dark depiction of the moon in the background, the tossed waves of the sea, the woman on shore and its general emphasis on age and debility (Horsman, xviii).

Mr Dombey and Carker – Carker employed as go-between to reduce proud Edith.

Mrs Pipchin installed.

Miss Nipper banished.

qy Mr Toots and Florence.   Yes. Through Miss Nipper.

qy Mr Morfin, and Harriet and John Carker.

No

Ediths hand, that Carker kissed. "She struck it on the marble chimney shelf"—&c

Number Plan

Chapter 42 *Confidential and Accidental*   409

(Dealings with the Firm of Dombey and Son — N.º XIV.)

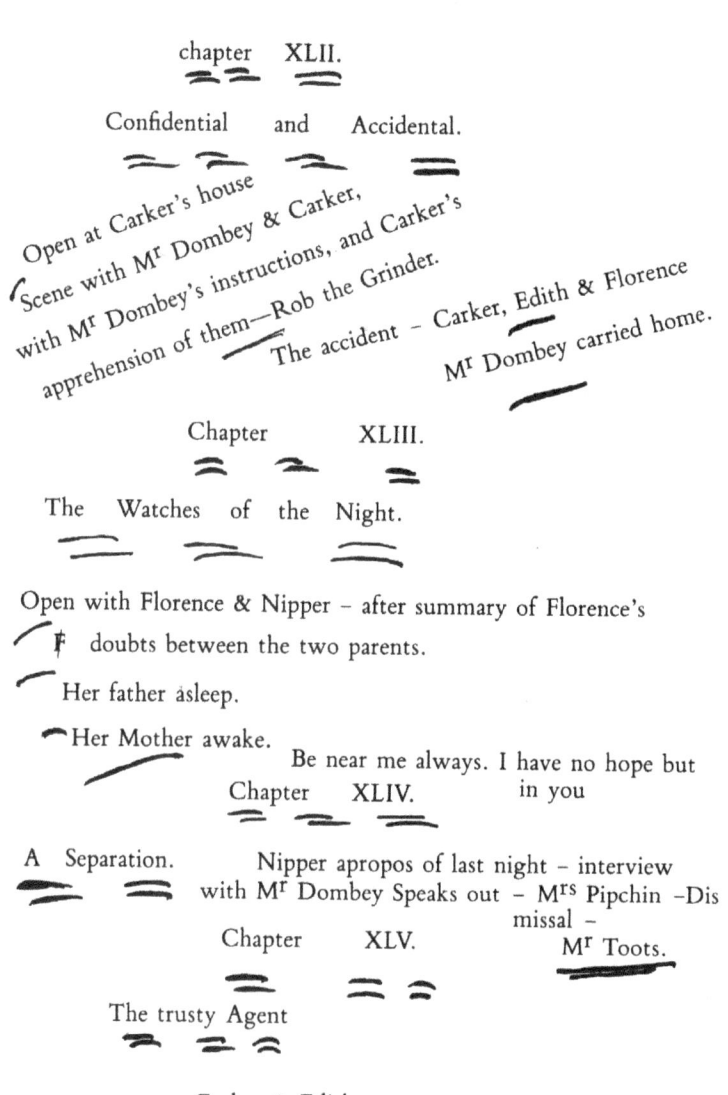

chapter   XLII.

Confidential   and   Accidental.

Open at Carker's house
Scene with Mr Dombey & Carker,
with Mr Dombey's instructions, and Carker's
apprehension of them—Rob the Grinder.
The accident – Carker, Edith & Florence
Mr Dombey carried home.

Chapter   XLIII.

The   Watches   of   the   Night.

Open with Florence & Nipper – after summary of Florence's
doubts between the two parents.

Her father asleep.

Her Mother awake.
Be near me always. I have no hope but in you

Chapter   XLIV.

A   Separation.   Nipper apropos of last night – interview
with Mr Dombey Speaks out – Mrs Pipchin –Dismissal –
Mr Toots.

Chapter   XLV.

The trusty Agent

Carker & Edith
The last view of them before the
elopement. She felt relenting by force.

Chapter Plan

Chapter 42 Fourteenth monthly number
November 1847

CONFIDENTIAL AND ACCIDENTAL

Attired no more in Captain Cuttle's

dressed in a substantial suit of brown livery ... Rob the Grinder, thus transformed as to his outer man] 2 Corinthians 4.16: 'but though our outward man perish, yet the inward man is renewed day by day.'

fear and trembling,] Ephesians 6.5: 'Servants, be obedient to them that are your masters according to the flesh, with fear and trembling, in singleness of your heart, as unto Christ'. The phrase also appears in 2 Corinthians 7.15 and Philippians 2.12.

He could not have quaked

The boy had a sense of power and authority in this patron of his that engrossed his whole attention and exacted his most implicit submission and obedience. ... Rob had no more doubt that Mr. Carker read his secret thoughts, or that he could read them by the least exertion of his will if he were so inclined ... his mind filled with a constantly dilating impression of his patron's irresistible command over him, and power of doing anything with him, he would stand watching his pleasure ... in a state of mental suspension,] The central feature of mesmerism was the mesmerist's power over his subject. Dickens's long involvement with mesmerism began in 1838, when he attended a large public demonstration conducted by the distinguished physician and mesmerist Dr John Elliotson, who had begun using mesmerism to treat patients at University College Hospital in 1837. Accounts of the demonstrations were published in *The Lancet* from May-September 1838, but Elliotson was forced to resign his post in December after his star patients had been shown to be imposters. Mesmerism nevertheless became more respectable during the 1840s, and in 1846 Elliotson was invited to give the Harveian oration at the Royal College of Physicians (*Letters* 1.461, n.2; 4.243, n.2).

Dickens became good friends with both Elliotson and another leading proponent of mesmerism, Chauncy Hare Townshend, author of the influential *Facts in Mesmerism* (1840). Another work that helped to advance the popularity of the phenomenon was Harriet Martineau's *Letters on Mesmerism* (*Athenaeum*, November-December 1844), which describe how she was miraculously cured of chronic ill health by mesmerism. Although Dickens refused to be mesmerized himself, he enthusiastically mesmerized others, beginning with his wife in April 1842: 'In six minutes, I magnetized her into hysterics, and then into the magnetic sleep. I tried again next night, and she fell into the slumber in little more than two minutes ... I can wake her with perfect ease'.

('Mesmerism' and 'animal magnetism' were used interchangeably at the time.) He later mesmerized his sister-in-law and gave many treatments to his friend, Mme de la Rue, from December 1844 and during 1845 (letter to Townshend, 23 July 1841, *Letters* 2.342; 3.180; 4.243, n.2, ff.).

The relationship of power, submission and obedience between Carker and Rob illustrates that Dickens subscribed to the notion that mesmerism was a spiritual, transcendental force at work between the mesmerist and his patient, and not merely a physical system involving fluids, chemicals and metals acting as magnetic transmitters. This latter view was held by Elliotson, a follower of Anton Mesmer's theories, first published in France from the 1770s onwards. Mesmer was a showman and confidence trickster, and his ideas were scoffed at by his contemporaries, including Elizabeth Inchbald in her farce about a deceitful servant disguised as a mesmeric doctor, *Animal Magnetism* (1788). Dickens himself played the quack doctor in several amateur theatrical performances of *Animal Magnetism* between 1848 and 1857 (*Letters* 5 *passim*, 8.207 n.8, 8.240, 8.254, n.1; Steven Connor, ' "All I Believed is True": Dickens Under the Influence', *Interdisciplinary Studies in the Long Nineteenth Century*, 10 [2010]). The craze for mesmerism began to decline in the 1850s, and Browning's poem, 'Mesmerism' (*Men and Women*, 1855) depicts a mesmerist who is both a manipulator and also possibly insane. For mesmerism as represented in Dickens's novels, including *DS*, see Fred Kaplan, *Dickens and Mesmerism: the Hidden Springs of Fiction* (1975).

"Yes, Sir," replied the abject Grinder,

golden guineas."] The guinea, a gold coin equivalent to 21 shillings, was last minted in 1813, though the term survived until 1971 for professional fees, horse-racing purses, auction prices and rents for more up-market premises.

"But perhaps to you,

"Just as monarchs imagine attractions in the lives of beggars."] An allusion to the proverb dating from the sixteenth century: 'Content lodges oftener in cottages than palaces.'

Mr. Carker bowed his head,

looked down at Mr. Dombey with the evil slyness of some monkish carving, half human and half brute;] The term 'monkish' is used here in a distinctly derogatory manner, reflecting Dickens's own anti-Catholic bias, and denoting 'corruption, pedantry, or other disagreeable characteristics, features, or tendencies attributed to medieval monasticism' (*OED*). Dickens claimed to have 'no sympathy with the Romish Church' in the preface to *BR*, attacked Catholic ritualism in *PI* ('Rome') and condemned Popish plots and Catholic bishops in *CHE*.

Mr. Dombey being insensible,

menders of the road,] Each parish was legally obliged to mend its own roads. A contemporary describes the typical duties of a road-mender:

> He clears the pathway from weeds, trims the hedges, sees that the watercourses are clear, looks to the drains, scrapes the horse manure into little heaps by the roadside to be carted away by the agencies appointed for the purpose; levels the roadway wherever it gets worn into holes or ruts, by shovelling in the necessary amount of macadam; and every day has enough to occupy him in all these matters, and fill up the requisite number of hours that he is bound to labour. (Mackay 6–7)

as vultures are said to gather about a camel who dies in the desert.] This was a scene mentioned in the accounts of British travellers in Egypt. For example: 'some of the camels employed by his party were left to perish; and he observed the skeletons of many more which had previously been left to feed the vultures in the wilderness' (Charles Frederick Partington, *British Cyclopædia of Natural History*, 1835, 1.673); and another traveller in Egypt and the Holy Land described seeing 'a solitary tree, long conspicuous on the horizon ... which dwindled, long before we reached it, into a stunted thorn. The half-eaten carcase of a camel lay beneath it, and the vultures that had been garbaging on it flew heavily away at our approach' (*Tait's Edinburgh Magazine*, 1838, 5.661).

He rode direct to Mr. Dombey's

it was not Mrs. Dombey's hour for receiving visitors,] Ladies customarily let it be known that they were 'At Home' (the phrase used on invitation cards) on a particular afternoon of each week in order to receive formal social calls (see note to chapter 36, p. 371).

Mr. Carker, who was quite prepared

a morning-room upstairs,] A 'morning-room' is a moderately-sized sitting-room that ladies used to receive intimate friends, to give orders to the household and to write letters. It is usually located at the front of the house, and has a 'pleasing prospect', often with a large bay window to let in the morning light. *The Gentleman's House* (1865) recommended that the morning-room be 'readily accessible from the Entrance for the reception of the more intimate class of visitors during the day', and that a 'door of communication' connect the morning-room with the drawing room, to provide 'for the ladies what is called *escape* in a manner the most legitimate of all, inasmuch as these two apartments become ... the best possible ante-rooms to each other' (Kerr 103–05).

About the time of twilight,

Mrs. Pipchin ... freshened the domestics with several little sprinklings of wordy vinegar,] In *The Domestic Management of the Sick-Room* (1841), Dr Anthony Todd Thomson explains the several uses of vinegar:

> Vinegar is, not without reason, regarded as possessing some chemical influence in decomposing infectious and contagious matters; and, consequently, it is almost invariably sprinkled over the floor of the rooms of those suffering under infectious diseases; or the vapour of hot vinegar is diffused through their apartments. It is thought to be still more salubrious, and a more powerful disinfectant, when it holds Camphor or Aromatic Oils in solution. ... Vinegar, in this state of combination, is extremely agreeable and refreshing, both to the invalid and the attendants of the sick-room. (397)

Chapter 43

THE WATCHES OF THE NIGHT

THE WATCHES OF THE NIGHT] Psalms 68.5–6: 'My soul shall be satisfied as with marrow and fatness; and my mouth shall praise thee with joyful lips: When I remember thee upon my bed, and meditate on thee in the night watches'. The phrase 'night watches' also appears in Psalms 119.148 and *BCP* (1662): 'Mine eyes prevent the night-watches: that I might be occupied in thy words.' A 'watch' was one of the periods into which the night was divided by the Hebrews, Greeks and Romans.

"Oh, it's very well to say

keeping guard at your Pa's door like crocodiles (only make us thankful that they lay no eggs!)] It was commonly believed that female crocodiles zealously guarded their eggs because 'A great many animals ... seek out and devour' them, though the distinguished naturalist Baron Georges Cuvier noted that 'this assertion does not appear to be very well founded' (*The Animal Kingdom*, 1817; 1831, 9.189).

There was a cut upon his forehead,

they had been wetting his hair,]

> It is important that the head should be kept cool by wetting the hair, and placing cold wet cloths upon the forehead and temples, and renewing them frequently; as when this precaution is not observed, during the application of the wet sheets to the other parts of the body, congestions to the head may take place when the fever is high. (J. Kost, *Domestic Medicine*, 1859, 41)

Awake, doomed man, while she

Awake, doomed man, while she is near! The time is flitting by; the hour is coming with an angry tread; its foot is in the house. Awake!] An echo of St Paul's exhortation in Romans 13.11–12:

> And that, knowing the time, that now it is high time to awake out of sleep: for now is our salvation nearer than when we believed. The night is far spent, the day is at hand: let us therefore cast off the works of darkness, and let us put on the armour of the light. (identified by Larson, 1985, 81)

Dickens may also be influenced by Carlyle's plea to the Captains of Industry in *Past and Present* (1843): 'Awake, O nightmare sleepers; awake, arise, or be forever fallen!' (4.4.269).

Chapter 44

A SEPARATION

With the day, though not

With the day, though not so early as the sun, uprose Miss Susan Nipper.] For this allusion to Dryden's translation of Chaucer, see note to chapter 19, p. 231.

"I have been in your service,

Meethosalem,] Methuselah lived 969 years according to Genesis 5.21–7, making him the oldest figure in the Bible:

And Enoch lived sixty and five years, and begat Methuselah: And Enoch walked with God after he begat Methuselah three hundred years, and begat sons and daughters: And all the days of Enoch were three hundred sixty and five years: And Enoch walked with God: and he was not; for God took him. And Methuselah lived an hundred eighty and seven years, and begat Lamech. And Methuselah lived after he begat Lamech seven hundred eighty and two years, and begat sons and daughters: And all the days of Methuselah were nine hundred sixty and nine years: and he died.

"There never was a dearer or

the more I was torn to pieces Sir the more I'd say it though I may not be a Fox's Martyr."] The *Actes and Monuments of these latter and perilous days, touching matters of the Church*, popularly known as Foxe's (or Fox's) *Book of Martyrs*, was first published in English in 1563. This huge anti-papist work traces the history of the Christian Church and its martyrs in a vivid, homely fashion, accompanied by grisly illustrations of tortures and executions. The description of the execution of Ignatius is typically horrific: 'he was compelled to hold fire in his hands, and at the same time, papers dipped in oil were put to his sides, and set alight. His flesh was then torn with red-hot pincers, and at last he was dispatched by being torn to pieces by wild beasts' (1.15).

"Begging your pardon, not even

I may not be a Indian widow Sir and I am not and I would not so become but if I once made up my mind to burn myself alive, I'd do it!] Suttee, the Hindu practice of burning widows alive on the funeral pyre of their husbands, was a recurrent topic in newspapers, periodicals and books from the 1820s into the 1840s. The British public first learned of the practice through the published accounts of Christian missionaries, travellers in India and members of the British East India Company. The British government tried to suppress suttee throughout the 1820s, and in 1829 Lord William Bentinck, Governor General of India from 1828–35, succeeded in making it illegal in Bengal. But elsewhere, the British permitted it, provided the act was voluntary and prior notice had been given to a magistrate, who was required to attend. Although suttee was finally abolished in 1839, it continued to be practised in territories under the control of Indian princes; in Jaipur, for example, suttee was not prohibited until 1846 ('Regulation for the Abolition of Suttees. AD 1829. Regulation XVII', *The Calcutta Magazine and Monthly Register* 1 [January 1830]: i; *The Penny Cyclopædia of the Society for the Diffusion of Useful Knowledge* 23 [1842]: 359; 'The Suttee, or, the Custom of Burning the Women', *The Gleaner* 24 [May 1845]: 257; Horace Hayman Wilson, 'Widow Burning', *The History of British India*. Rpt. in *The Living Age* 31 [November 1851]: 356–63).

"I have seen," said Susan Nipper,

ordering one's self lowly and reverently towards one's betters, is not to be a worshipper of graven images,] An allusion to that part of the Catechism which questions the child about the Ten Commandments. The child is first required to recite the Commandments, the second of which is: 'Thou shalt not make unto thee any graven image, or any likeness of any thing that is in heaven above, or that is in the earth beneath, or that is in the water under the earth' (Exodus 20.4). Then the child is asked what he has learned from the Commandments, specifically, 'What is thy duty towards thy Neighbour?' Part of the reply is: 'To order myself lowly and reverently to all my betters'.

"I left my dear young lady

I may not be a Peacock; but I have my eyes –] A reference to the iridescent eyespot, ringed with blue and bronze, at the tip of each feather of a peacock's tail. Greek mythology attributes the eyespots to Hera, who supposedly transferred the eyes of Argus – the vigilant watchman with a hundred eyes – to the tail of her favourite bird, the peacock, after Zeus had Argus destroyed. In *OCS*, Codlin remarks, 'I was attending to my business, and couldn't have my eyes in twenty places at once, like a peacock …' (37).

as if it was a guilty thing to look at her own Pa,] An allusion to the Ghost in *Hamlet* (1.1.144–6):

> *Bernardo.* It was about to speak when the cock crew.
> *Horatio.* And then it started, like a guilty thing,
>   Upon a fearful summons.

"Why, hoity toity!" cried the voice

the black bombazeen garments of that fair Peruvian Miner] See notes to chapter 8, pp. 128, 129.

"Do you call it managing

A gentleman – in his own house – in his own room – assailed with the impertinencies of women servants!"] *The Servant's Behaviour Book; or, Hints on Manners and Dress for Maid Servants in Small Households* (1859) advised servants to keep their voice low and respectful when they addressed ladies and gentlemen; to frequently use 'Sir' or 'Ma'am'; and to be tactful. The author of the book, 'Mrs Motherly' [Emily Augusta Patmore], cautions: 'Every girl who wishes to live in a gentleman's family must learn, sooner or later, to keep guard over her tongue' (vii, 11, 29). Both Susan and Mrs Pipchin violate several other rules of correct behaviour:

> NEVER BEGIN TO TALK TO YOUR MISTRESS, UNLESS IT BE TO DELIVER A MESSAGE, OR ASK A NECESSARY QUESTION. … Many young girls who are fond of talking will make a common message an excuse for a long conversation. … be sure you are careful to talk only as much as you see is agreeable to your mistress, and take the first hint to stop. (12, 15)

> NEVER TALK TO ANOTHER SERVANT, OR PERSON OF YOUR OWN RANK, OR TO A CHILD, IN THE PRESENCE OF YOUR MISTRESS, UNLESS FROM NECESSITY; AND THEN DO IT AS SHORTLY AS POSSIBLE, AND IN A LOW VOICE. (23–4)

"I intend to go this minute,

Mrs. P."] Susan is intentionally offending Mrs Pipchin by adopting an over-familiar form of address:

> A wife should not address her husband by the initial letter of his surname, as "Mr. B." or "Mr. P."; neither should a husband address his wife by the initial letter of his surname.
> When intimate friends address each other by the initial letter of their names it is by way of pleasantry only, and such cases, of course, do not come within the rules of etiquette. (*Manners and Rules of Good Society*, 1888, 54)

"You saucy baggage!" retorted

How dare you talk in this way to a gentlewoman who has seen better days?"] *As You Like It* 2.7.113–20:

> *Orlando*   If ever you have look'd on better days …
> And know, what 'tis to pity and be pitied …
> *Duke*   True is it that we have seen better days …

In the 1820s, the expression 'seen better days' began to be used for people like Mrs Pipchin, for example: 'the Friendly Female Society for relieving poor aged and infirm Women of good character who have seen better days' (*The Gentleman's Magazine* [1823] 93.645); 'If you have seen better days, and are by misfortune, or by extravagance and imprudence, reduced to indigence, manfully reject every temptation of indulgence' ('Useful Advice', *Christian Telescope and Universalist Miscellany* [August 1826–February 1827]: 3.68).

"I've got a brother down

a farmer in Essex,"]

> The fertility of the arable land, and the good husbandry practised, enable Essex to rank high among the agricultural counties of England; its proximity to the metropolis affords it great advantages, and the various agricultural societies that have been established have given a stimulus to improvement hitherto without example. The cultivation of potatoes and vegetable crops is extensive in the vicinity of London. Carraway, coriander, rape, canary, and white and brown mustard seeds occupy a considerable portion of the marshy districts, and fine tracts of grazing marshes extend from the mouth of the Thames northward to Bradwell Point, on which small Highland cattle and Welsh "runts" are fed, with numerous flocks of Southdown and Romney-marsh sheep. (Lewis, 1848)

Essex, a county in the southeast of England, is bounded by the counties of Suffolk, Cambridge, Hertford and Middlesex, and separated by the River Thames from Kent.

I've got money in the Savings Banks my dear, and needn't take another service just yet,] The savings bank movement started in 1814–15 with the establishment of banks in Bath, Edinburgh and Southampton. By November 1829, there were 487 savings banks in England, Wales and Ireland, with 409,945 accounts and capital of about £15 million. By 1844, savings banks had attracted more than a million depositors.

Savings banks gained in popularity when they abolished the requirement for minimum deposits and also made it easier for depositors to make withdrawals. A Glasgow bank formed in 1836 cited its large number of withdrawals as an indication that it was being used as intended: 'not so much with a view to increase, as to safe custody and preparation against rent day and other periodical disbursements'. According to a contemporary historian, 'One great advantage of a Savings Bank is, that it holds out to the lower classes fixed advantages, and preserves their little property from the fluctuations of value to which the Public Funds are liable' (Alborn, 2002; Pratt, 1830, xii).

"Why, come home to my place,

"Her son," said Mr. Toots, as an additional recommendation, "was educated in the Blue-coat School, and blown up in a powder mill."] Presumably a reference to the most famous 'Blue-coat school', Christ's Hospital, founded by King Edward VI on 26 June 1553, and intended to educate, clothe and maintain 'the children of the deserving poor' (Pascoe, 1877, 111; also see note to chapter 5, p. 90 and Plate 6, p. 91). The children had to be 'between 8 and 10 years of age, and free from disease as well as from any physical defect which would render them unable to take care of themselves'. In order to be admitted, the children first had 'to pass an examination as to their attainments' (112). The boys were generally instructed in a 'thorough Classical and Mathematical Education', though a mathematical education 'to fit boys for entering the Navy and Mercantile Marine' would be given to those boys 'of the Mathematical Foundations', and a commercial education would be 'given to boys who show no aptness for Classical study, and are at a certain age not prepared to take a place in the Upper Grammar School' (111). The boys, who were lodged in dormitories and who could only leave school on special 'Leave Days', wore a distinctive uniform:

> a long blue coat, reaching to the ankles, and girt about the waist with a leather strap; a yellow cassock, or petticoat, now worn under the coat only during winter, though originally an inseparable appendage throughout the year, and stockings of yellow worsted. A pair of white bands round the neck are a compromise for the rigid ruff, or collar, which of old was a part of the dress of all ranks except the lowest. (Staunton, 1863, 445)

Charles Lamb, himself a 'blue-coat boy', remarked upon

> the respect, and even kindness, which [the blue-coat boy's] well-known garb never fails to procure him in the streets of the metropolis. ... His very garb, as it is antique and venerable, feeds his self-respect: as it is a badge of dependence, it restrains the natural petulance of that age from breaking out into overt acts of insolence. This produces silence and a reserve before strangers. ... Within his bounds he is all fire and play; but in the streets he steals along with all the self-concentration of a young monk. ('Recollections of Christ's Hospital'; a later piece, 'Christ's Hospital Five and Thirty Years Ago' [November 1820], is much more critical of the school.)

Gunpowder mills were occasionally the sites of large and often fatal explosions, sometimes sparked by lightning strikes. The *Insurance Cyclopædia,* for instance, recorded a number of explosions in the early nineteenth century, including explosions at Waltham Mills in 1843 ('7 men killed, and buildings destroyed') and at Hounslow Mills in 1850 ('8 persons killed') (Walford, 1871, 129). The Waltham explosion was particularly horrific. As described in the *Annual Register,*

> the building blew up with a loud explosion; not one of the men escaping death. In a few moments the second part of the building blew up with another explosion – a minute more, and one part of the granulating-house blew up – and in a few more moments, a fourth explosion destroyed the second part of that. Of the seven men, five were carried to a great distance across the river, the body of one rising to such an height as to make an indentation some inches deep in the ground where it fell; heads were blown off, legs broken, and one body was ripped up! (1844, 46)

Susan accepting this kind offer,

his visage was in a state of such great dilapidation, as to be hardly presentable in society .... The Chicken himself attributed this punishment to his having had the misfortune to get into Chancery early in the proceedings, when he was severely fibbed by the Larkey one, and heavily grassed. But it appeared from the published records of that great contest that the Larkey boy had had it all his own way from the beginning, and the Chicken had been tapped, and bunged, and had received pepper, and had been made groggy, and had come up piping,] The blows would have been struck with bare fists, inevitably causing the loss of a great deal of blood, particularly in such vulnerable regions as the nose, and often leading to permanent injury and early death. Indeed, the damage was so great that few fighters fought more than once or twice a year, and a dozen times in their careers (Ford, 1971, 125).

The Chicken uses boxing slang to explain that his head had been trapped under his opponent's arm (put in 'Chancery') – a common move that was permitted by the rules – and then beaten by a rapid series of blows ('fibbed'). He was then knocked to the ground ('grassed'). The 'published records', however, indicate that the Chicken's nose was bloodied ('tapped') and his eyes closed by repeated blows ('bunged'), and that he had received a severe beating ('pepper'), been made groggy, and then stood up, panting hard ('piping') (*OED*; *Boxiana*, 1824). According to the *Modern Art of Boxing* (*c*. 1792), the most harmful blows were to 'the eye-brows, on the bridge of the nose, on the temple arteries, beneath the left ear, under the short ribs or in the kidneys ...' (qtd. in Ford, 1971, 124).

Reports of prizefights were occasionally published in major newspapers, such as *The Times* and *The Morning Post*, and, more commonly, in weekly publications, such as *Bell's Life in London and Sporting Chronicle*, *The Weekly Dispatch* and *Pierce Egan's Life in London* (Ford, 1971, 168, 176).

After a good repast, and

he would never leave Mr. Toots ... for any less consideration than the goodwill and fixtures of a public-house;] Prizefighters often became publicans. In 1820 alone, Tom Cribb was the keeper of the Union Arms, Panton Street, Haymarket; Jem Belcher ran the Castle Tavern, Holborn; Jack Randall, the Hole in the Wall, Chancery Lane, Fleet Street; and Harry Harmer, the Plough, West Smithfield. In the late eighteenth century, *The Times* thought 'it worthy of the notice of the magistracy to consider whether a man who breaks the peace should be a fit person to have a licence as a publican'. Other publican prizefighters suffered from similar problems. So Tom Johnson became the publican at the Grapes in Lincoln's Inn Fields, 'but the customers proving too flash, the licence was taken away'. He also lost his licence for a Dublin pub 'from this house not proving so consonant to the principles of propriety as were wished' (qtd. in Ford, 1971, 52–3). For the tendency of prizefighters to become alcoholics and more on Hen Pearce, see note to chapter 22, p. 271.

After a good repast,

the moral weight and heroism of his character,] Though Dickens intends the comment to be read ironically, proponents of prizefighting often made the case for its essential morality. In 1820, Henry Alken characterized a boxing match as 'so excellent a system of ethics as no other country can boast, and which has chiefly contributed to form the characteristic humanity of the English nation' (qtd. in Ford, 1971, 30). In 1840, an instructional book entitled *Defensive Exercises* concurred:

> In fact, it is to pugilistic schools, and their displays, that we owe "the whole of that noble system of ethics – fair play, which distinguishes and elevates our commonality, and which stern and impartial reason herself must hail as one of the honors of Britain." ... There can in fact be no better preparation for making effective combatants in our army and navy, than the national practice of boxing. "It teaches a man to look his adversary in the face while fighting; to bear the threatening looks and fierce assaults of an antagonist without flinching; to watch and parry his intended blow; to return it with quickness, and to follow it up with resolution and effect; it habituates him to sustain his courage under bodily suffering; and, when the conflict has ceased, to treat his enemy with humanity."

The same writer added defensively, 'What a contrast exists between all those barbarous modes of fighting, and the order which prevails whenever a fight occurs in this country! ... Thus boxing is really useful to society as a refinement in natural combat' (Walker 38–9). In *DC*, Steerforth instructs David in the art of boxing (21), one of the acquirements for a young gentleman at the time, and Mr George teaches boxing in *BH*.

Chapter 45

THE TRUSTY AGENT

"At least it was natural,"

yoked to his own triumphal car like a beast of burden,] Triumphal cars – lavishly and expensively decorated chariots drawn by animals or slaves – were used by Roman emperors in processions to celebrate a victory or a great event. In mythology, gods and goddesses frequently ride in triumphal cars, and the image is recurrent in classical monuments and Renaissance art. As theatrical props, triumphal cars were used in court masques and seventeenth-century plays (e.g. James Shirley's *The Triumph of*

Peace, 1633, and Nathaniel Lee's *The Rival Queens*, 1677). The practice continued in later centuries: for example, at the Coronation of George IV in July 1821, the greatest spectacle in the celebrations in Hyde Park appeared floating on the Serpentine:

> a splendid triumphal car drawn by two elephants, one before the other ... and caparisoned after the Eastern manner, with a young woman dressed as a slave seated on the back of each. The machine was constructed on a large raft, which was towed by three or four boats manned with watermen in blue uniform. (*Gentleman's Magazine* 91 [July–December 1821]: 78)

"But he will know it now!"

he unfolded one more ring of the coil into which he had gathered himself.] Reminiscent of Satan, in the guise of the serpent, in book 9 of *Paradise Lost*:

> ... not with indented wave,
> Prone on the ground, as since, but on his rear,
> Circular base of rising folds, that tow'red
> Fold above fold a surging maze, his head
> Crested aloft, and carbuncle his eyes;
> With burnished neck of verdant gold, erect
> Amidst his circling spires, that on the grass
> Floated redundant ... (496–503)

"I am forgiven, and have

May I ... take your hand before I go?" She gave him the gloved hand ... He took it in one of his, and kissed it,] Although Carker follows etiquette in requesting Mrs Dombey's hand – 'A man has no right to take a lady's hand till it is offered' (*The Habits of Good Society*, 1869, 827) – he offends when he kisses her hand. According to the *Treasury of Manners, Customs, and Ceremonies* (1855), kissing the hands of ladies in Great Britain and Italy 'is regarded as a mark of familiarity, which is permitted only to the nearest relations' (Anderson 29). Isaac Disraeli, paraphrasing a Frenchman in 1807, remarked that the practice is 'become too gross a familiarity, and it is considered as a meanness to kiss the hand of those with whom we are in habits of intercourse' (*The Curiosities of Literature* 2.351; the 1859 edition, edited by Benjamin Disraeli, seems to attribute the idea to Isaac Disraeli himself).

Chapter 46 Fifteenth monthly number
December 1847

RECOGNIZANT AND REFLECTIVE

Among sundry minor alterations in

the Price Current] A printed list of the market prices of merchandise, 'published weekly in London and other commercial cities' (Roberts, 1841, 36). In the view of Thomas Tooke, the *London Price Current*, which was established in 1782, 'is the oldest and best authenticated' of the lists (*A History of Prices*, 1838, 2.394).

The same increased and sharp attention

the minnows among the tritons of the East,] A reversal of Coriolanus's sarcastic rejoinder to Sicinius Velutus: 'Hear you this Triton of the minnows?' (3.1.88). In Greek myth, Triton was a merman, with a human head and shoulders and a fish tail from the waist down. He is usually represented blowing a conch-shell, in order to calm or stir the waves. For more on Dombey's business, see note to chapter 1, p. 25.

the Stock Exchange] See note to chapter 13, p. 181.

Walking his white-legged horse

Walking his white-legged horse thus, to the counting-house of Dombey and Son one day, he was as unconscious of the observation of two pairs of women's eyes,] The illustration for the scene, 'Abstraction and Recognition', depicts several posters on the wall, which echo themes in the novel (Plate 19, p. 427). One of these – 'Theatre/City/Madam' – alludes to Philip Massinger's play *The City Madam* (1632), which had been produced in London as recently as 1844, and which may have inspired several elements of Dickens's plot. In Massinger's play, a wealthy City merchant, Sir John Frugal, lacks a male heir, which is said to be 'a great pity', and has a wife who, like Mrs Skewton, pretends to be younger than her actual age. Sir John's younger brother Luke has squandered a fortune and has had his debts paid by Sir John, who employs him and who treats him like a servant, reminding him of his disgrace. Like John Carker, Luke thinks of himself as an 'example' (unlike John Carker, though, Luke is a scoundrel). The play also contains a bawd named 'Secret', who is reproached by her prostituted daughter for not caring 'upon what desperate service you employ me, / Nor with whom, so you have your fee', which parallels the relationship between Alice and her mother (see Steig, 1978, 100–1).

Mems.

Edith's elopement with Carker

on her wedding–Day.

Florence's flight from her father's house.

and taking refuge with the Captain

these
transposed

Mem.

The Thunderbolt chapter originally intended for the last of the N⁰ and the middle chapter meant to have led up – but the Thunderbolt chapter being written first, plan altered, to leave a pleasanter impression on the reader.

Number Plan

(Dealings with the Firm of Dombey and Son — N.º XV.)

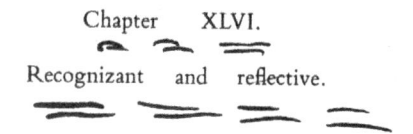

Chapter XLVI.

Recognizant and reflective.

Rob the Grinder waiting to take his masters horse

Carker recognized by Mrs Brown and her daughter. He himself abstracted, and not seeing them

Rob claimed as an old acquaintance by Mrs Brown, & means of future communication between them, established.

Carker and his brother – shewing Carker's state of mind — Dark indication of Edith's state of mind

Chapter XLVIII.

~~The Thunder~~   The Flight of Florence

To the little Midshipman's

Appearance of Diogenes, on the way there.

The good Captain – someone at the door – Mr Toots. – Preparation for Walter

chapter XLVIII.

The Thunderbolt.

Opening ~~reflectio~~ matter – sanatory.

Description of Florence's state of mind, and how her idea of her father whom she loves, becomes an abstraction

Her separation from Edith — Edith's last interview with Mr Dombey; Carker present.

Carker on the stairs — Edith and Florence on the stairs — The Night — The break of day – Elopement – blow – Florence flies –

Chapter Plan

Rob the Grinder ... as a demonstration of punctuality, vainly touched and retouched his hat to attract attention,] Anthony Trollope observed that 'the refined gentlemen and ladies of England ... are very apt to prefer the hat-touchers to those who are not hat-touchers. ... We argue to ourselves that the dear, excellent lower classes receive an immense amount of consoling happiness from the ceremony of hat-touching, and quite pity those who, unfortunately for themselves, know nothing about it' (*North America*, 1862, 5th ed., 1.57–8).

"Poor in not being able

the harm we owe him,"] According to William Tait's *Magdalenism* (2nd ed., 1842),

> ... seduction may be said to be a frequent cause of prostitution. This appears the more distressing, as the active agents in the accomplishment of this unjustifiable crime in general belong to the middle or highest ranks, whose education, wealth, and influence should be directed to the promotion of virtue and morality, rather than to rendering themselves conspicuous and powerful as promoters of vice, sorrow, and wretchedness. So far as can be ascertained, about eighteen per cent of all the common women have become prostitutes in consequence of seduction, and eighty per cent of all who have been seduced, have been led astray by individuals moving in a higher sphere than themselves. The means which, in many instances, are used by the seducers to accomplish their object, are such as are unworthy of any one aspiring to the name of gentleman. He who can unblushingly, by falsehood and artifice, seduce a virtuous and unsuspecting female from her friends and home for a moment's gratification to his animal appetite, and afterwards desert her to a life of misery, wretchedness, poverty, and suffering – which perhaps may be terminated by self-destruction – has no claim to any such title. Yet such individuals have the effrontery to mingle in society, and affect a sensibility of honour and integrity of moral principle which would prevent them from doing any thing in the least derogatory to their reputation and station in life. (131–2)

"Oh! Why can't you leave

a horse you'd go and sell for cats' and dogs' meat if you had *your* way!] Worn-out, diseased or useless horses were sold to knackers' yards, where they were slaughtered. The knacker sold the different parts of the carcass (skin, hoofs, bones, flesh, etc.) to other second-hand traders, such as dealers in hide, glue, oils and food for pet cats and dogs. The flesh, after being boiled, was bought by cats'-meat-men and dogs'-meat-men for 2 ½ pence per pound, and they sold it on in small quantities (Mayhew, 2.7, 9; 'knacker' in David Booth, *An Analytical Dictionary of the English Language*, 1835, 301).

19   'Abstraction and Recognition', by H. K. Browne, in the fifteenth monthly number

"This is the way," cried

the pigeon-fancying tramps and bird-catchers."] For pigeon-fancying, see note to chapter 23, p. 280; for bird-catchers, see note to chapter 22, p. 264.

"Stop, Misses Brown!" cried the

his master's prad] A slang term for a horse. Compare *OT*: 'He's in the gig minding the prad' (31).

Turning into a silent little

Turning into a silent little square or court-yard that had a great church tower rising above it, and a packer's warehouse, and a bottle-maker's warehouse ... a quaint stable at the corner;] The location appears to be what was then known as Crosby Square, and the church is the Church of St Helen's (now St Helen's Bishopsgate), between Bishopsgate Street and Leadenhall Street, and diagonally opposite Threadneedle Street. Many early-nineteenth century plates show St Helen's and its tower. For St Helen's as, apparently, the church where Florence and Walter are married, see note to chapter 56, p. 487. There was a well-known packer's warehouse in Crosby Square in the early nineteenth century, formerly the great hall of a celebrated sixteenth-century mansion with royal associations, Crosby Place. Following a fire in the seventeenth century, Crosby Place deteriorated, houses were built on the ruins, and the great hall of the mansion became a Presbyterian meeting-house. According to Charles Knight's *London* (1841), 'After the disuse of the hall as a meeting-house it was degraded into a packer's warehouse, and whilst thus occupied, received the most serious injury from the alterations which were made in it. In 1831 the lease ... expired' and restoration work to return the structure to its former grand state began in June 1836 (1.328).

At packers' warehouses, goods from suppliers were packed for transit or delivery to purchasers (Waterson 636). Bottle-makers, also called glass-blowers, made bottles partly by blowing and partly by manual working, molding or casting. George Dodd describes the process in detail and illustrates a bottle-maker in his *Days at the Factories: or, the Manufacturing Industries of Great Britain* (1843, 267).

"I don't know," said Rob,

Least said, soonest mended."] A proverbial phrase; see chapter 48 of *PP* for a similar use of the phrase.

He turned the white-legged

the darkening and deserted Parks] Green Park, St James's Park and Hyde Park, just to the south of Dombey's house (located either in the Portman Estate or the Portland Estate – see note to chapter 3, p. 46).

In fatal truth, these

In fatal truth, these were associated with a woman, a proud woman, who hated him. ... Upon the dangerous way that she was going, he was, still; and not a footprint did she mark upon it, but he set his own there, straight.] The characterization of Edith in these last four paragraphs is sketched in a memo added to the Number Plan for chapter 46: 'Dark indication of Edith's state of mind'. For Dickens's conception of Edith's relationship with Carker in the final chapters of the novel, see notes to chapter 47 and 54, pp. 429 and 471.

Chapter 47

THE THUNDERBOLT

On 9 (or 19) November 1847, Dickens wrote a letter to Forster which suggests that he had originally intended Edith Dombey to die a penitential death, in the conventional way for fictional adulteresses: 'Of course she hates Carker in the most deadly degree. I have not elaborated that, now, because ... I have relied on it very much for the effect of her death'. Forster, however, suggested a revision involving 'a nice point in the management of her character and destiny' (2.33–4). Horsman describes this suggestion as a 'clarification of Edith's motives' (xxxv). Dickens replied, 'I have no question that what you suggest will be an improvement' (*Letters* 5.197) and seems to have reordered his chapters accordingly. Originally, he had written chapter 46, left a gap for chapter 47 and then written chapter 48, 'The Thunderbolt', intended as the climax of the fifteenth number. Because of Forster's suggestion, presumably, he moved 'The Thunderbolt' into the gap he had left for chapter 47, and then wrote an additional chapter to conclude the number, the present chapter 48, 'The Flight of Florence'. As the Pilgrim editors observe, 'the missing middle chapter might well have accounted more closely for Edith and Carker' (*Letters* 5.197–8 n. 7). All of this suggests that Dickens compressed the interaction between Edith and Carker, originally planned for chapter 47, including eliminating any hint of adultery. In the Number Plan for number 17, Dickens notes definitively: 'Edith not his mistress'. For more on Dickens's revising his conception of Edith as an adulteress, see note to chapter 54, p. 471.

Was Mr. Dombey's master-vice

It might be worth while, sometimes, to inquire what Nature is, and how men work to change her, and whether, in the enforced distortions so produced, it is not natural to be unnatural.] The suggestion, in this passage and the ones that follow, is that behavior is not 'natural' but socially determined. In *LD*, Dickens also adopts the environmentalist position, in this case about a young prostitute who 'spoke coarsely, but with no naturally coarse voice' (1.14). Elsewhere, he praised William Hogarth, the eighteenth-century painter and engraver, for showing that the corruption of the poor was not inherent but the result of social conditioning:

> I think it a remarkable trait of Hogarth's picture ['Gin Lane'], that, while it exhibits drunkenness in the most appalling forms, it also forces on attention a most neglected wretched neighbourhood, and an unwholesome, indecent, abject condition of life that might be put as frontispiece to our sanitary report of a hundred years later date. (Forster 2.42)

Dickens's views were probably influenced by his close friend, Thomas Southwood Smith, the physician and sanitary reformer, who argued that the immorality and ill-health of the poor derived from their insanitary surroundings, and thus could 'be avoided by no prudence, and removed by no exertion, on the part of the poor' (qtd. in Cullen 54; Schacht, 1990, 78).

By adopting this position, Dickens is countering the views of contemporary political economists and evangelicals, who argued that environment played little or no part in determining human behaviour. In the view of Thomas Malthus, for instance, the poor 'are themselves the cause of their own poverty; and the means of redress are in their own hands and in the hands of no other persons whatsoever' (*On Population* 498); the political economist J. R. McCulloch insisted, 'the happiness or misery of the labouring classes depends almost wholly on themselves' (*A Treatise* 16); and the Reverend Thomas Chalmers claimed, 'the remedy against the extension of pauperism ... lies in the hearts and habits of the poor' (qtd. in Pope, 1978, 5–6; Schacht, 1990, 77–8).

Alas! are there so few things

Breathe the polluted air, foul with every impurity that is poisonous to health and life; and have every sense ... offended, sickened and disgusted, and made a channel by which misery and death alone can enter. Vainly attempt to think of any simple plant, or flower, or wholesome weed, that, set in this foetid bed, could have its natural growth, or put its little leaves forth to the sun as GOD designed it.] For contemporary theories about poisonous air, see notes to chapter 8, p. 125, and chapter 29, p. 324. This passage, written about a month before it was published, in late October or November 1847, seems to have been motivated by a series of letters by Dr John Charles Hall warning of a new outbreak of cholera, which had recently appeared in *The Times*. A leading article, written in support of the letters, observed, 'The cholera will pay but little heed to the schemings and intrigues of commissioners and corporations', adding that, while the wealthy could escape the disease, the poor of Bethnal Green, Shoreditch and St Giles's could not (15 October, 3; 20 October, 3; 30 October, 4; 2 November, 5; 17 November, 4). Shortly after the publication of the letters, Dickens subscribed £10 to the Health of Towns Association, which automatically made him a member.

Throughout the 1840s, there was considerable agitation for sanitary reform, led by evangelicals such as Lord Ashley, 7th Earl of Shaftesbury, and by pressure groups such as the Health of Towns Association, the Health of London Association, the Metropolitan Sanitary Association and the Society for Improving the Condition of the Labouring Classes. Dickens seems to have been a proponent of sanitary reform from the mid-1840s, though his first public statements on the subject do not appear until 1848, at the time of the cholera epidemic. His brother-in-law, Henry Austin, was one of the founders of the Health of Towns Association and wrote a paper for Edwin Chadwick's 1842 sanitary report. Dr Southwood Smith (see previous note) sent Dickens reports and pamphlets on the subject of the people's health. In 1846, Dickens first visited the recently completed Model Houses in Pakenham Street, constructed by the Society for Improving the Condition of the Labouring Classes (SICLC).

In 1848–9, the cholera epidemic arrived in London, contributing to the deaths of about 14,000 people in London alone, and to over 70,000 in England and Wales as a whole. Among the dead were 180 pauper children from the Juvenile Pauper Asylum at Tooting, which inspired Dickens to write four scathing articles on the Tooting deaths for the *Examiner*. In the years that followed, in his speeches, journalism and fiction, Dickens continued to promote sanitary reform and to castigate self-interested local authorities whose antipathy to centralization blocked reform (see Pope, 1978, 200–42).

Those who study the physical sciences,

Those who study the physical sciences ... tell us that if the noxious particles that rise from vitiated air, were palpable to the sight, we should see them lowering in a dense black cloud above such haunts, and rolling slowly on to corrupt the better portions of a town.] Scientists believed that the wind could push miasmic clouds from one location to another, although the exact range was debated. *The London Medical Gazette* remarked in 1827, for instance, 'If a gentle, but steady breeze (such, I mean, as is calculated to move on the cloud or fog which contains the miasma, without dissipating it), be blowing from the shore which produces it, we may conceive that the deleterious influence in question would be found in activity at a much greater distance from the land than if there were no wind, or too much wind, or wind in the opposite direction' (Chambers 5).

HW carried a poem entitled 'Miasma' (8.348) that described the terrible effects of the poisonous particles arising from 'a festering drain' that lay near 'a cotter's back door':

> And his children would play by the poisonous pool,
> For they liked it much better than going to school.
>
> Then Miasma arose from his reeking bed,
> And around the children his mantle spread –
>   "To save them from harm," Miasma said.
>
> But they sighed a last sigh. He had stolen their breath.
> And had wrapped them in Cholera's cloak of death. (ll. 14–20)

When we shall gather grapes from thorns, and figs from thistles;] From the Sermon on the Mount:

> Beware of false prophets, which come to you in sheep's clothing, but inwardly they are ravening wolves. Ye shall know them by their fruits. Do men gather grapes of thorns, or figs of thistles? (Matthew 7.15–16)

Oh for a good spirit who would

Oh for a good spirit who would take the house-tops off, with a more potent and benignant hand than the lame demon in the tale,] From *Le Diable boiteux* (1707), a collection of satirical sketches on contemporary society by the prolific French novelist and dramatist Alain-René Le Sage, which was translated into English as *The Devil upon Two Sticks* in 1708. It was considered one of the first picaresque novels. Many translations were published in London in the nineteenth century, sometimes under alternative titles, such as *The Devil upon Crutches, Asmodeus's Crutches* and *Asmodeus, or the Devil on Two Sticks* (he became lame when he was thrown down to earth from heaven). Asmodeus, who appears in Jewish tradition as the 'king of demons', characterizes himself in Le Sage's novel as 'the dæmon of luxury, or, to express it genteeler, the god Cupid' (ch. 1; 1815 ed.). He was frequently alluded to in the nineteenth century, often for satirical effect, as in Bulwer Lytton's *Asmodeus at Large* and Carlyle's *The French Revolution*.

In the passage alluded to by Dickens, Asmodeus addresses his companion, a young student named Don Cleofas:

> I intend from this high place to shew you whatever is at present doing in Madrid. By my diabolical power I will heave up the roofs of the houses, and, notwithstanding the darkness of the night, clearly expose to your view whatever is now under them. At these words he only extended his right hand, and in an instant all the roofs of the houses seemed removed: and the student saw the insides of them as plainly as if it had been noon-day; as plainly, says Louis Velez de Guevara, as you see into a pie, whose top is taken off.
>
> This view was too surprising not to employ all his attention; his eyes

run through all parts of the city, and the variety which surrounded him was sufficient to engage his curiosity for a long time. Signior Student, said the dæmon, this confusion of objects which you survey with so much pleasure, affords really a very charming prospect; but in order to furnish you with a perfect knowledge of human life, it is necessary to explain to you, what all those people which you see are doing. I will disclose to you the springs of their actions, and their most secret thoughts. (ch. 3; 1815 ed.)

On 7 October 1849, when Dickens was considering options for his new journal, *Household Words*, he conceived of a similar demon:

> I want to suppose a certain SHADOW, which may go into any place, by sunlight, moonlight, starlight, firelight, candlelight, and be in all homes, and all nooks and corners, and be supposed to be cognisant of everything, and go everywhere, without the least difficulty. Which may be in the Theatre, the Palace, the House of Commons, the Prisons, the Unions, the Churches, on the Railroad, on the Sea, abroad and at home: a kind of semi-omniscient, omnipresent, intangible creature. ... a sort of previously unthought-of Power going about. (*Letters* 5.622–3)

In *OMF*, Silas Wegg 'felt it to be quite out of the question that he could lay his head upon his pillow in peace, without first hovering over Mr Boffin's house in the superior character of its Evil Genius. ... [T]he mere defiance of the unconscious house-front, with his power to strip the roof off the inhabiting family like the roof of a house of cards, was a treat which had a charm for Silas Wegg' (3.7).

Her voice died away into silence

She did not lay her head down. ... She held it up as if she were a beautiful Medusa, looking on him, face to face, to strike him dead.] For Medusa, see note to chapter 18, p. 228. Unlike the other Gorgons, she was sometimes represented as beautiful.

Thus living, in a dream

the council in the Servants' Hall ... had plenty to say of Mr. and Mrs. Dombey, and of Mr. Carker,]

> The servants' hall, in which both men and maid servants have dinner and supper, is also the place to which all the men below the butler repair, when disengaged from their several occupations. In this place the kitchen maid, and the boy who cleans the servants' knives and forks, wait at table. After each dinner and supper the parties separate, and adjourn ... to the several places appointed for them. (Webster, 1845, 352)

'Servants' Hall gossip' or 'the gossip of the Servants' Hall' were clichés in the nineteenth century. A character in *The School for Wives* (1841), for instance, is said to have 'a horror of any thing being said before the servants – "it was so vulgar to let one's conversations become the gossip of the servants' hall" ' (Gascoigne 1.40).

The general visitors who came

Mr. Dombey's wearing a bunch of gold seals to his watch, which shocked her very much, as an exploded superstition.] Seals were sometimes attached to watch-chains as a talisman or charm. Napoleon III, for instance, wore a carnelian seal on his watch-chain, which had once been in the possession of Napoleon I, and which he willed to his son, the Prince Imperial, along with the injunction to keep it as a 'talisman'. Heeding his father's wishes, the son carried the carnelian seal on a string fastened about his neck ('The Late Emperor's Superstition', *The Spectator*, qtd. in *Littell's Living Age*, 5th Series, 1873. 2.571). The French novel *Cœur Volant!* (*Fickle Heart!*) notes of gamblers, 'All heavy players believe in some kind of *fetish*. Some put faith in a ring, others in the pendants of a watch-chain' (trans. Sir Gilbert Campbell; qtd. in *Notes and Queries* 31 March, 1883: 246).

She laughed. The shaken diamonds

the shaken diamonds in her hair] For formal evening wear, fashionable women would dress their hair with diamonds, pearls, artificial grapes, feathers, lace, and similar adornments, which would either encircle the head or be attached to the side or back of the head (de Courtais, 1973, 104, 114).

There are fables of precious stones that would turn pale, their wearer being in danger.] The ruby, in particular, 'was supposed ... to foretell evil by growing pale, and to indicate that the danger was past by recovering its vivid color' (McClintock and Strong, 1889, 148).

"Tell him, said Edith, addressing

I wish for a separation between us. ... Tell him it may take place on his own terms – his wealth is nothing to me – but that it cannot be too soon."] English laws relating to separation and divorce remained unchanged from the Reformation until the nineteenth century, when the Divorce Act of 1857 enlarged if not equalized the rights and responsibilities of spouses. Prior to the Divorce Act, exclusive jurisdiction of all matrimonial matters was exercised by the ecclesiastical courts of the Church of England, which assiduously applied canon law, established before the Reformation and incorporating Roman Catholic legal practices. Canon law insisted on the Christian tenet of the sanctity and indissolubility of marriage, and its legal remedies in matrimonial causes reflected the sacramental nature of wedlock. This religio-legal stance consistently formed the basis of controversy from the time of the Reformation up until the parliamentary debates on the divorce bill in the 1850s.

Church courts heard four kinds of matrimonial suit: nullity (in cases of incest, physical or mental incapacity, or marriage without parental consent to someone under 21 years of age); jactitation of marriage (a petition to obtain a decree of perpetual silence against a person who publicly made a claim to a marriage – a type of suit that had almost disappeared by the late eighteenth century); restitution of conjugal rights; and divorce *a mensa et thoro* 'from bed and board', granted on the grounds of adultery or extreme physical cruelty. This was, in effect, a judicial separation since neither spouse was allowed to re-marry.

From the eighteenth century up to 1857, the standard legal practice to obtain a 'full' divorce was for the petitioner firstly to have a decree of divorce *a mensa et thoro* granted in the ecclesiastical court. If this were successful, the husband would then issue proceedings in a common-law court for damages against his wife's lover. Only after a man could prove that adultery ('criminal conversation') had taken place would damages be assessed and awarded. Finally, for a divorce *a vinculo* (from the bonds of marriage), a private bill had to be presented to the House of Lords, and, if it survived a third reading, the bill then went to the House of Commons. Royal assent was given only after the success of these three actions. Inevitably, this expensive procedure ensured that parliamentary divorce was the privilege of wealthy men and that divorce with the right to remarry was a remote possibility for the majority of the population.

Major changes in the divorce law did not occur until 1850, two years after Dickens completed *DS*, when a Royal Commission was appointed to look into the law of divorce. The commissioners' recommendations of 1853 included the complete transfer of all matrimonial cases then heard by the church courts to new civil courts that would also be commissioned to grant divorces *a vinculo matrimonii* ('from the bond of marriage') previously only possible by an Act of Parliament. They also proposed to maintain the distinction between divorce *a mensa et thoro* and divorce *a vinculo matrimonii*. Divorces *a vinculo* would be granted for adultery only, and generally on the suit of the husband. A wife, however, could apply for divorce *a vinculo* 'in cases of aggravated enormity, such as incest or bigamy'. Grounds for divorce *a mensa et thoro* were adultery, gross cruelty, or willful desertion. In June 1854, Lord Chancellor Cranworth submitted a divorce bill to the House of Lords based substantially on the 1853 proposals. After a second reading on 13 June 1854, the bill was withdrawn owing to lack of agreement about an appropriate and professional tribune. Two similar bills were introduced in 1856 and 1857, and on 28 August 1857 the Matrimonial Causes Bill received the royal assent.

The fictional separation between Mr and Mrs Dombey may be influenced by the case of Caroline Sheridan Norton (1808–77). In 1836, Caroline Norton separated from her husband, who had absconded with their three children and filed a suit of 'criminal conversation' against the Prime Minister, Lord Melbourne, accusing him of adultery with his wife. Although Norton's suit was dismissed, his wife's name suffered irreparable damage. And because an unsuccessful petitioner in a 'crim. con.' action could not go to the third (parliamentary) stage towards divorce *a vinculo matrimonii*, the Nortons were legally bound together for life.

Mrs Norton began her first campaign to reform the law by publishing three pamphlets: *The Natural Claim of a Mother to the Custody of her Children as Affected by the Common Law Right of the Father* (1837); *The Case of the Hon. Mrs. Norton* (1838); and *A Plain Letter to the Lord Chancellor on the Law of Custody of Infants* (1838). Her close friends, Lord Lyndhurst and Thomas Noon Talfourd, Serjeant-at-Law, urged her cause in Parliament, and in 1839 the Custody of Infants Act was passed. In August 1853, Mrs Norton was back in court, fighting over the validity of a financial deed of separation signed by her husband and herself. This case exposed the anomalous position of separated married women who were still legally bound by the common-law principle of coverture (i.e. 'covered' by their husbands in all contracts, debts, and a few criminal laws). All property which belonged to a woman at the time of marriage was afterwards regarded as the husband's property; thus she was legally non-existent and, like criminals, the mentally ill, and minors, she was excluded from many civil, and all political rights in England (Cobbe, 1868, qtd. in Dennis Skilton, 1987, 148; Gravesend and Crane 11; James 272; Holcombe 12–13; Horsman, 1985, 47; Shanley 34–5; Stone 353–4; Simpson, 1997, 130–6).

Heaping them back into

The deed of settlement he had executed on their marriage,] See note to chapter 30, p. 330.

Chapter 48

THE FLIGHT OF FLORENCE

With this last adherent,

Florence hurried away ... to the City. The roar soon grew more loud, the passengers more numerous, the shops more busy, until she was carried onward in a stream of life setting that way, and flowing, indifferently ... like the broad river, side by side with it, awakened from its dreams of rushes, willows, and green moss, and rolling on, turbid and troubled, among the works and cares of men, to the deep sea.] Florence has left her father's house in the fashionable area just south of Regent's Park (see note to chapter 3, p. 46) and is walking eastward to the Wooden Midshipman, in the City of London. The figure of 'the stream of life' was a common one, as in the sermon by the well-known hymn writer, Bishop Heber

(1783–1826). His words on the river of life were frequently reprinted in collections such as *The Christian Remembrancer* (vol. 9, 1827), *Classic Cullings and Fugitive Gatherings* (1831) and *McGuffey's Rhetorical Guide ... Containing Elegant Extracts in Prose and Poetry* (1844) and many other volumes published on both sides of the Atlantic:

> Life bears us on like the stream of a mighty river. Our boat, at first, glides down the narrow channel, through the playful murmurings of the little brook, and the windings of its grassy border. The trees shed their blossoms over our young heads; the flowers on the brink seem to offer themselves to our young hands. ...
>
> Our course in youth and manhood is along a wider and deeper flood, amid objects more striking and magnificent. We are animated by the moving picture of enjoyment and industry which passes before us. ... The stream bears us on, and our joys and our griefs alike are left behind us; we may be shipwrecked, but we cannot anchor; our voyage may be hastened, but it cannot be delayed; whether rough or smooth, the river hastens towards its home, till the roaring of the ocean is in our ears, and the tossing of his waves is beneath our keel, and the ... floods are lifted up around us ... and of our further voyage there is no witness but the Infinite and Eternal! (Bishop Heber's Farewell Sermon to his Parishioners at Hodnet, April 20, 1823, on his departure for India. Qtd. in Heber's posthumously published *Sermons*, 1837, 3.224–5)

"It's Heart's-delight!" said the

Heart's-delight!"] For the song by Thomas Dibden, see note to chapter 23, p. 283.

At this stage of her recovery,

an imperfect association of a Watch with a Physician's treatment of a patient,]

> Invalids, supposing that the state of the pulse throws great light on the nature of their afflictions, as well as the probability of their recovery, the pompous class of legitimate physicians make a most imposing exhibition of a large watch, with dashing chain and seals, profound looks and attitude, during the time of examining the pulse. The poor sufferer supposes that the use of the watch is to ascertain, with precision, the state of the pulse; he little thinks that it is mere "chamber effect". ... the practitioner who has studied medicine as a science, and not its arts as a trade or a means of obtaining wealth, is able, on commencing practice, to know the rate at which a pulse beats without a watch. (Richard Reece, 'The Pulse'. *The Monthly Gazette of Health*, 1824, 9.852)

"What cheer, my pretty?"

a watch as can be ekalled by few and excelled by none.] An encomium dating from the eighteenth century; see, for example, the praise (in a history book of 1748) for the Emperor Tiberius's 'thorough knowlege of mankind; a knowlege in which he has been equalled by few, and excelled by none'; and a remark inspired by the tomb of Sir Francis Vere in the Tower of London: 'he made the art of war his peculiar study in which he was equalled by few, excelled by none' ('The Roman History' in: *An Universal History ... Compiled from Original Authors*, 1748, vol. 12, bk 3, ch. 17, p. 191; David Henry, *An Historical Account of the Curiosities of London and Westminster*, 1785, 51).

"Here, pretty!" returned the Captain.

"Though lost to sight, to memory dear, and England, Home, and Beauty!"] A conflation of two quotations. The first is from the opening stanza of 'To Memory You Are Dear' (1840), a song with words by George Linley:

> Tho' lost to sight, to memory dear
> Thou ever wilt remain;
> One only hope my heart can cheer, –
> The hope to meet again.

The second is from 'The Death of Nelson', a song with words by Samuel James Arnold, music by John Braham, written for the Lyceum opera, *The Americans* (1811). Captain Cuttle is quoting the supposed last words of the dying Lord Nelson: 'In honour's cause I fell at last, / For England, home and beauty.' Braham, a celebrated tenor and theatre-manager, produced and acted in the comic operetta, *The Village Coquettes*, at the St James's Theatre in 1836. Dickens wrote the words for the production and John Pyke Hullah the music.

"Send you away, my lady lass!"

We'll put up this here dead-light,] A 'dead-light', a nautical term, is a strong wooden or iron shutter, which is fixed outside a cabin window or porthole in a storm, to prevent water from entering (*OED*).

"My lady lass!," said the Captain,

yes verily, and by God's help, so I won't, Church Catechism,] An inversion of the response at the beginning of 'A Catechism', *BCP*:

Question. Dost thou not think that thou art bound to believe, and to do, as they have promised for thee? *Answer.* Yes verily: and by God's help so I will.

Nothing would induce the Captain

a great watch-coat.] A thick, heavy coat worn in bad weather by sailors, soldiers and watchmen. Robinson Crusoe converts several watch-coats into lighter-weight jackets.

"My lady lass!" said the Captain,

'you're as safe here as if you was at the top of St. Paul's Cathedral, with the ladder cast off.] As rebuilt by Wren after the Great Fire of London, the cathedral is surmounted by a dome crowned with a golden ball and cross. Visitors could ascend steep stairs for a view from the highest of three galleries, the Golden Gallery at the top of the outer dome (280 ft, 85 metres), and could also go higher still:

> If your head is steady enough, to master the feeling of dizziness which overpowers most people at so great an elevation … you may even ascend by ladders into the lantern itself, and from the *Bull's Eye Chamber,* extend your survey far into the country on every side. (Percy, 1824, 2.63)

that there balsam for the still small woice of a wownded mind!] A conflation of *Macbeth* 2.2.37, 39 – 'Sleep … Balm of hurt minds' – and I Kings 19.12 – 'and after the fire, a still small voice'.

The Captain concluded by kissing the hand that Florence stretched out to him, with the chivalry of any old knight-errant, and walking on tiptoe out of the room.] Because the term 'knight-errant' is frequently used to characterize Don Quixote, Dickens may well be alluding to a specific scene in Cervantes' novel:

> In fine, the princess recovers, and reaches her fair hand through the rails to the knight, who kisses it a thousand times, and bathes it with his tears; … he swears solemnly to comply with her request, kisses her hand again, and bids her farewell with such affliction as well nigh deprived him of life; from thence he retreats to his chamber. … (trans. Smollett, 1811 ed., 1.7)

"Why, you see, my lad,"

clap on] 'Clap on!' is 'The order to lay hold of any rope, in order to haul upon it' (Smyth, 1867, 189). Also, more generally, the phrase means to apply oneself with energy, or to hurry up (*OED*).

"But I was going to say,

As to sleep, you know, I never sleep now. I might be a Watchman, except that I don't get any pay, and he's got nothing on his mind."]

> The night watch for the most part consisted of helpless old men, or ... labourers, appointed by way of charity to keep them and their families off the poor-rate. They were paid from 10s. to 15s. a week, and they usually eked out their wages by taking hush-money, gifts from street-walkers, and contributions from publicans. ('The Police of London', *Quarterly Review*, 1870, 120.92)

For more on London watchmen, see note to chapter 39, p. 394.

"Not to me, Captain Gills,"

The state of my feelings towards Miss Dombey is of that unspeakable description, that my heart is a desert island, and she lives in it alone. I'm getting more used up every day, and I'm proud to be so. If you could see my legs when I take my boots off, you'd form some idea of what unrequited affection is.] Although Mr Toots has many early-nineteenth century forerunners, his self-consciously romantic type ultimately derives from *Die Leiden des jungen Werthers* (*The Sorrows of Young Werther*, 1774), Goethe's novel about unrequited love and passionate yearning. Werther is a sensitive young man who suffers terribly when he learns that the object of his affection loves another. As he grows increasingly desperate, he withdraws from the world and finally kills himself. The novel inspired countless imitations, parodies and pictorial descriptions. There were Werther bread-boxes, gloves, jewels, fans, china and even a perfume. The Wertherian type was melancholic, intensely self-absorbed and world-weary, usually escaping into a more rural or exotic world where he could indulge his passionate longings and languish in isolation. The Werther type influenced Byron's Childe Harold and Chateaubriand's René, and perhaps Shelley's Alastor, Keats's Endymion and Hölderlin's Hyperion. Young John Chivery is another Dickensian example of this type (see *LD* 1.18) (Sondrup 163–79; Philpotts, 2003, 227).

I have been prescribed bark, but I don't take it, for I don't wish to have any tone whatever given to my constitution.]

> In England, the bark is now universally allowed to be a powerful and permanent tonic, superior to all other remedies in counteracting the diseased actions of intermittent fever, and of eminent utility in restoring strength and vigour to the human frame, when weakened by hectic, remittent, or typhus fever, periodical pains, and acute rheumatism. ... It is given in the form of powder, decoction, infusion, or tincture. The form of powder is that which is

in general the most efficacious, but the compound tincture is without doubt an elegant and effectual preparation ... in diluted wine or water, with ten drops of the elixir of vitriol in each dose. The dose of the powder is from ten grains to two drachms. ... Its taste is best covered by milk, or a strong solution of liquorice, and the dose should be taken directly after it is mixed.

(Graham, 1827, 8–9)

Although *Modern Domestic Medicine* (1827) designates bark 'This heroic medicine', it also points out that 'warm controversies have at different times been carried on respecting its virtues, and the most injurious consequences have been attributed to its employment, even by respectable physicians' (8).

Chapter 49

Sixteenth monthly number
January 1848

THE MIDSHIPMAN MAKES A DISCOVERY

What to do, or where to live,

She had indistinct dreams of finding ... some little sisters to instruct, who would be gentle with her, and to whom, under some feigned name, she might attach herself, and who would grow up in their happy home, and marry, and be good to their old governess, and perhaps intrust her, in time, with the education of their own daughters.]

> We know of no class in society more pitiable than that of governesses; we mean those who are so from necessity. ... Oh, the loneliness of heart; the isolation of feeling so frequently experienced, so incomprehensible to those who have passed their lives in love and happiness, *in a home*! They know not the restraint of manner, thought, feeling, imposed upon "the governess."... Why is woman considered to degrade herself, to lose *caste*, by endeavouring to support herself, and that by the all-important office of education? ('On the False Position a Governess Holds in Society', *The New Monthly Belle Assemblée*, 1846, 25.362–3)

> [I]n no case, does any one think of inquiring whether a young lady who finds it necessary to 'take a situation as governess' is capable of educating successfully; neither are any pains bestowed on her 'training.' She has only to say she is competent, and that is usually sufficient: she is required to profess and undertake to be universally accomplished. We constantly see advertisements

Return of Walter.

Number Plan

(Dealings with the Firm of Dombey and Son — N.º XVI.)

chapter XLIX.

The Midshipman makes a discovery.

Florence and the Captain
Little picture of sunset.
Going out to buy clothes
"Drownded, an't he pretty?"
So to the Captain's narrative and the shadow in the little parlor
Walter changed in manner.

Chapter L.

M.ʳ Toots's complaint.

Walter more changed in manner. – Discourses about Uncle Sol, with the Captain.

M.ʳ Toots in a tremendous state — dispatched after Susan.

Florence and Walter – brother and sister &c Innocent love scene – Captain concludes the chapter

chapter LI.

M.ʳ Dombey and the World.

His feelings ~~towards~~ about Florence
The Major & Cousin Feenix.
The clerks – the city – ~~the~~ Perch–
Miss Tox –
The Servants.

Chapter Plan

in which a governess is required to teach everything. This being the fact, there is really nothing left for the unfortunate daughters of reduced gentility but saying they *are* able to teach everything. As to the general management of children, nobody ever supposes *that* requires any particular knowledge or habitude. It is evident that people think young ladies possess an instinctive power to educate; whereas it is a very rare talent, and depends on a peculiar order of sympathies and tastes, which require skilful cultivation. There must, therefore, necessarily be many inefficient governesses: and the good ones have all acquired their art by experience, and after many mistakes. (Miss Winter, 'The Family Governess' in *Heads of the People*, 1840, 210)

In the mid-nineteenth century, the term 'governess' might refer to a woman who taught in a school, a woman who lived at home and travelled to her employer's house to teach, or, as here, a woman who lived with her employer, taught the children and served as their companion. As the above quotations suggest, governesses occupied an ambiguous position in Victorian middle-class households, a fact reflected in Florence's desire to work 'under some feigned name'. Although most governesses prided themselves on being gentlewomen, their lack of an independent income compelled them to endure the social stigma of paid private employment, although this was preferable to working as a seamstress or as a domestic servant. The stigma was such that governesses preferred to advertise for 'a comfortable home', not daring to mention such mercenary or practical considerations as pay or qualifications (Hughes *passim*; Vicinus 4–19).

Governesses were paid between £25 and £45 a year, out of which they had to cover their expenses, such as laundry, travel and medical care. A highly educated lady in a wealthy family might demand £100; Mrs General, the governess for the wealthy Clennams in *LD*, earns a generous £400. (The minimum income of most middle-class families has been estimated by modern historians at figures ranging from £100 to £300).

Her little stock of money

She was too desolate to think how soon her money would be gone – too much a child in worldly matters to be greatly troubled on that score yet,] According to *A Guide to the Unprotected in Every-Day Matters Relating to Property and Income* (1863), 'Ladies rarely have any business to attend to before they attain the age of twenty-one' (vii). As a daughter in an upper-middle-class household, Florence would have been sheltered from many of the practical realities of the world, especially financial considerations. In one instance, the late-Victorian mother of a minor Bloomsbury figure, Gwen Raverat, struggled with simple household accounts: 'no one, least of all herself, ever understood them ... [A]fter my father's death The Accounts became a constant menace to everyone in the family. ... It was so hopeless and useless' (*Period Piece* 96–7; qtd. in Flanders, 2003, 89). For girls from a less privileged background, those who were compelled to work, matters were even more serious. 'A Choice of a

Business for Girls', a pamphlet published in 1864, cautions:

> The power of making out a bill with great rapidity and perfect accuracy is also necessary, and this is the point where women usually fail. A poor half-educated girl keeps a customer waiting while she is trying to add up the bill, or perhaps does it wrong, and in either case excites reasonable displeasure. (qtd. in Flanders, 2003, 90)

The Captain had spread

The Captain ... was making some delicate egg-sauce in a little saucepan: basting the fowl from time to time]

> EGG SAUCE. This agreeable accompaniment to *roasted Poultry* ... is made by putting three Eggs into boiling water, and boiling them for about twelve minutes, when they will be hard ... cut the Whites into small dice, – the Yolks into bits about a quarter of an inch square, – put them into a Sauce-boat; pour to them half a pint of melted Butter, and stir them together. (Kitchiner, *The Cook's Oracle*, 1836, 228)

The dinner being at

Unscrewed his hook, screwed his fork into its place,] On this type of prosthesis, see note to chapter 4, p. 470.

"My lady lass," said the

Liver wing it is.] 'In helping, recollect that the *liver-wing* is commonly thought more of than the other' (*The Housekeeper's Book ... for Economical Domestic Cookery*, 1837, 213).

"The whole row o' dead lights

dead lights] See note to chapter 48, p. 438.

"The wery planks she walked on,"

"The wery planks she walked on ... was as high esteemed by Wal'r, as the water brooks is by the hart which never rejices!] Captain Cuttle confuses Psalm 42.1 – 'As the hart panteth after the water brooks, so panteth my soul after thee, O God'

– with the proverb, 'It is a poor heart that never rejoices'. Dickens had used the proverb several years earlier in *BR*: 'What happened when I reached home you may guess. Ah! Well, it's a poor heart that never rejoices' (4).

rated on them Dombey books,] See note to chapter 25, p. 296.

The fowl and sausages

The Captain's delight and wonder at the quiet housewifery of Florence in assisting to clear the table, arrange the parlour, and sweep up the hearth ... as if she were some Fairy, daintily performing these offices for him;] One of the types of fairy was the brownie, who performed household chores:

> Every manor-house had its ... brownie, and in the kitchen, close by the fire, was a seat which was left unoccupied for him. ... Though, on the whole, a lazy, lounging hobgoblin, he would often bestir himself in behalf of those who understood his humours, and suited themselves thereto. When in this mood, he was known to perform many arduous exploits in kitchen, barn, and stable ... with marvellous precision and rapidity. These kind turns were done without bribe, fee, or reward, for the offer of any of these would banish him for ever. Kind treatment was all that he wished for; and it never failed to procure his favour. ('Brownies', *The Mirror of Literature, Amusement and Instruction*, 1826, 8.110)

Unlike as they were externally –

Faith, hope, and charity,] 'And now abideth faith, hope, charity, these three; but the greatest of these is charity' (1 Corinthians 13.13).

A wandering princess ... in a story-book] The earliest known appearances of this figure are in an oriental tale, 'Adventures of Prince Abdulselam and Princess Chelnissa. A Turkish Novel' (in *An Entire New Collection of Romances and Novels, Never Before Published*, 1780) and *The Letters of a Solitary Wanderer: the Story of Corisande* (1801) by the successful poet and novelist, Charlotte Turner Smith. Both Chelnissa and Corisande are described in the course of their journeys as a 'wandering Princess' (102) and 'the wandering Princess of Romance' (139), respectively. Then in 1817, a pamphlet exposing a celebrated imposter who pretended to be 'Princess Caraboo, from the island of Javasu' explained how an illiterate girl from Devon had persuaded people 'that she was no less a personage than an unfortunate, unprotected, and wandering Princess from a distant Eastern Island' (*Caraboo. Narrative of a singular imposition, practiced upon the benevolence of a lady residing in the vicinity of the City of Bristol, by a young Woman of the name of Mary Willcocks, alias Baker ... alias Caraboo, Princess of Javasu*. [J.M. Gutch], 1817, 54). The phrase, 'wandering princess' was taken up by other authors; for example, Amédée Pichot (*Historical and Literary Tour of a Foreigner in England and Scotland*, 1825, 1.366) and Letitia Elizabeth Landon ('Rebecca', *Heath's Book of Beauty*, 1833, 195).

The Captain was not troubled

a Ward in Chancery,] The female ward hypothesized here would be a legatee under the age of 21 who derived her subsistence from an estate that was in Chancery – the court that considered cases involving disputes over legacies, wills and trusts – and who thus would be directly subject to the authority of the court. In 1844, Dickens sued a number of small publishers, booksellers and printers, and became the plaintive in five Chancery actions to restrain breaches of copyright. He won his case, but 'after infinite vexation and trouble, he had himself to pay the costs incurred on his own behalf' (Forster 1.306). Dickens attacked the abuses of Chancery in *PP* (Mr Pickwick, imprisoned in the Fleet, encounters a Chancery prisoner who dies of consumption after twenty years, and a cobbler, imprisoned for twelve years, who was ruined by having money left him) and, most famously, in Ada Clare and Richard Carstone, the wards in Chancery in *BH*.

The pride Captain Cuttle had,

the Captain felt it a point of delicacy to retire during the making of the purchases, as they were to consist of wearing apparel;] Ready-made dresses and costumes were not sold until the 1850s, so Florence's purchases must be underclothes (such as camisoles, petticoats, chemises, drawers, crinolines, corsets) and nightdresses. In the early nineteenth century, most women made their own (or had them made by their servants), but there were specialist shops that sold ready-made, but always hand-sewn, underclothes and nightdresses. In the 1830s, Graham's Family Linen Warehouse at 207 Regent Street specialized in 'Marriage and Outfitting Orders' and ready-made linen for both ladies and gentlemen ('Outfitting' was a euphemism for underclothes). Before the 1850s, there was also the Maison Brie, *Specialité de Lingerie,* at 43 Conduit Street, Mayfair (Adburgham, 1981, 123, 130). For some of the *trousseau* being purchased in the 1830s and 1840s and some of it being hand-made at home, see note to chapter 56, p. 486.

"Poor Wal'r!" said the

Welcome to all as knowed you, as the flowers in May!] 'As welcome as flowers in May' was a traditional saying (Richardson, *The Local Historian's Table-Book*, 1844, 2.255).

The Captain did not go

read out of a Prayer-book the forms of prayer appointed to be used at sea.] The *BCP* (1662 version) contains a section entitled 'Forms of Prayer to be Used at Sea', though the indefinite article indicates that Captain Cuttle might be reading from one of a number of books that collected prayers for various occasions. *Family Prayer-book* (1829), for instance, contains suitable prayers for people going on a sea voyage, including 'The Seaman's Prayer': 'O thou, who stillest the raging of the sea, and the noise of the waves! All powerful God! ... Thou holdest the winds, and at thy command they go forth. Thou art God of the sea' (Brooks 177). Or the Captain may be reading from a prayer-book intended exclusively for sailors and their families, such as *The Sailors' Prayer Book* (1852), which contains prayers for each day of the week, for five weeks, as well as 'Special Services for Particular Occasions' (e.g. 'During a Storm at Sea').

"Aye," said the Captain, reverentially,

when the winds is roaring and the waves is rowling. ... 'A stiff nor-wester's blowing, Bill; hark, don't you hear it roar now! Lord help 'em, how I pity's all unhappy folks ashore now!' "] From 'The Sailor's Consolation': see the note to chapter 32, p. 350 which quotes the first stanza.

as if you was a-driving, head on, to the world without end, evermore, amen,] From 'The Order for the Burial of the Dead' (*BCP*): 'Glory be to the Father, and to the Son: and to the Holy Ghost; As it was in the beginning, is now, and ever shall be: world without end. Amen'.

"There's perils and dangers

"There's perils and dangers on the deep,] A phrase used as a proviso in legal and formal documents to describe risks at sea; for example,

> the said Ship (being already laden) shall, with the first good Wind and Weather, after the Date hereof (God permitting) sail directly from the said River of *Thames* to the Port of *Leghorn* in *Italy* (the Perils and Dangers of the Seas excepted) ... and from thence shall sail, and take her direct Course, as Wind and Weather shall serve, with as much Speed as may be (the Perils and Dangers of the Sea excepted) to *Venice*. (Wyndham Beawes, *Lex Mercatoria Rediviva: or, the Merchant's Directory*. 6th ed., 1781, 104; see also John Weskett, *A Complete Digest of the Theory, Laws, and Practice of Insurance*, 1783, 475)

There was a shadow

There was a shadow of a man upon the wall close to her.] The dramatic unfolding of this scene recalls the dénouement of *The Tempest*. Prospero has been describing an apparent shipwreck to Ferdinand's father, who has been mourning the loss of his son. Suddenly, Prospero pulls back a curtain and 'discovers' the lovers Ferdinand and Miranda (5.1.173) (Westland, 2004, 102–03).

Chapter 50

MR. TOOTS'S COMPLAINT

There was an empty room

the Tartar frigate,] See note to chapter 4, p. 60.

The Captain could be induced

"I've made that there little property over, jintly." These words he repeated with great unction and gravity, evidently believing that they had the virtue of an Act of Parliament, and that unless he committed himself by some new admission of ownership, no flaw could be found in such a form of conveyance.] This suggests that Cuttle has made a Will in order to nominate 'specific legacies', legacies of specified articles or property that are not pecuniary legacies. People were advised to '[m]ake a Will as soon as you have any property to dispose of' (*A Guide to the Unprotected in Every-day Matters Relating to Property and Income* [1863; 1891], 118).

It was an advantage of

so much excitement had been occasioned in the neighbourhood, by the shutters remaining unopened, that the Instrument Maker's house had been honoured with an unusual share of public observation. ... The idlers and vagabonds had been particularly interested in the Captain's fate; ... an opposite faction ... were of opinion that he lay murdered with a hammer, on the stairs.] An allusion to the Ratcliffe Highway murders of 1811. On 7 December 1811, a hosier named Timothy Marr, his wife and their baby, and a young apprentice, were found murdered in their shop in the Ratcliffe Highway, near the docks in London's East End. Marr, his wife and his apprentice had been beaten to death with a mallet, and the Marr baby was found with his throat slit. Of particular interest in the inquest and trial were eyewitness statements about the shop shutters. Late in the evening of 7 December, the hosier shuttered his shop after learning that a mysterious man was peeping through the windows. About ten minutes later, the local watchman discovered that some of the shutters were loose and called out to Marr. Someone inside the shop (it was later thought to be the murderer) answered, 'We know it!' At about 1 a.m., Marr's servant returned to the shop, discovered that the lights had been turned off and heard scuffling and someone breathing on the other side of the door. She told the pawnbroker next door, who entered Marr's shop by climbing over a brick wall in the backyard, and found the bodies. Twelve days later, on 19 December, there were more murders: the bodies of a publican, John Williamson, his wife and his servant, were discovered with their heads beaten in and their throats cut. Eventually, the murder weapon found at the scene of the latter crime, a 'peen maul' (a hammer used by a ship's carpenter) was traced to an Irish sailor, John Williams, who was arrested and who shortly after committed suicide in Coldbath Fields Prison (Flanders, 2011, 1–19).

The Ratcliffe Highway murders were talked and written about for years afterwards. They were mentioned by Thomas de Quincey in his famous essay, 'On Murder Considered as one of the Fine Arts' (*Blackwood's Magazine*, February 1827), and described at greater length in the 1854 postscript. Dickens was familiar with de Quincey's essay and postscript and owned a copy of an illustration 'representing the horrible creature [Williams] as his dead body lay on a cart, with a piece of wood for a pillow, and a stake lying by, ready to be driven through him' (*Letters* 11.247). In October 1866, *AYR* carried its own account of the event: 'Old Stories Re-Told: The Two Great Murders in the Ratcliffe Highway (1811)' (16.350–3).

the Beadle ... who had expected to have the distinction ... of giving evidence in full uniform before the coroner,] Upon the discovery of a suspicious death, the coroner was required to conduct an inquest:

> ... the coroner is to go to the place where any person is slain or suddenly dead, and shall by his warrant to the bailiffs, constables, &c., summon a jury out of the four or five neighbouring towns, to make inquiry upon view of the body; and the coroner and jury are to inquire into the manner of killing, and all circumstances that occasioned the party's death; who were present, whether the dead person was known, where he lay the night before, &c. Also all wounds ought to be viewed and inquiry made with what weapons, &c. And the coroner may send his warrant for witnesses, and take their examination in writing: and if any appear guilty of the murder, he shall inquire what goods and lands he hath: and then the dead body is to be buried. A coroner may likewise commit the person to prison who is by his inquisition found guilty of the murder; and the witnesses are to be bound by recognizance to appear at the next assizes, &c. (Tomlins and Granger, *The Law-Dictionary*, 4th ed., vol. 1, 1835, 'Coroner 2.1')

Deaths and inquests provided an income for beadles: a Parliamentary report in 1840 listed their fees: 'attending the coroner with notice of death, about 4s. 6d. or 5s.; summoning jury and attending inquest, 6s. 8d.' (*Report from Select Committee on the Office of Coroner for Middlesex*, 1840, 4). For the office of beadle, see note in chapter 5, p. 83.

"I have been thinking

that spice of the marvellous which was always in his character] The phrase 'spice of the marvellous' was associated with the tall tales told by sailors. In *A General History and Collection of Voyages and Travels* (1811), Robert Kerr characterized a tale about pet dancing snakes as having 'a sufficient spice of the marvellous' (37). And Herman Melville used the phrase in *Omoo: a Narrative of Adventures in the South Seas* (1847): 'Tonoi abounded in bullock stories; most of which, by the by, had a spice of the marvellous' (54.209).

I have often heard and read of people who ... have even gone upon her track to the place whither she was bound,] A contemporary example in the news was the disappearance of Sir John Franklin's arctic expedition in search of the North-West Passage in 1845. It was believed that the ships had become trapped in ice in September 1846. There was continual discussion in the press and in the government from February 1847 onwards (the year in which Dickens was composing this number) about the loss of the expedition and proposals for finding it. For example, on 23 February 1847, a naval officer wrote to the Admiralty 'that the time has arrived when due preparation should be made for instituting, if necessary, an active search for the ships' ('Papers and Correspondence Relative to the Arctic Expedition under Sir John Franklin', *Parliamentary Papers*, 1847, 41.23–47 [23]). Several search parties set out in the spring of 1848, the first of many over the next two decades. Dickens himself wrote a two-part article on the Franklin expedition – 'The Lost Arctic Voyagers' – which appeared in *HW* in 1854 (10 [2 and 9 December]: 361–5, 385–93).

"If my uncle had been

"If my uncle had been a heedless young man, likely to be entrapped by jovial company to some drinking-place, where he was to be got rid of for the sake of what money he might have about him ... or if he had been a reckless sailor, going ashore with two or three months' pay in his pocket, I could understand his disappearing, and leaving no trace behind.]

> 'I visited ... a short time ago, some of the houses at Wapping and its neighbourhood, into which the sailors are decoyed. These houses are kept by crimps, who waylay the unsuspecting sailors; they are by them conducted to these places, where they find music and dancing going forward; they are induced to take up their abode there, and are often plundered of every

farthing they possess. In some houses, I saw several foreigners; and in the days when burking was common, many of these unfortunates were made away with. In Bristol, when a ship arrives, the sailors are surrounded by a set of miscreants, who are called "runners," and are taken by them to houses of the lowest description. ... Instances innumerable might be stated of the horrible state of the dens to which seamen are obliged to resort for want of more respectable residences; robberies are of frequent occurrence; and in one, I fear not a solitary case, murder was committed.' (Montague Gore, qtd. in 'Sailors' Homes', *Chambers's Edinburgh Journal* 18 [4 September 1852]: 154)

In 'Jack Alive in London', George Augustus Sala describes the popular reputation of the sailor:

He is often a profligate, and a drunkard, and a swearer ... because abominable and vicious customs make him so; because, ill cared for on board ship, he no sooner lands than he becomes the prey of the infamous harpies who infest maritime London. He is robbed by outfitters ... he is robbed by the tavern-keepers, the crimps, and the boarding-masters. He is robbed by his associates, robbed in business, robbed in amusement. "Jack" is fair game to everybody. (*HW* 4.258)

In *OMF*, John Harmon is dressed as a 'common sailor' when he is drugged by Rogue Riderhood at his London shop, attacked by George Radfoot, and then thrown into the Thames to drown. Rogue Riderhood, we learn, 'had been previously taken up for being concerned in the robbery of an unlucky seaman, to whom some poison has been given' (bk 2, ch. 13).

"Hope, you see, Wal'r,"

your Little Warbler, Sentimental Diwision,] Song books of the eighteenth and nine-teenth centuries frequently contained 'Warbler' in their titles, e.g. *The Musical Char-mer, or Warbler of the Woods* (1785); *The Little Warbler. Scotch Songs* (1820); *The Cheer-ful Warbler, or, Juvenile Song Book* (1820); and *The Warbler, A New Song Book* (n.d.).

"Only one word more about

written in the ordinary course – by mail packet, or ship letter,] Packet-boats were passenger boats so-called because they carried letters, dispatches and bankers' parcels in sealed bags to and from foreign countries. In 1849, English mail-packets ran back and forth from England to 'France, Hamburg, Holland, Belgium, North America, Mexico, India, China, the Peninsula, Mediterranean, Brazils, West Indies, and the south-western coast of America', with postage varying between 8*d.* and 2*s.* 7*d.*, depending on distance and the quantity of correspondence between the locations. If the country was a British dominion, the sea postage was a flat 1*s.*, regardless of distance (except Heligoland). There were, however, several 'important parts of the British dominions abroad' – 'the Cape of Good Hope, Australia, Van Diemen's Land, and New Zealand' – that mail-packets did not visit. In these instances, correspondence was conveyed more slowly by merchant ship at a cost of 8*d.* for each letter, with a gratuity of twopence going to the captain of the ship. *Chambers's Edinburgh Journal* remarked, 'The universal complaint amongst emigrants and their friends is the failure of their correspondence in reaching its destination. This is caused principally by defective post-office arrangements in the interior of colonies, and to loss of ships and accidents at sea' ('Ocean Penny-Postage', 7 July 1849, 12.79).

Captain Cuttle, without quite understanding

the wind was right abaft.] 'Abaft' is a nautical term for a following wind.

"Wal'r my lad," said the Captain,

"prowiding as there is any just cause or impedemint why two persons should not be jined together in the house of bondage ... I hope I should declare it as promised and wowed in the banns.] Cuttle conflates passages from the *BCP* and the Bible. He alludes to the section of the Solemnization of Matrimony that describes the Banns, the public notice announcing an intended marriage:

> *First the Banns of all that are to be married together must be published in the Church three several Sundays, during the time of Morning Service, or of Evening Service, (if there be no Morning Service,) immediately after the second Lesson; the Curate saying after the accustomed manner,* I publish the Banns of Marriage between *M.* of —— and *N.* of ——. If any of you know cause, or just impediment, why these two persons should not be joined together in holy Matrimony, ye are to declare it. This is the first *[second,* or *third]* time of asking. (*BCP*)

In the Old Testament, Egypt is repeatedly referred to as 'the house of bondage' (for example, Exodus 20.1–2, 'God spake all these words, saying, I am the Lord thy God, which have brought thee out of the land of Egypt, out of the house of bondage').

"Well, my lad," growled the Captain

"I find myself wery much down by the head ... I've gone clean about.] To be or go 'down by the head' is to have the bow riding deeper than the stern which can be a useful manoeuvre but can also cause the ship to sink. To 'go (or come) about' is to change tack, that is, to steer the vessel across the eye of the wind to the opposite tack.

This dramatic manoeuvre can cause the ship to capsize if not done correctly.

"Lieutenant Walters," said Mr. Toots,

I am well aware that the most agreeable thing I could do for all parties would be to put an end to my existence,] For Mr Toots's Wertherism, and the tendency of the type to melancholia and suicide, see note to chapter 48, p. 503. In a similar comical way, Young John Chivery imagines his tombstone in *LD*.

"Captain Gills and Lieutenant Walters

"I should sink into the silent tomb with a gleam of joy."] A poetic cliché that shows up in many poems in the eighteenth and nineteenth centuries, the phrase 'silent tomb' is perhaps most famous from Wordsworth's poem about his dead daughter Catherine, 'Surprized by Joy' (1815):

> Surprized by joy – impatient as the Wind
> I turned to share the transport – Oh! with whom
> But thee, long buried in the silent Tomb,
> That spot which no vicissitude can find?

He caught her to his heart,

He caught her to his heart,] It is presumably this scene – what the Number Plan calls an 'Innocent love scene' – that Dickens was thinking of when he told Forster on 21 December 1847, 'One of the prettiest things in the book ought to be at the end of the chapter I am writing now'. Shortly after, he wrote Angela Burdett Coutts, 'I hope you liked the little loves of Florence and Walter? If you had seen [Francis] Jeffrey crying over them the other night, you would have been charmed with *him* at all events' (*Letters* 5.211, 5.223).

Chapter 51

MR. DOMBEY AND THE WORLD

The world. What the world

The world. What the world thinks of him, how it looks at him, what it sees in him, and what it says – this is the haunting demon of his mind.] 'The World' was a synonym for 'fashionable society' and 'everyone of account' much used by eighteenth-century writers like Addison and Swift and later by 'silver fork' novelists. Disraeli mocked the term in *Tancred; or, the New Crusade* (1847):

> To the great body, however, of what is called "the World" – the world that lives in St. James's Street and Pall Mall, that looks out of a club window, and surveys mankind as Lucretius from his philosophic tower … the Duke and Duchess of Bellamont were absolutely unknown. … It was clear, therefore, that the Bellamonts might be very great people, but they were not in "society." (1.2)

"Damme, Sir," says the Major,

His Royal Highness the late Duke of York did me the honour to say,] For the Duke of York, see note to chapter 1, p. 32; for Bagstock's name-dropping as a characteristic of his fictional model, Thackeray's Major Gahagan, see note to chapter 10, p. 150.

"I beg your pardon,"

her criminality] If she had actually committed adultery with Mr Carker, Mrs Dombey would have been liable to the charge of 'criminal conversation', a civil action that allowed a husband to sue his wife's lover and to claim damages because of her infidelity. For more on divorce law, see note to chapter 47, p. 434.

"I don't know about

when people meet with trials, they must bear 'em.] A hackneyed Christian precept (deriving from 1 Peter 4.12–13); see, for example, Scott, *Kenilworth* (1821): 'we will bear our trials manfully' (12).

But Miss Tox is not a part

she, a by no means bright or particular star, moves in her little orbit in the corner of another system,] ''Twere all one / That I should love a bright particular star / And think to wed it, he is so above me' (*All's Well that Ends Well* 1.1.79–81). Dickens also alludes to this quotation in *MC* (17), *DC* (51, 60, 61) and *BH* (40).

At the counting-house,

a little dinner ... takes place at a neighbouring tavern; the wit in the chair; the rival acting as Vice-President.] An 'Harmonic meeting', a popular musical evening held in public houses or 'song and supper rooms'. Refreshments were served during the programme, which was announced by the landlord of the house, who acted as chairman and sat surrounded by his friends at a table below the platform. A harmonic meeting is depicted in *SB* ('Scenes'), in *PP* 20, *BH* 11 and, another one, of a rougher sort, features in chapter 26 of *OT*, which describes the chairman, the singers and the low company of men and women who comprise the audience. For the comic singing at these occasions, see note to chapter 58, p. 504.

Recent occurrences ... which have not been altogether without notice in some Sunday Papers, and in a daily paper which he need not name (here every other member of the company names it in an audible murmur),] The earliest Sunday papers were established in the 1780s. By the 1830s, there were twelve Sunday papers published in London with a total circulation of 40,000. In the 1840s and early 1850s, several new Sunday papers were founded, including *Lloyd's Weekly Newspaper* (1842), *News of the World* (1843), *Weekly Times* (1847) and *Reynolds's Newspaper* (1850). Because such papers were cheap to produce and to purchase, and emphasized sensational subjects such as crime and scandal, they had a particular appeal to working-class audiences. 'I read *Lloyd's Weekly Newspaper* on a Sunday, and what murders and robberies there is now! What will there be when the Great Exhibition opens!', a street-stationer told Mayhew. Although some papers, edited by reputable, literary men, were well regarded, most were considered to inhabit 'the lower regions of the press – the stews'. One of Dickens's friends, Douglas Jerrold, was the editor of *Lloyd's Weekly Magazine* (*Parliamentary History of England*, 1819, 34.1006; *Cottager's Monthly Visitor*, 1830, 10.270–72; Mayhew, 1.291; Berridge, 1978, 247–64; Clarke, 2004, 246).

Sunday newspapers were particularly offensive to conservatives and the pious, who associated them with radicalism and immorality. According to the Dean of Chichester, 'it is notorious that the newspapers which are issued on the Sunday are of all others the most outrageous in their principles, the most intemperate in their language, seeming to combine and concentrate in themselves all the bitterness that can be extracted from the weekly press; while not a few tend directly to the subversion of all order, all government, all morality, all religion' (qtd. in *The District Visitor's Manual*, 1840, 177). The Bishop of London compared Sunday newsrooms (where papers could be read) to 'moral dram-shops, where doses of the most deleterious poison are imbibed by thousands of persons who ought to be engaged in reading and hearing the word of God' (*Cottager's Monthly Visitor*, 1830, 272).

Daily papers were published either in the morning or the evening, represented different political points-of-view and had varying degrees of political influence. In the 1830s there were five morning papers, foremost of which was 'that monarch of periodical literature – the all-powerful *Times*'. There were four evening papers: the *Globe, Courier, Sun* and *Standard* ('Private History of the London Newspaper Press', *Tait's Edinburgh Magazine* for 1834, 1.788–92).

Robinson replies to this like a man and a brother;] See headnote to chapter 3, p. 44.

Mr. Dombey's servants are

They have hot suppers every night, and "talk it over"] The futility of settling any matter by 'talking it over' was often mocked; see, for example, Henry F. Harrington, 'Is't my Nephew, or Not?' (1839):

> "No, no! I'll answer for his further good order," exclaimed Tidworth, to the foaming Baronet: "Let us be calm, and talk it over."
> "Be calm, ha, ha! Be calm! Talk what over? Isn't here a case of attempt at swindling, first, and aggravated assault and battery, afterwards? Talk what, over?" (ch. 5, in *The Ladies Companion*, 1839, 11.261)

Mr. Dombey's servants are becoming

no good would ever come of living in a corner house]

> The superstition that corner houses are unlucky is very common in Herefordshire. I once resided next to a corner house, and was frequently congratulated on having escaped that unenviable position, while, if I had been in any way unfortunate, my friends would exclaim, "No wonder – living next to a corner house." ('Corner Houses', *Notes and Queries*, 5th ser., vol. 4, July–December 1875, p. 216)

Chapter 52   Seventeenth monthly number
                                                                February 1848

SECRET INTELLIGENCE

"Board wages perhaps,

"Out of place now, Robby?" … "Board wages perhaps, Rob?"] On being dismissed, servants were entitled to be paid their usual wages plus board wages, which they received to pay for their support and maintenance during service. In a large household, for example, 'The Board Wages of Servants in general … may be reckoned at an average of 10s. per head, per Week, expense, for Board. The Men are allowed a

Pursue the connexion of Rob with the old woman and alice, to get Mr Dombey in pursuit of Carker.

The brother and sister Carker and Mr Morfin – Take up that thread – Relenting of alice.   Still carry Mr Dombey's pursuit through; pervading the number

Edith and Carker. Edith not his mistress –

Number Plan

(Dealings with the Firm of Dombey and Son — N.º XVII)

Chapter LII.

Secret Intelligence.

Alice & good Mrs Brown

To them Mr Dombey.

Rob the Grinder — The screw applied by the old woman

D.I.J.O.N.

Pursuit-ending

chapter LIII.

More Intelligence.

Mr Morfin and Harriet & John Carker
He tells them about James Carker, and shadows forth Mr Dombey's ruin.

alice relents. Pursuit-ending still carried through, quick and fierce.   Chapter LIV.

The Fugitives.

Edith alone at Dijon – Frenchmen laying supper. To her,

Carker - Scene between them. Pursuit still carried

through, quick and fierce.

Chapter Plan

Pot of Ale per day, and the Women a Pint, besides table-beer' (Adams, *The Complete Servant*, 1825, 8).

Mrs. Brown, moved as it seemed

expressive physiognomical revelations] Interest in physiognomy, or the discrimination of character by outward appearance, has existed since antiquity. In the nineteenth century, the most influential exponent of physiognomy was the Swiss pastor and religious writer Johann Caspar Lavater (1741–1801), whose *Physiognomische Fragmente* (4 vols, 1775–8) was published in twenty English versions and five translations by 1816. Although physiognomical study was most popular from about 1775 to 1810, interest in the subject continued into the 1870s. The pseudo-science received an apparently scientific basis in 1806 with the publication of Sir Charles Bell's Essay on the *Anatomy of the Expression*, the first scientific study to show the effect of muscles on human emotions. In 1855, Herbert Spencer speculated on the connection between physical actions and the psychic state in *Principles of Psychology*. Dickens himself had faith in physiognomy, holding it 'to be infallible; though all these sciences demand rare qualities in the student' ('A Little Dinner in an Hour', *AYR* 21.109).

"Lord, Misses Brown, no!

You expect a cove to be a flash of lightning. I wish I *was* the electric fluency ... I'd have a shock at somebody,] Rob has just been asked if he is 'dumb' and he seems to confuse 'fluent' (or 'fluency') with 'fluid' (electricity was once thought to be a fluid) or with 'current', or with both.

In 1748, Jean-Antoine Nollet first remarked on the similarities between electricity and lightning, and several years later Jacques de Romas proposed bringing an atmospheric charge to earth by using a kite. At about the same time, Benjamin Franklin showed that an iron rod could be used to collect lightning, which proved that clouds were electrified and which led to the invention of lightning-rods to protect buildings and ships.

In 1868, *AYR* warned its readers against playing with 'intensified electricity', remarking, 'Familarity made that ['intensified electricity'] an amusement which at first had given much alarm. Everybody took to giving and receiving electric shocks. The Abbé Nollet administered them to three hundred men of Louis the Fifteenth's guard, who, hand in hand, felt simultaneously the new sensation' (20.275). A 'galvanic blasting apparatus' is used to kill a crocodile in 'The Crocodile Battery', *HW* 2.540–3, and a similar device is employed to punish a fakir in 'A Fuqueer's Curse', *HW* 3.310–12. For more on electricity, see note to chapter 36, p. 378.

"What, haven't we talked enough

being on the rack,]

> The rack is a large open frame of oak, under which the prisoner was laid on his back, upon the floor, with his wrists and ancles attached by cords to two rollers at the end of the frame. These rollers were moved by levers in opposite directions, till the body rose to a level with the frame; questions were then put, and, if the answers were not satisfactory, the sufferer was gradually stretched, till the bones started from the sockets. (*The Popular Encyclopedia*, 1846, 6)

The rack was said to have been introduced to England by the Duke of Exeter, under Henry VI, and was sometimes referred to as the 'duke of Exeter's daughter' (6). For Dickens's association of the past with 'such frightful instruments of torture' (*Letters* 4.220), see note to chapter 27, p. 309.

"Neither," said the Grinder.

But take your solemn oath now, that you'll never tell anybody." ... This Mrs. Brown very readily did: being naturally Jesuitical;] Dickens is drawing on one of the negative connotations attributed to the Jesuits, their supposed tendency to dissemble, to prevaricate or to refrain from telling the truth (*OED*). For Dickens's antipathy to the Catholic Church, and for a similarly derogatory use of the term 'monkish', see note to chapter 42, p. 411.

Muttering to himself, and returning

D.I.J.O.N.] Situated in Eastern France, between the rivers Ouche and Suzon and about 196 miles from Paris, Dijon is the capital of the department of the Côte-d'Or. Its population, in 1832, was about 25,000, and its main manufactures included 'hosiery, blankets, coloured woollen-yarn, cotton-yarn, cotton-velvets, printed calicoes, muslins, linen, leather, hats, vinegar, mustard, which last is in high repute with epicures, and starch'. Dijon, which was 'surrounded by ramparts; which, being well planted, and commanding fine and extensive views, form an excellent promenade', contained several attractive walks as well as baths, a botanic garden and a mineral spring. It was also famous 'for the cultivation of science and literature', primarily because of its 'académie universitaire, comprehending faculties of law, sciences, and literature', its 'academies of sciences, belles letters, and arts', a drawing school and its society of jurisprudence. 'It is of an oval form, the circumference of its walls, exclusive of the suburbs, being about a mile and a quarter. ... The streets are regular, and well paved; and the houses in general neat and commodious'. Another contemporary account remarked on the 'air of life and gaiety' about Dijon 'not very common in the provincial towns of France' (Agassiz, 1833, 40; *Encyclopædia Metropolitana*, 1845, 18.10; *Penny Cyclopædia*, 1837, 8.496–7; Raffles, 1833, 410). For more on Dijon and travelling there from England, see note to chapter 54, p. 468.

Chapter 53

MORE INTELLIGENCE

"Then I shall wish you

The Papers ... is more eager for news of it than you'd suppose possible. One of the Sunday ones ... that had previously offered to bribe me ... was dodging about our court last night ... Another one ... is in the parlour of the King's Arms all the blessed day. I happened ... to let a little obsewation fall there, and next morning, which was Sunday, I see it worked up in print, in a most surprising manner."] For the low reputation of the Sunday papers, see note to chapter 51, p. 455. Reporters who specialized in the sensational were not well regarded and were even known to invent stories in the absence of actual news. According to an article in *Chambers's Edinburgh Journal* (1836):

> There is another class of newspaper reporters. ... These are the reporters of police cases, of accidents, Inquests, and all the other miscellaneous news with which it is hoped to entertain the public. From these men being paid so much per line for their articles – from a penny to three-halfpence – they have been designated "penny-a-line men." Some of them are permanently attached to a newspaper establishment; the rest are mere skirmishers upon the public common, and are ... to the newspapers what the Cossacks are to a regular army. It is these personages who are generally the inditers of the "mysterious occurrences," "most distressing affairs," "desperate accidents," &c. which appear in the London journals, and whose productions may be recognised by the inflated style in which they are usually written. ... If the subject of the report is thought interesting, he is well paid; for a report of half a column in each of the morning papers will produce him in the whole more than £ 1.3s. 3d. ('The London Press', *Chambers's Edinburgh Journal*, 1836, 4.19)

'The King's Arms' has been identified with several actual locations (in Cheyne Walk, in Leadenhall Street and in Little Britain), but without any conclusive evidence.

with his eye at the counting-house keyhole, which being patent is impervious.] Numerous patents were granted for locks during the first half of the nineteenth century, the most celebrated being the 'Detector Lock' patented by Charles and Jeremiah Chubb in 1818. They were granted another patent in 1824 for an improvement on it, and by the 1840s Chubb had become a household name:

> There can be no doubt but that the construction and arrangement of the parts in Chubb's invention do combine in a very high degree the four principal requisites of a good lock, viz. security, simplicity, strength, and durability. The

first, particularly, is increased beyond calculation by a contrivance which not only renders it impossible to be picked or opened by any false instrument, but also detects the first attempt to open it, – thereby preventing those repeated efforts to which even the best locks are sometimes exposed. ('Locks', *The Cabinet Cyclopædia. Useful Arts. Vol 2: Iron and Steel*, 1833, 11.263–84, *passim*)

"I have whistled, hummed tunes,

the whole of Beethoven's Sonata in B,] The manuscript reads 'Beethoven's Sonata Number three'. Beethoven's cello sonata number 3 (op. 69) is in A major, however. Although he wrote no cello sonatas in the key of B, Beethoven was the first great composer of cello sonatas and composed five sonatas for cello and piano as well as other pieces for the cello.

"That he has abused his trust

"that he has oftener dealt and speculated to advantage for himself, than for the House he represented; that he has led the House on, to prodigious ventures, often resulting in enormous losses;] Although Dickens does not specify the exact nature of the speculation, he is doubtless drawing on his public's knowledge of the 'Railway Panic' of 1845, which resulted in countless failed speculations. This association between the 'Panic' and Carker's speculation would have been reinforced by Browne's frontispiece to *DS*, with its depiction of an anthropomorphic locomotive rushing headlong upon Carker. Such a locomotive, with terrifying eyes in place of headlamps, was used several times in 1845 to symbolize the 'Panic' and the damage inflicted on speculators (for more, see note to chapter 55, p. 481 and Plate 20, p. 482) (Steig, 1971, 148). As for railways speculators such as George Hudson, the 'Railway King', Dickens came to feel

> a burning disgust against Mister Hudson. His position seems to me to be such a monstrous one, and so illustrative of the breeches pocket side of the English character, that I can't bear it. There are some dogs who can't endure one particular note on the Piano. In like manner I feel disposed to throw up my head, and howl, whenever I hear Mr Hudson mentioned. He is my rock ahead in life. (*Letters* 4.410–11)

Dickens later branded Hudson 'the Great Humbug of England' (5.65).

Undertakings have been entered on, to swell the reputation of the House for vast resources, and to exhibit it in magnificent contrast to other merchants' houses, of which it requires a steady head to contemplate the possibly ... ruinous consequences.] In this respect, John Sadleir, the model for Mr Merdle in *LD*, is typical. He made his early reputation as a solicitor in Dublin, as a parliamentary agent for Irish railways and as a director of the Tipperary Joint Stock Bank. In 1847 he was elected to Parliament for the borough of Carlow and served as a junior Lord of the Treasury under Lord Aberdeen. He was also chairman of the London and County Joint Stock Banking Company, chairman of the Royal Swedish Railway and a large purchaser of land in the Encumbered Estates Court in Ireland. He was also involved with the Grand Junction Railway of France, a Swiss railway and the East Kent Line. Shortly after his suicide on Hampstead Heath on 16 February 1856, it was discovered that the deed he had given in security on the purchase of an estate in the Encumbered Estates Court was a forgery. Immediately, other frauds came to light. Sadleir had over-issued shares and obligations in the Royal Swedish Railway to the amount of at least £150,000. He had been permitted by his brother, the manager of the Tipperary Bank, to overdraw more than £200,000 which, with other fraudulent practices, resulted in the deficit in the bank exceeding £400,000. In a particularly reprehensible move, on 1 February 1856, Sadleir issued a balance sheet and report that represented the Tipperary Bank as flourishing and declared a dividend at the rate of 6 per cent with a bonus of 3 per cent (Philpotts, 2003, 249–50).

The brother and sister sat

feeling like two people shipwrecked long ago, upon a solitary coast, to whom a ship had come at last, when they were old in resignation, and had lost all thought of any other home.] Shipwreck narratives, both fictional and real, were common in the early nineteenth century, including rewritings of one of Dickens's favourite novels, *Robinson Crusoe*. A brief sampling includes William Falconer, *The Shipwreck* (1825); *Sir Edward Seaward's Narrative of his Shipwreck* (2nd ed., 1832); *Melancholy Shipwreck and Remarkable Instance of the Interposition of Divine Providence* (1834); *The Rival Crusoes; or, the Shipwreck* (4th ed., 1836); and *The Shipwreck, or The Desert Island. A Moral Tale* (1840).

John Carker had gone out,

she had no more power to divest herself of these vague impressions of dread, than if they had been stone giants, rooted in the solid earth.] Accounts of the 'colossal statues' on Easter Island had been published since the eighteenth century, following the visit of a Dutch navigator in 1722. The statues were described by Captain James Cook, on his visit to the island in 1774:

> The attention of the voyagers was, however, forcibly attracted to some fine specimens of ingenuity, namely, the colossal statues. ... About fifteen yards from the landing place, within a space enclosed by stone walls, was a pillar consisting of a single stone, about 28 feet high, and 5 feet wide, representing the human head and bust. The workmanship was rude; but the features were not ill-formed, though the ears were disproportionably long. On the top of

the head was placed upright a huge circular piece of stone, about five feet in height, and the same in diameter, which resembled the head-dress of an Egyptian divinity. It was difficult to explain how the natives of this island could carve such huge statues with tools made of bone or shell, or how they could raise them upon pedestals when finished. Neither was the purpose more obvious for which the statues were set up. (*The Life, Voyages, and Discoveries, of Captain James Cook,* 1837, 71)

Dickens also may have in mind other stone giants, such as the ones in Honduras described by John L. Stephens in his *Incidents of Travel in Central America* (1841). The statues are mentioned in a review of the book in *Chambers's Edinburgh Journal,* 1842, 10.267, and they are described in *HW* in 1851:

We ... find at our first plunge into the forest a colossal figure frowning down upon us; it is a stone statue twelve feet high, loaded with hieroglyphic and with grotesque ornament. The grand face seems to be a portrait – but of whom? We explore farther, and find more and more of these stone giants, elbowed from their places by the growth of the trees, some of them buried to the chest in vegetation, staring through the underwood with their blind eyes. ... Who are these gods or heroes buried in the dark recesses of the wood? Who raised their monuments? ('Our Phantom Ship. Central America', 2.518)

The imagery may also owe something to the many accounts of 'the colossal bust of Memnon', the pharaoh Ramesses II, discovered in Egypt and transported to the British Museum in 1818 (*The British Museum. Egyptian Antiquities,* 1832, 1.234–96). The statue's fame preceded its arrival in London and inspired Shelley's sonnet, 'Ozymandias' (1818):

> Two vast and trunkless legs of stone
> Stand in the desert. Near them, on the sand,
> Half sunk, a shattered visage lies ...
> And on the pedestal these words appear:
> 'My name is Ozymandias, King of Kings:
> Look on my works, ye mighty, and despair!' (2–4, 9–11)

"Why do you tremble?" rejoined

I was concerned in a robbery ... and was found out, and sent to be tried. ... Though I was but a girl, I would have gone to Death,] Between 1819 and 1832, 160 people were executed for robbery in England (16% of the total number of executions). After 1837, though the death penalty still applied to several serious crimes, including burglary aggravated by violence, and robbery that involved cutting or wounding, the only criminals actually executed in England were convicted murderers (Gatrell 618).

Chapter 54

THE FUGITIVES

The time, an hour short

so large an Hotel ... the square court-yard in the centre,] This was probably the Hotel de la Cloche, judging from the proximity of the hotel to the 'Cathedral clock' (see note below) and the fact that it has a courtyard. Writing in 1823, Marianne Colston described its particular attractions to British visitors:

> I shall venture to say very little of this city, as we entered it rather late in the day, and the rain prevented my quitting the Hotel de la Cloche, where we found most comfortable accommodations. ... In fact, the card of the master of the house informed us in English, that the Hotel had been fitted up with a particular reference to the visitors from our country; and at the same time that I enjoyed the comforts which the inn afforded, I sighed to think that so many natives of our glorious island, should "make themselves a country" in foreign climes, and that we should be among the number of these unpatriotic absentees. (*Journal of a Tour in France ...*, 2 vols, 1.37)

The Hotel de la Cloche, described by a contemporary as 'a large and splendid establishment with a spacious promenade' (Reichard 244), was also recommended by Mariana Starke in 1833, by the *Handbook for Travellers in Switzerland and the Alps of Savoy and Piedmont* in 1838 and by Murray's *Handbook for Travellers in France* in 1844, the latter remarking that the hotel is 'good, well situated, near the Cathedral, close to the Paris gate' (524). The other hotel in Dijon recommended by Starke and Murray is the Hotel du Parc, but the *Handbook for Travellers in Switzerland* describes this hotel as being 'in a sort of park outside the town', whereas the Hotel de la Cloche was 'in the midst of the town' (33; 129).

At some point during his stay in France in late 1846, while he was writing the first numbers of *DS*, Dickens may have visited Dijon. Dickens was staying with his family in Lausanne, Switzerland from June to November 1846 and twice visited Geneva. He travelled to Paris in November 1846, and was again in Paris in December 1846 and January and February 1847. He may have also stopped in Dijon two years earlier, in July 1844, on his way from London to Genoa (though he does not mention the visit in *PI*).

"A thousand pardons! The sudden

"A thousand pardons!] An Anglicized version of the French phrase, *Mille pardons*, which is rare in contemporary French but was common in the nineteenth century;

for example, compare Jules Sandeau, *Sacs et parchemins* (1851): 'Mille pardons, monsieur; mille excuses, mademoiselle'. In the scenes with the French servants in this chapter and chapter 55, English dialogue is understood to represent French – a device Dickens later used extensively in *LD* and *TTC*. Other ways in which he signifies French are: the use of actual French words (*en route, restaurant, Monsieur, Madame*); the literal translation of French words or phrases into their inexact English equivalents ('It should be eaten on the instant', 'The supper will be here this moment', 'I am much hurried'); and the narrator's explicit comment that the characters are speaking French ('The answer was in French', 'Monsieur … addressed her in the French tongue as his charming wife'). For Dickens's familiarity with French and other similar instances of his signifying French in English dialogue, see Philpotts, 2003, 506–14.

the Golden Head] In French, *le tête d'or*. It is possible that Dickens knew the English hotel in Calais, The Albion, which was located in the Rue du le tête d'or, as mentioned by Francis Coghlan in *A Guide to France, or, Travellers their Own Commissioners*, 4th ed., 1829, 20.

"Pardon! There was the

the English nation had so grand a genius for punctuality.] English punctuality was proverbial. In Susan Ferrier's *Destiny; Or, The Chief's Daughter* (1831), tradespeople make the rounds of a village, 'with true English punctuality' (1.142). And a British traveller in the Austrian valley of the Durrenstein describes his holiday:

> I ranged the region during a whole summer, until the doubt with the peasantry lay between my being a magician, a madman, or an agent of Napoleon. … But, luckily, the native love of tranquility prevailed; and as I paid for my provisions with English punctuality, and without Austrian remonstrance at the little tax which they added to their price … I was suffered, at pleasure, to ramble, draw, eat, and pay. (*The Atheneum; or Spirit of the English Magazines*. 3rd series. 1 [October to March 1829]: 129–30)

"I came here alone,"

I want no attendance.] Before the late nineteenth century, a woman travelling alone, without a maid, and without a family to shelter and protect her, would have been thought eccentric. 'Daughters can travel alone … occasionally', Anthony Trollope acknowledged in 1866, 'but such feminine independence is an exception to the rule, and daughters are generally willing to submit themselves to that paternal and maternal guidance from which the adult male tourist so stoutly revolts'. Even women travelling in pairs or groups would have been considered 'unprotected' (*Travelling Sketches* 3). William Dean Howell remarked upon the fact that the English always seemed to travel in families (*Venetian Life*, 1867, 1.152). Miss Wade, in *LD*, is another solitary female traveller (see 1.2, in particular).

As the sound of Carker's fastening

the Cathedral clock striking twelve] The church of Notre-Dame in Dijon is reputed to be 'one of the most perfect models of Gothic architecture in Europe'. The church, which was built in the thirteenth century, has at its top the famous fourteenth-century Jacquemart chiming clock, surmounted by two iron automata of a man and a woman which strike the hours on the bell. The clock is said to be 'one of the earliest specimens of a regulated horological machine, which history mentions' (*Edinburgh Encyclopædia,* 1830, 742; 'The Church of Notre-Dame at Dijon', *Saturday Magazine,* 1834, 4.42).

"I say," he at length repeated,

You were to have engaged an attendant at Havre or Rouen,] Presumably, a courier, a travelling attendant hired to carry luggage, obtain passports, make arrangements for lodging and generally to see to the needs of his employer. Dickens was pleased with the couriers he employed on his two trips to Italy – characterizing Louis Roche, who accompanied him during the 1844–5 trip to Italy and the 1846 trip to Switzerland, as 'my gem of couriers', and Edward, the courier for the 1853 trip to Italy, as 'a very steady fellow', though 'a little too bashful' and with a 'painfully defective' knowledge of Italian (*Letters* 4.326, 7.206).

Edith Dombey would have taken a steamboat from Brighton or Southampton to Le Havre – 'the port of the Seine and of Paris, one of the most thriving maritime towns of France ... situated on the N. side of the estuary of the Seine, and [containing] 25,618 inhabitants [in 1844]' – and continued to follow the course of the Seine to Rouen, one of the main manufacturing towns in France, and then to Paris and finally to Dijon. Alternative routes between England and France were: Dover to Calais; Newhaven to Dieppe; Margate to Ostend; and by steam packet from the port of London to Calais and Boulogne (*A Handbook for Travellers in France,* 1844, 61; Coghlan, *A Guide to France, or, Travellers their Own Commissioners,* 1829).

Mid-nineteenth century travellers could choose between several different types of land transport in France: they could hire a carriage, as Mr Carker does on his return trip to Paris in chapter 55; they could take their own private carriage; they could pay to be transported in a diligence, a large unwieldly vehicle that moved slowly but was cheap; or they could travel by rail (Reichard, 1829, 24). A contemporary said of the hired carriage or *voiture*

> This mode of travelling by the voiturier is now generally adopted by travellers of the first respectability; and, where the whole voiture is engaged, differs in no respect from travelling in a private carriage, except that the right of property in the horses and carriage is but temporary, and the coachman does

not wear a livery. I am acquainted with persons, who would not choose to be considered otherwise than as persons of distinction, who have travelled in this way. ... In France and Italy there are but few stage-coaches, and no good ones but between the towns on the Channel and Paris. The post-houses furnish no carriages, but horses only. ('Four Years in France', qtd. in *The New Monthly Magazine and Literary Journal*, 269 –70)

"Hard, unrelenting terms they

they ... make the present more delicious ... Sicily shall be the place of our retreat. In the idlest and easiest part of the world,] Carker has in mind the Italian phrase used by Lady Blessington and often by the English when talking about Italy, *dolce far' niente*, usually translated as 'delicious idleness' or 'sweet it is to do nothing'; see, for example, 'It is true that we hear at times, from the Italians, of the *dolce far' niente,* or the delight of having nothing to do' (*Museum of Foreign Literature*, 1829, 14.151). In the 1840s, Sicily was a part of the kingdom of the Two Sicilies, which included the kingdom of Naples. Sicilians, like Italians more generally, were frequently figured as indolent (for Dickens's opinion of southern Italy, see note to chapter 61, p. 524). In 1836, Mariana Starke noted this prejudice in her description of the citizens of Palermo, who, she said, 'stand accused of being very idle' (420). Lady Blessington, on the other hand, rejoiced in the repose induced by the climate:

> Who that has seen Naples can wonder that her children are idle, and luxuriously disposed? To gaze on the cloudless sky and blue Mediterranean, in an atmosphere so pure and balmy, is enough to make the veriest plodder ... abandon his toil. ... Men, women, and children, all appear to feel the influence of the delicious atmosphere in which they live; an atmosphere that seems to exclude care and sorrow. ... It engenders a dreamy sort of reverie, during which, the book or the pen is often thrown down, and the *dolce far' niente* is indulged in even by those who, in their native land, have never known its effeminate pleasure. Italy is the country to which a person borne down by care, or overworked by business, should resort. Its climate will serve as an anodyne to induce the required repose. ... To live, is here so positive an enjoyment, that the usual motives and incentives to study and usefulness are forgotten. (*The Idler in Italy*, 1839, 2.194, 243–4)

"And calculated on it," she rejoined,

I suffered myself to be sold, as infamously as any woman with a halter round her neck is sold in any market-place.] The public sale of wives was a traditional method of divorce among the rural working-class. A French prisoner of war in England described having seen such a ceremony in Derbyshire and quotes an account of another divorce at Canterbury in 1814:

A husband, dissatisfied, wishes to be divorced; there are proofs of the misconduct of his wife, they are both agreed; they both present themselves, on a market day in the public square. The husband leads his wife by a cord tied around her neck, and then fastens her to the place where cattle are sold, and there he publicly sells her before witnesses. When the price is determined upon, and it seldom exceeds a few shillings, the purchaser unbinds the woman, leads her tied in the same manner, holding by the end of the cord, and he does not untie her until they have paraded over nearly half the square.

I have seen one of these auctions at Ashburn in Derbyshire, and have been an eyewitness of the circumstances I relate. These sales are very common in every part of England; the purchaser, always a widower or single man, is generally a lover of the commodity sold, and is well acquainted with it. She is only brought into the market place for the sake of form. The wife thus purchased, becomes the lawful wife of the buyer. ...

Besides my evidence of the fact which I assert, I can cite authorities which can remove every doubt: I mean the public papers. The editor of one of these periodical papers, in the number of February 18, 1814, thus expresses himself:

"A scene of a disgusting and very reprehensible nature, although authorized by custom, took place on Wednesday morning, in the castle market at Canterbury. A postillion, named Samuel Wallis, led his wife to the marketplace, having tied a halter around her neck, and fastened her to the posts which are used for that purpose for cattle. She was then offered by him at public auction. Another postillion, according to a previous agreement between them, presented himself, and bought the wife thus exposed for sale, for a gallon of beer and a shilling, in presence of a large number of spectators. The seller had been married six months to this woman, who is only nineteen years old." (Pillet, 1818, 181–4)

He watched her closely

she stood before him in the very triumph of her indignant beauty. She was resolute ... undauntable; with no more fear of him, than of a worm.] Browne's illustration of the scene, 'Mr. Carker in his hour of triumph', visually echoes the theme of Judith slaying Holofernes, the biblical story suggested by Edith's pose and in the large painting behind her. Judith, the heroine of the apocryphal book of Judith, used her beauty to rescue the Hebrew people from the revenge of Nebuchadnezzar's Assyrian army. She enticed Holofernes, leader of the army, into a private meeting and, once he was drunk, beheaded him in two strokes, concealing his head in her maid's sack. Upon learning of the death of their leader, the Assyrian troops panicked and were routed by the Bethulians and Israelites. It was during the nineteenth century – in works like Friedrich Hebbel's tragedy *Judith* (1840) and in paintings by Vernet – that the sexual implications of the story became noticed (Steig, 1978, 104–05; Jeffrey, 1992, 423–4). In *LD*, it is Mrs Merdle who evokes Judith (21).

On 21 December 1847, Dickens wrote Forster about a letter from his friend, Lord

Jeffrey, the judge and literary critic:

> Note from Jeffrey this morning, who won't believe (positively refuses) that Edith is Carker's mistress. What do you think of a kind of inverted Maid's Tragedy, and a tremendous scene of her undeceiving Carker, and giving him to know that she never meant that? (*Letters* 5.211)

The allusion is to Beaumont and Fletcher, *The Maid's Tragedy* (1619), though Dickens may have been more familiar with Macready and Sheridan Knowles's adaptation, *The Bridal*, which he saw on 26 June 1837. The Pilgrim editors point out that '*Dombey* inverts *The Maid's Tragedy* in more than one way':

> Evadne, the King's mistress, rejects her newly wedded husband from loyalty to the King; whereas Edith uses her seducer, Carker, as a means to humiliate her husband. Evadne returns to her husband after stabbing her royal paramour; whereas Edith chooses to live, though her husband is "dead" to her. Evadne is rejected and kills herself; Aspatia, the "Maid", is more honourably betrayed, but also takes her own life. *The Bridal* was similar to *The Maid's Tragedy*, but Evadne kills herself from shame and Aspatia survives. (*Letters* 5.211 n. 7)

Dickens carefully considered the characterization of Edith in her last scenes, as shown in the Number Plans, his letters to Forster and his re-working the order of chapters 46–48 (see headnote to chapter 47, p. 429). As the Pilgrim editors observe, Dickens and Forster 'were well aware that the conception of Edith's intended adultery and deception of Carker was fraught with difficulty' (*Letters* 5.197, n.6). How he began to prepare for Edith's renunciation and rejection of Carker in the present chapter is evidenced in a note added to the Number Plan for chapter 46 in number 15: 'Dark indication of Edith's state of mind', a reference to the last four paragraphs of chapter 46. And in the Number Plan for number 17, Dickens notes definitively: 'Edith not his mistress'.

"All stratagems in love – "

"All stratagems in love ... The old adage – "] 'All stratagems / In love, and that the sharpest war, are lawful' (Fletcher, *The Lovers' Progress,* produced 1623; revised 1634 as *The Wandering Lovers* by Massinger, printed 1647).

"Their name is Legion," she replied,

"Their name is Legion,"] In Mark 5.2–13, Christ heals a man possessed by devils: 'For he said unto him, Come out of the man, thou unclean spirit. And he asked him, What is thy name? And he answered, saying, My name is Legion: for we are many' (8–9).

"Too late!" she cried,

"I have thrown my fame and good name to the winds! ... I'll die, and make no sign.] *2 Henry VI* 3.3.29–30:

> King Henry: He dies and makes no sign. O God, forgive him.
> Warwick: So bad a death argues a monstrous life.

Chapter 55   Eighteenth monthly number
                                                                     March 1848

ROB THE GRINDER LOSES HIS PLACE

Some other terror came

an electric shock,] See notes to chapters 36 and 52, pp. 378, 457.

like Death upon the wing.] 'Death is on the wing' was a contemporary cliché, often showing up in a Christian context; e.g. 'Death is on the wing, and the feet of those may be at the door who shall carry you out dead' (John Nelson, 'A Series of Sermons and Lectures', 1830, 29); 'Death is on the wing, and darkness covers the land' ('Romanism in Ireland', *Evangelical Christendom*, 1847, 1.62).

He raised his wicked face,

in Italy, or in Sicily, where men might be hired to assassinate him,] Italians were commonly characterized as dangerous (as well as lazy, dirty, dishonest and superstitious). In 1826, William Hazlitt complained of the English readiness 'to *dub* the Italians (without any further inquiry) a nation of assassins and banditti' (*Notes of a Journey through France and Italy*, 310). A contemporary remarked more specifically, 'There are few persons among the Calabrians, of any class, from the highest to the lowest, who are not stained with many murders' (*Calabria* 144; Brand 22).

    For most of the 1840s, the security of Sicilian roads was the responsibility of Neapolitan *gendarmes*. During the revolution of 1848, however, the *gendarmes* were driven out of power and replaced by their predecessors, the Companies at Arms, a 'body of rural police ... established in 1812, during the English occupation of Sicily' (Dennis, *A Handbook for Travellers in Sicily*, 1864, lii).

He muttered Edith's name,

bargaining for the hire of an old phaeton, to Paris.] A phaeton was a low-slung, light-weight carriage that had a high seat and a folding hood. It was elegant and expensive, and most fashionable in the late eighteenth and early nineteenth centuries (it was the favourite carriage of the Prince of Wales) (Nimrod, 1851, 55; Sparkes 121–2). For more on travel in France, see note to chapter 54, p. 468.

"No matter. Every one to

horses ordered at the Post-house?"] Travellers could privately arrange to rent fresh horses at a posting-house or inn, a fast but expensive means of travelling. A contemporary described French posting-houses (*Poste aux Chevaux*):

> There is one of this kind of inns [*sic*], at every few leagues, on all the posting roads in this country. It is situated most commonly, in a town or a village; but, in cases where there are no considerable number of houses together … you meet with the inn in a lone situation. The *Poste aux Chevaux* is where the diligence always changes horses. The words, "*Post Royale*," (royal post-house), are generally written on the sign of the house. … There is allowed to be but one inn of the kind in any town. … The *Poste aux Chevaux* is, almost in every case, the public house of best accommodation that is to be met with upon the road. (Cobbett, 1824, 91–2)

A postilion, or post-boy, would ride the left-hand side horse drawing the carriage. *A Descriptive Road-Book of France* (1829) remarked of French posting procedures:

> All the arrangements for posting are simple, and usually attended to with the most scrupulous exactness. The whole of it is completely in the hands of government. There is no competition on the road, and they who arrive first are uniformly first accommodated. (Reichard 25)

Distances were calculated 'by posts, each of which consists of two leagues, and is equal to about four English miles, and two-thirds'. The usual charge, which was paid in advance, was 'one franc and 50 cents. per post for each horse, and 15 sous to the postilion; but as the expedition of the traveller, and much of his convenience, depend on keeping the driver in good humour, it is usual to give him 30 sous'. Travellers would also have to pay any turnpike fees or road dues (Reichard 25–6).

"A thousand devils! –

"A thousand devils! – and pardons!] The French exclamation, *Mille démons!*, as used, for example, by Victor Hugo in *Bug-Jargal* (1826): ' "Mille démons!" s'écria-t-il

Death of Carker

return of Susan　　　　Toots.
　Reappearance of Uncle Sol
Florence's Marriage.

Number Plan

(Dealings with the Firm of Dombey and Son — N<u>o</u> XVIII)

Chapter LV.

Rob the Grinder loses his place.

Carker's progress –

  journey

   Death

" while others drove some dogs away, that sniffed upon the road, and ~~soap~~ soaked his blood up, with ~~it~~ a train of ashes."   Chapter LVI.

Several people delighted, and the Game chicken disgusted.

  Susan Nipper brought to Florence
   Toots.
    Marriage coming on. They going a long Voyage
     M<u>r</u> Toots in church on the last publication of the banns
      re-appearance of Old Sol
       M<u>rs</u> Mac Stinger
    chapter LVII.   The chicken. "Wy its mean"

Another Wedding.

Chapter Plan

en rugissant' (in *Œuvres Complètes de Victor Hugo*, 1837, 2.470). For *Mille pardons!* and Dickens's techniques of representing French in English dialogue, see note to chapter 54, p. 466.

The clatter and commotion echoed

Nothing clear without, and nothing clear within. Objects flitting past,]

> I had been travelling, for some days; resting very little in the night, and never in the day. The rapid and unbroken succession of novelties that had passed before me, came back like half-formed dreams; and a crowd of objects wandered in the greatest confusion through my mind, as I travelled on, by a solitary road. At intervals, some one among them would stop, as it were, in its restless flitting to and fro, and enable me to look at it, quite steadily, and behold it in full distinctness. After a few moments, it would dissolve, like a view in a magic-lantern; and while I saw some part of it quite plainly, and some faintly, and some not at all, would show me another of the many places I had lately seen, lingering behind it, and coming through it. This was no sooner visible than, in its turn, it melted into something else. ('An Italian Dream', *PI*)

the distant Jura,] About 60 miles southeast of Dijon, the Jura Mountains in eastern France and northwest Switzerland form part of the Alpine system. They extend for 225 miles from the River Rhine at Basel to the River Rhône, with the highest peaks (about 5600 feet) being in the south, near Geneva.

The lamps, gleaming on the medley

Hi! away at a gallop over the black landscape;] The illustration of the scene, 'On the dark Road', marks Browne's first use in Dickens of the so-called 'dark plate', which added mechanically ruled and closely spaced lines to the steel plate to produce a grayish shading or 'tint' (Steig, 1978, 106).

And now the stars faded,

to the taper tips of the extinguishers upon the turrets.] In other words, the turrets resemble conical-shaped extinguishers (cf. 'extinguisher-topped towers' in *TTC* 2.9).

It was a vision of long

It was a vision of long roads; that stretched away to an horizon, always receding

and never gained; of ill-paved towns, up hill and down, where faces came to dark doors and ill-glazed windows ... again of long, long roads, dragging themselves out, up hill and down, to the treacherous horizon.]

> It has been the custom of the English, who traverse France on their way to Italy or Switzerland, to complain of the tiresome and monotonous features of the country, and to ridicule the epithet "*La Belle* France," ... (*A Handbook for Travellers in France*, 1844, xxxiii)

Some of the least attractive parts of France were said to be along 'the routes between Calais and Paris, and thence to Lyons, Strasburg, and Dijon': 'To this district, and to a large part of the province of Champagne, the descriptions of "wearisome expanses of tillage, unvaried by hill or dale, and extent of corn-land or pasture, without enclosures, supremely tiresome," are almost exclusively applicable' (*A Handbook for Travellers in France,* 1844, xxxiv). The *Handbook* lists two alternate routes to Paris from Dijon: by way of Troyes and by way of Sens and Tonnerre (the latter route was four miles shorter). Although some of the towns are described as 'picturesque' and 'neat', several others are criticized – such as Montbard (an 'unimportant and dirty town') and Tonnerre ('an old and dull town') (529).

Of morning, noon, and sunset;

among a host of beggars – blind men with quivering eyelids, led by old women holding candles to their faces; idiot girls; the lame, the epileptic, and the palsied – of passing through the clamour, and looking from his seat at the upturned countenances and outstretched hands,] On his journey through France in 1844, Dickens remarked, 'Beggars innumerable there are, everywhere; but an extraordinarily scanty population' (*PI*, 'Going Through France'). The beggars in the countryside also struck Thomas Raffles, who contrasted the rural poverty with the 'air of life and gaiety' he found in Dijon:

> We have seen many beggars on the road, but certainly not so many as I expected, and by no means so many as besiege the traveller in Ireland; such as there are, are chiefly old men and children. The most troublesome fellows are the boys, who surround you whenever you leave your carriage or your inn, each eager to become your guide, to the cathedral, or other objects of curiosity in the place, which they run over with great rapidity. Whether you wish for their assistance or not, they continue to pursue you, and it is almost impossible to get a walk in any direction through a town, without some of these pests at your heels. ('Letters during a Tour of France ... in 1817', 1833, 410)

The support of the poor in the countryside was 'somewhat precarious': 'In large towns there are hospitals for the sick and aged poor, and these are chiefly supported by a toll laid on all provisions entering the town. But in the country places there are no such asylums, and the support of the indigent is less certain' (Raffles 410).

A troubled vision, then,

interminable streets ... great crowds of people,]

> THE BOULEVARDS ... form two grand divisions, called the *Boulevard du Nord* and the *Boulevard du Midi*. The former is 5,067 yards in length, and is subdivided into 12 parts. ... The *Boulevard du Midi* is 16,100 yards in length, and is divided into seven parts. ... The northern boulevards are the pride and glory of Paris. ... Their spacious extent, the dazzling beauty, the more than luxury, of the shops, the restaurants, the cafes, that are to be found on or near them ... the crowds of well-dressed persons who frequent them ... the sounds of music; the incessant roll of carriages; all this forms a medley of sights and sounds not a little perplexing, though anything but unpleasing to the eye and ear of the visitor who perambulates them, for the first time, on a fine evening. (*Galignani's New Paris Guide*, 1845, 123)

soldiers ... military drums,] According to one observer, visitors to Paris will discover before long

> that the military spirit is one of the most striking characteristics of the French people. It predominates over every other form of life in the picturesque capital of France. The population may be said to rise to the sound of the *reveille* as in a great camp, and the drums beat the evening "tattoo" in every part of the city. At night, as the solitary passenger proceeds to his home, he meets patrols of the municipal guard, or is perhaps challenged by sentinels on duty at the different posts. (*Penny Cyclopædia*, 1844, 13.265)

Of sunset once again,

coming down into a harbour ... and of being at last again in England. ... he remembered a certain station on the railway, where he would have to branch off to his place of destination,] In chapter 54, Carker tells Edith that 'You were to have engaged an attendant at Havre or Rouen'. Dickens does not specify Carker's journey to and from France, however (for the many routes, see note to chapter 54, p. 468). The fact that, once he is in England and on the train to London, Carker has 'to branch off to his place of destination' and that he is dreaming of 'going down into a remote country place he knew' suggests that he might be on the South-eastern Railway from Dover to London and that his 'place of destination' might be in Kent. By 1849, the South-eastern Railway had branch lines from London to Greenwich, Tonbridge to Tunbridge Wells, Paddock Wood to Maidstone, Canterbury to Whitstable, Ashford to Ramsgate and Margate, and Minster to Deal (see the list in *Thacker's Courser's*

Annual Remembrancer and Stud Book, 1849, 4). The South-eastern line was especially known for its 'circuitous' route through remote places:

> We now enter the county of Kent, and arrive at Edenbridge, thirty-one miles from London. It is called Edenbridge from the river Eden, which flows through it; and though it may be a little paradise in its way, with its couple of houses, covered with flowers, it is so completely out of the world, that one wonders what on earth was the use of making a station there. The traffic is characteristic of the spot, for the passengers who stop at this little Eden are as "few and far between" as angels' visits. We sincerely sympathise with the South Eastern Company, which in the days of the unpopularity of railways, had to carry a line into all sorts of out-of-the-way places, to avoid the suicidal opposition of the large towns, which were afraid of being ruined by that which it is now proved would have multiplied many times over their prosperity. Thus we find the South Eastern Company driven at an enormous expense to take a circuitous course, omitting important places, and making such stations as that we have just named, and Penshurst, which we now reach at a distance of six-and-thirty miles from London. (Beckett, 1846, 285)

"Very confusing, Sir. Not

"By rail, Sir? … Very confusing, Sir. … gentlemen frequently say so."] It was common to note that the railway had radically altered perceptions of space and time, and often caused travellers to feel disoriented and confused:

> What changes must now occur, in our way of looking at things, in our notions! Even the elementary concepts of time and space have begun to vacillate. Space is killed by the railways, and we are left with time alone. … Now you can travel to Orléans in four and a half hours, and it takes no longer to get to Rouen. Just imagine what will happen when the lines to Belgium and Germany are completed and connected to the railways! I feel as if the mountains and forests of all countries were advancing on Paris. Even now, I can smell the German linden trees; the North Sea's breakers are rolling against my door. (Heinrich Heine, 1843, qtd. in Schivelbusch 37)

> Economically, the railways' operation … causes distances to diminish … Lille suddenly finds itself transported to Louvres; Calais to Pontoise; le Havre to Poissy; Rouen to Sèvres or to Asnières: Reims to Pantin; Strasbourg to Meaux; Lyon to a place half-way between Melun and Corbeil; Marseilles to Nemours; Perpignan to Pithiviers; Bordeaux to Chartres or to Étampes; Nantes to Arpajon, etc. (Constantin Pecqueur, 1839, qtd. in Schivelbusch 33)

Dickens himself wrote about the disorienting effects of rail travel in 'A Narrative of Extraordinary Suffering', an article in which 'Mr. Lost' is befuddled by the complexities of railway guides and by the rapid speed of rail travel:

> But, this tremendous blow, the annihilation of time, the stupendous reversal of the natural sequence and order of things, was too much for his endurance – too much, perhaps, for the endurance of humanity. He quailed beneath it, and became insensible. (*HW*, 1851, 3.362)

Unable to rest, and irresistibly

the yet smoking cinders that were lying in its track ... dropping glowing coals;] Cinders from the funnels and furnaces of passing trains presented a fire hazard, both to passersby and to adjacent wooden structures. 'The cinders ejected from the smoke funnel of the engine', Dionysius Lardner remarked in 1850, 'are generally in a state of vivid ignition, and if they happen to fall on any combustible object, are liable to set fire to it' (345). The same year, a railway company was found guilty in Norwich 'in an action for compensation for injuries to a barn, stables and granary, by the burning cinders and coke projected from an engine passing on the Norfolk railway' ('Fire Caused by a Railway Engine' 8.7). 'With regard to ignited fuel falling from the furnaces of locomotives', *The London Journal of Arts, Sciences, and Manufactures* claimed, 'the only means known of preventing accidents which may result therefrom, is by employing an ash-pan to catch the cinders, and thereby preventing them falling to the ground', though he went on to discuss the disadvantages to this method (1846, 29.434).

A trembling of the ground,

A trembling of the ground, and quick vibration in his ears; a distant shriek; a dull light advancing, quickly changed to two red eyes, and a fierce fire, dropping glowing coals; an irresistible bearing on of a great roaring and dilating mass;]

> ... the station, where, as night comes on, the sights and sounds grow more strange and awful. Every now and then a great flaming eye makes its appearance in the distance: the gradual boom of its approach grows louder and louder; the thunder of its tread reverberates from afar; the sickly hue of the buffer light is surpassed by the red light of the furnace, as it glares below the wheels; or, the furnace-door being opened, the steam is lighted up till it looks like flame wreathing high up in the air. As the iron gullet of the monster vomits aloft red-hot masses of burning coke, the thundering, gleaming mass rushes past at some fifty or sixty, perhaps seventy, miles an hour; and as it rolls off into darkness again on the other side of the station, with its three red eyes gleaming behind, it seems to burn its way through the sable livery of night with the strength and straightness and fury of a red-hot cannon-ball. (Williams, *Our Iron Roads*, 1852, 235)

"At what time," he asked

Express comes through at four, Sir. – Don't stop."] In 1843, the average speed of express trains on the London to Dover line was 26.6 mph; in 1848, this had risen to 35.2 mph (Salt, *Railway and Commercial Information*, 1850, 213). At the time, the trip from London to Dover took 2½ hours by an express train and 4¼ hours by an ordinary train (Tuck 100).
 In 1850, Dionysius Lardner remarked that the

> causes of danger and injury are augmented to the highest conceivable degree by the express trains. These trains move with an enormous and exceptional speed. Collision becomes inevitable unless a warning be sent along the line to clear the way. Nor is it always practicable, even with the warning, to avert it. … an express train, moving at the usual rate of such trains, cannot safely pull up except within a considerable distance. … the traveler who desires to reach a distant point with speed, is seldom so well informed as to be enable to appreciate the degree of danger which must attend the attainment of his object. (201–02)

The air struck chill and

the signal-lights burning feebly in the morning, and bereft of their significance,] The variability in the brightness of signal-lights contributed to the number of fatal accidents. In 'A New Signal Light for Railways' (1841), a civil engineer proposed introducing a very powerful light and described the serious nature of the present problem:

> One of the most imperfect parts of the railway system is undoubtedly the uncertainty of the night signals, and to this it is well known many of the most fatal of the accidents which have occurred must be traced. The great object of these signal lights is, to announce that the train has reached a certain point of its course, and to forewarn the engine driver of his approach to a station, or the junction of a branch railway, so that the speed of the engine may be checked in proper time to prevent collision. The lights used for this purpose are generally exhibited at the place the approach to which they are intended to announce; but the distance at which light projected horizontally, may be seen by a person approaching in the line of its transmission is very variable according to the state of the atmosphere, which in our climate is subject to great and sudden changes, in regard to clearness and fog. … It is therefore obviously indispensable to safety that the signal-lights should be so constructed, that in all states of the weather they shall be constantly visible at the same point, and that this point shall be sufficiently distant from the station, the approach to which the signal is intended to announce, so as to allow ample time for checking the engine's speed before coming up to it; and

upon no other grounds can the confidence of the public as to their security be reasonably based. (*The Civil Engineer and Architect's Journal, Scientific and Railway Gazette*, 1841, 4.150)

He heard a shout – another –

the red eyes, bleared and dim,] An image perhaps influenced by illustrations in *George Cruikshank's Table Book* for 1845. Angus B. Reach's 'The Natural History of the Panic', contains an etching and a woodcut of a train with terrifying eyes in place of headlamps. In the etching, 'The Railway Dragon', the train which represents the monster 'Panic' is depicted with fiery eyes and breathing steam from its mouth, while devouring an Englishman's roast beef and pudding (Plate 20, p. 483). In the woodcut, a very similar-looking locomotive invades a kitchen, frightening the cook and her cat. Both images also may have influenced Mr Dombey's vision of the train as being similar to 'the remorseless monster, Death!' (20). Humphry House has speculated that the depiction of the train in this chapter is influenced by a John Leech cartoon entitled 'The Railway Juggernaut of 1845' (*Punch* 9.47) but, as Michael Steig has observed, the Leech image 'lacks the terrifying eyes, so important in Dickens's set-piece – no headlamps are shown at all' (Steig, 1971, 145–8; *Charles Dickens: An exhibition to commemorate the centenary of his death* [Victoria and Albert Museum catalogue], 1970, 64).

When the traveller who

others drove some dogs away that sniffed upon the road … soaked his blood up,] The religious imagery in the paragraphs leading up to Carker's death suggests that this reference to dogs is an echo of the death of Jezebel, who is killed by being thrown out of a window and her corpse left to be eaten by dogs:

> So they threw her down: and some of her blood was sprinkled on the wall, and on the horses. … And they went to bury her: but they found no more of her than the skull, and the feet, and the palms of her hands. … And he said, This is the word of the Lord … in the portion of Jezebel shall dogs eat the flesh of Jezebel. And the carcass of Jezebel shall be as dung upon the face of the field in the portion of Jezebel, so that they shall not say, This is Jezebel. (2 Kings 9.33–7)

Chapter 55 *Rob the Grinder loses his Place*

20 'The Railway Dragon'. From *George Cruikshank's Table-Book*, 1845

Chapter 56

SEVERAL PEOPLE DELIGHTED, AND THE GAME CHICKEN DISGUSTED

"Oh my own pretty darling

though I may not gather moss I'm not a rolling stone] 'A rolling stone gathers no moss', a proverbial saying from the mid-fourteenth century.

"He says," here Susan burst

he may not be a Solomon,"] In 1 Kings 4.30–1, King Solomon is said to have had a wisdom that 'excelled the wisdom of all the children of the east country, and all the wisdom of Egypt' and to be 'wiser than all men'.

"This, however," said Mr. Toots,

the Square at Brighton,] Probably Brunswick Square, on the west side of Brighton, characterized as 'one of the best parts of Brighton' (*Penny Cyclopædia*, 1836, 424).

"Why, aye, my lad.

Wal'r and sweetheart will be jined together in the house of bondage, as soon as the askings is over,"] See note to chapter 50, p. 453.

"And then," said the Captain

That there pretty creetur, as delicately brought up as a foreign bird,] Parrots, 'parroquets', cockatoos, 'minor-birds' and thrushes were among the birds imported from South America and Africa and sold in London, for the most part in the East End by Jewish street sellers (Mayhew, 2.48, 96, 118). Imported birds were difficult to keep because they required special accommodation and higher temperatures than native birds. An article on 'Ornamental Aviaries' explains that large aviaries should have

> wings on either side, protected by a roof, where delicate birds might retire, and where more complete shelter from rain or sunshine might be obtained

.... This apartment might be faced in glass, and have the advantage of being heated in winter to the temperature necessary for some of the foreign birds. (*Saturday Magazine*, 21 [July-December 1842]: 142)

"*Aye!" nodded the Captain.*

"**The ship as took him up ... was a China trader ... and so, the supercargo dying at Canton, ... now he's supercargo aboard another ship ... And so, you see ... the pretty creetur goes away upon the roaring main with Wal'r, on a woyage to China.**"] A supercargo is an officer aboard a merchant ship who manages the cargo and the commercial transactions of the voyage and who disposes of the cargo on its arrival at the destined port. In the China trade, British supercargoes needed to have an intimate knowledge of the goods being bought and sold, and they were also required to be diplomats in order to negotiate with local rulers and settle disputes. The job was demanding but well rewarded as the supercargoes were allowed to invest money on their own account. Although British trading contacts with China began in 1637, China remained closed to significant British influence and trade until the Opium War of 1840–2, which forced on China a system of treaties that guaranteed foreign access to major Chinese cities, set aside residential areas for private business interests and transformed China into what a modern historian has called 'an uncolonized extension of [the British] Empire' (Osterhammel 146–54; R. B. Forbes, *Remarks on China and the China Trade*, 1844, *passim*; Patrick Conner, *The China Trade 1600–1860*, 1982, *passim*).

"*What then?" said the Captain.*

Them as should have loved and fended of her, treated of her like the beasts as perish.] An allusion to Psalm 49, and its warning against pride:

> They that trust in their wealth, and boast themselves in the multitude of their riches. ... Their inward thought is, that their houses shall continue for ever, and their dwelling places to all generations; they call their lands after their own names. Nevertheless man being in honour abideth not: he is like the beasts that perish. ... Like sheep they are laid in the grave; death shall feed on them; and the upright shall have dominion over them in the morning. ... Man that is in honour, and understandeth not, is like the beasts that perish. (6–20)

"*Miss Dombey being so inexpressibly*

to see what o'clock it is by the Royal Exchange.] The 'excellent' clock on the clock-tower on the south or Cornhill side of the third (or New) Royal Exchange

(Thornbury 1.501, 503). For more on the third Royal Exchange, see note to chapter 4, p. 55.

The honest Captain, with his

Leadenhall Market,] See note to chapter 39, p. 394.

Limited and plain as

Limited and plain as Florence's wardrobe was – what a contrast to that prepared for the last marriage in which she had taken part! – there was a good deal to do in getting it ready, and Susan Nipper worked away at her side, all day, with the concentrated zeal of fifty sempstresses.] What was known as the 'bridal wardrobe' or *trousseau* essentially comprised underclothes, dresses and household linen, but depending on the wealth and rank of the bride's family, it could include entire outfits for day and evening, jewellery, furniture and even carriages. Although it was usual in the 1830s and 1840s for some of the *trousseau* to be sewn by maids, the bride herself, her mother and sisters, there were also specialists in ladies' under-linen from whom brides ordered their *trousseaux*, or bought them ready-made (see note to chapter 49, p. 447).

In *The Diary of a Désennuyée* (1836), the fashionable novelist Mrs Gore describes the emotions involved in assembling the *trousseau* of a beautiful heiress:

> "As if I had not derived sufficient mortification during the last ten days before I left London, from witnessing the preparations for Lady Alicia Spottiswoode's *trousseau*; jewellers, mantua-makers, milliners, *lingeres,* whichever way one turned, nothing was to be heard of but the wedding-clothes of the Duchess of Merioneth. One would suppose no one had ever been married before!" ('August 29th')

The *Ladies' Book of Etiquette and Manual of Politeness* (1872) advised middle-class brides,

> In preparing a bridal outfit, it is best to furnish the wardrobe for at least two years, in under-clothes, and one year in dresses, though the bonnet and cloak, suitable for the coming season, are all that are necessary, as the fashions ... change so rapidly. ... If you are going to travel, have a neat dress and cloak of some plain color, and a close bonnet and veil. Avoid, as intensely vulgar, any display of your position as a *bride*, whilst traveling. (Hartley 259)

Walter was busy and

Chapter 56 *Several People delighted, and the Game Chicken disgusted*

Oh wandering heart at rest!] An image predominantly used by Christian writers from the seventeenth century; compare, for example, John Donne, Lent Sermon: 'Except the Lord of heaven fix our resolutions … we have *cor vagum,* a various, a wandering heart' (cited in *The Works of John Donne,* ed. Henry Alford, 1839, 5.443).

Oh! Well might Mr. Toots leave

to take a little turn to Aldgate Pump and back!] Aldgate Pump, located at the junction of Aldgate High Street with Leadenhall Street and Fenchurch Street, marks the east end of the City of London. 'The water from Aldgate pump long enjoyed great local celebrity', Henry Wheatly observed in 1891, 'but being found by chemical analysis to be impure, the pump was closed by authority in 1876' (1.29).

"Florence, love, the lading

Shall we … stay in Kent until we go on board at Gravesend] Outward bound ships stopped at Gravesend, on the south bank of the River Thames, about 22 miles from London Bridge, to complete their cargoes and to clear Customs. Because of its ease of access by rail or river steamer, and because of its 'salubrious air and cheap living', Gravesend had 'become a sort of watering-place for the London citizens, and on Sundays in summer the place is literally overrun with swarms of Londoners who come down in the morning and return in the evening' (*Handbook for Travellers in Kent* 18). Indeed, in April 1836, Dickens spent his honeymoon in the village of Chalk, near Gravesend, and returned, the following February, for a four-month holiday.

Then into the quiet room

cribbage] 'Cribbage is, in all probability, the most popular English game at [*sic*] cards at the present day. It seems as if redolent of English comfort, a snug fireside, a Welsh-rabbit, and a little mulled something simmering on the hob' (Chambers, 1832, 2.779). Cribbage, which involves counting combinations that are scored by moving pegs on a special board, was invented in the 1600s by Sir John Suckling, the English poet, and derives from an earlier game know as 'Noddy'. In *OCS*, Dick Swiveller teaches the Marchioness how to play cribbage, and in *OT*, Mrs Bedwin teaches Oliver.

The Captain's visage on these

Lovely Peg,] See note to chapter 9, p. 140.

The church Walter had chosen

The church Walter had chosen for the purpose, was a mouldy old church in a yard, hemmed in by a labyrinth of back streets, and courts, with a little burying-ground round it, and itself buried in a kind of vault, formed by the neighbouring houses, and paved with echoing stones. ... But so far was this City church from languishing for the company of other churches, that spires were clustered round it, as the masts of shipping cluster on the river. It would have been hard to count them from its steeple-top, there were so many. ... In almost every yard and blind-place near, there was a church. ... There were twenty churches close together, clamouring for people to come in.] This would seem to be the Church of St Helen's (now St Helen's Bishopsgate), identified in chapter 46 (see note, p. 428). The square mile of the City of London contains the greatest concentration of churches in Britain: after the rebuilding programme that followed the Great Fire of London in 1666, there were around 75 churches, 51 of them designed by Sir Christopher Wren. The text describes the view looking south from St Helen's towards the Thames, a view taking in between twenty and thirty churches and their steeples (Knight, 1851, 5.177–208).

In his essay, 'City of London Churches', Dickens remarks on the deserted City churches:

> There are few more striking indications of the changes of manners and customs that two or three hundred years have brought about, than these deserted Churches. Many of them are handsome and costly structures, several of them were designed by WREN, many of them arose from the ashes of the great fire, others of them outlived the plague and the fire too, to die a slow death in these later days. No one can be sure of the coming time; but it is not too much to say of it that it has no sign in its outsetting tides, of the reflux to these churches of their congregation and uses. They remain, like tombs of the old citizens who lie beneath them and around them, Monuments of another age. (*AYR* 3.89)

The two stray sheep in question

The two stray sheep were penned by a Beadle in a commodious pew,] The Beadle, as the peace officer of the parish, kept order in the church and the churchyard during Divine Service, and would sometimes perform the role of verger, ushering church-goers to their seats and opening pew doors for them when they went to take the sacrament (Blunt, 1876, 295).

a shabby little old man in the porch behind the screen who was ringing the same, like the Bull in Cock Robin, with his foot in a stirrup.] The bell-ringer, who is using a stirrup – 'a separate loop of rope, or leather, attachable to the end of

Chapter 56 *Several People delighted, and the Game Chicken disgusted*

the rope for chiming with the foot' (*OED*) – to ring the bells, is compared to the bull who 'tolled the Bell, / For poor Cock Robin's funeral knell' in 'Who Killed Cock Robin?':

> "Who'll toll the bell?"
> "I," said the bull,
> "Because I can pull,
> I'll toll the bell." (*Tom Thumb's Pretty Song Book, c.* 1744)

Dickens's description seems to derive from an early nineteenth-century illustration to the nursery rhyme (Plate 21).

21   'The Bell-Toller', from *Courtship, and Marriage, of Cock Robin and Jenny Wren, c.* 1825

Mr. Toots, however, appearing

pew-opener] See notes to chapter 5, p. 84 and chapter 31, p. 332.

Walter Gay and Florence Dombey were read aloud as being in the third and last stage of that association,]

> And when the banns are published, it shall be in the following form: – I publish the Banns of Marriage between M. of —, and N. of —. If any of you know cause or just impediment, why these two persons should not be joined

together in holy matrimony, ye are to declare it. [This is the first, second, or third time of asking.] ('The Form of Solemnization of Matrimony', *BCP*, 1662 version).

Miss Nipper, feeling that the eyes

a free seat in the aisle,] See note to chapter 5, p. 86.

two elderly females who were in the habit of receiving their portion of a weekly dole of bread then set forth on a shelf in the porch.] Traditionally, wealthy parishioners would make a charitable bequest that a dole of bread be distributed (weekly, on certain dates, or annually) to the poor, or wayfarers, or those who lived in the parish almshouses.

to appear, like the conjuror's figure, where he was least expected] An allusion to Prospero's 'tricksy spirit', Ariel, who makes many sudden, surprising and often invisible appearances in *The Tempest*. For 'tricksy spirit', see note to chapter 39, p. 395.

"His wery woice," said the

lay to, my lad, upon your own wines and fig-trees, like a taut ould patriark as you are,] In the 'last days' described in Micah 4.4: ' ... they shall sit every man under his vine and under his fig tree; and none shall make them afraid; for the mouth of the Lord of hosts hath spoken it'. Patriarch – the father of a church or rite – is a Christian term of respect applied in the Old Testament to the chiefs of the tribes of Israel and, in the New Testament, to Abraham and David as well as to the bishops in Rome, Constantinople, Alexandria, Antioch and Jerusalem.

'Tis *the* woice ... of the sluggard, I heerd him com-plain, you have woke me too soon, I must slumber again. Scatter his ene-mies, and make 'em fall!"] A conflation of two quotations. The first is from Isaac Watts's song, 'The Sluggard' (*Divine and Moral Songs for Children*, 1720): ' 'Tis the voice of the sluggard; I heard him complain, / "You have wak'd me too soon, I must slumber again" '. The second is from the British national anthem, 'God Save the King [Queen]', the first recorded performance of which was in 1745: 'O Lord our God arise, / Scatter his enemies, / And make them fall'. For another allusion to 'The Sluggard', see note to chapter 25, p. 294.

"Lost to sight, to memory dear,"

"Lost to sight, to memory dear,"] See note to chapter 48, p. 438.

Chapter 56 *Several People delighted, and the Game Chicken disgusted*

"Hear him!" cried the Captain

" 'Tis woman as seduces all mankind. For which … you'll overhaul your Adam and Eve,] Captain Cuttle connects the story of Eve's tempting Adam in Genesis 3 with a ballad sung by Filch from John Gay's *The Beggar's Opera* (1728):

> 'Tis Woman that seduces all Mankind,
> By her we first were taught the wheedling arts:
> Her very eyes can cheat; when most she's kind,
> She tricks us of our money with our hearts. (1.2)

"Sol Gills! The observation

The observation as I'm a-going to make is calc'lated to blow every stitch of sail … clean out of the bolt-ropes, and bring you on your beam ends with a lurch.] A bolt-rope is sewed all around the edge of the sail. A ship 'on her beam ends' is in danger of capsizing, as she is heeled so far to one side that the deck is almost vertical (Smyth, *Sailor's Word-book*).

Mariner, of England, as lives at home at ease, and doth improve each shining hour!"] A conflation of Thomas Campbell, 'Ye Mariners of England, A Naval Ode' (1801; *The Complete Poetical Works*, 1907) (e.g. 'Ye Mariners of England / That guard our native seas' [st. 1]) with Isaac Watts, 'Against Idleness and Mischief', in *Divine Songs for Children* (1715):

> How doth the little busy bee
>   Improve each shining hour,
> And gather honey all the day
>   From every op'ning flow'r! (st. 1; *The Works*, 1810)

"Bless your heart, Wal'r,"

her angry passions rise –] From Isaac Watts, 'Against Quarrelling and Fighting', *Divine Songs for Children* (1715):

> But, children, you should never let
> Such angry passions rise;
> Your little hands were never made
> To tear each other's eyes. (st. 2, *The Works*, 1810)

Mr. Toots was accompanied by

he was more demonstrative of aggressive intentions ... than comported with a professor of the peaceful art of self-defence.] Prizefighters had a reputation for brutality. Jon Bee complained in 1823 that the popular press had 'wittingly suppressed ... the various domestic offenses of the rougher boxers'. He explained how one prizefighter, Tom Hickman, 'brutally broke the back of Davis's dog, and committed the more brutal practice of misbehaving to his wife'. In fact, it was commonly believed that Hickman's thrashing of an old man had caused the death of the Master of Ceremonies of the Fives Court, Old Joe Norton. Another prizefighter, John Kendrick, was charged with committing a violent assault and, still another, John Crockery, was convicted of highway robbery and transported for life (Ford, 1971, 63). Despite the claims of such writers as Pierce Egan, who praised the 'good effects' of the 'manly spirit' associated with boxing, and George Borrow, who insisted that 'prizefighters and pugilists are seldom friends to brutality and oppression', they had little social standing and, in the words of a modern historian, 'were generally looked down upon as blackguards by the upper and middle classes' (Ford, 1971, 60). For more on the positive associations of prizefighting, see note to chapter 44, p. 420.

"Come Master," said the Chicken.

"Is it to be gammon] 'Gammon' as defined by *Grose's Classical Dic-tionary of the Vulgar Tongue*, means 'Any assertion which is not strictly true, or professions believed to be insincere; as, I believe you're *gammoning*, or, that's all *gammon*, meaning, you are no doubt jesting with me, or, that's all a farce' (Egan, 1823, n.p.).

"It is," said the Chicken,

blow on this here match to the stiff 'un;"] In other words, to tell Mr Dombey about the match. 'To blow' means to expose or inform. A 'stiff 'un' is a slang term for a corpse, a word used by undertakers (Hotten, 1865, 77, 246).

all the kit of 'em] 'The whole kit of 'em' is a slang phrase for 'the entire lot' (Hotten, 1865, 167).

"My sentiments is Game and Fancy,

"My sentiments is Game and Fancy,] The Chicken is saying that his sentiments are 'game' – they are full of pluck and courage. 'The Fancy' was an early-nineteenth century slang term for pugilism, and he presumably means someone with the heart and spirit of a boxer.

I'm to be heerd on at the bar of the Little Helephant,] Presumably, the well known public house in south London, the Elephant and Castle (see note to chapter 12, p. 171).

Chapter 57

ANOTHER WEDDING

Mr. Sownds the Beadle,

Mr. Sownds the Beadle, and Mrs. Miff the pew-opener,] For the offices of beadle and pew-opener, see note to chapter 5, p. 86; for the beadle's role at inquests, see note to chapter 50, p. 450; and in church, see note to chapter 56, p. 488; for the pew-opener at weddings, see note to chapter 31, p. 332.

A yellow-faced old gentleman from India] Although a yellow complexion was recognised as a symptom of many illnesses and diseases – including cancer, yellow fever and jaundice – it was biliousness (*bile mal elaboré*, or 'liverishness') that was associated with soldiers and civilians who had been in India, and the cause was generally understood to be an habitual over-indulgence in alcohol. In *Vivian Grey* (1827), Disraeli facetiously describes the symptoms of a man about to fight a duel: 'You have no appetite for dinner. ... You pass a restless night, and rise in the morning as bilious as a Bengal general' (2.5). In *Vanity Fair* (1848), Dobbin has a yellow complexion as a result of having caught yellow fever in the West Indies (ch. 5), and in *Henry Esmond* (1852), Esmond's frequently remarked upon 'yellow countenance' is caused by smallpox (chs 7, 9).

the yellow-faced old gentleman could pave the road to church with diamonds and hardly miss them.] In 1817, James Mill remarked on the conventional view that vast fortunes could be made in India, referring to 'The officers, who, along with the rest of their countrymen, had formed unbounded notions of the wealth of India, and whose imaginations naturally exaggerated the fortunes which were making in the civil branch of the service ...' (*The History of British India* 2.250). A mid-nineteenth century account provides details:

> No fewer than 10,000 British officers, of the higher grade, are to be numbered in the civil and military service of the Government [of India], whose incomes range from 200*l.* to 25,000*l.* a year. All these are well-born and educated men, of the middle classes, who find an honourable provision out of the resources of India. The total sum they draw yearly cannot be less than six or seven million sterling. ('The English in India', 1857, 112).

Men who made large fortunes in British India were referred to as 'nabobs', a word coined in the middle of the eighteenth century (*OED*).

The nuptial benediction is to be a superior one, proceeding from a very reverend, a dean,] The style 'Very Reverend' distinguishes a Dean, a priest (usually the rector of the parish) who has a role in church government. The Dean is the chief cleric of a

General Mems:

The birth of Florence's child, and her relenting towards her father.

The scene in his ~~study~~ own room "Let him remember it in that room, years to come!"

Bunsby proceeding to Church, the slave of Mrs Mac Stinger. His marriage procession. Captain exhorts him to sheer off, but he proceds to church in a state of stupefaction.

Alice and her mother ✓

Edith – qy Edith and Florence – certainly, Edith and Cousin Feenix. Yes. All Three

Mr Toots and Susan. Married. Toots grown fat. ✓

Miss Tox. ~~Mr~~ Mrs Chick. The Major. The Native.

Mrs Pipchin ✓

The Toodles, and Rob the Grinder. ✓

The Blimber Family and Mr Feeder B.A. ~~and~~ Cornelia united to Mr Feeder B.A. ✓

~~qy The Barnet Skettleses~~ – Miss Pankey – ✓

Master Bitherstone. ✓

Mr Morfin, Harriet Carker, and John Carker

qy Order of chapters –

Number Plan

(Dealings with the Firm of Dombey and Son — N°s XIX & XX.)

Chapter LVIII.

after a lapse.

House fallen and, Mr Dombey ruined

Introduce Mr Morfin, & Harriet, & their inheritance – the brother having died intestate.

Alice – repentance and death.
chapter LIX.

Retribution

Progress of Mr Dombey's ruin.

The house is a ruin, and the rats fly from it
Servants go
Sale & clearance of the whole place
Mrs Pipchin goes
Truth of Miss Tox – Verge of suicide – Florence
chapter LX.

Chiefly Matrimonial.

Toots married to Susan
Mr Feeder B.A. married to Cordelia
Bunsby married to Mrs Mac Stinger

"Susan my dear, don't exert yourself. Remember the medical man!"

open with Blimber's – lead to Bunsby, through the Captain, & end with Susan and Florence. Susan's dress.

Chapter LXI.

Relenting

Cousin Feenix taking Edith abroad, to live with him
Mr Dombey in his illness and danger – Florence & Mrs Toots attending him.
Cousin Feenix comes to beg Florence to go somewhere with him – don't say where – takes her to the house in Brook Street
Edith there. The Scene between them. Edith softened – Writes the truth, & gives it her. Their parting; never to meet again Chapter LXII.

The last bottle of Final the old Madeira
General sketch of Mr Dombey's recovery– Progress of the Fortunes of Walter and Florence –and their xxx/ life
His devotion to her little child as it grows, –as if it were another Paul, acting on his better nature– The general deference to him –
The last bottle of the old Madeira drunk

End with the sea – carrying through, what the waves were always saying, and the invisible country far away.

Chapter Plan

cathedral and responsible for the cathedral fabric and the day-to-day management and finance. Anglican priests, who are either rectors or vicars, are styled 'The Reverend'.

somebody who comes express from the Horse Guards.] Located in Whitehall, the Horse Guards is a guard-house and public building used as a barracks for the elite mounted troops of the British Army. It was where the Secretary of War, the Commander-in-Chief, the Adjutant-General and the Quartermaster-General had their offices until 1872. The Horse Guards was constructed by John Vardy in 1751–3, from a design provided by William Kent. 'The Horse Guards' also refers to the cavalry brigade of the English Household Troops, specifically the third regiment of this body, which performs cermonial duties.

Mrs. Miff is more intolerant

free sittings.] See note to chapter 5, p. 84.

Mrs. Miff is not a student of political economy (she thinks the science is connected with dissenters; "Baptists or Wesleyans, or some o' them," she says), but she can never understand what business your common folks have to be married.] So called 'classical' political economy grew out of the Scottish Enlightenment of the eighteenth century, especially the writings of Adam Ferguson, David Hume, and, most importantly, Adam Smith, and was developed in the early nineteenth century by David Ricardo. In *Wealth of Nations* (1776), Smith argued that national prosperity derived from the unimpeded functioning of markets, which satisfied the needs of both the individual and the larger community (Calhoun).

Mrs Miff is particularly alluding to the theories of Thomas Robert Malthus (1766–1834), the political economist whose *An Essay on the Principle of Population* (1798; rev. 1803) strengthened the arguments of those who wanted to reform the Old Poor Law. In *An Essay*, Malthus argued that poor relief was counterproductive: it encouraged marriage among the poor, and thus increased the number of children on poor relief:

> A poor man may marry with little or no prospect of being able to support a family without parish assistance. They may be said, therefore, to create the poor which they maintain; and as the provisions of the country must, in consequence of the increased population, be distributed to every man in small proportions, it is evident that the labour of those who are not supported by parish assistance, will purchase a smaller quantity of provisions than before, and consequently more of them must be driven to apply for assistance. (3.365)

For more on Malthus, see note to chapter 47, p. 430.

Mr. Sownds the Beadle is

Chapter 56 *Several People delighted, and the Game Chicken disgusted*

We must have our national schools] These elementary schools were intended for the working class and were the main source of their formal education. A contemporary explains that the term 'National Schools' comprehended 'a great number of schools, both new and old, conducted under what is termed the National System. This system originated in the efforts of various district societies, in different parts of the kingdom, to apply the principles of Dr. [Andrew] Bell, of Madras, to the government of the existing parochial free schools'. National Schools were operated by the National Society for Promoting Education of the Poor in the Principles of the Established Church throughout England and Wales, which was established in 1811 by sponsors from the Church of England, and which was intended as a rival to the Royal Lancastrian Society (established in 1808 by dissenters and renamed the British and Foreign Schools Society in 1814). Both the Established 'national schools' and their dissenting counterparts relied on the monitorial system, under which older students, referred to as 'monitors', taught younger students a mixture of religious instruction, singing and basic literary skills. Besides the use of monitors, the chief characteristics of National Schools were 'the use of church catechism and attendance on [*sic*] church worship by the children'. By 1832, there were about 12,000 'national' schools (McCulloch, 1847, 313; *Encyclopedia of the Victorian Era*, 2004, 1.243–4).

we must have our standing armies.] Throughout most of British history, the standing army (as opposed to the militia, or regional volunteer armed forces) has been associated with despotism. In 1639–41, for instance, Parliament refused to finance an army to repel a Scots invasion, and would not give Charles I control of an army to suppress an Irish rebellion. The British prejudice against standing armies was reinforced, in some quarters, by Cromwell's New Model Army and its subjugation of Scotland and Ireland following the English Civil War. After 1689, the Declaration of Rights established that a standing army was illegal without Parliament's approval and, in fact, large standing armies became less necessary in Great Britain following the Act of Union with Scotland in 1707 and the subsequent defeat of Jacobite rebellions. The British military tended to rely, instead, on a small force to keep order at home, garrisons for overseas possessions and small forces to contribute to European wars. A writer in 1840 remarked on 'the instinctive hatred of the English people to a standing army', and in 1849, *Blackwood's Edinburgh Magazine* rehearsed the popular prejudice against standing armies:

> Standing armies, we are told, are of no earthly use in the time of peace, and their expense is obviously undeniable. If peace could be made universal and perpetual, there would be an end of standing armies. The best means for securing perpetual peace is to do away with standing armies, because without standing armies there would be no facilities for war. ('Peace and War Agitators' 584)

Blackwood's countered, however, that 'without the assistance of standing armies through-out Europe during the late critical juncture [a reference to the revolutions of 1848], anarchy would now have been triumphant, and civilisation have received

They are looking at a

you're a tidy pair!"] That is, decent, of a good sort, nice (*OED*); see, for example, the comment of a flower-seller to Henry Mayhew: ' "Parsons and doctors are often tidy customers" ' (1.133).

Her heart beats quicker now,

busy carmen] Carters or carriers (*OED*).

Youthful, and how beautiful,

a Worshipful Company who have got a Hall in the next yard, with a stained glass window in it that no mortal ever saw.] The livery companies of the City of London are individually known as 'Worshipful Company' (as in the Worshipful Company of Bakers, the Worshipful Company of Butchers, etc.). As these trade and craft associations grew more prosperous during the Middle Ages and Renaissance, they acquired splendid halls to use for meetings, to conduct business and to socialise. Access was restricted to members of the company. An example of the grandeur of livery companies' halls is the Ironmongers' Hall, which is faced in Portland stone, and has 'an elegant front', 'a large vestibule divided by six Tuscan columns'; an oval, geometrical staircase; a state-room and a stained glass window depicting 'Sir Christopher Draper, Mayor', eight times Master of the Ironmongers' Company, holding a roll of paper in one hand and his gloves in another (*Some Account of the Worshipful Company of Ironmongers*, 1851, 468–70). For more on Worshipful Companies, see note to chapter 5, p. 89.

the Master and Wardens of the Worshipful Company] Each livery company is governed by an elected court comprising a Master (or Prime Warden in some companies), an Upper Warden, Middle Warden, Lower Warden, between ten and twenty Court Assistants and a Clerk.

There is every possible provision for the accommodation of dust, except in the churchyard, where the facilities in that respect are very limited.] In 'City of London Churches' (*AYR*, 1860), Dickens complained of the smell of 'the rot and mildew and dead citizens' permeating City churches and the pervasive dust from 'the decay of dead citizens in the vaults below': 'Dead citizens stick upon the walls, and lie pulverised on the sounding-board over the clergyman's head, and, when, a gust of air comes, tumble down upon him' (3.85–9). Earlier, *HW* attacked the practice of burying the dead in and around churches in 'Heathen and Christian Burial', 1 (6 April 1850): 43–8, and 'An Enemy's Charge', 12 (20 October 1855): 265–70. In *LD*, Dickens makes a similar complaint about the danger of City churches: Arthur Clennam is said to be thinking 'of the secrets of the lonely church-vaults, where the people who had hoarded and secreted in iron coffers were in their turn similarly hoarded, not yet at rest from doing harm' (bk 2, ch. 10).

Between 1852 and 1857, Parliament passed a series of acts (collectively known as the 'Burial Acts') to regulate public burials throughout Great Britain and Ireland. One such measure, passed in 1853, at the urging of the Home Secretary, Lord Palmerston, prohibited burials within churches, despite protests that the measure was a direct attack on class distinction as well as on church tradition and profits (Ridley 407; Morley 32–40; Brooks 3, 47–50).

The Captain, Uncle Sol

A man with a wooden leg ... stumps off again, and pegs his way ... out of doors.] The 'classic peg leg', also called a 'pin leg', was the 'most simple means employed in the case of those persons who have submitted to an amputation of the leg'. The sole advantage of the peg leg was its cheapness: it was uncomfortable to wear; caused a stiff habit of walking ('stumps off again'); could easily slip on pavements; and sank into mud. Most wearers of peg legs in the early nineteenth century were old sailors and soldiers, veterans of the Napoleonic Wars. For example, in Marryat's *Jacob Faithful* (1834), 'Old Tom' Beazeley is a Trafalgar veteran with two peg legs. The peg leg here contrasts with the expensive and complicated cork leg mentioned in chapter 41: see note p. 406 (Grossmith, 1857, 22, 31; Watson, 1885, 422–3).

No gracious ray of light

The morning luminary is built out, and don't shine there.] That is, the neighbouring buildings are too close to allow in the sun. In chapter 56, the church is described as being 'buried in a kind of vault, formed by the neighbouring houses ... It was a great dim, shabby pile'.

The amens of the dusty clerk appear, like Macbeth's, to stick in his throat a little;] *Macbeth* 2.2.29–31:

> But wherefore could not I pronounce 'Amen'?
> I had most need of blessing, and 'Amen'
> Stuck in my throat.

What with the young

smiling through her tears,] An admired image from the *Iliad* 6.484 (Andromache 'smiling through her tears' as she quiets her baby whilst pleading with Hector not to depart for war). English writers adopted the image from the late eighteenth century: it was used by Charlotte Lennox in *Sophia* (1762; 1.15), then echoed by Ann Radcliffe in *The Romance of the Forest* (1791; ch. 5) and *The Mysteries of Udolpho* (1794; ch. 7). Coleridge, in his poem 'Domestic Peace' writes of 'Sorrow smiling through her tears' (*Poems*, 2nd ed., 1797).

Chapter 58 Nineteenth and twentieth monthly numbers
April 1848

AFTER A LAPSE

The year was out,

The year was out, and the great House was down.] A major shipwreck could have profound and widespread consequences. Not only might the ship and lives be lost, but also cargo, profits, jobs, mail, investment capital and insurance. As *The Monthly Review* explained in 1809:

> It happens, not unfrequently, that a shipwreck is the cause of bankruptcy; in that case, we can only blame chance. Commerce has its storms as well as the sea. The events of the world, political convulsions, war, peace, scarcity, and even plenty, bring unforeseen changes, cause sudden convulsions in commerce, and baffle the best concerted schemes. (59 [1809]: 456)

'The trader is exposed necessarily to great risks', *The Law Review* remarked, 'and risks against which he cannot by any exercise of prudence or of care protect himself. The acts of foreign powers, the legislative provisions of his own country, the measures of the executive power, the failure of correspondents and debtors at home or abroad, the seasons, the chances of fire and shipwreck, some or even all may conspire against him or involve him in ruin' (7 [February 1848]: 117).

One summer afternoon; a year,

One summer afternoon ... there was a buzz and whisper upon 'Change of a great failure.] The Royal Stock Exchange (see note to chapter 4, p. 55). The 'afternoon' is explained by the fact, that, in the words of a contemporary writing in 1837, 'our merchants have for some years past acted on the aristocratic principle of lying in bed in the morning, and postponing the transaction of business till a late hour. It is hardly thought respectable to appear on 'Change before four o'clock' (business would be finished quickly, 'a little before five') (Grant 2.97). Augustus Hare, writing later in the century, puts the peak hours slightly earlier, between 3 p.m. and 4 p.m. The Exchange was busiest on Tuesday and Friday (1878, 1.253).

The same contemporary described the characteristic 'buzz and whisper' of the Royal Exchange:

> In one place you see three or four all earnestly talking together: in another you see only two; but the conversation which is being carried on between those two may be of the most important kind. It may not only be about transactions of a very extensive nature; but it may be a conversation on the result of which the stability of some great commercial establishment hangs. You can see by the earnestness and seriousness of the parties' manner, that the matter of their conversation is of no ordinary importance. In other instances, you see twos and threes standing and conversing together in different places; but you can at once discern, from the levity of their manner, that their business, if indeed they be engaged in business matters at all, is of no very interesting kind. ... It is worthy of observation, that during the business hour – for it cannot be called hours – of the Royal Exchange, you very seldom see persons standing by themselves. You almost invariably see every body engaged with some or other of the thousands present. The topics, though almost exclusively of a commercial nature, are of necessity extremely varied. There is not a branch of commerce under heaven which has not its representative there; there is scarcely a commodity in the world which is not the daily topic of conversation on the Royal Exchange. ... [W]ere it possible to transfer to paper all the conversations which are being carried on at the same time during the busy moments there, they would certainly have the appearance of the most unintelligible jargon which ever escaped human lips. (Grant, 1837, 2.100–02)

a List of Bankrupts published,] *The London Gazette* – an official journal published twice weekly in London, Edinburgh and Dublin – contained the names of bankrupts, lists of government appointments and promotions, and other public notices. In the early nineteenth century, English law recognized two distinct means of debt collection. 'Bankruptcy', which was reserved for 'traders' or entrepreneurs, allowed the debtor to discharge his debts and escape imprisonment, provided he surrendered himself to his creditors and conformed to the requirements of the 'Acts of Bankruptcy'. 'Insolvency', which was applied to 'non-traders', usually required the imprisonment of the debtor ('non-traders' were deemed more culpable for their debts than 'traders', who, it was assumed, often suffered financial loss because of events beyond their control, such as shipwreck) (Lester 94). For more on bankruptcy, see note below and note to chapter 59, p. 503.

The world was very busy now,

The world] For this synonym for fashionable society, see note to chapter 51, p. 455.

Here was a new inducement

It was apparently the fate of Mr. Perch to be always waking up, and finding himself famous.] 'I awoke one morning and found myself famous' was Byron's response to the overnight success of *Childe Harold's Pilgrimage*, Cantos 1 and 2 (1812). The quotation from his Memoranda was first published by Thomas Moore in his *Letters and Journals of Lord Byron: with Notices of His Life*, 2 vols, 1830, 347.

moaning in his sleep, "twelve and ninepence in the pound, twelve and ninepence in the pound!"] In a case of bankruptcy, the creditors can agree to receive a percentage of the total owed them, a dividend of so much 'in the pound' (here, Perch imagines the amount will be 60%). This arrangement, a 'composition', allows the debtor a small amount of money to live on. In fact, Mr Morfin later tells Harriet that Mr Dombey has 'resolved on payment to the last farthing of his means': see notes below, pp. 503, 505–7.

Mr. Perch always closed these

a Fire Office,] A fire insurance company. The first fire insurance offices in England date from the late seventeenth century and were established in the wake of the Great Fire of London in 1666. In the early nineteenth century, most fire insurance companies also dealt with life insurance, for example: Atlas Fire and Life Assurance Company; Imperial Life and Fire Insurance Company of London; London Phoenix Fire, and Pelican Life Insurance Company (*The Treble Almanack for the Year 1832*, 15).

To Major Bagstock, the bankruptcy

their late Royal Highnesses the Dukes of Kent and York,] For the Duke of Kent, see note to chapter 31, p. 337; for the Duke of York, see note to chapter 1, p. 32; for Bagstock's name-dropping, see note to chapter 10, p. 150.

to retire to a tub and live in it ... he'd have a tub in Pall Mall to-morrow, to show his contempt for mankind!] To express his disdain for society and demonstrate his ideal of self-sufficiency, the fourth-century BC philosopher Diogenes the Cynic lived in a large tub (for more on Diogenes, see note to chapter 14, p. 200).

Pall Mall] The location of Bagstock's club (see notes to chapters 7 and 41 pp. 111, 405). Pall Mall, named after the croquet-like French game of *paille-maille*, is the fashionable avenue, about one-third of a mile long, that runs between St James's Palace and Trafalgar Square. In the eighteenth and nineteenth centuries, Pall Mall was the favourite haunt of the upper class, attracted by the many fashionable coffee-houses, clubs and fine shops that lined the spacious street. It was described in 1807 as 'a handsome street, but subject to the endless rattle of coaches, and the lounging place of strings – or rather links, or chains – of men of fashion, and their humble imitators, during the months in which London is tolerable, that is, from December to June' (Thornbury and Walford, 1873–8, 4.126).

Of all this, and many

so many apoplectic symptoms, such rollings of his head,] For Bagstock's apoplexy and chorea, see notes to chapter 20, pp. 233, 238.

Nobody's opinion stayed the misfortune,

Mr. Dombey freely resigned everything he had, and asked for no favour from any one. That any resumption of the business was out of the question, as he would listen to no friendly negotiation having that compromise in view; that he had relinquished every post of trust or distinction he had held, as a man respected among merchants;] Mr Dombey refuses a 'composition', a formal system whereby creditors could agree among themselves as to how a debtor's assets might be distributed:

> On the issuance of a bankruptcy commission and the debtor having passed his last examination, nine-tenths of the creditors in number and value could agree to accept an offer of the debtor to pay a certain amount in the pound. If accepted, a new contract came into effect. ... The debtor was then free to carry out his business, subject only to the payment agreed upon in the composition. Under a composition or a deed of arrangement, bankruptcy law now recognized that the debtor and his creditors could settle their affairs and avoid the filing of a formal bankruptcy. (Lester 36)

For more on the bankruptcy laws in England, see above, p. 500.

he was going melancholy mad,] 'Melancholy, mad' occurs several times in Robert Burton, *The Anatomy of Melancholy* (1621) and was much used by writers in the seventeenth and eighteenth centuries, including Ben Jonson, Samuel Butler and Daniel Defoe. In *HT*, the piston of a steam-engine is said to work 'monotonously up and down like the head of an elephant in a state of melancholy madness' (ch. 5).

The clerks dispersed after holding

a little dinner ... enlivened by comic singing,] This is an 'Harmonic meeting': see note to chapter 51, p. 456. Comic singers performed at theatres such as Drury Lane and Covent Garden and also in taverns. The jolly, 'Free and Easy' atmosphere that characterized an evening with comic singing is described by Pierce Egan in his account of the celebrated Queen's Arms Tavern at Margate:

> Everybody is welcome, first come, first served – there is no distinction of persons – it is all 'hail fellow, well met;' and the only acknowledged great man amongst them is the chairman, whose hammer is omnipotent. The songs, although of various descriptions, are in general excellent; and mirth and harmony are the leading features of the assembly. ... The lovers *of sentiment* come in for their share of delight – "For the love of Alice Gray." The admirers of comic singing are equally well pleased with "Okey Pokey, King of the Sandwich Islands". (Egan, 1832, 100)

Some music connoisseurs considered the comic style 'coarse and generally excessively vulgar' (*Quarterly Musical Magazine and Review*, 1827, 9.358). As a child, Dickens had a reputation for comic singing and was even considered a 'prodigy' (Forster 1.1, 1.13).

The principal slipper and dogs' collar seller,] See note to chapter 13, p. 180.

the ticket porter ... moralised good sound morality about ambition, which (he observed) was not ... made to rhyme to perdition, for nothing.] The words are rhymed by Christopher Harvey, *The Synagogue* ('The Journey') (1640): 'Envy, lust, avarice, ambition, / The crooked turnings to perdition', and by Byron, *Don Juan*, canto 16 (1824):

> Heaven, and his friends, knew that a private life
> Had ever been his sole and whole ambition;
> But could he quit his king in times of strife,
> Which threaten'd the whole country with perdition? (st. 74)

"*The extent of Mr. Dombey's resources*

Any man in his position, could, and many a man in his position would, have saved himself, by making terms ... But he is resolved on payment to the last farthing of his means. ... His pride shows well in this."] Mr Dombey's admirable decision to pay his creditors 'to the last farthing' is similar to Arthur Clennam's desire to take full moral and financial responsibility for the failure of Daniel Doyce's business in *LD* (though Clennam is an insolvent and not a bankrupt): 'his own share should revert to his partner [Doyce], as the only reparation he could make to him in money value for the distress and loss he had unhappily brought upon him ...' (bk 2, ch. 26).

vices are sometimes only virtues carried to excess!] 'Vices are virtues' was a common phrase, but this may be an echo of the sermon 'On Moderation' by Edmund Butcher in 1798: 'All our vices are virtues abused' (*Sermons for the Use of Families*, 3rd ed.,

1819, 1.353). This sentiment was quoted by Smollett in his favourable review of Butcher's *Sermons* in *Critical Review*, 1800, 28.443.

Such a look of exultation

Such a look of exultation there may be on angels' faces, when the one repentant sinner enters Heaven, among ninety-nine just men.] 'I say unto you, that likewise joy shall be in heaven over one sinner that repenteth, more than over ninety and nine just persons, which need no repentance' (Luke 15.7).

The violoncello lying on the

the Harmonious Blacksmith,] That is, the air and variations from Handel's Harpsichord Suite No. 5 in E Major (1720). The nickname, which has no connection with the circumstances of the work's composition, was first used after the composer died. In *GE*, Herbert Pocket gives Pip the nickname 'Handel' because of Pip's association with the blacksmith, Joe Gargery (ch. 22).

In truth, this was the

her serious qualities] For 'serious' as a term associated with Nonconformity, see note to chapter 18, p. 226.

Mrs. Wickam having clinked sufficiently

Mrs. Wickam then sprinkled a little cooling-stuff about the room, with the air of a female grave-digger, who was strewing ashes on ashes, dust on dust ... and withdrew to partake of certain funeral baked meats] For the sprinkling of vinegar in the rooms of patients suffering infections, see note to chapter 42, p. 413. The literary allusions link the 'Order for the Burial of the Dead' (*BCP*) with two scenes in *Hamlet*. At the end of the burial service, the priest intones: 'we therefore commit his body to the ground; earth to earth, ashes to ashes, dust to dust; in sure and certain hope of the Resurrection to eternal life, through our Lord Jesus Christ'. These lines are referred to in *Hamlet* 5.1, in which Hamlet and Horatio meet the two gravediggers (with whom Mrs Wickam is compared) preparing Ophelia's grave:

> *Hamlet.* To what base uses we may return, Horatio! Why may not imagination trace the noble dust of Alexander ... as thus, Alexander died, Alexander was buried, Alexander returneth to dust; the dust is earth; of earth we make loam; and why of that loam whereto he was converted might they not stop a beer-barrel? (196–206)

This allusion in turn gives rise to a comparison between Mrs Wickam leaving Alice's deathbed to go for her dinner and the wedding feast of Hamlet's mother that immediately follows his father's funeral: Hamlet wryly remarks to Horatio, 'Thrift, thrift, Horatio! The funeral baked meats / Did coldly furnish forth the marriage tables' (1.2.180–1).

"We shall all change, Mother,

"We shall all change, Mother, in our turn," said Alice.] 'Behold, I shew you a mystery, We shall not all sleep, but we shall all be changed' (1 Corinthians 15.51; suggested by Larson, 115).

"I have felt, lying here

as the seed was sown, the harvest grew.] Galatians 6.7–8: 'for whatsoever a man soweth, that shall he also reap. For he that soweth to his flesh shall of the flesh reap corruption; but he that soweth to the Spirit shall of the Spirit reap life everlasting'. These verses gave rise to the proverb, 'He that sows good seed shall reap good corn'.

Harriet complied and read –

the blessed history ... the ministry of Him, who, through the round of human life ... had sweet compassion for, and interest in, its every scene and stage, its every suffering and error.] The New Testament, which Dickens valued over the Old Testament:

> Half the misery and hypocrisy of the Christian world arises (as I take it) from a stubborn determination to refuse the New Testament as a sufficient guide in itself, and to force the Old Testament into alliance with it – whereof comes all manner of camel-swallowing and of gnat-straining. (*Letters* 8.718–19)

Dickens distrusted the Old Testament and the purposes for which Nonconformists and Evangelicals used it. He believed that the broad-church Anglican clergymen who wrote *Essays and Reviews* (1860) had adopted 'a very wise and necessary position' by arguing 'that certain parts of the Old Testament have done their intended function in the education of the world *as it was*; but that mankind ... advances' (*Letters* 8.718–19).

In 1868, he made sure to include the New Testament among the books his youngest son took to Australia, 'Because it is the best book that ever was, or will be, known in the world; and because it teaches you the best lessons by which any human creature, who tries to be truthful and faithful to duty, can possibly be guided' (Forster 2.379). Shortly before beginning *DS*, Dickens wrote 'A Life of our Lord' (primarily based on Luke) to read to his children.

Chapter 59

RETRIBUTION

Mr. Towlinson and company are,

the Bank of England's a-going to break, or the jewels in the Tower to be sold up.] For the Bank of England, see note to chapter 4, p. 56. The Tower of London, built by William the Conqueror, and enlarged by later kings, serves as a repository for the crown jewels, which includes the crown and other ornaments worn or carried by the sovereign on state occasions.

the Gazette,] The *London Gazette* (see note to chapter 58, p. 501). 'To be in the gazette' means to be published a bankrupt. For an act of bankruptcy to be considered complete, an Act of Parliament (6 Geo. 4. c.16) required:

> First, the Secretary of Bankrupts, or his deputy, must sign a memorandum, that the *declaration of Insolvency* has been duly filed, as an authority to insert an advertisement of it in the Gazette: 2dly. The advertisement *must* be inserted in the Gazette *within eight days* after filing the declaration; – after which proceedings, the declaration will be considered an act of bankruptcy, committed at the time when the declaration was filed. (Edward E. Deacon, *The Law and Practice of Bankruptcy*, 1827, 1.82–3)

For Mr Dombey's arrangements for settling his debts, see notes to chapter 58, pp. 503, 505.

As soon as there is no

The women ... often repeat "a hun-dred thou-sand pound!" with awful satisfaction – as if handling the word were like handling the money;] Compare the opening paragraph in Dickens's *HW* article, 'A Slight Depreciation of the Currency':

> It was said by the wise and witty SYDNEY SMITH, that many Englishmen appear to have a remarkable satisfaction in even speaking of large sums of money; and that when men of this stamp say of Mr. So-and-So, "I am told he is worth Two HUN-dred THOU-sand POUNDS," there is a relish in their emphasis, an unctuous appetite and zest in their open-mouthed enunciation, which nothing but the one inspiring theme, Money, develops in them. (12 [3 November 1855]: 313)

For a similar passage, see *LD* 1.21.

a foreigner would hardly know what to do with so much money, unless he spent it on his whiskers;] Compare Mrs Gore's novel, *Abednego the Money-Lender* (1843):

> [T]he house to which he was about to repair, had little charm for Basil. The husband of Madame Branzini was the Neapolitan consul, and the persons resorting to his society were almost entirely foreigners. ... Most of them were men of science, or memorable artists, who had brought letters of introduction to the consul. ... Still, the form of their beards, and whiskers, the cut of their coats, the nature of their salutations, rendered them ridiculous or disgusting in the eyes of Basil.

For more on the English prejudice against foreigners and whiskers, see note to chapter 31, p. 333.

But not to remain long absent;

to settle in Oxford Market in the general green grocery and herb and leech line;] Located east of Great Portland Street (and thus sometimes known as Portland Market), Oxford Market was a small, covered market for meat, fish and vegetables, established in 1721. In 1834, a contemporary source claimed that Oxford Market, 'does not contain any thing worthy of notice either in its form or architecture, and is rapidly falling into decay' (*National History and Views of London and its Environs* 39). Similarly, *Knight's Cyclopædia, 1851* observed that Oxford Market 'has lost all pretensions to be considered a market at all. It is, or was lately, a sort of warehouse, though it was one of the best planned of all the older market-houses – a square with all the shops in front, with slaughter-houses in the centre' (799). In 1848, *Mogg's New Picture of London* noted, 'that, with some few exceptions, markets are, generally speaking, on the decline' (1.43). Although the 'leech line' flourished in the 1820s ('people thought it necessary at the spring and fall of the year to have a little blood taken from them'), by the 1840s it had fallen on hard times ('About 1840 a change came over the medical profession; and, instead of bleeding so much, they began to abstain, and the demand for leeches became less and less'; 'Obituary', *Pharmaceutical Journal* 597).

Misfortune in the family without

a lobster salad] Costing 3 shillings and sixpence to make a salad sufficient for four or five people, lobster salad was not an expensive dish, except in winter when salad leaves were expensive. Fresh leaves were dressed with an oil, vinegar, mustard and anchovy dressing and mixed with 'nice square pieces' from the body of a hen lobster (Beeton, recipe no. 272; 137).

with about a quarter of a tumbler-full of mulled sherry; for she feels poorly.]

Spiced sherry. The spices – commonly cloves, nutmeg and cinnamon – are infused in boiling water for an hour. The mixture is strained, sugar is added and then the whole is poured over sherry. According to John James's *The Treasury of Medicine* (1854), mulled wine 'is a useful cordial in typhus and low fevers; and in the debility of convalescence from fevers' (82).

There is a little talk about

a refuge in one of them genteel almshouses of the better kind.] Conditions in almshouses varied widely and depended on the income of the charity that endowed them and also on how carefully, and honestly, the charity's finances were managed. It was usual for almshouses to provide a cash pension to almspeople, but the value varied according to each charity's wealth. Wealthy foundations could offer a secure retirement with a good pension, as well as extras such as fuel and medical aid, and some even enabled inmates to afford a servant. Poorer foundations that could only offer a small stipend compelled beneficiaries either to work to earn money or to approach the local parish overseer for poor relief. In some cases charities handed over the management of almshouses to vestries or overseers, thus blurring the distinction between the almshouse with the poor house or the workhouse (Tomkins 1–29). In 'Mistaken Charity', John Hollingshead criticizes this latter type of almshouse, one of 'at least a hundred in London and the outskirts' in 1861:

> The rudest idea of the charitable refuge is the almshouse. ... How can the inmates of such a place be happy? Neither broken-down haberdashers, decayed Turkey merchants, nor needy frame-knitters are grateful for such refuges. ... You may meet with them [almshouses] at every turn; – in Moorgate, Cripplegate, Bishopsgate, and Southwark. ... The old pensioners find themselves in everybody's way; and everybody is in their way. Their air, and their light, are half blocked out by a law of metropolitan progress, and their poor lives are doubtless shortened by the accidents of their position. They live daily and hourly in a way that their benefactors never meant they should live in; and the boards and corporations who manage their funds are as well aware of this as most people. Too much respect is paid to the assumed, not the real, wishes of the dead; and no one has courage enough to ask Parliament to remove these unfortunate almshouses. (*Ragged London in 1861* 224–7)

In 1861, Hollingshead estimated, 'In London and the outskirts there are at least a hundred of these charitable refuges, and more than one-third of this number are jammed up in and about the city' (224–7). Hollingshead's account contrasts with Dickens's affectionate description of better endowed foundations, one in the countryside and one in the east of London, comfortable almshouses with tidy and cheerful inmates who observe etiquette in dress and behaviour and compete with each other 'respecting the gentility of their visitors' (*AYR*, 'Titbull's Alms-houses' 205–10).

Where he'll have his little garden ... and bring up sweet-peas in the spring."]
Among a number of characteristics that betoken 'a wonderful sameness about all' almshouse buildings, Hollingshead notes that they typically have 'a cabbage-garden at the back, [and] an ornamental grass-plot (where the charity is rich) laid out in front' (224–5). He adds, though,

> No matter how picturesque the general view of their building may appear; no matter how healthy or delightful may be the locality in which they are placed; no matter whether you call their institution by the name of college or almshouse; there is a mixture of the workhouse and the penitentiary in its constitution which it will never lose while a single inmate remains.
>
> (1861, 225)

"and be one of the Brethren of something or another."] The residents of almshouses were referred to as 'brethren' and 'sisters'; see, for example, the account of the Dulwich College almshouse in a Parliamentary committee report in 1834: 'each of the six poor brethren and six poor sisters, at the time of admission, should be unmarried persons of the age of three score years at least, not decrepit nor infected with any offensive disorder, of religious and sober lives and conversations' (*Further Report of the Commissioners* 897).

"How are the mighty fallen!" ... "Pride shall have a fall, and it always was and will be so!"] Biblical quotations that have become proverbial: 'The beauty of Israel is slain upon they high places: how are the mighty fallen!' (2 Samuel 1.19); 'Pride goeth before destruction, and an haughty spirit before a fall' (Proverbs 16.18). The final phrase echoes Revelation 1.8: 'I am Alpha and Omega, the beginning and the ending, saith the Lord, which is, and which was, and which is to come, the Almighty'.

It is wonderful how

a young kitchenmaid ... in black stockings –] 'The Maid-Servant, in her apparel, is either slovenly and fine by turns ... or she is at all times snug and neat and dressed according to her station. In the latter case, her ordinary dress is black stockings, a stuff gown, a cap, and a neck-handkerchief' (Leigh Hunt, 'The Maid-Servant' *The Indicator*, 1822, 54).

After a few days, strange people

a gentleman, of Mosaic Arabian cast of countenance, with a very massive watch-guard ... there is going to be a Sale; and then more people arrive, with pen and ink in their pockets, commanding a detachment of men with carpet caps, who immediately begin to pull up the carpets, and knock the furniture about,] Henry Mayhew found that most of the second-hand dealers in London were Jewish (1851,

2.119–21). A similar scene is the auction held at the Sedley's house in Russell Square following Mr Sedley's bankruptcy in *Vanity Fair* (1848):

> How changed the house is, though! The front is patched over with bills, setting forth the particulars of the furniture in staring capitals. They have hung a shred of carpet out of an up-stairs window – a half-dozen of porters are lounging on the dirty steps – the hall swarms with dingy guests of oriental countenance, who thrust printed cards into your hand, and offer to bid. Old women and amateurs have invaded the upper apartments, pinching the bed curtains, poking into the feathers, shampooing the mattresses, and clapping the wardrobe drawers to and fro. Enterprising young housekeepers are measuring the looking-glasses and hangings to see if they will suit the new menage ... and Mr. Hammerdown is sitting on the great mahogany dining-tables, in the dining-room below, waving the ivory hammer, and employing all the artifices of eloquence, enthusiasm, entreaty, reason, despair; shouting to his people; satirizing Mr. Davids for his sluggishness; inspiriting Mr. Moss into action; imploring, commanding, bellowing, until down comes the hammer like fate, and we pass to the next lot. (ch. 17)

Similarities include the hanging rug, 'the gentleman of Mosaic Arabian cast of countenance' (cf. 'guests of oriental countenance'), the 'shabby vampires' who have 'over-run the house ... punching the squabs of chairs and sofas' (cf. 'Old women and amateurs have invaded the upper apartments, pinching the bed-curtains, poking into the feathers, shampooing the mattresses, and clapping the wardrobe drawers to and fro' and 'the gentlemen [who] sit upon pieces of furniture never made to be sat upon' (cf. 'Mr Hammerdown is sitting on the great mahogany dining-tables'). Chapter 17 appeared in Number 5 of *Vanity Fair*, published in May 1847. Chapter 59 of *DS* was published in April 1848. George Cruikshank's illustration of an auction in *The Comic Almanack* (1842) shows a Jewish man, identified by the long lock of hair on the side of his face, sitting with other second-hand dealers at a dining table below the auctioneer's rostrum. Below the rostrum stands one of the auctioneers' porters, identified by his carpet cap (see quotation below from *The Comic Almanack*).

The men in the carpet caps

the stair-wires, made into fasces, decorate the marble chimney-pieces.] Stair-wires, also known as stair-rods, are usually made of brass and are thus a valuable item for re-sale.

Then, all day long,

kitchen-range] Many varieties of 'new improved Kitchen-Ranges ... said to be "patented" ' were coming onto the market in the 1830s and 1840s (J.C. Loudon,

Gardener's Magazine, 1840, 39), and journals offered advice on what to look for:

> One of the chief points in housekeeping, is to cook victuals with the smallest possible quantity of coal. To effect this desirable object, let the range be of a small size, consisting of a fireplace in the centre, large enough for only one vessel, with an oven upon the one side and a boiler on the other; the boiler also going round the back of the fireplace. (*Chambers's Information for the People*, 1840, 770)

The Capital Modern Household Furniture, &c., is on view.] An advertising phrase used by auction houses. An 1871 advertisement reads, 'Mr. Bullock, respectfully announces for sale by auction at his House, 211, High Holborn, W.C. on Saturday the 21st last., at 12, Capital Modern Household Furniture of the most costly manufacture, supplied by an Eminent West End Cabinet-maker and Upholsterer' (*Notes and Queries*, 7 [January-June 1871]: 508).

Then there is a palisade

Then there is a palisade of tables made in the best drawing-room; and on the ... dining-tables ... the pulpit of the Auctioneer is erected; and the herds of shabby vampires, Jew and Christian ... and the stout men with the napless hats, congregate about it and sit upon everything within reach ... and begin to bid. ... Lots are going, going, gone;] *The Comic Almanack* has a similar scene of a house auction in 'Going! Gone!; the Auction-Here' (1842):

> Glasses, tables, pictures, chairs, Dutch ovens, and beds; – and knots of men upon the stairs, with knots upon their heads; – and the dining-room table put in the front drawing-room, and covered by the back parlour carpet, – supporting the auctioneer, and the clerk, and catalogues, and desk, altogether enough to warp it. – And each hale porter stout is "drawing lots" about, which, if brittle, you may think fortunate, if from the room they are thrust whole, – from the specimen post of the best front bed, and the *book* muslin covers, that once were *red*, to the cinder-sieve and knife-board, in the dusthole. – " Any advance upon seven – eight, nine, ten, eleven – going! – thank you, sir – twelve, thirteen. Tap! gone for thirteen – the cheapest bargain ever seen. ... (1.329)

Then the mouldy gigs and chaise-carts

spring–vans] Spring, or suspension, vans were first used early in the nineteenth century 'for the more rapid delivery of the lighter bales of goods'. According to Henry Mayhew, they 'came into more general use for the removal of furniture in 1830, or thereabouts; and a year or two after were fitted up for the conveyance of pleasure parties' (3.361–2).

porters with knots.] London porters used these 'porter's knots' for carrying burdens. They resembled horse collars, doubly padded at the shoulders, with a loop passing around the forehead (*OED*).

All sorts of vehicles of burden are in attendance ... a tilted waggon ... a donkey-tandem.] The type of heavy rustic waggon with a tilt or awning, described by Mary Russell Mitford as a 'monstrous machine' pulled by four horses, was used to convey people and goods (*Our Village: Sketches of Rural Character and Scenery*, 1824,1.264). In contrast was the two-wheeled donkey-tandem, a 'light little oblong waggon drawn by a tandem pair of donkeys', with the donkeys being harnessed one in front of the other (H. Ellen Browning, *A Girl's Wanderings in Hungary*, 2nd ed., 1807, ch. 5).

At last it is all gone.

Sticking up bills in the windows respecting the lease of this desirable family mansion,] The conventional phrase for such signs; compare: 'To let, this desirable family mansion' ('Piccadilly', *Blackwood's Magazine* 60 [March 1865]: 374).

"I don't know any more

I know no more about him than the man in the south who burnt his mouth by eating cold plum porridge."] From the nursery rhyme, 'The Man in the Moon':

> The man in the moon came tumbling down
> And asked his way to Norwich;
> He went by the south and burnt his mouth
> With supping cold pease porridge.

"Besides," says the discreet lady,

an ejectment, an action for Doe,] John Doe and Richard Roe were legal fictions used to denote the plaintiff and the defendant in an action of ejectment, a usage that was abolished in 1852. The procedure for ousting a person from a property in order to regain possession is explained in *The Westminster Review* (1825):

> Ejectment is the common, and indeed almost the only action, which occurs in practice, for the recovery of real property. "It commences," says Mr. Stephen, "by delivering to the tenant in possession of the premises, a Declaration framed as against a fictitious defendant (for example Richard Roe), at the suit of a fictitious plaintiff (for example John Doe). (4.82–3)

"I know what's to be the end

in a jiffy." … "In a which," Mrs. Pipchin?"] Mrs Pipchin has employed the rather common and vulgar term 'jiffy' (in a very short space of time). Its earliest use in print seems to have been in 1785; it was first defined in Grose's *Dictionary of the Vulgar Tongue* (1796) (*OED*).

"It would be pretty much

I had a very fair connection at Brighton when I came here – little Pankey's folks alone were worth a good eighty pound a-year to me –] For Brighton and Mrs Pipchin's 'scale of charges', see note to chapter 8, p. 132.

"I tell you what, Polly

"Being, now, an ingein-driver, and well to do in the world,] In the 1840s, engine-drivers earned a wage on an authorized scale of between 4 shillings and twopence to 8 shillings per day, based on their service. The *Railway Times* and the *Railway Record* give 7 shillings per day as a typical amount. As a fireman in his previous job (see chapter 15 and note, p. 211), Mr Toodles would have earned about 3 shillings and 4 pence a day, with the range running from 2 shillings and 6 pence to 4 shillings and twopence. In the early years of the railway, promotion was often rapid but, almost certainly, in the case of Mr Toodles, would have stopped at the level of engine driver (Kingsford, 1970, 97–8, 138).

Mrs. Pipchin by this time

Fly Van,] A light vehicle that carried passengers and goods, renowned for its speed.
In his pride – for he was proud

Day after day uttered this speech; night after night showed him this knowledge.] Psalm 19.1–2: 'The heavens declare the glory of God; and the firmament sheweth his handywork. Day unto day uttereth speech, and night unto night sheweth knowledge'.

"Upon my soul I will,

as a cove's – " … "If you please, Miss, as a chap's – " … "I should prefer individual."] Both are slang terms; for 'cove', see note to chapter 22, p. 265. Grose's *Classical Dictionary of the Vulgar Tongue* (1823) defines 'chap' as: 'A fellow. An odd chap; a strange fellow'.

" – and if I hadn't been

But it's never too late ... to mend;] 'Never too late to mend' is a proverb dating from the sixteenth century.

Chapter 60

CHIEFLY MATRIMONIAL

The grand half-yearly festival

Wellington boots] Edmund Yates, writing about dress fashions in the 1830s and 1840s, remarked, 'No gentleman could wear anything in the daytime but Wellington boots, high up the leg, over which the trousers fitted tightly, covering most of the foot, and secured underneath by a broad strap' (1.46).

on a par with a genuine ancient Roman in his knowledge of English:] Cicero (see note to chapter 11, p. 163).

The fruit laboriously gathered from the tree of knowledge] Genesis 2.9, 2.17: 'And out of the ground made the Lord God to grow every tree … But of the tree of the knowledge of good and evil, thou shalt not eat of it: for in the day that thou eatest thereof thou shalt surely die.'

a kind of ... Norfolk Biffin,] A cooking apple, rusty red in colour, extensively cultivated in Norfolk. In *CC,* Dickens describes Norfolk Biffins as 'squab and swarthy' and 'in the great compactness of their juicy persons, urgently entreating and beseeching to be carried home in paper bags and eaten after dinner' (Stave 3).

When Doctor Blimber, in pursuance

when our friend Cincinnatus retired to his farm, he did not present to the senate any Roman whom he sought to nominate as his successor.] A hero of the Roman Republic, the patrician Cincinnatus (519–438 BC) was considered a model of civic virtue, humility and simplicity. Whilst living in modest circumstances on his own farm, he was invited back to Rome by the senators to serve as dictator and quell an invasion. When the invading tribes had been defeated, Cincinnatus immediately resigned his post and returned to his ploughing. The story is told by Cicero (*De Senectute* 56) and charmingly recounted by Oliver Goldsmith in *The Roman History,* *from the Foundation of the City of Rome, to the Destruction of the Western Empire*, 2 vols (1769), of which many nineteenth-century editions appeared under the title, *The History of Rome* (1817). A copy of the 1821 edition (2 vols) was in Dickens's Gad's Hill library (Stonehouse, 51).

"*adolescens imprimis gravis et doctus,*"] 'A serious and well-educated young man' (Cicero; *Lexicon Ciceronianum*, 1820, 1.54).

Dictator.] The name of the chief magistrate who was elected during emergencies in Rome: 'As his power was absolute, he could proclaim war, levy forces, conduct them against an enemy, and disband them at pleasure. He punished as he pleased; and from his decision there was no appeal, at least till later times' (*Lemprière's Classical Dictionary*, 1820).

The Doctor with his learned legs,

Cornelia with her orange-flowers]

> The custom of introducing orange blossom into wedding posies and wreaths is comparatively of modern date, although orange trees were growing in England in the time of Henry VII. Orange flowers at weddings is [*sic*] said to have been derived from the Saracens, or at least from the East, where they were emblems of a prosperous and fruitful marriage. (Wood, 1869, 2.197)

"Well, old Buck!" said Mr. Feeder

"Well! Here we are! Taken in and done for. Eh?"] An expression used by lodging houses and private boarding schools:

> I had not gone far before I espied a bill in a window announcing, "*Single men taken in and done for.*" The singularity of this announcement occasioned me to pause before the house. ... My recent adventure ... being uppermost in my mind, induced me to ask the good woman what she meant by single men being "done for." She replied that sometimes her lodgers wished to have breakfast got for them, or a chop or steak cooked, or little matters of that kind, for which she made but a trifling extra charge ... (Fagg, 1836, 136)

> ... at the age of eight years ... [I was] placed under the fostering care of Mr. Whippington; who was deemed the most learned pundit and pedagogue in the whole county, and in whose establishment, owing to the extraordinary combination which he had made of "comfort and economy," young gentlemen were taken in and done for, all for the small charge of forty guineas per year.
> (*The Monthly Magazine, or, British Register*. 24 [1837]: 629)

"Accordingly," resumed Mr. Toots,

Nobody but myself can tell what the capacity of that woman's mind is. If ever the Rights of Women, and all that kind of thing, are properly attended to, it will be through her powerful intellect.] A current topic while Dickens was composing *DS*. Women's equality with men in intellectual matters and the founding of a university for women are the concerns of Princess Ida, the heroine of Tennyson's *The Princess*, published in 1847. In the same year, announcements appeared about the founding of Queen's College, London, 'established for the promotion of female education, and for granting certificates of qualifications to Governesses'. On 29 March 1848, the founder of Queen's College, F. D. Maurice, delivered a lecture in Hanover Square entitled 'Queen's College, London: its Objects and Method' (*English Journal of Education* [1847], 1.395–6; *Freemasons' Quarterly Review* [1847], 332; *Gentleman's Magazine* [1848], 183.635; *Publishers' Circular* [1848], 11.163). Queen's College, London opened on 1 May 1848, the month following the publication of the last number of *DS*.

Echoes of the phrase 'Rights of Women', which gained fame with the publication of Mary Wollstonecraft's *A Vindication of the Rights of Woman, with Strictures on Political and Moral Subjects* (1792), were recurrent in the 1840s. For example, *Woman's Rights and Duties; Considered with Relation to their Influence on Society and on her Own Condition*, by 'A Woman', was published in 1840 (2 vols). Charlotte Elizabeth Tonna's four-part *The Wrongs of Woman* (London, 1843–4) documented the abuses of women, and children dressmakers and milliners. Both titles were widely reviewed and attracted sympathy and hostility alike, including the contemptuous and anti-feminist review, 'The Wrongs of Woman', in *Blackwood's* (1843): 54.597–607.

Mr Toots's praise for his wife's intellect and his willingness to allow her to express his opinions for him are in agreement with the beliefs advocated by the American transcendentalist and critic, Margaret Fuller, in *Woman in the Nineteenth Century* (first published 1843; London, 1845). Fuller repeatedly argues that women must be allowed to speak for themselves – 'But women ... will speak now, and cannot be silenced; their characters and their eloquence alike foretell an era when such as they shall easier learn to lead true lives' (70). She also maintains that women can only gain equality in marriage by becoming more independent, which requires men to become less dominating. Fuller visited England in 1846 and met Wordsworth, Harriet Martineau, Thomas and Jane Carlyle and Mazzini before travelling to France and Italy. (*HW* published an article, 'Margaret Fuller', which, while praising her energy and genius, criticised the unwomanly sentiments of *Woman in the Nineteenth Century*; 5 [April 1852]: 121–4).

The ceremony was performed

"went in," as the Chicken might have said,] Usually, the phrase meant 'went *back* into the ring', following the thirty-second break at the end of a round, though the phrase also seems to have more generally meant 'engage with'. In an account of a fight with Jem Belcher, Hen Pearce, the historical 'Game Chicken', 'continued to bleed freely from the blow he received in the first round. He smiled with confidence, however, went in, and rallied' (Miles, 1906, 1.176).

Cicero in his retirement at Tusculum,] See note to chapter 11, p. 168.

"To Mrs. Feeder, my love!"

" 'whom God hath joined,' you know, 'let no man' – don't you know?] 'Those whom God hath joined together let no man put asunder' (*BCP*, 'The Form of Solemnization of Matrimony'). Dickens satirizes the compulsive use of 'you know', a habit associated with vapid young men, in *DC*:

> 'Oh, you know, deuce take it,' said the gentleman, looking round the board with an imbecile smile, 'we can't forgo Blood, you know. We must have Blood, you know. Some young fellows, you know, may be a little behind their station, perhaps, in point of education and behaviour, and may go a little wrong, you know, and get themselves and other people into a variety of fixes – and all that – but deuce take it, it's delightful to reflect that they've got Blood in 'em. (25)

Dickens also caricatures the use of the phrase in *LD*: 'Upon my SOUL you mustn't come into the place, saying you want to know, you know!' (1.10).

the torch of Hymen] In Greek mythology, Hymen, the son of Apollo, is the god of marriage and the marriage song. He is frequently represented with a marriage feast torch in his hand.

Doctor Blimber, who had a

in the pastoral style, relative to the rushes among which it was the intention of himself and Mrs. Blimber to dwell, and the bee that would hum around their cot.] For Dickens's frequently mocking pastoralism, see note to chapter 21, p. 257. Doctor Blimber may be thinking of the 'cry' of Daphnis from Virgil, *Eclogue* 7:

> "O Meliboeus! goat and kids are safe;
> And, if you have an idle hour to spare,
> Rest here beneath the shade. Hither the steers
> Will through the meadows, of their own free will,
> Untended come to drink. Here Mincius hath
> With tender rushes rimmed his verdant banks,
> And from yon sacred oak with busy hum
> The bees are swarming."

time was made for slaves,] 'Time was made for slaves (and not for freedmen)' is proverbial. The phrase provides the caption for one of George Cruikshank's *Illustrations of Time* (pl. 3, 1827; G. W. Reid's *A Descriptive Catalogue of the Works of George Cruikshank*, i, London 1871, p. 123, no. 1411). The illustration depicts a white man whipping three black men (according to Cruikshank, 'Flogging them by the Hour').

The Captain, having seen Florence

his old neighbourhood, down among the mast, oar, and block makers, ship-biscuit makers, coal-whippers, pitch-kettles, sailors, canals, docks, swing-bridges, and other soothing objects.] For the canal, swing-bridge, coal-whippers and the area south of the West India Docks, see note to chapter 9, p. 140. For ship's biscuit, see note to chapter 4, p. 60. 'Block makers' made 'the pulley or system of pulleys mounted in a case, used to increase the mechanical power of the ropes running through them; employed esp. for the rigging of ships, and in lifting great weights'. When Dickens was a boy, living on Bayham Street, he paid visits to his godfather, 'who was a rigger, and mast, oar and block maker' (Forster 1.1.14). 'Pitch-kettles', large vessels used to heat or boil pitch, were commonly used on ships (*OED*).

These peaceful scenes, and particularly

Limehouse-Hole] Limehouse, which lies along the bend of the River Thames, known as Limehouse Reach, is situated between the Regent's Docks and the West India Docks. Limehouse Hole is the part of Limehouse Reach between the western entrance of the West India and Limehouse docks which was often crowded with foreign vessels. 'Along this part of the banks of the river are several merchant dockyards' (*North Sea Pilot*, Part 4, 1863, 21). In *OMF*, Rogue Riderhood, and his daughter Pleasant, 'dwelt deep and dark in Limehouse Hole, among the riggers, and the mast, oar and block makers, and the boat-builders, and the sail-lofts' (bk 2, ch. 12).

a triumphal procession that he beheld advancing towards him.] Browne's illustration, 'Another Wedding', includes several details that comment ironically on Dickens's scene and refer to earlier elements in the novel. Among these, in the left foreground, are a poster advertising productions of *She Stoops to Conquer* and *Black-Eyed Susan* (which includes the lines 'O Susan, Susan, lovely dear, / My vows shall ever true remain') and, immediately above Captain Cuttle, a sign reading 'Wanted/ Some Fine Young Men'. For a discussion of these details, see Steig, 1978, chapter 4.

The Captain made many attempts

the chapel ... recently engaged by the Reverend Melchisedech Howler, who had consented, on very urgent solicitation, to give the world another two years of existence, but had informed his followers that, then, it must positively go.] For the Reverend Howler's Primitive Methodism and the millenarianism often associated with the evangelical movement, see note to chapter 15, p. 225.

One of the most frightful circumstances

The Master Mac Stingers ... being chiefly engaged ... in treading on one anothers' half-boots;]

> For children, a kind of half boots, such as may be laced above the ancles, are superior to shoes, as they not only have the advantage of fitting the leg, but are likewise not easily trodden down at the heels, and children can walk more firmly in them than in shoes. (Mary Eaton, *The Cook and Housekeeper's Complete and Universal Dictionary*, 1822, 353)

"He is very, very ill," said Florence.

Your old cap, curls, and all?"] It was fashionable in the early decades of the nineteenth century for both ladies and women servants to wear a row of false curls, also called a 'front', beneath their cap. That the curls were patently artificial is indicated in the description of Miss Flint in *The Anglo-Irish of the Nineteenth Century: a novel* (1828): 'her cap and curls (the latter, as has already been insinuated, only *called* hers)' (Banim 2.11).

Chapter 61

RELENTING

He remained like this for

to feel a sympathy with shadows. It was natural that he should. To him, life and the world were nothing else.] An anticipation of the quotation from *Hamlet* at the end of this chapter (p. 525).

"I could have wished,

so many painful occurrences have happened, treading, as a man may say, on one another's heels,] *Hamlet* 4.7.163–4: 'One woe doth tread upon another's heel, / So fast they follow. Your sister's drowned, Laertes'.

The fact is,' said Cousin Feenix,

As in my parliamentary time, when a man had a motion to make of any sort – which happened seldom in those days, for we were kept very tight in hand] In the House of Commons, motions tabled by a back-bench MP for debate at an unspecified date in the future are in fact only rarely debated because the Parliamentary timetable is tightly controlled by the leadership of the parties, including the whips, MPs appointed by each party who help organise the party's contributions to parliamentary business. Motions can be tabled on trivial or important topics and may be regarded as merely gestures or as serious statements of an MP's ideology.

Mr. Pitt; the pilot ... who had weathered the storm.] For William Pitt and George Canning's poetic tribute to him, 'The Pilot that Weathered the Storm' (1802), see note to chapter 5, p. 82.

these fellows, being under orders to cheer most excessively whenever Mr. Pitt's name was mentioned, became so proficient that it always woke 'em.] The 'orders' would have come from the party whips (see note above). When a member speaks in the House of Commons, especially on party questions, he is often cheered and applauded by members of his own party. A writer claiming to be 'of no party' observed in 1836, 'In applauding their respective favourites, hon. members give full play to their lungs. Their cheers are sometimes deafening in the house, and are often distinctly heard at a great distance from it' (Grant, 1835, 43).

In a speech to the Administrative Reform Association, on 27 May 1855, Dickens commented on the somnolence of the House of Commons:

> in order to preserve it in a real state of usefulness and independence, the people must be ever watchful and ever jealous of it; and it must have its memory jogged; it must be kept awake; when it happens to have taken too much ministerial narcotic, it must be trotted about, and must be hustled and pinched in a friendly way. (*Speeches* 202–3)

In *LD*, Dickens remarked on 'the sleepy member who had gone out into the lobby the other night, and voted the wrong way' (2.12), and, in 'Mr Bull's Somnambulist', Dickens characterized Lord Aberdeen, the Prime Minister (1852–5), as 'a heavy sleeper, and difficult to awaken' (*HW* 10 [25 November 1854]: 337–9).

Conversation Brown – four bottle man at the Treasury Board,] 'Conversation Sharp' was the nickname of Richard Sharp (1759–1835), the wealthy merchant, critic, radical MP and member of the Holland House circle who was renowned for his conversational talents. A friend of the most eminent literary men of the day, Sharp was described by Byron as '*the Conversationist*, as he was called in London, and a very clever man' (letter of 9 January 1821 in Moore 2.403). In *BH*, the lawyer Mr Kenge is 'generally called Conversation Kenge' (ch. 3).

A 'four-bottle man' refers to someone who can drink four bottles of wine without much visible effect. So, R. H. Barham's *The Ingoldsby Legends*, first published in *Bentley's Miscellany* (beginning in 1837) and *The New Monthly Magazine*, mentions 'a four-bottle man in a company "screw'd," / Not firm on his legs, but by no means subdued'. A correspondent, writing for *The Dublin Review* in 1884, remarked on 'The difference of habits, especially in the matter of hard drinking, between the present generation and our great-grandfathers', and claimed that 'The "four-bottle man," who was so conspicuous a figure in the last century, is now as extinct as a Plesiosaurus' ('Science Notices' 448).

The Treasury Board, a 'board of five members of equal authority, any two of them being competent to execute the authority of the whole', ostensibly conducted the business of the Treasury Office, 'regarded as the highest branch of executive government. It has the entire control and management of the public revenue and expenditure; and exercises a supervision over all the revenue officers and public accountants of the kingdom; and, so far as receipt and expenditure are concerned, over every department of the public service' (Todd, 1869, 2.438). Since about the middle of the nineteenth century, the Treasury Board 'practically ceased to exist ... although still in theory a power it never assembles, and its functions are now exercised by the secretary and the permanent officials, acting under the general directions of the Chancellor of the Exchequer' (Todd, 1869, 2.438–9). The Treasury Office seems to serve as the model for The Circumlocution Office in *LD*.

Honourable Member] 'Honourable' is a courtesy title applied to Members of Parliament (also to Privy Councillors and certain ranks of the peerage). Dickens often used the title ironically, as when he referred to 'Our Honourable Friend' as 'the honourable member for Verbosity' (*HW* 5.453). Dickens's knowledge of Parliament derives, in part, from his time as a parliamentary reporter. He first worked as a freelance shorthand reporter in 1828, when he was 16, and from some time in early 1831 as a shorthand reporter for his uncle's publication, the *Mirror of Parliament*, for at least two years. From March to July 1832, Dickens reported for the ultra-Whig or Radical *True Sun*, and from August 1834 to late 1835 for the Whig *Morning Chronicle*, noted for the excellence of its parliamentary reporting. Dickens was later characterized by William Howard Russell, the famous Crimean correspondent, as 'the best reporter in London' (Atkins 1.58).

"I will leave," said Cousin Feenix,

who lived pretty freely in the days when men lived very freely,] An allusion to the Regency era, strictly 1811–20, when the Prince of Wales served as Regent on behalf of George III, but more generally used to describe the years between 1795 and 1837.

The Regency was characterized in the succeeding years as a period of excess and immorality, especially among the aristocracy. Dickens's well-known detestation of George IV and the values he represented is epitomized in the way the king is virtually effaced from history in the last chapter of *CHE*, which mentions him only in passing.

the yolk of an egg, beat up with sugar and nutmeg, in a glass of sherry, and taken in the morning with a slice of dry toast.] Egg-wine – made with sherry – is one of the drinks recommended for invalids by Mrs Beeton. She suggests that egg wine be served warm, 'with sippets of toasted bread or plan crisp biscuits' (para. 1867). In *LD*, the concoction is said to work 'like a charm' upon 'a depression' (1.21). Mrs Beeton also lists sherry as an ingredient in a number of concoctions recommended for invalids, including arrowroot, gruel, and 'nourishing lemonade'. She remarks, 'Sherry has of late got much into fashion in England, from the idea that it is more free from acid than other wines' though ' some careful experiments on wines do not full confirm this opinion (para. 1416, note).

Jackson, who kept the boxing-rooms in Bond-street – man of very superior qualifications, with whose reputation my friend Gay is no doubt acquainted – used to mention that in training for the ring they substituted rum for sherry.] Gentleman John Jackson (1769–1845) – who was described by Lord Byron as 'Professor of Pugilism' and 'Emperor of Pugilism' and by others as 'Commander-in-Chief' – conducted a school of self-defence at 13 Bond Street:

> He taught his pupils to feel that personal confidence and the contempt of danger were the first and best qualities of a pugilist. He showed them, that to hit with effect, they must first judge their distance, that is to say, to judge when the delivery of a blow would produce the most conclusive consequence. ... He showed that men ought to fight as well with their legs as with their hands. ... He decried all stiffness of position. ... Ambidexterity ... he also strongly inculcated. ... The lessons were conveyed in such as way as to produce conviction. (Vincent Dowling, qtd. in Ford, 1971, 135–6)

Jackson, who only appeared in three public matches, defeated Daniel Mendoza in 1795 for the championship of England. According to Pierce Egan, Jackson possessed,

> an uncommon fine person – his symmetry of form is attractive in the extreme, and he is considered one of the best made men in the kingdom, standing 5 ft. 11½ in., in height, and weighing about fourteen stone; with limbs elegantly proportioned, and an arm for athletic beauty that defies competition. (1812, 287)

Besides his physical impressiveness, Jackson, who was 'personally known to some of the first characters in the kingdom', was said to possess 'good breeding' and had 'acquired considerable proficiency in his manners and address'. He was 'one of the best behaved men also; in fact, Jackson possesses a *mind* that penetrates farther than the surface'. Once he retired from boxing, he '*practically* realized the character of a gentleman, equally respected by the rich and poor – and ever ready to perform a good action' (288, 290). For more about Jackson, and the drinking habits of prizefighters, see note to chapter 22, p. 271.

Their ride was six or eight

Their ride was six or eight miles long. ... they drove through certain dull and stately streets, lying westward in London,] A reference to the Georgian style of architecture, which the Victorians generally disliked, common in the West End of London. For example, in *Tancred* (1847) Disraeli complained of

> your Gloucester Places, and Baker Streets, and Harley Streets, and Wimpole Streets, and all those flat, dull, spiritless streets, resembling each other like a large family of plain children, with Portland Place and Portman Square for their respectable parents. (2.10)

In *In Memoriam* (1850), Tennyson described Wimpole Street as 'the long unlovely street', and in *LD*, Dickens noted the 'expressionless uniform' houses in Harley Street (1.21).

"I trust," said Cousin Feenix,

this world – which is remarkable ... for being decidedly the most unintelligible thing within a man's experience –] Wordsworth, "Lines Composed a Few Miles above Tintern Abbey" (1798): 'the heavy and the weary weight / Of all this unintelligible world' (ll. 39-40).

"My lovely and accomplished relative,"

going to the South of Italy, there to establish ourselves ... until we go to our long homes,] Ecclesiastes 12.5: '... man goeth to his long home, and the mourners go about the streets'. As a result of his own travels, Dickens came to dislike southern Italy, particularly Naples. He told Forster that 'The condition of the common people here [in Naples] is abject and shocking'. 'Except Fondi, he added, 'there is nothing on earth that I have seen so dirty as Naples' (*Letters* 4.266). For more on southern Italy, see note to chapter 54, p. 469.

"I am devilish sorry," said

all I can say is, with my friend Shakespeare – man who wasn't for an age but for all time ... that it's like the shadow of a dream.] 'He was not of an age, but for all time!' is Ben Jonson's description of Shakespeare in his preface to the *First Folio* (1623). The second allusion is to *Hamlet* 2.2.257–64:

> *Guildenstern*: Which dreams indeed are ambition; for the very substance of the ambitious is merely the shadow of a dream.
> *Hamlet*: A dream itself is but a shadow.
> *Rosencrantz*: Truly, and I hold ambition of so airy and light a quality that it is but a shadow's shadow.
> *Hamlet*: Then are our beggars bodies, and our monarchs and outstretch'd heroes the beggars' shadows.

Chapter 62

FINAL

The Captain, who is

There is a very halo of delight round his glowing forehead.] From 'To My Muse', by J. Player: 'Such were the dreams which once were wont to shed /A halo of delight around my head' (*The Pocket Magazine of Classics and Polite Literature*, 1819, 3.51). The poem gave rise to frequent uses of 'halo of delight' in the next few decades.

"Because, you know," says Mr. Toots,

the tender passion. ... "as makes us all slue round –] 'Love makes the world go round' is a proverbial saying from a traditional French song, '*C'est l'amour, l'amour, l'amour, Qui fait le monde A la ronde*' (*Oxford Dictionary of Phrase and Fable*). Dickens is probably thinking of the comical English version of the song, which was popular in the early to mid-nineteenth century:

> Oh! 'tis love, 'tis love, 'tis love,
> That makes the world go round;
> Ev'ry day, beneath his sway,
> Fools, old and young, abound;
> Love often turns young ladies' brains,
> At which mamma will scold,
> So, in revenge, Love thinks it fair
> To shoot sometimes the old;
> With love some folks go mad,

> 'Tis love makes some quite thin,
> Some find themselves so bad,
> The sea they must jump in.
> (*Universal Songster; Or, Museum of Mirth*, 1826, 3.369)

It is this version that Dickens alludes to in *OMF*: 'And oh, what a bright old song it is, that oh, 'tis love, 'tis love, that makes the world go round!' (bk 4, ch. 4). 'Slue' is a nautical term meaning 'to turn anything round or over' (Arthur Young, *Nautical Dictionary*, 1863, 358).

"I shall certainly do so,

I was what you may call a Blighted flower,] 'Blighted flower' was a sentimental cliché often used figuratively in the early nineteenth century; e.g. 'When Louisa returned to Dunbarrow, it was an early blighted flower, withered by unkindness and misfortune!' ('The Bachelor's Beat. No. III. *The Bachelor's Christmas.*' *Blackwood's Edinburgh Magazine* 23 [January 1828]: 16). 'My blessed Edith! Oh! So pale! so changed! / My flower, my blighted flower! ... (*The Works of Mrs Hemans*, vol. 7, *Scenes and Hymns of Life. The English Martyrs*, 1840, Sc. 2, 137–8).

The Captain approves of this

The Captain ... murmurs that no flower as blows, is like the rose.] An allusion to a popular English air, 'No Flower that Blows', composed by Thomas Lindley from his dramatic piece *Selima and Azor* (1776): 'No flow'r that blows is like is like [sic] this rose, / Or scatters such perfume' (*The Beauties of Melody*, 1827, 77).

He only answers, "Little Florence!

her earnest eyes.] MS and the first proof (A) contain the following passage, which was not used because this final number was seven lines too long. The passage recalls the conclusion of chapter 16:

> The voices in the waves speak low to him of Florence, day and night – plainest when he, his blooming daughter, and her husband, walk beside them in the evening, or sit at an open window listening to their roar. They speak to him of Florence and his altered heart; of Florence and their ceaseless murmuring to her of the love, eternal and illimitable, extending still, beyond the sea, beyond the sky, to the invisible country far away.
> Never from the mighty sea may voices rise too late, to come between us and the unseen region on the other shore! Better, far better, that they whispered of that region in our childish ears, and the swift river hurried us away!

SELECT BIBLIOGRAPHY

(i) *Works by Dickens*

The Clarendon Dickens. Oxford: Clarendon Press, 1966–. Edition cited in quotations from
    David Copperfield. Ed. Nina Burgess. 1981.
    Dombey and Son. Ed. Alan Horsman. 1974.
    Great Expectations. Ed. Margaret Cardwell. 1993.
    Little Dorrit. Ed. Harvey Peter Sucksmith. 1979.
    Martin Chuzzlewit. Ed. Margaret Cardwell. 1982.
    The Mystery of Edwin Drood. Ed. Margaret Cardwell. 1972.
    The Old Curiosity Shop. Ed. Elizabeth M. Brennan. 1997.
    Oliver Twist. Ed. Kathleen Tillotson. 1966.
    The Pickwick Papers. Ed. James Kinsley. 1986.

The Penguin English Library, Harmondsworth: Penguin. Edition cited in quotations from
    Barnaby Rudge. Ed. Gordon Spence. 1973.
    Bleak House. Ed. Norman Page. 1971.
    The Christmas Books. Ed. Michael Slater. 2 vols, 1971.
    Hard Times. Ed. David Craig. 1969.
    Nicholas Nickleby. Ed. Michael Slater. 1976.
    Our Mutual Friend. Ed. Stephen Gill. 1971.
    A Tale of Two Cities. Ed. George Woodcock. 1970.

The Oxford Illustrated Dickens. 21 vols. London: Oxford UP, 1947–58. Edition cited in quotations from
    '*American Notes*' and '*Pictures from Italy*'
    Master Humphrey's Clock (includes *A Child's History of England*)
    Sketches by Boz (this volume includes *Sketches of Young Gentlemen, Sketches of Young Couples, The Mudfog Papers* and '*The Pantomime of Life*')
    '*The Uncommercial Traveller*' and '*Reprinted Pieces*' (this volume includes *Sunday Under Three Heads, To be Read at Dusk, Hunted Down, Holiday Romance* and *George Silverman's Explanation*)

Memoirs of Joseph Grimaldi, edited by Dickens. Ed. Richard Findlater. London: MacGibbon & Kee, 1968
Charles Dickens' Book of Memoranda. Transcribed and annotated by Fred Kaplan. New York: New York Public Library, 1981

Dickens' Working Notes for His Novels, ed. Harry Stone. Chicago: U of Chicago Press, 1987.
The Letters of Charles Dickens. Pilgrim Edition. 12 vols. Oxford: Clarendon, 1965–2002. Vols 1 and 2. Ed. Madeline House and Graham Storey. Vol. 3. Ed. Madeline House, Graham Storey and Kathleen Tillotson. Vol. 4. Ed. Kathleen Tillotson. Vol. 5. Ed. Graham Storey and K. J. Fielding. Vol. 6. Ed. Graham Storey, Kathleen Tillotson and Nina Burgis. Vol. 7. Ed. Graham Storey, Kathleen Tillotson and Angus Easson. Vol. 8. Ed. Graham Storey and Kathleen Tillotson. Vol. 9. Ed. Graham Storey. Vol. 10. Ed. Graham Storey. Vol. 11. Ed. Graham Storey. Vol. 12. Ed. Graham Storey, Margaret Brown and Kathleen Tillotson.
The Letters of Charles Dickens. edited by his Sister-in-law and his Eldest Daughter. Vol. 1. 1833–1856. London: Chapman & Hall, 1880
Charles Dickens as Editor: Being letters written by him to William Henry Wills his sub-editor, ed. R. C. Lehmann. London: Smith, Elder. 1912
The Speeches of Charles Dickens: A Complete Edition, ed. K. J. Fielding. Hemel Hempstead: Harvester, 1988

(ii) *Articles in 'Bentley's Miscellany'*

Dickens, Charles. 'Some Particulars Concerning a Lion.' 1 (May 1837): 515–18.

(iii) *Articles and Poems in 'Household Words'*

Buckley, Theodore. 'Hampstead Heath.' 4 (27 September 1851): 15–18.
Buckley, Theodore. 'Quarter-Day.' 5 (26 June 1852): 342–5.
Cape. 'Miasma' [verse]. 8 (10 December 1853): 348.
Capper, John. 'Chip: Our Russian Relations.' 10 (18 November 1854): 333.
Capper, John. 'Underwriting.' 5 (4 September 1852): 585–9.
Collins, Wilkie. 'A Rogue's Life. Written by Himself. Chapter the Third.' 13 (15 March 1856): 205–14.
Dickens, Charles. 'A Flight.' 3 (30 August 1851): 529–33.
Dickens, Charles. 'From the Raven in the Happy Family [II].' 1 (8 June 1850): 241–2.
Dickens, Charles. 'The Heart of Mid-London.' 1 (4 May 1850): 121–5.
Dickens, Charles. 'Home for Homeless Women.' 7 (23 April 1853): 169–75.
Dickens, Charles. 'Insularities.' 13 (19 January 1856): 1–4.
Dickens, Charles. 'Mr. Bull's Somnambulist.' 10 (25 November 1854): 337–9.
Dickens, Charles. 'A Monument of French Folly.' 2 (8 March 1851): 554–8.
Dickens, Charles. 'A Narrative of Extraordinary Suffering.' 3 (12 July 1851): 361–3.
Dickens, Charles. 'The Noble Savage.' 7 (11 June 1853): 337–9.
Dickens, Charles. 'Our Commission.' 12 (11 August 1855): 25–7.
Dickens, Charles. 'Our Honourable Friend.' 5 (31 July 1852): 453–5.
Dickens, Charles. 'Our School.' 4 (11 October 1851): 49–52.
Dickens, Charles. 'A Slight Depreciation of the Currency.' 12 (3 November 1855): 313–15.

Dickens, Charles. 'An Unsettled Neighbourhood.' 10 (11 November 1854): 289–92.
Dickens, Charles, and W. H. Wills. 'The Old Lady in Threadneedle Street.' 1 (6 July 1850): 337–42.
Dodd, George. 'Bouquets.' 8 (5 November 1853): 230–3.
Dodd, George. 'Dolls.' 7 (11 June 1853): 352–6.
Dodd, George. 'Exploring Expedition to the Isle of Dogs.' 7 (21 May 1853): 273–7.
Dodd, George. 'India-Rubber.' 7 (12 March 1853): 29–33.
Dodd, George. 'Music Measure.' 7 (28 May 1853): 297–301.
Dodd, George. 'Wire-drawing.' 9 (22 April 1854): 217–21.
Head, John Oswald. 'Signals and Engine-Drivers.' 14 (6 September 1856): 179–80.
Hogarth, George, and W. H. Wills. 'Heathen and Christian Burial.' 1 (6 April 1850): 43–8.
Horne, R. H. 'Dust; or Ugliness Redeemed.' 1 (13 July 1850): 379–84.
Howitt, William. 'The Queen's Tobacco-Pipe.' 2 (4 January 1851): 355–8.
Mitchie, Archibald, and Henry Morley. 'Going Circuit at the Antipodes.' 4 (3 January 1852): 344–8.
Morley, Henry, and W. H. Wills. 'Ice.' 3 (16 August 1851): 481–4.
Morley, Henry. 'An Enemy's Charge.' 12 (20 October 1855): 265–88.
Morley, Henry. 'Foreign Airs and Native Places.' 3 (2 August 1851): 446–50.
Morley, Henry. 'Infant Gardens.' 11 (21 July 1855): 577–82.
Morley, Henry. 'Need Railway Travellers Be Smashed?' 4 (29 November 1851): 217–21.
Morley, Henry. 'Our Phantom Ship: Central America.' 2 (22 February 1851): 516–22.
Morley, Henry. 'Self-Acting Railway Signals.' 7 (12 March 1853): 43–5.
Murray, Grenville. 'The Roving Englishman: His Hints to Travellers.' 6 (13 November 1852): 211–14.
Payn, James. 'Her First Appearance.' 19 (11 December 1858): 29–33.
Sala, George A. 'Jack Alive in London.' 4 (6 December 1851): 254–60.
Sala, George A. 'Last Words with Philip Stubbes.' 12 (1 September 1855): 117–20.
Sala, George A. 'Things Departed.' 4 (17 January 1852): 397–401.
Speight, Thomas Wilkinson. 'Up and Down the Line.' 15 (27 June 1857): 601–7.
Thornbury, George Walter. 'The Stoker's Poetry.' 15 (31 January 1857): 114–16.
Wills, W. H. 'Baptism Rituals.' 1 (27 April 1850): 106–8.
Wills, W. H. 'A Little Place in Norfolk.' 1 (7 September 1850): 575–6.
Wills, W. H. 'The Monster Promenade Concerts.' 2 (19 October 1850): 95–6.

(iv) *Articles in 'All the Year Round'*

Ashby, J. Sterry. 'The Wooden Midshipman.' 28 (29 October 1881): 173–9.
Dickens, Charles. 'City of the Absent.' 8 (18 July 1863): 493–6.
Dickens, Charles. 'City of London Churches.' 3 (5 May 1860): 85–9.
Dickens, Charles. 'A Little Dinner in an Hour.' 1 (2 January 1869): 108–11.
Dickens, Charles. 'Night Walks.' 3 (21 July 1860): 348–52.
Dickens, Charles. 'Nurse's Stories.' 3 (8 September 1860): 517–21.
Dickens, Charles. 'Shy Neighbourhoods.' 3 (26 May 1860): 155–9.

Dickens, Charles. 'Titbull's Almshouse. By The Uncommercial Traveller.' 10 (24 October 1863): 205–10.
Dickens, Charles. 'Tramps.' 3 (16 June 1860): 230–4.
'Gardens by Gaslight.' *New Series*. 4 (29 October 1870): 519–22.
'Indian Servants.' 9 (27 June 1863): 416–20.
'Infallible Physic.' 2 (3 March 1860): 448–52.
'Lightning.' 20 (29 August 1868): 274–6.
'Military Mismanagement.' 10 (5 December 1863): 349–52.
'Music and Misery.' 20 (15 August 1869): 230–3.

(v) *Other Material*

à Beckett, Gilbert Abbott. 'Charts for Railway Travellers. No. II.—London to Dover.' *The Almanack of the Month* 1 (May 1846): 281–8.
Ackermann, Rudolph, Pyne, W. H., and William Combe. *Microcosm of London*. 3 vols. London: T. Bensley, 1808–10.
Acton, Eliza. *Modern Cookery, in all its Branches*. 2nd ed. London: Longman, Green, 1845.
Adams, Dr A. Mercer. 'Is Shaving Favorable to Health? A Plea for Beards.' *Edinburgh Medical Journal*. December 1861; rpt. in *The Dental Cosmos*. New Series. 4 (October 1862): 158–60.
Adams, Samuel and Sarah. *The Complete Servant*. London: Knight & Lacey, 1825.
Adams, William Bridges. *English Pleasure Carriages*. London: Charles Knight, 1837.
Adams, William Bridges. *Roads and Rails and Their Sequences, Physical and Moral*. London: Chapman and Hall, 1862.
Adburgham, Alison. *Shops and Shopping, 1800–1914*. 1964. 2nd ed. London: George Allen and Unwin, 1981.
Adolphus, John. *The Political State of the British Empire, Containing a General View of the Domestic and Foreign Possessions of the Crown; The Laws, Commerce, Revenues, Offices, and Other Establishments*. 4 vols. London: T. Cadell & W. Davies, 1818.
Agassiz, L. *A Journey to Switzerland, and Pedestrian Tours in that Country*. London: Smith, Elder, 1833.
'Aids to Beauty, Real and Artificial.' *The Cornhill Magazine*. 7 (January–June 1863): 391–400.
Alborn, Timothy. 'The Thrift Wars: Savings Banks and Life Assurance in Victorian Britain.' Paper presented at the Thirteenth Congress of the International Economic History Association, Buenos Aires, 25 July 2002.
Allen, Michael. *Charles Dickens' Childhood*. New York: St. Martin's Press, 1988.
Altick, Richard D. *The Presence of the Past: Topics of the Day in the Victorian Novel*. Columbus, Ohio: Ohio State UP, 1991.
Altick, Richard D. *The Shows of London*. Cambridge, Mass./London: Harvard UP, 1978.
Ancient and Modern Scottish Songs, Heroic Ballads, etc. 2 vols. Edinburgh: John Wotherspoon; James Dickson and Charles Elliot, 1776. Rpt. 1869.
Anderson, William, ed. *Treasury of Manners, Customs, and Ceremonies. For the Young*.

Edinburgh: Paton and Ritchie, 1855.
The Annual Register, or a View of the History and Politics of the Year 1843. London: F. & J. Rivington, 1844.
The Arabian Nights Entertainment. Trans. Jonathan Scott. 6 vols. London: Longman, Hurst, 1811.
Ariès, Philippe. *The Hour of Our Death.* New York: Vintage, 1981.
The Art of Preserving the Hair. [James Rennie]. London: Septimus Prowett, 1825.
Ashton, John. *The Dawn of the XIXth Century.* London: T. Fisher Unwin, 1906.
Ashton, John. *Modern Street Ballads.* London: Chatto & Windus, 1888.
Atkins, John Black. *The Life of Sir William Howard Russell.* 2 vols. London: John Murray, 1911.
Babbage, Charles. *The Ninth Bridgewater Treatise: A Fragment.* Vol. 9. *The Works of Charles Babbage*, ed. Martin Campbell-Kelly. New York: New York UP, 1989.
Baldick, Christopher, ed. *The Concise History of Literary Terms.* Oxford: Oxford UP, 1996.
Baldwin, Edward. *The Pantheon: or Ancient History of the Gods of Greece and Rome.* 4th ed. London: J Godwin, 1814.
Banham, Joanna, Sally Macdonald and Julia Porter. *Victorian Interior Design.* New York: Crescent, 1991.
Banim, John. *The Anglo-Irish of the Nineteenth Century: a novel.* 3 vols. London: Henry Colburn, 1828.
Barratt, Alfred. *Physical Ethics; or, The Science of Action.* London: Williams and Norgate, 1869.
Bascom, John. *The Principles of Psychology.* New York: G. P. Putnam and Sons, 1869.
Beawes, Wyndham. *Lex Mercatoria Rediviva: or, the Merchant's Directory.* 6th ed. Dublin: James Williams, 1773.
Beckmann, Johann. *A History of Inventions, Discoveries, and Origins* [trans. from the German]. 2 vols. 4th ed. London: Henry G. Bohn, 1846.
Bedford, Gunning S. *The Principles and Practice of Obstetrics.* New York: William Wood, 1863.
'Jon Bee.' [John Badcock]. *A Living Picture of London, for 1828, and Stranger's Guide Through the Streets of the Metropolis.* London. W. Clarke etc., 1828.
'Jon Bee.' [John Badcock]. *Slang. A Dictionary of ... the Sporting World.* London. T. Hughes, 1823.
Beeton, Isabella. *Beeton's Book of Household Management.* 1859–61. Facsimile rpt., London: Jonathan Cape, 1868.
Bell, Robert, ed. *The Story-teller; or, Table-book of Popular Literature.* London: Cunningham and Mortimer, 1843.
Bentham, Jeremy. *Book of Fallacies.* London: John & H. L. Hunt, 1824.
Bentham, Jeremy. *Constitutional Code.* Vol. 1. London: Robert Heward, 1830.
Berridge, Virginia. 'Popular Sunday Papers and mid-Victorian Society.' *Newspaper History from the Seventeenth Century to the Present Day.* Ed. George Boyce, James Curran and Pauline Wingate. London: Constable, 1978.
Best, Geoffrey. *Mid-Victorian Britain, 1851–1875.* New York: Schocken Books, 1971.
Bickersteth, Henry. *Medical Hints, Designed for the Use of Clergymen, and Others.* 3rd ed,

revised. London: R. B. Seeley and W. Burnside, 1829.

Bicknell, Algernon Sidney. *In the Track of the Garibaldians through Italy and Sicily*. London: George Manwaring, 1861.

Billington, J. D. 'Mr. Dombey Travels by Rail.' *Dickensian*. 28 (1932): 205–8.

Billington, J. D. 'A Note.' *Dickensian*. 29 (1932/3): 30.

Binney, Marcus, and David Pearce, eds. *Railway Architecture*. London: Bloomsbury Books, 1985.

Binns, John. *Recollections of the Life of John Binns: Twenty-Nine Years in Europe and Fifty-Three in the United States*. Philadelphia: the author, 1854.

Black's Guide to Kent. Edinburgh: Adam and Charles Black, 1874.

Blake, William P. *Production of the Precious Metals: or Statistical Notices of the Principle Gold and Silver Producing Regions of the World*. New York: George P. Putnam, 1869.

Blessington, Marguerite, Countess of. *The Idler in Italy*. 2 vols. London: Henry Colburn, 1839.

Blomfield, C. J. 'A Letter on the Present Neglect of the Lord's Day.' London: B. Fellowes, 1830.

Bloom, Ursula. *Victorian Vinaigrette*. London: Hutchinson, 1956.

Blunt, John Henry. *The Book of Church Law, being an Exposition of the Legal Rights and Duties of the Parochial Clergy and the Laity of The Church of England*. Revised by Walter G. F. Phillimore. 2nd ed. London: Rivingtons, 1876.

Book of English Trades and Library of the Useful Arts. London: J. Souter, 1818.

Boswell, James. *Boswell's Life of Johnson*. Ed. George Birkbeck Hill. Revised and enlarged by C. F. Powell. 6 vols. Oxford: Clarendon, 1934.

Bowditch, Nathaniel. *The New American Practical Navigator*. New York: Edmund M. Blunt, 1821.

Brand, C. P. *Italy and the English Romantics: The Italianate Fashion in Early Nineteenth-Century England*. Cambridge: Cambridge UP, 1957.

Bregion, Joseph, and Anne Miller. *The Practical Cook, English and Foreign*. London: Chapman and Hall, 1845.

Brewer, E. Cobham. *Dictionary of Phrase and Fable*. New edition. Philadelphia: Henry Altemus Company, 1894.

Briggs, Katharine M., ed. *A Dictionary of British Folk-Tales in the English Language, incorporating the F. J. Norton Collection*. Parts A and B. London: Routledge, 1970.

Brilliant, Richard. *Portraiture*. London: Reaktion Books, 1991.

Britain in the Hanoverian Age. 1714–1837, an Encyclopedia. Ed. Gerald Newman. New York/London: Garland, 1997.

The British Cyclopædia of the Arts, Sciences, History, Geography, Literature, Natural History, and Biography. Ed. Charles F. Partington. 10 vols. London: Wm. S. Orr, 1838.

The British Metropolis in 1851. A Classified Guide to London. London: Arthur Hall, 1851.

Britton, John. *A Dictionary of the Architecture and Archaeology of the Middle Ages: Including Words Used by Ancient and Modern Authors in Treating of Architecture and Other Antiquities*. London: Longman, Green, 1838.

Brooks, Charles. *Family Prayer Book, containing Forms of Morning and Evening Prayers for a Fortnight*. Hingham: Farmer and Brown, 1829.

Brooks, Chris. *Mortal Remains: The History and Present State of the Victorian and Edwardian Cemetery.* Exeter: Wheaton, 1989.

Brown, R. Weir. *Kenna's Kingdom: A Ramble through Kingly Kensington.* London: David Brogue, 1881.

Brown, Captain Thomas. *Biographical Sketches and Authentic Anecdotes of Dogs.* Edinburgh: Oliver & Boyd; London: Simpkin and Marshall, 1829.

'Brownies.' *The Mirror of Literature, Amusement and Instruction.* 8 (1826): 110–11.

Buckland, Theresa Jill. 'Edward Scott: The Last of the English Dancing Masters.' *Dancing Research: The Journal of the Society of Dance Research.* 21 (Winter 2003): 3–35.

Bull, Thomas. *Hints to Mothers, for the Management of Health during the Period of Pregnancy, and in the Lying-In Room.* 8th ed. London: Longman, Brown, 1853.

Bull, Thomas. *The Maternal Management of Children, in Health and Disease.* 2nd ed. Philadelphia: Lindsay and Blakiston, 1853.

Bulwer-Lytton, Edward. *England and the English.* 2 vols 1833. London: Routledge, 1876.

Bureaud-Riofrey, A. M. *Treatise on Physical Education; Specially Adapted to Young Ladies.* 2nd ed. London: Longman, Orme, 1838.

Burn, Robert Scott. *Practical Ventilation as Applied to Public, Domestic, and Agricultural Structures.* Edinburgh and London: William Blackwood, 1850.

Burnett, John. *Idle Hands: The Experience of Unemployment, 1790–1990.* London and New York: Routledge, 1994.

Burnett, John. *Plenty and Want: a Social History of Diet in England from 1815 to the Present Day.* London: Methuen, 1979.

Burnett, John. *A Social History of Housing.* 2nd ed. London: Methuen, 1986.

The Busy Hives Around Us: a Variety of Trips and Visits to the Mine, the Workshop and the Factory. London: James Hogg & Sons, 1861.

Butler, Mrs [Fanny Kemble]. *A Year of Consolation.* 2 vols. London: Edward Moxon, 1847.

Butt, John, and Kathleen Tillotson. 'Dickens at Work on *Dombey and Son*.' *Essays and Studies* (1951): 70–93.

C. G. *The King of Saxony's Journey through England and Scotland in the Year 1844.* London: Chapman and Hall, 1846.

Calhoun, Craig, ed. *Dictionary of the Social Sciences.* Oxford: Oxford UP, 2002.

Campbell, Lady Colin, ed. *Etiquette of Good Society.* London: Cassell, 1893.

Campbell, Thomas. *The Complete Poetical Works.* Oxford: Oxford UP, 1907.

Cannon, J. A., ed. *The Oxford Companion to British History.* Oxford: Oxford UP, 1997.

Cannon. John, ed. *Dictionary of British History.* Oxford: Oxford UP, 2009.

Caraboo. Narrative of a singular imposition, practiced upon the benevolence of a lady residing in the vicinity of the City of Bristol, by a young Woman of the name of Mary Willcocks, alias Baker ... alias Caraboo, Princess of Javasu. [J. M. Gutch]. London: Baldwin, Cradock, 1817.

Carlisle, Nicholas. *An Historical Account of the Origin of the Commission Appointed to Inquire Concerning Charities.* London: Payne and Foss, 1828.

Carlyle, Jane Welsh. *Newly Selected Letters.* Ed. Kenneth J. Fielding and David R. Sorensen. Aldershot, Hampshire: Ashgate, 2004.

Carlyle, Thomas. *History of Friedrich II of Prussia, called Frederick the Great.* 6 vols.

London: Chapman and Hall, 1858–65.

Carlyle, Thomas. *Past and Present*. 1843. Ed. Richard D. Altick. Boston: Houghton Mifflin, 1965.

Carus, G. C. *The King of Saxony's Journey through England and Scotland in the Year 1844*. London: Chapman and Hall, 1846.

Cassell's Household Guide to Every Department of Practical Life: Being a Complete Encyclopædia of Domestic and Social Economy. 4 vols. New and rev. ed. London: Cassell, Petter, 1877–8.

Central Society of Education. Second Publication. London: Taylor and Walton, 1838.

Chambers, R., ed. *The Book of Days: a Miscellany of Popular Antiquities*. 2 vols. London and Edinburgh: W. & R. Chambers, 1832.

Chambers's Encyclopædia. A Dictionary of Universal Knowledge for the People. 10 vols. London: W. and R. Chambers, 1868, 1870, 1872, 1874, 1883.

Chambers, William and Robert, eds. *Chambers's Information for the People*. Edinburgh: William & Robert Chambers, 1840, 1842, 1849, 1874.

Chambers, Thomas King. *Manual of Diet in Health and Disease*. 2nd ed. London: Smith, 1876.

Change for the American Notes: in Letters from London to New York. 'By An American Lady' [Henry Wood]. London: Wiley & Putnam, 1843.

Chronicles of the Sea: or, Faithful Narratives of Shipwrecks, Fires, Famines, and Disasters. Vol. 1. London: William Mark Clark, 1838.

'The Church of Notre-Dame at Dijon.' *Saturday Magazine*. 4 (1 February 1834): 42.

Churchill, Fleetwood. *On the Diseases of Infants and Children*. 2nd American Ed. Philadelphia: Blanchard and Lea, 1856.

Churchill, Fleetwood. *On the Diseases of Women; including those of Pregnancy and Childbed*. A New American Edition, with Notes and Additions by D. Francis Condie, M. D. Philadelphia: Blanchard and Lea, 1857.

Cirlot, J. E. *A Dictionary of Symbols*. 2nd ed. London: Routledge and Kegan Paul, 1971.

'The City of Coventry: Local government and public services: Public services.' *A History of the County of Warwick: Volume 8: The City of Coventry and Borough of Warwick* (1969): 275–98.

'The City of Coventry: Social history from 1700.' *A History of the County of Warwick: Volume 8: The City of Coventry and Borough of Warwick* (1969): 222–41.

Clarke, B. *The British Gazetteer, Political, Commercial, Ecclesiastical, and Historical*. 3 vols. London: H. G. Collins, 1852.

Clarke, Bob. *From Grub Street to Fleet Street: an Illustrated History of English Newspapers to 1899*. Aldershot, Hampshire: Ashgate, 2004.

Clarke, M. L. *Classical Education in Britain, 1500–1900*. Cambridge: CUP, 1959.

Clarke, William. *The Boy's Own Book*. 4th ed. London: Vizetely, 1829.

'Club-Life.' *Chambers's Edinburgh Journal*. 1 [October 1845]: 241–4.

Cobbett, James Paul. *A Ride of Eight Hundred Miles in France*. London: C. Clement, 1824.

Cobbett, William. *Eleven Lectures on the French and Belgian Revolutions, and English, and English Boroughmongering*. London: W. Strange, 1830.

Cobbold, Richard. *Valentine Verses: or, Lines of Truth, Love and Virtue*. Ipswich: E.

Shalders, 1827.
Cockburn, Henry Thomas, Lord. *Life of Lord Jeffrey, with a selection from his correspondence*, 2 vols., Edinburgh: Adam and Charles Black, 1852.
Cocoa and Chocolate: A Short History of Their Production and Use. Revised ed. Dorchester, Mass: Walter Baker, 1917.
Coghlan, Francis. *A Guide to France, or, Travellers their Own Commissioners*, 4th ed., London: J. Onwhyn, 1829.
Collins, Philip. *Dickens and Education*. London: Macmillan, 1964.
Collins, Philip, ed. *Dickens: The Critical Heritage*. New York: Barnes and Noble, 1971.
Collins, Philip. 'Dombey and Son–Then and Now.' *Dickensian*. 63 (1967): 82–94.
Colston, Marianne. *Journal of a Tour in France, Switzerland and Italy*. 2 vols. London: G. & W. B. Whittaker, 1823.
Colton, Calvin. *Four Years in Great Britain, 1831–1835*. 2 vols. New York: Harper & Brothers, 1835.
Combe, George. *A System of Phrenology*. 2 vols. 2nd ed. Edinburgh: Maclachlan & Stewart, 1853.
The Comic Almanack. 1st series: 1835–43. London: John Camden Hotten, 1843.
Complete Book of Trades; or, The Parents' Guide and Youths' Instructor. London: John Bennett, 1837.
Conner, Patrick. *The China Trade 1600–1860*. Brighton: Royal Pavilion, Art Gallery & Museums, 1982.
Cooke, Henry T. *An Historical and Descriptive Guide to Warwick Castle, Kenilworth Castle, Guy's Cliff, Stoneleigh Abbey, the Beauchamp Chapel, and Other Places of Interest in the Neighbourhood*. Warwick: Henry T. Cooke, 1849.
Copeland, James. *A Dictionary of Practical Medicine*. 3 vols. London: Longmans, Brown, 1858.
Cotterell, Arthur, ed. *A Dictionary of World Mythology*. Oxford: Oxford UP, 1997.
de Courtais, Georgine. *Women's Headdress and Hairstyles in England from AD 600 to the Present Day*. London: B. T. Batsford, 1973.
Crabb, George. *Dictionary of General Knowledge*, Boston: Gray & Bowen, 1830.
Craik, Dinah Mulock. *A Woman's Thoughts about Women*. London: Hurst and Blackett, 1858.
Cripps, Henry William. *A Practical Treatise on the Laws Relating to the Church and Clergy*. London: S. Sweet, 1845.
Crosby, Frances Jane. *Monterey, and Other Poems*. New York: R. Craighead, 1851.
Cruchley's London in 1865: A Handbook for Strangers. London: G. F. Cruchley, 1865.
Cruchley's Picture of London. 16th ed. London: G. F. Cruchley, 1851.
Cullen, M. J. *The Statistical Movement in Early Victorian Britain: The Foundations of Empirical Research*. Sussex: Harvester, 1975.
Cunningham, Peter. *Handbook of London, Past and Present*. London: John Murray, 1850.
Cunningham, Peter. *Modern London; or, London As It Is*. London: John Murray, 1851.
Cunnington, C. Willet. *Feminine Attitudes in the Nineteenth Century*. 1935. Rpt. New York: Haskell House, 1973.
Cunnington, C. Willett, and Phillis Cunnington. *Handbook of English Costume in the*

Nineteenth Century. London: Faber & Faber, 1966.

Cunnington Phillis, and Catherine Lucas. *Charity Costumes of Children, Scholars; Almsfolk, Pensioners*. New York: Barnes & Noble, 1978.

Cyclopædia of Practical Medicine. Ed. John Forbes, Alexander Tweedie, John Conolly. Vol. 2. London: Sherwood, Gilbert and Piper, 1833.

Dalgairns, Mrs. *The Practice of Cookery adapted to the business of everyday life*. 3rd ed. Edinburgh: Robert Cadell, 1830.

Darnton, F. J. Harvey. *Children's Books in England: Five Centuries of Social Life*. Cambridge: Cambridge UP, 1932.

Davey, Henry. 'Dickens at Brighton.' *Dickensian*. 6 (1910): 257–61.

David, Elizabeth. *Harvest of the Cold Months: the Social History of Ice and Ices*. London: Penguin, 1994.

de Courcy, Margaret, and Beatrice de Courcy. *The Ladies' Cabinet of Fashion, Music, and Romance*. Vol. 3. London: George Henderson, 1840.

Dennis, George. *A Handbook for Travellers in Sicily*. London: John Murray, 1864.

de Stasio, Clotilde. 'Starving vs Cramming: Children's Education and Upbringing in Charles Dickens and Herbert Spencer'. *Dickens Quarterly*. 27 (2010): 299–306.

De Tocqueville, Alexis. *Journeys to England and Ireland*. Ed. J. P. Mayer. New Brunswick, New Jersey: Transaction, 1988.

Dexter, Walter. 'Some Midland Towns and their Association with Dickens.' *Dickensian*. 24 (1928): 178–84.

Dickens, Charles, Jr. *Dickens's Dictionary of London*. London: Charles Dickens, 1879.

Dickens, Mary [Mamie]. *Charles Dickens: by his Eldest Daughter*. London: Cassell, 1886.

Dickens's Dictionary of the Thames: From Oxford to the Nore. London: Charles Dickens, 1883.

Dictionary of Dates, and Universal Reference. 3rd ed. London: Edward Moxon, 1845.

The Dictionary of Trade, Commerce, and Navigation. London: Britain, 1844.

Disraeli, Benjamin. *Tancred; or, The New Crusade*. 3 vols. London: Henry Colburn, 1847.

Disraeli, Isaac. *Curiosities of Literature*. 5th ed. 2 vols. London: John Murray, 1807.

The District Visitor's Manual, 2nd ed. London: John W. Parker, 1840.

Dobson, Michael, and Stanley Wells, eds. *The Oxford Companion to Shakespeare*. Oxford: Oxford UP, 2001.

Dodd, George. *Days at the Factories: or, the Manufacturing Industries of Great Britain. Series I.—London*. London: Charles Knight, 1843.

Dodd, George. *Dictionary of Manufacturers, Mining, Machinery, and the Industrial Arts*. New York: D. Van Nostrand, 1869.

Domestic Servants, As They Are and As They Ought to Be. Brighton: W. Tweedie, 1859.

Doveton, Captain. 'Entrance upon Military Life; or, My First March, and My First Station.' *Colburn's United Service Magazine*. Part 3. London: Henry Colburn, 1844. 101–09.

Dowling, A. J. *A Treatise on the Theory and Practice of Landscape Gardening*. 6th ed. New York: A. O. Moore, 1859.

Drabble, Margaret, ed. *The Oxford Companion to English Literature*. Oxford: Oxford UP, 1985.

Dyos, H. J. 'Railways and Housing in Victorian London.' *Journal of Transport History.* 2 (1955–6): 11–21, 90–100.

Eaton, Mary Eaton. *The Cook and Housekeeper's Complete and Universal Dictionary,* Bungay: J. & R. Childs, 1822.

Eberle, John. *A Treatise on the Practice of Medicine.* 2 vols. Philadelphia: Grigg & Elliot, 1835.

Edgecombe, Rodney Stenning. 'The Heroine of Quiet Service in *Dombey and Son.*' *Dickens Quarterly.* 25 (June 2008): 73–89.

Edinburgh Encyclopædia. Ed. David Brewster. Vol. 7. Edinburgh: William Blackwood and John Waugh, 1830.

Egan, Pierce. *Boxiana; or Sketches of Ancient and Modern Pugilism.* London: G. Smeeton, 1812.

Egan, Pierce. *Life in London; or, The Day and Night Scenes of Jerry Hawthorn, Esq., and His Elegant Friend Corinthian Tom, in their Rambles and Sprees through the Metropolis.* London: Sherwood, Neely & Jones, 1821.

Egan, Pierce. *Pierce Egan's Book of Sports, and Mirror of Life.* London: T. T. and J. Tegg, 1832.

Ellis, Sarah Stickney. *The Women of England, their Social Duties, and Domestic Habits.* New York: D. Appleton, 1843.

Emmerson, George S. 'The Hornpipe.' *Folk Music Journal.* 1970. 12–34.

Encyclopedia Metropolitana; or, Universal Dictionary of Knowledge, on an Original Plan. Ed. Edward Smedley, *et al.* Vol. 18. London: B. Fellowes, 1845.

'The English in India.' *The Westminster Review.* 68 (July 1857): 99–116.

Etiquette, Social Ethics, and the Courtesies of Society. London: Wm. S. Orr, 1854.

Eversley, William Pender, and William Feilden Craies. *The Marriage Laws of the British Empire.* 1910. Rpt. Littleton, Colorado: Fred B. Rothman, 1989.

'Expense of Funerals.' *Knight's Penny Magazine.* 13 (9 March 1844): 94–6.

Fagg, Michael. *The Life and Adventures of a Limb of the Law.* London: A. Hancock, 1836.

Fairburn, John. *The Universal Songster; or, Museum of Mirth.* Vol. 3. London: John Fairburn, 1826.

Fairfax, John. *New Guide and Directory to Leamington-Spa and its Environs.* 3rd ed. Leamington: John Fairfax, 1835.

Farrington, Karen. *Dark Justice: A History of Punishment and Torture.* Toronto: Reed Consumer Books, 1996.

Ferrier, Susan. *Destiny; or, The Chief's Daughter.* 2 vols. Philadelphia: Carey and Lea, 1831.

'A Few Thoughts on Small-Talk.' *The New Monthly Magazine and Literary Journal.* No. 27. 1 March 1823: 217–22.

Fielding, K. J. "The Monthly Serialisation of Dickens's Novels." *Dickensian.* 54 (1958): 4–11.

Fields, James T. 'Some Memories of Charles Dickens.' *The Atlantic Monthly.* 26 (August 1870): 235–45.

Fifty-Two Sermons by the Late Rev. William Howels. London: R. B. Seeley, and W. Burnside, 1836.

'Fire Caused by a Railway Engine.' *The New York Legal Observer.* 8 (1850): 7.
Fitzgerald, Percy. *The Royal Dukes and Princesses of the Family of George III.* 2 vols. London: Tinsley Brothers, 1882.
Flanders, Judith. *Inside the Victorian Home: A Portrait of Domestic Life in Victorian England.* New York: Norton, 2003.
Fletcher, W. J. 'The Captain of the Tartar.' *Macmillan's Magazine.* 86 (September 1902): 345–54.
Forbes, R. B. *Remarks on China and the China Trade.* Boston: Samuel N. Dickinson, 1844.
Ford, John. *Prizefighting: The Age of Regency Boximania.* South Brunswick and New York: Great Albion Books, 1971.
'Four Years in France.' *The New Monthly Magazine and Literary Journal.* Part II. Original Papers. 1826. 268–72.
Foxe's Book of Martyrs. A Universal History of Christian Martyrdom from the Birth of our Blessed Saviour to the Latest Periods of Persecution. 2 vols. Philadelphia: E. C. Biddle, 1840.
Francis, John. *A History of the English Railway: Its Social Relations and Revelations, 1820–1845.* 2 vols. London: Longman, Brown, 1851. Rpt. New York: Augustus M. Kelley, 1968.
Freer, Martha Walker. *Elizabeth de Valois, Queen of Spain and the Court of Philip II.* 2 vols. London: Hurst and Blackett, 1857.
Fuller, Margaret. *At Home and Abroad.* 1856. New and Complete Edition. New York: The Tribune Association, 1869.
Further Report of the Commissioners Appointed ... to continue the Inquiries concerning Charities in England and Wales ... Dated 19th July 1834. Part II. House of Commons: 1835. 895–924.
Gager, Valerie L. *Shakespeare and Dickens: The Dynamics of Influence.* Cambridge: Cambridge UP, 1996.
Gamble, John. *Views of Society and Manners in the North of Ireland.* London: Longman, 1819.
Gardiner, Juliet, and Neil Wenborn. *The History Today Companion to British History.* London: Collins & Brown, 1995.
Gascoigne, Caroline Leigh. *The School for Wives.* 3 vols. London: Henry Colburn, 1841.
Gatrell, V. A. C. *The Hanging Tree: Execution and the English People: 1770–1868.* Oxford: Oxford UP, 1994.
Gavarni, Paul, and Albert Smith. *Gavarni in London: sketches of life and character.* London: D. Bogue, 1849.
Gilbart, James W. *Principles and Practice of Banking.* New Edition. London: Bell & Daldy, 1871.
Gilbert, E. W. 'The Growth of Brighton.' *The Geographical Journal.* 114 (July–September 1949): 30–52.
Gleig, George Robert. *The Subaltern's Log-Book.* 2 vols. New York: J. & J. Harper, 1829.
Goffe-Stoner, Martha. ' "She Was Very Young, and Had No Mother": An Unnoticed Browning Allusion in *Dombey and Son.*' *Dickens Studies Newsletter.* 13 (1982): 97–9.
Goldberg, Michael. *Carlyle and Dickens.* Athens, Georgia: U of Georgia Press, 1972.

Goldsmith, Oliver. *The Collected Works of Oliver Goldsmith*. 5 vols. Ed. Arthur Friedman. Oxford: Clarendon Press, 1966.

Graham, Thomas John. *Modern Domestic Medicine*. 3rd ed. London: Simpkin and Marshall, 1827.

Graham, Thomas John. *Modern Domestic Medicine*. London: the author, 1827, 1835.

Grant, James. *The Great Metropolis*. 2 vols. London: Saunders and Otley, 1837.

Grant, James. *Lights and Shadows of London Life*. 2 vols. London: Saunders and Otley, 1842.

Grant, James. *Random Recollections of the House of Commons, from the Year 1830 to the Close of 1835*. 5th ed. Philadelphia: E. L. Carey & Hart, 1836.

Grant, Judith Skelton. 'Italians with White Mice in *Middlemarch* and *Little Dorrit*.' *English Language Notes*. 16 (1979): 232–4.

Greenwood, James. *The Seven Curses of London*. London: S. Rivers, 1869.

Greenwood, James. *In Strange Company: being the experiences of a roving correspondent*. London: H. S. King, 1874.

Greenwood, James. 'Studies of Street Life. The Coalheaver, Ancient and Modern.' *London Society*. 21 (April 1872): 333–40.

Griffin, James. *Memories of the Past; Records of Ministerial Life*. London: Hamilton, Adams, 1883.

Grose's Classical Dictionary of the Vulgar Tongue. Revised and Corrected … by Pierce Egan. London: Sherwood, Neely, 1823.

[Grose, Francis]. *A Dictionary of Buckish Slang, University Wit, and Pickpocket Eloquence*. London: C. Chappel, 1811.

Grossmith, William Robert. *Amputations and Artificial Limbs*. London: Longman, 1857.

Grove, Sir George, ed. *A Dictionary of Music and Musicians*. 4 vols. London: Macmillan, 1880, 1883 and 1889.

Grove, J. S. P. 'Walter's Enthusiasm for "The Admiral." ' *Dickensian*. 12 (1916): 74–5.

Guide to Kenilworth and its Neighbourhood. London: T. Nelson, 1858.

A Guide to the Unprotected in Every-day Matters Relating to Property and Income [1863]; 6th ed, revised. 'By a Banker's Daughter.' London: Macmillan, 1891.

Guizot, François. *Memoirs of Sir Robert Peel*. London: Richard Bentley, 1857.

The Gulistan: Being the Rose-garden of Shaikh Sa'di. Trans. Edwin Arnold. New York: Harper & Bros, 1899.

The Habits of Good Society: A Handbook for Ladies and Gentlemen. New York: Carlton, 1869.

Hale, Sarah Joseph. *The Ladies' New Book of Cookery: a Practical System for Private Families in Town and Country*. 5th ed. New York: H. Long and Brother, 1852.

Hall, James. *Dictionary of Subjects and Symbols in Art*. London: John Murray, 1974. Revised ed. 1979.

Hallam, Henry. *The Constitutional History of England*. 2 vols. London: John Murray, 1827.

Hancock, David. 'Commerce and Conversation in the Eighteenth-Century Atlantic: The Invention of Madeira Wine.' *The Journal of Interdisciplinary History*. 29 (Autumn 1998): 197–219.

A Handbook of Rome and its Environs. 7th ed. London: John Murray, 1864.

A Handbook for Travellers on the Continent: being a Guide through Holland, Belgium, Prussia, and Northern Germany. 3rd ed. London: John Murray, 1838.
A Handbook for Travellers in France. London: John Murray, 1844.
A Handbook for Travellers in Kent. 4th ed. London: John Murray, 1877.
A Handbook for Travellers in Switzerland and the Alps of Savoy and Piedmont. London: John Murray, 1838.
Hankey, Thomson. *The Principles of Banking, its Utility and Economy; with Remarks on the Working and Management of the Bank of England*. London: Effingham Wilson, 1867.
Hare, Augustus J. C. *Walks in London*. 2 vols. New York, George Routledge and Sons, 1878.
Harrison, Stephen. 'Horace and the Victorians.' *Perceptions of Horace: a Roman Poet and his Readers*. Ed. L. B. T. Houghton and Maria Wyke. Cambridge: CUP, 2009: 290–304.
Harrison, W. H. *Waldemar: A Tale of the Thirty Years' War*. London: Smith, Elder, 1833.
Hartley, Florence. *Ladies' Book of Etiquette, and Manual of Politeness: a Complete Hand Book for the Use of the Lady in Polite Society*. Boston and New York: Lee & Shepard, 1872.
Hazlitt, William. *Notes of a Journey through France and Italy*. London: Hunt and Clarke, 1826.
Heads of the People: Or, Portraits of the English. Drawn by Kenny Meadows. London: Robert Tyas, 1840.
Heads of the People: Or, Portraits of the English. Drawn by Kenny Meadows. London: Willoughby, 1841.
Hebert, Luke. *The Engineer's and Mechanic's Encyclopædia*. 2 vols. London: Thomas Kelly, 1846.
Henderson, Andrew. *Scottish Proverbs*, Edinburgh: Oliver & Boyd, 1832.
Hill, Nancy K. *A Reformer's Art: Dickens' Picturesque and Grotesque Imagery*. Athens, Ohio: Ohio UP, 1981.
Hitchins, Fortescue. *The History of Cornwall*. 2 vols. Helston: William Penaluna, 1824.
A History of the County of Warwick. Volume 7—The City of Birmingham. Ed. W. B. Stephens. Victoria County History. Woodbridge, Suffolk: Boydell & Brewer, 1969.
'History of Royal Leamington Spa'. <http://www.royal-leamington-spa.co.uk/htmlfiles/frame.htm> Royal Leamington Spa.
Hole, S. Reynolds. *Then and Now*. London: Hutchinson, 1902.
Hollingshead, John. *Ragged London in 1861*. London: Smith, Elder, 1861.
Hollington, Michael. 'Dickens and the Dance of Death.' *Dickensian*. 74 (1978): 67–74.
Hollington, Michael. *Dickens and the Grotesque*. London: Croom Helm, 1984.
Holt, Alfred H. 'Captain Cuttle's Quotations.' *Dickensian*. 28 (1932): 303–08.
Hone, William. *The Every-Day Book and Table Book; or, Everlasting Calendar of Popular Amusements* … 3 vols. London: Thomas Tegg & Son, 1838.
Hood, Thomas. *The Comic Annual for 1842*. London: Henry Colburn, 1842.
Hood, Thomas. *Poems*. New York: Wiley and Putnam, 1846.
Horn, Pamela. *The Rise and Fall of the Victorian Servant*. Dublin: Gill & Macmillan/New York: St Martin's, 1975.
[Hotten, John Camden]. *Charles Dickens: The Story of his Life*. New York: Harper &

Brothers. 1870.
[Hotten, John Camden]. *The Slang Dictionary; or, the Vulgar Words, Street Phrases, and "Fast" Expressions of High and Low Society.* London: John Camden Hotten, 1865.
The Housekeeper's Book ... for Economical Domestic Cookery. [Frances Harriet Green]. Philadelphia: William Marshall, 1837.
Howells, William Dean. *Venetian Life.* 2 vols. 2nd ed. Boston, Mass.: Houghton, Mifflin, 1895.
Hughes, Katherine. *The Victorian Governess.* London: Hambledon Press, 1993.
Hunt, Leigh. *The Autobiography of Leigh Hunt.* 2 vols. New York: Harper & Brothers, 1850.
Hurst, Isobel. *Victorian Women Writers and the Classics: the Feminine of Homer.* Oxford: OUP, 2006.
Hutton, R. H. 'The Genius of Dickens.' Rpt. in *Brief Literary Criticism.* Ed. E. M. Roscoe. London: Macmillan, 1906. 56–7.
Hutton, W. *The History of Birmingham.* 6th ed. London: George Berger, 1835.
Hymns ... a Supplement to Dr Watts' Psalms and Hymns. William Bengo Collyer. London: The Author, 1812.
'Indian Servants.' *Chambers's Journal.* 3 (27 March 1886): 202–5.
Infant Education. 3rd ed. London: Simpkin & R Marshall, 1825.
Ingoldsby Legends; or, Mirth and Marvels. (1837). [Richard Harris Barham]. Philadelphia: Willis P. Hazard, 1856.
Jalland, Pat. *Death in the Victorian Family.* Oxford: Oxford UP, 1996.
James, G. P. R. *The Step-mother. A Tale.* New York: Harper & Brothers, 1846.
James, John. *The Treasury of Medicine; or, Everyone's Medical Guide.* London: George Routledge, 1854.
James, Lawrence. *Raj: The Making and Unmaking of British India.* New York: St. Martin's Press, 1998.
Jeffrey, David Lyle, ed. *A Dictionary of Biblical Tradition in English Literature.* Grand Rapids, Eerdmans, 1992.
John, Juliet. *Dickens's Villains: Melodrama, Character, Popular Culture.* Oxford, Oxford UP, 2001.
Johnson, Cuthbert W. 'On the Improvement of the Cottages of the Agricultural Labourers.' *The British Farmer's Magazine.* New Series. 11 (1847): 208–11.
Johnson, Steven. *The Ghost Map.* New York, Penguin, 2006.
Jones, William. *How to Make Home Happy: or, Hints and Cautions for All.* London: David Bogue, 1857.
The Journey-Book of England in Hampshire. London: Charles Knight, 1841.
Kellett, John R. *The Impact of Railways on Victorian Cities.* London: Routledge & Kegan Paul; Toronto: U of Toronto Press, 1969.
Kemp, Dixon. *A Manual of Yacht and Boat Sailing,* 9th ed. Revised by B. Heckstall Smith. London: Horace Cox, 1900.
Kemp, Peter, ed. *The Oxford Companion to Ships and the Sea.* London: Oxford UP, 1976.
'Kenilworth Castle.' *The Penny Magazine.* 4 (31 July 1835): 289–96.
Kennedy, Carol. *Mayfair: A Social History.* London: Hutchinson, 1986.

Kerr, James. *The Land of Ind; or, Glimpses of India*. London: Longmans, Green, 1873.
Kerr, Robert. *A General History and Collection of Voyages and Travels*. Edinburgh: Blackwood, London: John Murray, [1811].
Kerr, Robert. *The Gentleman's House; or, How to Plan English Residences, from the Parsonage to the Palace*. London: John Murray, 1865.
Kingsford, P. W. *Victorian Railwaymen: The Emergence and Growth of Railway Labour 1830–1870*. London: Frank Cass, 1970.
Kiple, Kenneth F., ed. *The Cambridge World History of Human Disease*. Cambridge, Cambridge UP, 1993.
Kirkup, John. *A History of Limb Amputation*. London: Springer-Verlag. 2007.
Kitchiner, William. *The Cook's Oracle, Containing Receipts for Plain Cookery*. A new edition. Edinburgh: Robert Cadell, 1843.
Kitton, Frederic G., *Charles Dickens by Pen and Pencil, with Supplement*. London: F.T. Sabin, 1890.
Knight, Charles. 'Geography; or, the First Division of 'The English Cyclopædia.' 1866, 1.1109. London: Bradbury, Evans, 1866.
Knight, Charles. *London*. 6 vols. London: Charles Knight, 1841–4, 1851.
Knight's Cyclopædia, 1851. London: Charles Knight, 1851.
Kost, J. *Domestic Medicine. A Treatise on the Practice of Medicine, adapted to The Reformed System.'* Cincinnati: J. W. Sewell, 1859.
Lamb, Charles, John Bull, Thomas Hood. *The Laughing Philosopher*. London: Sherwood, Jones. 1825.
Landes, David. *The Unbound Prometheus. Technological Change and Industrial Development in Western Europe from 1750 to the Present*. Cambridge: Cambridge UP, 1969.
Lardner, Dionysius. *Railway Economy*. London: Taylor, Walton, 1850.
Larson, Janet L. *Dickens and the Broken Scripture*. Athens, Georgia: U of Georgia Press, 1985.
Larwood, Jacob, and John Camden Hotten. *The History of Signboards from the Earliest Times to the Present Day*. London: John Camden Hotten, 1866.
Lawson, John, and Harold Silver. *A Social History of Education in England*. London: Methuen, 1973.
Leigh's New Picture of London. London: W. Clowes, 1819.
Le Sage, Alain-René. *The Devil upon Two Sticks*. Translated from *Le Diable boiteux of M. Le Sage*. London: J. Walker, 1815.
Lester, V. Markham. *Victorian Insolvency: Bankruptcy, Imprisonment for Debt, and Company Winding-Up in Nineteenth-Century England*. Oxford: Clarendon Press, 1995.
Levinge, Captain R. G. A. 'The Atlantic—A Winter's Passage.' *Echoes from the Backwoods; or, Sketches of Transatlantic Life*. 2 vols. London: Henry Colburn, 1846.
Lewis, Samuel, ed. *A Topographical Dictionary of England*. 7th ed. London: the author, 1848.
Ley, J. W. T. 'The Sea Songs of Dickens.' *Dickensian*. 27 (1931): 255–66.
Ley, J. W. T. 'Sentimental Songs in Dickens.' *Dickensian*. 28 (1932): 313–21.
Ley, J. W. T. 'The Sporting Songs of Dickens.' *Dickensian*. 28 (1932): 187–9.
Lichten, Frances. *Decorative Art of Victoria's Era*. New York: Bonanza Books, 1950.
Lieber, Francis, ed. *Encyclopædia Americana*. Philadelphia: Desilver, Thomas, 1835.

Lightwood, James T. *Charles Dickens and Music*. 1912. London: C. H. Kelly, 1912.
Litvack, Leon. *Charles Dickens's 'Dombey and Son': an Annotated Bibliography*. The Dickens Bibliographies. Duane DeVries. General Ed. New York: AMS Press, 1999.
Lockhart, J. G. *Memoirs of the Life of Sir Walter Scott, Bart*. London: Ticknor and Fields, 1861.
Loftie, W. J. *In and Out of London; or, the Half-Holidays of a Town Clerk*. London/New York: Society for Promoting Christian Knowledge/Pott, Young, 1875.
Lohrli, Anne, ed. *'Household Words': A Weekly Journal, 1850–1859, Conducted by Charles Dickens. A Table of Contents, List of Contributors and their Contributions Based on the 'Household Words' Office Book*. Toronto: U of Toronto P, 1973.
London in 1838. By An American. New York: Samuel Colman, 1839.
London in the Sixties: (with a few digressions), by One of the old brigade. [Donald Shaw]. London: Everett, 1908.
London Encyclopædia. 22 vols. London: Thomas Tegg, 1829.
'The Love of the Country.' *The New Monthly Magazine*. 'Part the Third.' 1842: 87–94.
Macaulay, Alexander. *A Dictionary of Medicine: designed for popular use*. Edinburgh: Adam Black, 1831.
Mackay, Charles. *Under the Blue Sky*. London: Sampson Low, 1871.
Maddon, R. R. *The Literary Life and Correspondence of the Countess of Blessington*. 2nd ed. 3 vols. London: T. C. Newby, 1855.
Magazine of Domestic Economy. Vol. 2. London: W. S. Orr, 1837.
Mallet, Robert. 'Polyzonal Lens for Railway Signals.' *Mechanics' Magazine, Museum, Register, Journal, and Gazette*. 41 (17 August 1844): 104.
Malthus, Thomas Robert. *The Works of Thomas Robert Malthus*. 8 vols. Ed. E. A. Wrigley and David Souden. London: William Pickering, 1986.
Mangnall, Richmal. *Historical and Miscellaneous Questions, for the Use of Young Persons*. New Edition. London: Partridge and Oakey, 1848.
Manners and Rules of Good Society, or, Solecisms to be Avoided. 14th ed. London: Frederick Warne, 1887.
'The Map of London a Hundred Years Ago.' *The Gentleman's Magazine*. 42 (July 1854): 17–23.
McCalman, Iain, ed. *An Oxford Companion to the Romantic Age. British Culture 1776–1832*. Oxford: Oxford UP, 1999.
M'Clintock, John, and James Strong. *Cyclopædia of Biblical, Theological, and Ecclesiastical Literature*. New York: Harper & Brothers, 1889.
McCulloch, J. R. *A Descriptive and Statistical Account of the British Empire*. 2 vols. London: Longman, Brown, 1847, 1854.
McCulloch, J. R. *A Treatise on the Circumstances Which Determine the Rate of Wages and the Condition of the Labouring Classes*. 2nd ed. London: Routledge, 1854.
McKenna, Frank. *The Railway Workers, 1840–1970*. London: Faber and Faber, 1980.
Major, Gwen. 'Miss Tox's Dwelling Place.' *Dickensian*. 62 (1966): 122–4.
Mason, Michael. *The Making of Victorian Sexuality*. Oxford: Oxford UP, 1995.
Mayall, David. *Gypsy-travellers in Nineteenth-Century Society*. Cambridge: Cambridge UP, 1987.
Mayhew, Henry, and John Binny. *The Criminal Prisons of London and Scenes of Prison Life*.

London: Griffin, Bohn, 1862.
Mayhew, Henry. *London Labour and the London Poor*. 4 vols. London: Griffin, Bohn and Company, 1851.
The Melodist, and Mirthful Olio; an Elegant Collection of the Most Popular Songs. Vol. 3. London: H. Arliss, 1829.
Mermin, Dorothy. *Godiva's Ride: Women of Letters in England, 1830–1880*. Bloomington: Indiana UP, 1993.
The Metropolitan Charities. London: Sampson Low, 1844.
Metz, Nancy Aycock. *The Companion to 'Martin Chuzzlewit'*. Helm Information, 2001.
Miles, Henry Downes. *Pugilistica: The History of British Boxing Containing Lives of the Most Celebrated Pugilists*. 3 vols. Edinburgh: John Grant, 1906.
Milliken, W. E. 'The Little Midshipman.' *The Antiquary*. 4 (July–December 1881): 85–6.
Mills, James. *The History of British India*. 3 vols. London: Baldwin, Cradock, 1817.
Mirth in Miniature; or Bursts of Merriment. Derby: H. Mozley, 1825.
Mitch, David. 'Literacy and Mobility in Rural versus Urban Victorian England.' *UMBC Economics Department Working Papers* (October 2003): 1–35.
Mitch, David. *The Rise of Popular Literacy in Victorian England: the Influence of Private Choice and Public Policy*. Philadelphia: U of Pennsylvania Press, 1992.
Mitchell, B.R. *British Historical Statistics*. Cambridge: Cambridge UP, 1988.
Mitchell, Sally. *Daily Life in Victorian England*. Westport, Conn.: Greenwood Press, 1996.
Mogg's New Picture of London; or Strangers' Guide to the British Metropolis. London: E. Mogg, 1848.
Moncrieff's Guide to Leamington Spa, and its Vicinity. Leamington & Warwick: John Merridew, 1833.
Money, J. W. B. *Java; or, how to Manage a Colony*. 2 vols. London: Hurst and Blackett, 1861.
Moore, Thomas. *Letters and Journals of Lord Byron: with Notices of His Life*. 2 vols. London: John Murray, 1830.
Morier, James. *The Mirza*. 3 vols. London: Richard Bentley, 1841.
Morley, John. *Death, Heaven and the Victorians*. Pittsburgh, Pa.: U of Pittsburgh Press, 1971.
Mosse, Henrietta Rouvière. *A Father's Love and a Woman's Friendship*. 5 vols. London: J. Darling, 1825.
'Mrs. Bib's Baby.' *Punch*. 10 (1846): 53.
Mumford, Lewis. *Technics and Civilization*. 1934. New York: Harcourt, Brace, 1963.
National History and Views of London and its Environs. 2 vols. London: Allan Bell, 1832.
Nenadic, Stana. 'The Small Family Firm in Victorian Britain.' *Business History*. 35 (October 1993): 86–114.
Nevile, George. *Horses and Riding*. 2nd ed. London: Longmans, Green, 1877.
A New and Enlarged Military Dictionary. 2 vols. Charles James. London: T. Egerton, 1810.
A New System of Practical Domestic Economy. New Edition. London: Henry Colburn, 1827.

Newman, Gerald, ed. *Britain in the Hanoverian Age, 1714–1837, an Encyclopedia*. New York/London: Garland, 1997.
Nightingale, J. *An Historical Account of Kenilworth Castle, in the County of Warwick*. London: Wetton & Jarvies, 1821.
Nimrod. *The Road*. New Edition. London: John Murray, 1851.
North Sea Pilot. Part 4, River Thames and Medway, and the Shores of the North Sea. ... London: Hydrographic Office, 1863.
'Obituary.' *Pharmaceutical Journal and Transactions*. Third Series. 6 (1875–6): 597.
'Ocean Penny-Postage.' *Chambers's Edinburgh Journal*. 12 (7 July 1849): 79.
Olmsted, Denison. *A Compendium of Natural Philosophy*. New Haven, Conn.: S. Babcock, 1842.
Olsen, Donald J. *The Growth of Victorian London*. New York: Holmes & Meier, 1976.
'On the Conditions of Divine Forgiveness.' *The Christian Examiner*. 3 (September and October 1826): 379–90.
'On the False Position a Governess Holds in Society.' *The New Monthly Belle Assemblée*. 25 (December 1846): 262–3.
Opie, Mrs Amelia. *The Works of Mrs Amelia Opie, Complete in Three Volumes*. Philadelphia: James Crissy, 1843.
'Opticians' Signs.' *Notes and Queries* (23 May 1903): 412–14.
Ormond, Leonée. 'Dickens and Painting: the Old Masters.' *Dickensian*. 79 (1983): 130–51.
Osborne's London & Birmingham Guide. Birmingham: E. C. & W. Osborne, 1840.
Osterhammel, Jürgen. 'Britain and China, 1842–1914.' *The Oxford History of the British Empire*. Vol. 3. *The Nineteenth Century*. Ed. Andrew Porter. Oxford: Oxford UP, 1999.
Ostrogorski, M. *Democracy and the Organization of Political Parties*. 2 vols. New York: Macmillan, 1902.
Otis, Laura. *Networking: Communicating with Bodies and Machines in the Nineteenth Century*. Ann Arbor: U of Michigan Press, 2001.
The Oxford Companion to British History. Ed. John Cannon. Oxford: Oxford UP, 1997.
Palmer, William J. *Dickens and New Historicism*. New York: St. Martin's Press, 1997.
Parker, Richard G., and J. Madison Watson. *The National Third Reader: Containing Exercises in Articulation, Accent, Pronunciation, and Punctuation; Numerous and Progressive Exercises in Reading, and Notes Explanatory of Different Words and Phrases, on the Pages Where They Occur*. New York: Barnes & Burr, 1865.
Parkes, Mrs William. *Domestic Duties; Or, Instructions to Young Married Ladies, on the Management of Their Households, and the Regulations of Their Conduct in the Various Relations and Duties of Married Life*. Third American edition from the third London edition. New York: J. J. Harper, 1829.
Parkinson, James. 'An Essay on the Shaking Palsy.' 1817. Rpt. in *Journal of Neuropsychiatry and Clinical Neurosciences*. 14 (2002): 223–36.
Paroissien, David. *The Companion to 'Great Expectations'*. East Sussex: Helm Information, 2000.
Paroissien, David. *The Companion to 'Oliver Twist'*. Edinburgh: Edinburgh UP, 1992.
Pascoe, Charles Eyre, ed. *A Practical Handbook to the Principal Schools of England, based

for the most part on the Statutes, Schemes, and Regulations made under the Public Schools' Acts by the Public School Commissioners; under Various Schemes of the Endowed Schools Commissioners; and also upon Information Furnished by the Head Masters. London: Sampson Low, 1877.

Patten, Robert L. *Charles Dickens and his Publishers*. Oxford: Clarendon Press, 1978.

Patterson, R. H. *The Economy of Capital or Gold and Trade*. Amended Edition. Edinburgh and London: William Blackwood and Sons, 1865.

'Peace and War Agitators.' *Blackwood's Edinburgh Magazine*. 66 (November 1849): 581–606.

Pebody, Charles. 'Life in London. VIII.—At Tattersall's.' *The Gentleman's Magazine*. July–December 1873: 35–48.

Peck, John. *Maritime Fiction: Sailors and the Sea in British and American Novels, 1719–1917*. Basingstoke, Hampshire: Palgrave, 2001.

Pemble, John. *The Mediterranean Passion: Victorians and Edwardians in the South*. Oxford: Clarendon Press, 1987.

Penny Cyclopædia of the Society for the Diffusion of Useful Knowledge. London: Charles Knight, 1836, 1837 and 1843.

Percy, Sholto and Reuben. *London: or Interesting Memorials of its Rise, Progress and Present State*. 3 vols. London: T. Boys, 1824.

'Peruvian Silver Mines.' *The Merchants' Magazine*. 17 (July–December 1847): 433–6.

Peterson, M. Jeanne. *The Medical Profession in Mid-Victorian London*. Berkeley: U of California Press, 1978.

Philpotts, Trey. *The Companion to 'Little Dorrit'*. East Sussex: Helm Information, 2003.

Philpotts, Trey. 'Mad Bulls and Dead Meat: Smithfield Market as Reality and Symbol.' *Dickens Studies Annual*. 41 (2010): 25–44.

'Piccadilly: An Episode of Contemporaneous Autobiography.' *Blackwood's Magazine*. American Edition. 60 (March 1865): 374–86.

Picard, Liza. *Victorian London: The Life of a City 1840–1870*. New York: St. Martin's, 2006.

Picker, John M. *Victorian Soundscapes*. Oxford: Oxford UP, 2003.

Piesse, G. W. Septimus. *The Art of Perfumery and Method of Obtaining the Odors of Plants*. Philadelphia: Lindsay and Blakiston, 1857.

Pillet, René Martin. *Views of England, during a residence of ten years; six of them as a prisoner*. Boston: Parmenter and Norton, 1818.

Pimlott, J. A. R. *The Englishman's Holiday: A Social History*. London: Faber & Faber, 1947.

A Pinch – of Snuff. Composed of curious particulars and original anecdotes of snuff taking … 'By Dean Snift of Brazen-Nose' [Benson Hill]. London: Robert Tyas, 1840.

Pinto, Erasmus [Latham Smith]. *Ye Outside Fools! Glimpses Inside the Stock Exchange*. London: Samuel Tinsley, 1876.

Plain Observations on the Management of Children during the First Month, Particularly Addressed to Mothers. London: Underwood, 1828.

The Poetical Works of Miss Landon. Philadelphia: E. L. Carey and A. Hart, 1839.

Political Dictionary; Forming a Work of Universal Reference, both Constitutional and Legal. 2 vols. London: Charles Knight, 1845.

Poovey, Mary. *A History of the Modern Fact: Problems of Knowledge in the Sciences of Wealth and Society*. Chicago: U of Chicago Press, 1998.
Pope, Norris. *Dickens and Charity*. New York: Columbia UP, 1978.
The Popular Encyclopedia. Vol. 1. Pt 2. Glasgow: Blackie & Son, 1836.
The Popular Encyclopedia; or, "Conversations Lexicon:" Vol. 6. Glasgow: Blackie & Son, 1846.
Porter, G. R. *The Progress of the Nation, in its Various Social and Economical Relations. From the Beginning of the Nineteenth Century to the Present Time*. 3 vols. London: Charles Knight; John Murray, 1836, 1847.
Porter, Roy. 'Nervousness, Eighteenth and Nineteenth Century Style: From Luxury to Labour.' Eds. Marijke Gijswijt-Hofstra and Roy Porter. *Cultures of Neurasthenia from Beard to the First World War*. Amsterdam, NY: Rodopi, 2001. 31–49.
The Ports, Harbours, Watering-Places, and Coast Scenery of Great Britain. 2 vols. London: George Virtue, 1842.
A Practical Treatise on Breeding, Rearing and Fattening All Kinds of Domestic Poultry. [John Lawrence]. London: Sherwood, Neely & Jones, 1816.
Pratt, John Tidd. *The History of Savings Banks in England, Wales, and Ireland*. London: C. J. G. & F. Rivington, 1830.
Prichard, M. F. Lloyd, ed. *The Collected Works of Edward Gibbon Wakefield*. Glasgow: Collins, 1968.
Pückler-Muskau, Hermann. Trans. Sarah Austin. *Tour of England, Ireland and France, in the Years 1826, 1827, 1828, and 1829*. Philadelphia: Carey, Lea & Blanchard, 1833.
Raffles, Thomas. 'Letters during a tour of France, Savoy … in the summer of 1817.' *Christian Library*. 1 (1833): 389–438.
Von Raumer, Frederick. *England in 1835*. Philadelphia: Carey, Lea, 1836.
Raverat, Gwen. *Period Piece: A Cambridge Childhood*. 1952. London: Faber & Faber, 1987.
Read, Newbury Frost. 'Did Mr. Dombey Take his Chariot?' *Dickensian*. 29 (1932/33): 25–30.
Redding, Cyrus. *Every Man His Own Butler*. London: Whittaker, 1839.
Redding, Cyrus. *Fifty Years' Recollections, Literary and Personal, with Observations on Men and Things*. 3 vols. London: Charles J. Skeet, 1858.
Redding, Cyrus. *A History and Description of Modern Wines*. 2nd ed. London: Whittaker, 1836.
Reichard, M. *A Descriptive Road-Book of France*. New Edition. London: Samuel Leigh, 1829.
Report … From the Poor Law Commissioners, on an Inquiry into the Sanitary Condition of the Labouring Population of Great Britain. Vol. 27. London: W. Clowes and Sons, 1842.
'Researches Respecting the New Planet Neptune' [review of books on astronomy]. *North British Review* 7 (May 1847): 110–31.
Richardson, Henry S. *Greenwich: Its History, Antiquities, Improvements, and Public Buildings*. Greenwich: Harriet Richardson, 1834.
Richardson, M. A. *The Local Historian's Table-Book of Remarkable Occurrences…* 2 vols. London: J. R. Smith, 1844.

Ridley, Jasper. *Lord Palmerston*. New York: E. P. Dutton, 1970.
Ripley, George, and Charles A. Dana, eds. *The New American Cyclopædia: A Popular Dictionary of General Knowledge*. 16 vols. New York / London: D. Appleton and Company, 1860.
Roberts, George. *The Terms and Language of Trade and Commerce, and the Business of Every-day Life, Alphabetically Arranged, and Fully Explained*. London: Longman, Orme, 1841.
Robinson, N. 'The British House of Commons.' *Frank Leslie's Popular Monthly*. 10 (July 1880): 2–11.
Rodes, Robert E. *Law and Modernization in the Church of England: Charles II to the Welfare State*. Notre Dame: U of Notre Dame Press, 1991.
Roscoe, Thomas. *The London and Birmingham Railway*. London: Charles Tilt, 1839.
Routledge's Manual of Etiquette. 1860. Charleston, SC: BiblioBazaar, 2006.
Ruskin, John. *Praeterita: The Autobiography of John Ruskin*. Oxford: Oxford UP, 1989.
Russell, Norman. *The Novelist and Mammon: Literary Responses to the World of Commerce in the Nineteenth Century*. Oxford: Clarendon Press, 1986.
Sadie, Stanley, ed. *The New Grove Dictionary of Music and Musicians*. 2nd ed. 29 vols. UK and Europe: Macmillan; US and Canada: Grove's Dictionaries, 2001.
'Sailors' Homes.' *Chambers's Edinburgh Journal* 18 (4 September 1852): 153–5.
The Sailors' Prayer Book; A Manual of Devotion. London: John Snow, 1852.
Sala, George Augustus. *Daylight and Gaslight, with Some London Scenes They Shine Upon*. London: Chapman and Hall, 1859.
Sala, George A. *Dutch Pictures, with Some Sketches in the Flemish Manner*. London: Tinsley, 1861.
Salmon, Edward. 'Domestic Service and Democracy.' *Fortnightly Review*. 49 (March1888): 408–17.
Sanders, Andrew, ed. *Dombey and Son*. London: Penguin, 2002.
Sanderson, Michael. 'Literacy and Social Mobility in the Industrial Revolution in England.' *Past and Present* 56 (1972): 75–103.
Schacht, Paul. 'Dickens and the Uses of Nature.' *Victorian Studies*. 34 (Autumn 1990): 77–102.
Schlesinger, Max. *Saunterings in and about London*. London: N. Cooke, 1853.
'Science Notices.' *The Dublin Review* 40 (April 1884): 444–8.
'Scientific Notices.' *The London Journal of Arts, Sciences, and Manufactures*. London: W. Newton, 1846.
Scott, Charles Henry. *The Baltic, the Black Sea, and the Crimea: Comprising Travels in Russia, A Voyage down the Volga to Astrachan, and a Tour through Crim Tartary*. London: Richard Bentley, 1854.
Sea Songs and Ballads. By Dibdin and Others. London: Bell and Daldy, 1863.
The Servant's Behaviour Book; or, Hints on Manners and Dress for Maid Servants in Small Households. By 'Mrs Motherly' [Emily Augusta Patmore]. London: Bell & Daldy, 1859.
Shatto, Susan. *The Companion to 'Bleak House'*. London: Unwin Hyman, 1988.
Sheppard, Francis. *London 1808–1870: The Infernal Wen*. Berkeley and Los Angeles: U of California Press, 1971.

Sherwood, Mrs. *The Infant's Progress, from the Valley of Destruction to Everlasting Glory.* 3rd ed. Wellington, Salop: F. Houlston and Son, 1823.

Shivelbusch, Wolfgang. *The Railway Journey: the Industrialization of Time and Space in the Nineteenth Century.* Berkeley and Los Angeles: U of California Press, 1977, 1986.

Sickelmore, Richard. *History of Brighton and its Environs.* 5th ed. Brighton: C. and R. Sickelmore, 1827.

Silver, Carole G. *Strange and Secret People: Fairies and Victorian Consciousness.* Oxford: Oxford UP, 1999.

Simmons, Jack. *The Victorian Railway.* New York: Thames and Hudson, 1991.

Simmons, Jack, and Gordon Biddle, eds. *The Oxford Companion to British Railway History From 1603 to the 1990s.* Oxford: Oxford UP, 1997.

Simpson, Jacqueline, and Steve Roud. *A Dictionary of English Folklore.* Oxford: Oxford UP, 2000.

Simpson, Margaret. *The Companion to 'Hard Times'.* East Sussex: Helm Information, 1997.

Slater, Michael. *Charles Dickens.* New Haven and London: Yale UP, 2009.

Slater, Michael, ed. *The Dent Uniform Edition of Dickens' Journalism.* Vol. 2. *'The Amusements of the People' and Other Papers.* London: J. M. Dent, 1996.

Slater, Michael. *Dickens and Women.* J. M. Dent, 1983.

Smith, Eugene R. *The Gospel in All Lands.* New York: Missionary Society, 1888.

Smith, Charles Manby. *Curiosities of London Life; or, Phases, Physiological and Social, of the Great Metropolis.* 1853. London: F. Cass, 1972.

Smith, Horace. *The Poetical Works of Horace Smith.* 2 vols. London: Henry Colburn, 1846.

Smith, John Thomas. *An Antiquarian Ramble in the Streets of London.* Ed. Charles Mackay. 2 vols. London: Richard Bentley, 1846.

Smith, Sydney. *The Works of the Rev. Sydney Smith.* London: Longman, Brown, 1850.

Smith, Thomas. *A Topographical and Historical Account of St Mary-le-Bone.* London: John Smith, 1833.

Smyth, William Henry. *The Sailor's Word-Book: An Alphabetical Digest of Nautical Terms.* London: Blackie and Son, 1867.

Some Account of the Worshipful Company of Ironmongers. Compiled by John Nicholl. London: John Bowyer Nichols & Son, 1851.

'Some Hints on the Most Efficient Modes of Administering Medicines. By a Practitioner of Half a Century.' *Medico-Chirurgical Review* 82 (1 October 1844): 585–6.

Sondrup, Steven P. 'Wertherism and *Die Lieden des jungen Werther.' European Romanticism: Literary Cross-Currents, Modes, and Models.* Ed. Gerhart Hoffmeister. Detroit: Wayne State UP, 1990.

Songs of the Late Charles Dibdin. 3rd ed. London: Henry G Bohn, 1850.

Southey, Robert [under the pseudonym 'Don Manuel Alvarez Espriella']. *Letters from England. Translated from the Spanish.* 1807. New York: George Dearborn, 1836.

Sparkes, Ivan George. *Stagecoaches and Carriages: An Illustrated History of Coaches and Coaching.* Bourne End: Spurbooks, 1975.

Speake, Jennifer, ed. *The Oxford Dictionary of Proverbs.* Oxford: Oxford UP, 2003.

'Special Collections: Playbills. Theatre Royal, Brighton.' University of Kent at Canterbury.

<http://library.kent.ac.uk/library/special/icons/playbills/brightontheatreroyal.htm>

Staples, Joseph. *A Few Practical Observations on the Art of Cupping*. London: Longman, Rees, 1835.

Starke, Marianne. *Travels in Europe for the Use of Travellers on the Continent, and Likewise in the Island of Sicily*. London: John Murray, 1833; Paris: A. and W. Galignani, 1836.

Starke, Thomas. *A Treatise on the Law of Slander and Libel*. 2nd ed. 2 vols. London: J. & W. T. Clarke, 1830.

Staunton, Howard. *The Great Schools of England: an Account of the Foundation, Endowments, and Discipline of the Chief Seminaries of Learning in England; including Eton, Winchester, Westminster. St. Paul's, Charter-House, Merchant Taylors', Harrow, Rugby, Shrewsbury, etc. etc.* London: Sampson Low, 1865.

Steig, Michael. *Dickens and Phiz*. Bloomington: Indiana UP, 1978.

Steig, Michael. '*Dombey and Son* and the Railway Panic of 1845.' *Dickensian*. 67 (1971): 145–8.

Steel, John William. *A Historical Sketch of the Society of Friends in Newcastle and Gateshead, 1653–1898*. London: Headley Brothers, 1899.

Stocqueler, J. H. *The Military Encyclopedia; a Technical, Biographical, and Historical Dictionary*. London: Wm. H. Allen & Co., 1853.

Stonehouse, J. H. *Catalogue of the Library of Charles Dickens from Gadshill … .* London: Piccadilly Fountain, 1935.

'Summary of Occupations of Persons Enumerated in England and Wales …'. *Abstract of the Answers and Returns … Occupation Abstract*. London: W. Clowes, 1844.

The Supplement to the Penny Cyclopædia of the Society for the Diffusion of Useful Knowledge. Vol. 2. London: Charles Knight, 1846.

Surtees, Robert Smith. *Mr Romford's Hounds*. London: Bradbury, Agnew, 1865.

Survey of London: The Grosvenor Estate in Mayfair. Vol. 39. London: Athlone Press, 1977.

Sutherland, John. 'Does Carker Have False Teeth?' *Who Betrays Elizabeth Bennet? Further Puzzles in Classic Fiction*. Oxford: Oxford UP, 1999.

Sutherland, John. *The Longman Companion to Victorian Fiction*. Harlow: Longman, 1988.

Syme, James. *Principles of Surgery*. 3rd ed. London: H. Baillière, 1842.

Tait, William. *Magdalenism: An Inquiry into the Extent, Causes and Consequences of Prostitution in Edinburgh*. 2nd ed. Edinburgh: P. Ricard, 1842.

Talbot, James Beard. *The Miseries of Prostitution*. London: James Madden, 1844.

Tallis, John. *Tallis's London Street Views*. London: John Tallis, [1839].

Tappan, Henry P. *A Step from the New World to the Old, and Back Again*. 2 vols. New York: D. Appleton, 1852.

Tayler, Charles Benjamin. *May You Like It*. Philadelphia: John Conrad, 1822.

Taylor, J. *The Wonders of Nature and Art, Comprising Upwards of Three Hundred of the Most Remarkable Curiosities and Phenomena in the Known World*. 8th ed. London: J. Chidley, 1838.

Tennyson, Hallam. *Alfred Lord Tennyson: a Memoir*. 2 vols. London: Macmillan, 1897.

Thames Haven Dock and Railway; Incorporated by Act of Parliament; with Observations on Their Anticipated Advantages. London: W. Lewis and Son, 1841.

Thompson, M. W. *The Decline of the Castle*. Cambridge: Cambridge UP, 1987.

Thomson, Anthony Todd. *The Domestic Management of the Sick-Room*. London: Longman, Orme, 1841.

Thomson J., and Adolphe Smith. *Street Life in London*. New York: B. Blom. 1877. Rpt. 1969.

Thornbury, George Walter, and Edward Walford. *Old and New London*. 6 vols. London: Cassell, Petter & Galpin, 1873–8.

Thorne, James. *Handbook to the Environs of London*. 2 vols. 1876. Rpt. Godfrey Cave Associates, 1983.

Thornton, Edward. *Illustrations of the History and Practices of the Thugs, and Notices of Some of the Proceedings of the Government of India, for the Suppression of the Crime of Thuggee*. London: Nattali and Bond, 1851.

Thornton, Peter. *Authentic Décor: The Domestic Interior 1620–1920*. 1984. London: Seven Dials, Cassell, 2000.

Thornwell, Emily. *The Lady's Guide to Perfect Gentility*. New York: Derby and Jackson, 1856.

Tillotson, Kathleen. 'Louisa King and Cornelia Blimber.' *Dickensian*. 74 (1978): 91–5.

Tillotson, Kathleen. 'Steerforth's Old Nursery Tale.' *Dickensian*. 79 (1983): 31–4.

Timbs, John. *Curiosities of London*. London: John Camden Hotten, 1867.

Timbs, John. *Popular Errors Explained and Illustrated*. London: Tilt and Bogue, 1841.

Todd, Alpheus. *On Parliamentary Government in England: Its Origin, Development and Practical Operation*. 2 vols. London: Longmans, Green, 1869.

Tomkins, Alannah. 'Retirement from the Noise and Hurry of the World?: the Experience of Almshouse Life, 1650–1850.' Paper presented at the Voluntary Action History Society Seminar, 22 April 2008.

Tomlins, Sir Thomas Edylne. *The Law-Dictionary, Explaining the Rise, Progress, and Present State of the British Law*. With extensive additions … by Thomas Colpitts Granger, Esq. 2 vols. London: J. and W. T. Clarke, 1835.

Tooke, Thomas. *A History of the Prices and of the State of Circulation, from 1793 to 1837*. 2 vols. London: Longman, Orme, 1838.

Toynbee, William, ed. *Diaries of William Charles Macready, 1833–1851*. New York: Putnam's, 1912.

Trollope, Anthony. *North America*. New York: Harper & Bros., 1862.

Trollope, Anthony. *Travelling Sketches*. London: Chapman and Hall, 1866.

Trollope, Thomas Aldophus. *A Summer in Brittany*. 2 vols. London: Henry Colburn, 1840.

Tuck, Henry. *The Railway Shareholder's Manual*. 8th ed. London: Effingham Wilson, 1847.

Ure, Andrew. *A Dictionary of Arts, Manufactures, and Mines*. 2 vols. New York: D. Appleton, 1844.

The Useful Arts Employed in the Production of Clothing. 2nd ed. London: John W. Parker, 1851.

Vance, Norman. *The Victorians and Ancient Rome*. Oxford: Blackwell, 1997.

Velpeau, Alfred. *An Elementary Treatise on Midwifery*. Trans. from the French. 3rd American edition. Philadelphia: Lindsay & Blakiston, 1845.

Vicinus, Martha. *Suffer and Be Still: Women in the Victorian Age*. Bloomington: Indiana UP, 1973.
Vitali, Miroslaw, K. P. Robinson *et al. Amputations and Prostheses*. London: Baillière Tindall, 1978.
Walford, Cornelius. *The Insurance Cyclopædia*. London: Charles and Edwin Layton, 1871.
Walker, Donald. *Defensive Exercises*. London: Thomas Hurst, 1840.
Walkowitz, Judith R. *Prostitution and Victorian Society: Women, Class, and the State*. Cambridge: Cambridge UP, 1982.
'Walks in the Neighbourhood of London.' *The London Saturday Journal* 1 (30 March 1839): 193–5.
Walpole, Spencer. *The Electorate and the Legislature*. London: Macmillan, 1881.
Warwick Castle: An Illustrated Survey of the Historical Warwickshire Home of the Earls of Warwick. Warwick Castle Estate Office: Leamington Spa, n.d.
Waterston, William. *A Cyclopædia of Commerce, Mercantile Law, Finance, Commercial Geography and Navigation*. A New Edition. London: Henry G. Bohn, 1847.
Watkins, Gwen. *Dickens in Search of Himself*. Totowa, NJ: Barnes and Noble, 1986.
Watkins, John. *A Biographical, Historical and Chronological Dictionary*. London: Richard Phillips, 1806.
Watson, B. A. *A Treatise on Amputations of the Extremities* … . Philadelphia: P. Blakiston, 1885.
Watts, Isaac. *The Works of the Reverend and Learned Isaac Watts, D.D.* London: J. Barfield, 1810.
Webb, R. K. *Modern England*. 2nd ed. New York: Harper & Row, 1980.
Webster, Thomas, and Mrs. Parkes. *An Encyclopædia of Domestic Economy*. New York: Harper & Brothers, 1855.
Weale, John. *The Pictorial Handbook of London*. London: H. G. Bohn, 1854.
Weinreb, Ben, and Christopher Hibbert, eds. *The London Encyclopedia*. 2nd ed. London: Macmillan, 1993.
Wells, Stanley, ed. *A Dictionary of Shakespeare*. Oxford: Oxford UP, 1998.
Weskett, John. *A Complete Digest of the Theory, Laws, and Practice of Insurance*. London: Frys, Couchman, 1783.
Westland, Ella. 'Dickens's *Dombey* and the Storied Sea.' *Dickens Studies Annual*. 35 (2004): 87–108.
Wheatley, Henry B. *London Past and Present. Its History, Associations, and Traditions*. 3 vols. London: John Murray, 1891.
White, Walter. *A Month in Yorkshire*. London: Chapman and Hall, 1861.
Whitehead, Jack. *The Growth of Camden Town: AD 1800–2000*. 2nd ed. London: Jack Whitehead, 2000.
Whytt, Robert. *The Works of Robert Whytt*. Edinburgh, J. Balfour,1768.
Wilderspin, Samuel. *On the Importance of Educating the Infant Poor*. 2nd ed. London: Simpkin & R. Marshall, 1824.
Wiley, Margaret. 'Mother's Milk and Dombey's Son.' *Dickens Quarterly*. 13 (1996): 217–28.
Williams, Frederick S. *Our Iron Roads: Their History, Construction, and Administration*.

London: Ingram, Cooke, and Co., 1852; 2nd ed. revised. London: Bemrose & Sons, 1883. Rpt. Frank Cass, 1968.

Willis, Hal. 'The "Pop" Visit.' *Bentley's Miscellany.* 9 (1841): 150–7.

Wilson, Charles. *Observations on Gout and Rheumatism.* 3rd ed. revised. London: The Author, 1833.

Wollaston, William. 'On Sounds Inaudible by Certain Ears.' *Philosophical Transactions of the Royal Society.* 110 (1820): 306–14.

'Wonderful Trees, No.3 – the India Rubber Tree.' *Robert Merry's Museum.* 17 (1849): 131–3.

Wood, Edward J. *The Wedding Day in All Ages and Countries.* 2 vols. London: Richard Bentley, 1869.

Woodforde, John. *The Strange Story of False Teeth.* London: Routledge, 1968.

'The World of London. Part III.' *Blackwood's Edinburgh Magazine.* 50 (July 1841): 60–71.

'Wreckage.' *Littell's Living Age.* 35 (October–December 1852): 174–7.

Wright, Brian. *Firemen's Uniforms.* Haverfordwest: Shire Publications, 1991.

Wyld, J. W. *The London and Birmingham Railway Guide.* London: James Wyld, 1838.

Yates, Edmund. *His Recollections and Experiences.* 2 vols. London: Richard Bentley, 1884.

Young, John H. ed., *Our Deportment or the Manners, Conduct and Dress of the Most Refined Society.* Detroit: F. B. Dickerson, 1880.

Zucchi, John E. *The Little Slaves of the Harp: Italian Child Street Musicians in Nineteenth-Century Paris, London, and New York.* Montreal/Kingston: McGill-Queen's UP, 1992.

INDEX

Page numbers in *italic* refer to illustrations

Aberdeen, George Hamilton Gordon, 4th Earl of, 521
accidents: railway, 6, 480–1; reported in newspapers, 462; at sea, 106, 266, 286, 300, 349, 453; street, 100; as subject of small talk, 198
accomplishments (of ladies), 262
accounts (household), 444–5
acrostics, 273
Acton, Eliza: *Modern Cookery*, 384
Adam, Robert and James, 46
Adams, Samuel and Sarah: *The Complete Servant*, 88, 115, 132, 366
Adams, William Bridges, 255
Addison, Joseph, 139, 187, 300, 354, 455
Administrative Reform Association, 521
Aesop, 332
Afghan War, first (1838–42), 137
Agnew, Sir Andrew, 225
ailments, *see* diseases and ailments
Ainger, Alfred, 161
Ainsworth, William Harrison: *Crichton*, 310
air pollution, *see under* sanitary reform
Alcott, Bronson, 159
Aldgate, 54; Pump, 487
Alfred the Great, King, 195
Alken, Henry, 421
Allestree, Richard, 35, 362
allusions, literary, *see under* author of work referred to; for books of the Bible, *see under* Bible; for anonymous works, *see* title
almshouses, 490, 509–10
Alphington, Devon, 319
Alston, J. W.: *Hints on Landscape Painting*, 262
American Journal of Education, 159
American War of Independence (1775–83), 360
Americans, The (opera), 438
amputations, *see* prostheses
anæsthetics, 51
Anderson, John Henry, 190
angels, fallen, 365
Anglicans, *see* Church of England
Anglo-Irish of the Nineteenth Century, The, 520
Anglo-Norman architecture, 405–6
animals: bears, 304; bulls, 4, 100–1, 138; camels, 412; cattle, 93, 100–1, 418, 470; cows, 146, 257; crocodiles, 413; dolphins, 142; donkeys, 513; elephants, 57, 171, 254, 422; guinea pigs, 312; horses, 36, 248, 343, 426, 473; lions, 135; mice, 49; monkeys, 49; peacocks, 416; pigs, 100; porcupines, 48, 49; rabbits, 312; rats, 306; sheep, 93, 96, 100, 131, 134; snails, 131; snakes, 311-12, 327–8; squirrels, 49; tigers, 57; tortoises, 49; wolves, 131, 214, 418; *see also* birds; dogs
Annual Register, The, 290, 294, 397, 419
Anti-Slavery Society, 44
antiquarianism, 405–6
apothecaries, 194-5; *see also* physicians; surgeons
Arabian Nights' Entertainments, The, 2, 179, 183–4; *see also* oriental tales
archæology, 2, 83
army: standing, 497–8
Army List, 153
Arne, Thomas, 69
Arnold and Dent, Messrs, 58
Arnold, Samuel James, 438
Articles of War, 152
artificial limbs, *see* prostheses
Ashbourne, Edward Gibbon: *Pitt: Some Chapters of His Life and Times*, 82
Ashby, J. Sterry, 57–8
Asmodeus (demon), 432
'at home', 371, 412; *see also* visiting-cards; weddings: cards
attorney's clerks, 84–5
auctions, 81, 182, 381, 470, 510–2
Aulnoy, Marie-Catherine Le Jumel de Barneville, baronne d': *Fairy Tales and Novels*, 131
Austen, James, 139
Austin, Henry, 431
Australia, 4, 96–7, 360, 365

Babbage, Charles: 'On the Permanent Impression of Our Words and Actions on the Globe We Inhabit', 290–1
babies: breast-feeding, 28, 35–9, 43, 73; care of, 19, 22, 76; clothing, 114; development, 80; pincushions, 32; *see also* children
Babylon, 83
Backhouse, James, 93
Bacon, Francis: *Essays*, 221
Baden-Baden, 338–9, 371
Bahadur Shah II, Mughal Emperor, 316
Baillie, Captain William, 196
Baines, Edward, 89
baize: Bible covers, 133; doors, 170
Baldwin, Edward, 106
Ball, John, 224
ballads: 6, 62, 230, 283, 491; street, 2, 34, 35, 140; *see also* songs
Ball's Pond, Islington, 223–4, 337

ballooning, 71
Bank of England, 55–6, 348, 373, 375
bankers, banking: 26, 46, 56; records and books, 64; savings banks, 418; *see also* Bank of England
bankruptcy, 26, 500–3
baptism *see* children: christening
Baptists, 496
Barbados, 4, 25, 185
Barclay, Perkins, & Co., Messrs, 43
Barham, R. H.: *The Ingoldsby Legends*, 522
bark (medicinal), 440–1
Barnaby Rudge, 200, 411, 446
Barnum, Phineas T., 187
Baroni, Pompeo, 166
barons, 312–3
barrel-organs, 49, 164, 170; *see also* street musicians
Barrymore, William, 401
basket-making, 306
Bass, Michael Thomas, 164, 277
Bath chair, 253
Batt, Thomas, 266
Battle Bridge, London, 337
Battle of Life, The, 2
Bayham Street, Camden Town, 3, 93, 519
Bayswater, 190
beadles: 83, 90, 236, 488; in church, 86, 332; at inquests, 450–1
beards, *see* whiskers 333
Beaumont, Francis and John Fletcher: *The Lovers' Progress*, 471; *The Maid's Tragedy*, 471
Beckford, William: *Modern Novel Writing*, 310
Bedlam (Bethlehem Hospital), 79, 307
Beethoven, Ludwig van: cello sonatas, 463
Beeton, Isabella Mary: on food, 92, 186, 192, 200, 237, 260, 296, 320, 508, 523; household advice, 45, 115, 367, 372, 378–80
beggars: 83, 181, 305–6, 34; in France, 477–8
beheading, 327
Belcher, James (Jem), 236, 270, 518
Belcher, Tom, 420
Bell, Dr Andrew, 497
Bell, Sir Charles, 108, 460
bell-ringers, 488–9, *489*
bellows-mending, 306
Bengal, 56, 110, 136, 137, 402, 415, 493
Bentham, Jeremy, 90, 119
Bentinck, Lord William, 415
Bentley's Miscellany (magazine), 88, 310
Berkeley, G. C., 98
Berkshire, 377
Bethlehem Hospital, *see* Bedlam
betting, 182, 267
beverages: beer, 26, 97, 145, 282–3, 289, 349, 470; brandy, 30, 325; champagne, 379; chocolate, 382, 347, 407; coffee, 138, 146, 347, 379; currant wine, 138; egg-wine, 523; gin, 343; ginger beer, 321; grog, 72, 283; lemonade, 26, 523; Madeira, 64, 67, 146, 379; milk, 259–60, 282, 283, 382, 441; mulled wine, 509; negus, 200; port wine, 200; porter, 43, 192; punch, 34; rum, 61, 145, 146, 347; sherry, 379, 508–9, 523; table beer (small beer), 192, 460; tea, 88, 128, 133, 154, 177, 194, 320, 325, 329; wine, 26, 97, 152, 208, 238, 325, 329, 347, 378–80, 522; *see also* drinking
Bible: 2, 87, 89, 90; 133; taught in school, 392; Acts, 226, 327; Chronicles, 363; 1 Corinthians, 358, 399, 446, 506; 2 Corinthians, 358, 410; Ecclesiastes, 362, 524; Ephesians, 173, 410; Exodus, 153, 332, 416, 453; Galatians, 506; Genesis, 134, 201, 264, 305, 354, 414, 491, 515; Hebrews, 343; Isaiah, 214, 365; James, 358; Job, 346; John, 393; Joshua, 292; 1 Kings, 484; 2 Kings, 154, 439, 482; Luke, 267, 505; Mark, 471; Matthew, 282, 389, 432; Micah, 232, 490; New Testament, 389, 506; Old Testament, 81, 506; Peter, 455; Philippians, 410; Proverbs, 204, 232, 293; Psalms, 28, 250, 328, 338, 413, 445, 485, 510, 514; Revelation, 214, 365, 510; Romans, 293, 414; 2 Samuel, 510; Sermon on the Mount, 389, 432
biblical characters: Adam and Eve, 491; Cain and Abel, 264; Jezebel, 482; Joshua, 292; Judah (tribes of), 389, 392; Judith and Holofernes, 470; Nebuchadnezzar, 470; Melchizedek, 201; Methuselah, 414–5; Moses, 332; Noah, 305; Patriarchs, 490; Paul, St (Saul of Tarsus), 293, 327, 414; Potiphar's wife, 354; prodigal son, 267; Solomon, 293, 484
Bickersteth, Edward, 202
bill-discounters, 26
billiard-marker, 271–2
Binny, John, 103
bird-catchers, 264–5, 280, 355, 428
birds: 57, 172; cage birds, 114, 346, 355; caught by bird-catchers, 264–5, 280, 355; exotic, 353–4, 484–5; food, 346; parrots, 353–4, 370, 484; peacocks, 416; pigeons, 265, 280–1, 394, 428; performing, 49; *see also* animals
Birmingham, 7, 242, 246–8, 268; *see also* London and Birmingham Railway
Birmingham and Midland Institute, 291
Bishop, Samuel: *Poems on Various Subjects*, 387
Blackstone, William: *Commentaries on the Laws of England*, 331
Blackwood's Edinburgh Magazine, 18, 84, 417, 497
Blake, William: *Jerusalem*, 55
Bleak House, 54, 81, 163, 200, 214, 272, 292, 392, 421, 447, 455–6, 522
Blessington, Marguerite, Countess of, 81, 469
block-makers, 146, 519
Blonde, HMS, 229
Blue-coat School (Christ's Hospital), 90–1, *91*, 418–9

'Boarding House, The', 309
boiler, *see under* railways
bolt-rope, 491
bombazeen, 33, 130
Bond Street, 269, 337, 523
bonds (deeds), 144
bone-house, 295
Book of Common Prayer (*BCP*): 2, 250, 413; Baptism, 86–7; Burial of the Dead, 399, 448, 505; Catechism, 71, 76, 90, 148, 284, 416, 438–9, 497; on Gunpowder Plot, 86; Prayers to be used at Sea, 351, 448; 'Psalter', 250; Solemnization of Matrimony, 71, 284, 338, 339, 453, 489–90, 518
Book of English Trades, The (1818), 43
Book of Trades (1837), 194
Borrow, George, 492
Boston Blind School (Massachusetts), 90
Boswell, James: *Life of Samuel Johnson*, 130
bottle-makers, 428
Bourne, J. C., *207*
Bow Bells, 54–5, 72
boxers, boxing: brutality, 492; drinking, 271, 420; Jackson and, 523; morality, 421; nicknames, 269; practice, 268–71; as publicans, 420; purses (prizes), 233, 236; as science, 268, 269, 270, 338; slang, 401, 420, 517–8
Boyce, William, 146
Bradbury and Evans (publishers), 14, 18
Bradshaw's Guide, 241
Braham, John, 438
Bramhall, J.: *Defence of True Liberty of Human Actions*, 41
brass bands, *see under* street musicians
Brayley, Edward: *The Graphic and Historical Illustrator*, 406
breakfast: after marriage ceremony, 340
breaking on wheel, 177
Brewer, James Norris: *The Picture of England*, 406
brick-fields, 355
'bricks-and-mortar', 205, 355, *356*
brides: 66, 101, 339–40; trousseau, 486; visiting etiquette, 371, 383; *see also* marriage and divorce; weddings
Bridgewater Treatise, Ninth, 290–1
brig, 347
Brighton, 6, 120, 125–6, 131–2, *160*; Bedford Hotel, 152, 404; Brunswick Square, 484; Royal Pavilion, 133; Theatre Royal, 196
Britain: 26, 177, 190, 193, 199, 246, 307; imperial ambitions, 334; and India, 137, 254; lighthouses, 285; manufacturing, 246; possessions abroad, 150, 272; railways, 209; slavery, 403; standing armies, 497
British Association for the Advancement of Science, 199
British Empire, 272, 485

British and Foreign Schools Society, 497
British Gazetteer, The, 352
British Metropolis, The, 210
Britton, John: *The Beauties of England and Wales*, 406
Broadstairs, Kent, 61, 288
Brocken (Hartz mountains), 362
brokers, 58, 142, 144
'Broker's Man, The', 144
Brontë, Anne: *Agnes Grey*, 120
Brontë, Charlotte, 121
Brontë, Emily, 121
Brook Street, Grosvenor Square, 328
Brooks's Club, London, 405
brothels, 359; *see also* prostitution
Brothers Grimm, 332
Brougham, Henry, Baron, 403
Brown and Lenox, Messrs, 146
Browne, Hablot Knight: accompanies CD to Leamington, 247–8, 251; CD's directions to, 2, 22, 83, 174, 240, 247–8, 253, 256; dark plate technique, 476; illustrations, 6, *12*, *23–4*, 53, 82, 101, *127*, 138, 196, 255, 304, *427*, 463, 470, 519
Browne, Mary Anne: 'The Moorland Child', 348
brownies (household), 446
Browning, Robert, 2; *A Blot in the 'Scutcheon* (play), 278
Brummell, George Bryan ('Beau'), 377, 407
Brunel, Isambard Kingdom, 256, 287
Bryanstone Square, 46, 268, 329
Buchan, William: *Domestic Medicine*, 125
budget (collection), 396
Builder, The (magazine), 353
Bull, Thomas: *The Maternal Management of Children*, 38, 43, 73
Bunyan, John: *The Life and Death of Mr Badman*, 354; *Pilgrim's Progress*, 236
burden (ship's), 347
Burdett Coutts, Angela, Baroness, *see* Coutts, Angela Burdett
Burke, Edmund: *Thoughts on the Cause of the Present Discontent*, 305
Burnett, Harry, 3, 120
Burnett, Henry and Fanny, 120
Burnett, Sir William, 146
Burney, Fanny (Mme d'Arblay): *Camilla*, 123; *Cecilia*, 82
Burney, James: *A Chronological History of Voyages and Discoveries in the South Sea*, 141
Burns, Robert: 'The Deil's Awa' wi' the Exciseman', 335
Burton, Robert: *The Anatomy of Melancholy*, 503
Bury, Lady Charlotte Campbell: *The Manoeuvring Mother*, 170
business: 25–7; family owned, 26–7; for girls, 444–5; 'wholesale, retail and for exportation', 14;

see also under type of business
Butcher, Edmund: 'On Moderation' (sermon), 504
Butler, Joseph, Bishop of Durham, 119
Butler, Samuel, 503
butlers, *see under* servants 329
Butt, John and Kathleen Tillotson, 2, 26, 105
Byrom, John: 'Enthusiasm, a Poetical Essay', 310
Byron, George Gordon, 6th Baron, 2, 17, 198, 231, 269, 522–3; *Beppo*, 357; *Childe Harold's Pilgrimage*, 168, 395, 440, 502; *Don Juan*, 354, 504; *The Prisoner of Chillon*, 261; 'So We'll Go No More A-Roving', 311; 'The Waltz', 81, 113

Calais, 467, 468, 477, 479
Caledonia (ship), 286
Camden Town, 3, 93–4, 95–7, 98, 205, 207–8, 212, 355
Campbell, Lady Colin: *Etiquette of Good Society*, 76, 87
Campbell, Thomas: 'Ye Mariners of England', 284, 491
cannibals, 395
Canning, George: 'The Pilot that Weathered the Storm', 82, 521
Cannon, Tom, 236
capital punishment, 327, 465; *see also* beheading; executions
capitalists, 4, 25, 97, 98
Capper, John: 'Our Russian Relations', 198
'Caraboo, Princess', 446
card games: cribbage, 487; piquet, 262–3, 304; whist, 317, 400
Cardigan, James Thomas Brudenell, 7th Earl of, 233
Carême, Anton: *Le Cuisinier Parisien*, 92
Carlton Club, London, 407
Carlton, William J., 128
Carlyle, Thomas, 2, 98, 185, 290, 324; *The French Revolution*, 238, 432; *Latter Day Pamphlets*, 82, 98, 222; *On Heroes, Hero-Worship and the Heroic in History*, 356–8; *Past and Present*, 39, 308, 351, 414; *Sartor Resartus*, 201
Caroline of Ansbach, Queen, 191
carmen, 498
carriages and coaches: on the Continent, 335, 468–9, 473, 477, 478; barouche, 78, 255; carriage (private), 355, 380; chariots, 248, 421; diligence, 468; donkey-carts, 260; fly-van, 514; gig, 355, 512; hackney (cab), 36, 44, 78–9, 94, 100, 208, 232, 342, 381; omnibuses, 100, 208, 341-2, 355; phæton, 6, 473; post-chaises, 78, 241, 248; spring-vans, 512; stage-carriage, 342; stage-coaches (-carriages), 152, 171, 208, 247, 258, 342, 384; waggons, 513
case bottles, 60
Cassell's Household Guide, 47, 181
catechisms (children's books), 121, 122, 176, 187;

see also under Book of Common Prayer
Catholicism, *see* Roman Catholicism
cathedrals: 244, 405–6; dean (ecclesiastical), 493, 496; in France, 466, 468, 477; *see also* St Paul's
Caxton, William: *The Golden Legend*, 105
Central Society of Education, 154, 164, 264, 266
Cervantes Saavedra, Miguel: *Don Quixote*, 2, 82, 282, 439
Chadwick, Edwin, 324; *The Poor Laws in London and Berkshire*, 192; *The Practice of Interment in Towns*, 45, 120; *Report on the Sanitary Conditions of the Labouring Population of Great Britain*, 45
chair-mending, 306
Chalk, near Gravesend, 487
Chalmers, Revd Dr Thomas, 202, 430
Chalmers, Dr Thomas, 202
Chambers, William: *About Railways*, 208
Chambers, William and Robert: *Chambers's Information for the People*, 160
Chambers's Edinburgh Journal, 17, 100, 110, 242, 453, 462, 465
Chancery court, 447
chandlers (ship's), 52, 146, 321, 347
changelings, 42, 121
Chantry, Sir Francis, 222
Chapman, George: translates Homer, 163
charity: almshouses, 509–10; and 'Hen' Pearce, 271; and night watchmen, 440; *see also* charity schools; hospitals
charity schools: 89–92, 264, 266, 386, 388, 392, 419; Charity Hospital (Blue-Coat School), 90–1, *91*, 418, 419; Christ's Hospital, 91; Royal Military College, 152
Charles I, King, 497
Charming Sally (ship), 67
Chartism, 4
Chatham, 3, 93; dockyard, 286–7
Chaucer, Geoffrey: Dryden translates, 231, 414; *Canterbury Tales*, 2; *The Knight's Tale*, 231
Cheapside, 54, 104, 182, 205, 277
Cherry, Andrew, 397
cherubs, 338
Chesterfield, Philip Dormer Stanhope, 4th Earl of, 200
chickweed, 346
childbirth, 19, 22, 29–30, 35, 36; muffled door-knockers, 29
children: 'child-stripping' (clothes), 103; christening, 76–7, 83, 85–7; and death, 212; didactic literature, 136; diet, 132; education, 89, 121–2, 135–6, 154, 264; employment, 248; sent home from India, 137–8; upbringing ('management'), 39, 51, 80, 129, 132, 155; *see also* babies; catechisms
Child's History of England, A, 309, 313, 523
Chimes, The, 182, 324
chimney-boards, *see under* furniture

China, 4, 52, 61, 88, 372; labourers (coolies), 4, 403; trade, 485
'Chinese Junk, The', 52
Chinese language, 220
Chinese Saloon, 124
Cholmondeley, George Horatio, 2nd Marquess of, 227
Christmas Carol, A, 64, 325
Christ's Hospital, *see* Blue-coat School
Chronicles of the Sea, 68, 294
chronometers, *see* nautical instrument makers
Chubb, Charles and Jeremiah, 462
Church of England: 76, 82, 85, 187, 343, 506; and divorce, 434–5; forms of addressing clergy, 493, 496; and National Schools, 497; *see also* cathedrals
churches: 90, 95, 195, 206, 244, 291, 415; and burial, 498–9; in City of London, 84, 408; *see also under name of church*
Cicero, Marcus Tullius, *see under* classical authors
cigars, *see under* tobacco
Cinderella, *see under* Perrault, Charles
City Canal, 144–5
City of London: business hours, 348; churches, 84, 408; Corporation, 54; Court of Common Council, 63; livery companies, 64, 498; Lord Mayor and office holders, 55, 63, 297; *see also* London
'City of London Churches', 84, 488, 498
City Road, 99–100
'civilization and improvement', 95
Clarke, Mary Anne, 33
classical authors: 163; Apollonius Rhodius, 295; Aristotle, 163, 402; Cicero, 163, 167–8, 515–6; Empedocles, 378; Herodotus, 404; Hesiod, 25, 239; Homer: 166; *Iliad*, 25, 59, 162, 295, 500; *Odyssey*, 2, 66, 69, 123, 177; Horace, 167–8, 172, 353; Menander, 292; Ovid, 99, 162, 167, 172; Persius, 286; Petronius, 172; Plato, 166; Plautus, 165, 167; Pliny the Elder, 172; Plutarch, 143–4, 227, 229, 256; Socrates, 166; Suetonius, 171–3; Tacitus, 172–3; Terence, 165, 167, 292; Theocritus, 257; Tibullus, 162; Virgil, 155, 162, 163, 165, 167, 170, 257, 404, 518; Zeno, 169
classical historical figures, events, places: Alexander the Great, 227; Alexandria, 291; Archimedes, 229; Cincinnatus, 515; Cleopatra, 255–6, 260, 382; Colossus of Rhodes, 297; Cornelia (Mother of the Gracchi), 167, 223; Curtius, 165; cynics, 200; Diogenes, 200, 227–8, 502; Marcellus, 229; Mark Antony, 163; Oracle of Delphi, 288; 349; peripatetics, 163, 402; Portico, 402; Ptolemy I Soter ('the Great'), 291; Punic Wars, 187; Ramesses II, Pharaoh, 465; Roman dictator, 516; Roman emperors, 171–3, 271, 404, 421, 438; Rubicon, 404; Scipio Africanus the Elder, 167; *stoa pœcile*, 168; Stoics, 169; Tusculum, 168
classical mythology: Amazons, 279–80; Apollo, 271; Arcadia, 257; Argonauts, 66, 295; Atlas, 115; Cupid, 381; Cyclops, 69; Danæ, 39; Eumenides, 148; Golden Fleece, 276, 295; Gorgons, 228, 273, 360; Hesperides (Golden Apples of), 276; household gods, 366; Hymen, 518; Jason, 66, 295; Juno, 165, 354; Lares and Penates, 366; Medusa, 228, 433; Minerva, 166; Momus, 124; Morpheus, 169; Oedipus, 161; Sisyphus, 260; Sphinx, 161; Taurus, 176; Titans, 115; Triton, 283, 423; Venus, 381; Zeus, 115; *see also under* education
Cleopatra, 255–6, 260, 382
clock-mending, 306
clubs: burying, 398; gentlemen's 111, 337, 405, 407, 455, 502; Pugilistic Club, 236; rowing, 317
coaches, *see* carriages and coaches
coachmen, *see under* servants
coal-heavers, 349–50
coal-whippers, 140, 519
Cobbett, William, 81, 473
Cobbold, Richard, 'The Farewell', 203–4
Cock Lane Ghost, 133
Cockburn, Henry Thomas, Lord: *Life of Lord Jeffrey*, 17
coffee-houses, 208, 266, 502
Coghlan, Francis: *A Guide to France*, 467
Coke, Sir Edward: *Institutes of the Lawes of England*, 147
Coleridge, Samuel Taylor, 2, 81, 308; 'Domestic Peace', 500; 'Rime of the Ancient Mariner', 230, 341
colliers, 38, 140
Collins, Philip, 18, 90, 214
Collins, Wilkie: 'The Last Stage-Coachman', 258; *The Woman in White*, 86
Colston, Marianne, 466
Combe, George and Andrew, 330
Combe, William, 309
Comic Almanack. The, *see* Cruikshank, George
Commandments (Ten), 416
Commercial Road, 140, 285
commission (law), 115
Commons, House of, *see under* Parliament
Congreve, William: 'The Birth of the Muse', 268
Conington, John, 155
conjurers, *see under* exhibitions 190
Constable, John: *Chain Pier, Brighton* (painting), 160
constitutional (walk), 175
'Conversation Sharp', *see* Sharp, Richard 198
convicts: on hulks, 192; transportation, 4, 296, 360, 362, 365
Cook, Captain James, 464
cooks, *see under* servants

Cooke, William Fothergill, 210
coolies, 4, 403
Cooper, James Fenimore, 3, 141, 325; *The Headsman*, 112
Copland, James: *A Dictionary of Practical Medicine*, 383; *Of the causes, nature and treatment of palsy and apoplexy*, 108, 233
Corn laws, 4
Cornhill, 55, 58, 66, 104, 142, 301, 485
Cornhill Magazine, 253–4
Cornuel, Anne-Marie Bigot de, 357
coroners, 450–1
cosmetics, 253–4; *see also* eau de Cologne
costermongers, *see under* street-sellers
costume and appearance: ankle-jacks, 205; artificial aids, 254–5, 303, 520; beadles, 83; bombazeen, 33, 130; charity school, 90–1, 266, 386, 392, 419; coachmen's, 258–9, 361; Company of Watermen and Lightermen's, 317; cravats, 28, 371; dreadnought, 285; false eyebrows, 254, 303; firemen's, 318; fly-away bonnet, 399; gentleman's, 515; gloves, 50, 175, 239, 381–2; gorget, 265; greatcoats, 239, 271; half-boots, 520; hats, 349, 374, 399; 'inexpressibles', 61, 387; Hessian boots, 376–7; knee breeches, 160; maids', 510; mantua makers, 33; mourning, 50, 83, 114, 130, 224–5, 349; naval (seamen's), 57, 59, 61, 70, 142, 145, 232, 285, 439; nankeen, 61, 372; patterns, 282; ready-made clothes, 447; slopsellers' shops, 145, 349; small-clothes, 229; sou'westers, 145, 349; tippets, 32; trousers, 61, 387; *trousseau*, 486; tuckers, 31, 261; underclothes, 447; velveteen, 265; waistcoats, 265, 372; watch-coats, 439; Wellington boots, 515; Welsh wigs, 59; wristbands, 197, 380, 405; *see also* cosmetics; hair; whiskers
Cottager's Monthly Visitor, The, 399
cottages ornées, 352–3, *352*
country houses, 373
couriers, *see under* servants
'Court Ceremonies', 65
Coutts, Angela Burdett, 1, 3, 45, 151, 214, 360–1, 363, 454
Covenanters (Scottish), 400
Covent Garden, 180, 326, 374, 402, 504
Coventry, 7, 242, 244, 246, 401
Cowper, William: *Conversation*, 300; *The Task*, 357, 395; 'Truth', 357
Crabbe, George: *The Village*, 357
Crace, J. G. & Sons, 318
Craik, Dinah Muloch, 121
Cranworth, Robert Monsey Rolfe, Baron (Lord Chancellor), 435
Cribb, Tom, 420
cribbage, 487
cricket, 204
Cricket on the Hearth, The, 17

Crimean War (1854–5), 199
Cromwell, Oliver, 497
Crosby, Frances Jane: 'Monterey', 78
Crosby Square, 428
crossing-sweepers, 225
Crown Jewels, *see under* jewellery 507
Cruikshank, George, 92, 174; *The Comic Almanack*, 98, 511–2; *Illustrations of Time*, 519; *London Characters*, 83; 'London going out of Town', 355, *356*; 'The Railway Dragon' (etching), 482, *483*; *Table Book*, 98
Cunningham, Peter: *Handbook of London*, 349, 394
cupping, *see under* health
curfew bells, 195
currency, *see* money
Custody of Infants Act (1839), 436
Custom House, 193, 325
Customs Department, 325
Cutlers' Company, 171
cut-paper work, 113
cutters (boats), 317
Cuvier, Baron Georges, 413

Daily News, 1, 17, 68
dairies, 259–60
Dalby's Carminative, 76; *see also* opium
Dana, Charles Henry: *Two Years Before the Mast*, 141
Dance of Death, 315–6
'Dancing Academy, The', 197
dandyism, 193, 381–2
Dante Alighieri, 358; *Divine Comedy*, 2, 277
Darwin, Erasmus: *Zoonomia*, 192
David Copperfield, 3, 32, 34, 36, 110, 114, 136, 141, 152, 169, 312, 388, 421
Davies, Sir John: 'Hymns to Astroea', 273
Davy, Sir Humphry, 123, 168; Davy-lamp, 168
Davy, John, 397
Day, Thomas: *The History of Sandford and Merton*, 122
day-book, 393
dead: burial, 4, 295, 498–9; *see also* funerals
dead-light, 438
dean (ecclesiastical), 493, 496
death, 213–5, 328, 331, 472; beheading, 327; bone-houses, 295; children and, 212; executions, 465; images, 315–6, 401; and inquests, 450; suicide, 450, 454, 464; widow burning (suttee), 4, 415
death penalty, *see* capital punishment
death's head, 306
debtors, 144, 500–4, 505, 507
Declaration of Rights (1689), 497
dedication of *DS*, 15
Defensive Exercises, 421
Defoe, Daniel, 2, 503; *Robinson Crusoe*, 66, 68, 395, 439, 464

dentistry, 50–1; *see also* teeth
de Quincey, Thomas: *Confessions of an English Opium-Eater*, 83; 'Dinner, Real and Reputed', 297; 'On Murder Considered as one of the Fine Arts', 450
'Detective Police Party, A', 31
Devil, 399; lame, 432
Devis, Arthur William: *The Death of Nelson* (painting), 67
Devon, 256, 352, 446
Dibdin, Charles: 'The Sailor's Consolation', 350, 448; *Songs, Naval and National*, 146; *The Waterman*, 317; 'The Whim of the Moment', 159–60; *see also* songs
Dibdin, Thomas, 202, 283, 325
Dickens, Alfred (CD's brother), 128
Dickens, Catherine (CD's wife), 35
Dickens, Charles: anti-Catholic bias, 411–12; autobiographical fragments, 115, 126, 128; background, 3; on behaviour and social conditioning, 430; in Brighton, 126; on children's observation, 134; comic singing as child, 504; criticizes mediævalism, pastoralism, picturesque, romanticism and sentimentality, 139, 257, 303, 308–10, 418, 440, 454; edits *Daily News*, 1, 17, 68; financial security, 1; lodges with Mrs Roylance, 126, 128; lost in London as child, 101; love of dogs, 228; on material change, 65; on New and Old Testaments, 506; in Paris, 335, 366–7, 466; as parliamentary reporter, 522; practises mesmerism, 410–1; praises Browning play, 278–9; sanitary reform, 5–6, 81, 431; on schooling, 89–90, 165–6; sickliness in boyhood, 178; on slavery, 231; ridicules spiritualism, 133; travels in Europe, 1, 15, 335, 466, 468, 477; and Urania Cottage (for fallen women), 360–1; values cleanliness and order, 37; visits Leamington with Hablot Browne, 247–8, 251; in Warren's blacking factory, 3, 126; works as attorney's clerk, 85
Dickens, Charles Culliford Boz (Charley; CD's son): education, 5, 151, 161, 163
Dickens, John (CD's father), 3, 126, 162, 287
Dickens, Mamie (CD's daughter), 134
Dickens, Walter Landor (CD's son), 161
Dijon, 461, 477; Hotel de la Cloche, 466; Notre-Dame church, 468
dining conventions: *à la française*, 378; *à la Russe*, 378; bills of fare, 378–9; caterers and confectioners, 329, 379; etiquette, 198, 367, 372; 'ice', 379; invitations, 379–80; table decorations, 376; times, 297, 300
diseases and ailments: apoplexy, 40, 108, 150, 233, 238, 303, 503; caused by miasma, 125, 324, 431; chickenpox, 118; cholera, 430–2; chorea, 7, 108, 233, 302; cyanosis (blue jaundice), 7, 109, 150, 233, 400; dropsy, 402; dyspepsia, 40; emphysema, 7, 108–9; exophthalmia, 7, 108–9, 150, 233; gout, 108–9, 149–50, 233, 238; hypochondria, 301; hysteria, 301–2; indigestion, 43; low fever, 509; nervous complaints, 7, 40, 43, 301–2, 383; palsy, 7, 109, 150, 233, 261, 383, 399; paralysis, 7, 108, 382; puerperal fever, 30; railway-induced, 38; rheumatism, 386; syphilis, 109; thrush, 115; typhus ('gaol fever'), 192, 324, 440, 509; whooping cough, 118; yellow fever (West India fever), 149, 185; *see also* health; miasma theory
dispensaries, *see under* hospitals ~~227~~
Disraeli, Benjamin, 98, 308; *Coningsby*, 325; *Endymion*, 15; *Miscellanies of Literature*, 98; *Sybil, or, The Two Nations*, 98, 281; *Tancred*, 376, 455, 524
D'Israeli, Isaac: *The Curiosities of Literature*, 422; *Miscellanies of Literature*, 98
dissenters, 351, 496, 497
'Diurnal Revolutions of Davie Diddledoft, The', 197
divan, 268
diving-bells, 71–2
divorce, *see* marriage and divorce
Döbler, Herr (conjurer), 190
doctors, *see* apothecaries; physicians; surgeons
Dodd, George: *Days at the Factories*, 428; *Dictionary of Manufactures ... and the Industrial Arts*, 405; *The Food of London*, 180
Doe, John and Richard Roe (legal fictions), 513
Doggett, Thomas, 317
dogs: 228, 482; dogs'-meat-men, 426; of Montargis, 401–2; performing, 49; sold by street-sellers, 180, 181; stealing, 227
Dolby, Richard: *The Cooks's Dictionary and Housekeeper's Directory*, 379
dolls' dressmakers, 339
Domestic Duties, or, Instructions to Young Married Ladies, 39
Donne, John, 487
D'Orsay, Alfred Guillaume Gabriel, Count, 227, 381
double-knocks, 107–8, 379
Douce, Francis, 315–6
Downs, the (anchorage), 62, 287
dragons, 276
Draper, Sir Christopher, 498
Dreadnought (ship), 286
dreams, 2, 169, 370, 476
'Dreams', 370
dress, *see* costume and appearance
drinks, *see* beverages
drinking: and the British in India, 137; 'four bottle man', 522; and robbing sailors, 451–2; and Sabbatarians, 225
Dryden, John: translates Chaucer, 231, 414;

translates *Plutarch's Lives*, 144, 228, 229;
translates Virgil, 163; *All for Love*, 256;
'Eleonora', 356; *Lives of Eminent and Illustrious Englishmen*, 123
drysalters, 282
Dulwich College almshouse, 510
Dutch clocks, 48
dwarfs, *see under* exhibitions 187
Dyer, John, 56, 139
Dyos, H. J., 94

Eagles, John, 18
Earl, George Windsor: *The Eastern Seas*, 350
East India Company, 56, 81, 111, 137, 140, 153, 372
East India Docks, 58, 140, 145
East India House, 55–8, 394
Easter Island: statues, 464–5
eau de Cologne, 381–2
Eberle, John, 233
Economist, The (journal), 17
Edgeworth, Maria: *Patronage*, 112
Edinburgh Medical and Surgical Journal, 108
Edinburgh Review, 158, 162
education: books and catechisms, 121–2, 135–6, 169; and child management and discipline, 121–2, 129, 135, 154; classical, 5, 124, 155, 161–9, 173, 175–6, 419; ignorant teachers, 99; methods, 158–65, 175, 388–9; military, 151, 152; naval, 58, 59; reforms, 88–90; required by railway workers, 40; as theme in *DS*, 5; scientific, 162; women's, 163, 177–8, 262, 444–5, 517; *see also* charity schools; schools
Edward (CD's courier), 468
Egan, Pierce, 492, 504, 523; *Boxiana*, 270–1, 401; *Life in London*, 359
Eglinton Tournament (1839), 308
Egypt, 291, 453, 463, 465, 484
electricity, 377–8, 458; *see also* magnetism; telegraph
elephant and castle, 171
Elephant and Castle public house, 492
Eliot, George: *The Mill on the Floss*, 169
Elizabeth I, Queen, 63, 273, 312, 313
Elliotson, Dr John, 410–1
Ellis and Blackmore (solicitors), 85
Ellis, Sarah Stickney: *The Women of England*, 52–3
Elliston, Robert William, 130
Ely, Thomas Turton, Bishop of, 227
emigration: 4, 58; Australia, 296–7, 453; coolies, 403
Encyclopædia of Domestic Economy, An, 186
entertaining, *see under* dining conventions
enthusiasm, 310
environment: effect on human behaviour, 430
epitaphs, 225, 397–8
Erasmus, Desiderius, 364

esquire, 170–1
Essex, 289, 418
etiquette: 'at homes', 371, 412; forms of address, 34, 170–1, 259; kissing hands, 422; small talk, 198; touching hats, 426; visiting cards, 101, 272; wedding cards, 371, 383; *see also* dining conventions; weddings
Eton College, *see under* schools
Eton Latin Grammar, 169; *see also under* education: classical
Euston Station, 93, 205, *206*, 212, 239–40, 243
Evangelicals, 506
Examiner, The (journal), 17, 214, 431
executions, 465; *see also* beheading
Exeter, Henry Holland, 3rd Duke of, 461
exhibitions: on China, 52; conjurors, 187, 190; dwarfs, 187, 190; electricity, 377–8; giants, 187, 190; 'Living Skeleton', 123–4

Faber, Frederick William: *The Blessed Sacrament*, 130
factories, 88, 198, 258, 279, 281, 355; Midlands, 244, 247; Warren's blacking, 3, 126; wood-turning, 405
Fairfax's New Guide and Directory to Leamington Spa and its Environs, 259
fairies: and changelings, 121
fairy tales: *The Arabian Nights' Entertainments*, 2, 179, 183–4; 'Dick Whittington', 55, 72, 102, 105, 140, 220; 'Hop-o-my-Thumb', 131, 326, 356; *Mother Goose's Tales*, 105, 131, 276; motifs in *DS*, 2, 7, 121, 131, 166, 332; 'Princess Zamea', 131; 'Puss in Boots', 131; 'Sleeping Beauty', 2, 273, 278; 'Story of the Fisherman', 179; *see also* nursery rhymes; Perrault, Charles
Family Prayer-book, 448
fancy (pugilism), 492; *see also* boxers, boxing
Fanny Parkinson, or, My Brother's Funeral, 33
Faraday, Michael, 123, 377–8
farming, farmers, 42, 306, 377, 418; Australian, 296–7; Marie Antoinette's *hameau*, 257–8
Faust, 241, 399
Fawkes, Guy, 176–7; *see also* Gunpowder Plot
fencing, 271–2
Fenn, Charles: *Compendium of the English and Foreign Funds*, 98
Fenning, Daniel: *Universal Spelling Book*, 135
Ferguson, Adam, 496
Ferrier, Susan: *Destiny*, 467
Field, Inspector Charles, 31
Fielding, Henry: *Joseph Andrews*, 354; *Tom Jones*, 106
Fields, James T., 128, 228
financiers, 25, 27
Finchley, 346
fire-buckets, 183
fire-fighting, 318

fire office, 502
fire-ships, 284
flat iron, 37
Fleet prison, 31, 447
Fletcher, Angus, 150
flower and root-sellers, 48, 320–1, 326, 498
fly-cages, 321
Flying Dutchman, 2, 283
food: aspic, 92; beefsteak and kidney pudding, 296; caterers, 329, 379; children's, 132; confectionery, 379; devilled dishes, 237, 380; diet for nursing mothers, 43; dried fruits, 154; egg sauce, 296, 445; eggs and muffins, 233; fruit, 180, 380; game, 237; ginger, 186, 347; gravy, 138; herrings and roe, 260; 'ice', 379; kidneys, 237; lamb's fry, 223; lobster salad, 508; mutton, 237; naval rations, 349; nuts, 347; oranges, 44; ox tail soup, 384; pastry-cook's shop, 384; pineapples, 180, 373; poultry, 237; rabbit, 237; roast fowl and veal stuffing, 296; rolls, 138; savoury pies, 237; sheep's heart, 296; ship's biscuit, 60, 519; steak, 138; sugar, 146, 347; veal, 237; Welsh rabbit, 487; of working class, 43; *see also* recipes
footmen, *see under* servants
foreigners: English view of, 4, 333–4; Indian servants, 109–10, 237, 239
Forster, John: on Bayham Street, 3, 93; and Brighton, 126; on CD in Paris, 367; on CD's education, 162; and CD's engaging upholsterer for parents, 319; on CD's finances, 1; and CD's intentions for *DS*, 16, 26, 54, 114, 186, 429, 454; and CD's living abroad, 2; and CD's scepticism over political efficacy in reform, 324–5; and CD's trip to Birmingham, 248; and CD's views on christening, 83; and Edith's relations with Carker, 429, 470–1; on Lamert at Sandhurst, 152; reads CD's drafts, 19, 22; reviews for *Examiner*, 214; sends Browning play to CD, 278; on sickly young CD, 178; and success of *DS*, 18; and title of *DS*, 14; *The Life of Dickens*, 15, 22, 57
Foxe, John: *Book of Martyrs*, 415
France: beggars, 477; British prejudices, 4, 334; customs, 213, 367; dances, 113, 194; landscape, 477; railway development, 6, 479; travel to and in, 335, 468–9, 473, 476–7
Francis, John: *A History of the English Railway*, 95–6
Franck, R.: *Northern Memoirs*, 286
Franklin, Benjamin, 458
Franklin, Sir John, 451
French language, 466–7, 476
Frick, George: *A Treatise on the Diseases of the Eye*, 109
Friedrich II (the Great), King of Prussia, 290
Friendly Societies, 38
Froebel, Friedrich Wilhelm August, 5, 159

'From the Raven in the Happy Family', 124, 224
Fulham, 279, *280*, 289
Fuller, Margaret: *Woman in the Nineteenth Century*, 517
Fuller, William, 269
funds (public securities), 297
funerals, 44–5, 124, 224, 351, 505; *see also* mourning
furniture: 319, 347, 405, 486; chimney-boards, 220–1; eighteenth-century, 111; second-hand, 142–3, 511–2; *see also* interior decoration
Fuseli, Johann Heinrich: 'The Nightmare' (painting), 174

Gall, Franz Joseph, 330
Galt, John: *The Ayrshire Legatees*, 224
gardens, gardening: of almshouses, 110; of cottages ornées, 352–3; flower and root-sellers, 48, 320–1, 326, 498; hothouses, 158–9; houseplants, 320–1; pinery, 373; window boxes, 48, 320
Gardener's Magazine, 320
Gas Light and Coke Company, 49
gas lighting, 49, 130, 380
Gaskell, Elizabeth, 121, 379
Gay, John, 2; *The Beggar's Opera*, 491; 'Sweet William's Farewell to Black-Eyed Susan', 63
Gentleman's House, The, 45, 412
Gentleman's Magazine, The, 133, 182, 208
gentlemen's clubs, *see under* clubs
Gentlemen's Magazine of Fashion, 28
Geoffrey of Monmouth: *Historia Regum Britanniæ*, 55
George IV, King (*earlier* Prince of Wales), 4, 32, 71, 125, 193, 337, 422, 473, 522–3
George, St, 105
Germany, 113, 177, 324, 338–9, 362, 367, 479
ghosts: 35, 86; Cock Lane, 133; in *Hamlet*, 178–9, 327, 416; in *Macbeth*, 32
giants, *see under* exhibitions
Gibbon, Edward, 169
gill (liquid measure), 221
Gillray, James, 32, 81; 'The Old Lady of Threadneedle-Street in danger', *375*
Gilpin, William, 309
girls, *see* women
'Globus, Septimus': *Der Freischutz Travestie*, 92
God Save the King (Queen) (British national anthem), 490
Godfrey's Cordial, 76; *see also* opium
godparents, 76, 87
Godwin, William: *An Enquiry Concerning Political Justice*, 95; *Fleetwood*, 112
Goethe, J.W. von, 358; *Faust*, 241; *The Sorrows of Young Werther*, 440
Gog and Magog, 55, 101
Goldsmith, Oliver, 2, 65, 346; *The Deserted Village*, 210; *History of England*, 95; *The Roman History*

(*The History of Rome*), 515–6; *She Stoops to Conquer*, 92
'Gone Astray', 101
Goodwin Sands, 62, 287–8
Gore, Catherine Grace Frances: *Abednego the Money-Lender*, 508; *The Banker's Wife*, 27; *The Diary of a Désennuyée*, 486
governesses, *see under* servants
Graham, Thomas John: *Modern Domestic Medicine*, 43, 402, 441
Graham's Family Linen Warehouse, Regent Street, 447
grampus, 85
Grampus (ship), 286
Grand Junction Canal, 244
Gravesend, Kent, 487
Gray, Thomas: 'Elegy Written in a Country Churchyard', 357
'Great Exhibition and the Little One, The', 52
Great Expectations, 505
Great North Road, 354–5
Great Portland Street, 508
Great Western Railway, 208, 210
Greek language, *see under* education: classical
Greek War of Independence, 284
Green, Charles, 71
Greenwich, 678
Greenwich Mean Time, 208–9
Greenwich Seaman's Hospital, 286–7
Greenwood, James, 26
Gresham's College, 55
Griffin, Revd James, 120
Grinfield, Charles: *A Century of Acrostics*, 273
grocers (general dealers), 52, 154, 508
Grose's Classical Dictionary of the Vulgar Tongue, 492, 514
Grossmith, William Robert, 70, 406
Grosvenor, Lord Robert, 225
Grosvenor Square, 328
Guide to the Unprotected ... Relating to Property and Income, A, 330, 444, 449
Guildhall, 55, 101
guinea (coin), 411
gunpowder mills, 419
Gunpowder Plot (1605), 86, 176–7
Gunter (caterer), 329
gypsies, 48, 305–6, 400

Hackney, 326
hair: curl papers, 178, 196; decoration, 434; dressing, 196, 381–2; false curls, 303, 520; trading, 104; wigs, 183, 254, 380; *see also* whiskers
Hale, William, 359
Hall, Anna Maria: *Marian, or a young maid's fortune*, 154
Hall, Dr John Charles, 430

Hallam, Henry, 393
Hampstead, 205, 207, 355
Hampstead Heath, 205, 464
Hampstead Road, 129, 326
Handbooks for Travellers (John Murray): on the Continent, 334–5, 339, 362; in Devon and Cornwall, 256; in France, 477; in Switzerland, 466
Handel, George Frederick: 'The Harmonious Blacksmith' (from Harpsichord Suite no.5), 505; *Saul*, 92
handkerchiefs: printed with maps, 93
Hard Times, 27, 362, 503
Harding, J. D., 262
Hardwick, Philip, 205
Hare, Augustus, 55, 501
Harlequin, 302
Harley Street, 30, 524
Hampstead, 207, 326, 355, 464
Harmer, Harry, 420
harmonic meetings, 456, 503–4
harpsichord, *see* musical instruments ~~113~~
Harrington, Henry F.: 'Is't my Nephew, or Not?', 457
Harrison, Frederic, 161
Harrison, W. H.: *Waldemar*, 78
Harrogate, 256
Hartley, David: *Essay on the Origin of the Passions*, 187; *Observations on Man*, 370
Harvey, Dr William, 404
hatchments, *see under* mourning ~~331~~
Hawthorne, Nathaniel: *Twice-Told Tales*, 112
Haydon, Benjamin Robert: *Curtius Leaping into the Gulf* (painting), 165
Hazlitt, William, 472
Heads of the People, 25, 29, 84, 98, 197, 332
health (cures, treatments): anæsthetics, 51; bark, 441; cupping, 131–2; electric shocks, 378; emetics and purges, 73, 75–6, 115, 118; ginger, 186; for infections, 413, 505; leeches, 508; mesmerism, 410; moral 'cures', 115; opium, 30, 76; for palsy, 382–3; quackery, 125; restorative drinks, 382, 508–9, 523; stimulants, 30; teething remedies, 76; vinegar, 413, 505; *see also*: diseases and ailments; sea air, sea water; spas, watering places; water-cures
Health of London Association, 431
Health of Towns Association, 431
Heath, James, 253
Heather, William, 57
Hebbel, Friedrich: *Judith*, 470
Heber, Reginald, Bishop of Calcutta, 436–7
heel-taps, 341
hemp, 266
Henry VIII, King, 4, 313
Her Majesty's Theatre, Haymarket, 373–4
heroes: concept of, 356–8

Hickman, Tom, 492
Highgate, 207, 354, 355
History of Signboards, The, 97
Hodder, George, 215
Hogarth, William, 430; 'Gin Lane' (print), 363
Hogg, Sir James, 57
Holbein, Hans, 313; *Dance of Death*, 315
Holborn, 260, 420, 512
Hollingshead, John: 'Mistaken Charity', 509–10
Holloway, 72, 207, 354
home: concept of, 162, 366 366
Homer, *see under* classical authors
Homes, John: *Douglas, a Tragedy*, 71
Honduras, 2, 465
Hone, William: *The Every-Day Book and Table Book*, 14, 92, 124, 180, 318
Honourable (title), *see under* etiquette: forms of address
Hood, Thomas, 130, 254; 'The Bridge of Sighs', 292; 'The Double Knock', 107; *Up the Rhine*, 237
Hook, Theodore: *Jack Brag*, 373
hooks (prosthetic hands), *see under* prostheses
Horace, *see under* classical authors
Horne, Richard Hengist, 29, 103
hornpipes, 34
Horse Guards, see Household Cavalry
horse-road, 343
Horsman, Alan, 3, 8, 19, 41–2, 128, 153, 226
hospitals: 149, 227, 410, 477; Bethlehem, 79, 307; dispensaries, 227; lying-in, 35, 36–7; for prostitutes, 361; Seamen's, 286–7
hothouses, *see under* gardens, gardening
House of Commons, *see under* Parliament
House, Humphry, 482
House of Lords, *see under* Parliament
Household Cavalry, 47, 272, 496
Household Narrative of Current Events (monthly), 68
Household Words (magazine articles cited), 31, 38, 45, 52, 55, 56, 57, 65, 68, 72, 87, 89, 94, 96, 101, 103, 104, 113, 124, 125, 129, 133, 138, 146, 159, 162, 198, 205, 208, 224, 227, 232, 241, 243, 259, 263, 266, 267, 269, 272, 277, 285, 288, 300, 301, 309, 318, 334, 335, 339, 360, 370, 373, 374, 376, 380, 387, 402, 433, 451, 452, 460, 465, 480, 498, 507, 517, 521, 522
houses: built by speculators, 95–7; as castles, 147; corner, 457; cottages ornées, 352–3; country houses, 373; demolished for railways, 94, 205–6, 355; mews, 49; middle class, 39, 279, 320, 412; for railway employees, 211; West End, 25, 46–7, 268, 276, 319, 328;
housekeeping: associated with morality, 37; cleaning fires, 175; ironing, 37–8; kitchen ranges 511–12; scouring floors, 282; washing day, 146–7

How to Make Home Happy, 100
Howell, William Dean: *Venetian Life*, 467
Howitt, William: 'The Queen's Tobacco-Pipe', 52
Hudson, George, 463
Hudson, Josh, 233
Huffam, Christopher, 67, 145
Hughes, Thomas: *Tom Brown at Oxford*, 53
Hugo, Victor: *Bug-Jargal*, 473
Hullah, John Pyke, 438
Hume, David, 106, 496; *Treatise of Human Nature*, 187
Hurd, Richard: *Letters on Chivalry and Romance*, 308
Hyde Park, 190, 225, 328, 422, 429

Iceni, 187
illnesses, *see* diseases and ailments
immigrants, 164, 268
Inchbald, Elizabeth: *Animal Magnetism* (play), 411
India: British in, 4, 136–7, 237, 254; children from, 137–8; effect on complexion, 493; making fortunes in, 493; Mughal emperors, 316; servants, 109–10, 233, 239; suttee (widow-burning), 4, 415; Thugs, 4, 403; *see also* East India Company
India Docks, 140, 144–6, 201
India rubber, 263–4
insolvency, 501
'Insularities', 334
insurance: fire, 318, 502; ships, 266, 348–9, 500; *see also* Lloyd's of London
interior decoration, 113, 318–20, 376; houseplants, 320–1; *see also* upholsterers
inventions, 65, 111, 123, 378, 406, 460, 462
Ireland, 4, 193, 464, 477, 497, 499
Ironmonger's Hall, 498
Irving, Washington, 120
Isle of Dogs, 144, 145, 146, 285
Islington, 14, 99, 184–5, 208, 223, 227, 354–5
Italy: 104, 404, 422, 448; and CD, 1, 15, 335, 468, 524; British notions of Italians, 472; travelling in, 469, 477, 517, 524

Jackson, Gentleman John, 269, 523–4
Jamaica, 25, 221, 347
James, G.P.R.: *The Step-mother*, 339
James I, King, 360
James, John: *The Treasury of Medicine*, 509
Jeffrey, Francis, Lord, 17, 215, 454, 470
Jericho, 292
Jerrold, Douglas, 85, 309, 456; *Black-Ey'd Susan*, 62
Jesuits (Society of Jesus), 461
jewellery: 223, 387, 389, 434, 440, 486; Crown Jewels, 507; mourning, 50, 204–5
Jews: 84; bird-sellers, 484; boxers, 268; hat-furriers, 102; old clothes sellers and dealers,

47–8; second-hand dealers, 510–12
Johnson, Samuel, 133, 201, 357
Johnson, Tom, 420
jointure, 259
Jones, William, 162
Jonson, Ben, 503, 524; *Epicene, or the Silent Woman*, 386
Joule, James Prescott, 378
Journal of Mining and Manufactures, 129
jugglers, *see* street performers
junctions, *see under* railway
Jura Mountains, 476
Juvenile Pauper Asylum, Tooting, 431

Kauffmann, Angelica: 'Cornelia, Mother of the Gracchi' (painting), 167
Kay-Shuttleworth, Dr James, 5
Kean, Edmund, 302
Keats, John, 139
Kemble, Charles, 196
Kemble, Fanny, 334
Kemble, John Philip, 130, 256, 258
Kenilworth Castle, 247–8, 304, 315
Kensington 190, 371
Kent (county): 91, 171, 289, 306, 406, 418, 487; and CD, 61, 287, 487; railways, 478–9
Kent, Charles, 17
Kent, Elizabeth: *Flora Domestica*, 320
Kent and Strathern, Edward Augustus, Duke of, 4, 337, 502
Kerr, Robert: *A General History and Collection of Voyages and Travels*, 451
Ketch, Jack, 367
Kilsby Tunnel, 245
King, Joseph Charles, 3, 161
King, Louisa, 3, 161–2
King's College School, London, 5
King's Cross, 337
Kingsley, Charles: *Westward Ho!*, 399
Kingston-upon-Thames, 6, 373
Kitchiner, William M.D.: *The Cook's Oracle*, 223, 445
knackers, 426
knife-grinding, 306
Knight, Charles, 44, 191; *London*, 46, 428
Knight, William Payne, 309
Knighthood, Orders of, 42, 236
Knight's Cyclopædia, 508
knocking-up (mornings), 281, 394
Knowles, Sheridan, 471
Koran, Holy, 184, 307

Ladies' Book of Etiquette and Manual of Politeness, 486
Ladies' Magazine of Gardening, 320
Lamb, Charles, 419
Lamert, James, 152

lamplighters, 49
Lancet, The (journal), 382, 410
Landon, Letitia Elizabeth: 'The Indian Girl', 78
Langham, Nat, 269
Langland, William: *Piers Plowman*, 286
Langley, Batty: *Gothic Architecture Improved by Rules and Proportions*, 308
Langton, Robert: *The Childhood and Youth of Charles Dickens*, 294
Laplace, Pierre Simon, marquis de, 290
Lardner, Dionysius, 480–1
Larson, Janet, 354
'Last Cab Driver, The', 79
Latin: CD learns, 162; *see also under* education: classical
Lausanne, 1, 227, 466
Lavater, Johann Caspar: *Physiognomische Fragmente*, 458
Law Review, The, 500
Law Times, The, 295
Leadenhall Market, 394, 486
Leadenhall Street, 56, 57, 58, 66, 182, 205, 462, 487
Leamington Spa, 7, 246–8, 250–1, 259, 315; Copp's Royal Hotel, 247–8, *249*, 250
leather: British market in, 26
Lee, Nathaniel: *The Rival Queens*, 422
Leech, John: 'The Railway Juggernaut of 1845' (cartoon), 482
leeches, 508
legs: wooden and cork, *see under* prostheses
Le Havre, 468, 478, 479
Leigh's New Picture of London, 63–4
Lemon, Mark, 215
Lennox, Charlotte: *Sophia*, 500
Le Sage, Alain-René: *Le Diable boiteux*, 432
Leslie, C. R., 304
letters *see* post
levee, 238
Lewis, Matthew Gregory ('Monk'), 106
Liddell, Henry George and Robert Scott: *A Greek-English Lexicon*, 402
Life Guards, see Household Cavalry
Life of Our Lord, The, 1, 506
lighthouses, 68, 285
Limehouse, 3, 144, 145, 232, 285, 519
Lind, Jenny, 384
Lindley, Thomas: *Selima and Azor*, 526
link-men, 380–1
Linley, George: 'To Memory You Are Dear', 438
Lisson Green (now Marylebone Road), 36
literacy, 40, 178
Littell's Living Age, 68
Little Britain, 462
'Little Dinner in an Hour, A', 458
Little Dorrit, 27, 31, 82, 201, 257, 269, 272, 309, 328, 363, 396, 440, 453, 463, 467, 504, 522

'Living Skeleton, the': see Seurat, Claude Ambroise
Lloyd, Edward, 266
Lloyd's List, 68, 266–7
Lloyd's of London, 55, 266, 300–1, 348, 349
Lloyd's Register of Shipping, 284
Lock Asylum for the Reception of Penitent Female Patients, 361
Lockhart, Capt. John, 61
locks (patent), 462
lodging houses, 103, 128, 136, 208, 259, 516
Loftie, W. J., 279
Lohrli, Anne, 162
London: displaced population, 94; docks, 3, 52, 58, 140, 144–6, 193, 201, 204, 449, 519; expansion, 107, 355–6; fashionable neighbourhoods, 30, 46, 107, 190, 328, 337; gentlemen's clubs, 111, 337, 405, 407, 455, 502; Great Fire (1666), 55, 502; Great Plague (1665), 325; immigrants, 164, 268; maps, 93; migrants, 358; omnibuses, 100, 208, 341-2, 355; prostitutes, 359–61, 363–4, 426, 430; suburbs, 3, 6, 7, 48, 93, 181, 206, 326, 329, 342, 354, 355; traffic, 100, 182, 354; *see also* City of London; and individual places and institutions
London and Birmingham Railway, 7, 93, 95, 205–8, *206–7*, 211–2, 239–46
London Bridge, 65, 182, 355, 487
London Encyclopædia, 104
London Gazette, The, 501, 507
London Journal of Arts, Sciences, and Manufactures, 480
London Magazine, 32
London Medical Gazette, The, 431
London Price Current, 423
London Society for the Protection of Young Females, 358–9
long arm of the law, 364–5
Long's Hotel, Bond Street, 337
Lord Mayor's Show (London), 55, 63
Lord's Day Observance Society, 225
Lords, House of, *see under* Parliament 341
'Lost Arctic Voyagers, The', 451
Loudon, J.C., 373; *Encyclopædia of Gardening*, 320, 353
'Louis, Monsieur' (giant), 187, 190
Louis Philippe, King of the French, 367
Lugar, R.: *Architectural Sketches*, 353
Lyndhurst, John Singleton Copley, Baron, 436
Lytton, Edward Bulwer-, 1st Baron, 328; *Asmodeus at Large*, 432; *The Last Days of Pompeii*, 163

Macaulay, Alexander: *A Dictionary of Medicine, designed for popular use*, 30, 149
Macaulay, Thomas Babington, Baron, 17; *Lays of Ancient Rome*, 163
McCulloch, J. R., 119, 130
Mackenzie, Henry: *The Man of Feeling*, 346

Mackenzie, William: *A Practical Treatise on the Diseases of the Eye*, 109
Macready, William Charles, 161, 256, 374, 471
magic circle, 251
magnetism, 2, 123, 374, 377–8, 410; *see also* electricity
maids, *see under* servants
Maison Brie, Conduit Street, 447
Malcolm, Sir John, 110
Mallett, David and James Thomson: *Alfred: A Masque*, 69
Malthus, Thomas Robert, 430; *Definitions in Political Economy*, 95; *An Essay on the Principle of Population*, 496
Man in the Moon, The (magazine), 18
man-traps, 113
Manchester Square, 46, 276
Mandeville, Bernard, 119
Mangnall, Richmal, *Historical and Miscellaneous Questions*, 392
maps: London, 93
Marat, Jean Paul, 238
Margate, 468, 479, 504
Marie Antoinette, Queen of France, 257–8
Marine Chronicle, The, 68
markets: Covent Garden, 180, 326; Leadenhall, 394, 486; leather, 26; Oxford ('Portland'), 226, 508; Rag Fair, 48; Smithfield, 4, 100–1, 324; street markets, 181, 281
market gardens, 65, 94, 113, 279
Marlowe, Christopher: *Doctor Faustus*, 241
Marr, Timothy, 449–50
marriage and divorce: adultery, 455; banns, 453; contracts, 27, 330, 436; form of address, 34, 417; jointure, 259; legal procedure for divorce, 434–6; marriage market, 4, 27, 377; public sale of wives, 469–70; *see also* brides; weddings
Marryat, Captain Frederick, 3, 66, 141; *Jacob Faithful*, 499; *Mr Midshipman Easy*, 239; *The Phantom Ship*, 283
Marsh, Revd Samuel, 202
Marsh(-Caldwell), Anne: *The Old Men's Tales*, 215
Marshalsea prison (CD's father imprisoned), 3, 126, 162
Martin Chuzzlewit, 1, 17, 25, 28, 231, 455
Martineau, Harriet, 318, 517; *Letters on Mesmerism*, 410
'Martyr Medium, The', 133
Marylebone, 36, 107, 329
Marylebone Road, 46
Mason, William: *The English Garden*, 245
Massinger, Philip: *The City Madam*, 423
Maurice, F. D., 517
Mavor, William: *A General Collection of Voyages and Travels*, 141
Mayfair, 81, 371, 447
Mayhew, Henry: on air pollution, 47; on ballad-

and street-singers, 34, 140; on bird-catchers, 264, 355; on carriages abroad, 335; on chickweed, 346; on costermongers, 180; on dog-collar men, 181; on ginger-beer sellers, 321; on Jewish second-hand dealers, 48, 510; on jugglers, 224; on missing people, 295; on mudlarks, 293; on omnibuses, 342; on oranges, 44; on 'parrot-duffing', 353; on parsons and doctors, 498; on rabbit-skin buyers, 102; on rag-gatherers and bone-pickers, 102–3; on flower and root sellers, 326; on spring-vans, 512; on street musicians, 336; on street tumblers, 225; on wagging, 266
Mayne, Sir Richard, 359
mechanical toys, 277–8
medicines, *see under* health
mediævalism, 308, 139; *see also* Eglinton Tournament; Pugin
Meeting House Lane, Peckham, 65
Mélampe (French frigate), 61
melancholy, 139, 440, 454, 503
Melbourne, William Lamb, 2nd Viscount, 4–5, 435
Melville, Herman: *Omoo*, 451
Mendoza, Daniel, 269, 523
Mesmer, Anton, 411
mesmerism ('animal magnetism'), 2, 410–11
Methodists, 310; *see also* Primitive Methodists
Metropolitan Police, *see under* police
Metropolitan Sanitary Association, 81, 431; *see also* sanitary reform
mews, 49
miasma theory, 2, 125, 324, 430–1; *see also* sanitary reform
'Miasma' (poem), 431–2
Mickle, William: 'The Sorceress', 362
midshipman (wooden), 57–8, 59
midshipmen, *see under* Royal Navy
Mile-End Turnpike, 66
militia: substitutes, 119
milk-shops, *see* dairies
Mill, James, 493
Mill, John Stuart, 119, 155, 185
millenarianism, 520; *see also* Primitive Methodists
Miller, John: *The Beulah Spa* (play), 67–8
Miller, Joseph, 171
Milliken, W. E., 58
Milton, John: *Paradise Lost*, 2, 268, 293, 422
Mirror of Literature, The, 229–30
Mirror of Parliament, The, 522
missing persons, 295
missionaries, 389
Mitford, Mary Russell, 305, 513
Modern Domestic Medicine, 43, 402, 441
Mogg's New Picture of London, 223, 394, 508
Mogg's Strangers' Guide to London, 93
Molloy, Charles, 85
money: earnings of supercargoes, 485; explained for children, 121–2; in marriage settlements, 330; Savings Banks, 418; stolen from sailors, 451–2; Sydney Smith's witticism, 507; women's ignorance of accounts, 444–5
'monkish', 411–12
Montague Square, 46, 329
Montargis, Dog of, 401–2
Monthly Review, The, 500
Moore, Peter, 111
Moore, Thomas, 502
morality: associated with housekeeping, 37; and wet-nurses, 38–9
Morgan, George Osborne, 155
Morison's Pills, 125
Morley, Henry, 159
Morning Chronicle, 522
Morning Chronicle Survey of Labour and the Poor, 103
morning-rooms, 412
Morpeth, George William Frederick Howard, Viscount (*later* 7th Earl of Carlisle), 5
Morton, Thomas: *Cure for the Heartache*, 31; *Speed the Plough*, 31; *The Way to Get Married*, 31
Moses, E. & Sons, 253
Mosse, Henrietta Rouviere: *Father's Love, and a Woman's Friendship: A Novel*, 331
Mother the Best Governess, The, 262
Mother Goose's Tales, *see under* fairy tales; *see also* Perrault, Charles
mother-in-law (jokes), 381
Mottley, John: *Joe Miller's Jests*, 171
mourning: dress, 50, 83, 114, 130, 224–5, 349; hatchments, 331; jewellery, 50, 204–5
moustaches, *see* whiskers
'Mr Bull's Somnambulist', 521
'Mrs Lirriper's Lodgings', 80
mudlark, 293
Mulgrave, George Augustus Constantine Phipps, Earl of, 15
Mulock, Dinah Maria: *Two Marriages*, 171
murder: malice aforethought, 331; Ratcliffe Highway, 449–50; Thugs, 403
Musical World, The, 113
musical instruments, 113, 143, 404, 405, 463; *see also* street musicians
musicians, *see* street musicians
mutes, 45, 124, 224

nabobs, 493
Nairne, Edward: *Poems, Miscellaneous and Humorous*, 387
nankeen, 61, 372
Naples, 309, 469, 524
Napoleon I (Bonaparte), Emperor of the French, 184, 198, 290, 333–4
Napoleon III, Emperor of the French, 434
'Narrative of Extraordinary Suffering, A', 479

Nash, John, 46, 97, 133
National Society for Promoting Education of the Poor in the Principles of the Established Church, 497
nautical costume, *see under* costume and appearance: naval
nautical instrument makers, 52, 57–8, *59*, 60
nautical melodrama, 2, 62, 67
nautical novels and novelists, 66–7
nautical superstitions, 2, 283
nautical terminology: abaft, 453; avast, 287; beam ends, 491; bearings, 149; broaching, 348; clap on, 439; dead-light, 438; good roads, 288; head to the wind, 220; hove down, 148; overhaul, 396; points, 202; sheer off, 343; stand by, 72; stand out, 287; slue, 526; to wear, 286; *see also* Royal Navy; *see also under* songs: nautical
Naval Chronicle, The, 68
Nelson, Admiral Horatio, Viscount, 67, 231
New Model Army, 497
New System of Practical Domestic Economy, A, 132
Newcastle-upon-Tyne, 140
Newgate Street, 104
newspapers: 83, 121, 179, 185, 415, 420; as curlpapers, 178; ironed by servants, 50; missing persons, 295; reporters, 462; sanitary reform, 324; shipping intelligence, 68, 346 Sunday, 456, 462
Nicholas Nickleby, 99, 118, 214, 226, 302, 402
nicknames: boxers, 269–70
Niebuhr, Barthold Georg, 308
'Night Walks', 291
Nollet, Jean-Antoine, abbé, 458
Nonconformists: 505–6; 'serious', 226
Nore anchorage, 204
Norfolk Biffin (apple), 515
Norie, J. W. and Charles Wilson (shopkeepers), 57–8
Normanby, Constantine Henry Phipps, 1st Marquess of, 15
Normanby, Maria, Marchioness of (*née* Liddell), 15
North British Review, 215
North, Christopher, *see* Wilson, John
North-West Passage, 451
Northampton, Charles Compton, 4th Earl of, 166
Norton, Caroline Sheridan, 4–5, 435–6
Norton, Old Joe, 492
Norwich Union Insurance Company, 318
Norwood, Surrey, 351–2
nurses, *see under* servants
'Nurse's Stories', 80
nursery rhymes: 'The Man in the Moon', 513; 'Ride a Cock Horse', 99; 'Who Killed Cock Robin?', 489, *489*; *see also* fairy tales; Perrault, Charles

oakum, 285

office hours, 62
officers (military and naval): 66, 111, 142, 151, 152, 193, 232, 236, 333, 348, 451; China Trade, 485; Indian Army, 112, 153, 493
old clothes sellers, 47–8, 181; *see also* street sellers
Old Curiosity Shop, The, 214, 247–8, 346, 487
Old Lady of Threadneedle Street, 375; *see also* Bank of England
Old and New London, 107
Oliver Twist, 359, 363, 456, 487
omnibus, *see under* carriages and coaches
opera, *see* theatres
Opie, Amelia, 254
opium, 30, 76
Opium Wars, 52, 485
orange blossom, 516
orders and honours, 42, 236; military, 153, 313
oriental tales, 183; 'Adventures of Abdulselam and Princess Chelnissa', 446; *see also Arabian Nights' Entertainments*
ornaments: cut-paper work, 113; table, 376
Ørsted, Hans Christian, 123, 377
Osborne's London and Birmingham Guide, 246
Ottoman Empire, 184
'Our Commission', 241
Our Mutual Friend, 37, 214, 339, 363, 433, 452, 519, 526
'Our Parish', 83
'Our School', 138, 162, 402
'Our Watering Place', 288
Oxford, 53, 161, 195, 300, 402, 406
Oxford Market (or Portland Market), 226, 508
Oxford Movement, 308
Oxford Street, 46, 182, 205, 277, 324, 337

packet-boats and steam packets, 232, 452–3, 468; *see also* steam vessels
Pakenham Street, 431
Pall Mall, 111, 124, 405, 455, 502
Palmerston, Henry John Temple, 3rd Viscount, 499
pantomimes, 96, 258, 302
Paris: 6, 46, 152, 334, 461, 468, 469, 473, 477–9; and Dickens, 15, 214, 243, 335, 366–7, 466
Parker, Martyn: 'The Gallant Seamen', 61
Parkinson, Dr James, 7, 383; *Essay on the Shaking Palsy*, 261
Parliament, Houses of: 86, 115, 125, 176, 179, 204, 208–10, 222, 225, 238, 313, 451, 497, 509, 510, 521, 522; Bills and Acts, 88–9, 101, 198, 225–6, 403, 449, 497, 499, 507; committees, 47, 79, 324; Commons, 58, 63, 88–9, 198, 209, 210, 341, 377, 403, 433, 435; debates, 94, 435–6; Lords, 341, 435; reports, 40, 58, 236, 394, 450
Parr, Thomas ('Old Parr'), 404
Parsons, Richard, 133
pastoralism, 257, 303, 308, 518

pastry-cook shops, 384
Patmore, Emily Augusta: *The Servant's Behaviour Book*, 416
Paxton, Joseph, 125
Payn, James: 'Her First Appearance', 376
Peacock, Thomas Love: *Nightmare Abbey*, 139
Pearce, Hen ('the Game Chicken'), 236, 270–1, 270, 420, 518
Peckham, 65
Peel, Sir Robert, 227
Peninsular Wars, 174, 193
Penny Cyclopædia, 125, 137, 143, 204–5, 256, 372, 386, 406
Penny Magazine, The, 315
Pentonville, 337
Pepys, Samuel: *Diary*, 106
Percy, Thomas: *Reliques of Ancient English Poetry*, 308
Pereira, Dr Jonathan, 192
Perrault, Charles: *Histoires, ou Contes du Temps Passé* (transl. as *Mother Goose's Tales*), 332; 'Cinderella', 105; 'Hop-o'-my-Thumb', 131, 356; 'Puss in Boots', 131; 'The Sleeping Beauty in the Wood', 2, 273, 276, 278
Persiani, Giuseppe, 374
Peru: silver mines, 128–9
Pestalozzi, Johann Heinrich, 159
Peter Parley's Annual, 304
pew-openers, 86, 90, 332–3
Phelps, Samuel, 256
philosophers (modern), 119, 222, 290–1, 378
Philosophical Transactions (Royal Society), 149
photography, 65
phrenology, 2, 330
physicians: 247, 271, 351, 382, 397–8, 437, 441; and children's health, 35, 115, 132, 382; CD's friendships with, 410, 430; education and status, 29–30, 194–5; *see also* apothecaries; surgeons
physiognomy, 2, 237, 330, 460
pianos, 113, 143, 405
Pickford & Co. (carriers), 209
Pickwick Papers, The, 2, 31, 124, 316, 339, 428, 447
Picture of London, The, 36
Pictures from Italy, 17, 168, 411, 466, 476
picturesque (style), 139, 258, 262, 308–10, 353, 405
pieman, tossing the (game), 388
pigeons, *see under* birds
Pilgrimage to Parnassus, The (play), 166–7
pincushions, 132, 375
'Pindar, Peter' (pseud. of John Wolcot), 32
pinery, 373
piquet (picquet), 262–3, 304
pitch-kettles, 519
Pitt, William, the Younger, 4, 81–2, *375*, 521
Pixérécourt, Guilbert de: *The Forest of Bondy*, 401

Plain Observations on the Management of Children, 22
Player, J.: 'To My Muse', 525
plumbers, 319–20
police: 38, 49, 63, 118, 225, 295, 462; detective police, 31; knocking-up, 281; Metropolitan Police established, 83, 394; and prostitute numbers, 359
'Political Catechism, A', 122
political economy, 121, 430, 496; *see also* Utilitarians
Polyphemus, HMS, 69
Pope, Alexander, 139, 257, 300; (transl.) *Odyssey*, 123, 163, 177
porters, 182, 192, 319, 511, 513
Portland Market, *see* Oxford Market
Portland Place, 46, 107, 226, 268, 329, 429, 524
Portman Square, 46, 205, 329, 429, 524
Portsea, 3
Portsoken Ward, Houndsditch, 48
post: letters, 185–6; at Lloyd's of London, 266–7; office, 210; overseas, 452–3; postmen's knocks, 107; service, 225, 385
post-captains (naval), 142
postilion, 6, 248, 473
posting-houses, 473
potboys, 282–3
poverty: and charitable giving, 490; in France, 477; and Malthus, 430, 496; and prostitution, 363, 365, 426
Pre-Raphaelite Brotherhood, 308
Presbyterians, 400
Preventive Service (Water-Guard), 179
Price, Uvedale, 309
Primitive Methodists, 201–2, 343, 520; *see also* Methodists
Prince Imperial (Louis Napoleon), 434
Prior, William Henry, 280
prisons: 31, 363–4, 433; Coldbath Fields, 450; Fleet, 31, 447; Marshalsea, 3, 126, 162; Newgate, 135; prison colonies, 360
prostheses: for hands, 70, 147, 445; for legs, 406–7, 499
prostitution: 359–61, 363–5, 426, 430; rehabilitation, 36, 361; *see also* Urania Cottage
Prout, Samuel, 262
pseudo-sciences, 2, 460; *see also* mesmerism; phrenology; physiognomy
public-houses: 101, 145, 282, 388, 492; boxers manage, 420; and dog stealing, 227; French, 473; harmonic meetings, 456, 503–4
public schools, *see under* schools
Pückler-Muskau, Prince Hermann, 49, 164, 367, 378
pugilism: as science, 268, 269, 270, 338; *see also* boxers, boxing
Pugilistic Club, The, 236

Pugin, Augustus Welby: *Contrasts*, 351; *see also* mediævalism
Punch and Judy show, 48–9, 340
Punch (magazine), 18, 32, 71, 97, 381, 482
punctuality: and the English, 467

quackery, 125
quadrant, *see under* nautical instrument makers
quadrille, 194
quarter days, 296, 366
Queen Charlotte's Lying-in Hospital, 35, 36–7
Queen's College, London, 517
'Queer Street', 400

rabbit skins, 102
race walkers, 267
rack, 461
Radcliffe, Ann: *The Mysteries of Udolpho*, 500; *The Romance of the Forest*, 500
Radicals, radicalism, 81, 198, 210, 521, 522
Raffles, Thomas Stamford, 477
Rag Fair, Rosemary lane, near Tower Hill, 48
rag-and-bone collectors, 102–3, 361
Ragged Schools, *see under* schools
railways: accidents, 6, 481–2; boilers, 38, 43–4; businesses resulting from, 95, 97, 206, 208; carriages, 206, 212, 240, 241, 243, 245; carriage of goods, 209; cause decrease in road traffic, 354–5; and 'civilisation and improvement', 95; construction, 93–8, 205–8, 355; demolition of houses, 94, 205, 206, 355; diseases contracted by employees, 38; drivers, 38, 211; fire danger, 480; firemen, 38, 115, 211; in France, 6, 479; guards, 38; houses for employees, 211; and geology, 233; gradients, 242; junctions, 208, 385, 481; in Kent, 478–9; maps, 208; noise and vibration, 6, 242–3; objections to, 95–7, 98; patents, 209; psychological effects, 479–80; signal lights, 6, 481–2; special engines, 385; speculators, 95–6, 97–8, 355, 463–4; speed, 6, 241, 384, 481; status of employees, 38, 108, 211; stokers, 38; taverns, 97; and telegraphy, 210; time standardized, 208; tunnels, 212, 242–3, 245, 384; wages, 514; whistles, 384
'Railway Panic' (1845), 463
rainbows, 25
Randall, Jack, 420
Ranke, Leopold von, 308
Ranters, *see* Primitive Methodists
Raphael Sanzio: 'The School of Athens' (painting), 402
rat-catching, 306
Ratcliffe, Stepney, 284–5
Ratcliffe Highway murders (1811), 449–50
Raverat, Gwen: *Period Piece*, 444
Rayer, P.: *Treatise on diseases of the skin*, 109
Reach, Angus B.: 'The Natural History of the Panic', 482
recipes: aspic, 92; beef steak and kidney pudding, 296; devilled dishes, 237; egg sauce, 296, 445; egg wine, 523; herrings and roe, 260; kidneys, 237; lamb's fry, 223; lobster salad, 508; negus, 200; ox tail soup, 384; preserved ginger, 186; roast fowl and veal stuffing, 296; tea, 320; *see also* food
Redding, Cyrus, 253; *A History and Description of Modern Wine*, 64; *Every Man His Own Butler*, 64, 67
Reform Act (1832), 198
Regency era: 258; 316, 522–3; dandyism, 381–2
Regent's Canal, 98, 243, 285
Regent's Park, 93, 205, 312, 329, 436
Regent's Street, 181, 337, 447
Rembrandt van Rijn: 'Aristotle Contemplating the Bust of Homer' (painting), 166; 'Christ Healing the Sick' (engraving), 195–6, 213
reporters, *see under* newspapers
Reverend: title, 493, 496
Reynolds, Capt. (of 11th Hussars), 236
Ricardo, David, 496
Rich, Claudius James, 83
Richardson, Samuel, 106
road-menders, 412
robbery: 492; and death penalty, 465; of drunken sailors, 452; by Thugs, 403
Roche, Louis (CD's courier), 468
Roman Catholicism, 308, 411–12, 461
romanticism, 303, 308–9, 440
Romas, Jacques de, 458
root-and-branch men, 210
root-sellers, 326; *see also* gardens, gardening
Roscoe, Thomas: *The London and Birmingham Railway Guide*, 241–2, 245–6
Rottingdean, 136
Roundell, William, 213
Rousseau, Jean-Jacques: *Emile*, 5, 159
Rowe, Nicholas: *The Tragedy of Jane Shore*, 261
Rowlandson, Thomas: 174; *The English Dance of Death* (prints), 316
Rowlandson, Thomas and William Combe: *The Tour of Dr. Syntax in Search of the Picturesque*, 309
Royal College of Physicians, 29
Royal College of Surgeons, 29
Royal Colosseum Saloon, Albany Street, 378
Royal Exchange, 55, 56, 233, 236, 266, 485–6, 500–1; *see also* Stock Exchange
Royal General Theatrical Fund, 165
Royal Horse Guards, see Household Cavalry
Royal Italian Opera, *see under* theatres
Royal Lancastrian Society, 497
Royal Leamington Spa Courier and Warwickshire Standard, 250
Royal Military College, Sandhurst, 152
Royal Navy: 3, 141, 179, 184, 287, 396, 419;

clubs, 111; colours, 142; costume, 57, 59, 61, 142, 232; daily rations, 349; hospitals, 149; midshipmen, 57–9, 66; victualling, 60, 72, 349
Royal Opera House, Covent Garden, *see under* theatres
Roylance, Elizabeth, 3, 126, 128
Rubens, Peter Paul: *Ambrosio, Marquis de Spinola* (painting), 314; *St Ignatius Loyola* (painting), 314
Rundell, Maria Eliza Ketelby: *A New System of Domestic Cookery*, 192
Ruskin, John, 214, 404; *Præterita*, 134; *The Seven Lamps of Architecture*, 309; *The Stones of Venice*, 308
Russell, Lord John, 1, 5
Russell, Norman, 25, 26, 27
Russell, Dr Richard: *Dissertation on the Use of Sea Water in Diseases of the Glands*, 125
Russell, (Sir) William Howard, 522
Russell Square, 511
Russia: 56, 334; campaigns into India and Turkey, 4, 37, 184; fairs, 4, 88; trade with Britain, 198–9, 347

Sabbatarianism, 225–6
Sadleir, John, 463–4
Saffron Hill, 206
Sailors' Prayer Book, The, 448
sailors: robbed in public houses, 451–2; *see also* Royal Navy; *see also under* costume
sailors' yarns, 451
St George's Channel, 287
St Giles (parish), 324
St Helen's church, Bishopsgate, 428, 488
St Mary Ovary church, Southwark, 406
St Mary-le-Bow church, 54
St Paul's Cathedral, 55, 130, 439
Sala, George Augustus, 133, 304, 374, 377; *Gaslight and Daylight*, 165, 194; 'Jack Alive in London', 52, 452
Samber, Robert, 105, 131, 276
Sandeau, Jules: *Sacs et parchemins*, 467
Sandhurst, *see* Royal Military College
Sandwich Islands, 229, *230*
sanitary reform, 5–6; air pollution, 4, 47, 81, 125, 430–2; Metropolitan Sanitary Association, 81, 431–2; miasma theory, 2, 125, 324, 431
savings banks, *see under* bankers, banking
Scarborough, 256
scari (fish), 172
School for Wives, The, 434
schoolmasters: in CD's novels, 99–100; cruelty of, 266
schools: Eton College, 151, 158, 162–3, 175, 132, 137; girls, 177–8; globes, 166; military, 151; national, 497; and new boys, 402; preparatory and boarding, 129–30, 164; private

venture, 158; public, 2, 5, 137, 151, 158, 187; pugilism, 523; Ragged, 5, 89; Sunday, 178; truancy, 266; *see also* charity schools; *see also under* education: classical
science, 2, 222, 286, 291, 437, 460; and air pollution causes, 431; sound waves, 290–1; statistics, 199; *see also* pugilism
Scotland: Act of Union (1707), 497
Scott, Sir Walter, 17, 308, 374, 400; *Heart of Midlothian*, 400; *Kenilworth*, 315, 455; *Rokeby: a Poem*, 283; *Waverley*, 198; *Woodstock*, 354
Scottish Enlightenment, 496
sea air, sea water: as cure, 125, 135; *see also* spas and watering places; water cures
sea monsters, 169
sea stories, *see* nautical novels and novelists
Seamen's Hospital, 286–7
Selborne, Roundell Palmer, 1st Earl of, 155
selfishness: and Utilitarians, 119–20
sentimentality, 2, 139, 140, 310
Serpentine, The, 191, 422
servants: behaviour towards employers, 416–7; board wages, 457; butlers, 192, 329, 433; character references, 394; coachmen, 36, 108, 248, 258, 377, 468; on the Continent, 334, 468; cooks, 17, 118, 226; couriers, 334–5, 468; employment agencies, 118; footmen, 45, 226, 276; governesses, 4, 177, 191, 441, 444, 517; Indian, 109–11, 233, 237, 239; lady's maids, 366; link-men, 380–1; maids, 118, 132, 175, 510; monthly nurses, 28; nursery maids, 26, 28–9, 46, 73, 88, 226; pastry cooks, 335, 340, 384; postilions, 248, 473; servants hall gossip, 433–4; servants' quarters, 45–6, 170; quarter days, 296, 366; wet-nurses, 28, 35–9, 43
settlement, deeds of, 330, 436
Seurat, Claude Ambroise ('the Living Skeleton'), 123–4
Seven Dials, 48
Seven Years War (1756-63), 60
Sèvres porcelain, 258
sexton, 87, 167
Shaftesbury, Anthony Ashley Cooper, 3rd Earl of, 119
Shaftesbury, Anthony Ashley Cooper, 7th Earl of (*earlier* Lord Ashley), 5, 431
Shakespeare, William: 7, 222, 231, 312, 313, 386; Ben Jonson on, 524; *All's Well that Ends Well*, 455; *Antony and Cleopatra*, 255–6, 260, 382; *As You Like It*, 77, 417; *Coriolanus*, 423; *Hamlet*, 84, 106, 114, 178, 238, 291, 306, 327, 341, 385, 416, 505, 520–1, 525; *Henry IV, Pt.1*, 136, 311; *Henry IV, Pt.2*, 147; *Henry V*, 284; *Henry VI, Pt.1*, 236; *Henry VI, Pt.2*, 472; *Julius Caesar*, 236, 399; *Macbeth*, 32, 108, 120, 130, 268, 306, 384, 439, 499; *The Merry Wives of Windsor*, 176; *Othello*, 303, 340; *Richard III*, 316; *The Tempest*,

251, 395, 449, 490; *Twelfth Night*, 311; *The Winter's Tale*, 139
Sharp, Richard ('Conversation'), 521–2
Shelley, Percy Bysshe: 'Alastor', 268; 'Lines', 261; 'Ozymandias', 465; 'To a Sky-Lark', 139
Shelton, Tom, 271
Sheppard, Francis, 358
Sheridan, Richard Brinsley, 2, 111; *The Duenna*, 200; *School for Scandal*, 354; *A Trip to Scarborough*, 132
Sheridan, Thomas, 111, 130
Sherwood, Mary Martha: *The History of the Fairchild Family*, 136
Shillibeer, George, 342
ship-chandlers, see chandlers 60
shipping intelligence, 68, 266, 300, 301, 346
ships: insurance, 266, 330, 348–9, 500; log, 348; wrecks and losses at sea, 266, 286, 300–1, 349, 448, 453, 500; *see also* Lloyd's of London
ships' biscuits, 60, 519
'Shipwreck, The', 68
Shirley, James: *The Triumph of Peace*, 421–2
Shoe Lane, 206
shower baths, 39–40
Shropshire, 377
'Shy Neighbourhoods', 265
Sibthorp, Col. Charles, 98
Sicily, 257, 469; assassins, 472
Sidney, Samuel, 296
Sidney's Emigrant Journal, 296
sign-manual, 398
Sketches by Boz, 456
slaves, slavery, 25, 230–1, 239, 354, 421, 422, 519; abolition, 403; campaign against, 44, 95
Sleeman, W. H.: *The Thugs*, 403
'Slight Depreciation of the Currency, A', 507
Sloman, Charles, 358
slopsellers, 145, 349
small talk: art of, 198
Smart, B. H.: *Walker Remodelled*, 191
Smeeton, George, 268
Smith, Adam, 119, 122, 496; *Wealth of Nations*, 496
Smith, Charles Manby, 94, 352
Smith, Charlotte Turner, 446; *Emmeline*, 112
Smith, John: *The Fairy Book*, 131
Smith, Sydney, 151, 507
Smith, Thomas: *A Topographical and Historical Account of the Parish of St Mary-le-Bone*, 46
Smith, Thomas Southwood, 430–1
Smithfield, 133
Smithfield Market, 100–1, 324
Smollett, Tobias: reviews Butcher's *Sermons*, 505; translation of *Gil Blas*, 106; *The Expedition of Humphry Clinker*, 106, 251, 400; *Peregrine Pickle*, 82, 106; *The Reprisal*, 220; *Roderick Random*, 220

smugglers, 179, 192–3
snuff, *see under* tobacco
soap, 154, 198, 282; soap-boilers, 103; Windsor, 180, 181
Society for Improving the Condition of the Labouring Classes, 431
Society for Promoting Christian Knowledge (SPCK), 90
'Some Particulars Concerning a Lion', 135
songs: 'As I was a-walking one May summer's morn', 396; 'C'est l'amour, l'amour, l'amour', 525; 'The Jolly Young Waterman', 317–8; 'May we ne'er want a Friend', 202; 'To Memory You Are Dear', 438; 'Old Towler', 92
songs, comic: 34–5, 503–4; 'A Cobbler there was', 34; 'The Exciseman', 335
songs, nautical: 'The Bay of Biscay O', 397; 'Cheerily Man', 203; 'The Collier's Bonny Lassie', 140; 'The Collier Swell', 140; 'I'm Afloat', 140; 'In the Whim of the Moment', 159–60; 'A Life on the Ocean Wave', 140; 'The Sailor's Consolation', 350, 448; 'Sweethearts and Wives', 283, 437
songs, patriotic: 'The Death of Nelson', 438; 'God Save the King (Queen)', 490; 'Hearts of Oak', 146; 'Rule Britannia', 69, 393; *see also* ballads
songbooks, 452
sound waves, 290–1
South Devon Railway Company, 256
Southampton, 347
Southey, Robert, 247; *Life of Nelson*, 67
Southsea, 128
Southwark, 289, 337, 406, 509
Southwark Bridge, 182
Southwood, Dr Thomas, 37
sou'westers, 145, 349
sovereign (coin), 65
spas and watering places, 198, 338–9, 351, 487; *see also* sea air, sea water; water cures
Speaker, The (House of Commons), 198
speculators: 26,128, 312, 349, 352; railway, 95–6, 97–8, 355, 463-4
Spencer, Herbert, 132
Spenser, Edmund, 327; *The Faerie Queene*, 55, 261
Sphinx, 161
spiritualism, 133
Spurzheim, Johann Gaspar, 330
stair-wires, 511
standing army, 497–8
Stanfell, Frank, 396
Stanfield, Clarkson, 70, 396
Stanhope, Philip Henry, 5th Earl, 227
Starke, Mariana, 466, 469
statistics, 38, 199, 325
statues and busts: Blue Coat charity school boy, 91; classical, 166, 297; Easter Island, 2, 464–5;

George IV, 337; Gog and Magog, 55, 101; Pitt the Younger, 82; public, 174, 222; wooden midshipman, 59
Statute of Apprentices (1563): repealed (1814), 58
Staunton, Howard: *The Great Schools of England*, 165
steam engines: manufacturing and mining, 58, 60, 65, 128, 158, 247, 405, 503; railways, 38, 41, 44, 207, 209, 211, 243, 245, 480, 482
steam vessels: 294, 300, 347, 452–3, 468; coastal and cross-channel, 6, 232, 336, 366, 468–9, 487
Steel, John William, 93
Steig, Michael, 304, 423, 463, 470, 476, 482, 519
Steinmetz, Andrew: *Slavery and the Internal Slave Trade in the United States of America*, 231; *A Voice in Ramah*, 231
Stephens, John L.: *Incidents of Travel in Central America*, 465
Stephenson, George, 209–12
Sterne, Laurence: *Tristram Shandy*, 1, 304, 316
Stewart, Dugald: *Elements of the Philosophy of the Human Mind*, 370
Stock Exchange, The, 25, 55, 98, 181–2, 423, 500; *see also* Royal Exchange
Stockton and Darlington Railway, 211
Stone, Thomas, 370
Stowe Park, Buckinghamshire, 244
Strand, The, 182, 269, 378
strait-waistcoats, 79
Strauss, Johann the Elder, 113
Strawberry Hill, Twickenham, 353
street lighting, 49, 130, 380–1
street musicians, 48–9, 335–7; barrel organs, 49, 164, 170, 404; brass bands, 277, 335, 337
street performers, 277, 304; jugglers, 224; Punch and Judy, 48–9, 340; tumblers, 225
street sellers, 102–3, 180–1; costermongers, 26, 98, 180, 326, 380, 388; traditional cries, 48, 180; *see also under* Jews; *see also* Mayhew, Henry
street-walkers, *see* prostitution
Stretch, L.M., 393
Stubbes, Philip: *The Anatomie of Abuses*, 104
substitute (militia), 119
Suckling, Sir John, 487
suicide, 450, 454, 464
Sunday, 141, 145, 242, 487; markets, 180; newspapers, 456, 462; Sabbatarianism, 225–6; schools, 178
supercargo, 485
superstitions: Brocken, 362; changelings, 121; corner houses, 457; Flying Dutchman, 283; gold seals, 434; walking on a grave, 294
surgeons, 29, 50, 143, 247; *see also* apothecaries; physicians
Surtees, Robert Smith: *Mr Romford's Hounds*, 253
suttee (widow-burning), 4, 415
swearing, 398, 452; children's punishment for, 135; 'demi-swearing', 199–200
Swift, Jonathan, 455; *Polite Conversation*, 194, 221
swivel-bridges, 281
Sydney, Sir Philip: *Arcadia*, 257
Syme, James: *Principles of Surgery*, 50–1

Tait, Archibald Campbell, Bishop of London (*later* Archbishop of Canterbury), 212
Tait, Catherine, 212
Tait, William: *Magdalenism*, 359–60, 426
Talbot, James Beard: *Miseries of Prostitution*, 358–9, 361, 363
Tale of Two Cities, A, 467
Talfourd, Thomas Noon, 436
tallow, 198, 199, 347
Tartar, HMS (frigate), 60–1
Tartars, 51
Taverner, Richard, 365
Taylor, John: *The Olde, Olde, very Olde Man*, 404
Taylor, (Philip) Meadows: *Confessions of a Thug*, 403
teeth: children's teething remedies, 76; false, 185, 254; *see also* dentistry
telegraph (electric), 209, 210, 385, 387
Tennyson, Alfred, 1st Baron, 2, 168; 'Buonaparte', 334; *In Memoriam*, 524; *Maud*, 255; *The Princess*, 517
Thackeray, William Makepeace, 2, 97, 125, 169, 215, 339; *Henry Esmond*, 493; *The Newcomes*, 27, 329; *The Tremendous Adventures of Major Gahagan*, 112, 142, 150, 337, 455; *Vanity Fair*, 18, 151, 331, 493, 511; *The Virginians*, 292
Thames, River: Company of Watermen and Lightermen, 317; flooding, 4, 289; picturesqueness, 279, 289; rowing clubs and matches, 289, 317–8; steam boats, 232
Thames Street, 181, 193, 325
theatres, 130, 198, 336; Adelphi, 215, 302; Astley's, 302; Covent Garden, 190, 402, 503; Drury Lane, 130, 302, 503; English Opera House, 92; Her Majesty's Theatre, Haymarket, 373–4; Lyceum, 258, 438; New Strand, 190, 241; Prince's, 241; Princess's, 302; Royal Italian Opera, 374; Sadler's Wells, 241, 302; Theatre Royal, Brighton, 196
Thirlwall, Connop, 155
Thomson, Dr Anthony Todd: *The Domestic Management of the Sick-Room*, 413
Thomson, James, 2; *The Seasons*, 51, 164
Thornbury, Walter, 46
Thorne, James: *Rambles by Rivers: The Thames*, 289
Thornwell, Emily: *Lady's Guide to Perfect Gentility*, 34
'Thoughts about People', 376
Threadneedle Street, 55–6, 375, *375*, 428
Thugs, 4, 403
ticket-porters, *see* porters ~~182~~

Tillotson, Kathleen, 112; *see also* Butt, John and Kathleen Tillotson
time: standardized for railway, 208–9
Times (newspaper), 5, 199, 222, 295, 431, 456
tinkering, 306
Tipperary Joint Stock Bank, 464
Tippoo Sultan, 57
Tite, Sir William, 55
title of *DS*, 14
tobacco: 61, 268, 289, 325; cigars, 192–3, 197; snuff, 193–4, 290
Tocqueville, Alexis de, 247
Tom Brown at Oxford, 53
'Tom Thumb, General' (Charles Sherwood Stratton), 187
Tom Tiddler's Ground, 375–6
Tonna, Charlotte Elizabeth: *The Wrongs of Women*, 517
Tooke, Thomas, 423
Tower Hill, 48, 54
Tower of London, 52, 438, 507
Townshend, Chauncy Hare, 410
Tracey, Lieut. Augustus, 7, 67
Trade, Board of, 44, 199
tramping, 365, 305–6
'Tramps', 305
transportation (of convicts), 266, 360, 365, 492
'Travelling Abroad', 134
Treasury Board, 522
Trimmer, Sarah, 392
triumphal cars, 421–2
Trollope, Anthony, 53, 426, 467; *Can You Forgive Her?*, 303; *The Last Chronicle of Barset*, 354; *The Way We Live Now*, 27
trousseau, 486
troy weight, 176
truants, 266
True Sun (journal), 522
Truman, Hanbury & Co., 43
tumblers (street performers), 225
Turkey, *see* Ottoman Empire
'Twenty-four Hours in a London Hospital', 227
Two Pilgrims, a Romance, The, 341

umbrella-menders ('mushfakers'), 48, 306
'Uncommercial Traveller, The', 51
underclothes, *see under* costume and appearance
underwriters, 348–9; *see also* Lloyd's of London
United Service Club, 111
'Unsettled Neighbourhood, An', 93
upholsterers, 319; *see also* interior decoration
Urania Cottage, Shepherd's Bush, 3–4, 359–61, 363; *see also* prostitution
Ure, Andrew, 43
Utilitarians, 119; *see also* political economy

vacations: midsummer, 187

vagabonds, 264, 305
Vanbrugh, Sir John: *The Relapse*, 132
Vardy, John, 496
Venice, 309, 448
Vere, Sir Francis, 438
Vernet, Carle (Antoine Charles Horace), 470
Versailles: Petit Trianon, 257–8
Via Dolorosa, 317
Victoria, Queen, 4, 15, 125, 153, 337
Village Coquettes, The (operetta), 438
Virgil, *see under* classical authors
'Visit to Newgate, A', 4, 363
visiting-cards, 110, 272; *see also* 'at home'; weddings: cards
Visitors' New Guide to to the Spa of Leamington Priors, and its Vicinity, 310
Vulgarities of Speech Corrected, The, 53

wagers, *see* betting
Wakefield, Edward Gibbon, 365
Walker, John: *A Critical Pronouncing Dictionary and Expositor of the English language*, 191
walking-matches, 264–5
Waller, Edmund, 222
Wallis, Samuel, 470
Wallis's Guide for Strangers through London, 93
wallpaper, 318–9; *see also* interior decoration
Walpole, Horace, 353
Waltham Mills: explosion, 419
waltz, 81, 113–4, 277, 336
Wapping, 285, 289, 451
'Wapping Warehouse', 58
warming pan, 376
Warren's blacking factory, 3, 126
Warton, Thomas the Younger, 139
Warwick Castle, 247, *249*, 304, 307–8, 310, 313–5
Warwickshire, 239, 312, 401
washing-day, 146–7
watches, 60, 209, 438, 510; CD's, 265; as exports, 347; physicians', 437; seals, 434; stands, 183
watchmen, 281, 394, 439, 440
water-carts, 47
water-cures, 40; *see also* sea air, sea water; spas and watering places
watering places, *see* spas and watering places
Waterloo Bridge, 171
watermen, 232, 422
Watson, Mrs Richard, 362
Watts, Isaac, 350; 'Against Idleness and Mischief', 491; 'Against Quarrelling and Fighting', 491; *Divine Songs for Children*, 167; 'Fire, Air, Earth, and Sea', 350; 'The Sluggard', 294, 490
Weber, Carl Maria Friedrich von: *Der Freischutz*, 91
weddings, 71, 195, 332–3, 338, 371; banns, 489–90; cards, 371, 383; mourning dress, 331; orange blossoms, 516; *trousseau*, 486; *see also* brides; marriage

Wedgwood, Josiah, 44
Weise, Leopold, 165
'Well-authenticated Rappings', 133
Wellington, Arthur Wellesley, 1st Duke of, 4, 130, 174
Wellington House Classical and Commercial Academy, 34, 138, 162
Wesley, Charles, 154
Wesleyans, 496, 201
West End (London), 30, 46, 48, 103, 107, 276, 337, 512
West India Docks, 58, 144–6, 201
West Indies, 347, 403, 452; export trade, 4, 25, 186, 347, 353; fever, 185, 493
Westmacott, Sir Richard, 222
Westminster, 89, 91, 289; *see also* Parliament, Houses of
Westminster Abbey, 404
Westminster Bridge, 171
Westminster Review, The, 17, 513
wet nurses, *see under* servants
Wheatstone, Charles, 210
whiskers: and Englishmen, 183–4; and foreigners, 183–4, 333–4, 508; and railway workers, 38; *see also* hair
whist, 317, 400
Whitby, 204
White, Francis, 407
White, John, 97
White's Club, London, 407
Whitley Hall, 246
Whittington, Sir Richard (Dick), 55, 72, 105, 220
Whytt, Robert: 'Of the Predisposing Causes of Nervous ... Disorders', 301
widows, 223, 303, 304; burning in India, 4, 415; income, 132; mourning, 114
Wilberforce, William, 95
Wilderspin, Samuel, 5, 129, 159, 163; *Infant Education*, 130
Wilkie, Sir David, 32
William I ('the Conqueror'), King, 195, 307, 327
William III (of Orange), King, 55
William IV, King, 98
Williams, Frederick S., 98
Williams, John, 450
Williamson, John, 450
wills (testamentary), 449
Wills, W. H., 56, 100; 'A Little Place in Norfolk', 373; 'The Monster Promenade Concerts', 277
Wilson, George, 57
Wilson, John ('Christopher North'), 272
Wimpole Street, 524
Windsor soap, 181
wire-drawing, 387
Wisdom of our Ancestors, The (CD's fake books), 325
witches, 362
Woburn Abbey, Bedfordshire, 244

Wolcot, John, *see* 'Pindar, Peter'
Wollaston, William Hyde, 123, 290
Wollstonecraft, Mary: *Mary*, 112; *A Vindication of the Rights of Woman*, 517
Wolverton, Buckinghamshire, 211–2
Woman's Rights and Duties (by 'A Woman'), 517
women: attributes of wet-nurses, 38–9; childbirth diseases, 29–30; education, 163, 177–8, 262, 444–5, 517; equality debate, 517; hysteria and hypochondria, 301–2; ideals of womanhood, 52–3, 356–7; and marriage as a market, 27; travelling alone, 467–8; *see also* prostitution
Woodway House, Teignmouth, Devon, 352
Wordsworth, William, 2, 139, 308; 'Lines Composed a Few Miles above Tintern Abbey', 524; 'Ode: Intimations of Immortality', 205, 263; 'On the Power of Sound', 261; 'Surprized by Joy', 454
'World of London, The', 58
world, the: society as, 455
Worshipful Companies, *see* City of London: livery companies
Wren, Sir Christopher, 84, 439, 488

Yates, Edmund, 515; *His Recollections and Experiences*, 269, 271
yellow jack, *see under* diseases and ailments: yellow fever
York and Albany, Frederick Augustus, Duke of, 4, 32–3, 150, 238, 455, 502
Young England Movement, 308